The Balkans

from Constantinople
to Communism

DENNIS P. HUPCHICK

palgrave

THE BALKANS
© Dennis P. Hupchick, 2002

First published 2001 by PALGRAVE™
175 Fifth Avenue, New York, N.Y. 10010 and
Houndmills, Basingstoke, Hampshire RG21 6XS.
Companies and representatives throughout the world

PALGRAVE is the new global publishing imprint of St. Martin's Press LLC
Scholarly and Reference Division and Palgrave Publishers Ltd (formerly
Macmillan Press Ltd).

ISBN 0-312-21736-6 hardback

Library of Congress Cataloging-in-Publication Data

Hupchick, Dennis P.
   The Balkans : from Constantinople to communism / Dennis P. Hupchick.
      cm.
   Includes bibliographical references and index.
   ISBN 0-312-21736-6
   1. Balkan peninsula—History. I. Title: From Constantinople to communism. II. Title.

DR36 H87 2001
949.6—dc21   00-062590

A catalogue record for this book is available from the British Library.

Design by planettheo.com

First edition: January 2002
10 9 8 7 6 5 4 3 2 1

Printed in the United States of America.

In memory of my mentor,
James F. Clarke
(1906-1982)

Contents

Preface

On a late-September evening in 1938, British Prime Minister Neville Chamberlain went on radio to address the nation regarding the growing international crisis surrounding events in Czechoslovakia. The Nazi-influenced Sudeten German minority in that state had precipitated a situation that threatened to result in a German invasion of the country. France had signed an alliance guaranteeing Czechoslovakia's security, and Britain was closely allied with France in case of any future hostilities. An invasion by Hitler's Germany would force both to live up to their treaty responsibilities. The frightening possibility of a costly and bloody European war loomed large, and naturally the British people were concerned. In the course of his address, Chamberlain, desperate to avoid a conflict, made the following comment: "How horrible, fantastic, incredible it is that we should be digging trenches and trying on gas masks here because of a quarrel in a faraway country between people of whom we know nothing." The next day Hitler notified Chamberlain that he was willing to discuss a diplomatic solution to the crisis. The day after that, the British prime minister flew off to Munich, where he and French Premier Edward Daladier, under the delusion that peace thus would be assured, essentially caved in to Hitler's demands to dismember France's East European ally. Fear of spilling British blood to uphold Britain's moral responsibilities and ignorance of East European realities led Chamberlain to the Munich appeasement. Far from preventing the war he feared, his actions ultimately guaranteed its outbreak a year later.

One cannot help but be struck by similarities between Chamberlain's reaction to the Sudeten crisis sixty-odd years ago and those of Western leaders to the war in Bosnia-Hercegovina that raged between 1992 and 1995. The same ignorance, befuddlement, and fear reflected in Chamberlain's telling remark characterized their efforts to end the Bosnian debacle. Apparently lacking any concrete understanding of the situation on the ground, caught off guard by the rapid and violent disintegration of Yugoslavia, and afraid that the resulting regional instability would threaten relationships in the North Atlantic Treaty Organization (NATO) and the European Union (EU), the Western powers vacillated among inactivity, half measures, and appeasement of nationalist aggressors—anything to avoid costly, and potentially bloody, direct intervention—before finally manipulating the parties involved in the war into signing a tenuous agreement at Dayton, Ohio.

Later, in 1999, fear of casualties and, once again, a lack of understanding of Balkan realities led the West to resort to an airwar half measure against Serbia in an avowed effort to protect the Albanian minority in the Serbian province of Kosovo from Serbian ultranationalist "ethnic cleansing." NATO's bombing campaign did not spare the Kosovar Albanians from the atrocities that it supposedly sought to prevent. Ultimately Serbia's leadership was bludgeoned into submission and most of the Kosovar Albanian refugees originally forced out of the region by the Serbs returned to their devastated homes, whereupon they began perpetrating their own round of atrocities on those Kosovar Serbs who did not flee when Serbian forces withdrew.

The befuddlement and fear demonstrated by Western leaders during the Bosnian and Kosovo crises were a direct reflection of an ignorance of Balkan history. But the leaders merely mirrored the more widespread ignorance of their respective constituencies. The majority of westerners had little knowledge of, or interest in, Balkan affairs beyond a rudimentary, generalized, and frequently oversimplified awareness of assorted cold war-related situations: Yugoslavia was a "good" Communist country ever since Marshal Josip Tito broke with Joseph Stalin in 1948 and mixed capitalism with socialism; Bulgaria was the blind puppet and lackey of the Soviet Union; Romania under Nicolae Ceauşescu was a "friendly" Communist state that frequently opposed Soviet imperialism; rarely noticed Albania was akin to Tibet, isolated in its mountains and in its affinities to Red China; Greece was part of NATO, a member of the West that was not considered part of the Balkans; and Turkey, another NATO ally, was Middle Eastern and not a part of Europe. When Yugoslavia disintegrated in 1992, unfamiliarity with pre-cold war Balkan history made it easy for Western politicians and journalists to blame the resulting warfare on "centuries-old" ethnic or religious conflicts—again, an oversimplification rooted in a fundamental misunderstanding of Balkan history—and to tag the fighting inaccurately as the "Third" Balkan War (assuming, of course, that their Western audiences were aware that there once had been two others).

Perhaps the unfamiliarity with Balkan history displayed by English speakers can be blamed partly on a certain lack of general education dealing with the region. Except for a few occurrences that have played important roles in determining the course of Western European developments (such as the fall of Constantinople to the Ottoman Turks in 1453 and the 1914 assassination of the Austro-Hungarian Archduke Francis Ferdinand in Sarajevo), events in the Balkans rarely have found their way into English-language secondary education textbooks. At the level of higher education, the same often holds true for courses in general European and world history.

This "Balkan gap" in recent English-language education can be attributed in some measure to continuing vestiges of Western European cultural antipathy toward the Orthodox European and Islamic civilizations that have held historical sway in the region as well as to a certain lack of available, sound general studies of Balkan history. When discussing Orthodox Europe and Islam, westerners frequently portray them as either threatening or as inferior with regard to the West. As threats, both provide westerners with their most long-standing cultural bogymen: Orthodox Europe spawned the Byzantine Empire, Russia, and the Soviet Union; Islam begot the Arab Caliphate, the Spanish Moors, the Saracens, the Ottoman Empire, and, most currently, Islamic "fundamentalism," Libya, Iran, and Iraq. Less concrete (but more insidious because of their casualness) are the consistent Western portrayals of Orthodox European and Islamic inferiority in texts and in the media by using culturally negative or pejorative descriptive terms (such as "underdeveloped," "backward," "Asiatic," "fossilized," among others) when discussing them and by categorizing their political and social structures as innately flawed (such as being politically "autocratic" or "authoritarian" and socially "inequitable" or "tradition-bound").

As birthplace for the Orthodox European civilization and dominated for close to half a millennium by Islamic civilization, the Balkan Peninsula suffers accordingly. Its very name seems unconsciously associated in Western minds with "otherness," since it derives from a colloquial Turkish term for mountain. This perceptual foreignness has been reinforced further by the late-nineteenth- and early-twentieth-century chaos and divisiveness characterizing the rise of modern nation-states in the region, epitomized in the term "balkanization." So tangible is the negative perception of the Balkans in Western minds that many peoples native to the region—Greeks, Romanians, Croats, and Slovenes, in particular—adamantly reject the use of the term, thus hoping to escape the impression of inferiority in the West. Some Western scholars of the region do so as well because of an awareness of the cultural implications of the word. Instead, the term "Southeastern Europe" has become a common substitute.

One might posit that, if the Balkans received the volume of English-language general historical coverage approaching that given most areas of Western Europe, then at least westerners' ignorance of the region would be mitigated and the cultural biases dampened. This, of course, is conjecture. As it stands, few book-length general studies of Balkan history have been published in English. Even if the comparison is limited to English-language books specifically treating Eastern Europe, the Balkans place far behind those devoted to Central-Eastern and Northeastern European topics. It would appear that the Balkans enjoy copious coverage only when events in the region cause some sense of crisis in the West. Both the "Eastern Question" (1875-78) and the Balkan Wars (1912-13) produced outpourings of predominantly superficial or subjective publications on the Balkans that ceased once the crises ended. The current rash of mostly journalistic and memoir publications generated by the collapse of Yugoslavia, the war in Bosnia-Hercegovina, and the humanitarian debacle in Kosovo follows in their mold.

Because the prospects are likely that post-Communist turmoil in the Balkans will continue for some time to come, raising serious security and foreign policy issues for the United States and Europe, westerners will need to know as much as possible about the region, especially about its history. The number of reliable and comprehensive general histories of the Balkans readily available in English at present can be counted on one's fingers and toes, and most of these are limited in scope, dated, or written almost exclusively for specialists. Supplementing these works are some English-language studies devoted to important stages in Balkan history, such as the Byzantine, Ottoman, and modern national periods. For much of the later national and Communist periods in Balkan history, the reader is forced to cull information from general studies of Eastern Europe. Augmenting such general studies are a number of English-language, national-oriented histories spanning all of the periods. Taken as a whole, however, their coverage is uneven because English-language histories of states that have been of intrinsic cultural or political interest to the West (such as Greece and Yugoslavia) far outstrip in number those of the other Balkan states (including pre-Yugoslavia Bosnia-Hercegovina, Croatia, Macedonia, Montenegro, Serbia, and Slovenia). Also, most of these works have as their focus the modern national and, especially, Communist periods rather than the Byzantine or Ottoman, and many of them suffer from nationalist or ideological biases. In any case, their total numbers are few relative to those available for the rest of Eastern Europe, let alone to those treating with Western European states.

On the whole, few comprehensive studies of the Balkans exist. More narrowly directed general works of all kinds tend to emphasize periods in which Western influences play a significant role. Times in which non-Western forces predominated in Balkan history are de-emphasized or ignored. Yet it is precisely the non-Western influences that have made the Balkans "the Balkans"—that region of Europe that has proven so befuddling to westerners over the years.

The historical survey that follows is an attempt to assist the English-speaking student and general reader in gaining a basic introductory understanding of Balkan history in all of its varied cultural stages, from the end of antiquity through the collapse of communism (but without the usual pro-Western biases) and to provide them with a resource for launching further, more in-depth study should they so desire. As the title proclaims, it is a survey history of *the Balkans*. The term intentionally and consistently is used throughout the text to emphasize the region's cultural and historical uniqueness relative to Western Europe without any implied qualitative connotation—and nothing more.

The text constitutes an interpretive narrative organized into large, subdivided sections corresponding to important developmental periods—"eras"—in Balkan history, beginning with the advent of Slav and Turk settlement in the region and ending with the collapse of Communist governments in 1991. Post-1991 developments have not been included, since the "facts" surrounding them are still too sketchy, or partisan, or not at present fully understood regarding their future significance to provide any definitive insight into the fundamental nature of the new, post-Communist era. The text represents an interpretive synthesis of ideas and observations gained by years of extensive reading and research in the fields of history and Balkan studies and by extended periods of firsthand experience in the region itself.

In an effort to aid those interested in pursuing study of the Balkans at greater length, extensive lists of further readings and a selected general bibliography supplement the text. Rather than fill the text with footnote references to general data that essentially are well known to specialists, a detailed list of reference readings pertinent to the material presented is appended at the end of each major text division. Selected listing of general studies as well as some collections of primary sources translated into English immediately follow the body of the text. Each of the listings is organized topically, first by general works and then by state/region.

The references included in the listings are extensive but selective. First, since this study is targeted specifically at English-speaking introductory students and general readers, the works listed are published exclusively in English. Thus, many important source studies have been omitted because they are available only in non-English languages. Those possessing the ability to read foreign languages will find more than adequate references to such studies in the notes and bibliographies of the works cited.

Second, for reasons both of intent and space, only book titles have been included, most of which represent monographs. It seems unlikely that this book's intended readership will be able to jump immediately into digesting the narrowly focused and highly specialized literature represented by scholarly articles. The titles listed provide the general in-depth exposure to various issues in Balkan history usually needed before plunging into the available periodical literature.

As a final, personal note, I wish to extend acknowledgment and thanks to those who lent support and assistance over the time involved in bringing the following study to fruition. The completion of the manuscript's final draft was facilitated through a sabbatical leave granted me by President Christopher N. Breiseth and the trustees of Wilkes University. President Breiseth's enthusiastic support for the project was inspirational and greatly appreciated. A number of colleagues and friends at Wilkes University were particularly helpful. Harold E. Cox, a historian who contributed expert cartographic collaboration on three of my previous book projects, once again produced the maps supplementing this text. I feel truly fortunate to enjoy his willing cooperation. J. Michael Lennon, vice president for academic affairs, and Robert J. Heaman, expert in literary culture, kindly gave of their time to critique portions of the manuscript to help make it more readable for nonspecialists, for which I am grateful. Kathleen J. Diekhaus, departmental secretary, rendered useful clerical aid, and Brian R. Sacolic, reference and database librarian, provided valuable bibliographic search assistance. At Palgrave Press, Michael J. Flamini and Amanda Johnson demonstrated genuine tolerance and great understanding over delays caused by unforeseen health problems and revisions. Finally, I wish to thank my wife, Anne-Marie, for suffering through three years of her husband's assorted preoccupations, obsessions, and agonies surrounding the project.

Dennis P. Hupchick
Wilkes-Barre, PA, 2001

Note on Spelling and Pronunciation

An attempt has been made in the following text to render most proper names and foreign terms in or near their native spellings. Exceptions to this approach are terms generally better known to English speakers in their Anglicized forms (such as the names of states, certain cities, and various geographic elements) and the first names of Greek, Russian, and Western European individuals. Place-names (other than Constantinople/Istanbul, Adrianople/Edirne, and Nicæa/İznik) are given in their contemporary forms, with variants provided in parentheses following their initial appearances in the text. In the case of languages written in non-Latin alphabets, a "phonetical" transliteration system, generally following that used by the U.S. Board on Geographic Names, is employed for Bulgarian and Russian, while for Serbian and Macedonian a system based on the Latin, Croat form of Serbo-Croatian (utilizing diacritical marks and familiar in the West for transliterating "Yugoslav" languages), is used. Turkish terms are spelled in the Latin characters currently used in Turkey, with appropriate diacritics.

A guide to the simple phonetical pronunciation of certain foreign letters follows.

ai (Greek), **é** (Hungarian):	as **long a** in b*ay*
á (Hungarian), **a** (in all cases *except* Hungarian):	as **a** in *ah*
c (in all cases *except* Turkish), **ţ** (Romanian):	as **ts** in bea*ts*
č, ć (Serb, Croat, Macedonian), **cs** (Hungarian), **ç** (Turkish):	as **ch** in *ch*urch
dj (Serb, Croat, Macedonian), **gy** (Hungarian), **c** (Turkish):	as **dzh** in ba*dge*
e (in all cases):	as **short e** in l*e*t
ğ (Turkish):	as **silent h** in o*h*
h (Bulgarian, Serb, Croat, Macedonian, Turkish, Russian):	as **ch** in Ba*ch*
i (in all cases), **oi** (Greek), **yi** (Hungarian):	as **ee** in sw*ee*t
j (in all cases *except* Romanian):	as **y** in *y*et
ó (Hungarian):	as **long o** in s*o*
ő (Hungarian), **ă** (Romanian):	as **ur** in p*ur*ge
š (Serb, Croat, Macedonian), **s** (Hungarian), **ş** (Romanian, Turkish):	as **sh** in *sh*eet
sz (Hungarian):	as **s** in *s*ay
u (in all cases), **ou** (Greek):	as **oo** in z*oo*
ü (Turkish, Hungarian):	as **yoo** in mil*ieu*
ŭ (Bulgarian), **â** (Romanian), **ı** (Turkish), **ë** (Albanian), **ö, a** (Hungarian):	as **short a** in b*u*t
x (Albanian):	as **dz** in bu*ds*
y (Russian), **î** (Romanian):	as **short i** in *i*t
ž (Serb, Croat, Macedonian), **zs** (Hungarian), **j** (Romanian):	as **zh** in mea*s*ure

Map 1. Balkans — Physical

Northern Border of the Balkan Peninsula

Land from 1,500 ft (458 m) to 3,000 ft (915 m)

Land from 3,000 ft (915 m) to 6,000 ft (1,830 m)

Lands above 6,000 ft (1,830 m)

Map 2. Balkans — Political and Ethnic

MILES
0   50   100   150   200

0   100   200   300
KILOMETERS

South Slavs

Major Ethnic Minorities:
AL Albanians   HU Hungarians
BG Bulgarians   MA Macedonians
CR Croats   MN Montenegrins
GK Greeks   SB Serbs
GR Germans   TK Turks

Map 3. Rise of the First Bulgarian Empire

Border of Bulgar State, 681

Territories Acquired by Krum (803-814)

Territories Acquired by Malamir-Presyan (831-852)

Territories Acquired by Boris I (852-889)

Territories Acquired by Simeon I (891-927)

Territories under Nominal Bulgar Control, 803-895

Map 4. Rise of Medieval Serbia

HOLY ROMAN EMPIRE

Danube R.

POLAND

KIEV

GOLDEN HORDE

MOLDAVIA

HUNGARY

VENICE

Venice

SLAVONIA

SREM

BOSNIA

CROATIA

HUM

Belgrade

Braničevo

WALLACHIA

PAPAL STATES

Raška

RAŠKA

Peć

Kotor

Dubrovnik

Zeta

KOSOVO

Vidin

Niš

Danube R.

BULGARIA

Tŭrnovo

KINGDOM OF THE TWO SICILIES

Naples

Kyustendi

Sofia

Plovdiv

Skopje

Durrës

Ohrid

MACEDONIA

Serres

BYZANTINE

THRACE

Constantinople

ALBANIA

Vlorë

Thessaloniki

EPIRUS

Ioannina

Larissa

Mt. Athos

EMPIRE

THESSALY

To Byzantium

SICILY

EUBŒA

SELCÜK

MILES

0   50   100   150   200

0   100   200   300
KILOMETERS

Patras

PR. OF ACHAIA

Mystra

MOREA

D. OF ATHENS

Athens

EMPIRE

Monemvasia

To Byzantium

CRETE
To Venice

- - - - Serbian Border under Stefan Uroš II Milutin (1282-1321)
▬▬▬ Serbia under Stefan Uroš IV Dušan (1331-1355)

Map 5. Ottoman Expansion in the Balkans, 1354–1566

Map 6. The Ottoman Balkans, Late 17th – 18th Centuries

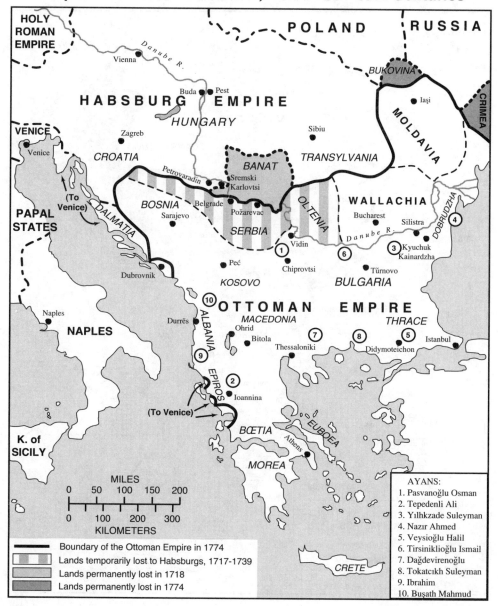

HOLY ROMAN EMPIRE

POLAND

RUSSIA

Danube R.

Vienna

BUKOVINA

CRIMEA

Buda · Pest

Iaşi

HABSBURG EMPIRE

HUNGARY

MOLDAVIA

Sibiu

VENICE

Zagreb

Venice

CROATIA

TRANSYLVANIA

BANAT

Petrovaradin

Sremski Karlovtsi

(To Venice)

DALMATIA

BOSNIA

Belgrade

Požarevac

OLTENIA

WALLACHIA

PAPAL STATES

Sarajevo

SERBIA

Bucharest

Silistra

④

DOBRUDZHA

Danube R.

① Vidin

③ Kyuchuk Kainardzha

Dubrovnik

Peć

Chiprovtsi

⑥

Tŭrnovo

KOSOVO

BULGARIA

⑩ OTTOMAN   EMPIRE

Naples

Durrës

MACEDONIA

THRACE

NAPLES

Ohrid

Bitola

⑦

⑧

⑤ Istanbul

Thessaloniki

Didymoteichon

ALBANIA

⑨

EPIROS

②

Ioannina

(To Venice)

BŒTIA

EUBOEA

Athens

K. of SICILY

MOREA

MILES
0 50 100 150 200

0   100   200   300
KILOMETERS

CRETE

AYANS:
1. Pasvanoğlu Osman
2. Tepedenli Ali
3. Yılhkzade Suleyman
4. Nazır Ahmed
5. Veysioğlu Halil
6. Tirsiniklioğlu Ismail
7. Dağdevirenoğlu
8. Tokatcıkh Suleyman
9. Ibrahim
10. Buşath Mahmud

——— Boundary of the Ottoman Empire in 1774

Lands temporarily lost to Habsburgs, 1717-1739

Lands permanently lost in 1718

Lands permanently lost in 1774

Map 7. Emergence of Balkan States, 1830–1862

BAVARIA

Danube R. Vienna

RUSSIA

HABSBURG EMPIRE

Buda Pest

BESSARABIA

HUNGARY

Iaşi

MOLDAVIA

SLOVENIA

Zagreb

TRANSYLVANIA

Venice

CROATIA - SLAVONIA

VOJVODINA

ROMANIA
(United 1861)

Galaţi

BOSNIA

Zemun

DALMATIA

Sarajevo

Belgrade

WALLACHIA

SERBIA

Bucharest

PAPAL
STATES

HERCEGOVINA

Vidin *Danube R.*

BULGARIA

Dubrovnik

MONTENEGRO
Cetinje

Niš

Sofia

Plovdiv

(To Habsburgs)

Naples

Skopje

Edirne

MACEDONIA

THRACE Istanbul

Thessaloniki

ALBANIA

KINGDOM

Ioannina

OF

EPIROS

THESSALY

THE

TWO SICILIES

Mesalóngion
Thebes
Patras Epidavros Athens
Navplion
GREECE Navarino

CYCLADES
ISLANDS

MILES

| 0 | 50 | 100 | 150 | 200 |

| 0 | 100 | 200 | 300 |
KILOMETERS

OTTOMAN   EMPIRE

Border of Ottoman Empire
Autonomous Serbia, 1830
Independent Greece, 1830
Autonomous and united Romania, 1856

CRETE
(To Egypt)

Map 8. San Stefano – Berlin Balkans, 1878–1885

Borders set at the Treaty of San Stefano, lost at Berlin, 1878
San Stefano Bulgaria, 1878
Final border of Bulgaria, Berlin, June 1878
Border of Bulgaria, 1885
Occupied by Austria-Hungary after Berlin, 1878
Gains of Greece, 1881

Map 9. Balkan Wars, 1912–1913

BORDERS BEFORE THE FIRST BALKAN WAR, 1912

BORDERS AFTER THE FIRST BALKAN WAR, 1912

BORDERS AFTER THE SECOND BALKAN WAR, 1913

Map 10. The Balkans, 1923

CZECHOSLOVAKIA

POLAND

SOVIET UNION

AUSTRIA

Danube R.

Vienna

Bratislava

Klagenfurt

Budapest

HUNGARY

BUKOVINA

BESSARABIA

MARAMURES

CRISANA

Cluj

Iaşi

Kishinev

Odessa

SLOVENIA

Venice

Trieste

Ljubljana

Zagreb

Rijeka

CROATIA

SLAVONIA

VOJVODINA

Novi Sad

Timişoara

BANAT

TRANSYLVANIA

Alba Iulia

MOLDAVIA

R O M A N I A

DALMATIA

Zadar

BOSNIA HERCEGOVINA

Sarajevo

Belgrade

K. OF SERBS, CROATS AND SLOVENES

SERBIA

WALLACHIA

Craiova

Ploieşti

Bucharest

Danube R.

Silistra

Rome

ITALY

Dubrovnik

MONTENEGRO

Cetinje

Niš

Sofia

Varna

Naples

KOSOVO

Skopje

B U L G A R I A

Plovdiv

Shkodër

ALBANIA

MACEDONIA

Edirne

Durrës

Tiranë

Ohrid

Kavala

THRACE

Istanbul

Vlorë

Thessaloniki

EPIROS

T U R K E Y

Ioannina

CORFU

GREECE

SICILY

Izmir

MILES
0 50 100 150 200

0 100 200 300
KILOMETERS

Athens

DODECANESE IS.

To Italy

CRETE

Borders of "New" states at Versailles, 1919-1920
Regional borders within "New" States
Region of Klagenfurt plebiscite zone, 1920

Map 11. The Balkans, 1941–1943

Ribbentrop-Molotov Line, 1939

Occupied by Romania, 1941-1944

Second Vienna Award, 1940

Acquired by Bulgaria, Craiova Treaty, 1940

ALBANIA
(To Italy) States annexed or occupied by Axis Powers, 1938-1941

Map 12. The "Cold War" Balkans

Glossary

Ahi	Islamic urban fellowship.
Akçe	Silver coin used in the Ottoman Empire.
Akıncı	Ottoman irregular cavalry used for scouting, raiding, and pillaging.
Askeri	Ottoman military-administrative (ruling) class.
Avaris	Ottoman extraordinary tax, often collected on a regular basis.
Ayan	Ottoman semi-independent provincial strongman or governor.
Bakşiş	"Gift" (Turkish); a bribe.
Ban	"Leader" (Croatian); Hungarian title for a nominally subordinate Croatian or Bosnian provincial ruler.
Banovina	Post-1929 province of Yugoslavia.
Başıbazuks	Ottoman irregular troops recruited from Muslim villagers and Circassians.
Bey	Turkish title for lord, notable, or governor.
Beylerbeyi	Highest ranking original Ottoman provincial commander-governor.
Boier	Romanian landholding aristocrat.
Bojar	Serbian landholding aristocrat.
Bolyar	Bulgarian landholding aristocrat.
Călăraşi	Romanian free peasants.
Car	Serbian medieval imperial title.
Celep	Livestock breeder or dealer; deliverer of food to Istanbul or to military depots.
Četnik	Serbian anti-Ottoman guerrilla; Serbian World War II nationalist partisan.
Çift	Land plot on Ottoman military fiefs reserved for the fief-holder's personal use.
Çiftlik	Privately owned Ottoman capitalistic farm or estate.
Cizye	Ottoman poll-tax levied on non-Muslim subjects.
Comes/Knez	Dubrovnik head of state.
Dervenci	Ottoman mountain pass, road, or bridge guard.
Derviş	Islamic mystical order; wandering Muslim holy man.
Devşirme	Periodic Ottoman child levy; Ottoman slave administrator class.
Divan	Ottoman imperial state council.
Djed	"Grandfather" (Slavic); head bishop of the Bosnian church.
Doge	Venetian head of state.
Dorobanţi	Romanian landless peasants; Romanian serfs.
Dragoman	Ottoman foreign trade agent for westerners holding capitulations.
Emir	Turkish prince or dignitary.
Esnaf	Ottoman artisan or merchant guild.
Eyalet	Largest original Ottoman provincial military-administrative unit.
Fraţia	"Brotherhood" (Romanian); nineteenth-century Romanian nationalist organization.

Gaza	Ottoman holy war.
Gazi	Ottoman holy warrior; Ottoman border warrior.
Haiduk	Slav bandit; sometimes an anti-Ottoman resistance fighter.
Han	Ruler of Turkic or Mongol-Tatar peoples.
Hane	"Hearth" (Turkish); household originally constituting the smallest Ottoman tax unit.
Haraç	Ottoman land-use tax.
Has	Largest Ottoman *sipahilık* fief, usually granted out of imperial lands (see *Sipahilık*).
Hatti Hümayun	Ottoman imperial edict, issued by a sultan (which see).
Hisba	Islamic religious injunction against undue profiteering, fraud, and speculation among artisans.
Hospodar	"Governor" (Turkish); Phanariote-era Romanian ruler.
Janissary	Ottoman slave standing infantry, recruited through the *devşirme* (which see).
Kadı	Ottoman judge.
Kadıasker	Highest Ottoman judge.
Kaghan	Avar ruler.
Kaghanate	Avar confederative state.
Kanun	Ottoman secular law, issued by a sultan (which see).
Kapıkulu	Ottoman military-administrative slave household of the sultan (which see).
Kaza	Smallest original Ottoman provincial military-administrative unit.
Klepht	Greek bandit; sometimes an anti-Ottoman resistance fighter.
Knez	"Leader" (Serbian); Serbian princely title; head of a Serbian village commune.
Krajina	Border zone.
Kralj	Serbian royal title.
Kul	Ottoman slave.
Madancı	Ottoman metal ore miner or processor.
Mahalle	Ottoman residential quarter.
Martolos	Local Ottoman militiaman.
Medrese	Islamic mosque school of higher theological learning.
Millet	"Nation" (Turkish); a group of Ottoman subject people considered by the authorities as a legal-administrative unit, based on religious affiliation.
Mir	Russian village commune.
Miri	Ottoman Government owned properties, usually land.
Mufti	Islamic legal scholar.
Mülk	Ottoman private property, usually land.
Müsellem	Ottoman landholding light cavalry.
Narodna Odbrana	"National Defense Society" (Serbian); early twentieth-century Serbian nationalist organization supporting nationalist activities outside of Serbia.
Nazami Cedid	Early nineteenth-century westernized Ottoman military force.
Paşa	High, honorific Ottoman title of rank; high military rank (e.g., a general).
Philike hetairia	"Society of Friends" (Greek); nineteenth-century Greek émigré nationalist-revolutionary organization.
Posveta	"Enlightenment" (Bosnian Serb); early twentieth-century Bosnian Serb nationalist-cultural organization primarily supported by *Narodna Odbrana* (which see).
Pronoia	Byzantine conditional military landholding.

Reaya	"Flock" (Turkish); originally all subjects of the Ottoman state, later restricted to non-Muslims only.
Samizdat	"Self-published" (Slavic acronym); anti-Communist dissident literature.
Sancak	"Banner" (Turkish); Ottoman original military-administrative unit forming a major subdivision of a province.
Sancakbeyi	Commander-governor of a *sancak* (which see).
Securitate	Romanian Communist security and secret police force.
Şeriat	Islamic Sacred Law.
Şeyülislam	"Leader of Islam" (Turkish); chief judge and enforcer of Islamic laws.
Sipahi	Ottoman cavalryman, either fief-holding or salaried.
Sipahilık	Ottoman military fief system.
Skupština	Serbian national assembly.
Sporazum	Yugoslavian Croatian autonomous territory (1939).
Sŭbranie	Bulgarian national assembly.
Sufi	Mystical school of Islam.
Sultan	Ottoman imperial title.
Sunni	Muslim belief based on the four recognized "orthodox" legal schools of Islam.
Tanzimat	Ottoman nineteenth-century adaptive reform movement and reform group.
Theme	Byzantine regional army; Byzantine province.
Timar	Ottoman small-size *sipahilık* fief (see *Sipahilık*).
Tsar	Bulgarian and Russian male imperial title.
Tsarina	Bulgarian and Russian female imperial title.
Ulema	Islamic learned religious leadership class.
Ustaše	Croatian ultranationalist terrorist organization.
Vakıf	Ottoman income-producing property bestowed on religious establishments as endowments in perpetuity.
Vali	Highest ranking Ottoman provincial commander of professional military forces.
Veliki Knez	Medieval Serbian ruling prince.
Veliki Župan	Early medieval Serbian ruling prince.
Vezir	Ottoman governor-general or commander-in-chief.
Vilayet	Nineteenth-century Ottoman province.
Vladika	Montenegrin title for the ruling prince-bishop.
Voievod	Romanian princely title.
Voynuk	Horse breeder for the Ottoman imperial stables and the military.
Yamak	Ottoman auxiliary Janissary.
Yaya	Ottoman irregular (auxiliary) infantry.
Yürük	Turkic nomadic pastoral tribe.
Zadruga	Serbian extended communal family.
Zakonik	Medieval Serbian civil law code, issued under Car Stefan Dušan.
Zeamet	Medium-size Ottoman *sipahilık* fief (see *Sipahilık*).
Zimma	Guarantee of protection granted by Muslim authorities to their non-Muslim subjects under the *şeriat* (which see).
Zimmi	"Protected persons" (Turco-Arabic); non-Muslims subject to Muslim rule and protected by *zimma* (which see), usually denoting an inferior status.
Župan	Serbian princely title.

Land, People, and Culture

Before launching directly into the survey of Balkan history, it is necessary to place the study into context by addressing the question: What *are* "the Balkans"?

They constitute the geographical region of Europe called the Balkan Peninsula and are often labeled Southeastern Europe. Although apparently straightforward, such a description suffers from the inability of geographers to separate definitively the so-called continent of Europe from that of Asia. Despite this problematic uncertainty, few would disagree that the Balkans are part of Eastern Europe. Most fundamentally, the Balkans are defined by the assorted human societies who live there, most especially by their culture. Culture is a particular society's shared perception of reality, which is shaped by the people's mundane physical and human environments and provides a common group identity that transcends individual personal traits. When treating particular societies that inhabit a specific region, one must consider their culture. Culture itself, however, is a complex issue, existing on the small-group level as ethnicity and on the large-group level as civilization. It makes little sense to concentrate primarily on ethnic culture when compiling a general history of the ethnically variegated Balkans. More useful is the focus on the three major civilizations—the "native" Orthodox Eastern European and the two "imposed" Islamic and Western European—that have thrived there over the course of the past two millennia. Their "origins" and unique interplay among the region's inhabitants are what actually lend definition to "the Balkans."

Land

The Balkan Peninsula is a rugged, irregular, inverted triangle of land jutting southward from the European landmass into the eastern Mediterranean Sea. It is bounded on the west by the Adriatic Sea, on the east by the Black Sea, and on the southeast by the Aegean Sea. The northern land border of the Balkan triangle is partially defined by mountain ranges. The Carpathian Mountains provide a limited boundary to parts of the north and northeast, while the Julian Alps delineate the peninsula's extreme northwestern corner. Roughly 300 miles (480 kilometers) of open land carved by the Danube, Sava, and Drava rivers divide these two chains in the northwest while, in the northeast, the plains and tablelands of the Danube and Prut rivers separate the Carpathians from the Black Sea by some 125 miles (200 kilometers). In the northwest, the Sava River often has been designated a boundary because it once constituted the Ottoman Empire's most stable border in the area. Likewise, the Drava River served the same function because it formed a border for Yugoslavia. Similarly, the Prut River has been used as a Balkan boundary in the northeast, since it delineated a border of Romania. Using the Drava and Prut rivers as part of the geographical boundaries, the Balkan Peninsula encompasses some 276,700 square miles (716,650 square kilometers) of territory. (See Map 1.)

Close to 70 percent of the Balkans is covered by mountains. The name "Balkan" derives from a colloquial Turkish word for a forested mountain. Now the term also is the name of a string of mountains just south of the Danube River in today's Bulgaria, known in classical times as the Haimos (Hæmus), that stretches from the Black Sea for half the east-west width of the peninsula. To their south stretch a densely grouped series of mountain ranges—the Rila (with the highest peak in the Balkans: 9,592 feet [2,926 meters]), the Rhodope, the Pindos, and the Taigetos—to the tip of the peninsula in the Greek Peloponnese. The peninsula's west is dominated by the ruggedly limestone Dinaric and Albanian Alps, which run parallel to the Adriatic coastline but spread extensively inland. The mountains furnish an assortment of metal ores and minerals, especially in the central and northern regions. Iron, zinc, chrome, lead, antimony, copper, nickel, gold, and silver ores are present as well as such minerals as bauxite, lignite, and chromite. The oil deposits of the Carpathian foothills in the peninsula's extreme north are the largest in continental Europe.

Except for the mostly narrow coastal plains, most of the peninsula's lowlands are river valleys. The Danube's is the largest, cutting a wide swath between the Dinaric Alps and the Carpathian Mountains, narrowing at the so-called Iron Gates east of Belgrade, where the river carves a gorge separating the Balkan and Carpathian mountains, before again widening into a broad plain extending to the Black Sea. Others, such as the Drava, Sava, Morava, and Iskŭr river systems (important branches of the Danube watershed), the Aliakmon, Vardar, Struma, Mesta, and Maritsa river valleys (which run to the Aegean Sea), and the Neretva, Drin, Shkumbin, and Vijosë river valleys (which flow to the Adriatic), provide the interior with both a modicum of arable land and the primary natural lines of overland communication.

Climatically, the Balkan Peninsula is not a unit. It enjoys a Mediterranean climate along most of its seacoasts and a continental one throughout its interior.

Vegetation and land use vary with the natures of the dual climate. Along the Adriatic, Mediterranean, and Aegean coasts, the land mostly is rocky and denuded, supporting such crops as olives, grapes, figs, lemons, and oranges, and the herding of sheep and goats. In the interior, most of the mountains are forested; cereal crops predominate in the river valleys and lowlands; vineyards are found in some areas of the Danubian Plain, in the Maritsa River valley, and along the upper Sava; and livestock breeding mostly involves pigs and cows, although sheep and goats are fed on highland pastures. The line separating the two climate zones lies close to the coastline in most of the peninsula, since the mountains, which form the climatic border, push close to the seas almost everywhere. (See Map 1.)

Regarding political geography, the Balkan Peninsula historically is of strategic significance. Its location in the eastern Mediterranean makes it a crossroads of three continents—Europe, Asia, and Africa—and, since earliest recorded times, its accessibility by both sea and land opens it to political, military, and cultural incursions and contentions from all directions. In the past, six foreign empires—the Persian, Roman, Byzantine, Ottoman, Habsburg Austrian, and Russian—sought to possess, whole or in part, the benefits offered by the peninsula's strategic location and natural resources with varying degrees of success.

Interspersed among the foreign imperial efforts were those of indigenous Balkan states. Because of the peninsula's rugged geography and harsh climate, political life in the Balkans historically has been far from stable. Small states, beginning with the classical Greek city-states, have been the rule because of the mountainous topography, which tended to separate human habitation among isolated river valleys and highland plateaus, and resulted in centuries of fierce competition among the states for control of the geographically restricted available natural resources. The fact that Balkan states nearly always proved vulnerable to outside empires competing for sway in the region meant that those resources rarely benefited the inhabitants. Minerals and ores were either extracted directly by the foreigners or provided to them by regional states at their mercy.

When Balkan states managed to survive for any length of time, they did so mostly in the peninsula's interior, where the geographic division between coast and mountains had economic consequences. Often the coast, with its important seaports, was controlled by foreign states that frequently were at odds with those in the interior, thus effectively barring the latter from secure outlets to the seas. For this reason, the economies of Balkan states primarily remained agricultural long into the twentieth century.

Today the Balkan Peninsula is home to nine states as well as a small portion of a tenth—Turkey. (See Map 2.)

Albania lies in the west, along the Adriatic Sea, and encompasses 11,097 square miles (28,489 square kilometers) of territory divided into two zones: The north and central coastal plains and the much more extensive interior and south coastal highlands (Albanian Alps), which in places reach heights of over 6,550 feet (2,000 meters). Most river systems run from the highlands to the sea; chief among them are the Drin, Shkumbin, and Vijosë. Cereal production and some Mediterranean-type agriculture take place on the coastal plains, while forests and livestock pasturing predominate in the highlands. Chromium and copper represent the most important mineral resources. The capital for the state's population of 3.3 million people is Tiranë.

Bosnia-Hercegovina, with its capital at Sarajevo, was home, before the war of 1992 to 1995, to an ethnically and religiously mixed population of 4.6 million people inhabiting 19,776 square miles (51,233 square kilometers) in the peninsula's northwest. The state lies almost completely within the folds of the Dinaric Alps, some peaks of which are over 6,550 feet (2,000 meters) high. Most of the sparsely available arable land lies in the valleys of the Neretva, Bosna, and Drina rivers and in scattered small mountain basins and plateaus. Much of the terrain is covered by forest, making timber products economically important. Livestock is herded in upland pastures. Lignite, iron, and manganese are mined in Bosnia, while bauxite and lignite are worked in Hercegovina. In former times, eastern Bosnia was an important gold and silver mining region.

Bulgaria, encompassing 42,855 square miles (110,994 square kilometers), controls nearly half of the eastern Balkans and is home to 8.8 million people. Geographically, it is fairly well defined: Most of the northern border is determined by the Danube River, but the extreme northeastern portion that crosses the Dobrudzhan Plain is undefined; the Black Sea coast serves in the east; the southern slopes of the Rhodope Mountains partially define the southern frontier, but the line is arbitrary on the Thracian Plain in the southeast; and the western slopes of the Struma River valley, along with the northern bend in the Balkan Mountains, roughly form the western border. Within these boundaries lie the Balkan, Rila, and Rhodope mountain ranges and an extensive network of river systems, which generally flow north into the Danube or south to the Aegean. The plain and tablelands of Thrace and the Danube are excellent for cereal and fruit cultivation. A uniquely important crop is roses, grown in one particular mountain valley, the attar of which is a crucial and expensive ingredient in many top-of-the-line perfumes. Pigs, sheep, cows, and goats commonly are herded. Coal (both black and brown), iron, copper, zinc, and lead are important mineral resources. The capital city of Sofia has been an urban settlement since pre-Roman times.

Croatia is populated by 4.7 million people residing on 21,824 square miles (56,538 square kilometers) of territory in the northwest of the peninsula. Its crescent-shape physical configuration consists of three regions: Croatia Proper, with the state's capital of Zagreb, serves as the central core, from which stretch the two horns, composed of Slavonia, the northern lowlands lying between the Sava and Drava rivers, and Dalmatia in the south, which comprises the Adriatic coastline and the adjoining Dinaric highlands. Peaks in the mountains exceed elevations of 4,950 feet (1,500 meters) in a few areas. The Sava and Drava are the primary river systems. Much of the land is forested in Croatia Proper and in the Dalmatian highlands. Livestock is herded on upland pastures while grains are sown in depressions and valleys. Mediterranean-type cultivation and scrub evergreens proliferate along the Dalmatian coast. In the lowlands of Slavonia, cereal and fruit crops predominate. Mineral resources are limited, consisting of relatively small pockets of iron, natural gas, oil, and bauxite.

Greece, including its Aegean island holdings and Crete, encompasses 50,962 square miles (131,990 square kilometers) and 10 million people. Its capital at Athens is built around the remains of the famous ancient acropolis. Mountains cover 80 percent of the triangular-shape mainland, which forms the southern tip of the Balkan Peninsula, making less than a third of the land suitable for cultivation. The Pindos Mountains, whose highest peak—Mt. Parnassos—rises to 8,059 feet (2,457 meters), run the north-south length of the central and southeastern regions, breaking at the Gulf of Corinth, only to be continued in the Peloponnese by the Taigetos range. The mountainous interior is linked to the surrounding seas through deep valleys cut by the Aliakmon and Acheloös river systems. Most cultivation is restricted to the narrow coastlines, where typical Mediterranean-type crops, including citrus fruits, are produced. Cereal crops are grown in scattered upland plateaus, the Thessalian Plain, and in the northern Macedonian-Thracian coastal plain, which is the most extensive lowland in the state. In the mountains, Mediterranean-type scrub and pasture predominate. Although a variety of mineral ores are present—bauxite and magnesite, especially, along with deposits of iron, copper, lead, zinc, and silver—they exist in such small amounts that they are of little economic benefit. Given the ruggedness of the terrain, the great extent of irregular coastline, and the paucity of natural resources, it is little wonder that the Greek economy historically has depended on maritime trade rather than on agriculture and manufacturing.

Macedonia, situated in the center of the peninsula, today covers 9,778 square miles (25,333 square kilometers) of territory and boasts a population of 2.2 million people, governed from the capital at Skopje. It is a mountainous region where the southern Dinaric and eastern Albanian Alps meet the northern projections of the Pindos Mountains. While a few peaks in the western, Albanian Alp range can top 6,600 feet (2,000 meters) in elevation, elsewhere summits rarely exceed 4,950 feet (1,500 meters). The Vardar River system, which bisects the state from north to south, provides it with its principal lowlands. On these are grown cereals, tobacco, cotton, and some fruits as well as wine-producing vines. Close to half of the total territory is heavily forested, but there is some upland pasture for sheep and goats, along with localized cultivation in valleys and depressions. Mineral resources include small deposits of zinc, lead, iron, chrome, and manganese. In times past, gold was mined in the eastern regions.

Romania, with a territory in the peninsula's northeast covering 91,699 square miles (237,499 square kilometers) and containing 23.1 million inhabitants, is the largest Balkan state. It is divided topographically into two basic arable zones—the plains and tablelands of the Danube and Prut rivers in the south and east and the rolling, forested Transylvanian Plateau—by the boomerang-shape and territorially extensive Carpathian Mountains. Geographically, and for the most part historically, Transylvania and its neighboring regions, situated north and west of the Carpathians, lie outside of the Balkan Peninsula. The southern arm of the Carpathians, often called the Transylvanian Alps, is higher and more precipitous than the eastern, with some peaks reaching elevations of over 6,500 feet (2,000 meters). All of the river systems draining the southern Wallachian Plain and eastern Moldavian Tableland flow from the Carpathians to the Danube, while those of the Transylvanian Plateau mostly run westward, emptying into the Tisza River on the Pannonian Plain of Hungary. The Carpathians and the Transylvanian highlands are thickly forested, providing pastureland for sheep and goats and some cultivation in depressions and valleys. The extensive Wallachian and Moldavian lowlands, as well as the western edge of Transylvania, are heavily cultivated, with grains, flax, hemp, tobacco, and grape-producing vines among the important crops. Romania possesses the richest and most diverse mineral resources in the Balkans. Europe's largest continental oil fields lie in the foothills of the southern Carpathians, and Transylvania is rich in natural gas. Large deposits of salt, lignite, black and brown coal, copper, and iron, supplemented by zinc, manganese, silver, gold, and mercury, are mined in the Carpathians and in the Transylvanian Plateau. Bucharest, the capital, sits on the Wallachian Plain.

Slovenia, with a territory of 7,834 square miles (20,296 square kilometers) and a population of 1.9 million people, edges out Macedonia as the smallest state in the peninsula. Governed from the capital at Ljubljana, it lies in the extreme northwest within the terminal ranges of the Julian Alps, among which the highest peak reaches 9,400 feet (2,863 meters). The mountains lend the state a truly "alpine" appearance reminiscent of Switzerland. Most all of the land not covered by mountains consists of highly forested foothills and depressions, cut through by the upper courses of the Sava and Drava rivers. The largest area of lowland is the Drava Basin in the east, where grains and some fruits and vines are grown. Elsewhere, cultivation is undertaken in the numerous depressions and valleys. Livestock pasturing and lumbering are widespread. Mineral resources include modest deposits of oil and natural gas, brown coal, lignite, zinc, lead, and mercury.

Yugoslavia, a federation today uniting the republics of Serbia and Montenegro that together comprise 39,507 square miles (102,350 square kilometers) of territory and 10.7 million people, occupies the north-central regions of the peninsula. Its capital at Belgrade is situated strategically at the confluence of the Danube and Sava rivers. The Dinaric Alps dominate the landscape in the south and southwest of the state, and Montenegro lies almost completely within their folds. Similar to the situation of Bosnia-Hercegovina, the state is landlocked, possessing only a short length of Adriatic coastline in Montenegro, although the Morava River, which originates in the extreme south, close to Macedonia, provides a relatively direct access route linking the interior to the Aegean Sea by way of the Vardar River valley. Serbia, much the larger of the two state partners, is only partially defined by geographic features. These exist only for its southern half. The Dinaric ranges mark out the boundaries to the south and west, while the northern bend of the Balkan Mountains and the Danube River delineate the east. The northern half of Serbia's borders is mostly drawn over lowlands (Vojvodina and Srem) forming part of the Pannonian Plain and generally bisects river lines, making it geographically arbitrary. South of Belgrade the land rises into somewhat forested hill country, known as Šumadija, which is drained by the extensive Morava River system. The full range of continental crops are cultivated on the Pannonian lowlands and in the valleys of Šumadija. The more densely forested mountain regions offer pasturing and some grain cultivation. In areas of mountainous and highly barren Montenegro, Mediterranean-type cultivation takes place. In terms of mineral resources, Montenegro boasts only bauxite as significant, while Serbia is endowed with numerous deposits of brown coal, lead, and zinc, along with lesser amounts of black coal and copper.

People

The Balkans' harsh and divisive geography played an important role in shaping the lives of its inhabitants. Mountainous terrain generally fragmented human settlement among the scattered lowlands and highland plateaus, contributing to the rise of strong ethnic group identities. In a rugged land where natural resources often were limited, group cohesiveness was crucial for survival. Competitive conditions bred ethnic cultures frequently typified by extremes in expression—communal generosity and stubborn territoriality; overt hospitality and brutal atrocity; bouts of fun-loving enjoyment and irrational violence. All Balkan peoples traditionally have exhibited one common characteristic: A sense of passionate, tenacious group pride.

While the ethnographic map of the Balkans is diverse, the peninsula's population of approximately 69.3 million people (not including the inhabitants of European Turkey and the millions who reside in Istanbul) essentially is comprised of three primary groupings: Historically *ancient peoples, South Slavs,* and *Turks.* In addition, there exist a smattering of numerically smaller groups of Gypsies, Jews, and an assortment of other ethnics, such as Italians, Hungarians, Germans, Ukrainians, and Russians. (See Map 2.)

Contrary to the common perception that South Slavs form the majority in the Balkans' total population, *ancient peoples* (that is, those who reasonably can trace

the presence of ethnic ancestors in the peninsula at least back to classical antiquity)
account for some 50 percent (roughly 35 million). The ancestors of these peoples
spoke Indo-European languages. The most familiar are the Greeks, who populate
the southern extremity of the peninsula as well as the Aegean and Ionian islands and
Crete. Their ancient origins are so well known, and their classical cultural impact
on Western Europe so recognized, that they need not be described here.

Today the Greeks generally occupy the same territories as they did in antiquity,
despite the sixth- and seventh-century Slavic invasions and settlements of their
mainland Balkan possessions, which forced most Greek speakers to the coastal
peripheries for survival. Only a long process of military reconquest by the Greek-
speaking Byzantine Empire, conducted over the subsequent two centuries, permitted the Greeks to regain control of their ancient homeland's interior. Even then,
pockets of Slavic-speaking populations survived as far south as the Peloponnese and
in the region of Macedonia. Although speculative arguments have been advanced
that the lengthy Slavic incursions into Greek-inhabited regions probably diluted the
direct genetic link between modern Greeks and their classical ancestors, these
arguments are irrelevant since language, and the self-identity that it conveys (not
DNA) is the fundamental measure of ethnic culture.

Albanians speak a unique language that is thought to have descended from
ancient Illyrian. If so, they then possess an ethnic heritage equaling that of the
Greeks. This heritage would place them among the oldest existing non-Greek ethnic
groups in all of Europe, akin in time to the Basques of Western Europe. Although
today they are confined mostly to a small territory hugging the western Balkan
coastline and its mountainous interior, in antiquity the Illyrians occupied a large
swath of the western Balkans lying to the north of the Greeks, which included
present-day Albania, northwestern Greece, Montenegro, part of Serbia, most of
Bosnia-Hercegovina, and a good part of western Macedonia.

Waves of Roman, Goth, Avar, and Slav invasions and settlements pushed the
Illyrians into the generally mountainous regions that the Albanians inhabit today.
In that rough and isolating environment, their Albanian descendants evolved as a
mostly tribalized, pastoral society divided into two distinct subgroups identified by
dialect: Ghegs and Tosks. The Ghegs, who inhabit the rugged northern regions,
developed as archetypical wild mountaineer tribes—pastoral, warlike, prone to
feuding, and resentful of outside authority. The Tosk tribes, who occupy the less
intimidating southern lowlands and their highland interior, are milder in temperament and more amenable to central authority. Four and a half centuries of Ottoman
rule over the Albanians did little to weaken the structure of their society or to
moderate their deep-rooted outlooks. Traditional aversion to unified, central
political authority retarded the growth of national consciousness among them until
late into the nineteenth century, a situation that made them vulnerable to threats
from highly nationalist neighbors. Only intervention by the European Great Powers

in the early twentieth century preserved the Albanians as a nation and a state, and they have persisted as the least modernized of all Balkan peoples into the present.

The Romanians claim an ethnic heritage as old as that of the Albanians. They speak a Latin-based language that, in Romanian national thinking, derives from the Roman occupation of ancient Dacia during the second and third centuries. Dacia once included the territories of present-day Romania and the Danubian Plain in northern Bulgaria. It was conquered and occupied by the Roman Emperor Trajan (98-117) in the early second century. According to Romanian ethnic theory, when Emperor Aurelian (270-75) withdrew his legions south of the Danube in 270, the Latinized native Dacians remained behind, surviving successive waves of Germanic, Slavic, and Turkic invaders by taking refuge in the Carpathian Mountains, from which they reemerged in the thirteenth century ethnically unscathed to occupy the Wallachian Plain, the Moldavian tablelands, and the Transylvanian Plateau, where they have remained to the present. This contention is contested by many non-Romanians, who reject the possibility of Latin-Dacian survival under the adverse ethnic conditions that held in the area during the centuries of foreign invasions. They suggest that the Romanians originated south of the Danube as nomadic pastoral Latin speakers who migrated into present-day Romania some time after the arrival of the Turkic Magyars in the Danubian Basin during the late ninth century. This contention partly is based on the continued widespread existence of pastoralists in every area of the Balkans known as Vlahs, who also speak Latin-based language. In fact, the name of the Romanian region of Wallachia is derived from that of those wanderers, meaning "Land of the Vlahs." The Romanians counter this argument by insisting that the Vlahs spread south into the Balkans from Romania. The question of Romanian ethnic origins is not yet definitively settled.

As for the Vlahs themselves, the theory of their Dacian origin is contested by one that considers them descendants of Latinized Thracians, an ancient people contemporaneous with the Greeks, Illyrians, and Dacians, who inhabited the Thracian Plain (to which they lent their name), the southern and western regions of today's Bulgaria, and the eastern portions of present-day Macedonia. They were a tribal people active in livestock breeding, farming, and ore mining. Close and continuous commercial contacts with ancient Greek colonies along the Black Sea coast initially led to their early partial Hellenization, but conquest by Rome in the first century B.C.E. and six centuries of continuous Roman imperial presence resulted in the Thracians' Latinization. The inundation of South Slavs into the Thracians' homelands during the sixth and seventh centuries led to their absorption into Slavic culture or their taking to the high mountains, where they subsisted as scattered, small groups of primitive pastoralists. By the thirteenth century they acquired the name Vlah. Their wandering lifestyle, small numbers, and wide geographical dispersion prevented them from forming a nation during the nineteenth and twentieth centuries. Today they constitute an ethnic minority in all of the central and southern Balkan states, and their total number is dwindling (perhaps less than 100,000) because of their continual assimilation into the dominant ethnic groups of those states.

South Slavs constitute the second major ethnic component of the Balkan population, numbering some 29 million people (over 41 percent of the peninsula's inhabitants), divided today among seven major groups: Bosnians, Bulgarians, Croats, Macedonians, Montenegrins, Serbs, and Slovenes. The South Slavs form one of the three primary branches of the Slavic-speaking family of peoples in Europe, the others being the West and the East Slavs. The ancestors of all three entered Eastern Europe during the fifth through seventh centuries from a common homeland thought to have been located somewhere in the vicinity of the great Pripet Marshes, which straddle the border separating today's Ukraine and Belarus. They came as part of the lengthy human migratory process that is commonly called the Barbarian invasions of Europe. Initially all of the Slav tribes must have spoken dialects of a common Slavic language shaped in the Pripet homeland. But the tribal migrations in three generally different directions and into three separate environments, coupled with the passage of time and the later intrusion and settlement of non-Slavic peoples into the central areas of Eastern Europe, resulted in the formation of three distinct subgroups of Slavic speakers, corresponding to the western, southern, and eastern tribal groups.

The South Slavic tribal groups moved south and southwest from their Pripet homeland, eventually entering the Byzantine-controlled Balkan Peninsula as either allies of or refugees from the invading Turkic Avars during the second half of the sixth century. Their search for a new, permanent homeland proved successful. Today their descendants solidly inhabit virtually all of the northwestern, central, and southeastern regions of the Balkans.

Turks comprise a third ethnic component of the Balkan population. Although today numerically small—a little over 1 million people (about 2 percent of the total population)—they have played a role in shaping the history of the Balkans far beyond their numbers.

In late antiquity the rolling plains of the Danube and Prut rivers in the Balkans' northeast served Turkic tribes from the Eurasian steppes as an open door into the heart of the peninsula and the riches of the Eastern Roman Empire. Huns and related tribes swept through the Balkans in the fifth and sixth centuries, followed by the Avars and their allies in the sixth and seventh. Among these latter were the Bulgars, who established a state south of the Danube. Unlike the Avars, whose settlements in the Balkans proved transitory, the Bulgar state persisted in the face of concerted Byzantine pressures. By the ninth century the Bulgars were challenging the Byzantine Empire for political hegemony in the Balkans, but by that time they also were well on the way toward ethnic assimilation into their Slavic-speaking subject population. The conversion of the Turkic Bulgar ruling elite to Orthodox Christianity at midcentury opened the gate to their rapid and total Slavic assimilation. Within a hundred years of the Bulgar conversion, most traces of their Turkic origins had disappeared, except for their name—the Bulgars had been transformed into Slavic Bulgarians.

Oğuz, Pecheneg, and Cuman Turkic tribes appeared in the Balkans between the ninth and eleventh centuries. Most of them eventually suffered an ethnic fate similar to the Bulgars and left little lasting impression, although the Gagauz Turks of Bessarabia, a region lying east of the Prut River (now known as Moldova), and some Turks living today in the eastern Balkans may be direct ethnic descendants of those medieval Turkic interlopers. Additionally, the Ottoman Turks' five-century rule over most of the Balkans established numerous scattered enclaves of Turkish-speaking groups throughout much of the southern portion of the peninsula, with a heavy concentration in the southeastern region of ancient Thrace.

Among the scattered additional ethnic groups that individually populate the Balkans in small numbers but cumulatively total a bit over 4 million people (usually lumped together under the category of "Other" in demographic statistical tables and accounting for approximately 6 percent of the peninsula's inhabitants), the Jews deserve notice. The Balkan Jews are predominantly of southern, Sephardic origin. While some are descendants of ancient Mediterranean Jewish merchant colonists, most are the heirs of Spanish Jews who were expelled from Spain following the late fifteenth century. Numerous Spanish Jews settled in the Ottoman eastern Mediter-ranean, where they were granted recognition of self-government (on an equal footing with the Christians of the empire) and additional privileges, primarily within the Ottoman commercial class. Centered on the old Byzantine Greek port of Thessal-oniki, the Sephardic Jews came to play an important role in the international maritime commerce of the Ottoman Empire in the eastern Mediterranean.

The lack of Ottoman anti-Semitism carried over into the post-Ottoman Balkan world. The independent Balkan states of the twentieth century continued to demonstrate a tolerance for Jews that was exceptional compared to conditions elsewhere in Europe. Anti-Semitism in Romania between the second half of the nineteenth century and the 1940s was caused by an inundation of Ashkenazi Jewish refugees fleeing rising Russian nationalist chauvinism during the first half of that period, the effects of the Bolshevik revolution and civil war in Russia, and the rabid Polish nationalism of newly refounded Poland. The influx of these Jews mixed with abominable social conditions in Romania to create a volatile situation. The difference in Romanian perceptions between these northern Jews, many of whom arrived as land managers for wealthy Romanian absentee landlords, and the southern Jews, who were considered traditionally benevolent trading partners, sparked a radical reaction on the part of the Romanian peasantry, who were then suffering under the region's most inequitable land distribution system. Of all the peoples of the Balkans, only the Romanians and the Croats, who historically were tied to

Catholic Central-Eastern Europe, spawned native neofascist, anti-Semitic movements before World War II and conducted Nazi-style anti-Semitic policies during that conflict. After the German takeover of the Balkans in 1941, tens of thousands of Jews in the peninsula perished, especially in Greece and Serbia, where German occupation freed the Nazis to work their will. As happened elsewhere in Eastern Europe following the war, the majority of the surviving Balkan Jews emigrated to the newly founded state of Israel.

All "Other" ethnic groups exist as minorities in the present Balkan states. Gypsies, who number around 400,000, are found in every state, predominantly as members of the more economically strapped social classes, often earning meager livelihoods as beggars, peddlers, musicians, or black marketeers. In the past, Ottoman and Habsburg defense policies resulted in settling thousands of military colonists, hailing from disparate ethnic backgrounds, on their borders to guard against possible enemy incursions. Today close to half a million Hungarians reside in the northern Serbian province of Vojvodina, where they are joined by fewer numbers of Czechs and Slovaks, to name just two groups. Significant numbers of Hungarians and Germans also are present in the Transylvanian regions of Romania. A large Italian population is found in the Istrian Peninsula of Croatia. Descendants of Mongol-Tatars live on the tableland of Dobrudzha in both Bulgaria and Romania. Russians, Ukrainians, Ruthenians—the list can go on—join those already mentioned in a crazy-quilt pattern of small enclaves scattered throughout all of the northern Balkan states, from Slovenia to Romania. The striking ethnic diversity that the "Other" group lends the Balkans provide the peninsula with one of its most distinctive characteristics.

Culture

Although consideration of ethnicity inescapably deals with culture on the most basic level, concentrating on ethnic culture alone offers historical study little more than a localized spotlight for comprehending the human past. An exclusively ethnic historical approach is acceptable if focused on a single society. Any attempt to understand the broader historical reality by relying exclusively on ethnicity becomes bogged down in the complexities of ethnic diversity, raising the problem of differentiating the proverbial forest from the trees. General history must approach ethnic diversity within a context that makes the development and interactions of numerous ethnic groups comprehensible. This approach can be achieved by dealing with human culture on the higher level of civilization. Civilization represents the cultural forest; its member ethnic cultural groups constitute the trees.

Three civilizations coexist among the peoples of the Balkans today: The Orthodox Eastern European, the Western European, and the Islamic, of which the Orthodox

European is primary. Orthodox civilization was born in the Byzantine Empire, in which the Balkans played an integral role. Following the Islamic Turkish conquest of Byzantine Anatolia in the eleventh century, the Balkans became the chief repository of Orthodoxy, seconded by Russia, to which the Balkan version of Orthodox civilization had been exported a century earlier. So ingrained was Orthodox civilization among the Balkan peoples that it survived, with some modifications, centuries of official Islamic preeminence during the era of Ottoman domination. The same can be said regarding the import of Western European civilization, which held firm sway in the region's northwestern corner since medieval times but entered the Orthodox lands in force with the national movements of the nineteenth century, movements with which the Orthodox Balkan populations still are contending.

That two European civilizations exist may strike some as odd. When westerners speak of Europe in cultural terms, they commonly apply certain assumptions. These assumptions are based on the historical developmental phases or periods that occurred in Western Europe, such as the Dark Ages, the Renaissance, the Reformation, the Counter-Reformation, the Scientific Revolution, the Enlightenment, and the rise of modern liberal democracy, nationalism, and the nation-state. If such assumptions are not applied, then economic ones, once again based on Western experiences, are—progression from slaveholding, through feudalism and mercantilism, to the Industrial Revolution and market capitalism.

In the Balkans, only the Slovenes and Croats who inhabit the northwestern corner can be included as European because of their lengthy ties to Western European developments. As for the other Balkan peoples, their historical experiences do not coincide with the Western pattern. Their heritage is bound directly to the Byzantine Empire, which was nothing less than the eastern half of the Roman Empire that survived the "decline and fall" of the western by a thousand years and in which the living traditions of the classical world never disappeared. Thus, they did not experience a Dark Ages or a Renaissance similar to that of the Western Europeans. The close partnership of church and state in Byzantine society precluded the emergence of a Western-style Reformation and Counter-Reformation, while the theocratic society imposed on the Byzantine Balkans by centuries of Ottoman Islamic rule hindered any sort of secular Scientific Revolution or Enlightenment. When in the nineteenth century the peoples of the Byzantine-Ottoman Balkans embraced Western European concepts of nationalism, the nation-state, and liberal democracy, along with their scientific industrial-capitalist economic foundations, they did so like botanists attempting to produce new plant strains—by grafting them onto a different but closely related cultural trunk. They could do so because neither they nor the Western Europeans doubted that they were European, despite their developmental differences.

A certain set of unique cultural attributes are European. One obviously is the Greco-Roman heritage. The hyphenation of the term is important. It expresses the cultural reality of the Hellenic legacy, in that it is composed of two related but different traditions. At its base lies the sense of human reality created by the classical Greeks: The perception that the individual human is the supreme expression of universal perfection, serving as a standard against which all elements of creation are measured. That reality was reflected in every manifestation of classical Greek culture, explaining its emphasis on ideal realism and sense of timeless universality in every art form; establishing the context for mythological and philosophical development; and spawning traits of humaneness and rationality in seeking to understand the physical world. It also created in the Greek mentality deep-seated propensities toward mysticism, ritualism, and symbolism concerning the human relationship with the supernatural world.

When the Romans began their conquest of the eastern Mediterranean world in the second century B.C.E., they recognized the superiority of Greek culture in the more esoteric realms of human experience. Because of their agrarian roots, the Romans' culture stressed the value of the individual but also of the need for the individual's strong commitment to a central authority that represented the will of society and was charged with ensuring the community's maintenance, territorial expansion, and defense. Individualism, coupled with civic responsibilities, nurtured in the Romans a practicality in dealing with the world. Out of those traits grew their highly developed predilections for legalism, organizational efficiency, militarism, administration—all of the qualities needed for upholding their centrally governed, agricultural world. Practicality also fostered in them superior engineering, planning, and technical skills unmatched by any of their contemporaries. The Greeks' realism and rationality sat well with the Romans' practicality and orderliness, so the Roman conquerors flung open the door to wholesale cultural partnership.

The combination of the two cultures was not completely harmonious. Roman copies of Greek originals displayed subtle but marked differences. The Roman copy had about it a noticeable sense of concrete photographic realism that was completely lacking in the elegant, refined, and idealized Greek original. This dual quality permeated all aspects of the Greco-Roman heritage. It was sustained through the use of both the Greek and the Latin languages in the Roman Mediterranean world, and the speakers of each considered those of the other culturally inferior. Latin speakers predominated in the western Roman provinces; Greek speakers did so in the eastern ones.

When the Emperor Diocletian (284-305) divided the Roman Empire into two administrative halves to stabilize the imperial succession and to better defend the empire's far-flung borders against foreign enemies, he did so along the invisible line marking the human cultural divide in the northwestern corner of the Balkan Peninsula separating the Greek East and Latin West. (This line ran through the territory of today's Bosnia-Hercegovina.) Although his administrative action failed to solve the grave military and administrative problems facing the empire, Diocletian's splitting of the Roman state succeeded in institutionalizing the demarcation—creating the hyphen—between the two branches of Greco-Roman civilization. After him, the two branches developed along increasingly divergent lines.

A second common European attribute is the vital role played by peoples new to the classical Hellenic world—the so-called barbarians—in forging the birth of a European cultural reality. Without the fifth- through ninth-century barbarian migrations into Roman territories, one cannot imagine Europe as anything other than a geographical term. The incursions destroyed much of classical Hellenism, but that which survived was injected with large doses of the barbarians' native cultures, creating a cultural mixture that became the alloy in which Europe was cast.

Mostly Germanic peoples inundated the western, Latin-speaking areas of the Greco-Roman world. Slavs and Turks settled in its eastern, Greek-speaking Balkan region. After the dust of the initial German invasions cleared, those interlopers established settled states of their own, loosely modeled after the Western Empire they had destroyed. The Germanic states retained a bastardized form of Latin Hellenism by means of the Roman Catholic church, which survived the disruption of the invasions to serve as the cultural cement that lent them a measure of cohesion.

The Slavs, who began entering the Eastern Roman Balkans in the sixth century, never managed to destroy that portion of the classical Hellenic state. Their inroads cost the empire some territory, but its political, military, and economic strength ensured its survival. The coming of the Slavs facilitated the transformation of the East Roman into the "Byzantine" Empire, and Hellenic continuity was preserved. When Slavic states developed in the Balkans, most did so under the strong cultural influence of neighboring Byzantium. A living Hellenic tradition was imposed on the newly settled Slavs by the sheer force of local Byzantine predominance. The Greek language gained sway over those Slavs whom the empire managed to incorporate directly within its borders. Those who remained outside of the empire were brought into close cultural association with it through the invention of a uniquely Slavic written language—the Cyrillic—which was inspired by Byzantine Christian missionaries and paralleled Greek literary forms.

One last and most crucial attribute defines Europe culturally: Christianity. Without it, the other two attributes are meaningless. Although Greco-Roman tradition and the input of new peoples are important components in Europe's cultural definition, their combination with Christianity is necessary to delineate it completely.

No one today considers Syria, Jordan, Egypt, or Libya European states, yet their inhabitants once were as Hellenized and overrun by outsiders as were those of France, Italy, Greece, or Bulgaria. In the former case, the outsiders were seventh-century Arabs, who brought with them the newly born worldview expressed by Islam. Although the Islamic civilization borrowed heavily from the Judeo-Christian and Hellenic traditions, equally heavy doses of Mesopotamian and native Arabic traditions ensured its unique core cultural identity. The stages of Islam's historical development bore little resemblance to those of Europe until relatively recent times.

Christianity is the seminal factor in identifying Europe. In fact, the term "Europe," as commonly used today, did not appear until the late eighteenth and early nineteenth centuries; prior to that time the traditional term was "Christendom." Only those peoples who have assimilated the Christian worldview completely have ever been considered European. Since the early Middle Ages, those non-Christian peoples who entered geographical Europe and found themselves in contact with the region's Christian societies were forced to choose between joining them by converting or risking possible annihilation at their hands. This fact explains the importance of Christian conversion for relative latecomers, such as Bulgarians, Czechs, Hungarians, Poles, and Russians, into the European world. Their conversions were their passkeys to membership in the European community. The borders of Europe became (and remain) synonymous with the limits of mainstream Christian culture.

Instead of a single European civilization stemming from the demise of Hellenism by Christianity and barbarian incursions, two basic European variants emerged because of the cultural division within the parent Greco-Roman civilization. They can be considered analogous to twins, since the two sibling civilizations share a preponderance of fundamental traits but are different enough in character and mentality to ensure their separate individuality. Both essentially express the same Christian perception of reality framed in common Hellenic terms, but the forms of expression differ. The difference depends on the branch of Greco-Roman tradition out of which each sprang.

That which emerged in the western part of the old Greco-Roman world couched Christianity in terms of the legality, practicality, and militancy peculiar to the Romans' hierarchical Latin Hellenic culture. Latin-based Roman Catholicism, which institutionalized these basic traits in a Christian context, epitomized the cultural nature of Western Europe at its most elemental level. Every ethnic society that espoused the Catholic form of Christianity and adopted the Latin alphabet for its written language became a human component of Western Europe. Its twin emerged from the eastern, Greek half of the Hellenic world, where Christianity was expressed in the highly mystical, ritualized, and symbolic universality of Greek culture. The Christian institutionalization of those traits occurred in the Byzantine Empire's Greek-based Orthodox Christianity. Unlike the Catholic West, which brooked no deviation from its Latin-based culture, more metaphysical Orthodoxy demonstrated a multicultural tolerance. Societies espousing Orthodox Christianity were free to do so in their various native languages, but collectively they constituted members of Orthodox Eastern Europe.

Today 64 percent (44.3 million) of the 69.3 million inhabitants of the Balkans are Orthodox Christians, constituting clear majorities in the populations of Bulgaria,

Greece, Macedonia, Romania, and rump Yugoslavia (Serbia and Montenegro), while in Albania and Bosnia-Hercegovina they represent the largest religious minority. Orthodox European civilization is the historically seminal civilized culture of the Balkan Peninsula's majority population. This fact, not geography or ethnicity, definitively places the Balkans in Eastern Europe.

PART ONE

Era of Byzantine Hegemony

600–1355

By the opening of the seventh century, the eastern half of the classical Roman Empire had nearly completed its evolution into the Greek-speaking Byzantine Empire. Its Hellenism was couched mainly in terms of a highly mystical and ritualized Orthodox Christianity. Its governance was conceived of as an organic partnership between state and church, personified by an emperor who was considered God's viceroy on earth and the thirteenth apostle of Christ. It epitomized the majesty of the divinely ordained Christian world-state, expressed by the motto: One God, one Emperor, one Empire. It was militarily and economically powerful. Little wonder, then, that it exerted an overwhelming attraction on the primitive Slavic and Turkic barbarians who came to settle in the Balkan Peninsula. The newcomers found the influence of Byzantium irresistible and thus were raised, over time, to the level of "civilized" societies. When they succeeded in founding their own states, these were modeled on the empire, ultimately creating a Byzantine-like multicultural commonwealth to which they made significant contributions in their own right. When Byzantium collapsed for half a century as the result of the Fourth Crusade, its Balkan satellites vied for its imperial mantle. And when the frail, resurrected empire underwent a lingering, slow death in the face of mounting Western threats and Ottoman assaults, its Balkan cultural offspring briefly surpassed it in regional preeminence.

CHAPTER ONE

East Romans, Slavs, and Bulgars

During the late third and fourth centuries the Eastern Roman Empire managed to weather the storm of successive incursions by peoples from the north. Survival came at a cost. When the Germanic Visigoths successfully sought refuge from the Huns within the Eastern Empire's borders in 376, the situation was unprecedented. Emperor Valens (364-78) bungled the job of peacefully integrating them and a war resulted, in which the mounted Goths crushed the Roman infantry and killed Valens in the Battle of Adrianople (378). Learning their lesson, subsequent eastern emperors used such assimilation policies as administrative and monetary bribery and inter-ethnic marriages to pacify the leaders of the various invading peoples. After initially ravaging wide areas of the empire's Balkan provinces, the Visigoth Alaric (395-410), the Hun leader Attila (445-53), and the Ostrogoth ruler Theodoric (471-526) all were successfully bribed by money or titles to move their activities into the Western Roman Empire. When the Avars, Slavs, and Bulgars appeared on the borders of the Balkan provinces in the sixth and seventh centuries, the Eastern Empire's leaders and Balkan subjects had little inkling that dealing with them would prove any different or that the newcomers would transform the demographic and political landscape of the Balkans.

The Balkans and Eastern Rome to the Mid-Sixth Century

The Eastern Roman Empire's success in escaping the fate of the Western Empire at the barbarians' hands was due to its superior economic and demographic situation. The Western Empire essentially was agrarian, sparsely populated, and commercially isolated relative to the Eastern. Rome's eastern provinces lay at the heart of millennia-old civilized human development; the western ones existed on the fringes. Populous Egypt, Syria, and Anatolia enjoyed abundant and varied food resources culled from a mild climate and extensive fertile lowlands. The smaller western populations mostly faced a harsh, cold climate, extensive dense forests, and rugged, mountainous terrain; their primary food resources lay in North Africa's coastal lowlands. The Eastern Empire served as the terminus for numerous trade routes stretching eastward to India and China and southward into East Africa, and cross-border trade directly tapped into the riches of Persia, Sudan, and Ethiopia. The western provinces not only were dependent on the eastern ones for access to the fruits of long distance trade but had as cross-border trading partners only primitive Germanic, Celtic, and Berber tribal societies, which faced even harsher environmental conditions than their own. All told, the Eastern Empire possessed decisive advantages over the Western for withstanding the lengthy inroads of invaders.

While this generalized picture held true for the Eastern Empire as a whole, it was only slightly relevant for the empire's Balkan provinces, where the prevalence of mountainous and forested terrain created a situation closely resembling that in the Western Empire—a fragmented population, limited agricultural lands, and a relatively harsh climate. The peninsula's significance for Rome lay in its roles as a land bridge linking the western to the eastern provinces and as a bulwark against northern threats to the chain of coastal trading centers in its south (such as Durrës [Dyrrachion], Thessaloniki, and Byzantion) that linked the western centers to the eastern markets by sea.

Nature favored the peninsula for both roles. The tightly packed mountain ranges permitted crossing in a limited number of places, where rivers cut passes that could serve as roadways. Otherwise, overland travel was restricted to narrow coastal lowlands where they existed. The road network built was simple by Roman standards and somewhat restricted. It consisted of three major routes. The oldest was the *Via Ignatia,* which began at the Adriatic port city of Durrës, climbed through the Albanian Alps along the Shkumbin River to Ohrid (Lichnidos) in Macedonia, where it then wended eastward through the northern Pindos ranges to Thessaloniki, continued along the Aegean coast, across southern Thrace, and terminated at Byzantion, on the shore of the Bosphorus Strait. This was the shortest, most direct route linking the Roman west and east. The second major highway was the Belgrade (Singidunum)-Byzantion military highway, which ran diagonally across the peninsula from northwest to southeast, starting at Belgrade. It then followed the Morava River valley to Niš (Naissos), traversed the southern outcrops of the western Balkan Mountains to Sofia (Serdika), after which it hugged the Maritsa River down to Thrace and joined the *Via Ignatia* west of Byzantion. Also called the Diagonal Highway, it was a strategic line of communication directly tying northern Italy and Gaul to the eastern provinces. These two routes were linked by a third running north and south, which used the Morava and Vardar river valleys through Macedonia to connect Niš and Thessaloniki. None of these routes was completely free of difficult passages. All suffered from adverse seasonal weather conditions and the potential for local banditry. The limited nature of the road network placed constraints on military, economic, and personal movement in the peninsula.

Although the mountains made overland communications difficult, they did provide military defense positions protecting the peninsula's interior against attacks from the north. The few primary invasion routes following existing major roadways could be blocked effectively by fortifications erected in the passes through which they ran. Lacking fortifications, planned ambushes could suffice. The Balkan Mountains stretched across half of the peninsula like a natural fortress wall, and the northern faces of the Dinaric and Albanian Alps could be used for the same purpose. A military drawback to the mountain defenses was that not all of the numerous small passes cut by lesser tributaries of the major rivers and scattered throughout all of the ranges could be fortified. An enemy with knowledge of them could outflank the principal fortifications guarding the main roadways. Thus defensively, the peninsula's mountains were both a blessing and a curse. (See Map 1.)

By the mid-sixth century the Balkan Peninsula's populations mostly were acculturated into Rome's Hellenic civilized society. In the south, the Greeks and the Greek language predominated. To their northeast, the Thracians were Hellenized. The Illyrians, who lived north and west of the Greeks, fell heavily under Latin cultural influence from Italy. Their Dalmatian and Istrian lands in the northwest formed part of the Latin-speaking Roman prefecture of Italy, although Illyrians in the central regions of the peninsula were under the sway of the Greek-speaking prefecture of Illyricum. Numerous Illyrians isolated in the high mountains probably escaped serious contact with either Latins or Greeks and retained their native language. In the far north, the Dacians may have preserved a corrupted Latin linguistic legacy stemming from a long Roman military presence that ended in the third century.

Except for the Greek-inhabited south, the Balkans constituted little more than a transit zone for west-east military movements and an economic backwater before the early fourth century, when Emperor Constantine I the Great (306-37) established his imperial capital at ancient Byzantion in 330. The city was enlarged and renamed Constantinople (the City of Constantine). The situation then changed. With the center of imperial power relocated to the region's southeast, the peninsula's inhabitants living close to the major roadways enjoyed a brief period of commercial prosperity and expanded urbanization, as traffic to and from the capital increased. In regions away from major routes, however, local barter trade in kind remained the norm.

Despite Rome's reputation as a highly urbanized society, the majority of the empire's Balkan population was rural. Land was divided among individual free smallholdings, free village holdings, and large estates owned by magnates and worked by serfs. The exact proportion of each in the landholding scheme is unclear, but most likely the share of great landed estates generally rose at the expense of the others throughout the fourth through sixth centuries. This trend was aided by ever-escalating state taxes levied to pay for military expenses. Numerous freeholders fled into the mountains to evade rapacious tax collectors, and their properties were expropriated by the government or the magnates.

Most taxes went to support the defensive army established by Constantine I in the fourth century. The empire's borders were manned by frontier forces recruited from local inhabitants, fugitives, pensioned army veterans, refugees, and captives. Their task was to hinder an invading enemy until a mobile elite force under the emperor's command arrived to deliver the decisive blow. The elite force was comprised of paid professionals (usually barbarian mercenaries) organized into formal military units stationed strategically in the interior. In the early sixth century the frontier forces in the northern Balkans included a mixed ethnic bag of Illyrians, Thracians, Dacians, Goths, Sarmatians, Alans, and Scythians, while the mobile professional army primarily consisted of Goths and Huns.

Despite the increased prosperity of the Balkan provinces after the fourth century, their intrinsic value to the empire never equaled that of the West Asian provinces, nor did they match Italy in terms of imperial prestige. If troops were needed to bolster the frontier defenses in the east against Persia, the peninsula's elite forces were dispatched. When Emperor Justinian I the Great (527-65) set out to reconquer North Africa and Italy from the Goths, his professional forces mostly were drawn from the Balkans. When the elite forces were absent, the peninsula lay vulnerable to attacks from the north. Justinian's gamble in the west was destined to have lasting significance for Balkan history.

Risks were run in the Balkans because Justinian felt that he could depend on the frontier forces, using extensive fortifications and mountain defenses, to slow an enemy incursion until the elite units were freed from duties in the west and returned to deal with the situation. A large share of the ruinously high taxes imposed by Justinian was devoted to constructing new fortresses, renovating and enlarging older ones, and fortifying cities throughout the Balkans as compensation for the transfer of the mobile elite forces to combat fronts in the west. If the strategy of in-depth frontier defense proved insufficient and an enemy broke through before the elite forces returned, the emperor believed that he could depend on his capital to play the delaying role of last resort.

Constantinople was the largest and strongest fortress-city in Europe. It was situated on an easily defensible triangular bit of land on the European shore at the point where the Bosphorus Strait met the Sea of Marmara. Directly on its north was the large, crescent-shape mouth of a small river emptying into the Bosphorus known as the Golden Horn. On the city's south stretched the Sea of Marmara, which found access to the Mediterranean through the Dardanelles Strait. The Bosphorus-Marmara-Dardanelles seaway separated Europe from West Asia and linked the interior of Eurasia beyond the Black Sea directly to the Mediterranean. Geography lent Constantinople enormous advantages. The city was located at the most direct point along the continental divide for overland traffic to cross into the interiors of two continents, and it controlled the maritime traffic between Central Asia and the eastern Mediterranean. Constantinople was the economic and military crossroads of Europe and Asia.

By the Romans' fortifying the triangle of land on which the city sat, Constantinople became impregnable. A seawall built at the water's edge girded its southern and northern sides. Protecting the wide western land side was the most extensive and strongest set of medieval walled defenses ever erected in Europe, incorporating a series of three successively higher and thicker stone ramparts protected by a moat. For a thousand years the land walls of Constantinople saved the empire from defeat or even utter destruction by its enemies. When the Ottomans blasted holes in the land walls with artillery in 1453, the event signaled the end of Europe's Middle Ages.

Constantinople's walls protected more than the empire's capital; they guarded the womb of an emerging Orthodox European civilization. The city gave concrete expression to Constantine's policy of reconstituting the Roman Empire on a Christian moral basis. Constantine was convinced that the empire's third-century problems stemmed from a collapse of inner morale, which the traditional Hellenic religions did little to correct. Christianity was different. It provided adherents with a consistent meaning for human life and possessed a strong ethical-moral system with the necessary sanctions for its enforcement. During his bloody rise to sole rule over an empire recently divided by Diocletian, Constantine recognized the utility of tying the outlawed Christian sect to the interests of his empire—Christianity could help strengthen and perpetuate the empire by morally unifying its people.

For Christianity to serve Constantine's political purposes, it had to be correct—orthodox—in its beliefs, since a religion divided in its fundamental precepts offered little to a ruler who sought its use to reinvigorate a declining empire. Unfortunately, in Constantine's time Christianity was divided fanatically over its central issue of faith—the baffling and illogical nature of its godhead, the Trinity—between two rival Christian camps, the Arians and Alexandrines.

Within a year of becoming sole Roman emperor in 324, Constantine decided that a divided Christian church would not serve his purpose of buttressing his centralized imperial authority as the official state religion. Using the imperial position of *Pontifex Maximus,* in 325 Constantine determined to bring order to the Christian church by calling a general meeting of all leading church officials in the city of Nicæa. Constantine ordered them to settle the Arian/Alexandrine problem, set the agenda, presided over the sessions, and participated in the theological discussions. By the close of Christianity's First Ecumenical Council, an official creed was proclaimed and the high bishops (patriarchs) of Rome, Alexandria, Jerusalem, and Antioch were given canonical privileges that elevated them equally to the highest level of authority within the church. The Christian church emerged from Nicæa as the accepted state religion, with an administrative organization mirroring that of the empire.

Nicæa had important consequences for the emperor and his authority within an increasingly Christian Roman Empire. Constantine's prominent role in the council demonstrated his intention to link the spiritual authority of Christianity closely to the civil authority of the state. Nicæa made Christianity an important component of the Roman Empire, and the active participation of the emperor in church matters made it hard to distinguish between politics and religion. The Christian leadership felt indebted to him for their church's meteoric rise from persecuted sect to favored faith. He was hailed as the Thirteenth Apostle of Christ and God's viceroy on earth. While initially these Christian accolades were bestowed on Constantine personally, they thereafter were transferred to the imperial office itself, as Constantine's successors continued to solidify bonds with the church as a matter of state interest.

The founding of Constantinople gave symbolic but concrete reality to a new imperial political ideology: The Christian state church represented the true believers' temporal community whose borders were synonymous with the Roman Empire. State and church were united in an indissoluble partnership that reflected a divinely ordained world order. The emperor's role in this partnership was obvious. To guarantee the divine temporal order, the Roman emperor acted as God's supreme civil representative, governing along Christian precepts and protecting the Christian empire against all enemies. He was assisted in this by an innate alliance with the Christian patriarchs, to whose number a fifth—that of Constantinople—was added in the early fifth century.

While there existed only one Christian emperor of the Christian empire, no single patriarch was recognized as unqualified head of the church. Spiritual authority was shared equally among them and was exerted collectively through ecumenical councils. Collective spiritual authority was extended somewhat to the emperor's office, in recognition of its divine preference, but decisions in matters of faith could be made only by the councils, with or without the emperor's participation. One fact was apparent, however: The Roman emperor emerged as the dominant authority figure in the Christian state. Thanks to Constantine, East Roman Christian Europe received a divinely sanctioned framework for strong, highly centralized, autocratic political authority.

Constantine may have laid the groundwork for the emergence of a new Orthodox European civilization within a transformed East Roman (Byzantine) Empire governed from Constantinople, but Emperor Justinian I assured its success. Justinian was a ruler determined to solidify the autocratic power of his office and to realize the grandiose pretensions implied by the official Christian imperial ideology that equated the divine world order with the extent of the empire. Justinian spent his reign relentlessly pursuing imperialist goals in both domestic and foreign policy, to the point of driving the empire into near bankruptcy by the time of his death.

Internally, Justinian concentrated on consolidating his supreme authority over the state by legal and religious means. He ordered the great collection and codification of Roman law that entrenched Christian precepts and eventually came to serve as the legal foundation for state government in much of both Eastern and Western Europe until the late eighteenth century. While the code and its summary were published in Latin, the supplemental books, consisting of Justinian's imperial decrees, appeared in Greek, officially demonstrating that Greek culture was supplanting the Latin in the Eastern Roman Empire. The Justinian Code not only furnished the state with a unitary body of justice, it also entrenched as law the will of the absolute monarch.

To further his policy of cementing autocratic power through Christianity, Justinian sponsored expensive building campaigns. While much effort and resources were expended on practical civil projects, such as defensive fortifications, Justinian devoted particular attention to creating and propagating a new form of Christian church architecture intended to express the power and glory of the partnership between Christianity and the Roman imperial office. The result was epitomized in Justinian's magnificent imperial cathedral in Constantinople, Hagia Sophia (The Holy Wisdom). The domed structure epitomized the all-embracing, mystical Greek order of cultural reality and exuded symbolic representations of the emperor's supremely central role in the divinely ordained Christian universal order.

The mystical persona of the Christian emperor was reinforced further by Justinian's copious borrowings of autocratic court rituals from neighboring Persia, the final incarnation of the ancient Mesopotamian civilization. The practice became commonplace in Constantinople and served to ritualize all aspects of the imperial office. By removing consideration of the person of the ruler and ritualizing his mystical inner spiritual character, Justinian fashioned the final step in shaping the ideological structure for Eastern Christian autocratic political power, giving the Hellenic tradition of deified Roman emperors its conclusive Christian facade.

Girded with this mystical Christian aura, Justinian sought to assert his claim to supreme earthly authority in the religious sphere. He attempted to legislate theological matters in the same manner as he had the civil. Although his efforts ultimately failed, Justinian set a dangerous precedent that never disappeared completely from Orthodox European political ideology. Justinian's pretension to supreme spiritual authority has been branded Caesaropapism—control of the church by the state. Western historians and theologians often have applied the term to Byzantine (Orthodox European) political realities, but, except for Justinian's failed effort and a few cases among later Byzantine and Balkan rulers, the term has been inappropriately used outside of Russia. The traditional church-state relationship characterizing Byzantine (Orthodox European) political realities was one of union, harmony, and synthesis of the two rather than the domination of one by the other.

Using the reestablishment of Orthodox religious unity as a pretext, Justinian set out to re-create the undivided empire of the past by conquering former Western Roman lands from heretical Arian Germanic control. Between 535 and 554 he waged near-constant warfare in the west. At its successful conclusion, his empire encompassed the western lands of Italy, Sicily, most of North Africa, and the southern regions of Spain. His Vandal and Ostrogoth enemies were utterly eradicated. Administrative and religious unity of East and West was reestablished, and, over it all, Justinian briefly reigned supreme from his capital at Constantinople.

Justinian's reconquests in the west were the swan song for a unified Christian Hellenic world-state. Costs for success were prohibitive, and the empire lay militarily and financially exhausted. In 568, fourteen years after Justinian's victory, the Germanic Lombards successfully invaded Italy, and within four years the empire lost most of the peninsula, except for Rome, Ravenna, and the southern regions around Naples. Justinian died in 565 before the futility of his western policies was revealed fully, but signs of insuperable strain in maintaining them arose even prior to his death. Already, in the last decade of his life, Avar and Slav forces penetrated the empire's Balkan possessions in a prelude to the inundations that followed during the next century and a half.

Arrival of the Avars and Settlement of the Slavs

A sophisticated art of diplomacy permitted the eastern emperors to risk defending their Balkan provinces with frontier forces and fortifications alone using elite units elsewhere. Selective bribes or subsidies often bought security by playing various threatening groups off against each other. The game worked well through the first half of the sixth century, when Justinian neutralized the Germanic Lombard and Gepid threat to the Balkans, permitting him use of the peninsula's professional forces in the west.

Other raiders, however, proved more troublesome. As early as the first decade of the sixth century, Slav tribes migrating south from their Pripet homeland arrived on the empire's Balkan borders. They may have been loosely divided into two different but related groups, Antes and Slaveni, but those groupings lacked any sort of sophisticated political organization. While they often conducted destructive local raids into the empire, those Slav tribes essentially were disunited, posing more of a nuisance than a major threat to the imperial Balkan provinces. That situation changed with the arrival of the Avars in the 550s.

The Avars were a highly organized and powerful Turkic tribal confederation governed by a central ruler (*kaghan*). Justinian's attempts to enlist them as puppet allies against other Turkic and Germanic threats north of his Balkan borders backfired. Instead, by the end of the 560s the Avars crushed their German and Turk competitors, conquered the Slav tribes north of the Danube, and created a large confederated tribal state centered on Pannonia. Rather than facing fragmented and feuding tribal groups amenable to manipulation, the empire was presented with a powerfully unified state controlling the entire frontier beyond its Balkan borders.

The full import of that situation rapidly became apparent. In the early 580s the Avars outflanked the empire's Danube defenses in Mœsia by breaking across the Sava River west of Belgrade. With the Balkans' elite forces absent in the east fighting Persia, the mounted Avars freely attacked along the three major roadways into the heart of the peninsula for the rest of the decade. Thrace and the environs of Constantinople itself were ravaged. Fortunately for the empire, its major centers withstood the Avar assaults and the frontier defenses in Mœsia remained in imperial hands. Initially the imperial authorities did not view the Avar menace as fatal so long as Constantinople and the primary cities held out.

In terms of imperial prestige, however, the Avar depredations were an embarrassment for a state considering itself the divinely ordained world order. Particularly galling was the fact that large numbers of the formerly disorganized and primitive Slavs pushed south into the peninsula, either in flight from the Avars or as their infantry allies. The Slavs' disunity and lack of state structure made them difficult for the empire to deal with in the traditional manner. They had no important or sufficiently powerful tribal leaders who could be bribed or subsidized with any assurance of effectiveness. Nor could any binding treaties be signed with them for the same reason. Their primitiveness actually permitted them to exist in harsh environments that more sophisticated populations avoided, and it became apparent that the Slavs were seeking new territories to settle as much as simple plunder. The Slavs were not viewed by the imperial authorities as particularly dangerous militarily, but the lack of military forces to root them out of their Balkan footholds was distressing.

In 591 Emperor Maurice (582-602) concluded a peace with the Persians that freed him to send elite forces back to the Balkan Peninsula. Avar and Slav inroads were stopped and imperial authority was restored over most of the Balkan provinces by 602. Maurice's success, however, was short-lived. He was overthrown and killed by his own mutinous troops, sparking a Persian invasion of the empire's West Asian provinces to take advantage of the situation. The subsequent war dragged on for some twenty-five years, draining the Balkans of its elite forces. With their departure, the empire lost its former advantage over the Avars and Slavs in the peninsula. The Avars collected themselves, reasserted their control over the neighboring Slavs, and renewed their incursions. Only a huge tribute payment in 623 made by Emperor Herakleios (610-41) persuaded them to cease plundering the environs of Constantinople; it did nothing to guarantee against future depredations.

In 626 the Persians launched a concerted assault on Constantinople through Anatolia in an attempt to crush the stricken Eastern Empire. They were joined in the attack by the *kaghan*'s massed Avar and Slav forces, who threatened the capital from the European side. Avar assaults on the city's powerful land walls were smashed by the defenders, and attempts to ferry Persian troops across the Bosphorus in small Slav boats were defeated by the imperial navy using Greek fire. Immediately thereafter, Avar operations disintegrated, and the horde scattered northward in confusion, compelling the Persians to retreat. Within six years the tables were turned—the crushing defeat that the Persians had hoped to inflict on the empire was, instead, dealt them by Herakleios.

The collapse before Constantinople was a fiasco from which the Avar *kaghanate* never fully recovered. The Avar confederation slowly began disintegrating. The West Slav tribes living to the north of the *kaghanate*'s Pannonian heartland rebelled against continued Avar control, and a number of allied Turkic steppe tribes broke away. So too did the South Slav tribes who, as a consequence of their involvement in Avar activities, now lay scattered in settlements spread throughout the Balkan Peninsula from the Danube to the Peloponnese.

Probably about the time of the Avar defeat before Constantinople, two related but different tribes of Iranian (or, perhaps, mixed Iranian-Slav) ethnicity threw off Avar authority and pushed across the Danube into the northwestern and north-central territories of the Balkans—the Croats and the Serbs. Those regions already were colonized heavily by some Avars but mostly Slavs of the Slaveni group, while most of the Hellenized population had fled to the safety of the Dalmatian coastal cities and offshore islands, where they founded new cities, such as Dubrovnik (Ragusa). The newly arrived Croats and Serbs fell on the Avars and drove them northward into Pannonia, after which they brought the assorted local Slaveni Slavs under their control. Tradition credits Emperor Herakleios with encouraging and blessing the achievements of the Croats and Serbs and with rewarding them with legal rights to the lands that they occupied. This view probably is a myth. It is unlikely that imperial policy played any direct role in the events. The Croats and Serbs established two loosely structured tribal confederations comprised of the already settled Slavs. Both peoples swiftly lost their Iranian ethnic characteristics as they underwent assimilation into the Slavic culture of their more numerous subjects.

With Persia decisively defeated and the Avars in decline, the East Roman Empire should have had little trouble in assimilating the primitive Antes Slavs, who had settled in the eastern and southern Balkans, into its highly developed Hellenic culture. Unforeseen circumstances in the east, however, stifled the opportunity. In 636 the imperial forces in Syria, exhausted by the long, victorious war with Persia and largely unsupported by the heretical Monophysite population of the provinces, suffered a stunning defeat at the hands of Muslim Arab tribal armies from out of the Arabian Peninsula. The Arab forces swept rapidly through Syria, Palestine, and

Egypt, where the disaffected populations often hailed them as liberators and converted to the new Islamic faith in droves.

Herakleios could do nothing to stem these disastrous events. He had exhausted the empire's military resources in defeating Persia and, with no time to recoup, had nothing left to use against the Arab onslaught. All that he managed was a reform of the empire's military. The Constantinian frontier-mobile elite formations were disbanded and then reconstituted as combined professional territorial units of approximately 10,000 men each (*themes*), whose strength was maintained by recruitment among the inhabitants of districts in which they were stationed. In later years the territories supporting *themes* evolved into a new provincial administrative system, in which civil and military authority was combined and land tenure was dependent on service in the ranks. Herakleios's stopgap military reform, assisted by the ramparts of the Taurus Mountains in Anatolia's southeast, prevented the Arabs from conquering Anatolia, the last remaining region wholly under imperial control, and dealing the empire a fatal blow.

The calamity inflicted by the Arabs, however, nearly proved mortal. Syria, Palestine, and Egypt were lost permanently, and with them went huge tax revenues, lucrative trade centers, vast food supplies, and large reservoirs of human resources. Catastrophic economic consequences were immediate. The imperial treasury dried up, commerce collapsed, and urban life, which depended on the monetary supply and trade, contracted. The Balkan provinces, reeling from recent Avar depredations and Slav settlement, were particularly hard hit. A number of interior urban centers in the peninsula already were depopulated. Others found themselves surrounded by Slav settlements and cut off from local or long-distance trade, in which case they either withered and died or shrunk into villages. Once the impact of the Islamic eastern conquests was felt from the 640s on, urban contraction accelerated.

Although recent scholarship suggests that the collapse of urban life in the Balkans during the seventh century was not as extensive as previously believed, there is no doubt that the total number of cities declined. Because imperial administration and traditional Hellenic culture were tied closely to an urban environment, the primary foundations for Hellenizing the large number of Slavs colonized throughout the peninsula were crippled to the point of ineffectiveness. It appears that cultural assimilation mostly operated in the opposite direction, with Hellenized inhabitants holed up in walled cities, surrounded by rural Slav settlements, that slowly were being acculturated into the more primitive culture of their encirclers. Exceptions to this picture were found in the stronger walled coastal cities (e.g., Thessaloniki and Durrës), a number of cities in Thrace and the southern Balkan Mountain highlands (Plovdiv [Philippopolis] and Sofia), and some of the major cities in the Greek south (Athens and Corinth). Yet the sad truth was apparent: By the second half of the seventh century, the empire had lost any semblance of real control over most of the Balkans.

Large numbers of Slavs now inhabited extensive areas of the peninsula, especially the districts served by the major highways. But significant numbers of the Hellenic populations survived. In many places the two coexisted, usually in the more out-of-the-way regions, such as in the Dinaric Alps. The Hellenic populations did not simply disappear because of widespread Slavic settlement. Undoubtedly many were killed in the turmoil of the Avar campaigns. Others fled into the mountains, where they either founded small hill towns or turned to a more village-oriented pastoral life; in some cases, as with the Illyrians, they joined already present ethnic relatives and preserved their identity intact, emerging historically centuries later as distinct ethnic groups—such as the Albanians and Vlahs. Still others sought refuge along the coastlines in cities and on islands, where, thanks to imperial maritime resources, traditional Hellenic existence was maintained and the authorities readily provided them with protection and support. Such especially was true along the Dalmatian and Albanian Adriatic coastlines and in the Greek-inhabited Adriatic and Aegean southern regions.

That Greeks survived in the south proved fortuitous for the Eastern Empire. Thessaloniki, the second largest imperial port city in the Balkans after Constantinople, held out as a major center of Greek habitation and culture despite being surrounded by Slav settlements. So too did fortified cities such as Athens and Corinth. While many Slavs established themselves in the region of Macedonia, their numbers progressively grew smaller as they settled into areas farther south; conversely, the numbers of indigenous Greeks remaining in the countryside increased proportionally. It is probable that villages in entire localities remained exclusively Greek-speaking in the interior of central and southern Greek districts, while some villages were mixed Slav and Greek.

A high level of ethnic intermixing occurred between Greeks and Slavs in the southern interior. Nevertheless, a large enough pool of Greek speakers remained in the region to serve as the springboard for the southern Balkans' re-Hellenization, which commenced in the eighth century and continued in earnest throughout the ninth, after imperial administration largely was reestablished. Hellenic survival and recovery in the southern Balkans, coupled with the reduction of imperial territory in the east to heavily Hellenized Anatolia, were crucial factors in the transformation of the Eastern Roman into the "Byzantine" Empire. Despite retaining an ethnically diverse population within its constricted borders, the empire essentially became Greek in language, ideals, and spirit.

The Establishment of the Bulgar State

A political void existed in the Balkans during the second half of the seventh century following the successive blows of Avar depredations, Slav settlement, and imperial military, administrative, and economic contraction resulting from the empire's losses to the Arabs in the east. Into that Balkan void rode the Bulgars in the late 670s.

The Bulgars were a confederation of steppe nomadic Turkic tribes who formerly were part of successive tribal confederations centered on Ukraine, particularly those headed by the Gök Turks and the Avars. Those associated with the Gök Turks were reduced to Khazar tributaries in the 630s, while the Bulgar tribes previously tied to the Avars broke away after the *kaghanate*'s defeat before Constantinople. One of the latter was the Onogur Bulgars, led by Han (ruler) Kubrat (605-65), who established the mixed ethnic confederation of Great Bulgaria in the northern Caucasus and the southern Ukrainian steppe. In 635 Kubrat drove the Avars from his lands and forged friendly relations with Eastern Rome. Another Bulgar rebellion against Avar control was led by the chieftain Kuber (ca. 675-ca. 88) in the late 670s. He headed a "tribe" of mixed ethnicity (composed of Avar war prisoners) in Slavonia. Kuber rebelled and led his small force south into the central Balkans, where they settled in northern Macedonia. Although his followers were a mixed bag of Bulgars, Thracians, Illyrians, and possibly Franks, the imperial authorities collectively identified them as "Bulgars."

Kubrat's Great Bulgaria was shattered by the Khazars in the early 640s, and, on his death, leadership of the Bulgar tribes was divided among his surviving sons. One tribal group moved northeast and settled in the upper Volga-Kama River region, becoming the future Volga Bulgar state. Two smaller groups traveled westward to Pannonia and northern Italy, where they fell under the control of the Avars and the East Roman governor of Ravenna, respectively. The main branch of Bulgars, led by Asparuh (died 701), pushed southwestward along the Black Sea coast to the Danube delta in the Balkans' extreme northeast and subdued the Slavs and Avars on the Wallachian Plain. Sometime in the late 670s Asparuh's Bulgars crossed the Danube into Dobrudzha, a region nominally under imperial authority, where they built a fortified encampment and settled.

Despite previous good diplomatic relations between the Eastern Empire and Asparuh's father Kubrat, Emperor Constantine IV (668-85) felt ill-disposed to lose even a small portion of his already shrunken imperial territory to the intruders. He attacked the Bulgars with the limited military forces that he could muster, hoping to expel them from their bridgehead south of the Danube, but he was defeated. Unable to keep his military away for long from the more vital Anatolian front against the Arabs, Constantine signed a peace treaty with Asparuh in 681. By the agreement's terms, the emperor officially recognized the existence of a Bulgar state in Dobrudzha, Asparuh was granted control over Mœsia between the Danube and the Balkan Mountains, and the empire undertook to pay the Bulgar ruler an annual tribute. The treaty was signally significant. Throughout the previous decades of turmoil in the Balkans, the empire never relinquished its claim to nominal control of the entire peninsula. Now, for the first time, the empire surrendered specifically designated regions to outsiders. Asparuh's Bulgar state became the first barbarian state to receive official recognition in the Balkans (and in Eastern Europe).

Little is known concretely about the early Bulgar state. It seems it was typically Turkic steppe nomadic and ruled by an autocratic *han* (a title associated with the sky-god Tengri and directly inherited from the Gök Turks). Another Gök Turk association was the ruling clan's name, Dulo—a leading clan among the Western Gök Turks. Also typical was the Bulgars' political structure, with authority divided between inner and outer clans and all Bulgars elevated above the non-Bulgar tributary populations, who initially participated in the state only as subjects. In Asparuh's state, the tributaries mostly were Slavs, most of whom were collectively known as the Seven Tribes, living on the Danubian Plain in Mœsia.

Further evidence culturally linking the Balkan Bulgar state to Turkic steppe traditions was the layout of the Bulgars' new capital of Pliska, founded just north of the Balkan Mountains shortly after 681. The large area enclosed by ramparts, with the rulers' habitations and assorted utility structures concentrated in the center, resembled more a steppe winter encampment turned into a permanent settlement than it did a typical Roman Balkan city.

There is evidence for Late Roman/Byzantine cultural influences on the early Bulgar state. Asparuh's father Kubrat had been an imperial ally and had received an official court ranking (*patrikios*). Kubrat may even have been baptized an Orthodox Christian on a visit to Constantinople as a child (although Asparuh and his followers were staunchly pagan). Kuber, probably one of Asparuh's brothers, unsuccessfully attempted to preserve his ephemeral state in Macedonia by tying himself to imperial clientage. The fact that Asparuh received an annual subsidy from the empire confirmed his position as a tributary client of the emperor, in many respects similar to his father's previous situation.

Additional evidence for Roman/Byzantine influences in the early Bulgar state were stone commemorative inscriptions carved during the early eighth through ninth centuries. These mostly were written in Greek, using Greek letters rather than Turkish runes. Their content included names of Bulgars bearing Roman/Byzantine titles, Roman/Byzantine terminology, and Roman/Byzantine dating systems. Apparently the Bulgars commonly mimicked some political and administrative imperial models, maintained close direct relations with the imperial court, and, given their own low level of literacy, used some Hellenized subjects as functionaries from an early date.

Both the Turkic and the Roman/Byzantine traditions helped shape a viable Bulgar state. The former provided an elite warrior ruling class headed by an autocratic *han*. Their responsibility was to uphold the ruler's undisputed central authority, defend and expand the borders of the state, and ensure that the subject populations remained loyal and productive. In return, the ruler guaranteed their dominant position within the state, their monopoly on all important governing-military offices, and their well-being vis-à-vis their peers and others. The latter tradition imparted an imperial ideal to the rulers that was geared toward fashioning a sedentary, sophisticated state, which could take advantage of skills possessed by its non-Bulgar subjects. Such skills were reflected in record keeping, court ceremonies and bureaucratic talent. Together, the two traditions forged a Bulgar *state* in the true sense of the word.

The borders of Asparuh's state stretched from the Black Sea in the east to the northern bend of the Balkan Mountains in the west, and from the Carpathian Mountains and Dniester River in the north to the Balkan Mountains in the south, encompassing the regions of southern Bessarabia, Dobrudzha, Wallachia, and Mœsia. The Bulgars acquired a string of imperial Danube frontier fortresses, including Vidin (Bononia), Nikopol (Nikopolis), and Silistra (Durostolon), but they seem to have died out, with their ruins serving as quarries for new Bulgar towns built close by. The important Black Sea port of Varna (Odessos) remained under imperial control. (See Map 3.)

The state's population was divided unevenly between Bulgars and non-Bulgars. The number of Bulgars was low—probably no more than 10,000 warriors and their families—generally concentrated on the Danube's southern bank and throughout Dobrudzha. They conducted a mixed pastoral and agricultural economy and established a lively barter trade with imperial territories to the south. The non-Bulgars constituted the majority population and consisted of sedentary Slavs living in villages and pursuing agriculture, providing infantry forces and paying tribute in kind to their Bulgar overlords. They lived in tribal groups led by native chiefs, who gradually were admitted into the ruling elite's lower ranks. Some Slav tribes on the state's peripheries were more Bulgar tributaries than outright subjects. Almost nothing is known about the continued existence of Hellenized Thracians and Dacians in the state's territories. Initially the Bulgars maintained their own settlements segregated from the subject Slavs. The inevitable ethnic interbreeding, however, apparently began at an early date.

Within a decade of its establishment, the Bulgar state began to play an important role in Byzantine Balkan affairs. Using new *theme* forces introduced into the Balkans by Emperor Constantine IV, in 688 Constantine's heir Justinian II (685-95, 705-11) set out to punish the Slavs and Kuber's "Bulgars" in the region around Thessaloniki. Although he succeeded in subduing a number of Slav tribes, he was ambushed by Kuber and lost most of his army, prisoners, and booty. Asparuh, at peace with the empire, did not intervene in the campaign. Soon thereafter Justinian II was deposed and banished. After a decade in exile, in 705 Justinian enlisted the military aid of Bulgar Han Tervel (701-18), whom he considered a client, and won back his throne in Constantinople. In a display of official gratitude, Justinian brought Tervel to the imperial palace, where he was invested with both a court robe and a high ceremonial imperial rank, enthroned next to Justinian, and received the obeisance of the imperial court hierarchy.

Tervel's treatment by Justinian was more display than true sentiment. Justinian quickly tired of paying the annual tribute to the Bulgars stipulated in the 681 treaty and prepared for war. Forewarned of the emperor's hostile intentions, Tervel unleashed a surprise attack on the empire and thwarted Justinian's plans. When Justinian was overthrown for a second time in 711, Tervel used the occasion as grounds for ravaging the empire's Thracian territories until a treaty was signed with Emperor Theodosios III (715-17) in 716. The commercial terms in that document spoke for a sophisticated and effective administration in the Bulgar state that could control and regulate commerce. By treaty arrangement, the Bulgars opened a market in Constantinople.

Both parties needed peace to jointly face the impending threat of an Arab invasion. In 717 that invasion materialized, and the Arabs laid siege to Constantinople. The Bulgar-Slav troops sent by Tervel proved instrumental in forcing the Arabs' withdrawal. In terms of saving medieval Europe from Islamic conquest, many historians consider the Arabs' defeat by the Byzantines and Bulgars before Constantinople an achievement equal to, or greater than, that of Charles Martel in defeating the Moors in France at the Battle of Tours (731/32).

Affairs in the Bulgar state are sketchy for the half-century period following Tervel's reign. With the death of Han Sevar (725-39), the house of Dulo ended and a civil war erupted between two factions of Bulgar warrior-aristocrats (*bolyars*). One side held a pro-Byzantine stance, advocated peace with the empire, and may have been allied with Slav tribal leaders. The other side was anti-Byzantine, sought war with the empire, and may have been committed to preserving exclusive Bulgar elite status within the state. It appears that the peace party dominated until 755 and the war party thereafter.

The Byzantine authorities apparently knew little about the workings of Bulgar society and generally treated the Bulgars with contempt, hostility, and fear. Expediency alone had led them to recognize the Bulgars' state on what they still considered imperial territory, and they bided their time hoping for an opportunity to destroy them. The chance came in the mid-eighth century when the Bulgars' internal civil strife coincided with the fall of the Arab Umayyad imperial dynasty, which freed Anatolian military forces for use against the divided Bulgar state. Between 756 and 775 Emperor Constantine V (741-75) conducted a series of nine wars against the Bulgars in which he oftentimes came close to obliterating their forces. Yet despite consistent victories in the field, Constantine failed to destroy the Bulgar state. It survived because, protected on the south by the ramparts of the Balkan Mountains, its core northern territories remained unconquered.

The rise of the Arab Abbasid caliphate in the east generally kept Constantine's successors preoccupied throughout the remaining quarter of the eighth century, but warfare in the Balkans did not completely cease. Emperor Constantine VI (780-97) and his mother Empress Irene (797-802) conducted Balkan campaigns whenever possible, targeting small Slav tribal groups, whom the Byzantines collectively called *Sklavinai,* in hopes of winning easy military victories for propaganda purposes in the capital. Their operations focused on regions well away from Bulgar interest, such as Thessaly, Attica, the Peloponnese, and Thessaloniki, and intentionally avoided any serious engagement with the Bulgars.

One of Constantine's and Irene's campaigns did, however, initiate the successful Byzantine recovery of the Greek south. In 782 and 783 the eunuch general Stavrakios attacked the Slavs near Thessaloniki, marched southward through Thessaly, winning victories against Slav opponents along the way, and raided into the Slav-held Peloponnese. The campaign won few concrete gains, but the imperial triumph accorded Stavrakios in the capital presaged the emphasis that the authorities soon placed on regaining the Greek southern Balkans. Further emphasis came with the creation of a new Balkan *theme*—Macedonia—carved out of the already existing Thracian and Helladic *themes* and centered on western Thrace, with its commander (*strategos*) stationed at Adrianople.

The recovery of Greece began in earnest with Emperor Nikephoros I (802-11). Around 805 imperial forces operating out of Corinth extended Byzantine authority over the northern Peloponnese. Patras was recovered and rebuilt, and a new *theme* was created to encompass the regained territory. Soon afterward the Slavs in the Peloponnese unsuccessfully revolted against the growing Byzantine presence. In response, Nikephoros transferred Greek-speaking populations from other regions of the empire to the Peloponnese and central Greece, forcibly settling them in Slav-inhabited areas. To ensure the successful Hellenization of the Slavs living in Greece, an Orthodox church organization using the Greek language exclusively was imposed throughout the region. It conducted an intensive campaign of Slav religious conversion. Aided by the church, the newly arrived Greek-speaking colonists inexorably absorbed and dominated the neighboring resident Slavs. In less than a century after Nikephoros's efforts, Greece once again predominantly was Greek.

CHAPTER TWO

The First Bulgarian Empire

Byzantine-Bulgarian relations dominated Balkan affairs between the ninth and early eleventh centuries. Asparuh's small Bulgar state was transformed into a large and powerful Slavic Bulgarian empire controlling the central and eastern Balkans. By officially embracing Orthodox Christianity and creating a Slavic literary language and culture, Bulgaria became both the primary Balkan political rival of the Byzantine Empire and Byzantium's chief competitor for the mantle of leadership in the Orthodox world. But the late ninth- and early tenth-century "Golden Age" of Bulgaria proved ephemeral. The Bulgarian decline that set in soon after preserved Byzantine political and cultural hegemony in the Balkans and opened the door to the political development of other Balkan peoples, particularly the Croats and Serbs.

Bulgaria's Rise to Empire

During the 790s forces of Frank King Charlemagne (771-814) attacked the Avar *kaghanate,* inflicting on it a crushing defeat and winning Charlemagne control over western Pannonia, northern Dalmatia, and Slavonia, which were inhabited mainly by Croats. Those Avars remaining in Pannonia may have been dealt a second blow around 803 by a group of former Bulgar clients led by Krum (ca. 803-14), who by 807 was undisputed *han* of all the Bulgars. Much historical speculation surrounds Krum's reign. He supposedly expanded the Bulgar state to the Tisza River and a common border with Charlemagne's Frank Holy Roman Empire. He is portrayed as cementing centralized autocratic power and as favoring the Slav tribal leadership over the traditional Bulgar *bolyar* elite. Sadly, primary sources supporting such contentions are lacking.

An attack on the Bulgar state by Byzantine Emperor Nikephoros I in 807 gained only Krum's animosity and seven more years of unrelenting warfare, during which Krum captured large swaths of the empire's lands south of the Balkan Mountains. In 811 Krum ambushed and destroyed Nikephoros's army in those mountains and the emperor was killed. It is said that, after the battle, Krum had Nikephoros's skull fashioned into a silver-lined ceremonial drinking cup, from which he and his chiefs drank—a traditional steppe nomadic ritual assertion of military dominance over a defeated enemy. Krum quickly capitalized on his victory and overran much of Thrace and Macedonia. Cities and fortresses either were captured or abandoned by their inhabitants, and large numbers of Byzantine troops voluntarily deserted to Bulgar service or were taken prisoner. Byzantium fell into political turmoil.

In 812 Krum offered the empire mild peace terms, given his military position: The return of all lands taken during the war in exchange for an annual tribute, an exchange of war prisoners, and free bilateral trade relations. The imperial authorities refused and the Bulgars continued their depredations, plundering the environs of Constantinople and threatening to assault the city. Unable to breech the land walls, however, the Bulgars could not force a peace on the empire. Krum was still menacing the capital at his death in 814, but a military impasse had developed.

Two years later the stalemate was broken. In 816 Emperor Leo V (813-20) negotiated with Krum's successor Han Omurtag (814-31), essentially agreeing to the terms Krum had originally offered. The ensuing peace lasted for thirty years, during which time the Bulgar state underwent significant expansion. Omurtag and his successor, Malamir (831-36) (who may have reigned until 852 under another name, Presyan), benefited greatly from the peace. They took advantage of the Avars' collapse to enlarge their state in the north and west, acquiring Belgrade, eastern Slavonia, and the northern territories of future Serbia. A firm hold on Pannonian territories east of the Tisza River was secured and efforts made to secure control over Transylvania. (See Map 3.)

By the time the Bulgars appeared in the Balkans' northwest, two fluid Croat states in western Pannonia and northern Dalmatia lay under Frankish authority. The Franks recognized the Croats' native rulers as tributaries and pursued active Roman Catholic missionary efforts among them. In 819 the Pannonian Croats rebelled against Frank rule and were joined by a group of Slav tribes hailing from the Timok River region, who technically were under Bulgar authority. This event led Omurtag to campaign in the northwest during the 820s to prevent the Franks from pushing eastward and threatening Bulgar lands. When hostilities ended, Omurtag's state bordered on the Franks' Croatian tributaries.

In the mountains south of Dalmatian Croatia and west of the Morava River, a small Serb state ruled by one Vlastimir arose by the ninth century. Bulgar westward expansion may have inspired some Serb tribes to unite defensively under Vlastimir's authority. The Byzantines, seeking potential allies against the Bulgars, sent agents and gold to encourage Serb unification. Sometime after 839 the Bulgars invaded Serbian territory, and fighting continued for a number of years, ending only when the Serbs agreed to pay the Bulgars tribute. In the end, the newly unified Serbian state retained its independence and Bulgar westward expansion beyond the Morava was blocked.

While enlarging his state northwestward, Omurtag faced a growing domestic problem involving Christianity. The Bulgar state contained significant numbers of Christians from the beginning, and the many Byzantine refugees and captives settled during Krum's wars increased the Christian population further. Although the Bulgars originally took a syncretistic approach to non-Bulgar deities to ensure having as many gods on their side as possible, by Omurtag's time the Bulgars associated Christianity with the Byzantine Empire. The pagan Bulgar *bolyars* viewed the religion as a threat to their sociopolitical order, which was based on rights derived from divine pagan totems. Moreover, the Orthodox Christian hierarchy was controlled by the Patriarchate of Constantinople, so subject Christians might be considered Byzantine agents who threatened the state's continued independence. Mass conversions to Christianity raised the specter of future Byzantine clientage. Omurtag therefore persecuted Christians as a matter of state policy. In spite of his efforts, however, the religion continued to spread.

The 816 peace treaty remained intact until it expired in 846, after which the Bulgars invaded Byzantine Macedonia and pushed west of the Vardar River for the first time. By the early 860s Bulgar Han Boris I (852-89) had clear possession of northern and western Thrace (including an outlet on the Aegean Sea), the best part of Macedonia (including Ohrid), and a corridor extending from Macedonia to the Adriatic Sea, near the Byzantine port city of Vlorë (Valona).

Bulgar territorial gains in the Balkans represented Byzantine losses, and the empire's holdings shrank to the Greek-speaking southern regions, the Adriatic city of Durrës, and nominal control over the Dalmatian coastline. Those lands in the western Balkans not held by Croats and Serbs were controlled by the Bulgars. (See Map 3.)

The "Golden Age" of Bulgaria

By the mid-ninth century the Bulgar state was the dominant power in the Balkans and extended northward to the rim of the Bohemian Plateau, where it bordered on the newly arisen Slavic Great Moravian state. Its size, however, did not ensure security. The Balkans' rugged terrain and restricted road system made administrative control difficult, and the ruler's authority in his far-flung lands was uneven and oftentimes questionable. While Byzantium remained the Bulgars' primary rival in the south, northward expansion created new outside threats—the Frank Kingdom and Moravia—from the opposite direction, placing the Bulgars at a strategic disadvantage. After unsuccessfully attempting to deal with that situation militarily, Boris I devoted the rest of his reign to skilled diplomatic maneuvers intended to secure his state both domestically and internationally.

Internally, the Bulgar state's population was divided among the ruling Turkic-speaking Bulgars, a hodgepodge of Slavic-speaking tribes, and a smattering of Greek-speaking former Byzantine subjects. The Bulgars appeared destined to lose the military advantages lent them by their steppe traditions because the number of elite Bulgars was declining steadily, and they faced inevitable assimilation by their sedentary subject peoples. Externally, the Bulgar state contended with an implacable Byzantine enemy on its south, the potentially dangerous Frank Kingdom to its northwest, and, after the 830s, a new Turkic steppe nomadic threat from the northeast—the Magyars. The latter were clients of the Khazars, who, in turn, were allies of the Byzantines. The Magyars' appearance raised the specter of a possible Byzantine-coordinated two-front war.

Boris was aware of the innate and potential dangers to his state. While he could do little to correct the administrative problems imposed by the mountainous terrain, in an inspired decision he deftly addressed the dangers of both a divided population and possible Byzantine aggression by turning to Christianity. Christian conversion could eliminate the religious-cultural barriers separating his polyglot population and cement a new common cultural bond in their place, producing a unified Bulgarian people more loyal to the central government and far easier to administer. By adopting Christianity as the official state religion, the Bulgars also would gain recognized membership in the Christian European community, which would permit normal international relations with other European states and stave off possible extinction as an alien threat by either the Byzantine or East Frank/Holy Roman empires. A transcendent consideration for Boris also may have been the universal validity that Christianity lent a ruler, who, as God's representative on earth, stood above the rest of society, like the emperor in Constantinople.

Boris's active efforts to adopt Christianity for his state were precipitated in 862 when Great Moravian Prince Rostislav (846-70), aware of the political implications of Christian conversion, requested from Emperor Michael III (842-67) Byzantine missionaries to counteract similar German activities in Moravia in an attempt to escape Frank political suzerainty. Michael, quick to grasp the opportunity for forging a new anti-Bulgar alliance in the northwest proffered by Rostislav's petition, happily complied. In 863 he dispatched to Moravia two Greek brothers from Thessaloniki, Constantine and Methodios.

The two missionaries were sons of an imperial official. Both were well educated and fluent in the Slavic dialect spoken in the immediate neighborhood of Thessaloniki. Constantine, an accomplished linguist, philosopher, and diplomat, already had at hand a Slavic alphabetical system of his own creation. Known as Glagolitic, it consisted of a complicated series of signs rooted in a mixture of Greek, Phoenician, and assorted original letters, into which Constantine had translated some basic Orthodox liturgical texts using the local Macedonian dialect. The fact that he and Methodios promptly set out for Moravia with a number of texts already translated meant that Glagolitic was created prior to the Moravian mission. The most plausible explanation is that the alphabet originally was intended for a planned future mission to the Bulgar state.

Once in Moravia, the two missionaries proved so successful that the German Catholic church leadership vehemently denounced them to the pope. At that time the growing split between Catholic and Orthodox Christianity had not yet reached breaking point, and Orthodox clerics still considered the pope an honored Christian patriarch. Moreover, the Byzantines acknowledged ultimate papal jurisdiction over Moravia, since it lay well north of the ecclesiastical line in the northwestern Balkans separating the spiritual domains of the pope and the patriarch of Constantinople. Constantine and Methodios were summoned to Rome by the pope and they complied.

The row instigated by the Germans over the Byzantine Moravian mission became known as the Three Language Heresy. The German church claimed that only Hebrew, Greek, and Latin were acceptable "sacred" languages for the divine Scriptures. In Rome, Constantine eloquently defended his new Slavic alphabet, stressing that, while Greek and Latin originally were pagan and Hebrew the language of Jews, Glagolitic was Christian from its inception. The papacy, threatened by increasing German efforts at church autonomy, sided with Constantine, who then entered a monastery in Rome, took the monastic name of Cyril, and died in 869 without returning to Moravia. Methodios was made Moravian bishop and did return, but a pro-Frank coup there in 870 ushered in a flood of German clerics who used Latin exclusively and overwhelmed Methodios's diocese. After his death in 885, his followers were expelled from Moravia by the dominant German church authorities. Various later ninth-century popes agreed with the German argument that Glagolitic was uncanonical, and its use soon died out in Moravia.

While the Byzantine Moravian mission floundered, developments in the Balkans took an important turn. In 864 Emperor Michael attacked the Bulgar state with his combined Balkan and Anatolian forces while most of Boris's troops were concentrated in the north facing Moravia. Unable to offer effective resistance, Boris immediately accepted Michael's conditions for a quick ending to the hostilities. He agreed to adopt Christianity from Constantinople, to permit Greek clergy into his state to undertake the conversion of his people, and to break off permanently an alliance with the Franks. As a friendly concession from Michael, Boris was permitted to annex a piece of territory southeast of the Balkan Mountains, called Zagora, that he already controlled.

In 865 Boris was baptized a Christian and adopted the name Michael, in honor of his godfather, the emperor. A number of leading Bulgars followed Boris's example.

Pagan temples throughout the Bulgar state either were destroyed or were converted into Christian churches. The Greek clergy sent by the Byzantines established a Greek-speaking ecclesiastical organization and set to converting the population. Terrified of losing their sky-god Tengri's protection, and concerned over rapidly increasing Byzantine influence, a number of Bulgar *bolyars* rebelled in 866 but were suppressed. In retaliation, Boris liquidated many of the old *bolyar* clans, strengthened his authority by creating a new class of dependent service nobility, and imposed a new legal system modeled on the Byzantine, leaving Bulgar ethnic dominance broken.

Boris shared the *bolyars'* worries about the growing Greek presence in his state. He was aware that a Greek-speaking church organization in his lands operating under the authority of the patriarch of Constantinople might result in clientage to the Byzantine Empire. Bulgar independence stood under direct threat. In 866 circumstances provided Boris with an opportunity to overcome the dire political situation created by conversion. An emotional schism dividing the churches of Constantinople and Rome had developed over the uncanonical election of the Constantinopolitan patriarch. Photios (858-67; 877-86), a noted philosopher, was rushed through the clerical orders for eligibility to replace an illegally deposed predecessor. Pope Nicholas I (858-67) originally tolerated Photios's election because he sought jurisdiction over the western Balkans and Byzantine-controlled southern Italy in return for his support. When Photios proved ungrateful and did not make the payment, Nicholas excommunicated him as a usurper in late 866, and Photios reciprocated in kind.

Seeking both recognition of his royal authority and ecclesiastical autonomy for his state's Christian church, Boris was not particular whether they came from Constantinople or Rome. He capitalized on the split between the two by playing a masterful diplomatic game. Boris requested missionaries from Rome to replace the Greek clergy already in his state. Pope Nicholas, however, refused Boris both a royal crown and an authorized autonomous state church organization. Then, after Michael III was overthrown by Basil I (867-86), Photios was deposed as Byzantine patriarch, and Basil determined that the Bulgar church must be prevented from falling under papal authority. He called an ecumenical council in Constantinople during 869-70 to heal the Photian schism and packed it in favor of the Byzantine clergy. Over the objections of the small papal delegation, the Bulgars easily won recognition of an autonomous Bulgarian Orthodox church from the Byzantine ecclesiastical authorities, carrying with it implied de facto recognition of Boris's royal prerogatives.

Boris immediately sought to turn church autonomy into real political advantage. He needed some way of countering the increased Greek clerical presence following the council, but the pope's adamant refusal to grant him state church autonomy precluded help from Rome. Once again events transpired in Boris's favor. Some of Methodios's disciples expelled from Moravia following his death arrived at the Bulgar state's borders in 886, bringing with them their Glagolitic liturgy. Boris welcomed the refugees with open arms, offered them his patronage, and helped them establish a missionary operation centered on Ohrid in Bulgar Macedonia, where they trained youths for the clergy and translated the entire Orthodox liturgy into Slavic. The newly trained Slavic-speaking priests then were sent among the state's Slav subjects. As their influence spread and the numbers of converts multiplied, a new sense of community and state was created within the population. Separate ethnic identities slowly merged into a common Bulgarian one, and regional or tribal loyalties perceptibly shifted to the state, personified by its now-Christian ruler. A state of Bulgaria, as opposed to a Bulgar state, was born.

Leading the successful Slavic mission in Bulgaria was Kliment, Methodios's former disciple and head of the Ohrid mission, and his assistant Naum. Besides translation work, Kliment established a school in Ohrid that trained students exclusively in the Slavic alphabet. Boris appointed him first archbishop of a Bulgarian Orthodox church independent from the Greek archbishop seated in the capital at Pliska. While at first the new church used the Glagolitic alphabet originally designed by Constantine-Cyril, a more simplified Slavic writing system was needed to increase the numbers of trained native Slavs in the church's ranks.

Kliment and Naum led the effort to design and propagate a new Slavic alphabet based on modified Greek letters, which they named Cyrillic in honor of their mentor. Cyrillic was precise in representing all Slavic phonics. The Greek liturgical texts in Bulgaria soon were translated into Slavic using the new letters, and native Bulgarian clergy were trained in Cyrillic literacy. From Macedonia the new alphabet spread throughout the extensive territories under Boris's control, permitting him to displace the Greek clergy in Bulgaria and to create an officially independent state church organization on the Byzantine model. Bulgarian independence from Byzantium thus was fortified.

The Christianization of the Bulgarian population by Slavic-language missionary activity may have signaled the collapse of Turkic Bulgar culture in Bulgaria and the victory of ethnic Slavicization, but concrete supporting evidence regarding those processes is lacking. Ultimately the Turkic Bulgars were assimilated by the Slavs. The total Slavicization of the Bulgar elite most likely was a gradual result of the Slavic Cyrillic alphabet's success rather than its cause. In any event, Christianity swept away the pagan beliefs of both Slavs and Bulgars, and its propagation in Slavic lent the state and its population a common language that bound them together into a single people and culture.

Boris emerged from his struggle for a Slavic church as the divinely ordained autocratic ruler of a culturally unified state with a loyal population. He adopted the trappings of an Orthodox Christian autocrat, based on the only available model—the Byzantine emperor. As Christian autocrat, he issued law codes (heavily influenced by Byzantine examples), revamped the state administration, erected churches, founded monasteries, and patronized religious arts. While he used Christianity for political purposes, he also was devout in his personal Christian beliefs. Members of his family, including his sister, already were Christians at the time of his baptism, and he took seriously his founding of Christian monastic communities. Boris was so deeply religious that, after a serious illness in 889, he abdicated the throne and retired to a monastery that he had established outside of Preslav.

The legacy of Boris to both Bulgaria and the Orthodox world in general was important. His Christianizing efforts laid the foundation for a Slavic literary culture of far-reaching portent. All of Helleno-Christian culture was opened to Slavic speakers through translation. Moreover, the new Bulgarian literary workers soon produced original works of their own, demonstrating that the Cyrillic alphabet was the most significant cultural tool created for the Slavs of Eastern Europe. Through it they could advance and expand their indigenous cultures in their native terms, permitting them to hold their own against foreign pressures that often threatened their very existence as ethnic entities. Because of Boris's astuteness, the future of the Serbs, Russians, Macedonians, and even of the non-Slavic Romanians was affected significantly.

Vladimir (889-93), Boris's eldest son and successor, sympathized with the anti-Christian and anti-Byzantine stance of the remaining Bulgar *bolyar* elite. When he actively attempted to revive paganism in Bulgaria, Boris emerged from retirement and toppled him. A state council was convened in Preslav, a Slavic and Christian center, unlike traditionally pagan and *bolyar*-dominated Pliska. The council recognized Vladimir's deposition, released Simeon, Boris's younger son, from monastic vows, and proclaimed Simeon ruler. Christianity was declared the official state religion, and Preslav was designated as the state's new capital. The council also may have installed Cyrillic Slavic as the official language of both church and state. Having saved his life's work, Boris then retired permanently to his monastery.

Simeon I (893-927) became the greatest of all Bulgarian rulers. He successfully overcame a series of state-threatening situations, won Byzantine recognition of Bulgaria's equal imperial status, and ultimately guaranteed forty years of Bulgarian-Byzantine peaceful coexistence following the stormy warfare between them that characterized much of his reign. He was a consummate diplomat and a skilled military strategist as well as religiously devout and cultured. He excelled in patronizing monasticism, building projects, and, particularly, literary activity. Simeon apparently took a personal interest in historical writings and sponsored the first original Bulgarian literary works, such as those of Chernorizets Hrabŭr and Ioan Ekzarh.

Ironically, Simeon was not groomed in childhood for the throne—that had been his elder brother's upbringing. Boris intended an Orthodox church vocation for his younger son, culminating in his becoming Bulgarian archbishop or, if fortunate, patriarch. Simeon had been sent off to Constantinople as a teenager, where he became a monastic novice, took the name of Simeon, and spent a decade in religious study. He became fluent in Greek, and, on his return to Bulgaria, he took up residence in a monastery outside of Preslav, where he led a Greek-to-Slavic literary translation project before being elevated to the throne in 893.

One of Simeon's first acts as ruler was the complete elimination of the Greek church hierarchy inside of Bulgaria. He confirmed Kliment Ohridski as western Bulgarian archbishop and raised the Bulgarian cleric Konstantin to the bishopric of Preslav, which encompassed eastern Bulgaria. Greek authority was undercut completely, and the Greek clergy fled the state in droves. They were replaced by Slavic-speaking Bulgarian clerics, thus virtually assuring Bulgaria's complete religious independence. Preserving Bulgaria's political independence, however, was another matter.

A trade conflict over changes in long-standing Byzantine-Bulgarian commercial relations initiated by Emperor Leo VI (886-912) in 894 escalated into war. Early Bulgarian victories compelled Leo to seek Magyar assistance. While Leo's forces kept Simeon pinned in the south, his navy ferried the Magyars south across the Danube, after which they ravaged northeastern Bulgaria as far south as Preslav. Taken completely by surprise and tottering on the brink of defeat, Simeon demonstrated that he had learned Byzantine ways well. He appealed for help to the Pechenegs, a powerful Turkic steppe people and traditional enemies of the Magyars, who attacked them in their rear and drove the main body of Magyars west into Pannonia. With the northern threat neutralized, Simeon concentrated his forces on Byzantine Thrace, where he won a major victory near Adrianople in 896. A treaty confirming Simeon's control over most of the Balkans and granting him an annual tribute payment from the Byzantines was finalized in 897. Sixteen years of peace with Byzantium followed the treaty, permitting Simeon to conduct the munificent Slavic cultural patronage for which he became noted. By staging military threats during that period, Simeon was able to negotiate new territorial acquisitions in Macedonia and Thrace from Byzantium without actually fighting. (See Map 3.)

War with the Byzantines resumed in 912 after Emperor Alexander (912-13) refused to pay Simeon the annual tribute stipulated in the 897 treaty. Alexander's death soon after hostilities commenced, however, threw Byzantine state affairs into chaos. A hastily arranged regency council for young Emperor Constantine VII Porphyrogenitos (913-59), headed by Patriarch Nicholas Mystikos (901-7, 912-25), was forced to deal with Simeon, whose army was before Constantinople's walls by late 913. Negotiations led to major concessions on the part of the regents and to Mystikos meeting Simeon outside of the city's walls and performing some sort of coronation ceremony. What that "coronation" of Simeon actually signified remains uncertain to this day.

There are four interpretations of the event's meaning. One is that Simeon was adopted as the emperor's spiritual son. A second is that he was bestowed the rank of "caesar," as Tervel had been by Justinian II a century earlier. A third view is that, since young Constantine VII apparently became betrothed to one of Simeon's daughters, he was crowned the official imperial father-in-law—the *basileopater*. The fourth and most probable interpretation is that Mystikos actually crowned Simeon emperor of the Bulgarians. It certainly was a title—*tsar* in Slavic—that Simeon used after the event, and it made perfect sense once Bulgaria became a Christian state.

The traditional pagan Bulgar title of *han* had little appeal to Christian rulers, while that of emperor encompassed the rank and prestige of the old title but linked them to the Christian Byzantine political model. Byzantine political philosophy permitted the acceptance of such a title for non-Byzantine rulers because, no matter the titles of others, the Byzantine emperor remained the supreme earthly authority figure. The fly in the ointment for Simeon was that his new title was conferred by a weak regency council and not by an emperor in person. Early in 914 Mystikos and his coregents were overthrown by Zoe, young Constantine's mother, who attempted to negate the coronation agreement. Simeon compelled Zoe to recognize the arrangement by military force. Yet Zoe's government was as unstable as the former regency, so her acknowledgment of Simeon's imperial title carried no guarantee of permanent official Byzantine legitimization.

Proof soon came in 917, when Zoe attempted to renege on her peace with Simeon. She enlisted the Pechenegs for a joint assault on Bulgaria in an attempt to shore up support for her regime. The war was completely unprovoked. Zoe sent a fleet to ferry the Pechenegs across the Danube in coordination with the landing of the main Byzantine army on Bulgaria's Black Sea coast. Perhaps bought off by their old ally Simeon, the Pechenegs failed to appear. Simeon then smashed the invading army outside of Pomorie (Anchialos), inflicting the most crushing Byzantine defeat since Krum's massacre of Nikephoros a century earlier.

Having cleared Thrace of Byzantine forces, Simeon found himself in a dilemma similar to that which had faced Krum. He consistently won on the battlefield, but without a fleet to cut the capital off from the sea, he could not force a conclusive decision on the Byzantines, who could hold out behind the protection of Constantinople's impregnable land walls. To make matters worse, for three years after Pomorie Simeon had no set government in Constantinople with which to negotiate. Zoe was deposed in early 919, and there followed a period of instability until Romanos I Lekapenos (920-44) was installed as senior emperor to the teenager Constantine VII. Meanwhile, Simeon was distracted during the early 920s by events in the small Serbian state on his western border.

After the death of its first ruler, Vlastimir, Serbia suffered from a protracted succession struggle. In the 890s Petr Gojniković (892-917) secured both the princely throne and Simeon's protection. Peace between Serbia and Bulgaria lasted until 917, during which time Slavic Christianity penetrated among the Serbs from their powerful neighbor. In 917 Petr was ousted by Pavel Branović (917-21), who allied himself with the Byzantines once on the throne. In a confusing welter of local border military operations, the Serbs briefly managed to preserve their state's independence from Bulgarian control under Knez (Prince) Zaharije Prvoslavljević (921-24), although Simeon won clientage from numerous Serb tribes not part of the Serbian state.

While Simeon toyed with the Serbs, he continued inflicting bloody defeats on the Byzantines and ravaging the empire's territories as far as Constantinople and Corinth. Byzantine diplomacy foiled his attempt to gain a North African Arab fleet for a combined assault on Byzantium's capital. In 923 Simeon once again brought his army before Constantinople, pillaged its suburbs, and successfully demanded a meeting with Emperor Romanos. To forestall any ambushes by either side, the two wary rulers met outside of the city walls on a jetty built out over the Golden Horn. What exactly was discussed is unknown but apparently a peace was agreed on (but no document signed), and Romanos recognized Simeon's imperial title and status as equal to his own. Simeon then marched north, and in 924 he launched a military avalanche on Serbia to settle affairs there. Defeated Serbia was ravaged and annexed to Bulgaria.

Romanos refused to ratify the agreement he had reached with Simeon. He was willing to pay Simeon an annual tribute but balked at Simeon using the title "Emperor of the Bulgars and Romans." Whether Simeon actually *used* that specific title is unknown; the only sources are hostile Byzantine ones. If Simeon did, it may not have signified a claim to the Byzantine throne so much as a proclamation of his right to rule over former "Roman" (Byzantine) subjects and lands that the Bulgars had won from the Byzantine Empire since the late seventh century; in such a case, the title's use was a claim to Bulgarian territorial legitimacy. Just as likely, however, Simeon's alleged use of the title may have proclaimed his intention of replacing Byzantium with his Bulgarian empire as the divinely ordained Christian world-state.

Serbia's annexation brought Bulgaria a shared border with the Kingdom of Croatia in the Balkans' northwest, which was governed by its greatest medieval ruler Tomislav (ca. 910-28), an ally of Byzantium. Throughout the ninth century Dalmatian Croatia, although technically under Frank suzerainty, drew closer to the Byzantine orbit. A rebuilt Byzantine navy brought most of the Dalmatian coastal cities back under direct imperial control in the ninth century. The Croats remained entrenched surrounding the cities and in the hinterlands under a prince of their own. Although some Croat tribes accepted Byzantine suzerainty, an active Byzantine presence in Dalmatia declined as a result of Byzantium's bitter struggle with Simeon's Bulgaria, and the region essentially was left to its own devices.

A Dalmatian Croat rebellion in 875 ended Frank suzerainty and an independent state was created, although the Franks retained control of Pannonian Croatia for a while longer. The princely throne of the new state proved unstable, with occupants following one another in rapid succession. The most significant development occurred in 879 when, as a result of one of the normal coups that determined Croat leadership, the successful claimant Branimir (879-92) pledged his state's loyalty to the pope. From that time on Dalmatian Croatia received papal recognition of its independence in return for Rome's spiritual jurisdiction within the state.

Tomislav gained the throne of Dalmatian Croatia sometime around 910, consolidated an army and navy, and liberated Pannonian Croatia from depredations inflicted by the Magyars, who had settled on the Pannonian Plain after 895 and were terrorizing their neighbors. Tomislav incorporated Pannonian Croatia under his rule and established a border with the Magyars along the Drava River, creating the first united Croat state. His Croatia probably included Dalmatia, what is today Croatia Proper, Slavonia, and the greater part of Bosnia. There was no permanent capital but Tomislav's chief residence appears to have been Biograd on the Dalmatian coast. Around 923 Tomislav concluded an alliance with Byzantium against Simeon. Fearful of being caught between the Byzantines in the south and Croatia in the northwest, Simeon invaded Tomislav's lands in 926 but suffered a resounding defeat. Tomislav was crowned king about that time and emerged as the ruler of a militarily strong state. With his death in 928, however, united Croatia disintegrated in civil war.

As one of his final political acts, in 926 Simeon proclaimed his imperial status by elevating the Bulgarian archbishopric of Ohrid to the level of an independent patriarchate, thus completing the Byzantine Orthodox cultural model in Bulgaria. The all-powerful Orthodox Christian Bulgarian *tsar* now ruled in partnership with an official native patriarchal Orthodox church. Both were cloaked in all of the outward trappings of Byzantine ceremonial. The Byzantine forms couched in the Slavic cultural dress of Simeon's Bulgaria became the model for all future non-Byzantine states within Orthodox European civilization—in particular, Serbia and Russia. Many historians refer to the rise of a Byzantine Commonwealth in describing the phenomenon. If so, Simeon's Bulgaria set the precedents and standards for its future membership.

While on his way to beleaguer Constantinople once again in 927 and to force the Byzantine authorities to recognize his imperial status officially, Simeon died. Although imperceptible at the time, his demise marked the beginning of Bulgaria's decline.

Bulgaria Falls

When news of Simeon's death reached Serbia, the Serbs successfully threw off Bulgarian rule and restored an independent state under Časlav Klonimirović (ca. 927-ca. 960), who immediately allied himself with Byzantium. During Časlav's reign cultural influences, religious from Byzantium and Slavic from Bulgaria, permeated Serbia. Despite later efforts by the Roman Catholic church to win the Serbs for western Christendom, the Slavic Orthodox Christianization that accelerated during this period virtually guaranteed the Serbs' lasting membership in Orthodox civilization.

On gaining the Bulgarian throne Tsar Petŭr I (927-67) immediately invaded Byzantine Thrace to display Bulgaria's continued military strength. His show of force worked. Emperor Romanos, preoccupied with the Arabs in Anatolia, swiftly made peace. By the terms of the agreement, Petŭr's imperial title officially was recognized, he received an annual tribute, and he married Romanos's granddaughter Maria Lekapena. The autocephalous Ohrid Bulgarian patriarchate was recognized, and so too was Bulgarian control of Macedonia. In return, Petŭr agreed that his imperial title was valid in Bulgaria alone, and he recognized the imperial primacy of the Byzantine ruler. In one short campaign Petŭr gained virtually all that Simeon had struggled for during his entire reign.

Romanos's generosity in 927 is a matter of scholarly debate. Perhaps Romanos feared that the pope would recognize the titles of the Bulgarian ruler and patriarch, which would have resulted in increased papal influence in Bulgaria and, thus, restriction of Byzantine influence in the heart of the Balkans. By granting recognition first, the Byzantines forestalled such possible papal infiltration.

The presence of a Byzantine-born *tsarina* (empress) in Bulgaria increased Byzantium's influence at Petŭr's court. Bulgarian officials began using Byzantine court titles, although the underdeveloped nature of the Bulgarian bureaucracy at the time makes it unlikely that they conducted the same duties as their titular Byzantine counterparts. Byzantine influences also were apparent in religious cultural activities, such as in church structures and decoration, literature, architecture, and music. These developments, however, appear almost wholly confined to court circles surrounding Maria Lekapena and did not filter down to the general population in the forms of heretical religious movements or antigovernment opposition, as some socialist scholars once contended.

Little is known concretely about much of Petŭr's reign. Until the final years, virtually everything written about his Bulgaria is somewhat conjectural. Extant evidence indicates that pagan religious practices and the number of ethnic Bulgars declined to insignificance. Only Orthodox Slavic Bulgarians appear in the sources. Slavic-speaking Christian *bolyar* landlords held elite status in Bulgarian society, serving as officials in the central government, local provincial administrators (possibly possessing considerable autonomy depending on their distance from the capital), military commanders, and high church prelates. Important issues sometimes were dealt with by state or church councils of high officials, but these probably were not a regular part of the governing institution. The *tsar* ruled both through edicts, insofar as they could be enforced on the *bolyars* in the countryside, and through Byzantine-like law codes.

Christian conversion had brought with it assorted Christian institutions. Besides the hierarchical structure of the Byzantine Orthodox church, monasticism particularly was popular and widespread. Petŭr's reign apparently nourished monastic growth in both number and landholding. Bulgaria's most venerated and popular native saint, Ivan Rilski, lived during the period. He founded the greatest monastic center of medieval Bulgaria, Rila Monastery, in the wilds of the Rila Mountains sometime in the late 930s. His reputation for holiness, his renunciation of worldly materialism, and his rigorous monastic testament to his followers won him undying admiration among the common people, renown among the ruling elite (including Petŭr himself), and numerous imitators on all social levels.

Rural peasants formed the majority in Bulgaria's population. Some were small landholders living in free villages while others were bound to large estates owned by *bolyars* or monasteries. The proportional balance of the two within the overall rural population is undetermined. Taxes were paid in kind since Bulgaria did not mint its own coins at the time. A small urban population existed, undoubtedly including numerous foreigners, such as Greeks and Armenians. Many were involved in trade and crafts since Bulgaria's geographic location made it an important commercial transit center between Byzantium and European or Eurasian markets. In terms of acquiring goods and hard currency, trade was important for Bulgaria.

One Bulgarian development during Petŭr's reign was the rise of the Christian Bogomil dualistic heresy, an Asian Manichæan variant probably imported through Armenian Paulician intermediaries who earlier had been resettled in Thrace by the Byzantines for use as border guards against the Bulgars. Bogomilism was founded by the mythical priest-preacher Bogomil (a name meaning "worthy of God's pity"), who operated in Bulgaria. Bogomil concepts spread from Bulgaria into Byzantium and then to West Asia. They also moved through the Balkans to Dalmatia and on into Italy and southern France, where they acquired new names—Patarinism, Catharism, and Albigensianism.

The Bogomils certainly believed in some form of dualistic spiritual reality pitting a metaphysical "good" against a material "evil"; rejected established Christian church institutions; preached the value of poverty, simplicity, and asceticism; and espoused antiestablishment concepts condemning most existing political and social institutions. Historical scholarship long held that Bogomilism became a popular vehicle for mass political and social protest among the Bulgarian peasants. Unfortunately, the only sources regarding Bogomilism were produced by its Bulgarian and Byzantine theological enemies, whose venom may have blown its popularity and significance out of proportion. Recent scholarship purports that such an elevated theological system was unlikely to have inspired the illiterate peasant population, whose religious beliefs traditionally were tied to elemental materialism. No evidence exists for Bulgarian Bogomils leading or massively participating in any known political or social protests. In fact, no sources prove that Bogomilism actually enjoyed a mass following. It appears that the heresy was confined to a small number of literate believers scattered throughout Bulgaria who played an active role in propagating dualist concepts among others of their ilk in the central and western Balkans. The Bogomils probably were little more than a nuisance to the devout religious and state authorities.

Petŭr's good relations with Byzantium did not prevent Byzantine efforts to reduce Bulgaria's presence in the Balkans. During Petŭr's reign the Byzantines rebuilt their old alliance with the Magyars, who now occupied the Pannonian Plain to Bulgaria's north. This union again threatened Bulgaria with a possible coordinated attack on two fronts. The death knell of the First Bulgarian Empire, however, did not originate in that alliance but in another forged by Byzantine Emperor Nikephoros II Phokas (963-69) with the rising state of the Kievan Rus' on the Ukrainian steppe to Bulgaria's northeast.

An outstanding general and leader, Nikephoros brought Byzantium exceptional military successes, recovering Crete from the Arabs in 961 and conducting a series of victorious campaigns against the Arabs in the east. Personally he was an ascetic who patronized the emergence of organized monasticism on Mount Athos—the Holy Mountain—in the Chalcedon Peninsula east of Thessaloniki. In the centuries that followed, the monasteries of Mount Athos collectively evolved into the greatest and most influential religious center in the Orthodox world. The Athonite monastic communities became the recruiting ground for patriarchs, set the trends in most Orthodox cultural spheres—art, literature, architecture—and imposed their precepts indelibly on the church in general. All Orthodox states eventually founded their own monastic communities on Athos, linking themselves to the most important existing wellspring of official Orthodox culture.

Fresh from victories in the east, in 965 Nikephoros refused Petŭr the annual tribute stipulated in the 927 treaty and mobilized his Balkan forces in Thrace against Bulgaria. He called on his Rus' ally Svyatoslav (962-72) to harry the Bulgarians from the north. Svyatoslav did more than requested; in 967 his troops crushed the Bulgarians and occupied extensive Bulgarian territories. Petŭr suffered a stroke and abdicated, dying in 969. Nikephoros became concerned over Svyatoslav's decision to remain in Bulgaria, which was not part of their arrangement. To speed a Rus' withdrawal, Nikephoros released Petŭr's son, a hostage in Constantinople, who returned to Preslav and immediately was hailed by the *bolyars* as Tsar Boris II (967-71). He served as a Byzantine client charged with expelling Svyatoslav from his Balkan foothold.

Boris was in no position to do the job on his own, so Nikephoros, again preoccupied with eastern affairs, summoned the Pechenegs to attack Svyatoslav in the rear. Their assault on Kiev forced the Rus' ruler to retire northward, but, contrary to expectations, Svyatoslav defeated them. Attracted to the wealth and civilization of Bulgaria, he swiftly returned, capturing Preslav, reducing Boris to a subservient vassal, and incorporating Bulgarian forces into his army. Meanwhile, Nikephoros was replaced as emperor by another general, John I Tzimiskes (969-76), who, tiring of Svyatoslav's activities in Bulgaria and Thrace, determined to expel him completely from the Balkans.

In 971 Tzimiskes sent a fleet to the Danube while he led his army against Svyatoslav from the south, easily traversing the unguarded Balkan Mountains and taking Preslav. The impotent Tsar Boris was captured and Svyatoslav's forces were bottled in the Danube River port city of Silistra. Rus' efforts to break the Byzantine siege in open battle failed, forcing Svyatoslav to surrender on terms. The Rus' ruler was permitted to withdraw as a "friend" of Byzantium in return for agreeing never again to attempt a permanent lodgement in the Balkans.

The Rus' episode was a disaster for the Bulgarian state. Boris was paraded through the streets of Constantinople as part of Tzimiskes's official triumph and subsequently publicly divested of his imperial regalia. The autocephalous Bulgarian Ohrid patriarchate was abolished, reduced to an archbishopric, and placed under the authority of the Patriarchate of Constantinople. Bulgaria itself was dismembered. Tzimiskes annexed its eastern regions, Mœsia and Dobrudzha, and integrated them directly into the Byzantine administrative system. By this time the Magyars had stripped away all of Bulgaria's Pannonian and Transylvanian holdings, leaving Wallachia an administrative no-man's land. Only the western regions centered on Macedonia remained in Bulgarian hands.

Western Bulgaria largely was unaffected by the Rus' invasion and Tzimiskes's conquests. Tzimiskes made no effort to extend his authority into the region, and soon his full attention once again turned to the perennial Arab problem in the east. Beyond manning the Bulgarian forts along the lower Danube and installing two military governors in Mœsia and Dobrudzha, there apparently was little direct Byzantine presence in annexed eastern Bulgaria, and in Macedonia the Bulgarians virtually were independent.

Bulgarian leadership in Macedonia coalesced around a certain Count Nicholas's four sons, David, Moisei, Aron, and Samuil. Wary of the talented military emperor, the brothers waited for Tzimiskes to die in 976 before moving to unite all of the western Bulgarian lands under their collective authority. Word of their activities reached former Tsar Boris II and his brother Roman, captives in Constantinople since the 971 debacle. They escaped and set out for Macedonia, but Boris was killed by a Bulgarian border guard who failed to recognize him. Roman may have been accepted as ruler by the four brothers, but this is uncertain. By 988, however, Samuil alone ruled over western Bulgaria.

Although modern Macedonian nationalists claim Samuil's state as their own, there is no historical support for the assertion. Macedonia was strictly a geographical term at the time. Samuil himself called his state Bulgarian, as did his Byzantine enemies. It was considered by all the direct continuation of the Bulgarian Empire with a new capital at Ohrid, which was somewhat protected from direct Byzantine assault and lay at the heart of Samuil's primary western power base. A seemingly conclusive argument for Samuil's conscious sense of Bulgarian continuity was his reestablishment of the Bulgarian Ohrid Patriarchate and appointment to its seat of the prelate who had held patriarchal office at the time of Tzimiskes's conquest of eastern Bulgaria.

Tzimiskes's earlier humiliation of the Bulgarian *tsar* made it impossible for his imperial successors to accept the old Byzantine-Bulgarian imperial relationship of near equality, and an independent Bulgaria was considered unacceptable. The Byzantines grew even more determined to obliterate Samuil's state after he attacked the regions of Thessaloniki and Thessaly in the late 970s. Taking advantage of a civil war over the succession to the Byzantine throne, Samuil moved to expand his control over all of the western Bulgarian lands, and his success in pushing as far south as Thessaly spoke for a collapse of Byzantine authority in the central Balkans. By 986 Samuil asserted control over half of the eastern Bulgarian lands lost in 971, including the city of Sofia.

Emperor Basil II (976-1025), sitting unsteadily on the throne following the civil war, could ill afford the affront to imperial prestige by permitting Samuil's successes to go unpunished. He invaded Bulgaria in 986 at the head of his armies but failed to capture Sofia, his objective. During Basil's retreat, the Bulgarians ambushed him in the mountains and slaughtered his forces. Basil barely managed to escape. His hope for swift revenge on Bulgaria was foiled because he lacked troops and faced a rebellion in Anatolia. In desperation, Basil concluded an alliance with the Rus' ruler Vladimir I (ca. 980-1015) that ultimately resulted in Vladimir's conversion to Orthodox Christianity and Basil acquiring a large contingent of Rus' troops. With Rus' aid, Basil gained uncontested hold on his throne, while Vladimir received the ready-made Cyrillic Orthodox culture created in Bulgaria a century earlier, which elevated his primitive state to a civilized society.

Meanwhile, Samuil continued his expansionary policies in the Balkans, regaining most of Tzimiskes's Bulgarian conquests by the early 990s. Samuil's forces raided almost at will deep into Byzantine territory, as far south as the Peloponnese and west to Durrës and Epiros. Thessaly was conquered and a large portion of its population transferred north to resettle depopulated Bulgarian regions. By 997 Samuil controlled all of Macedonia (except Thessaloniki), Mœsia, Epiros, Thessaly, western Thrace, Durrës, and much of present-day Albania. Byzantium's Balkan possessions teetered on the verge of complete collapse.

Until he settled matters in the east, Basil had to counter the Bulgarians in the Balkans mostly by diplomatic means. In the early 990s he concluded an alliance against Samuil with Jovan Vladimir (died 1016), who ruled a renewed Serbian state centered on Zeta (present-day Montenegro), but the move proved fruitless. Samuil turned his attention to Jovan in 997 and defeated him, gaining control over Zeta and Raška, which were transformed into client vassal states. He then pushed farther into the Balkan northwest, bringing Zahumlje (today's Hercegovina) and Bosnia into his growing Serbian client-state menagerie. Following those successes, in 997 Samuil had himself crowned *tsar,* ruling an enormous empire stretching from the Adriatic to the Black seas and from the Aegean Sea to the Danube River.

In his search for anti-Bulgarian allies, Basil also turned to the ruler of Croatia, Stjepan Držislav (969-97), in an attempt to reassert an active Byzantine presence in Dalmatia, which by Basil's time essentially had disappeared. Držislav, however, proved ineffective as a counterforce against the Bulgarians. Samuil pushed to the border of Dalmatia, and Držislav died in 997. Soon thereafter Croatia was weakened by a power struggle among the dead ruler's sons. Byzantium, too occupied with Samuil in the south, could do nothing to stabilize the situation. The Byzantines left it to their Venetian allies to intervene in the region, which proved of great consequence for Dalmatia's future.

At the turn of the millennium, Basil at last could undertake a concerted effort to crush Samuil. Again Basil placed himself at the head of his troops and advanced on Sofia, which this time fell into his hands. Determined to obliterate Bulgaria, Basil unleashed a relentless, sustained, year-round military offensive. From Sofia, he reoccupied most of Mœsia. Then he sent forces south into eastern Macedonia and opened the way to Greece. Soon eastern Macedonia and Thessaly were returned to Byzantine control. Basil then turned north once again, marched to the Danube, and captured the fortress city of Vidin, despite Samuil's diversionary attack on Adrianople. By 1004 Basil was back in Macedonia, where he defeated Samuil in battle outside of Skopje. In the following year Durrës was betrayed back to Basil. Four years of Basil's resounding campaigning demonstrated that, when free from threats in the east, the Byzantines could concentrate overwhelming force in the central and southern Balkans against any possible Bulgarian threat. In turn, Samuil lost half of his territories and his troops proved unequal to the Byzantines in standup combat. His Macedonian heartland was now caught in a pincers between Basil's gains along the Danube and the Byzantine forces in Thessaly.

After 1005 the war dragged on for another decade, but its details are lacking. Finally, in 1014 Samuil was forced to make a stand with his main army in a fortified position blocking the Belasitsa Pass through the eastern Macedonian mountains. Basil attacked, found a way to outflank the Bulgarian position and crushed Samuil's forces. Although the Bulgarian ruler escaped, some 14,000 of his men were said to have been captured. Basil supposedly had them blinded, except for one out of every hundred men, who was spared one eye so that he could lead the rest back to Samuil's camp. Samuil, stricken by the sight of his blinded army, suffered a massive stroke and died two days later. The victory and its grisly aftermath won Basil the sobriquet of *Boulgaroktonos*—"the Bulgar-Killer."

Some recent scholarship dismisses the blinding story as a fiction concocted nearly two centuries after the fact. In any event, the Belasitsa battle did not prove decisive, since the war dragged on for another four years. After the battle, Basil actually retreated, probably because his forces were only one part of a two-pronged pincer attack and the Bulgarians had defeated the other. Moreover, the loss of 14,000 men should have proven catastrophic for the Bulgarians, yet fighting continued for four years afterward without any significant Byzantine success. It is certain that Samuil's death, from whatever cause, brought on a leadership crisis in Bulgaria, resulting in internal discord between successors possessing only localized power bases. Samuil's immediate successor, Gavriil Radomir (1014-15), was murdered by his cousin Ivan Vladislav (1015-18), who claimed the throne and continued fighting the Byzantines. When he was killed besieging Durrës in 1018, Bulgarian resistance finally crumbled; apparently the *bolyars* concluded that rule by Basil was the most preferable option available.

Basil offered the Bulgarians a relatively magnanimous peace settlement. All Bulgarian territories were annexed by Byzantium. The *bolyars,* however, were brought into the local imperial administrative system, but many of the powerful and potentially dangerous ones were expatriated to Anatolia. Existing Bulgarian taxation in kind was preserved. (Elsewhere in the empire taxes were paid in gold coin.) Although the Bulgarian Ohrid patriarchate again was reduced to an archbishopric, it was granted autonomy, controlling all of its existing sees, and native Bulgarian prelates continued to hold their offices.

Basil divided his conquered Bulgarian lands into three provinces—Bulgaria (Macedonia, with its capital at Skopje), Sirmium (the client Serb Bulgarian lands, with its capital at Srem), and Paristrion (Mœsia and Dobrudzha, with its capital at Silistra)—all of which were commanded by generals appointed by the emperor. Byzantine garrisons were stationed in key cities to maintain order. Those fortresses that could not be garrisoned were destroyed to prevent them from being used as bases for future rebellions. Despite various regional uprisings, the annexed Bulgarian territories were firmly fixed in Byzantine hands.

The demise of Samuil's Bulgaria brought nearly all of the Balkan Peninsula back under Byzantine control. All of the former imperial Balkan provinces were reconstituted. Zeta (Serbia), Bosnia, Zahumlje, and Croatia were ruled by native princes who were Basil's vassals. For the first time since the mid-sixth century, the Balkans were united under the aegis of the Orthodox Christian Roman Empire.

CHAPTER THREE

Byzantium Declines

Despite the apparent resurgence of Byzantine power in the Balkans during the early decades of the eleventh century, with the death of Basil II Byzantium began to weaken internally. A series of ineffective emperors and palace coups, reflecting the growing dominance of the empire's bureaucratic functionaries over the military leadership class, led to a decline in the state's ability to hold and defend Basil's extensive territorial legacy. By the third quarter of the eleventh century Byzantium lost all of its Italian and much of its Anatolian possessions to Western Normans and Muslim Turks, respectively. Its army was shattered in the process and the empire verged on collapse. The assorted Balkan populations took advantage of the situation to reassert themselves while the empire called on the Christian West for military reinforcement. The resulting Crusades aided the separatist trends of the Balkan peoples, temporarily destroyed the Byzantine Empire, and opened the door to independence for the Balkans' non-Greeks.

Fragmenting Byzantine Control: The Eleventh Century

About the time of Bulgaria's destruction, Serbian Zeta (then known as Duklja) was brought under Byzantine control. During the mid-1030s, however, a Serb rebellion placed Stefan Vojislav (ca. 1034-43) on the Zetan throne. Although the Byzantines initially suppressed the uprising and captured Vojislav, he managed to escape imprisonment in Constantinople, return to Zeta, and lead a successful guerrilla war against the imperial troops sent against him. An uprising in the Byzantines' western Bulgarian lands during 1040 kept them distracted and aided Vojislav's resistance.

Typifying the poor political judgment of Basil's successors, the taxes paid by the subject Bulgarians had been converted from in kind to cash and then their rates were increased, causing increasing discontent. Exacerbating rising Bulgarian unrest, Emperor Michael IV (1034-41) had replaced the Slav Bulgarian archbishop of Ohrid with a Greek appointee without consulting the Bulgarian bishops. In 1040 in the northern Bulgarian lands, a rebellion erupted led by a certain Petŭr Delyan, who claimed to be Samuil's grandson. Delyan was crowned *tsar* in Belgrade amid widespread local popular support, after which he pushed south into Macedonia and the empire's Greek territories. To counter Delyan, a Bulgarian pro-Byzantine agent joined Delyan, came to share the leadership, and split the rebellion. Within a year Delyan was eliminated and the rebels intentionally led to defeat.

Byzantine preoccupation with Delyan's uprising permitted Vojislav, from his capital at Shkodër (Scutari), to assert Zeta's independence. Failed imperial attempts to oust him resulted only in Vojislav expanding his territories to include Zahumlje and part of northern Epiros. When he died in 1043 Zeta was the leading Serbian state in the Balkans, but its strength was fragile. Joint rule by his five sons degenerated into sibling rivalries and political instability until one brother, Mihajlo (ca. 1046-81), emerged as sole ruler. Mihajlo concluded a peace with Byzantium and married a relative of Emperor Constantine IX Monomachos (1042-55), thus preserving his independence and avoiding vassal status. His position buttressed, Mihajlo consolidated the state's territories in the hands of his sons at the expense of his brothers. Then he conquered Raška between 1060 and 1074.

Mihajlo's accommodation with Byzantium was more a matter of expediency than of sincerity. In 1072 he supported an anti-Byzantine rebellion in Macedonia led by Georgi Vojteh, a Slav landowner from Skopje. The uprising was timed to take advantage of two disastrous Byzantine defeats during the previous year—at Manzikert, to the Seljuk Turks, and at Bari, to the Normans. The empire was seriously damaged by both defeats, permanently losing most Anatolian and all Italian possessions, respectively, and its military capabilities plummeted to a new nadir. Despite their crippled military, the Byzantines managed to defeat three Zetan armies sent by Mihajlo to aid the rebels, and in 1073 the Macedonian rebellion collapsed.

Contacts with the papacy in 1077 brought Mihajlo a royal crown blessed by the pope. This diplomatic move gained him a powerful Western ally in the papacy. Through it he also received potential cooperation from the Normans in Italy, who were inveterate enemies of the Byzantines. Presumably this alliance also might constrain the Normans from attacking Zeta during their invasions of the Balkans' Adriatic coast. In addition, Mihajlo sought an independent church for Zeta, as all good sovereign Christian states theoretically needed. Zeta possessed no church metropolitanates; its Christians came under the authority of the Ohrid, Durrës, and Split prelates. Alienated from Constantinople, Mihajlo sought a Zetan archbishopric from the papacy. By Mihajlo's time, the Great Schism of 1054 had divided medieval

Christianity into two distrustful camps: The eastern Orthodox, led by the patriarch of Constantinople and supported by the Byzantine emperor, and the western Roman Catholic, headed by the pope and supported by most Western sovereigns. Since both Ohrid and Durrës were under the Orthodox Patriarchate's authority, Mihajlo expected the pope to leap at the chance for increasing Catholic jurisdiction in the western Balkans. Apparently the papacy did not immediately comply, and an archbishopric for Zeta was not forthcoming.

Elsewhere in the Balkans' northwest, Byzantium's troubles were compounded. During the ninth and tenth centuries Venice, a titular imperial possession, developed a powerful navy. Unable to maintain an active presence in Dalmatia because of the Bulgarian wars, and with their Croatian ally in internal disarray, the Byzantines became dependent on the Venetians to defend and administer the Dalmatian coast. Basil II named the *doge* (head of state) of Venice his official representative in Dalmatia, and the region's cities submitted loyalty oaths to the Venetian head of state, although they continued to be self-governing in practice. The relationship between Venice and the Dalmatian cities was uneasy, since many Dalmatians viewed Venice as a commercial competitor and its enhanced imperial position threatened their own trade interests.

A few Dalmatian cities, led by Dubrovnik, refused even nominal Venetian control. Possessing a growing merchant fleet of its own, Dubrovnik strengthened contacts with Byzantium and won recognition as an imperial province in its own right. Other Dalmatian cities joined with Croatian pirates in preying on Venetian ships in the Adriatic, but by 998 Venice had defeated the pirates and attempted to make Basil's recognition of Venetian imperial suzerainty over Dalmatia a reality.

In Croatia, Držislav's sons were at each others' throats over the state's rulership. Venice insinuated itself into the civil conflict by supporting the eldest brother, Svetoslav (997-1000), and holding his son hostage. Although Svetoslav was overthrown by his younger brothers Kresimir III (1000-30) and Gojislav (1000-ca. 1020), the fact that his son remained in Venetian hands meant that the new Croatian joint rulers faced the threat of Venetian intervention. A game of competing nominal suzerainty over Dalmatian coastal cities ensued between Venice and Croatia, dying down in 1019 when Basil II reclaimed all of imperial Dalmatia. Croatia submitted to Byzantine vassal clientage, and soon thereafter Venice fell into civil war.

Croat ruler Kresimir found the Venetian situation advantageous. He reasserted control over the Croatian Dalmatian cities, and, after Basil's death and the neglect of Dalmatian matters by his successor Constantine VIII (1025-28), he ceased paying homage to Constantinople. The Venetians won some territory from him, however, and the Magyars, pressing from the north, took Slavonia. Kresimir's successor Stjepan I (1030-58) preserved Croatian control over its Dalmatian coastal cities by means of an expanded Adriatic navy. He increased Croatian territory, and authority of the Croat bishop of Knin was extended northward to the Drava River.

Byzantium restored good relations with Croatia during the reign of Petr Kresimir IV (1058-75). The empire, in military decline, needed the Croats to defend Dalmatia from a rising Norman threat. In 1069 Kresimir was named commander of Byzantine Dalmatian forces. In his own lands, he loosely ruled over three provinces—Bosnia, the Slavic Dalmatian coast, and Slavonia. The latter, it appears, was highly autonomous and governed by a son-in-law of Hungarian King Béla I (1061-63), Zvonimir Trpimirović. Zvonimir accepted Croatia's annexation of his province in return for his continued autonomous rule, an important voice in Croat state matters, and his own succession to the throne should Kresimir die childless. In 1075 Zvonimir (1075-90) was crowned Croatian king following Kresimir's death without a direct male heir.

An interesting cultural development in Croatia was its complete acceptance of Roman Catholicism with the use of the Slavic Glagolitic liturgy, which had spread to northern Dalmatia from Moravia. During the 1060s the use of Glagolitic by some Croatian churches became a major issue. At the time, Catholic reform was on the papal agenda, and a number of traditionally Latin-speaking high clergymen, seeking to standardize the liturgy, demanded the abolishment of Slavic. Kresimir IV favored the Latin liturgy. The Catholic reformers considered the Croatian church corrupt, since many of its priests knew no Latin, wore beards, and married (all characteristic of Orthodox clergy). A 1060 synod in Split declared Latin the Croatian church's official language and condemned the Slavic liturgy, along with priests' beards and marriages. Unrest grew among the Croats, with the nobles and high clergy supporting Latin and the lower clergy and general population sympathetic to the Slavic. A pro-Slavic revolt in 1064 was crushed. Although the Glagolitic liturgy persisted for centuries in isolated pockets, the Catholic church in Croatia remained grounded in the Latin organization headed by the pope.

In addition to the troubles in distant Serbia and Dalmatia during the eleventh century, the Byzantines faced unrest in regions under their more direct authority. In 1066 Vlahs and Bulgarians in Thessaly rebelled against high taxation and irregularities in its collection. Emperor Constantine X Doukas (1059-67) had ignored prior warnings of the rebellion, and, when it came, only deft negotiations with its secretly pro-imperial leader prevented its spread into Byzantine Macedonia and Bulgaria. Although a minor event, the Thessalian uprising demonstrated the utter lack of touch that the bureaucratic functionary rulers in the capital had with realities in the provinces. They forced their Balkan subjects to pay taxes in gold coin when hard currency had all but disappeared following the seventh-century Slav and Bulgar settlements. They compounded the problem by progressively increasing tax rates and resorting to heavy-handed collection tactics. Their taxation policy only fostered despair and discontent.

Another problem springing from the central government's insensitivity to provincial conditions was the rise of great magnates who owned private armies and fortresses. The increasing military neglect and ineptitude demonstrated by the functionary emperors, caused by their fear of the powerful families who monopolized command of the provincial troops, only succeeded in privatizing military forces throughout the empire. Beginning in the tenth century the provincial military magnates increasingly grew independent of the central authorities and, by the opening of the thirteenth century, essentially held large areas of Macedonia and Greece as autonomous family domains. Their absorption of villages obligated to supply troops to the provincial forces greatly weakened the military capabilities of the traditional *theme* system and led to increased use of mercenaries in the Byzantine army.

Outside threats to the Byzantine Balkans caused serious problems once Byzantium's military decline became obvious. Particularly troublesome was the mayhem caused by the Turkic Pechenegs. Following the conquest of Bulgaria they became the empire's immediate neighbors in the northeast Balkans. Former Byzantine allies used to harassing the Bulgarians, the Pechenegs saw no reason to cease raiding south of the Danube after the Byzantine victory. Unable to defend its Danubian border adequately, Byzantium enlisted some outlawed Pecheneg rebels to serve as frontier defense troops. Their continuous raiding north of the Danube against the main Pecheneg body sparked a retaliatory invasion of the empire. Although the Pecheneg invaders were defeated and many were captured and used as either mercenary frontier guards or settlers, the Byzantines found themselves with a large and unruly horde of Turkic nomads within their borders.

The ineffectual Emperor Constantine Monomachos let himself be drawn into the continued squabble between the former rebels and the main branch of Pechenegs with unfortunate results. His intervention in Pecheneg affairs served only to unite them in rebellion against imperial authority. Three Byzantine armies led by inept courtiers met defeat at the hands of the rebel Pechenegs, who proceeded to pillage and plunder Thrace and Mœsia with impunity. Only after mercenary units composed of Varangian (Rus') imperial guardsmen and Anatolian mountaineers finally defeated a large Pecheneg force did the rebellion officially end in 1052. Pecheneg raiding and brigandage, however, continued for decades afterward, causing untold economic disruption in the Balkans and forcing the government to make repeated extortion payments in return for protection or peace.

The establishment of the Pechenegs within the empire also had repercussions for Byzantine foreign relations. When the now-resident Pechenegs began raiding northward into Hungary, the Magyars retaliated by attacking Byzantium in 1059. Although peace was swiftly restored, continued Pecheneg incursions into Magyar territories led the Magyars to attack the empire again in the late 1060s, which resulted in their capturing several Danubian cities. A third Magyar attack in the early 1070s, for the same reasons, ended with the Hungarians briefly in possession of Belgrade and firmly in control of eastern Slavonia.

To add to the Byzantines' woes, during the mid-1060s a new Turkic steppe nomadic people—the Oğuz—crossed the Danube into the empire and proceeded to ravage Mœsia, Thrace, Macedonia, and northern regions of Greece. An outbreak of plague struck down many of the invaders, causing the survivors either to flee or to join the imperial forces as mercenaries. The Oğuz had been pushed into the Balkans by yet another group of Turkic steppe people, the Cumans. They waited in the steppe-country wings north of the Danube delta for a future opportunity to raid the empire.

Another foreign threat to the Byzantine Balkans emerged in Italy during the 1060s. There the Normans, descendants of Vikings who had settled in France a couple of centuries earlier and had been fighting as allies of the pope, were busy expelling the Byzantines from southern Italy and Sicily. They succeeded completely when they captured Bari in 1071. Despite political differences with the pope, those master warriors were firmly committed to Catholicism and viewed the Orthodox Byzantines as schismatic, traitorous enemies of the faith. Having taken southern Italy, they naturally turned to continuing their struggle against the hated Eastern heretics by crossing the Adriatic and attacking them on their Balkan home soil.

The Normans moved first against northern Dalmatia in 1074 but were repelled by the Venetians after some transitory initial successes. As a consequence, Venice again claimed suzerainty over Dalmatia based on the old prerogatives granted it by Basil II. Stymied in the north, the Normans, led by Robert Guiscard (died 1085), turned their attention farther south in 1085 and assaulted Byzantine-controlled Durrës in a combined land and sea operation. The recently crowned Byzantine Emperor Alexios I Komnenos (1081-1118) moved against them with whatever forces he could muster, along with a Serb contingent led by Konstantin Bodin, the son of Zetan ruler Mihajlo and a former captive of the empire. As a gesture of Zetan Serb anti-Byzantine sentiment, Bodin had recently married an Italian princess whose family was pro-Norman, and he may have contracted a secret alliance with the Normans prior to their invasion. In any event, while the allied Venetian fleet succeeded in breaking the Norman invasion's naval component (in return for their services, Alexios essentially turned all Byzantine maritime carrying trade over to the Venetians and granted them total administrative and fiscal autonomy), Bodin and his troops sat out the land battle that resulted in Alexios's defeat, the loss of his army, and the Normans' capture of Durrës.

After their victory, the Normans pushed deep into the empire, passing through Epiros and Macedonia into Thessaly. Fortunately for the Byzantines, an uprising in the Normans' Italian possessions forced Guiscard and most of his men to return to Italy. Durrës was garrisoned and left as the Normans' Balkan foothold for renewed efforts against the Byzantines. Guiscard, however, died of the plague before he could renew his Balkan operations. Alexios managed to recapture Durrës and then attacked and defeated his treacherous Serbian ally in 1090. The loss sparked a civil war within

Zeta among Bodin's relatives, and, in the confusion, the local rulers (*župans*) of Raška, Bosnia, and Zahumlje broke free of Zetan control. Zeta itself was forced to accept Byzantine overlordship and lost its leadership role among those Serbs who continued to oppose the Byzantines. That mantle passed to the rulers of Raška.

In the early 1090s Raška was ruled by Vukan (1083-ca. 1122), who styled himself *veliki* (great) *župan*. He controlled a number of semiautonomous local *župans* from his capital at Novi Pazar. In 1090 he started raiding imperial territory around Kosovo against little Byzantine opposition because the Pechenegs were raising serious problems for Alexios at the time. When in 1092 the Byzantines were able to retaliate against him, Vukan defeated them, but a second Byzantine invasion forced him to sue for peace and swear homage to Alexios. Soon after the emperor departed from Raška, however, Vukan renounced the treaty and expanded southward, capturing Skopje. By 1095 Alexios once again marched on Vukan, who then swore to another peace with the empire, providing Alexios with hostages, including his son Uroš, as a guarantee of his word. In all of those affairs, Vukan obviously operated as an independent player and not a Zetan vassal.

A State of Flux: The Late Eleventh and Twelfth Centuries

Alexios Komnenos's post-Norman invasion military forces consisted of an assortment of mercenaries, great magnates' private troops, and impressed Balkan peasants. Besides Normans and Serbs in the west, he faced renewed Pecheneg problems in the central and northeastern Balkans during the late 1080s and early 1090s. He resorted to an alliance with the Cumans, who controlled the plains north of the Danube, to finally destroy the Pecheneg threat, but such an action left the empire vulnerable to Cuman incursions. Those developments, coupled with the Seljuk Turks' occupation of most of Anatolia, placed the Byzantine Empire in dire straits. In desperation, Alexios wrote to the pope in 1090 requesting Western mercenary troops to help bolster his faltering military. Pope Urban II (1088-99) used Alexios's letter to strengthen the papacy's temporal authority in the West by placing the pope at the head of a Christian crusading movement against the East. As a result, Alexios received more than he bargained for.

Scholars debate whether Alexios's request for military aid was necessary. By the time that the First Crusade arrived in the Byzantine Balkans in 1096, a series of military, administrative, and ecclesiastical reforms carried out by Alexios had stabilized the Byzantine position to the point that the empire not only could hold its own but was poised to win back much of its losses unassisted. Criticism from hindsight is easy. In 1090 the empire had been reduced mainly to its Balkan territories. Serbs, Croats, and Venetians steadily stripped away portions of the northwestern Balkans, and chaos caused by Pecheneg and Cuman incursions made

Byzantium's hold on its other Balkan lands shaky. Alexios cannot be faulted for believing that he needed serious military assistance.

Alexios initiated much-needed judicial, fiscal, and administrative reforms, but the most important involved the military. He won the support of provincial commanders by instituting the *pronoia* system of military landholding. Generally accepting existing provincial realities, Alexios provisionally distributed state lands to the great magnates on condition of their military service. The state retained ownership of the land grants, which could be revoked and redistributed if the holders did not fulfill their military obligations. Alexios counterbalanced the increased power of the magnates by playing off against them the high Orthodox clergy.

Although the Great Schism between Orthodox and Roman Catholic Christianity occurred in 1054, it initially was an ecclesiastical division only marginally affecting the general populations of East and West. That situation changed with the Crusades. Before the first Western feudal forces arrived in the Balkans on their overland trek to the East, there appeared an undisciplined horde of peasants, beggars, ruffians, and soldiers led by Peter the Hermit and Walter the Penniless, who swept through the Balkans along the Diagonal Highway to Constantinople like a plague of locusts. Alexios quickly ferried them across the Bosphorus to Anatolia and swift extermination by the Seljuks. The ill-will against Catholics that they spawned among the Orthodox inhabitants along their line of march became a lasting legacy.

Popular Orthodox anti-Catholic sentiment was reinforced when one of the four contingents comprising the First Crusade followed the same Diagonal route on its way to join the other three, who used the *Via Ignatia* route from Durrës, at Constantinople. Acting as if operating in enemy country, the troops looted their way south, fighting several skirmishes with local Serbian and Bulgarian inhabitants along the way. Although problems between crusaders and natives were fewer on the *Via Ignatia* route, the First Crusade's Balkan marches engendered a popular animosity between Orthodox and Catholics, rendering future compromise on religious differences problematic.

Alexios never desired the 50,000-strong crusader army that answered his appeal for mercenary troops. Unlike mercenaries, who fought under their employer's orders, the crusaders considered themselves independent of the emperor. Rather than reclaiming Anatolia for Byzantium, they sought only fighting, fame, and fortune in the Holy Land. Alexios and the crusade's leaders suspected one another's motives and intentions. This especially held true for the Normans, led by Guiscard's son Count Bohemond, Byzantium's inveterate enemies. Even though Alexios obtained Western-style feudal oaths from the crusaders' leaders and assisted them during their Anatolian operations against the Turks, Byzantine-crusader relations were strained almost from the beginning and would remain so throughout the crusading epoch, despite sporadic periods of cooperation between the leaderships of both sides. The growing mutual distrust and antagonisms that emerged among the crusaders' common ranks and Byzantium's general population ultimately intensified into mutual cultural animosity between European Orthodox and Catholic Christians.

The activities of the crusaders in the East occupied the attention of Alexios and his successors for close to a century. Such imperial preoccupation contributed to a decline in the already precarious Byzantine presence in the northwestern Balkans, ultimately permitting Croatia's absorption into Hungary and its Western European civilization, as well as Hungary's subsequent involvement in Balkan affairs.

In Croatia prior to the Crusades, Zvonimir had been crowned king by a papal legate, accepting vassal status under Pope Gregory VII (1073-85) and actively supporting papal reform policies, including the ban on the Slavic liturgy in the Croatian church. Zvonimir attempted to disempower the regional Croat nobility by removing local notables from government positions and replacing them with trusted supporters, including high Catholic clergymen. His attack on the local Croat nobles earned him their undying opposition, the consequences of which became apparent when Zvonimir died. He had married a sister of Hungarian King László I (1077-95), who bore him a son, but the child died soon after Zvonimir. His widow failed to win the Croat nobles' support, so László intervened in Croatia to protect her interests. Hungarian invasions and occupations of much Croatian territory, which continued under László's successor Kálmán I (1095-1114), and the death of Petr, the last independent Croat king, while resisting the Hungarians, led to the Croat notables negotiating a controversial deal with Kálmán in 1102, commonly called the *Pacta Conventa,* in which they agreed to accept a dynastic union with Hungary.

According to the agreement, the Croatian notables recognized the Hungarian monarch's sovereignty in exchange for retaining most of their political, legal, and social autonomy within Croatia. (Centuries later Hungarian nationalists claimed that the 1102 union represented a conquest completely incorporating Croatia within the Hungarian Kingdom; Croatian nationalists insisted that the union preserved an autonomous Croatian Kingdom in partnership with Hungary.) Recent scholarship has demonstrated that the *Pacta Conventa* was a fourteenth-century forgery and that what exactly transpired in 1102 remains unknown. In any event, after 1102 the history and fate of Croatia became linked to those of Hungary and Central Europe until the early twentieth century.

The incorporation of Croatia brought Hungary into direct contact with the Serbian states to its south and into competition with Byzantium over their possession. The two major Serbian states, Zeta and Raška, theoretically were Byzantine vassals. Zeta was in decline, disintegrating from a long civil war among its regional nobility for control of the throne following Bodin's death around 1101. Raška, after Vukan's reign, was an uneasy Byzantine client state. Through 1172 Byzantium and Hungary conducted a bewilderingly complex military and diplomatic relationship, in which they used the Serbs as pawns. Whole regions—Slavonia, Bosnia, Dalmatia—changed hands on almost a regular basis. The Hungarians consistently instigated anti-Byzantine Serb uprisings, while the Byzantines successfully put down the rebellions, often installed puppet rulers in Raška, and cultivated potential royal Hungarian heirs and pretenders in Constantinople.

Military campaigning by both sides was frequent. Emperor Manuel I Komnenos (1143-80), arguably the last great Byzantine military emperor, dispatched no less than thirteen expeditions against the Hungarians before he succeeded in placing his Hungarian protégé and sworn vassal Béla III (1172-96) on Hungary's throne. Once Hungarian king Béla, lived up to his oath, and Hungary remained a loyal Byzantine ally for as long as Manuel ruled. By 1172 Manuel's military efforts had won back Croatia, Bosnia, and Slavonia for the empire, and Béla accepted those conquests.

Sometime in the late 1160s the Nemanja family acquired Raška's throne, perhaps with Manuel's blessing. Although four brothers at first shared power, by 1171 one of them, Stefan I (1171-96), emerged as *veliki župan*. The next year Manuel marched on Stefan and forced him into sworn vassalage, after which time, like Béla in Hungary, Stefan ruled Raška as a loyal Byzantine client for as long as the emperor lived. During his period of vassalage, Stefan gained control of Hum (formerly Zahumlje) and Zeta.

Manuel died in 1180 and, almost immediately, his two former loyal vassals considered themselves free of further obligations to Byzantium. Anarchy reigned in Constantinople over the imperial succession, easily permitting Béla to retake Slavonia, Dalmatia, and the parts of Croatia formerly lost to Manuel. When Andronikos I Komnenos (1183-85) acquired the throne by massacring all of Manuel's surviving family, Béla retaliated by invading deep into the Byzantine Balkans, pushing south of the Balkan Mountains toward the imperial capital and sacking Niš and Sofia along the way. In the west, the Normans took advantage of the Hungarian drive to attack and capture Durrës in 1185. They then advanced on Thessaloniki, which was captured and sacked, before continuing toward Constantinople. The dual Hungarian and Norman assault sparked a revolt in the capital that overthrew Andronikos and enthroned Isaac II Angelos (1185-95). Béla recognized Isaac as the legitimate emperor and withdrew his forces, allowing the new emperor to concentrate on successfully driving the Normans out of the Balkans.

The turmoil of the early 1180s had important resonances inside of Byzantium's Bulgarian lands. There had been periodic Bulgarian revolts against Byzantine rule starting as early as Delyan's rebellion in 1040-41. Many of the uprisings seemingly were sparked by the anti-Slavic religious policies of the Byzantine authorities, especially after the later decades of the eleventh century. Slavic schools were closed, Greek-language religious services were imposed in some regional churches, and numerous Slavic books apparently were destroyed. (No Slavic works from the First

Bulgarian Empire survived in the Bulgarian regions [fortunately, many were preserved in Russia], while a number of Greek manuscripts from that period survived in Ohrid.) Byzantine control of the Bulgarian lands represented a serious cultural blow to the Bulgarians.

Precisely at the time when Isaac Angelos seemed in command of the Balkan situation, it began to unravel. In 1185 Isaac levied a special tax in the territories formerly occupied by Béla to pay for his grandiose wedding to Béla's daughter, which had been part of the agreement for Hungarian withdrawal. The Vlahs living in the Balkan Mountains refused to pay. At the same time, two Bulgarian notables and brothers, Petŭr and Ivan Asen, arrived in Isaac's camp seeking a *pronoia* grant in that region. Isaac refused their request in an insulting fashion, and the brothers returned to their home in Tŭrnovo bent on revenge. They issued a call for revolt that shrewdly allied to their cause the Orthodox religious cult of St. Demetrios, the traditional protector of Thessaloniki, venerated by Orthodox inhabitants throughout the Balkans. By appealing to the cult sentiments of both Bulgarians and Vlahs, the brothers were able to unite two populations that shared a common pastoral existence but were separated by different languages and traditions.

By proclaiming the favor of the popular saint, the Asen brothers successfully stirred up a widespread rebellion of Bulgarians and mountain Vlahs. Although Vlahs initially played a leading role in the revolt's early stages (Petŭr and Ivan even may have been ethnic Vlahs themselves), they rapidly were superseded by Bulgarians, whose imperial traditions the brothers adopted—Petŭr Asen assumed the title and regalia of Bulgarian *tsar* in Tŭrnovo. The rebellion sunk roots in the Balkan Mountains and spread to Bulgarian peasant villages in Mœsia. Popular discontent with high taxes and proliferating dues and tithes imposed by the Byzantine authorities swelled the rebels' ranks.

Isaac took a year to begin dealing with the Asens' rebellion. In 1186 he marched north and defeated the brothers in battle; they fled beyond the Danube and took refuge with the Cumans in Wallachia. After winning the support of those warriors, the brothers returned with a Cuman army in tow and reestablished themselves. The Cumans commenced raiding into Byzantine Thrace and along the Black Sea coastline. Isaac's efforts to repeat his former victory proved fruitless, and in 1188 he was constrained to recognize officially an independent Bulgarian state that included Mœsia and Dobrudzha, which the Asens governed from Tŭrnovo. The Cumans' Wallachian holdings fell under nominal Bulgarian control. To secure the Asens' promise to cease attacking Byzantine territories, a third brother, Kaloyan, was held hostage in Constantinople.

The Asens quickly concluded that, as was traditional in Orthodox political culture, their state needed its own church organization. Since the Bulgarian archbishopric of Ohrid lay in Byzantine hands, the brothers unilaterally raised the Tŭrnovo prelate to archbishop, removed him from Ohrid's jurisdiction, and placed all of their state under his ecclesiastical authority. Their actions were uncanonical and went unrecognized by the Patriarchate of Constantinople, but that mattered little to the brothers. The new head of the Bulgarian church then crowned Ivan I Asen (1187-96) *tsar* in Tŭrnovo, while Petŭr remained his uncrowned junior colleague residing in the old capital of Preslav.

The Asens' Second Bulgarian Empire was modeled heavily on Byzantium. Byzantine administrative and landholding systems operating at the time of the rebellion were retained, but the statewide centralization characteristic of Byzantium's bureaucracy could not be implemented completely. The new Bulgarian *bolyar* class was drawn from the rebel leadership, augmented by the brothers' direct appointees. Many were Cumans while others were service nobles. Despite their debt to the rulers for acquiring lands and power, over time significant numbers of *bolyars* succeeded in gathering to themselves large estates and considerable authority, which provided them with extensive local autonomy. The vast majority of the Bulgarian population remained rural peasants, most of whom lived as serfs on the estates of the rulers and their family, of the *bolyars,* or of the monasteries. For them, life did not change.

The success of the Bulgarian uprising signaled Byzantine military decline. The empire barely managed to retain the regions around Adrianople and Plovdiv against Bulgarian and Cuman raids. The disruption caused by the combative passage through the Balkans in 1189 of Holy Roman Emperor Frederick I Barbarossa's (1152-90) crusading army (part of the Third Crusade) served to emphasize Byzantine military ineffectiveness. Byzantium's hold on the Balkans obviously was slipping. Serbian ruler Stefan Nemanja threw off his alliance with the empire and attacked Byzantine Macedonia. In Dalmatia, Venice and Hungary competed for possession of the coastal cities unhindered by any concern for Byzantine intervention.

In 1190 Isaac Angelos again attempted to crush Bulgaria and regain the initiative for the empire. After failing to bring the Asens to battle, his army was trapped by the Bulgarians while retreating through a pass in the Balkan Mountains and defeated. Three years later the Bulgarians annihilated another Byzantine army near Arkadioupolis and took central Thrace. In desperation, Isaac forged an anti-Bulgarian alliance with his father-in-law, Béla of Hungary, for a combined assault on the Bulgarians, but Isaac was dethroned in 1195 before operations began. His brother Alexios III Angelos (1195-1203), needing revenues to gain support for his rule, immediately canceled the campaign. Instead, he exploited quarrels that emerged within the Bulgarian leadership. Ivan Asen was murdered by one of his *bolyars* in 1196, as was his brother Petŭr II Asen (1196-97) in the following year. Rule passed to the youngest Asen brother Kaloyan (1197-1207), the former hostage of the Byzantines. In 1201 Kaloyan lost his primary military support when the Cumans were defeated by the Russians of Galich and was forced to sign an agreement with Emperor Alexios III. The Byzantines were left in control of Thrace, the Rhodope Mountain region, and Macedonia (all of which the Bulgarians had been threatening to take) in return for Alexios's recognition of complete Bulgarian independence.

The Fourth Crusade and Its Aftermath

Mutual suspicions and growing antagonisms between the Orthodox East and the Catholic West, grounded in the Great Schism of 1054 and exacerbated by unfortunate incidents in their direct contacts with one another during the first three Crusades, combined in 1204 to bring catastrophe to the Byzantine Empire. The Balkan Orthodox world was affected deeply by the event.

Orthodox Byzantines, Serbs, and Bulgarians had experienced Catholic crusader looting and violence in locales through which those warriors marched. They had been forced to tolerate crusader disrespect for their traditions and insults to their faith, especially during the reign of Manuel Komnenos, who personally admired the westerners' military skills, supported the crusaders' efforts in the Holy Land, and gave some "Latin" crusader leaders important roles in Byzantine state affairs. Popular Orthodox animosity toward the interlopers led to a massacre of Catholics in Constantinople in 1182. The Angelos emperors had come to power on a wave of anti-Latin sentiment. During their reigns, rulers and ruled alike viewed the Latin crusaders as a papal threat to the Orthodox Byzantine state itself—a state that they believed personified the divinely ordained world order for all Christians.

Suspicion of the Orthodox easterners also grew in the West. Although the Crusades needed cooperation between both branches of Christendom to succeed, some westerners condemned the Byzantines as schismatics and considered Constantinople a legitimate target for a crusade, believing that fighting "heretics" was the spiritual equivalent of combatting Muslim "unbelievers." Therefore, assaulting Byzantium could be justified religiously as a "crusade."

Pope Innocent III (1198-1216) was determined to reunite the two branches of Christendom on Catholic terms and to launch a fourth crusade to recover the Holy Lands for Christianity. In 1199 he called for a new crusade, but his appeal was met enthusiastically only among the nobility of northern France. They contracted with Venetian Doge Enrico Dandolo (1193-1205) for ships to transport their anticipated crusading army to the East. A secret clause in the agreement designated Egypt, rather than Palestine, as the crusaders' target. In 1202 the participating crusaders gathered in Venice, waiting to board the large fleet into which the Venetians had invested a year of construction effort and much municipal money. The French crusaders were led by a northern Italian count, Boniface di Montferrat, who some years earlier, while in Constantinople, had played an important role in Byzantine affairs. Normans from the Kingdom of the Two Sicilies augmented the crusaders' ranks.

From pope to common warrior, the Fourth Crusade was riddled with enemies of the Orthodox Byzantine Empire. Innocent III personally was dedicated to bringing the Orthodox East under papal authority. The Normans were traditional antagonists of the Byzantines. The Venetians were angry over the economic discrimination that they suffered from the Byzantines, who showed increasing favor to Pisa and Genoa, Venice's commercial rivals. Dandolo, who emerged as the central figure and mainspring of the undertaking, thus had economic grievances to settle with Byzantium. Yet too much should not be made of the obvious anti-Byzantine antipathy among the crusade's participants in causing its misdirected culmination. A series of fateful circumstances combined with the crusaders' sentiments proved decisive in the matter.

The crusading army that gathered at Venice was smaller than expected, but its leaders had contracted ships in advance based on original estimates of need. Dandolo convinced Montferrat that the smaller force could make up Venice's enormous construction costs by helping him capture the Dalmatian port city of Zadar, which then technically lay under Hungarian authority. That feat was accomplished in 1202. While wintering at Zadar, the crusaders were approached by Alexios Angelos, son of Isaac II Angelos, who had been deposed and blinded in 1195 by Alexios III. Patronized by Philip of Swabia, a contender for the Holy Roman imperial throne and Isaac's son-in-law, young Alexios sought the crusaders' help in restoring his father to power in Byzantium. Although Pope Innocent opposed the idea by threatening them with excommunication, Alexios's promise to aid the crusaders' holy war once they restored Isaac won over the crusade's leaders.

Under the pretext of aiding Isaac, the crusaders descended on Constantinople in 1203. Although the effort succeeded, Isaac proved too much a creature of the Orthodox East to play the role of lackey for Catholic westerners, whom the Byzantines looked on (with some justification) as barbaric and culturally underdeveloped. Isaac did not feel bound by promises made in his name by his son, who now ruled as the more dominant coemperor Alexios IV Angelos (1203-4). Alexios IV himself had second thoughts about the matter and prevaricated in providing the crusaders with the promised support.

Forced to winter outside of Constantinople, the crusaders grew restless and suspicious. They raided the countryside to forage, and skirmishes with Byzantine troops multiplied. In 1204 an uprising in the capital placed the anti-Latin Alexios V Mourtzouphlos (1204) on the throne, and the crusaders finally turned their greed and frustration on the Byzantines, whom they considered (justifiably) to have reneged on promises of support. They assaulted the city by sea and land in April, breaking through the seawalls along the Golden Horn, and the Byzantine imperial and Orthodox courts fled. Once inside the capital, the crusaders gave vent to a venomous cultural animosity. The wholesale raping, pillaging, and plundering inflicted on the stricken city, the largest and wealthiest in the world at the time, were unprecedented. The Orthodox East never forgot or forgave the Catholic West for the sack of Constantinople, and the event sealed the gulf between the two European societies.

Illustrating the extent of Byzantium's internal decline preceding the catastophe was the ease with which Thrace, southern Macedonia, Thessaly, Attica, and the Peloponnese fell to the crusader forces following Constantinople's fall. In feudal fashion, the victors divided the conquered territories among themselves. Baldwin of Flanders was proclaimed emperor of Constantinople (1204-5), controlling Thrace and a small strip of northwest Anatolian territory. Montferrat received the Kingdom of Thessaloniki, encompassing the region around the city, part of southeastern Macedonia, and Thessaly. The rest of the territorial spoils—the Duchy of Athens (the city and the region of Attica) and the Principality of Achaia (the Peloponnese)—were distributed as vassal fiefs to leading warrior princes. Venice received control over a part of Constantinople, most of the Aegean islands, and small corners of the Peloponnese, Crete, and the cities along the Adriatic coast, while the Venetian Pier Morosini was raised to Latin (Catholic) patriarch of the East. Faced with a fait accompli, Pope Innocent III accepted the destruction of Byzantium as God's will. The resulting Latin Empire, weakened from inception by Western-style feudal rivalries, sank few roots in the hostile Orthodox East.

Three Orthodox states emerged as contenders for expelling the Latins and reestablishing the Orthodox Empire. The first was the so-called Empire of Nicæa, founded in Anatolia by refugees from Constantinople. Under Theodore I Laskaris (1204-22) the Nicæans effectively kept the Latins bottled up in their Anatolian coastal foothold. The other two contenders were located in the Balkans.

Bulgaria under Kaloyan became the strongest Slavic Balkan state by 1203. Serbia, ruled by Stefan II Nemanja (1196-1227), was reduced to dependency. Cuman forces again augmented the army. Hungarian holdings south of the Danube were taken, and, after Constantinople fell, Kaloyan acquired some Byzantine territory in Thrace and Macedonia. In late 1204 Kaloyan accepted nominal union with the papacy to gain official recognition for both his title of *tsar* and the self-proclaimed Tŭrnovo Patriarchate. Pope Innocent, however, recognized him only as "king" (not *tsar*) and the Tŭrnovo archbishop as "primate" (not patriarch). Kaloyan simply ignored the fine official distinctions and set about threatening the intruding Latins to his south.

In early 1205 Kaloyan intervened in Thrace on behalf of Greek landholders in revolt against their new Latin overlords. Latin Emperor Baldwin I marched against him and was defeated outside of Adrianople, taken prisoner, and brought to Kaloyan's capital at Tŭrnovo, where he died in captivity. Virtually all of Thrace fell into Bulgarian hands, except for the city of Adrianople, which the local Greeks held. Kaloyan then moved against the Kingdom of Thessaloniki and captured the fortress of Serres. Only a year after the westerners' stunning success at Constantinople, the Latin Empire was weakened seriously by the Bulgarians. Kaloyan, however, was assassinated in 1207 while besieging Thessaloniki, and his nephew Boril (1207-18) proclaimed himself ruler. Many *bolyars* refused to recognize Boril's accession, which threw Bulgaria into a decade of internal unrest until forces loyal to the sons of former Tsar Ivan I Asen overthrew Boril and placed Ivan II Asen (1218-41) on the throne. Personally mild, pious, and generous, Ivan also proved an effective military commander and statesman. His reign came to represent the apogee of the Second Bulgarian Empire.

Epiros, the other Balkan contender for Orthodox imperial restoration, was founded by Michael I Angelos Doukas (1204-15), a cousin of emperors Isaac II and Alexios III Angelos. Located in western Greece and southern Albania, with its capital at Arta, Michael's state retained the former Byzantine administrative system and a sound military base. Epiros consciously preserved Byzantium's heritage and stood in opposition to the Latin Kingdom of Thessaloniki to its east, the Venetians in the Adriatic, and the Slav Bulgarians to its north. Under Michael's successor Theodore Angelos Doukas Komnenos (1215-30), Epiros briefly achieved ascendancy in the Balkans.

Theodore spent a lengthy apprenticeship in Nicæa with Theodore Laskaris prior to acquiring the Epirote throne. While there, he had recognized Laskaris's supremacy through a sworn oath of fealty. Once in Epiros, however, Theodore embraced Michael's goal of reconstituting Byzantium from Arta, rendering conflict with Nicæa unavoidable. His first act was the capture of a new Latin Emperor Peter de Courtenay (1217). Peter was traveling to Constantinople from France via Rome, where he had been crowned by the pope, when Theodore seized him in the Albanian Alps and had him executed. Soon thereafter the Epirote ruler embarked on a sweeping campaign against his Bulgarian and Latin neighbors. In 1217 Theodore overran most of Macedonia and pushed on against the Thessalian territories of the Latin Kingdom of Thessaloniki. At the time of the Epirote attack, that kingdom was weakened: Its ruler, Boniface di Montferrat, had been killed fighting the Bulgarians; many of its warrior knights had returned to the West; and the temporarily leaderless Latin Empire could provide no concrete support. By 1220 all of mainland Greece west of the Pindos Mountains was in Epirote hands. Theodore finally took Thessaloniki itself in 1224, and the Latin Kingdom of Thessaloniki disappeared. By proclaiming himself emperor, Theodore placed himself in open opposition to the Nicæan Emperor John III Vatatzes (1222-54).

Although on the verge of collapse after the Epirote assaults, the Latin Empire's life was prolonged by the disunity among its three sworn enemies. In Anatolia, Vatatzes captured all of the Latins' territory except for the coast opposite to Constantinople. Nicæan troops crossed the Dardanelles into Thrace and occupied Adrianople. Just as the Latin Empire looked ripe for destruction, Theodore of Epiros attacked the Nicæans, defeated them, and advanced toward Constantinople. Theodore, in turn, was stymied by Ivan II Asen of Bulgaria.

Ivan aimed at nothing less than the creation of a Bulgarian-Byzantine empire centered on Constantinople. An anti-Nicæan alliance with Theodore of Epiros was patched together. In the Latin Empire, Emperor Baldwin II (1228-61) was a minor. The Latins offered Ivan the regency, and the young emperor was betrothed to Ivan's daughter. Theodore of Epiros then declared war on Bulgaria but was defeated decisively in 1230 by Ivan at the Battle of Klokotnitsa, in which Theodore was captured and blinded. After Klokotnitsa, Epiros's role in the struggle for Byzantine restoration became marginal. Ivan occupied all of western Thrace, Macedonia, and a portion of northern Albania, while Theodore's brother Manuel Angelos (1230-37) was permitted to retain Thessaloniki and Epiros as Ivan's vassal.

With Theodore of Epiros eliminated, the Latins grew frightened of their powerful Bulgarian regent, so the deal with Ivan was abrogated, and John de Brienne (1231-37) was named regent and coemperor for young Baldwin. In retaliation, Ivan declared war on the Latins and concluded an alliance with Vatatzes's Nicæa. Ivan renounced Kaloyan's nominal union of the Bulgarian church with the pope. The Orthodox Patriarchate in Nicæa recognized the Tŭrnovo primate as Orthodox Bulgarian patriarch, and the Bulgarians once again possessed an independent Orthodox church.

In the midst of a combined Bulgarian-Nicæan advance on Constantinople, Ivan realized that the fall of the Latin Empire would benefit the Nicæans more than he himself and ultimately result in Bulgaria facing a far more serious rival than the weak Latins. He turned on Vatatzes but hurriedly made peace in 1237, following an epidemic outbreak in Tŭrnovo that killed a number of Ivan's immediate family. (Ivan interpreted their deaths as God's wrath for his double-crossing a fellow Orthodox ruler.) Ivan died in 1241 and Bulgaria soon after was ravaged by a Mongol-Tatar invasion. The blow dealt by the invaders was so damaging that Bulgaria collapsed as a serious Orthodox imperial contender.

By the end of 1242 Nicæa found no serious rival remaining in the field. Bulgaria was weakened by two successive child-emperors under ineffectual regencies, anarchistic *bolyar* unrest, and Mongol-Tatar vassalage, which permitted Vatatzes to seize most Bulgarian territory south of the Balkan Mountains in Thrace and Macedonia. Vatatzes forced Epirote ruler John I Angelos (1237-44) to renounce his claim on the imperial title and to accept the position of despot under his suzerainty. Theodore II Laskaris (1254-58), Vatatzes's successor, continued military efforts against Bulgaria but lost Epiros to a revolt in 1257 led by Michael II Angelos (1236-71). By that time the Latin Empire was reduced to little more than the immediate environs of Constantinople itself.

When Laskaris was succeeded by a child, John IV Laskaris (1258-61), a military revolt in Nicæa led to the regency of Michael VIII Palaiologos (1259-82), who eventually imprisoned and ultimately blinded John in 1261. Michael forged an alliance with Bulgaria and concluded a treaty with Genoa, Venice's chief commercial rival in the eastern Mediterranean, granting it privileges similar to those enjoyed by the Venetians in the former Byzantine Empire. In July 1261 a Genoese fleet ferried a Nicæan army across the Straits to Thrace. A reconnoitering force of that army operating in the vicinity of Constantinople found the city virtually undefended—most of the Latin and Venetian forces were off besieging an island in the Black Sea. Sympathetic supporters inside the city informed the Nicæans of an undefended portal in the land walls, through which a small detachment entered and opened a main military gate for the rest of the army. Baldwin II and his followers fled, and the Latin Empire came to an anticlimactic end.

Michael VIII entered Constantinople in triumph and proclaimed the reestablishment of the Byzantine Empire. Although the coup immediately bestowed great international status, restored Byzantium was a hollow shell of its former self. Its territories encompassed a corner of northwestern Anatolia, Thrace, Macedonia, Thessaly, and a smattering of small holdings in the Peloponnese. To its north, Bulgaria was a wary ally. Most of Greece lay in Latin Frank hands. All of the northwestern Balkans was lost irretrievably. Venice and Hungary controlled Dalmatia and Croatia, Bosnia enjoyed an uneasy independence, and a new Orthodox power—Serbia—was on the rise.

CHAPTER FOUR

Serbia Preeminent

While the Fourth Crusade and its aftermath preoccupied the central and southern Balkans, new states were consolidated in the peninsula's northern regions. Two Slav states—Bosnia and Raška Serbia—emerged in the northwest, and, in the northeast, two Romanian states—Wallachia and Moldavia—were established. Of the four, Serbia eventually rose to preeminence among all of the Balkan states by the mid-fourteenth century. Restored Byzantium, after a brief period of initial vigor, slipped into progressive decline. Bulgaria never fully recovered from the effects of Mongol-Tatar clientage and growing political fragmentation. Bosnia barely held its own against the expansionary pressures of Hungary and the centripetal tendencies of its nobility. Wallachia and Moldavia, while heavily influenced by Bulgarian Orthodox political and religious culture, were isolated from the rest of the Balkan world south of the Danube and became virtual Hungarian satellites. Thus Slavic Orthodox Serbia came to lead the fourteenth-century Balkan Orthodox world, though its preeminence proved short-lived.

New States on the Peripheries

During the late twelfth and thirteenth centuries three new Balkan states emerged in the Balkans' north. The earliest to rise was Bosnia, a region within the Dinaric Alps in the northwest Balkans. Originally Bosnia was an inland component of Byzantine Dalmatia. It was separated from the Adriatic coastal area during the eleventh-century consolidation of Croatia, at which time it acquired the name "Bosnia"—the land centered on the Bosna River. Bosnia was a bone of contention between Croats and

Zetan Serbs, who frequently alternated in controlling the region. After Croatia's union with Hungary in 1102, Bosnia fell into Hungarian hands during the 1120s. Emperor Manuel I Komnenos, however, reestablished Byzantine authority in the 1160s. Following his death in 1180, an independent Bosnian state emerged under a certain Kulin (ca. 1180-1204).

Kulin acknowledged nominal Hungarian suzerainty, for which he received the title *ban* (Hungarian provincial ruler). He gained a certain amount of independence by commercially developing Bosnia's silver mining industry and by forging lucrative trade arrangements with the Adriatic port city of Dubrovnik. He may have tried to parry the powerful competing cultural-political influences in Bosnia of Roman Catholicism and Orthodoxy, emanating from Hungary-Croatia and Serbia, respectively, by favoring Bogomilism, but this is uncertain. Kulin and his family were accused of being devoted to the Bogomil belief and desirous of making it the state religion by both Catholic Hungarian and Orthodox Serbian rulers eager to gain Bosnia for themselves. When Pope Innocent III preached a crusade against Kulin and the heretics in 1203, the Bosnian ruler wisely announced his adherence to Catholicism. A Catholic synod convened in Bosnia and condemned Bogomilism before the pope's crusaders arrived.

Despite such efforts, Bosnia did not escape continued allegations of being riddled with Bogomilism by Catholic outsiders, especially Hungarians, who used the argument to justify repeated but unsuccessful so-called crusades in efforts to reassert their direct control over the region. The Hungarians did succeed in having the pope place all Bosnian Catholics under the authority of their bishop of Kalocsa. In response, the Bosnians rejected the new ecclesiastical administration and established an autonomous Bosnian church of their own, which both the papacy and the Hungarians stigmatized as Bogomil. Existing evidence from Bosnia itself, however, indicates that the Bosnian church was Roman Catholic in dogma, although intentionally schismatic from papal control.

Ban Stjepan Kotromanić (ca. 1318-53) made Bosnia an important player in the political affairs of the northwestern Balkans. Kotromanić gained recognition of Bosnia's continued autonomy under a very loose nominal Hungarian suzerainty. He solidified good relations with the Hungarians by marrying his daughter to Hungarian King Louis I de Anjou (1342-82). He also successfully resisted a Serbian invasion led by Car Stefan Uroš IV Dušan (1331-55) in 1350 and expanded the territory under his authority to include parts of Croatia and most of Hum, gaining control of the Neretva River valley to the Adriatic.

It was under Kotromanić that a full-fledged autonomous Bosnian church emerged. Headed by a bishop with the title *djed* (grandfather) and staffed by clergy drawn exclusively from Catholic monasteries, the Bosnian church enjoyed close ties with the *ban*. Outside of Bosnia, the papal claim that the Bosnians were heretics persisted. Franciscan missionaries were sent to reassert papal authority in Bosnia.

Kotromanić, originally Orthodox, converted to Catholicism, and, from that moment on, all Bosnian rulers were Roman Catholic. Despite the missionaries' success with the rulers, many of Bosnia's local nobility and population persisted in their autonomous Bosnian faith or in Orthodoxy.

Kotromanić developed Bosnia's mining industries further, opening new mines and expanding trade contacts with Dubrovnik. Saxon Germans were brought in from Hungary to provide technical expertise, and Dubrovnik colonists handled the mines' administrative and financial operations. Bosnia prospered as a primary European supplier of silver and lead. Towns flourished, craft industries mushroomed, and commerce thrived. Since the foreign colonists who predominated in the expanding and wealthy Bosnian urban population were Catholic, the Franciscan missionaries found ready support in the thriving towns. The native Bosnian church became restricted to the rural regions that were mostly unaffected by the ore mining boom.

Bosnia reached its apex under Ban Tvrtko I (1353-91). The beginning of his reign was inauspicious. Kotromanić had created a territorially large state but one governed through a weak central administration. At his death, Bosnia began to dissolve into numerous local principalities controlled by independent-minded lords. King Louis of Hungary stripped Tvrtko of much territory before confirming him as his hapless and seemingly dependent vassal *ban*. Contrary to Hungarian expectations, Tvrtko gradually consolidated his authority within Bosnia, despite a noble uprising. By the early 1370s he firmly controlled most of the region.

With his authority assured, Tvrtko began meddling in the affairs of the Serbs lying to his east. He took from them nearly all of Hum and the Adriatic coastline between the Gulf of Kotor and Dubrovnik. Having acquired a good deal of Serbian territory and playing on his maternal Serbian ancestry (his grandmother was of the Serbian royal Nemanja family), in 1377 Tvrtko claimed the royal crown of both Bosnia and Serbia. Although few Serb nobles outside of Bosnia's borders recognized his claim, all successive Bosnian rulers used the royal title rather than that of *ban*. Following the death of Hungarian King Louis I in 1382, Tvrtko took advantage of the subsequent regency to extend his control over much of Croatia and Dalmatia, adding the names of both to his assumed royal title.

On Tvrtko's death in 1391, his Bosnian kingdom remained intact, although the central power of his successors was weak relative to the strong regional authority of the local nobles, who sported their own subordinate vassals and military forces. Those lords seem to have maintained the state because they deemed it in their best interests to do so—small local principalities would have been easy prey for the neighboring Hungarians and Serbs. The king exerted effective authority only over the central territories of Bosnia, while the local nobility reigned in areas conquered by Kotromanić and Tvrtko. Such regional particularism was abetted by the existence of three separate Christian religions—Catholicism, Orthodoxy, and the Bosnian church. Each tended to dominate in given areas of the kingdom to the relative exclusion of the others, thus preventing any particular one from serving as a vehicle for strong state integration.

While a Bosnian state emerged in the Balkans' northwest, by the middle of the fourteenth century two new non-Slavic Romanian states appeared north of the Danube in the peninsula's extreme northeast. Often collectively identified as the Romanian (or Danubian) Principalities, Wallachia and Moldavia emerged as separate political entities. The political independence of both was precarious and preserved only by their status as veritable satellites of their powerful Hungarian neighbor. The shared Orthodox culture of the two, acquired through some of their populations' connections with the Second Bulgarian Empire, remained closely linked to developments south of the Danube.

Vlachs and Cumans living on the Wallachian Plain and on the southern Moldavian tablelands represented significant components of the Asen brothers' forces in their successful bid to restore an independent Bulgarian state in the 1180s. The extent to which the Bulgarian rulers in Tŭrnovo exerted direct authority over regions north of the Danube remains unclear. Given the fact that the Cumans were a steppe-nomadic people and that the Vlahs traditionally were identified as being at least semipastoralists, it seems doubtful that Bulgarian political control over them was anything but nominal. It is certain that the Slavic form of Orthodox Christianity prevalent in Bulgaria took firm hold among the Vlahs in the thirteenth century, at which time they also apparently adopted a more settled agricultural lifestyle. Since the Vlahs' native language was Latin-based, their ready acceptance of the Slavic liturgy and the use of the Cyrillic alphabet in writing their vernacular speaks for strong cultural ties with Bulgaria and with Orthodox European civilization in general.

Any Bulgarian control over the trans-Danubian regions was obliterated by the Mongol-Tatar devastation of Bulgaria and the Vlah-inhabited regions in 1241-42. By the end of the 1240s Hungary, already in control of Transylvania to the north of the Carpathian Mountains, began pushing southward onto the Wallachian Plain in efforts to stifle Cuman and Vlah threats to its borders. The Hungarians encountered a number of small Vlah political formations under the authority of local leaders (*voievods*). These possessed their own political organizations and demonstrated a certain amount of social differentiation between landowning notables and peasants. Their essentially strong internal organization helped preserve them in the face of persistent Cuman and Mongol-Tatar raiding expeditions in the region. As Hungarian movement south of the Carpathians intensified throughout the second half of the thirteenth century, these small Vlah entities were brought under Hungarian authority as vassal client districts.

By the late thirteenth century the Wallachian Vlah client districts commenced a gradual process of consolidation, which was accelerated by events inside of

Hungary. The end of the native Hungarian Árpád ruling dynasty threw the state into political disarray. The unsettled conditions in Hungary permitted Voievod Basarab (ca. 1310-52), possibly a Cuman prince, to unite the Vlah lands lying between the Carpathians and the Danube, and extending as far east as the Black Sea near the Danube Delta, under his authority. He negotiated alliances with Bulgaria and Serbia and broke his ties of vassalage to the new Hungarian King Charles Robert I de Anjou (1301-42). In 1330 Charles Robert invaded south of the Carpathians to reimpose Hungarian suzerainty over the region, but he was defeated and forced to recognize the independence of Basarab's state, which acquired the name of Wallachia—the "Land of the Vlahs."

From his capital at Curtea de Argeş in the southern foothills of the Carpathians, Basarab's successor Nicolae Alexandru (1352-64) obtained Byzantine recognition of an autonomous Wallachian Orthodox church in 1359, when his capital's bishop was elevated to the rank of Wallachian metropolitan by the patriarch of Constantinople, thus providing the Wallachian ruler with the state church organization required for fully independent status within Orthodox European political culture. The new metropolitan's jurisdiction was not confined to Wallachia alone but extended over all of the Orthodox Vlahs living in Hungarian-controlled Transylvania. Wallachian independence was strengthened under Alexandru's successor Vladislav I Vlaicu (1364-77), who issued the first Wallachian coins, forged increasing economic ties with Transylvania, and founded monasteries throughout his territories to serve as centers of Orthodox culture.

The political development of the Vlahs inhabiting the Moldavian tablelands and foothills east of the Carpathian Mountains was impeded somewhat, relative to those in Wallachia, because of their more direct vulnerability to incursions of Pechenegs, Oğuzes, Cumans, and Mongol-Tatars from the Ukrainian steppe. In addition, both East Slav Ruthenians and West Slav Poles were pushing gradually southward into the northern territory (later known as Bukovina) of the region. By the late thirteenth century, however, small political entities of Orthodox Vlahs headed by local notables were spread over Moldavia. During the first half of the fourteenth century the Hungarian presence in the region increased, as the Magyars attempted to create border marches east of the Carpathians to protect Transylvania against Mongol-Tatar raids. Although some local Vlah district *voievods* resisted Hungarian control by aligning themselves with the Poles in the north, while others in the southeast came under Mongol-Tatar control, by midcentury the Hungarians had established a vassal Vlah border march in western Moldavia.

Soon after the Hungarian border march in Moldavia was founded, some Maramureş Vlah notables, led by Voievod Bogdan I (1359-ca. 1365), staged an anti-Hungarian uprising. Pressured by the Hungarians, Bogdan and his rebels were forced to move east of the Carpathians, where they raised a number of Moldavian notable supporters, drove out the region's Hungarian vassal governor, and installed

Bogdan as *voievod*. King Louis I sent a Hungarian army to crush the rebellion in 1365 but it was defeated, resulting in the de facto establishment of Moldavian independence. Under Bogdan's successors during the remaining years of the fourteenth century, the young rebel state, ruled from its capital at Suceava, consolidated its control over the territories lying between the eastern Carpathian Mountains and the Prut River, as far south as the Danube frontier with Wallachia and as far north as the southern border of Poland.

Moldavian independence was precarious. Constant political and cultural pressures were exerted on the state by neighboring Roman Catholic powers— Hungary in the west and Poland in the north. The fourteenth-century Moldavian rulers attempted to counter the dual political threat by playing the two against each other through a complex foreign policy of shifting alliances. After Hungarian King Louis I acquired the Polish throne (1370-82), creating a dynastic union of Moldavia's two primary antagonists, the Moldavian rulers began lengthy negotiations with the Byzantine Patriarchate of Constantinople for the creation of an independent Moldavian Orthodox church. In 1401 Voievod Alexandru the Good (1400-32) finally won Byzantine recognition of his capital's bishop as metropolitan of an autonomous church organization. Thus Byzantium bestowed political recognition on Moldavia within the context of accepted Orthodox European political culture.

The Latin states founded in the Balkans by the French warriors of the Fourth Crusade certainly were peripheral culturally. Two Latin Frank states persisted in the Greek lands after the Kingdom of Thessaloniki's collapse in 1224—the Duchy of Athens and the Principality of Achaia. Created by blatant military conquest and governed in typical western feudal fashion by a small elite minority of warriors consciously and purposely isolated from their Orthodox Greek subjects in culture, the Latin Balkan states nevertheless managed to outlive most of their neighboring native Orthodox rivals.

From its inception in 1204, the Duchy of Athens, which included the regions of Attica and Bœotia, was locked in disputes over its northern border with the more powerful Kingdom of Thessaloniki. By the 1220s Athens virtually was cut off from direct access to the Adriatic coast and the West by the Greek Despotate of Epiros, which controlled the western half of mainland Greece beyond the Pindos Mountains and Thessaly to the city's north. Forced to shift for themselves, the Latin dukes of Athens cultivated relations with both Epiros and the Empire of Nicæa. Efforts to gain suzerainty over all of Greece involved them in the politics and conflicts surrounding possession of southern Thessaly and the Island of Eubœa in the 1260s and 1270s. At that time the previously more powerful Peloponnesian Principality of Achaia was in decline, following its defeat by the Nicæans in 1259 and the capture of its ruler, William de Villehardouin (1246-78). Byzantine Emperor Michael VIII campaigned in Epiros, Thessaly, and Eubœa during the 1270s, attempting to reassert imperial authority in those regions. He was resisted by the Latins of Athens as well as by a number of independent-minded local Greek lords, especially the despots in Epiros, who sought to strengthen their position vis-à-vis Byzantium through marriage alliances with the dukes of Athens. By 1278 Athenian Duke John de la Roche (1263-80) emerged as the leading Frank lord in Greece.

The dukes of the Duchy of Athens came to serve as bailiffs in Achaia for the relentlessly anti-Byzantine Anjevin rulers of the Kingdom of the Two Sicilies, Charles I (1262-85) and Charles II (1285-1309). Anjevin diplomacy built a powerful system of client states in the Balkans to serve as a springboard for decisive operations against the Byzantine Empire. After the extinction of its ruling Villehardouin family in the 1270s, Achaia fell into their hands, as did the port city of Durrës. By the end of the thirteenth century the Despotate of Epiros turned to the Anjevins for support against Byzantine encroachment, and the Anjevins successfully won the throne of Hungary after the extinction of the Árpáds in 1301.

When the ruling de la Roche family went extinct in 1308, the Duchy of Athens fell into civil war over the ducal succession. Titular Duke Walter de Brienne (1308-11) called for assistance from the Catalan company, who were then wreaking havoc in Thrace and Macedonia, to maintain his hold over the state. Unfortunately for Brienne, the Catalans turned on him and took control of the duchy for themselves, subsequently accepting nominal vassalage to the Aragonese kings of Sicily, who had expelled the Anjevins in 1309. Athens remained under Catalan rule until it was acquired by a powerful scion of the wealthy Italian Acciajuoli banking house, after which it devolved into backwater obscurity amid petty squabbles among family members until its capture by the Ottomans in 1456.

Much of the Peloponnese was conquered by Latin Frank knights in 1205, who carved out the Principality of Achaia. Its Villehardouin ruling princes commenced a long struggle to bring all of the Peloponnese—known at the time as the Morea—under their authority. The mountain-dwelling Slavs still present in the region, joined by most of the native Greek population led by their local nobles, offered stiff resistance to the spread of Frankish hegemony. In 1248, after a lengthy siege aided by the Venetians, William de Villehardouin captured the fortress city of Monemvasia, the key to the southeastern Morea. Its acquisition gave the Achaian principality control of the entire Peloponnese, except for a few port cities in the southwest that were in Venetian hands. To consolidate his authority over his conquests, in 1249 William built an imposing fortress in the foothills of the Taigetos Mountains just outside of Sparta, which he called Mystras.

In 1259 Epiros allied itself with William in an effort to evict the Nicæans from the Thessaloniki region. The Achaian ruler led his army into Macedonia but met defeat and capture by the Nicæans in a battle near Bitola (Pelagonia). As ransom, in 1262 William turned over to Byzantine Emperor Michael VIII Monemvasia, Mystras, and a fortress in the Morea's Mani Peninsula, which thereafter became bases for Byzantine efforts to recover the Peloponnese. The region deteriorated into one great battle-ground, and Achaia lost more land to local Greek nobles and Byzantines in the 1260s. To win western aid, William signed a treaty in 1267 designating the Sicilian Anjevins as his heirs. During the 1270s, as Anjevin direct interest in Achaia made itself felt, the Latins' situation stabilized, since the Byzantines were forced to concentrate on resisting a threatened invasion of the Balkans by Charles I, who was determined to reestablish the Latin Empire in the East.

The Anjevin invasion plan evaporated in 1282 amid a Byzantine-instigated uprising in Sicily known as the Sicilian Vespers and the subsequent lengthy Anjevin-Aragonese war for control of the Sicilian Kingdom. Thereafter, rule of Achaia degenerated into a revolving door of absentee westerners and weak local Franks, permitting the Morean Greeks to expand their holdings in the Peloponnese. By the mid-fourteenth century a thriving Byzantine state centered on Mystras—the Despotate of the Morea—controlled the greater part of the region and gradually was Hellenizing the surviving Latin territories in its north. In 1430 the last of those were captured by the despotate, and the Latin presence in southern Greece ended. The Orthodox Greeks again held firm sway.

Serbia, Bulgaria, and Byzantium in the Thirteenth Century

Stefan I Nemanja, self-proclaimed *veliki župan* of Raška Serbia, came to power as Byzantine Emperor Manuel I Komnenos's vassal. He succeeded in carving out independence of sorts for his state by playing neighboring Byzantium and Hungary against one another. By frequently allying himself with Hungary in its numerous conflicts with Manuel, Nemanja won renown among the Serbs as a great warrior struggling against Greek domination, but his military victories never proved decisive. Each was followed swiftly by Byzantine retaliation and the reimposition of Raška's client status.

Raška's position changed after Manuel's death. Succeeding Byzantine emperors proved less capable in quelling their rebellious Serb clients. The Asens' uprising in Bulgaria diverted Byzantine attention from the northern Danube frontier, permit-ting Nemanja to proclaim outright Serbian independence in 1190, after which he expanded his authority over surrounding Serb-inhabited regions—Zeta, northern Albania, southern Dalmatia, Hum, and much of present-day eastern Serbia.

Nemanja was a devout Orthodox Christian. Throughout his reign, he built numerous churches and monasteries, which also helped cement together his disparate lands, and actively fought heresy. (Whether that was Bogomilism, as some scholars suggest, is uncertain.) His youngest son, Rastko, became a monk on Mount Athos under the name of Sava, and Nemanja himself abdicated the throne in 1196 for the monastic life. He took the religious name of Simeon and joined Sava on

Mount Athos, where the two jointly founded the large and influential Slavic monastery of Hilandar. After his death in 1199, Nemanja was canonized an Orthodox saint. His actions favoring the Orthodox church solidified a strong partnership between state and church in Serbia and were continued by his successors. The church, in turn, supported the Nemanja ruling dynasty. A cult of Nemanja, fostered by his sons Sava and Stefan, sanctified the ruling house and bestowed on it a divine right to rule. For nearly a century after Nemanja, virtually all Serbian rulers carried the name "Stefan" as a tangible linkage to the dynasty's holy founding figure, who became the saintly protector of the state.

The true founder of the Nemanja dynasty was Nemanja's son and successor Stefan II Nemanja (1196-1227). His reign began amid conflict with his elder brother Vukan, prince of Zeta, whom Nemanja intentionally passed over in his abdication in favor of the younger Stefan. With Hungarian assistance, Vukan attempted to establish Zeta as a separate kingdom. He invaded Raška in 1202 and Stefan was forced to flee to Bulgaria, whose ruler, Kaloyan, supplied him with a Cuman army in exchange for territories around Belgrade and Niš. Stefan's continued struggle with Vukan and the Hungarians ended in 1207 through successful mediation by his saintly brother Sava; Stefan regained his throne.

Zeta remained independent for another decade, while Stefan, having extended his authority into Kosovo, continued his efforts to gain control of it. Constant involvement in Zeta's Adriatic regions brought Stefan into contact with the Catholic West. In 1216 he finally annexed Zeta. Recognizing that Stefan's Serbia was a growing force in the Balkans' northwest, and perceiving an opportunity to spread Catholic jurisdiction deeper into the Balkans, the pope sent Stefan a royal crown in 1217, for which Stefan acquired the title of "First Crowned." The Catholic coronation was opposed by many of Stefan's Orthodox clergy, including his brother Sava, who, having returned to Serbia, left for Mount Athos in protest.

In 1219 Sava traveled to Nicæa, where he managed to gain the Nicæan Orthodox patriarch's recognition of an autocephalous Serbian Orthodox archbish-opric, separate from that of Ohrid (which was under Epirote authority at the time). Sava was ordained the first Serbian archbishop, returned to Serbia, and reconciled with his brother Stefan, whom he promptly crowned Orthodox ruler of Serbia with a crown sent by the Nicæan patriarch. Stefan's second, Orthodox coronation effectively ended Catholic hopes in Serbia, and the partnership of the state and Orthodoxy was restored. Thereafter, church prelates enjoyed a voice in Serbian state affairs and literate clerics staffed the government's bureaucracy, while members of the ruling landed nobility monopolized the high church offices. An extensive building campaign planted churches and monasteries throughout Stefan's lands, spreading Orthodox education and cultural solidarity. Sava, from his seat in Žiča, shaped a code of canon law that stabilized the new Serbian church and served as the basis for civil law until the mid-fourteenth century.

Stefan's immediate successors were ineffectual rulers, unable to thwart the territorial ambitions of Serbia's powerful neighbors. Serbia fell heavily under Bulgarian influence, and more of its eastern territories passed into Bulgarian hands. A powerful secular and clerical Serbian aristocracy came to dominate the royal office. Vague legal notions of succession and inheritance led to dynastic conflicts and regional disturbances, exacerbated by continuing animosities between adherents of Orthodoxy in the central Serbian lands and of Catholicism in the western, more Adriatic-facing regions. The pro-Western ties of King Stefan Uroš I (1242-76), who married a daughter of deposed Latin Emperor Baldwin II and concluded an alliance with the Anjevin Sicilian King Charles I de Anjou, failed to deflect Hungarian expansion into northern Serbia and Bosnia.

While during most of the remaining decades of the thirteenth century the successors of Nemanja and Stefan II proved unable to maintain their predecessors' developmental pace, Serbia's neighbor, Bulgaria, experienced grave problems of its own. The Mongol-Tatars of the Golden Horde, having devastated Bulgaria during the 1240s, conducted nearly annual raids into Bulgaria, extorting tribute and causing widespread disruption. Reduced to tributary status by the Mongol-Tatars and cursed with weak central leadership after Ivan II's death, Bulgaria fell prey to growing disaffection among its regional *bolyars*. The Asen dynasty came to an ignominious end with the overthrow and death of Koloman II Asen (1256) at the hands of *bolyar* rebels from the Belgrade region.

The victor of the civil war that followed, Konstantin I Tih (1257-77), adopted the surname Asen to lend legitimacy to his rule and pursued a strong anti-Byzantine policy by concluding alliances with the Golden Horde and with the Byzantines' inveterate Anjevin enemy, Charles I of the Two Sicilies. Neither diplomatic move succeeded in the long run. The Mongol-Tatars were bribed by Byzantine Emperor Michael VIII into conducting raids into Bulgaria beginning in the mid-1270s, while Charles's invasion never materialized.

Incessant Mongol-Tatar incursions and Konstantin's efforts to stabilize ruined state finances by issuing devalued coins sparked a Bulgarian peasant rebellion in 1277. Headed by a swineherd named Ivailo, who claimed that God ordained that he be *tsar,* the rebels worsted a Mongol-Tatar raiding force, defeated Konstantin in battle, and placed their leader on the throne in Tŭrnovo. Tsar Ivailo (1277-80) was constrained to renew tribute payment to the Golden Horde and forced to fight a series of campaigns against the Byzantines. His troops exhausted by three years of constant combat, Ivailo was abandoned by his *bolyar* supporters. He fled to the Golden Horde, where he was murdered by the Mongol-Tatar *han,* Byzantium's ally.

To replace Ivailo, the Bulgarian *bolyars* chose Georgi I Terter (1280-92), possibly a Cuman in ethnic origin. Continued Byzantine-inspired Mongol-Tatar devastations of Bulgarian territories forced Terter to marry his daughter to their *han's* son Chaka in an attempt to buy peace. Despite the marriage, the Golden Horde increased its intimidation of Bulgaria, ultimately forcing Terter to seek asylum in Byzantium. The Mongol-Tatars then installed one Smilets (1292-98) as their Bulgarian puppet ruler. By that time Serbia was shaking itself out of its torpor under the rule of Stefan Uroš II Milutin (1282-1321), who annexed most of Macedonia to his state. Smilets married his daughter to Milutin's son and heir, Stefan Uroš III Dečanski (1321-31). The Bulgarian bride became the mother of medieval Serbia's greatest ruler, Stefan Uroš IV Dušan.

Smilets was killed in 1298, leaving a minor as his heir. After Milutin refused to head a regency, Terter's Mongol-Tatar son-in-law Chaka (1299) invaded Bulgaria, assisted by Terter's son Teodor Svetoslav, a hostage of the Golden Horde since Chaka's marriage. Svetoslav, by means of bribes and threats, convinced the Bulgarian *bolyars* to accept Chaka's rule. Toktai (1290-1312), the new *han* of the Horde and Chaka's sworn enemy, then invaded Bulgaria. Chaka was overthrown, and the newly proclaimed Tsar Teodor Svetoslav (1300-21) had him strangled and his severed head sent to the Mongol-Tatar ruler as a token of friendship. Toktai reciprocated by granting Svetoslav southern Bessarabia as an addition to the Bulgarian state. Thereafter, Bulgaria remained on friendly terms with the Golden Horde, and the two often joined together as allies against Byzantium.

The newly restored Byzantine Empire enjoyed two decades of resurgence after 1261 under the adept leadership of Emperor Michael VIII Palaiologos. On recovering the capital, Michael's Balkan territories consisted of southern Thrace, Thessaloniki, southern Macedonia, and a few offshore Aegean islands. The remaining pre-Latin imperial lands lay divided among the Despotate of Epiros, a Greek breakaway Duchy of Thessaly (Neopatras), the Latin states of Athens and Achaia, and the Venetian Duchy of the Archipelago, which included a few ports in the Peloponnese and numerous Aegean islands. Michael devoted his entire reign to recovering those lost territories.

A portentous start for his efforts came soon after Michael was installed in Constantinople. To purchase his ransom from Byzantine captivity in 1262, William de Villehardouin of Achaia turned over three important Peloponnesian fortresses—Mystras, Monemvasia, and Great Maina. These provided bases for Byzantine recovery operations in the region. Michael established a district of the Morea governed from Mystras. Although Michael himself undertook little expansion in the Peloponnese, after his death Mystras grew into a populous urban and cultural center, serving as the seat of both the Byzantine regional governor and the Orthodox Lakedaimonian bishopric. By the first decades of the fourteenth century, Byzantine Mystras controlled most of the southern Peloponnese.

After dealing with the Morea, Michael turned his attention to Epiros and Bulgaria. In 1262 he commenced a series of military campaigns against the Epirote Despotate, forcing it to recognize Byzantine suzerainty and bringing much of it under direct Byzantine control. Michael then moved against Bulgaria, and by 1265 much of northern Thrace, including Plovdiv, and the Black Sea coast once again were in Byzantine hands. His gains were consolidated by a skillful policy of marriage alliances contracted with the rulers of Epiros, Bulgaria, and the Golden Horde. Hungary was made an ally to serve as a Damocles sword should Serbia attempt to cause trouble from the northwest. To solidify his successes, in 1272 Michael had both the Bulgarian and Serbian Orthodox churches subordinated to the authority of the Patriarchate of Constantinople.

The greatest threat to Michael's policy of Balkan expansion came from the West. Both the papacy and the Anjevins of the Kingdom of the Two Sicilies were eager to reinstate the Latin Empire in Constantinople. Charles I de Anjou undertook lengthy preparatory operations for the venture by gathering an invasion fleet and creating a web of anti-Byzantine alliances with the various Balkan states. Michael attempted to counter such an onslaught in a number of ways. He attempted to reconstitute a Byzantine fleet of his own but, realizing that it was no match for the westerners, was forced to forge economically disadvantageous alliances with the Western maritime powers of Venice and Genoa, which were granted extensive commercial privileges and resident colonies in Constantinople in exchange for their naval assistance.

Despite the naval alliances, Sicilian Anjevin King Charles I made headway in paving the road for his planned effort to resurrect the Latin Empire by invading the Balkans along the *Via Ignatia* route. By the 1270s Corfu, some of the adjacent Greek coastline, and Achaia were in Charles's hands. He moved against Epiros and captured Durrës in 1272, driving Despot John Angelos (1271-72) into Thessaly, which he held until 1295. Charles then proclaimed himself king of Albania, which won him the support of the few Catholic Albanians, and he established alliances with Stefan Uroš I of Serbia and John of Thessaly.

Facing a seemingly overwhelming crisis, Michael VIII stymied the threat by adept diplomacy. Taking advantage of the pope's increasing anxiety over Charles's growing power in Italy and playing to the papacy's desire to reestablish Christian church unity under papal authority, Michael made overtures to the pope about placing Byzantium's Orthodox church into papal hands. Michael sent a delegation to the Catholic church Council of Lyon in 1274, where they acknowledged both papal primacy and the union of the churches. In exchange for agreeing to the union, Michael obtained papal assurance that he would be given a free hand to reconquer all formerly Byzantine territory in the Balkans, even if that meant fighting Latins.

Freed by the union, Michael launched an offensive against the Anjevin forces in Epiros and their Thessalian and Venetian allies in the Balkans. Internal opposition within the Byzantine Empire, however, blunted the advantages Michael briefly gained by the church union of Lyon. The majority of the empire's Orthodox clergy, including the patriarch, and population repudiated the union, causing a veritable schism within the Orthodox church. Venomous antiunion pamphlets were produced at churches and monasteries in Constantinople and Mount Athos, while

Michael and his adherents cruelly persecuted opponents. All of his Balkan Orthodox enemies joined in the opposition. Censure from the courts of Bulgaria, Serbia, Epiros, and Thessaly was unanimous. Byzantine prestige in the Orthodox Balkans suffered a blow from which it never truly recovered.

In 1281 a French clergyman was elected pope. Pope Martin IV (1281-85) immediately fell into line with Anjevin policy. He condemned Michael as a schismatic and declared him deposed, although the emperor consistently had proven dedicated to the union, even to the extent of antagonizing his subjects and jeopardizing his own policy interests. With Michael left isolated on all sides, the door seemed opened for Charles to initiate his long-planned Balkan invasion. The door slammed shut, however, when the wily Byzantine emperor pulled off one of his most stunningly successful diplomatic feats. In 1282 Byzantine gold stirred up the Sicilian Vespers revolt against Charles in Sicily, while Michael financed a fleet for King Pedro III (1276-85) of Aragon to assault Sicily and wrest the island's throne from Charles. Although Charles managed to retain his mainland Italian possessions, he was forced to abandon permanently his invasion plans.

Michael paid dearly for his unstinting efforts to reclaim and defend Byzantium's position in the Balkans. He antagonized his own people by swearing union with the hated Roman Catholics. On the sea, Michael's Byzantine navy melted away in the face of the superior Venetian and Genoese maritime presence. His constant military efforts, although successful in permitting the empire to hold its own in the short run, were conducted at the expense of its Anatolian defenses. The best of his Anatolian troops were used up fighting in the Balkans, and Byzantium's army was left dependent mostly on Latin and Turk mercenaries. Growing financial pressures forced Michael to skimp on fortifications and garrisons along the Anatolian border that faced an increasingly aggressive Ottoman Turkish neighbor. Although Michael's reign at the time appeared to herald the beginning of a Byzantine political renaissance, rapid decline soon followed his death in 1282.

Serbia's Rise to Empire

The reign of Stefan Uroš I lent a certain amount of stability to a Serbian state that, under his predecessors, suffered from centripetal aristocratic forces. Uroš's centralizing policy of not granting family appanages, in an effort to halt the internal political fragmentation, alienated his eldest son, Dragutin. After fruitless repeated attempts to change his father's policy, Dragutin sought aid from the Hungarians, who helped him overthrow Uroš in 1276 and ascend the throne as King Stefan Dragutin (1276-82). Dragutin reversed his father's policy, and strong aristocratic political influence reemerged. For reasons still unknown, Dragutin soon fell out of favor with the Serb *bojars.* In 1282 they deposed him and elevated his younger brother Stefan Uroš II Milutin, a pious but dissolute individual.

Milutin proved a shrewd political opportunist who restored central royal authority in Serbia. On acquiring the throne, he initiated lengthy attacks on Byzantine Macedonia, winning significant territorial gains, including the city of Skopje. Expansion into northern Macedonia had two important results. First, Serbia entered the Byzantine-centered south-central Balkans for the first time, which shifted Serbian foreign policy from its original northwestern Adriatic-Danubian focus to one oriented toward the southeast and Byzantium. Second, by acquiring Skopje, the Serbs possessed a strategically located, well-fortified city that could serve as capital for a territorially extensive state. Its central geographic location astride the important Vardar-Morava commercial route and its largely Greek population made it a natural political, economic, and cultural center. Skopje's benefits, combined with Serbia's flourishing mining and trade resources, guaranteed Milutin status as a major player in Balkan affairs.

Milutin also devoted attention to his northern border with Hungary. His deposed brother Dragutin governed the Belgrade region as a Hungarian client. Despite that fact, the two brothers often acted in concert as military allies: Dragutin aided Milutin in the south, while their roles were reversed in the north. By the early 1290s the two had expanded Serbian control south of the Danube as far as Bulgaria's northwestern border in the vicinity of Vidin. Threatened by Serbian expansion, Shishman, *bolyar* and lord of Vidin, who probably governed the region independent of direct central Bulgarian control, failed to repel the brothers' forces and accepted Serbian suzerainty. Soon afterward, the brothers' successful partnership dissolved and Milutin, fearing a military confrontation with Dragutin, sought peace with the Byzantines in Macedonia to avoid a two-front war.

Byzantine Emperor Andronikos II Palaiologos (1282-1328) failed to prevent territorial losses to Serbia in Macedonia and northern Albania. Although diplomatic steps, such as renouncing the Lyon church union and concluding peace with Venice, brought Byzantium internal reconciliation and a small measure of external security, the sad state of the military bequeathed him by Michael left Andronikos little choice but to end warfare with Milutin on any terms. With both rulers desirous of peace, a treaty was negotiated in 1299.

To seal the agreement, Milutin demanded the hand of an imperial princess-bride. Andronikos offered the only option available—his five-year-old daughter Simonis. Exceedingly flattered, Milutin accepted. It was an apt demonstration of his personal character. Milutin was a widower in his forties who maintained amorous relations with two kept concubines, a Greek Thessalian princess, and a nun (his former sister-in-law). In spite of Milutin's sordid love life and the strenuous objections of the Byzantine Orthodox church, Andronikos pushed the marriage through to its conclusion in Thessaloniki in 1299. Milutin retained most of his conquered Byzantine territory as his child-wife's dowry, and Skopje became the new Serbian capital. (See Map 4.)

Simonis brought a large entourage to Serbia, where she was kept in the royal nursery for some years before her husband consummated the marriage. With her arrival, Serbia received a massive injection of Byzantine culture. Byzantine-style court ceremonial and dress were adopted; Byzantine functional and honorary titles appeared; court offices were renamed; and Byzantine administrative, legal, and fiscal institutions were copied. Byzantinization was reinforced by Serbia's newly won populous Greek-speaking regions, in which Milutin retained all former Byzantine political, social, and cultural activities.

An important Byzantine import into Serbia was the system of land tenure based on the conditional *pronoia* military estates, which existed alongside of the traditional Serbian family patrimonial method of joint landholding among brothers. Just as *pronoia* estates in Byzantium were changing from conditional to hereditary grants by the time that they were copied in Serbia, the Serbs' version was hereditary from the start, although the holder's military obligations remained. How widespread the Byzantine-style system was during Milutin's time is uncertain. It probably remained less extensive than the traditional landholding scheme and flourished mostly in the former Byzantine territories.

The final two decades of Milutin's reign were disturbed by civil strife with his brother Dragutin and assorted regional nobles and territorial losses to the Hungarians. Milutin also had problems with his illegitimate son Stefan Dečanski, who was unhappy over his father's favoritism toward his legitimate younger brother Konstantin. When Milutin died without a testament, a civil war erupted among Dečanski, Konstantin, and their cousin Vladislav. Dečanski emerged victorious, ascending the throne as Stefan Uroš III Dečanski (1321-31).

During the civil war, both Hum and Vidin threw off Serbian suzerainty. Hum soon fell under Bosnian control, while Vidin, governed by Mihail Shishman, returned to the Bulgarian orbit. When Tsar Teodor Svetoslav died in 1322, the Bulgarian *bolyars* turned to Mihail as the strongest local notable capable of holding the throne in the face of Byzantine assault. Tsar Mihail Shishman (1323-30) reunited Vidin with Bulgaria and regained all territories lost in northern Thrace during recent Byzantine campaigns. In 1326 he signed a peace with Byzantium, which at the time was rent by civil war.

Matters had not progressed well for Byzantium following the 1299 peace with Serbia. The empire's poor financial situation had constrained Andronikos II to cut costs, with particularly devastating effect on the military. Economic dependence on Genoa led Andronikos to dismantle what remained of Michael VIII's navy, placing the empire's naval defenses completely into those foreigners' hands. Since the army was made up of paid mercenaries, Andronikos drastically reduced their numbers. In Anatolia, the Ottomans persistently encroached on imperial lands while, in the

Balkans, Byzantium was hard-pressed to withstand periodic Serbian and Bulgarian raids. Creative tax reforms had increased state revenues, but these were squandered on bribes intended to keep neighboring rulers in check. Byzantium no longer was a great power in its own right.

Andronikos continued his father's Balkan interests at the expense of the empire's Anatolian possessions. As catastrophe loomed in Anatolia over losses to the Ottomans, Andronikos employed the Catalan Grand Company from Sicily for service against the Turks. In 1304 the Catalan mercenaries arrived in Anatolia, where they demonstrated both their outstanding military skills by defeating the Turks and their cold-blooded rapaciousness by widespread and indiscriminate pillaging of Turkish and Byzantine regions. Andronikos induced them back to Europe, where disgruntlement over arrears in pay led to new excesses and rising Byzantine indignation. When their leader Roger de Flor was assassinated in 1305 by Byzantine agents, the Catalans ran amuck in Thrace.

For two years the Catalans ravaged the Thracian countryside unopposed; then, having exhausted Thrace's resources, they moved westward into Macedonia, where their depredations continued, oftentimes in partnership with Milutin's Serbia. By 1310 the Catalans moved southward into Thessaly, which they pillaged for a year before taking service with Duke Walter de Brienne of Athens. In 1311 they turned on Walter and seized control of Athens for themselves, holding it for over seventy years.

With the passing of the Catalans, the last Western threat to Byzantium ended, but the empire was left ravaged and weak. One bright spot was the military district of the Morea. There Andronikos Palaiologos Asen (1316-21) expanded imperial territory in the Peloponnese and elevated Monemvasia into a commercial center rivaling the Venetian ports of Methoni and Koroni. Any other positive progress, however, was forestalled by a civil war that erupted between Andronikos II and his namesake grandson.

The younger Andronikos, a frivolous and irresponsible individual, was irked by the tutelage of his grandfather. He had been excluded from the imperial succession by the emperor after his followers mistakenly murdered his brother. Enraged, young Andronikos found support among youthful aristocratic elements and in 1321 opened a civil war to dethrone his unpopular grandfather. The rebellion persisted in desultory fashion for seven years, during which the Bulgarians intervened on behalf of the younger Andronikos, while Serbia did so on the elder's side. Young Andronikos won the support of Byzantine Macedonia and was hailed emperor in Thessaloniki in early 1328. Support for the old emperor melted away and the younger Andronikos forced him to abdicate, assuming the throne himself as Andronikos III Palaiologos (1328-41).

By the end of the civil war, Serbia obviously was the dominant Balkan power. Byzantium consisted of little more than Constantinople, southern Thrace, southern

Macedonia, and a portion of the Peloponnese. Its ruler was weak, its small army demoralized, and its core Thracian territory exhausted from two decades of depredations. Bulgaria suffered from politically fragmenting *bolyar* regionalism, and Mihail Shishman was handicapped because of his alliance with the incompetent Andronikos III, who proved a liability once he attained the imperial throne. Dečanski had supported the elder Andronikos in the civil war to further Serbia's Macedonian interests, and, despite his ally's defeat, he managed to expand his holdings in that region. Possession of Macedonia became the bone of contention among the three neighboring rivals.

Viewing Dečanski as their common primary threat, in late 1328 Andronikos and Mihail forged an anti-Serbian treaty. Little action occurred until 1330, when a Bulgarian-Byzantine offensive was launched. Andronikos tentatively advanced into the Serbs' Macedonian frontier district. Meanwhile, Dečanski and Mihail met in a decisive battle near Kyustendil (Velbuzhd) in eastern Macedonia. The Bulgarian army was destroyed and Mihail fatally wounded. On learning the news, Andronikos quickly withdrew.

The Battle of Kyustendil had crucial consequences. Although the Bulgarian *bolyars* enthroned Mihail's nephew Ivan Aleksandŭr (1331-71), Bulgaria lay militarily crippled and politically subordinated to Serbia's interests. While Ivan Aleksandŭr was not officially a Serbian vassal, his ability to conduct independent Bulgarian policies was limited. He later styled himself "Emperor of Bulgarians and Romans" and carried out successful military campaigns against Byzantium, but he was barred completely from competing in the centrally crucial region of Macedonia, which became a Serbian preserve.

As for Byzantium, Andronikos was left alone to face the expansionist Serbs, who launched a war of Macedonian conquest in 1331. Although he negotiated a temporary peace with Serbia in 1334 that freed him to capture Thessaly and part of Epiros, Byzantine catastrophe in the Balkans had begun. In just over a decade after Kyustendil the empire slipped into another civil war, opening the door for Serbia's rise to Balkan hegemony.

Excited by their victory at Kyustendil, the Serb nobles were eager to deliver the coup de grâce to Byzantium, but Dečanski decided otherwise. His son, Dušan, taking advantage of the resulting alienation of the *bojars,* led a coup that deposed his father, who soon thereafter was strangled on his son's orders. The new ruler, Stefan Uroš IV Dušan, first made a peace and marriage alliance with Bulgaria's Ivan Aleksandŭr, freeing him to operate in Macedonia without concerns for his eastern border. His forces captured Ohrid and pushed as far south as Thessaloniki, where they were stopped by the city's strong walls. Since he was under threat from the Hungarians in the north, Dušan accepted Andronikos's peace offer in 1344 on terms permitting him to retain only part of his conquests. There matters stood until Andronikos's death in 1341 and the outbreak of renewed civil war in Byzantium.

John V Palaiologos (1341-76) was nine years old when his father, Andronikos, died. The regency of John Kantakouzenos, Andronikos's lifelong friend and supporter, was opposed by John's mother and the patriarch. With both the Serbs and the Bulgarians threatening the empire's northern and western borders, and Anatolian Turk raiders plundering the Thracian coast, Kantakouzenos raised troops with his own money, campaigned against those enemies, and checked them all. In his absence, the regency was taken over by his opponents. The deposed Kantakouzenos responded by declaring himself young John's coemperor and, with support from Thracian magnates, initiated a war against his enemies in the capital.

The new civil war soon became bound up with radical social reform and religious movements. A movement of Zealots voiced the frustrations of the impoverished peasants and urban poor, which they expressed in venomous hatred of the wealthy aristocrats who controlled Byzantine affairs. Kantakouzenos's enemies used the Zealots against him, since he obviously was linked to the magnates' interests. Civil war took on the character of class war. Mass Zealot risings broke out in the major Thracian and Macedonian cities, and in Thessaloniki the Zealots violently seized power in 1342. Simultaneously, the Orthodox church split over the issue of Hesychism, an ascetic mystical movement born on Mount Athos, whose adherents strove to reach direct spiritual contact with God through visions of a divine light induced by solitude and mental concentration. The patriarch and regency disapproved of Hesychism and persecuted its adherents soon after the civil war's outbreak. The Hesychists then threw in their lot behind Kantakouzenos.

By 1342 Kantakouzenos's fortunes were in decline and he appealed to Dušan for help. Dušan's *bojars* were eager to continue military conquests in Macedonia, so an alliance was concluded with Kantakouzenos, who was granted asylum inside of Serbia. The rebel's fortunes soon took a turn for the better when, in 1343, the governor of Thessaly, who also controlled southern Epiros, recognized him as emperor. Alarmed at the sudden improvement in Kantakouzenos's position, Dušan ceased supporting him and joined forces with the regency in Constantinople.

With Dušan now his enemy, Kantakouzenos left Macedonia and turned for assistance to an old friend from past diplomatic contacts, the Seljuk Turkish *emir* (prince) of Aydın, Umur *paşa* (honorific title of high rank) (1334-48). From that time on, he received continuous Turkish support, first from the Seljuks and then from the Ottomans. His Turkish allies tipped the military scales in Kantakouzenos's favor. Although he failed to take Zealot-governed Thessaloniki and was compelled to abandon Macedonia to Dušan, Kantakouzenos conquered Thrace. In return for their aid, he permitted his Turkish allies to plunder the newly won territories. When Bulgarian Tsar Ivan Aleksandǔr, in league with the regency in Constantinople, pushed southward into Thrace, Kantakouzenos unleashed his Ottoman forces on him. Thereafter, paralyzing Turkish raids into Bulgaria became frequent events. The regency in Constantinople also called on Seljuk aid from Anatolia in 1346, but, upon discovering that Thrace had been reduced to a wasteland by their predecessors, they turned on Bulgaria and Constantinople's environs for plunder without confronting Kantakouzenos.

The situations in Byzantium and Bulgaria favored Dušan's almost bloodless expansion into the Greek regions of the western Balkans. By 1346 he controlled all of Macedonia except Thessaloniki. From his capital at Skopje he proclaimed himself "Emperor of the Serbs, Greeks, Bulgars, and Albanians," a clear pronouncement of his determination to eliminate Byzantium and to create a new Balkan Orthodox empire under his authority. Dušan realized that only by attaining the supreme imperial office in Constantinople could his ambitions succeed. He unilaterally elevated the Serbian bishop to the throne of patriarch, earning the anathema of the Greek patriarchate, and established his new state primate's seat at Peć (Ipek), in Kosovo. Dušan now possessed the essential church partner for an Orthodox imperium. On Easter 1346 the Serbian patriarch crowned Dušan *car* (emperor), with representatives of most Balkan Orthodox church centers in attendance.

The following year Kantakouzenos entered Constantinople as Emperor John VI (1347-54), and young John V was reduced to junior imperial partner. To secure the Peloponnese, the district of Morea was elevated to a despotate and Kantakouzenos's son Manuel was installed as despot (1348-80). Those developments did little to obstruct Dušan's relentless advance on Byzantine lands. He completed his conquest of Albania and Epiros and capped his expansion by seizing Thessaly. Thessaloniki, however, remained beyond his reach. When the Zealot government fell in 1350, the city reverted to Kantakouzenos's control, but it proved the only lasting Byzantine foothold in Macedonia. (See Map 4.)

Dušan controlled an empire stretching from the Danube to the Gulf of Corinth, and from the Adriatic to the Aegean coasts. It was half Greek and half Slavic in language, and its center of gravity lay in the Greek-speaking lands of the south. Dušan delegated the governance of the northern, Serb-inhabited lands to his son Stefan Uroš, while he himself administered the former Byzantine territories from Skopje. His court entirely was Byzantine in character, and his administrative system was modeled on that of Byzantium. Many of the new Byzantine titles that Dušan bestowed on members of his family were those that, in Byzantium, only an emperor could grant. So Byzantine-like was the administration that life for the Greek-speaking populations in the state continued on as before their conquest; only the ruling class had changed.

Between 1349 and 1354 Dušan had a civil law code (*zakonik*) compiled, promulgated, and revised. This earliest extant secular Serbian law code combined Byzantine jurisprudence with Serbian customary law. In its details it has provided historians with insights into mid-fourteenth-century imperial Serbia. Just as in Byzantium, the emperor theoretically was considered the supreme authority figure in the state, owner of the lands and inhabitants under his control, and source of all law. In practice, however, powerful regional *bojars* and high church officials placed limitations on the ruler's authority by way of privileges guaranteed by the central government. A hierarchical class structure was defined and supported by the state, with each level assigned specific rights and punishments under the law. Overall, the code described a traditional Orthodox agrarian society, led by an autocratic ruler dependent on the support of a small but powerful secular and religious landholding elite, who, in turn, dominated, but were themselves dependent on, a mass majority of politically insignificant free and enserfed peasants.

After his 1346 coronation it appeared that Dušan need only make one last effort to enter Constantinople and satisfy his ultimate imperial pretensions. In 1351 he besieged Thessaloniki but again was unsuccessful; it was obvious that, without a fleet to seal off port cities, the Byzantines could withstand his land threats from behind their powerful defense walls. What was true for Thessaloniki was doubly so for Constantinople. Dušan attempted to win Venice's assistance, but the Venetians had no desire to replace a weak Byzantium with a powerful Serbia in the eastern Mediterranean. When the maturing Emperor John V raised a rebellion against Kantakouzenos in 1352, Dušan supported the imperial rebel but suffered defeat at the hands of Kantakouzenos's Ottoman Turkish mercenaries sent by Emir Orhan (1326-60).

In 1354 the Byzantine fortress city of Gallipoli was ruined by an earthquake and occupied by Ottoman troops serving Kantakouzenos. This was the first time that the Turks had not returned to Anatolia after fulfilling their mercenary duties in the Balkans. Led by Orhan's son Süleyman, they quickly established Gallipoli as a permanent European base for raiding operations into Thrace. Nearby Constantinople was thrown into panic, and its population blamed Kantakouzenos. Capitalizing on the situation, John V Palaiologos easily toppled the long-standing usurper, and Kantakouzenos was sent into monastic exile. Despite the return of legitimate rule, however, Byzantium was ruined politically, administratively, economically, and territorially.

Byzantium seemed ripe for Dušan's picking, but efforts against Constantinople were delayed by Hungarian attacks on Serbia's north in 1354. Any attempt to capture Constantinople required overcoming a number of strategic problems. Dušan had no ally who could provide the fleet necessary for a successful siege and assault. Furthermore, the Ottomans ensconced at Gallipoli posed a serious threat to his flank and rear if he settled in before Constantinople's walls. Dušan died in his own lands in late 1355, before he could march on Constantinople. Into the grave with him went his Serbian Empire. Stefan Uroš V (1355-71) lacked his father's talents and forceful personal character to hold the disparate elements of the empire together. Released from Dušan's control, the powerful regional *bojars* rapidly turned their provincial holdings into fully or semi-independent principalities, retaining only the most nominal ties to Dušan's impotent successor.

FURTHER READINGS

General

Boba, Imre. *Nomads, Northmen and Slavs: Eastern Europe in the Ninth Century.* The Hague: Mouton, 1967.

Dolukhanov, Pavel M. *The Early Slavs: Eastern Europe from the Initial Settlement to the Kievan Rus'.* London: Longman, 1996.

Dvornik, Francis. *The Making of Central and Eastern Europe.* London: Polish Research Center, 1949.

Fine, John V. A., Jr. *The Early Medieval Balkans: A Critical Survey From the Sixth to the Late Twelfth Century.* Ann Arbor: University of Michigan Press, 1983.

———. *The Late Medieval Balkans: A Critical Survey from the Late Twelfth Century to the Ottoman Conquest.* Ann Arbor: University of Michigan Press, 1987.

Lock, Peter. *The Franks in the Aegean, 1204-1500.* London: Longman, 1995.

Macartney, C. A. *The Magyars in the Ninth Century.* Cambridge: Cambridge University Press, 1930.

Obolensky, Dimitri. *The Bogomils: A Study in Balkan Neo-Manichæism.* Cambridge: Cambridge University Press, 1948.

Riley-Smith, Jonathan. *The First Crusaders, 1095-1131.* Cambridge: Cambridge University Press, 1997.

Runciman, Steven. *A History of the Crusades.* 3 vols. Cambridge: Cambridge University Press, 1951-54.

———. *The Medieval Manichee.* Cambridge: Cambridge University Press, 1967.

Sedlar, Jean W. *East Central Europe in the Middle Ages, 1000-1500.* Seattle: University of Washington Press, 1994.

Setton, Kenneth M., ed. *A History of the Crusades.* 4 vols. Madison: University of Wisconsin Press, 1955-77.

Spinka, Matthew. *A History of Christianity in the Balkans: A Study in the Spread of Byzantine Culture Among the Slavs.* Chicago, IL: American Society of Church History, 1933.

Vlasto, A. P. *The Entry of the Slavs into Christendom: An Introduction into the Medieval World of the Slavs.* Cambridge: Cambridge University Press, 1970.

Bosnia

Fine, John V. A., Jr. *The Bosnian Church: A New Interpretation. A Study of the Bosnian Church and Its Place in State and Society from the 13th to the 15th Centuries.* Boulder, CO: East European Monographs, 1975.

Bulgaria

Angelov, Dimitŭr. *Formation of the Bulgarian Nation: Its Development in the Middle Ages (9th-14th c.).* Translated by Ara Stoicheva. Sofia: Sofia Press, 1978.

Antoljak, Stjepan. *Samuel and His State.* Translated by Eran Frankel and Zoran Anchevski. Skopje: Macedonian Review Editions, 1985.

Browning, Robert. *Byzantium and Bulgaria: A Comparative Study Across the Early Medieval Frontier.* Berkeley: University of California Press, 1975.

Dimitrov, Bozhidar. *Bulgarians: Civilizers of the Slavs.* Translated by Marjorie H. Pojarlieva. Sofia: Borina, 1993.

Dinekov, Petŭr. *Cyril and Methodius and Bulgarian Culture.* Sofia: Sofia Press, 1981.

Duichev, Ivan. *The Uprising of 1185 and the Restoration of the Bulgarian State*. Translated by Nina Panova. Sofia: Sofia Press, 1985.

Gandev, Hristo. *Formation and Establishment of the Bulgarian Nation*. Translated by Rumyana Iosifova. Sofia: Sofia Press, 1987.

Gyuzelev, Vasil. *The Adoption of Christianity in Bulgaria*. Translated by N. Panova. Sofia: Sofia Press, 1976.

———. *The Proto-Bulgarians: Pre-History of Asparouhian Bulgaria*. Translated by Yuliya Stefanova. Sofia: Sofia Press, 1979.

Nicoloff, Assen. *Samuel's Bulgaria*. Cleveland, OH: Author, 1969.

Runciman, Steven. *A History of the First Bulgarian Empire*. London: G. Bell, 1930.

Sharenkoff, Victor N. *A Study of Manichaeism in Bulgaria with Special Reference to the Bogomils*. New York: Carranza, 1927.

Byzantine Empire

Angold, Michael. *The Byzantine Empire, 1025-1204: A Political History*. 2nd ed. London: Longman, 1997.

Bartusis, Mark C. *The Late Byzantine Army: Arms and Society, 1204-1453*. Philadelphia: University of Pennsylvania Press, 1992.

Brand, Charles M. *Byzantium Confronts the West, 1180-1204*. Cambridge, MA: Harvard University Press, 1968.

Bury, J. B. *The Imperial Administrative System in the Ninth Century, with a Revised Text of the Kletorologion of Philotheos*. London: H. Frowde, 1911.

Cheetham, Nicolas. *Mediæval Greece*. New Haven, CT: Yale University Press, 1981.

Clari, Robert de. *The Conquest of Constantinople*. Translated by Edgar H. NcNeal. New York: Columbia University Press, 1936.

Comnena, Anna. *The Alexiad of...* Translated by E. R. A. Sewter. Baltimore, MD: Penguin, 1969.

Dvornik, Francis. *Byzantine Missions Among the Slavs: SS. Constantine-Cyril and Methodius*. New Brunswick, NJ: Rutgers University Press, 1970.

Ferluga, Jadran. *Byzantium on the Balkans: Studies on the Byzantine Administration and the Southern Slavs from the VIIth to the XIIth Centuries*. Amersterdam: Hakkert, 1976.

Godfrey, John. *1204, the Unholy Crusade*. Oxford: Oxford University Press, 1980.

Gunther of Paris. *The Capture of Constantinople: The "Hystoria Constantinopolitana" of...* Translated by Alfred J. Andrea. Philadelphia: University of Pennsylvania Press, 1997.

Head, Constance. *Imperial Twilight: The Palaiologos Dynasty and the Decline of Byzantium*. Chicago, IL: Nelson-Hall, 1977.

Jenkins, Romilly J. H. *Byzantium: The Imperial Centuries, A.D. 610-1071*. New York: Vantage, 1969.

Kazhdan, A. P., and Ann W. Epstein. *Change in Byzantine Culture in the Eleventh and Twelfth Centuries*. Berkeley: University of California Press, 1985.

Liutprand [of Cremona]. *Mission to Constantinople (968 A.D.)*. Translated by Ernest F. Henderson. Lawrence, KS: Coronado, 1972.

Lowe, Alfonso. *The Catalan Vengeance*. London: Routledge and Kegan Paul, 1972.

Lurier, Harold E., ed. and trans. *Crusaders as Conquerors: The Chronicle of the Morea*. New York: Columbia University Press, 1964.

Magdalino, Paul. *The Empire of Manuel I Komnenos, 1143-1180*. Cambridge: Cambridge University Press, 1993.

McGeer, Eric. *Sowing the Dragon's Teeth: Byzantine Warfare in the Tenth Century*. Washington, DC: Dumbarton Oaks, 1995.

Miller, William. *The Latins in the Levant: A History of Frankish Greece (1204-1566)*. Reprint ed. Cambridge: Speculum Historiale, 1964.

Morris, Rosemary. *Monks and Laymen in Byzantium, 843-1118*. Cambridge: Cambridge University Press, 1995.

Nicol, Donald M. *The Despotate of Epiros, 1267-1479*. Cambridge: Cambridge University Press, 1984.

———. *The Last Centuries of Byzantium, 1261-1453*. 2nd ed. Cambridge: Cambridge University Press, 1993.

———. *The Reluctant Emperor: A Biography of John Cantacuzene, Byzantine Emperor and Monk, c. 1295-1383*. Cambridge: Cambridge University Press, 1996.

Psellus, Michael. *Fourteen Byzantine Rulers: The* Chronographia *of . . .* Translated by E. R. A. Sewter. Rev. ed. Baltimore, MD: Penguin, 1966.

Queller, Donald E., and Thomas F. Madden. *The Fourth Crusade: The Conquest of Constantinople*. Philadelphia: University of Pennsylvania Press, 1997.

Runciman, Steven. *The Eastern Schism: A Study of the Papacy and the Eastern Churches during the 11th and 12th Centuries*. London: Panther, 1970.

———. *The Last Byzantine Renaissance*. Cambridge: Cambridge University Press, 1970.

Setton, Kenneth M. *Catalan Domination of Athens, 1311-1388*. Cambridge, MA: Mediæval Academy of America, 1948.

Stephenson, Paul. *Byzantium's Balkan Frontier: A Political Study of the Northern Balkans, 900-1204*. Cambridge: Cambridge University Press, 2000.

Theophanes. Chronographia: *A Chronicle of Eighth Century Byzantium*. Translated by Anthony R. Santoro. Gorham, ME: Greek, Roman and Byzantine Studies Conference, 1982.

Tougher, Shaun. *The Reign of Leo VI (886-912): Politics and People*. Leiden: E. J. Brill, 1997.

Toynbee, Arnold. *Constantine Porphyrogenitus and His World*. London: Oxford University Press, 1973.

Treadgold, Warren T. *Byzantium and Its Army, 284-1081*. Stanford, CA: Stanford University Press, 1995.

Urbansky, Andrew B. *Byzantium and the Danube Frontier: A Study of the Relations between Byzantium, Hungary and the Balkans during the Period of the Comneni*. New York: Twayne, 1968.

Vacalopoulos, Apostolos. *Origins of the Greek Nation: The Byzantine Period, 1204-1461*. Translated by Ian Moles. New Brunswick, NJ: Rutgers University Press, 1970.

Villehardouin. *Memoirs of the Crusades*. Translated by M. R. B. Shaw. Baltimore, MD: Penguin, 1969.

Whittow, Mark. *The Making of Byzantium, 600-1025*. Berkeley: University of California Press, 1996.

Croatia

Guldescu, Stanko. *History of Medieval Croatia*. The Hague: Mouton, 1964.

Krekić, B. *Dubrovnik in the Fourteenth and Fifteenth Centuries: A City Between East and West*. Norman: University of Oklahoma Press, 1972.

Stuard, Susan M. *A State of Deference: Ragusa/Dubrovnik in the Medieval Centuries*. Philadelphia: University of Pennsylvania Press, 1992.

Serbia

Stewart, Cecil. *Serbian Legacy*. London: Allen and Unwin, 1959.

Soulis, George. *The Serbs and Byzantium during the Reign of Tsar Stephen Dušan (1331-1355) and His Successors*. Washington, DC: Dumbarton Oaks Papers, 1984.

PART TWO

Era of Ottoman Domination

1355–1804

In less than 150 years following their first permanent settlement in Europe, the militantly Islamic Ottoman Turks came to dominate most of the Balkan Peninsula and emerged as major players in general European affairs. During the early sixteenth century the Ottomans pushed beyond the Balkans, conquering Hungary and threatening Habsburg Vienna at the very heart of Central Europe. By that time the Balkan states of Byzantium, Bulgaria, Serbia, and Bosnia had been destroyed and the Romanian Principalities reduced to Turkish vassal clientage. The conquered Christian populations of the Balkans were submerged in a powerful, highly centralized, theocratic imperial state grounded in the precepts of Islamic civilization and Turkic traditions. While the subject Christians were reduced to second-class status in Ottoman society, those precepts and traditions offered them a certain measure of religious toleration, administrative autonomy, and economic well-being that was exceptional for nonaristocratic society in the rest of Europe. That condition changed during the seventeenth century, when the effects of Western European technological developments and global exploration began to inflict consistent military defeats and economic hardships on the Turks, resulting in the destabilization of Ottoman society and a progressive worsening in the overall situation of the Ottomans' non-Muslim subjects that continued through the eighteenth century.

CHAPTER FIVE

Ottoman Conquest

The weaknesses of the fragmented Balkan states following Dušan's death in 1355 opened wide the door to the conquest of the Balkan Peninsula by the Ottoman Turks. The Balkan states proved no match for those militantly expansive and highly motivated Islamic invaders, who conquered most of the Balkans (except for its extreme northwestern corner) by the mid-sixteenth century. Its conquest was accomplished in two stages, separated by a decade-long interregnum in the early fifteenth century. The first stage spanned the second half of the fourteenth century, during which Thrace, Bulgaria, Macedonia, and Thessaly were acquired outright and Byzantium, Serbia, Wallachia, and much of Morea were reduced to vassal clientage. The second stage, which extended over most of the fifteenth century, accomplished the destruction of Byzantium and the conquest of Constantinople; the total annexation of Serbia and Morea; the outright acquisition of Epiros, Albania, Bosnia, Hercegovina, and much of Croatia; and the imposition of vassal clientage on Moldavia.

Factors in the Ottomans' Rise and Balkan Conquests

The Ottomans emerged from a welter of small, independent Anatolian Islamic Turkish principalities that succeeded the Seljuk Empire following its defeat by the Mongols in 1243. Most of those states were founded by Turkic tribes previously pushed out of Central Asia into Seljuk territory by the Mongols. Each of them sought to emulate the Seljuks' former predominance, and all faced the political dilemma, common to nomad-based states, of reconciling nomadic traditions with settled, stable governing institutions. Failure to find a solution to that predicament was the bane of all previous nomad states.

As the nomad states lacked professional standing forces, their essential military foundation was continually threatened by the transitory loyalty of rank-and-file warriors, who followed a particular leader only for as long as he was successful. Nomadic traditions of inheritance, which subscribed to equal division among male heirs, worked against a ruler passing on his territorial possessions whole and to a single successor; a frequent result was civil wars among sons that weakened or destroyed the state. Moreover, the nomad warrior lifestyle worked at odds with settled agrarian and urban pursuits that generated the fiscal and economic resources on which governments depended for stability and longevity. While the rulers of the thirteenth-century Anatolian Turkish principalities primarily depended on nomad warriors for their military strength, they desired the benefits of controlling strong, settled, and organized states. Only the Ottomans ultimately succeeded.

Ottoman origins probably lay in the nomadic Turkic Kayı tribe that entered Anatolia from Iran in the early thirteenth century and became allied with the Seljuks. Their tribal leader—traditionally identified as Ertuğrul—was a Seljuk vassal and received a small piece of territory in northwestern Anatolia that abutted Byzantine lands. Although other Turkish principalities shared borders with Byzantium, only that of Emir Osman I (1281-1324), the first truly historical Ottoman ruler, lay astride the main route to Europe, passing through Byzantium's most populous and richest Anatolian territories. Throughout his reign, Osman pursued unrelenting warfare against the Christians lying directly across his border.

Islamic precepts combined with Turkic nomad warrior traditions and geography to make Osman's political situation unique. The concept of "holy war" (*jihad* in Arabic, *gaza* in Turkish) was central to militant Islam. Many Muslim warriors considered it their sacred duty to expand Islam's worldly domain by force, buttressed by the promise that those who died in the effort received the immediate reward of everlasting paradise. A Turk warrior fighting in the name of holy war was called a *gazi,* but all nomad warriors, whether *gazi* or not, sought to enjoy the benefits—plunder and loot—of the militant lifestyle. With most of Anatolia held by Islamic principalities, holy war could be found only in the northwest fighting Christian Byzantium, and the possibilities for the richest fruits of combat could be found only in Byzantine possessions opposite Osman's small state. A swelling number of Anatolian warriors was attracted to Osman's standard, eager to fight for both religious glory and worldly rewards. His principality quickly acquired a multi- or nontribal character, with loyalty to the house of Osman replacing strictly tribal allegiances.

The "house" of Osman was a crucial factor in the rise of the "Ottoman" (*Osmanlı*) state to preeminence among the Anatolian Turkish principalities. Beginning with Osman and ending with the death of Süleyman I the Magnificent (1520-66), it enjoyed an unprecedented succession of ten consecutive extraordinarily talented and successful rulers (*sultans*). No other contemporaneous Christian

Balkan or Muslim West Asian state was blessed with such continuity of effective leadership. Under the house of Osman, traditional nomad attachment to successful commanders became institutionalized as dynastic loyalty, and nomadic mentality gave way to state stability.

One important key to the Ottoman sultans' success was their capitalization on the holy war concept, which provided them with a large, highly motivated military force as well as with a mass following of itinerant peasants and townspeople who flocked to their state from throughout Anatolia seeking new homes and lives in the rich lands captured from Byzantium. The Ottoman principality quickly evolved into a large, heterogeneous, and dynamic frontier society, in which all inhabitants shared an amorphously eclectic lifestyle.

Popular Islamic culture held sway in the Ottoman border state. Holy war was viewed as an absolute duty to be conducted continuously against nonbelievers. None of classical Islam's conditional restraints on defining "true" holy war were given serious consideration. For Ottoman border society, Islam itself was more oral tradition and *sufism* (the mystical branch of Islam, technically considered orthodox) than scholarly theology and accepted law schools. Most Ottomans, rulers and ruled alike, were connected in some way with interrelated networks of religious mystical orders (*dervişes*), urban fellowships (*ahis*), and craft guilds (*esnafs*) found throughout Anatolia.

The early Ottoman rulers proved extremely adept at welding their diverse followers into a loyal, unified society. They succeeded because they themselves were full-fledged members of that society. Not only were they successful military commanders, they were *gazis* themselves. They were members of mystical *derviş* orders, leaders of *ahi* fellowships, and closely tied to the trade guilds. (Each ruler was trained in a particular craft until well into the imperial period of Ottoman history.) Those institutions' networks provided the rulers with financial support, intelligence information, recruiting pools for additional followers, and sometimes fifth-columnists within enemy states. Endowed with stout military and broad popular support, the early Ottoman rulers possessed unique tools for expanding their small border principality into an empire.

To consolidate a stable principality, the Ottoman rulers needed a capital city to serve as a political and economic center. This was accomplished when Osman's son and successor Orhan captured Bursa from the Byzantines in 1326. Possessing a capital of his own, Orhan began acting the ruler in the accepted classical Islamic traditions of the Seljuks, building mosques, patronizing fellowships and guilds, and attracting Muslim scholars. Soon after Orhan took Bursa, the rest of Byzantine Anatolia fell into his hands, and the Ottoman state became a recognized leading power among the Anatolian Turkish principalities.

By 1354 Orhan could stand on the Bosphorus shore of his lands and peer over at the towering walls and majestic domes of Constantinople on the opposite bank.

His state had arrived at an important crossroads, both geographically and figuratively. He controlled the Anatolian access to the most important overland European-Asian trade routes, whose central terminus was the Byzantine capital. He also faced a choice regarding the future road for Ottoman state expansion: To move into Christian Europe or to continue on in Islamic West Asia. The fortuitous acquisition of Gallipoli on the European side of the Dardanelles Strait in 1354 settled the question in favor of continued holy war in the Balkans.

A combination of factors accounted for the Ottomans' rapid and vast Balkan conquests. Once again, the Islamic holy war concept lent them a motivating morale that their European foes initially could not equal. Ottoman forces repeatedly overcame unfavorable battlefield odds to defeat their more numerous European enemies. The compact formations and lumbering shock tactics of the heavily armored Europeans were no match for the more lightly armored Ottoman nomadic horse-archers, who relied on speed, fluidity, and deception in combat. Perhaps more important, the Turk warriors' commitment to both holy war and their Ottoman commanders consistently gave them the combat advantage in terms of morale and unity of command (which military experts regard as utterly crucial for battlefield success). Their European enemies, on the other hand, fielded armies composed of independent-minded nobles (whose eagerness to fight for their ruler depended on the perceived advantages to themselves such action might bring) and impressed, untrained peasants (who had little to gain by risking their lives), which made high combat morale and obedience to the commander's orders somewhat problematic on the battlefield. The armies of state alliances and crusades were usually hastily constructed from forces led by rulers jealous of their own positions and often in direct competition with one another, whose motives for united action were based either on personally threatening circumstances or on political and spiritual benefit. Such forces demonstrated little unity of command and battlefield cohesion. The Ottomans consistently won those campaigns that mattered.

As the Ottomans' victories in the Balkans multiplied, increasing numbers of Anatolian warriors flocked to their ranks, and their territorial conquests grew. In the wake of the advancing armies arrived a steady stream of settlers from the Ottomans' cosmopolitan border society in Anatolia. Many came voluntarily, seeking new lives in a new land, settling in the cities and countrysides of the newly won territories. Some, such as the more nomadic pastoral tribes (termed *yürüks*), were colonized at the sultans' orders in regions depopulated by decades of warfare or to secure and protect strategic lines of communication. As Ottoman territory in the Balkans expanded, the new arrivals provided both a ready recruitment pool for the larger army needed to serve on the borders and a demographic base to ensure firm Ottoman control.

The sultans of the conquest proved to be master strategists and tacticians. They were open to advice from their subordinate commanders and knew how to delegate authority, with the assurance that their orders would be obeyed. The sultans learned lessons from their own successes and mistakes as well as from those of their adversaries, and they were pragmatic and willing to break with tradition whenever there was a practical reason for doing so (such as adopting early gunpowder weapons, especially artillery, over protests from subordinates that these were "unclean" and not in the tradition of classical Islamic warfare).

The Ottoman rulers' skills also were manifest in the political sphere. Unlike their European Christian enemies, who were fragmented politically and at odds with one another, the Ottoman sultans enjoyed centralized authority that facilitated consistent political action. The state itself was their personal possession, in which their will was law (so long as it did not conflict with Islamic sacred law, the *Şeriat*). To counteract the traditional nomadic Turkish system of shared inheritance and to guarantee that the state's unity would be preserved by orderly succession, the early sultans initially designated their eldest sons viceroys (*vezirs*) and top military commanders, thus giving them firsthand leadership experience and the opportunity to win the warriors' allegiance. When, by the mid-fifteenth century, that system proved disruptive, a system of fratricide was institutionalized: Upon a sultan's death, the son who received the allegiance of the key military, administrative, and religious leaders had all of his remaining brothers killed.

The sultans of the conquest successfully broke the innate restraints of nomadic tradition on their authority by making use of institutions adapted from the Byzantines and Seljuks. To impose some measure of permanent control over their nomad warriors, they created a "service nobility" of sorts by granting tribal leaders and notables lucrative land grants for their support in territories won from the Christians. Those endowments, modeled extensively on the *pronoia* military grants of Byzantium, involved revenues extracted from parcels of land rather than ownership of the land itself. They were conditional upon the recipients fulfilling continued military obligations to the ruler.

To further cement their independent authority, the sultans created an efficient administrative system to furnish a stable source of tax revenues. Initially staffed extensively by experienced Christian advisors from Byzantium and other Balkan states, the Ottoman central government became dominated by the sultans' personal household slaves, over whom the rulers held the power of life and death. Thus the Ottoman government became the most effectively centralized in all of Europe from the late fourteenth through mid-sixteenth centuries and the envy of many rulers of Christian European states.

Slaves also were key in the sultans creating their own military forces to augment (and counterbalance) the army's nomad warriors. Following Seljuk tradition, the Ottomans formed standing professional military units of Janissaries (*Yeni-çeri* in Turkish, meaning "New Troops") from enslaved prisoners of war, who fell under their direct personal control and were separate from the traditional nomad warrior army. As the empire expanded in the Balkans, so too did the number of Janissaries. Like the slave-administrators, the Janissaries were completely dependent on the will of their ruler-masters, rendering them the most effective standing military force in Europe until the mid-sixteenth century.

Institutionalized slavery provided the Ottoman sultans with the means of breaking the limitations imposed on centralized state development by nomadic traditions through creating an invulnerable power base of their own. Slavery, combined with the sultans' alliances with *derviş* orders, *ahi* fellowships, and guilds scattered throughout their territories, formed the foundation on which they built their strong, centralized state.

Also important in the Ottomans' rise was their rulers' mastery of diplomacy, coupled with their abilities to understand the inner workings of their enemies and to use that knowledge against them. Many of their Balkan conquests were accomplished through diplomatic, rather than violent, means. The sultans played the divided Balkan Christian states one against another through a series of temporary and shifting alliances, often sealed by deft political marriages with women from the ruling houses of their Christian opponents; Byzantine, Bulgarian, and Serbian spouses proliferated in the sultans' harems.

The early sultans also realized that the Christian states were disunited internally by the growing institution of feudalism, which they came to understand, respect, and use to their advantage. The peaceful acquisition of troops and revenues was far more preferable in the sultans' eyes than their attainment by costly and disruptive warfare. Typically, the Ottomans threatened their enemies with violent military actions in hopes that their rulers would accept vassalage to the sultans, which entailed paying annual tribute and supplying military forces on demand. Only when such hopes proved unattainable, or when vassals reneged on their obligations, did the Ottomans resort to all-out warfare. Throughout the period of the conquest, Balkan Christian rulers commonly embraced Ottoman vassal status in an effort to preserve their positions and possessions. The fact that Byzantine, Bulgarian, Serbian, and Bosnian rulers all eventually attempted to break their vassal pledges ultimately resulted in their military defeat and the Ottomans' outright expropriation of their states.

The sultans of the conquest also understood the religious divisions among their Christian enemies—between Orthodox and Roman Catholic and between mainstream Christians and heretics. For example, during their military operations against the Latins in Greece, Bosnia, and along the Adriatic, the Ottomans played to their own advantage on the Orthodox populations' deep-seated distrust of Roman Catholicism following the Great Schism of 1054 and the Crusades. When Byzantine Emperor John VIII Palaiologos (1425-48) agreed to reunite the Orthodox and Roman Catholic churches on papal terms at the Council of Florence in 1439, the Ottomans used the disaffection of the general Orthodox population in Byzantium to ease their way in conquering the Morea and the Byzantine capital of Constantinople itself.

A final factor aiding the Ottoman conquest of the Balkans was the international situation in Europe during the mid-fourteenth through mid-sixteenth centuries. The Balkan Christian states were weak and divided, while disruptive conditions hampered effective concerted action on the part of Western European states. The arrival of the Ottomans in Europe coincided with the ravages of the Black Plague throughout the West, which crippled the westerners' ability to respond to the Turkish threat. Moreover, Western Europe then was experiencing an era of intense political fragmentation that undercut its medieval order. The Avignon Captivity (1303-78) and the resulting Roman Catholic Great Schism (1378-1418) undermined traditional papal authority. The Holy Roman Empire was transformed into a disunited federation of independent German states by the Golden Bull of 1356, and its Italian city-state possessions broke free of imperial control. France and England were locked in the Hundred Years War (1338-1453). Poland-Lithuania had its hands full with the Teutonic Knights and a rabid internal conflict between the king and the aristocracy.

Only Venice and Hungary, which lay astride most of the Balkans' northern frontier, were in a position to oppose the Ottomans' advance. Venice, wracked by plague and demographically small, could do little more than defend its scattered Balkan coastal and offshore possessions. The Hungarians earned lasting national glory by standing against the Turks and taking the lead in three Balkan crusades, in 1396, 1444, and 1448. All three ended in defeat because of the lowered prestige of the papacy, which carried less weight in mobilizing Christian zeal for the fight, and the unwillingness of rulers in the larger Western states to participate, lest rival states prosper in their absence by attacking them at home. All told, Western Europe adopted a defensive posture regarding the Ottomans, effectively abandoning the Balkans to them until the seventeenth century.

The First Stage of Conquest, 1354-1402

Once Orhan decided to pursue holy war against the Christians in Europe, Anatolian Turks were settled in and around Gallipoli to secure it as a springboard for military operations in Thrace against the Byzantines and Bulgarians. Most of eastern Thrace was overrun by Ottoman forces within a decade and permanently brought under Orhan's control by means of heavy Turkish colonization. The initial Thracian conquests placed the Ottomans strategically astride all of the major overland communication routes linking Constantinople to the Balkans' frontiers, facilitating their expanded military operations. In addition, control of the highways in Thrace isolated Byzantium from direct overland contact with any of its potential allies in the Balkans or in Western Europe. Byzantine Emperor John V was forced to sign an unfavorable treaty with Orhan in 1356 that recognized his Thracian losses.

Soon after Orhan's death in 1360, his successor Murad I (1360-89) captured Adrianople, the most important Byzantine military, administrative, and economic center in Thrace. By transferring his capital from Bursa, in Anatolia, to that newly won European city, which he renamed Edirne, Murad signaled his intentions to continue Ottoman expansion in Europe. Before the fall of Adrianople, most Europeans regarded the Ottoman presence in Thrace as merely the latest unpleasant episode in a long string of chaotic events in the southern Balkans. After Murad designated Edirne as his capital, they realized that the Ottomans intended to remain in Europe at Christendom's expense.

The Balkan states immediately menaced by the Ottomans' conquests in Thrace—Byzantium, Bulgaria, and Serbia—were ill-prepared to deal with the threat.

Byzantium's territory was fragmented mostly among the capital at Constantinople and its Thracian environs, the city of Thessaloniki and its immediate surroundings, and the Despotate of the Morea in the Peloponnese. Contact between Constantinople and the two other regions was possible only by means of a tenuous sea route through the Dardanelles kept open by the fickle Genoese. None of Byzantium's components possessed the resources to defeat the Turks on its own, and concerted action on their part was impossible. The survival of Constantinople itself depended on its legendary defense walls, the lack of an Ottoman navy, and the willingness of the Turks to honor provisions in the 1356 treaty permitting the city to be provisioned.

Bulgaria under Tsar Ivan Aleksandŭr was in decline. To consolidate his authority over as much territory as possible, he divided the state into three appanages held by his sons. That policy proved only partially successful. In the 1340s a *bolyar* named Balik tore Dobrudzha away from Aleksandŭr's control. (Dobrudzha later received its lasting name from a Turkish corruption of the name of Balik's brother and successor, Dobrotitsa [ca. 1366-85].)

Bulgaria's cohesion was shattered further in the 1350s by a rivalry between the holder of Vidin, Ivan Stratsimir, Ivan Aleksandŭr's sole surviving son by his first wife, and Ivan Shishman, the product of Aleksandŭr's second marriage and the *tsar's* designated successor. The disunity caused by the half-brothers' antagonisms was magnified during the 1350s and 1360s in the religious sphere by the ascendancy of Hesychism within the Bulgarian Tŭrnovo Orthodox Patriarchate. Intolerant of mainstream Orthodox practices, heretics, and Jews, the Hesychasts, led by the fanatical monk Teodosii, initiated disruptive persecutions that caused popular unrest and a wave of emigrations precisely when the Ottoman threat to Bulgaria reached serious proportions.

In addition to internal problems, Bulgaria was further crippled by Hungarian attack. In 1365 Hungarian King Louis I invaded and seized Vidin province, whose ruler Stratsimir was taken captive. Despite the concurrent loss of most Bulgarian

Thracian holdings to the Turks, Ivan Aleksandŭr became fixated on the Hungarians in Vidin. He formed a coalition against them with Dobrudzhan ruler Dobrotitsa and Voievod Vladislav I Vlaicu of Wallachia. Although the Hungarians were repulsed and Stratsimir was restored to his throne, Bulgaria emerged more intensely divided than previously. Stratsimir proclaimed himself *tsar* of an "Empire" of Vidin in 1370, and Dobrotitsa received de facto recognition as independent despot in Dobrudzha. Bulgaria's efforts were squandered to little domestic purpose and against the wrong enemy.

Given Serbia's preeminence in the Balkans under Car Stefan Dušan, its rapid dissolution following his death in 1355 was dramatic. The powerful regional Serb nobles demonstrated little respect for his successor, Stefan Uroš V. Young, weak, and perhaps mentally handicapped, Uroš was incapable of ruling as his father had. The separatist-minded *bojars* were quick to take advantage of the situation, and Serbia fragmented.

First to throw off Serbian control were the Greek provinces of Thessaly and Epiros as well as Dušan's former Albanian holdings. A series of small independent principalities arose in western and southern Macedonia, while the Hungarians encroached deeper into Serb lands in the north. Uroš held only the core Serbian lands, whose nobles, although more powerful than their prince, generally remained loyal. These core lands consisted of: The western lands, including Montenegro (Zeta); the southern lands, held by Jovan Uglješa in Serres, encompassing all of eastern Macedonia; and the central Serbian lands, stretching from the Danube south into central Macedonia, coruled by Uroš and the powerful noble Vukašin Mrnjav-čević, who held Prilep in Macedonia. Far from preserving Serb unity, Uroš's loosely amalgamated domains were wracked by constant civil war among the regional nobles, leaving Serbia vulnerable to the rising Ottoman threat.

By 1370 Murad controlled most all of Thrace, bringing him into direct contact with Bulgaria and the southeastern Serbian lands ruled by Uglješa. Uglješa, the most powerful Serb regional ruler, unsuccessfully attempted to forge an anti-Ottoman alliance of Balkan states in 1371. Byzantium, vulnerable to the Turks because of its food supply situation, refused to cooperate. Bulgaria, following Ivan Aleksandŭr's death early that year, lay officially divided into the "Empire" of Vidin, ruled by Stratsimir (1370-96), and Aleksandŭr's direct successor Tsar Ivan Shishman (1371-93), who ruled central Bulgaria from Tŭrnovo. Young, his hold on the throne unsteady, threatened by Stratsimir, and probably pressured by the Turks, Shishman could not afford to participate in Uglješa's scheme. Of the regional Serb *bojars,* only Vukašin, protector of Uroš and Uglješa's brother, joined in the effort. The others either failed to recognize the Ottoman danger or refused to participate lest competitors attacked while they were in the field.

Uglješa and Vukašin, accompanied by the latter's son Marko, led their forces into Western Thrace in September 1371, advancing to the Maritsa River near the village of Ormenion (Chernomen), northwest of Edirne. There Murad launched a surprise attack with his outnumbered troops and annihilated the Serbian army. Both Uglješa and Vukašin perished in the carnage. So overwhelming was the Ottoman victory that the Turks referred to the battle as the Rout (or Destruction) of the Serbs.

What little unity Serbia possessed collapsed after the catastrophe at Ormenion. Uroš died before the year was out, ending the Nemanja dynasty, and large areas of central Serbia broke away as independent principalities, reducing it to half of its former size. No future ruler ever again officially held the office of *car,* and no single *bojar* enjoyed enough power or respect to gain recognition as a unifying leader. Vukašin's son Marko, who survived the slaughter, proclaimed himself Serbian "king" (*kralj*) but was unable to make good on his claim outside of his lands around Prilep in central Macedonia. Serbia slipped into accelerated fragmentation and internecine warfare among the proliferating regional princes.

In the aftermath of the Ormenion battle, Ottoman raids into Serbia and Bulgaria intensified. The enormity of the Turks' victory and the incessant Turkish raids into his lands convinced Tŭrnovo Bulgarian Tsar Shishman of the necessity for coming to terms with the Ottomans. By 1376 at the latest, Shishman accepted vassal status under Murad and sent his sister as the sultan's "wife" to the harem at Edirne. The arrangement did not prevent Ottoman raiders from continuing to plunder inside of Shishman's borders. As for Byzantium, Emperor John V definitively accepted Ottoman vassalage soon after the battle, opening the door to Murad's direct interference in Byzantine domestic politics.

The Bulgarians and Serbs enjoyed a brief respite during the 1370s and into the 1380s when matters in Anatolia and increased meddling in Byzantium's political affairs kept Murad preoccupied. In Serbia, the lull permitted the northern Serb *bojar* Prince Lazar Hrebeljanović (1371-89), with the support of powerful Macedonian and Montenegrin nobles and the backing of the Serbian Orthodox Patriarchate of Peć, to consolidate control over much of the core Serbian lands. Most of the Serb regional rulers in Macedonia, including Marko, accepted vassalage under Murad to preserve their positions, and many of them led Serb forces in the sultan's army operating in Anatolia against his Turkish rivals.

By the mid-1380s Murad's attention once again focused on the Balkans. With his Bulgarian vassal Shishman preoccupied by a war with Wallachian Voievod Dan I (ca. 1383-86), in 1385 Murad took Sofia, the last remaining Bulgarian possession south of the Balkan Mountains, opening the way toward strategically located Niš, the northern terminus of the important Vardar-Morava highway. Murad captured Niš in 1386, perhaps forcing Lazar of Serbia to accept Ottoman vassalage soon afterward. While he pushed deeper into the north-central Balkans, Murad also had forces moving west along the *Via Ignatia* into Macedonia, forcing vassal status on regional rulers who until that time had escaped that fate. One contingent reached the Albanian Adriatic coast in 1385. Another took and occupied Thessaloniki in

1387. The danger to the continued independence of the Balkan Christian states grew alarmingly apparent. (See Map 5.)

When Anatolian affairs forced Murad to leave the Balkans in 1387, his Serbian and Bulgarian vassals attempted to sever their ties to him. Lazar formed a coalition with Tvrtko I of Bosnia and Stratsimir of Vidin. After he refused an Ottoman demand that he live up to his vassal obligations, troops were dispatched against him. Lazar and Tvrtko met the Turks and defeated them at Pločnik, west of Niš. The victory by his fellow Christian princes encouraged Shishman to shed Ottoman vassalage and reassert Bulgarian independence.

Murad returned from Anatolia in 1388 and launched a lightning campaign against the Bulgarian rulers Shishman and Stratsimir, who swiftly were forced into vassal submission. He then demanded that Lazar proclaim his vassalage and pay tribute. Confident because of the victory at Pločnik, the Serbian prince refused and turned to Tvrtko of Bosnia and Vuk Branković, his son-in-law and independent ruler of northern Macedonia and Kosovo, for aid against the certain Ottoman retaliatory offensive.

Murad's expected assault materialized in 1389. The sultan personally led the largest Ottoman force mustered in the Balkans to that time, which included Christian contingents furnished by Bulgarian, Serbian, Albanian, and Macedonian vassals, Kralj Marko of Prilep among them. Likewise, Lazar himself commanded the coalition army comprised of troops of his loyal Serb *bojars,* Branković's Kosovar and northern Macedonian forces, a Bosnian contingent, and some allied Hungarian and Albanian units. The protagonists met at Kosovo Polje (the "Field of the Blackbirds") on 28 June 1389.

In military terms, the bloody Battle of Kosovo Polje technically was a draw. So much mythology surrounds the engagement that its details largely are obscured. It is certain that both Murad and Lazar were killed—Murad perhaps by a group of Hungarian knights and Lazar, possibly after he was captured, by order of Bayezid I (1389-1402), who replaced his dead father as commander on the battlefield. Both sides sustained huge casualties and, by the end of the day, the surviving Serbian and Bosnian troops withdrew, leaving the Turks in possession of the field. Decimated to the point that they could not pursue their enemies, the Turks also withdrew to their Thracian territories so that Bayezid could solidify his succession against opposition from his brothers.

Although a draw, Kosovo Polje proved an important Ottoman victory over the Serbs. While the Ottomans could count on an Anatolian reserve to replace their losses, the Serbs, who had mustered all of their able-bodied troops for the battle, were left irreparably weakened. In the three years following the battle, Ottoman raids forced one militarily ineffective Serb regional ruler after another to accept vassalage to Bayezid. Lazar's young and weak successor Stefan Lazarević (1389-1427) concluded a vassal agreement with Bayezid in 1390 to counter Hungarian moves into northern Serbia, while Vuk Branković, the last independent Serb prince, held out until 1392.

Bayezid, whose nickname was "the Thunderbolt," lost little time in expanding Ottoman Balkan conquests. He followed up on his victory by raiding throughout Serbia and southern Albania, forcing most of the local princes into vassalage. Both to secure the southern stretch of the Vardar-Morava highway and to establish a firm base for permanent expansion westward to the Adriatic coast, Bayezid settled large numbers of *yürüks* along the Vardar River valley in Macedonia.

The appearance of Turk raiders at Hungary's southern borders awakened Hungarian King Sigismund of Luxemburg (1387-1437) to the danger that the Ottomans posed to his kingdom, and he sought out Balkan allies for a new anti-Ottoman coalition. By early 1393 Tŭrnovo Bulgaria's Ivan Shishman, hoping to throw off his onerous vassalage, was in secret negotiations with Sigismund, along with Wallachian Voievod Mircea the Old (1386-1418) and, possibly, Vidin's Ivan Stratsimir. Bayezid got wind of the talks and launched a devastating campaign against Shishman. Tŭrnovo was captured after a lengthy siege, and Shishman fled to Nikopol. After that town fell to Bayezid, Shishman was captured and beheaded. All of his lands were annexed outright by the sultan, and Stratsimir, whose Vidin holdings had escaped Bayezid's wrath, was forced to reaffirm his vassalage.

Having dealt harshly and effectively with his disloyal Bulgarian vassals, Bayezid then turned his attention south to Thessaly and the Morea, whose Greek lords had accepted Ottoman vassalage in the 1380s. Their incessant bickering among themselves, especially those of the Greek Morean magnates, required Bayezid's intervention. He summoned a meeting of all his Balkan vassals at Serres in 1394 to settle these and other outstanding matters. Among the sultan's attending vassals were the Thessalian and Morean nobles, Byzantine Emperor Manuel II Palaiologos (1391-1425), and Serbian Prince Lazarević. At the meeting, Bayezid acquired possession of all disputed territories, and all of the attendees were required to reaffirm their vassal status.

When the Moreans later reneged on their Serres agreement with Bayezid, the angered Ottoman ruler blockaded the Morean despot's imperial brother Manuel II in Constantinople and then marched southward and annexed Thessaly. The Duchy of Athens accepted Ottoman overlordship when Turkish forces appeared on its border. Although a massive Ottoman punitive raid into the Peloponnese in 1395 netted much booty, events in the Balkans' northeast saved Morea from further direct attack at the time.

While Bayezid was occupied in Greece, Mircea of Wallachia conducted a series of raids across the Danube into Ottoman territory. In retaliation, Bayezid's forces, which included Serb vassal troops led by Lazarević and Kralj Marko, struck into Wallachia in 1395 but were defeated at Rovine, where Marko was killed. The victory saved Wallachia from Turkish occupation, but Mircea accepted vassalage under

Bayezid to avert further Ottoman intervention. The sultan took consolation for his less than victorious efforts in annexing Dobrudzha and in supporting a pretender, Vlad I (1395-97), to the Wallachian throne. Two years of civil war ensued before Mircea regained complete control of the principality.

In 1396 Hungarian King Sigismund finally pulled together a crusade against the Ottomans. Comprised primarily of Hungarian and French knights, but including some Wallachian troops, the crusader army, though nominally led by Sigismund, lacked command cohesion. The crusaders crossed the Danube, marched through Vidin, and arrived at Nikopol, where they met the Turks. The headstrong French knights refused to follow Sigismund's battle plans, resulting in their crushing defeat. Because Stratsimir had permitted the crusaders to pass through Vidin, Bayezid invaded his lands, took him prisoner, and annexed his territories. With Vidin's fall, Bulgaria ceased to exist, becoming the first major Balkan Christian state to disappear completely by direct Ottoman conquest.

Following Nikopol, Bayezid contented himself with raiding Hungary, Wallachia, and Bosnia. He conquered most of Albania and forced the remaining northern Albanian lords into vassalage. A new, halfhearted siege of Constantinople was undertaken but lifted in 1397 after Emperor Manuel II, Bayezid's vassal, agreed that the sultan should confirm all future Byzantine emperors. Soon thereafter Bayezid was called back to Anatolia to deal with continuing problems with the Ottomans' Turkish rivals and never returned to the Balkans. (See Map 5.)

Bayezid took with him an army composed primarily of Balkan vassal troops, including Serbs led by Lazarević. He soon faced an invasion of Anatolia by the Mongol ruler Timurlenk (Tamerlane) (1369-1405), and their armies met outside of Ankara in 1402. The Ottomans were routed and Bayezid was taken prisoner, later dying in captivity. The Ottomans were reduced to Mongol vassals. A civil war, lasting from 1402 to 1413, broke out among Bayezid's surviving sons. Known in Ottoman history as the Interregnum, that struggle temporarily halted active Ottoman expansion in the Balkans.

The Second Stage of Conquest, 1413–1521

The Ottoman Interregnum brought a brief period of semi-independence to the vassal Christian Balkan states. Süleyman, one of the late sultan's sons, held the Ottoman capital at Edirne and proclaimed himself ruler, but his brothers refused to recognize him. He then concluded alliances with Byzantium, to which Thessaloniki was returned, and with Venice in 1403 to bolster his position. Süleyman's imperious character, however, turned his Balkan vassals against him. In 1410 he was defeated and killed by his brother Musa, who won the Ottoman Balkans with the support of Byzantine Emperor Manuel II, Serbian Despot Stefan Lazarević,

Wallachian Voievod Mircea, and the two last Bulgarian rulers' sons. Musa then was confronted for sole control of the Ottoman throne by his younger brother Mehmed, who had freed himself of Mongol vassalage and held Ottoman Anatolia.

Concerned over the growing independence of his Balkan Christian vassals, Musa turned on them. Unfortunately, he alienated the Islamic bureaucratic and commercial classes in his Balkan lands by continually favoring the lower social elements to gain wide popular support. Alarmed, the Balkan Christian vassal rulers turned to Mehmed, as did the chief Ottoman military, religious, and commercial leaders. In 1412 Mehmed invaded the Balkans, took Sofia and Niš, and joined forces with Lazarević's Serbs. The following year Mehmed decisively defeated Musa outside of Sofia. Musa was killed, and Mehmed I (1413-21) emerged as the sole ruler of a reunited Ottoman state.

Mehmed faced a delicate political situation in the Balkans. His Serbian, Wallachian, and Byzantine vassals virtually were independent. The Albanian tribes were uniting into a single state, and Bosnia remained completely independent, as did Moldavia. Hungary retained territorial ambitions in the Balkans, and Venice held numerous Balkan coastal possessions. Prior to Bayezid's death, Ottoman control of the Balkans appeared a certainty. At the end of the Interregnum, that certainty seemed open to question.

Mehmed generally resorted to diplomacy rather than militancy in dealing with the situation. While he did conduct raiding expeditions into neighboring European lands, which returned much of Albania to Ottoman control and forced Bosnian King-Ban Tvrtko II Tvrtković (1404-9, 1421-43), along with many Bosnian regional nobles, to accept formal Ottoman vassalage, Mehmed conducted only one actual war with the Europeans—a short and indecisive conflict with Venice.

The new sultan had grave domestic problems. Musa's former policies sparked discontent among the Ottoman Balkans' lower classes. In 1416 a popular revolt of Muslims and Christians broke out in Dobrudzha, led by Musa's former confidant, the scholar-mystic Şeyh Bedreddin, and supported by Wallachian Voievod Mircea. Bedreddin preached such concepts as merging Islam, Christianity, and Judaism into a single faith and the social betterment of free peasants and nomads at the expense of the Ottoman bureaucratic and professional classes. Mehmed crushed the revolt and Bedreddin met a tragic death. Mircea then occupied Dobrudzha, but Mehmed wrested the region back in 1419, capturing the Danubian fort of Giurgiu and forcing Wallachia back into vassalage. Mehmed spent the rest of his reign reorganizing Ottoman state structures disrupted by the Interregnum. The renewed conquest of the Balkans was taken up by his successor, Sultan Murad II (1421-51).

After spending a year consolidating his position, Murad turned his attention to the Balkans. He initiated the sixth Ottoman siege of Constantinople in 1422, raided Wallachia, and, after Venice took Thessaloniki from Byzantium in 1423, besieged that city as well, forcing the Venetians to pay tribute. In a series of treaties signed during 1424 with Hungary, Byzantium, Wallachia, and Serbia, Murad gained those signatories' acceptance of vassal status and their agreement to pay tribute. Venice, its commercial predominance in the eastern Mediterranean threatened by the strong Ottoman Balkan presence, signed no treaty with Murad, so war persisted until 1430. In that year Murad captured Thessaloniki and forced the Venetians to sign a peace, in which they accepted tributary status and recognized Ottoman control of Macedonia in return for access to the Black Sea and retention of certain Balkan coastal ports. At the same time, the independent city-republic of Dubrovnik was pressured into paying similar tribute to Murad.

Of all the Christian states facing Murad in Europe, Hungary was by far the most dangerous, constituting the principle obstacle to continued Ottoman expansion in the Balkans and to future European conquests in the north and west. Murad became convinced of the need to eliminate Hungarian influence in Wallachia, Bosnia, and Serbia at all costs.

Wallachia fell into anarchy following Mircea's death in 1418. After 1420 control of the principality had changed hands some nine times between Dan II and Radu II Praznaglava before Voievod Alexander I Aldea (1431-36), an Ottoman vassal, ended the game of musical thrones. Sigismund later arranged for Aldea's overthrow and replacement by Vlad II Dracul (1436-42, 1443-47), who renounced Ottoman suzerainty. In Bosnia, Tvrtko II, although technically an Ottoman vassal, had once been the creature of Sigismund, and Hungarian pretensions to Bosnia remained strong.

As for Serbia, after Lazarević died in 1427 the state was weakened once again by dynastic problems, since the dead ruler left no direct heir. During the Interregnum, Lazarević had grown friendly toward Sigismund, accepting Hungarian suzerainty in 1411 and receiving land grants in Hungarian-held Balkan territory, including the silver mining town of Srebrenica in eastern Bosnia. After Mehmed reunited the Ottoman state, Lazarević renewed his vassalage to the sultan but retained his client status to Sigismund as well. As he grew ill in the 1420s, Lazarević designated Djordje Branković (1427-56), a powerful Kosovo *bojar*, as his successor and had him recognized as both Sigismund's and Murad's vassal. Murad invaded Serbia immediately on Branković's elevation to the Serbian throne, and Sigismund thereupon occupied the fortress city of Belgrade, Lazarević's former capital, to prevent Murad from acquiring that strategically located stronghold. Branković was forced to build the fortress of Smederevo on the Danube, southeast of Belgrade, to serve as Serbia's new and last capital.

Ottoman raids into Albania, Greece, and Morea intensified in the 1430s. Most local lords of those regions turned to Hungary for help. Therefore, beginning in 1432 Murad concentrated on harassing Sigismund's kingdom and its allies, paying particular attention to Transylvania. Ottoman military efforts intensified after Sigismund died in 1437. Extensive swaths of Serbian territory were occupied outright, but Murad's siege of Belgrade proved unsuccessful. His efforts to push on against the Hungarians were cut short in 1439 when he was called to Anatolia to deal with yet another Seljuk Turkish threat to his Asian holdings.

Murad's European enemies attempted to take advantage of his absence. Byzantine Emperor John VIII Palaiologos traveled to Italy in a desperate effort to win military assistance against the Ottomans from the papacy and other Western rulers. The price he paid for promises of aid was the union of his empire's Orthodox church to that of the Roman Catholic on papal terms. John signed the formal act of union at the Catholic Church Council of Florence in 1439. By the terms of the union, the Orthodox faithful were required to: Recognize the pope as the supreme head of the united Christian church instead of leadership by ecumenical councils alone; accept a Catholic modification to the definition of the Trinity in the Nicæan Creed (the so-called *filioque* clause); substitute unleavened for leavened bread in the sacrament of Holy Communion; and espouse the Catholic concept of Purgatory. In the end, however, John's effort failed. The pope and the Western rulers were so locked in their own power struggles that no practical material aid ever materialized for Byzantium, while the empire's general Orthodox clergy and population so vehemently opposed the union that John and his successors, who dutifully adhered to the agreement, lost most of their subjects' active support. Instead of strengthening Byzantium's position, the union ultimately only weakened it further.

Murad expended some effort in bringing Albania, Epiros, and the Adriatic coastline under direct Ottoman authority. With Venice, his principal protagonist in those regions, distracted by a war with its rival Genoa, in 1441 Murad captured the Epirote center of Ioannina, and the fractious central and southern Albanian petty lords were stripped of their independence. In 1443, with Murad in Anatolia and hoping to throw off Ottoman authority completely, the Albanian lords united under the leadership of George Kastriotis, an experienced Albanian warrior who had fought in the Ottoman ranks during Murad's previous campaigns. For the next two decades Kastriotis fought a fierce and successful guerilla war against the Ottomans in the rugged Albanian Alps, earning the name under which he became famous— Skanderbeg (Lord Alexander [the Great]).

The Hungarians, now ruled by Władisław I Jagiełło (1440-44) of the Polish-Lithuanian royal dynasty, saw Murad's absence in Anatolia as an opportunity for decisive action. Led by their greatest general, János Hunyadi, a Magyarized Romanian noble from Transylvania, in 1441 and 1442 they attacked Murad's skeleton Balkan forces and penetrated deep into Ottoman territory. Hunyadi's victories mobilized some enthusiasm in the West for a new crusade to expel the Islamic enemy from European soil. Pope Eugenius IV's (1431-47) efforts to raise a pan-European crusade failed because of the usual rivalries among the leading Western monarchs, so a smaller coalition was hastily formed. Nominally led by King Władisław but actually commanded by Hunyadi, the crusading force that took the field consisted of Hungarians, Wallachians under Dracul, Djordje Branković's Serbs, and a large contingent of German and French knights.

In 1443 Hunyadi and his crusaders crossed the Danube into Serbia, defeated two Ottoman armies, captured Niš, crossed the Balkan Mountains in winter, and advanced as far as Sofia. Weather and supply problems, however, forced Hunyadi to retire north of the Danube early in 1444. Murad, faced with Skanderbeg's rebellion and revolts in the Peloponnese, negotiated with the crusaders, signing a ten-year truce at Edirne in 1444 that recognized Serbia's independence under Branković and released Wallachia from Ottoman vassalage. Since he soon after struck a peace with his Anatolian rivals, Murad, sick of war and yearning for personal tranquility, abdicated in favor of his twelve-year-old son Mehmed, believing that the Ottoman state was secure.

The youthful Mehmed proved unable to control his high Ottoman officials and military commanders. Made aware of the situation, Pope Eugenius urged the crusade's renewal, and Hunyadi, under pressure from King Władisław but concerned over breaking the solemn oaths that bound the Edirne truce, reluctantly agreed. The new effort's quickly conceived plans entailed a rapid march of the crusader army into the Balkans, where it would be joined by Skanderbeg and his Albanian forces for an assault on Edirne. Meanwhile, the Venetians were to seal off the Straits to prevent Ottoman Anatolian forces from crossing over into the Balkans, and Byzantine troops in Morea were to conduct diversionary attacks. In the end, the plans mostly fell through.

Unfavorable winds prevented the Venetians from closing the Straits, and Murad, hastily emerging from retirement in Anatolia to serve as supreme Ottoman military commander, bribed the Genoese into transporting a large Ottoman force to the Balkans. The Byzantine diversions in the Peloponnese came off as planned, but the crusader army's main assault went awry. It began later than intended and its manpower was reduced by Branković's refusal to participate, lest he lose Serbia's newly regained independence. After crossing the Danube, the crusaders were forced to march eastward along its southern bank through northern Bulgaria toward the Black Sea because Branković refused them passage through Serbian lands. They arrived outside of the port city of Varna in November 1444 only to discover that Murad had returned and had assembled an army to meet them. In the ensuing battle, King Władisław was killed and the crusaders nearly were wiped out. Hunyadi survived only by ignominious flight. Skanderbeg and the Albanians never arrived and, on learning of the debacle, they retired to the fastness of their mountain strongholds.

The Crusade of Varna was the last concerted attempt by the medieval Christian West to drive the Ottomans from Europe. Its failure had profound consequences for the Balkans. As the only effort made to live up to the promises of aid given Emperor John VIII at Florence, its defeat abandoned Byzantium to its fate. The rest of the Balkan Christian states were left to fend for themselves as best they could. Divided, lacking significant military resources, and mostly dependent on Ottoman vassal status for their continued survival, they were in no position to resist serious Ottoman efforts to eliminate them entirely. Serbian Despot Branković reaffirmed his vassalage to Murad soon after the battle, and, in 1446, Wallachian Voievod Dracul, sensing the way that the political winds now blew, shifted his allegiance from Hungary to Murad and accepted Ottoman suzerainty.

Having dealt with the immediate danger, Murad resumed retirement but, once again, it was temporary. Mehmed remained incapable of controlling his high officials, and in 1446 a coup by the young sultan's grand vezir returned Murad to the throne. Resigned to his fate, Murad acted to secure definitive control over all of the Balkans. Morea was ravaged as punishment for its activities during the failed crusade, and its Palaiologian rulers were forced into tributary vassalage. Most of mainland Greece, except for Athens and a string of coastal ports and offshore islands held by Venice, was conquered outright. In 1447 Murad campaigned in Albania against Skanderbeg's rebels, but operations were cut short by news of a new crusader invasion led by Hunyadi.

The crusaders pushed through Serbia, despite Branković's refusal to participate or help, and advanced southward into Kosovo. They were joined by troops sent by Skanderbeg and Voievod Vladislav II (1447-56), Hunyadi's new Wallachian vassal. In October 1448 Murad intercepted the crusaders at Kosovo Polje, the site of Serbia's defeat almost sixty years earlier. After two days of battle, Hunyadi's troops were routed, dampening Western crusading zeal and crippling Hungarian offensive capabilities. Wallachia again accepted Ottoman suzerainty, Serbia was rewarded for its neutrality by another decade of vassal existence, and Skanderbeg was left isolated. The Second Battle of Kosovo Polje guaranteed Ottoman control over the Balkans south of the Danube. (See Map 5.)

Mehmed II (1451-81) again came to the Ottoman throne following Murad's death in 1451. Older and a good deal wiser, he made capturing Constantinople his first priority, believing that it would solidify his power over the high military and administrative officials who had caused him such problems during his earlier reign. Good reasons underlay his decision. So long as Constantinople remained in Christian hands, his enemies could use it as either a potential base for splitting the empire at its center or as an excuse for the Christian West's continued military efforts. Constantinople's location also made it the natural "middleman" center for both land and sea trade between the eastern Mediterranean and central Asia, possession of which would ensure immense wealth. Just as important, Constantinople was a fabled imperial city, and its capture and possession would bestow untold prestige on its conqueror, who would be seen by Muslims as a hero and by Muslims and Christians alike as a great and powerful emperor.

Mehmed spent two years preparing for his attempt on the Byzantine capital. He built a navy to cut the city off from outside help by sea; he purchased an arsenal of large cannons from the Hungarian gunsmith Urban; he sealed the Bosphorus north of the city by erecting a powerful fortress on its European shore to prevent succor arriving from the Black Sea; and he meticulously concentrated in Thrace every available military unit in his lands. A trade agreement with Venice prevented the Venetians from intervening on behalf of the Byzantines, and the rest of Western Europe unwittingly cooperated with Mehmed's plans by being totally absorbed in internecine wars and political rivalries.

In April 1453 Mehmed laid siege to Constantinople. Although the city's defenders, led by Emperor Constantine XI Palaiologos (1448-53), put up a heroic defense, without the benefit of outside aid their efforts were doomed. The formerly impregnable land walls were breached after two months of constant pounding by Mehmed's heavy artillery. In the predawn hours of 29 May 1453, Mehmed ordered an all-out assault on the battered ramparts. After a brief but vicious melee at the walls, in which Emperor Constantine died bravely, the Ottoman troops broke through and swept over the city. Constantinople, for a millennium considered by many Europeans the divinely ordained capital of the Christian Roman Empire, fell to Mehmed and was transformed into what many Muslims considered the divinely ordained capital of the Islamic Ottoman Empire. Renamed Istanbul by Mehmed, the fabled city's imperial legacy lived on.

After three days of obligatory sacking, Mehmed began consolidating and embellishing his new capital. Justinian's cathedral of Hagia Sophia was converted into an imperial mosque, as eventually were numerous other churches and monasteries. The rights of non-Muslim inhabitants were protected to ensure continuity and stability for commercial activities. Never fully recovered from the sack of 1204, and suffering from Byzantium's two centuries of near poverty, Constantinople by the time of Mehmed's conquest was but a hollow shell of its former self. Its population had dwindled, and much property was either abandoned or in a state of disrepair. The sultan immediately began to repopulate the newly renamed city. Civic and private properties were offered to the public to entice much-needed skilled artisans, craftsmen, and traders of all religions and ethnicities back to the city. Istanbul rapidly grew into a multiethnic, multicultured, and bustling economic, political, and cultural center for the Ottoman state, whose distant frontiers guaranteed it peace, security, and prosperity.

Mehmed, now known as "the Conqueror," determined to centralize his empire. In the Balkans, he decided to eradicate the last vestiges of Byzantium in Morea and to eliminate the surviving Christian vassal princes elsewhere. In 1454 he commenced a series of military campaigns, lasting until 1463, aimed at establishing a solid military defense line along the Danube and the Adriatic against Hungary and Venice.

Serbia ranked first on Mehmed's agenda. After two years of campaigning, Mehmed acquired southern Serbia and the lucrative silver and gold mines of Novo Brdo. In 1456 a cowed Branković permitted Mehmed to march through his remaining lands and besiege the Hungarians in Belgrade. Mehmed's efforts to take the fortress city were checked by Hunyadi, who arrived with reinforcements at the last moment and forced Mehmed to retire. Soon afterward Branković died, and the usual Serbian succession problems reemerged. In the anarchy that erupted, Mehmed laid claim to the Serbian throne, based on his having a Serb stepmother, but continuing problems with Skanderbeg in Albania and the Byzantine despots in Morea prevented him from acting immediately on his claim.

The wily Albanian commander attempted to drive out the Ottoman garrisons stationed in Albania, and Mehmed dispatched a number of expeditions to push Skanderbeg's forces back into the mountains. While the sultan was thus occupied, the Morean despots, the brothers Demetrios Palaiologos of Mystras (1449-60) and Thomas Palaiologos of Patras (1449-60), fell into civil war. Demetrios was well disposed toward the Ottomans, while Thomas sought help from the pope and other Western rulers against both his brother and the Turks. Their conflict reduced Morea to anarchy.

Mehmed arrived in Greece in 1458 and annexed its northern regions. By early 1459 Athens was taken, and a year later Thomas was forced to flee Patras. Demetrios then handed over Mystras to Mehmed. With the fall of Morea in 1460, the Byzantine Empire ceased to exist. All of Greece, with the exception of the Venetian-controlled ports of Methoni, Koroni, and Pilos in Morea, lay under direct Ottoman authority.

A year before Morea fell, Mehmed had moved swiftly north and invaded Serbia one final time, making good on his claim to the Serbian throne. What lands that remained of vassal Serbia were occupied outright by Mehmed's forces. At the time Hungarian King Matthias Corvinus (1458-90), Hunyadi's son, was more interested in Central European affairs than in the Balkans, so he gave scant attention to events occurring south of his border. The Serbs' last stand took place at Smederevo, which fell to Mehmed in June 1459. With its capture, the Serbian state completely disappeared. Only the city of Belgrade, still held by the Hungarians, lay beyond Mehmed's control south of the Danube.

Following the conquests of Serbia and Greece, Skanderbeg's Albania continued to cause Mehmed problems. A truce was arranged with the troublesome Albanian in 1461 in time for Mehmed to deal with a Wallachian incursion into Ottoman Bulgaria led by Voievod Vlad III Dracula (1456-62, 1476), a renegade Ottoman vassal (whose cruel pathological character was internationally infamous while he lived and would serve four centuries later as the model for the central character in the vampire novel that made his name immortal). In 1462 Mehmed invaded Wallachia and drove Dracula out. Instead of annexing the principality, he merely reduced it to vassal status under a new *voievod.*

Alarmed by the Ottomans' consolidation of their Balkan holdings and expansion along the Adriatic coast, Venice encouraged the redoubtable Skanderbeg to break his truce with Mehmed in 1462. Bosnian King-Ban Stefan Tomašević (1461-63), heartened by Skanderbeg's renewed activities, renounced Ottoman suzerainty and accepted Hungarian protection. Herceg Stefan Vukčić (1435-66), lord of Hercegovina, which had separated from Bosnia in the 1440s, followed suit. Their actions elicited Mehmed's quick response. He invaded Albania in 1463 and forced Skanderbeg to sign a new truce. Next, he turned north and overran both Bosnia and Hercegovina. Bosnia was conquered outright but Hercegovina, with Hungarian assistance, staved off a similar fate for another eighteen years, until finally falling to the Turks in 1481.

One territory closely linked to the Serbs was Montenegro, a mountainous region to Serbia's southwest with a small coastline on the Adriatic. In the early 1450s it achieved independence from Branković's Serbia under the leadership of Stefan Crnojević (ca. 1451-65), who enjoyed Venetian support. Assisted by his state's rugged terrain, Crnojević turned back the raiders Mehmed sent against him during the 1450s, although a number of his regional tribal chieftains accepted Ottoman vassalage. After his death, his son Ivan Crnojević (1465-90) swore vassalage to Mehmed in 1471, but that did not prevent the Ottomans from occupying large portions of his lands. When Ivan reneged on his tribute payments, Mehmed included an invasion of Montenegro in the massive assaults against Albania and its Venetian-held coastal cities that he dispatched in the years 1477 to 1479. Ivan was driven out and Mehmed annexed most of Montenegro.

Mehmed's moves in the western Balkans frightened the Venetians, who dreaded the continued Ottoman approach to the Adriatic coastline and its string of port cities. They patched together an anti-Ottoman alliance with Hungary and Skanderbeg in 1463. During the war, which lasted until 1479, Venice won possession of a number of Aegean islands but experienced terrifying Ottoman raids into its northeastern Italian holdings. Skanderbeg fought on until his death in 1468, after which Mehmed conquered Albania completely. Hungary held onto Belgrade by fending off Mehmed's second siege in 1464. Hungarian King Matthias injected a new player into the struggles with the Ottomans by securing an alliance with Moldavian Voievod Ştefan the Great (1457-1504).

Moldavia traditionally maintained a policy of vassalage toward Poland to preserve its independence from Hungary. Its location in the extreme northeast, beyond both the Danube and Wallachia, spared it problems with the Ottomans until 1420, when Mehmed I first raided Moldavia after suppressing the Bedreddin rebellion. During the 1430s and 1440s the principality was wracked by civil wars, of which Sultan Murad II took advantage. As the state weakened, Voievod Peter Aron (1455-57) accepted Ottoman suzerainty and agreed to pay tribute, but, given Moldavia's distance from Ottoman borders, his acts were more symbolic than concrete.

Ştefan the Great initially used the Ottoman vassalage inherited from his father as a tool against Hungary, Moldavia's traditional enemy. He participated in Mehmed II's invasion of Wallachia against Dracula because, at the time, Dracula was a Hungarian ally. An exceptional military commander and organizer, Ştefan captured the Danube commercial city of Kilia from Wallachia in 1465 and defeated a Hungarian invasion of his state two years later. As his successes both on the battlefield and in imposing his authority within Moldavia grew, Ştefan ceased paying the annual tribute to the Ottomans, and his relationship with Mehmed II deteriorated. He invaded Wallachia in 1474 and ousted its prince, who was Mehmed's abject vassal. In response, Mehmed demanded that Ştefan resume his tribute payments and turn over the city of Kilia as well. Ştefan refused and soundly repulsed Mehmed's subsequent punitive invasion of Moldavia in early 1475.

The victorious *voievod* realized that Mehmed would seek to avenge the defeat, so Ştefan sought Hungarian aid by becoming Matthias Corvinus's vassal. Mehmed personally led an invasion of Moldavia in 1476, and his forces plundered the country up to Suceava, Ştefan's capital. Lack of provisions and an outbreak of cholera among the Ottoman troops, however, forced Mehmed to retire, and Ştefan went on the offensive. With Hungarian help, he pushed into Wallachia and spent the next nine years fighting a heroic border war with the Ottomans. Ştefan's efforts were the primary reason that the two Romanian Principalities maintained their independence and did not suffer the fate of the other Ottoman vassal states south of the Danube.

In 1480 Mehmed dispatched an army to Italy that marched against Rome to punish the pope for supporting Venice and assorted anti-Ottoman coalitions. The invasion force captured Otranto and was advancing on Rome when news of the sultan's death in 1481 stopped their advance, sparing Rome almost certain capture.

When Mehmed died, the conquest of the Balkans essentially was complete. (See Map 5.) His successor Bayezid II (1481-1512) conquered few new territories. He did grant Ivan Crnojević's request to govern a small Montenegrin territory, centered on Cetinje, as a tributary vassal to forestall possible Albanian-like guerilla war in that forbiddingly mountainous region. After Djordje Crnojević (1490-96), Ivan's successor, was implicated in a failed Albanian uprising, Bayezid forced him out in 1496, and Montenegro was directly absorbed into the sultan's holdings.

Bayezid also faced a continuing war with Ştefan of Moldavia. In 1485, after the Ottomans captured all of Moldavia's Black Sea coastal territories, Ştefan was forced into renewed vassal status and accepted the Ottomans' gains. Acquisition of those territories linked Bayezid's lands to those of his Muslim vassals, the Crimean Tatars, and cut off the European Christian states from direct access to the Black Sea. The lucrative Black Sea trade passed completely into Ottoman hands.

So secure was the Ottomans' control over the Balkans that Selim I the Grim (1512-20), Bayezid's successor, concentrated almost exclusively on conquests in the Islamic Middle East. Only minor Balkan territorial gains were won, mostly on the border with Hungarian Croatia, by Selim's son Sultan Süleyman I the Magnificent, primarily as supplements to his dramatically extensive conquests in Hungary during the 1520s and 1540s, which brought the Ottomans to the gates of Vienna (1529) and helped earn Süleyman his sobriquet. Significantly, he laid the groundwork for his Hungarian campaigns by first accomplishing what Mehmed II had failed to do— capturing Belgrade in 1521. (See Map 5.)

CHAPTER SIX

The "Ottoman System"

By the early sixteenth century most of the Balkan Peninsula's Christians were submerged within the Ottomans' Islamic theocratic society. In traditional Islamic civilization, no separation existed between religious and secular matters, and religious considerations predominated in all state affairs. The Ottomans injected a number of unique traits into the scheme. Historians often label their sociopolitical construct the "Ottoman System," characterized by slave government administration and state power sharing between governing and religious "establishments." That term, however, conveys a sense of structural rigidity that probably was nonexistent throughout the Ottoman period, since it uses as its specific model the state organization operating in the first half of the sixteenth century under Süleyman I. While the slave administration predominated after its inception in the second half of the fourteenth century, it was persistently opposed by powerful Muslim warriors, religious leaders, and bureaucrats. The idea that two separate "establishments" shared state power was developed by outsiders attempting to understand Ottoman society and probably never entered the minds of the Ottomans themselves, since theocratic notions tended to preclude such categorical distinctions. To avoid these clichés, a general overview of the "Ottoman System" operating in the Balkans best concentrates on its three fundamental sectors: The military-administrative, the religious-legal, and the social-economic.

The Military-Administrative Sector

The Ottoman Empire was an Islamic, rather than a Turkish, state. Islamic principles regarding the state's nature were fundamental. All Muslims were considered members of a single community of "true believers" wholly governed by religious precepts found in the *Şeriat*. The territories in which Islam held sway were considered the "Domain of Islam." They stood in perpetual opposition to the "Domain of War," or those lands inhabited and ruled by non-Muslims. Therefore, the Islamic state required a structure enabling it to both defend and expand the Domain of Islam in the face of the Domain of War.

The Ottoman Empire essentially was structured as a vast army compound, in which the administrative organization was synonymous with that of the military. All those enjoying full participation in that organization were classified *askeri* (military) and members of the ruling elite. The capital served as both administrative center and military headquarters for the sultan, the state's ruler and supreme military commander. The empire's provinces were structured as encampments reflecting the military organization. Each territorial unit of a province, from the smallest townshiplike district (*kaza*) to that of the province (*eyalet*) itself, fielded a set number of cavalrymen (*sipahis*) for the army based on its territorial size. Each was governed by an officer possessing virtually indistinguishable military and civil authority and whose rank reflected its size.

The *sancak* ("banner" or "standard"), governed by a *sancakbeyi,* was the primary provincial unit, roughly representing an administrative county and a military regiment. *Sancaks* were subdivided into *kazas* (townships/companies), governed by *beys* (lords), while a number of *sancaks* were combined into *eyalets* (provinces/corps), the largest provincial units governed by *beylerbeyis* (governors/generals). *Sancaks* and *eyalets* were centered on towns or cities that served as the *beys'* seats, where Janissary detachments, religious judges (*kadıs*), and bureaucrats also were located for maintaining order, law, and taxation, respectively. Early in the Balkan conquest, the Ottoman Empire consisted only of two *eyalets*—Rumeli ("Europe," derived from the Turkish name for the Byzantine Empire, *Rum* ["Rome"]) and Anatolia. By the third quarter of the sixteenth century the empire consisted of thirty-one *eyalets,* five of which were located in Europe. Three were headquartered in the Balkans—at Sofia, Sarajevo, and Gallipoli.

The sultan was the linchpin of the empire's organization. Consistent military successes transformed the office from leading nomad warrior commander into the traditional Eastern Mediterranean–West Asian absolute, autocratic, God-ordained emperor. The sultan became the protector and proprietor of the state, the head of the Islamic community, the sole source of civil law, and the controller of all state offices. Only the precepts of Islam and the force of tradition effectively restrained the sultan's authority. Proprietary ownership of all state territories and control over all official offices together cemented the sultans' absolute power and central role in maintaining the empire's structure.

Ownership of the empire's lands permitted the sultans to support and field the army that played so crucial a role in Islamic state principle. Conquered territories were considered imperial lands (*miri*) at the sultans' disposal. While the sultans retained large tracts as private imperial property (*has*), part of which was dispensed among family, friends, and the highest officials, most *miri* was distributed in pseudofeudal fashion among *sipahi* warriors and their commanders as conditional military fiefs, providing for the recipients' maintenance without recourse to the state treasury.

The system of military fiefs, known as the *sipahilık,* was rooted in Seljuk tradition but generally followed the Byzantine *pronoia* model. At the time of their conquest Byzantine lands already were portioned out as *pronoia* holdings to powerful military families. Numerous *pronoia*-holders accepted Ottoman vassalage and joined the sultans' forces in exchange for retaining their holdings on former Byzantine terms. The sultans used similar terms in distributing vacant *pronoia* lands to their warriors. The practice was continued in the conquered Balkan non-Byzantine lands, since most of the Orthodox Christian states generally followed the Byzantine military landholding model. The Ottomans saw no reason to reinvent a well-established, working system. (The same held true for Ottoman provincial adminis-trative structure—*sancaks* and *kazas* often corresponded to former holdings of the vanquished Christian regional lords and nobles.)

Unlike medieval European feudal landholding, the Ottoman *sipahilık* system did not grant the recipient outright ownership of a land parcel or its inhabitants but strictly was financial in nature. A recipient had the right to collect all or a share of taxes due from a certain land parcel's inhabitants on condition that he fulfill fixed state service duties. That conditional arrangement was spelled out in a deed of investiture issued by the sultan, which specified the territorial extent, personal revenues (scaled relative to his military-administrative rank), and state obligations attached to the grant. The common cavalryman received the lowest-valued fief (*timar*), while *beys* and high-ranking commanders-officials received more valuable parcels (*zeamets*). Failure to fulfill the obligations or abusing the rights attached to the grant usually resulted in the holder being divested of the fief and its redistribution to another candidate. Thus the land on which the *sipahi* was dependent technically always remained the sultan's property.

During the Balkan conquest's early years the sultans used the distribution of military fiefs primarily to cement the loyalty of powerful warriors and their leaders by creating a kind of service nobility. Through the *sipahilık,* the sultans largely were able to cow the fickle nomad warriors on whom they initially depended and to forge them into an effective, settled military force generally obedient to the rulers' commands and committed to preserving the system on which their livelihoods depended.

Although the *sipahilık* tamed the warriors, it did not guarantee their absolute fidelity. Local military leaders might place loyalty to their followers or region ahead of that owed the sultan. The potential threat to the ruler's authority posed by the *sipahilık*-supported warrior class led the early sultans to establish a separate, personal military-administrative power base to serve as a counterweight. They did so by combining a long-held Islamic tradition of institutionalized slavery with their control of all imperial offices.

Orhan made the initial moves toward creating a nonnomad warrior military force. He formed paid, professional cavalry and infantry units mostly recruited from Balkan Christians (but by the close of the conquest's first stage, those units' ranks were almost exclusively Muslim). Although such units were more loyal than nomad warriors, loyalty based on pay was far from absolute. Murad I first realized that salary grounded in slavery could create the absolutely loyal military force necessary to balance the warrior class.

In the time-honored Islamic tradition of using slaves (*kuls*) as soldiers and administrators, Murad created the first Ottoman slave military-administrative system (*kapıkulu*) by taking captured troops as his share of war booty from victories over the Balkan Christians. Murad had them trained in Ottoman tactics and organized into military units under his direct command. The sultan's new soldiers— the Janissary infantry and the guard cavalry—existed outside of the Turkish warrior tradition and were dependent on the ruler alone, who owned, paid, fed, clothed, armed, housed, and led them in battle.

The most militarily capable slaves were appointed officers in the new units. The intellectually brightest were singled out for training in administrative functions and used as the sultan's high government officials (*vezirs*). Although initially their total number was small (no more than 4,000), Murad's use of slaves was the embryonic beginning of the Ottomans' hallmark slave military-administrative system and signaled a transformation in the nature of the state's government from one grounded in nomadic traditions to one based on strong central authority buttressed by a professional military and bureaucracy.

Bayezid I expanded on Murad's efforts, increasing the numbers of his slave military to some 7,000 men and creating a large, centralized governing bureaucracy. Headquartered in his palace, the new administration was comprised primarily of his household slaves and hired Christian advisors, whose main function was tax collecting. His slaves also were sent into the provinces as commanders-governors. To further cement his power vis-à-vis the warriors, Bayezid multiplied the use of vassalage toward the rulers of the Balkan Christian states, who supplied troops to the Ottoman forces under terms made directly with him.

The Turkish warrior class's discontent over the *kapıkulu*'s creation helped fuel the Interregnum and assisted Mehmed I in winning the Ottoman throne. He did not abolish the *kapıkulu* but he curtailed its power and authority, relying instead on leading Turk supporters to staff his military command and government offices. The slave system was not abandoned completely because the notion of controlling absolutely reliable military and government officials was too powerful for any sultan to relinquish.

Mehmed's son Murad II commenced rebuilding the *kapıkulu* soon after ascending the throne. Once again the sultan's slaves occupied high provincial military-administrative positions and were appointed to numerous offices in a reinvigorated central government, but the most important offices, such as those of grand *vezir* (the sultan's viceroy and second highest position in the state) and head of the treasury, remained in the hands of freeborn Turks. Murad also increasingly rejected the use of vassalage regarding Balkan Christian rulers in favor of outright annexation of their territories.

The rivalry between the *kapıkulu* and warriors underlay young Mehmed II's inability to rule before and after the Varna Crusade. Any chance for the warriors to predominate was thwarted by his conquest of Constantinople. Initially supported by the *kapıkulu,* Mehmed expanded the Janissaries to 10,000 men. Slaves all, they were forbidden to marry, live off barracks, or take up trades (which might provide income other than the salary paid them) to guarantee their unquestioned loyalty and obedience. Mehmed's Janissaries were the most reliable standing military force in Europe at the time. He used the Janissaries not only against his European enemies but also to intimidate his provincial *sipahis* against rebellion by garrisoning detachments in key locations throughout the provinces.

Mehmed further hobbled the warrior class by confiscating his most vocal opponents' lands and removing Turkish notables from high government offices in the palace. In their stead he placed members of his slave household. Mehmed's slaves held a majority of the central government's leading offices. Only in the imperial state council (*divan*), which consisted of all high government officials and served as the sultan's imperial cabinet, did freeborn Muslims continue to play any important administrative role.

The policy of using Janissaries to ensure order in the provinces and of relying almost exclusively on the *kapıkulu* for military-administrative leadership was continued by Bayezid II, Selim I, and Süleyman I. During the latter's reign, the Janissaries were expanded to some 12,000 to 14,000 men, and his slave household took near-exclusive control of the central administration. Only in the *divan* did freeborn Muslim religious leaders remain.

There were some notable exceptions to the predominance of either the warrior class or the *kapıkulu* in the Ottoman military-administrative system.

Throughout the period of the conquest, certain important military and governmental positions were held by hired Balkan Christians. Because the Turks originally were a land-based people, they initially possessed little maritime expertise. When it became obvious that expansion in Europe required a naval, as well as a land, force, the sultans turned to their Balkan Christian subjects who enjoyed maritime traditions for the ships and men needed to create and maintain a fleet. Although over time Turks and North African Arabs acquired maritime skills, Balkan Christians (notably Greeks) continued to play important roles in commanding and manning the Ottoman navy.

Likewise, as foreign relations with European protagonists grew increasingly important, those matters were delegated to hired Balkan Christians (mostly wealthy Greek merchants) commonly involved in international trade. The sultans realized that the cultural divide separating Muslims and Christians made using such Christian intermediaries more effective than using Turks in the diplomatic games played with European opponents.

While the *sipahılık* system was imposed throughout the Ottoman Empire, the sultans' use of institutionalized slavery in the military-administrative sector had consequences unique to their Balkan territories. These had to do with the *devşirme,* a periodic levy of youths from among the Balkans' Christian subjects used to fill the ranks of the sultan's slave household. First conducted on a limited scale during the late fourteenth century, it was instituted regularly in the fifteenth century by Murad II to provide a stable source of slaves in numbers large enough to staff his expanding *kapıkulu,* whose manpower needs outstripped the supply derived from military captives. Until the late seventeenth century the *devşirme* was the principal source of slaves for the Ottoman military-administrative system, and those slaves were drawn exclusively from the Balkans.

Depending on need, *devşirmes* were conducted at intervals of one to seven years, collecting 1,000 to 3,000 youths each time. When a child levy was desired, detailed orders and quotas were sent to the Balkan provincial authorities, who then dispatched Janissary detachments to the villages (towns were exempt to protect the craft industries and trade), each of which was required to provide for inspection a set number of youths between the ages of seven and fourteen. All eligible youths (sons of artisans or craftsmen were ineligible for economic reasons) were mustered in the village center and inspected, and a predetermined number was chosen for collection on the basis of demonstrated physical or intellectual promise. Selected youths immediately were considered enslaved by the sultan and marched off under guard to the capital or to Anatolia, where they were converted into devout Muslims, physically conditioned and mentally disciplined by a number of years labor in the countryside, and provided with the best available training for careers in either the Janissary military units (the fate of the majority) or the palace central administration (for the minority who exhibited exceptional intellectual capabilities).

On completing their training, the *devşirme* recruits entered their new careers at the lowest ranks. Promotion usually depended on individual talent and job performance, since advancement in the slave household theoretically depended on merit (although favoritism, political expediency, and bribery could influence individual promotions). Merit promotion, combined with dire consequences ranging from demotion to execution for incompetency or failure, helped make the *devşirme*-staffed military-administrative system the most efficiently centralized in Europe during the fifteenth and sixteenth centuries.

Modern Western Europeans and most modern Balkan nationalists usually envision the horrors of African slavery when the word "slavery" is mentioned. Slavery in the Ottoman context, however, little resembled that of the American South—there were no whips, chains, or other degrading aspects involved. Entry into the sultan's slave household opened the door to immense power, wealth, social position, and public honor for any slave with the natural abilities and dedication to rise through the ranks. The emphasis placed on individual merit for filling important offices, with little regard for birth status or social position, was advanced relative to conditions in contemporary European societies, where such considerations were paramount. To be the sultan's slave was to possess the opportunity to rise in military-administrative standing as far as skill and ability would permit, including the office of grand *vezir*—second only to the sultan in authority.

In an ironic way, slavery and the *devşirme* opened an avenue of social mobility to the Ottoman Islamic state's Balkan non-Muslim subjects that they theoretically should not have possessed. Many *devşirme* officials remembered their families and birth places by extending to them preferential treatment. Numerous Christian parents, especially in the poorer mountain districts and in ineligible urban centers, begged or bribed local authorities to take their sons because they realized the potential benefits offered by the *devşirme*. Even Muslims sometimes sought to have their children illegally collected. Some urban Muslims followed the example of their Christian counterparts and resorted to bribing local officials for that purpose. The Bosnian Muslims, originally Christians converted after their conquest by Mehmed II, arranged to have themselves and their descendants declared eligible for the *devşirme* as a condition for their conversion, with the stipulation that those children collected would serve only in the palace administration and not in the military.

By the late fifteenth century the Ottoman military-administrative system was firmly in the hands of the *kapıkulu*. Its ranks were filled almost exclusively by *devşirme* recruits. So dominant were they that the name "*devşirme*" was transformed from one simply identifying a child levy to one denoting a powerful and wealthy Ottoman social class.

The Religious-Legal Sector

Islam was more than a state religion, it was the heart of the Ottoman state. Islamic sacred law—the *Şeriat*—lay at the core of Ottoman society, and the Koran, its bedrock component, served as the state's official law code. Full-fledged members of Islamic society—Muslims—accepted as natural the notion that all law was religious and that their government necessarily must be Islamic. As an Islamic theocracy, the Ottoman Empire represented Islamic civilization's most dynamic and powerful component society.

The Ottomans espoused mainstream *sunni* (orthodox) Islam, as opposed to the minority *shiite* branch practiced primarily in Iran. *Sunni* Muslims adopted a set of the Prophet's traditions (*sunnas*) and sayings (*hadiths*) as legal supplements to the Koran. These were necessary since Koranic prophecy stopped with Muhammad's death, at which time Islam was deemed complete. Muhammad bequeathed to his followers a dynamic Islamic state for which many areas of law remained ill defined or completely untouched by the Koran. Because religious law was a matter crucial to the state, the religious leadership (the *ulema*), which was composed of the most literate and skilled legal scholars, was forced to fill the gaps. They extrapolated legal precedents from Muhammad's biography concerning situations not specifically covered in the Koran. Four collections of such precedents became accepted as canonical, and a school of interpretive law grew up around each. Although all four operated within the Ottoman Empire, only the Hanifid school enjoyed statewide recognition.

The authority of the Ottoman sultans always was tempered by Islamic legality. The Ottomans maintained the traditional Turkish governing concept, reinforced by Byzantine traditions after 1453, of an autocratic ruler possessing the right to issue legally binding secular decrees (*kanuns*). In all cases, such laws customarily were approved by the Islamic *ulema* leadership to ensure their compatibility with the Şeriat.

The members of the *ulema* were learned scholars of jurisprudence (*muftis*) who produced the law books, served as the government's legal advisors, and generally were responsible for the empire's Islamic administration. At their head stood the Şeyülislam ("Elder of Islam"), the chief *mufti*, who was appointed by the sultan. His duties included reviewing and approving the sultan's secular laws and overseeing the provincial *muftis* and judges who promulgated and dispensed both religious and secular law. He was assisted by two *kadıaskers*, one responsible for the European and the other for the Asian provinces, who were the only *ulema* members given official positions in the sultan's *divan* council.

The presence of the *ulema* was manifest throughout the empire by the network of provincial judges. *Kadıs* responsible for dispensing and upholding law sat in the administrative centers of all *kazas* and wielded great local authority. Just as the Şeyülislam served as the Islamic watchdog of the sultan's governance, the *kadıs* oversaw the operations of the various provincial administrators and possessed ultimate authority over the police function of the provincial Janissaries. They presided over courts charged with implementing the laws promulgated by the *muftis* and adjudicating local cases at issue with both the religious and secular laws among Muslim and Christian subjects alike.

Although enforcing the Şeriat was the primary function of the local *kadıs*, secular legal matters often figured prominently in their operations. The Ottomans displayed a practical adeptness in adopting and adapting preexisting secular legal statutes in conquered territories dealing with matters outside of the *Şeriat*'s jurisdiction. The sultans incorporated them in *kanuns* issued to enforce their authority as lands were acquired. By retaining the legal relationships already in force among conquered territories' populations, the transition from native to Ottoman rule was eased, economic disruption avoided, and the possibility of rebellion minimized. At the local level in the conquered Balkan lands, Byzantine, Bulgarian, Serbian, Bosnian, and Albanian laws continued in force.

That the Ottomans' non-Muslim Balkan subjects were permitted to retain their religious beliefs and thus their European cultural identities can be attributed to certain concepts of religious toleration embedded in Islamic precepts.

Muslims considered Islam the final divinely ordained correction for the waywardness that had crept into the two related monotheistic faiths of Judaism and Christianity. Both had received God's divine revelation—the Jews in their Torah and the Christians in their New Testament—but had strayed from its precepts. For that reason, God made a final attempt to bring humankind to the true path of faith through the last prophet, Muhammad, who recorded the revelation made to him in the Koran. Just as the Bible contained the older Jewish writings supplemented by the newer Christian revelation, the Koran retained a great deal of the Bible—both Old and New Testaments—augmented by new, highly specific corrective divine principles.

Possession of a book containing divine monotheistic revelation was extremely important in Islamic mentality. It demonstrated a people's direct and intimate relationship with the true deity and fundamentally served to differentiate them from irrevocably unrighteous pagan polytheists. Muhammad himself classified Jews and Christians as "Peoples of the Book" because of their written scriptures, and he treated them with religious tolerance as a result. Their scriptures were proof of their past direct intimacy with God, although their beliefs were considered flawed by Islam. Whether their continued adherence to their own precepts was wrong was a matter that only God could judge. Therefore, "Peoples of the Book" were permitted to practice their faiths within the Islamic state, while pagans could be forced to convert to Islam on pain of death.

Ottoman religious toleration of Christians and Jews was conditional. By definition, Islam was the supreme faith in an Islamic state. Under the *Şeriat,* the Ottoman Empire's Christian and Jewish subjects were afforded "protection" (*zimma*), that is, continued existence as practicing Christians and Jews, on condition that they acknowledged the domination of Islam and its temporal authorities and accepted inferior legal and social status. The *zimmis* ("protected ones"), as tolerated non-Muslim subjects were classified, were compelled by the Hanifid religious law school to pay discriminatory taxes, to which Muslim subjects were not liable, and to suffer a number of legally defined restrictions. Such taxes included the poll tax (*cizye*) and the *devşirme* (which was applicable to the empire's

Balkan Christian subjects alone). Discriminatory restrictions ranged from limiting the size, height, and conspicuousness of non-Muslim religious edifices to regulating the style, color, and textiles permissible in clothing. *Zimmi* ownership of horses and weapons was, with certain exceptions, forbidden. In legal proceedings, *zimmi* defendants and testimony were at a decided disadvantage in cases where they were opposed by Muslims.

The Ottomans also had pragmatic reasons for tolerating their non-Muslim Balkan subjects. From its beginnings, Islam was a civilization spread by conquest, and every Islamic state initially acquired a significantly large non-Muslim subject population. In West Asia and North Africa, their *zimmi* subjects predominantly were Christians and Jews. The discriminatory taxes paid by them often constituted the single most lucrative source of revenue for the Islamic state. Therefore, it was in the state's interest to preserve the numbers of its *zimmis* at the highest possible level. Until the early sixteenth century and the expansionary campaigns of Selim I in Islamic West Asia and Egypt, the Ottomans' non-Muslim Balkan subjects equaled or outnumbered the Muslims in the empire as a whole.

The numerous Balkan non-Muslims posed legal difficulties for the Ottoman governing authorities. In an Islamic state, the *Şeriat* was applicable only to Muslims and possessed no validity among *zimmis,* for whom *kadı* courts had no jurisdiction unless cases involved them with Muslims. The very process of Balkan conquest innately posed increasing administrative problems for the sultans, and by the close of the fifteenth century nearly half of the empire's subject population lay outside the law.

Until the fall of Constantinople, the problem was dealt with on an ad hoc basis. Laws already in force in conquered territories were incorporated into the sultans' secular *kanuns.* The Ottoman authorities often enlisted local Christian or Jewish religious leaders to settle mundane legal issues among their coreligionists. By the reign of Mehmed II, however, the *zimmis'* numbers had swelled to such an extent that the sultan found it necessary to create an institutional structure for administratively integrating this important segment of the empire's subject population into the theocratic Ottoman state. In 1454, one year after taking Constantinople, Mehmed instituted the *millet* (religious nation) system of *zimmi* administration.

Mehmed reasoned that the religious laws of the various non-Muslim groups could serve to govern them as the *Şeriat* did Muslims. Using the "Peoples of the Book" precept as justification, Mehmed divided his subject population into *millets,* based solely on religious affiliation and administered by the highest religious authorities of each. All *zimmis* were distributed among three *millets,* representing the most important existing non-Muslim faiths: The Orthodox Christians, headed by the patriarch of Constantinople and representing the single largest and economically most important non-Muslim group; the Jews, who were of great commercial and cultural significance, headed by an elected representative of the rabbinical council in Istanbul; and the

Armenian (Gregorian Monophysite) Christians, headed by an Armenian patriarch of Istanbul appointed by the sultan, who also represented the empire's Roman Catholic subjects. The Muslims constituted a de facto fourth *millet.*

The first officially founded *millet* was the Orthodox Christian in 1454. The Armenian was recognized in 1461, while the Jewish (officially constituted in 1839) was represented by a leader chosen from the Istanbul Jewish community by Mehmed himself in 1453.

Each non-Muslim *millet* represented its membership before the Ottoman court and was internally self-governing. They all were granted the rights to tax, judge, and order the lives of their members insofar as those rights did not conflict with Islamic sacred law and the sensibilities of the Muslim ruling establishment. The religious hierarchies of the *millets* thus were endowed with civil responsibilities beyond their ecclesiastical duties, and their head prelate was held accountable for their proper internal functioning. In effect, each *millet* became an integral part of the empire's domestic administration, functioning as a veritable department of the Ottoman central government. In return for ensuring the smooth administration of its non-Muslim subjects, the sultan's government granted each *millet* a considerable amount of autonomy in the spheres of religious devotion and cultural activity, judicial affairs not involving Muslims, and local self-government.

Although the term *millet* involved the idea of "nation" in the Turkish language, it shared little with the Western European concept. *Millet* identified people solely on the basis of religion; ethnicity played no role. Both the Armenian and Jewish *millets* were defined by belief, despite their names' apparent modern ethnic connotations. As for Orthodox Christians, the Ottomans made no distinctions among Greek, Bulgarian, Serbian, Macedonian, or Romanian Orthodox believers. All were lumped together in a single *millet,* even though it is certain that the Muslim authorities were aware that ethnic differences existed among them. Given the Muslim Ottoman rulers' theocratic mentality, ethnicity was thought relatively unimportant. It made little difference to them that the head of the Orthodox *millet* was, and would remain, a Greek.

By eliminating all consideration of ethnicity, *millet* identification entirely lacked the territorial connotations associated with the Western European concept of nation. No matter where one lived within the empire, no matter how mixed the population, *millet* affiliation governed one's life; all were members of their own self-contained administrative communities, complete unto themselves, with no claims whatsoever on the others. The homeland for all Ottoman subjects lay anywhere within the borders of the empire. This fact increasingly led to mixed ethnic populations throughout the Balkans.

Until the close of the eighteenth century, *millet* affiliation—that is, religious belief—was the fundamental source of group identity among all of the empire's subjects, demonstrating that the *millet* system possessed roots far deeper than simply

Islamic concepts of religious toleration. Since the fourth century, self-identity primarily was religious in nature for the populations of Christian Western Europe, the Balkans, West Asia, and North Africa. For Jews, their own religious identity was centuries older.

The Ottoman *millet* system was not a new concept—the Byzantine, Umayyad, Abbasid, and Seljuk states all had used the leadership of minority religions for administrative purposes. It merely institutionalized the practice and, by doing so, firmly cemented religious group identities among the Ottomans' general subject population. It also proved a shrewd political mechanism, providing the Ottomans with the ability to administer effectively their multireligious subject population within the precepts laid down for an Islamic state. At the same time, it solidified differences among the major groups of the empire's numerous non-Muslim subjects, making it difficult for them to organize concerted rebellious activities against the state. Ultimately, the *millet* system served as one of the pillars that perpetuated Ottoman control over the Balkans for centuries.

The Socioeconomic Sector

Religion and the military-administrative system provided the Ottoman Empire with its fundamental social categorizations: Society was divided religiously between superior Muslims and inferior non-Muslims and politically between military rulers and ruled. All those enjoying *askeri* (military) status (military-administrative officials, warriors, standing soldiers, bureaucrats, and members of the *ulema*) were ranked in the ruling class. All others, Muslims and *zimmis* alike, constituted those ruled, whose primary function was to support the rulers economically. Their status and purpose were expressed aptly in the rulers' official designation of them—*reaya* ("the flock"). The term bore the connotation of sheep that required careful shepherding, protection, and fattening so that they could be fleeced beneficially in the interests of the ruling class.

The Ottoman government espoused no concerted overall economic strategy in the modern sense. Its economic goals were state survival, internal order, and just social relationships within Islamic precepts that were attained through the principles of stability and self-sufficiency. Economic legislation and regulation were enacted without consideration of their broader implications or situations, and every economic activity was judged as either good or bad in itself. Fostering expanded markets and increased productivity had little appeal for the Ottoman government because their accompanying financial uncertainty and price fluctuations were viewed as potentially destabilizing.

Any intervention in the economy was made to guarantee production of absolute essentials (such as precious metals and salt) and military materials, or to enforce fairness in economic relations (combatting fraud, verifying weights and measures, equalizing raw material distribution, and such). The spirit of Islam was strongly laissez-faire in economic matters, and what regulation the Ottomans did impose often ran counter to traditional religious law. Many government taxes were legally questionable (especially the *devşirme* and most customs duties), and were justified to the religious leadership only by the most creative and convoluted type of casuistic arguments.

Military expenditures constituted the principal economic stimulus provided by the Ottoman state. The money spent on weapons and other military supplies returned income to the state in the form of conquered territories that provided plunder, new taxes, and new properties for *sipahilık* distribution. Even in the sphere of military spending, however, the Ottomans demonstrated narrow economic vision. Infrastructural expenditures (on roads, bridges, and mountain passes, for example) were limited to military expediency with little regard for broader civilian economic well-being. Instead of investing in a fleet of commercial transport ships to service international markets, the Ottomans depended on outsiders (primarily Venetians and Dubrovnik Dalmatians) for much of their maritime carrying trade, depriving themselves of higher profits and security.

Located at the center of the major maritime and overland trade routes linking Europe and Asia, the Ottoman Empire naturally was involved with international commerce. The sultans viewed creating a beneficial trading environment as a duty grounded in the best Islamic tradition. (Muhammad himself had been a merchant.) Foreign traders thus were offered relatively free access to the empire's ports so long as no political differences existed with them at any given time and customs duties were paid. By the mid-sixteenth century the empire flourished commercially as the middleman in the lucrative spice, silk, and other luxury trade carried on by Europe with Asia.

Those foreign traders deemed economically important by the Ottomans often were granted certain privileges (such as remission of customs duties) called "capitulations." In many respects, the capitulations granted through the mid-sixteenth century constituted the establishment of formal Ottoman diplomatic relations with various Western European states. Representatives of the Ottomans' privileged trading partners received diplomatic protection and immunity somewhat analogous to *millet* status, although they remained subject to Ottoman laws in cases involving them with the empire's subjects. If residing within the empire, they could own property, worship freely, and enjoy self-government. They usually dealt with the Ottoman authorities through intermediaries drawn from the empire's Christian *millets,* but direct interaction with Muslims was minimal.

Tax revenues, along with military considerations, were paramount for the Ottoman rulers. A stable economy meant guaranteed income to pay the general military expenditures, to support the military-administrative system, to fund public charitable activities, and to purchase luxury commodities. The government proved extremely adept at devising taxes. Anything that could be taxed was taxed. There were customs duties; trade taxes; market fees; sales taxes; land use (*haraç*) and pasturing taxes; livestock taxes; road, bridge, and mountain pass tolls; a household tax; court costs; fees for legal documents; and numerous other imposts for which all Ottoman subjects were liable. In addition, there were discriminatory taxes paid by *zimmis,* the most important and lucrative being the *cizye.* In crisis or emergency situations, temporary extraordinary taxes (*avaris*) were imposed. Most general taxes were levied using the household (*hane*) as the basic taxation unit rather than the individual to ensure revenue stability through group obligation.

Prolific tax registers were kept, serving to both regulate tax collection and provide census information of sorts. Interestingly, the Ottomans created no bureaucratic mechanism expressly for tax collection. Fiscal administrators developed records of taxes due and kept track of revenues received but left the actual collection to others. The tax collectors were fief-holders in most rural regions; otherwise, they were tax farmers. The latter agreed to pay the government fixed amounts of revenue at regular intervals. Since tax farming was open to obvious abuse, the sultans, understanding that economically ruined subjects provided little or no tax revenues, issued laws protecting their subjects against rapacious tax farmers and vigilantly applied them when necessary.

Tax revenues from the Balkans' *reaya* population were vital for maintaining the empire. Through the end of the fifteenth century, Balkan Christian *zimmis* constituted the largest single component of the Ottoman population. As late as the second decade of the sixteenth century, the European portion of the empire comprised over two-fifths of the total population (approximately 5 out of a total of 12 million people). Christian subjects, who numbered more than 4 million, accounted for over four-fifths of the empire's Balkan population and more than a third of all Ottoman subjects. Following the sixteenth-century military conquests of Islamic lands in West Asia and North Africa, the Balkan Christians' share of the empire's total population dwindled by almost 50 percent to less than a fifth. Still, the empire counted on the extra taxes paid by its Balkan *zimmis.*

The overwhelming majority of Balkan *reaya* were village-dwelling peasants living on military fiefs. Since the Ottomans primarily were urban, most Balkan peasants were Christian *zimmis.* Under the *sipahilık* system, the resident peasants enjoyed direct use of the land under terms contained in a lease issued to them by the fief's holder. The fief-holder was obliged to facilitate the uninterrupted cultivation and habitation of the land to guarantee a stable income. The peasants were obliged to sow and cultivate their land parcels and make timely tax payments. Tithes in kind and cash payments were the preferred methods of payment. Tithes ensured the *sipahi* of the basic food and craft necessities. Cash payments included tithes commuted to cash and taxes levied on most components of agrarian life, such as on livestock, mills, forges, and milking facilities.

Other than the small plot granted each fief-holder as personal income-producing property (*çift*), the land was divided into numerous autonomous plots parceled among the peasants with rights to hold and work them. Thus the peasants were not left landless. Neither were they enserfed. The price for retaining use of the land and their personal freedom was certain obligations owed the fief-holder, such as working on his *çift* three days during the year (which often was commuted to a cash payment). Compared to the deplorable situation of peasants living under late-feudal conditions in neighboring European states, Ottoman *zimmi* peasants enjoyed a far better lot, which helped to account for the immigration of numerous Christian peasants into the Ottoman Balkans during the fifteenth and sixteenth centuries from Hungary and southern Poland.

By the sixteenth century the most important fiscal obligation owed by the Ottomans' non-Muslim peasantry was the annual *cizye,* the head tax paid by all males over the age of twelve and capable of work. A peasant's listing in the *cizye* tax registers carried with it legal obligations to the land, to *corvées,* and to various labor services. Service demands usually had a military purpose, such as furnishing transport for military supplies, undertaking construction projects, performing courier service, or working on road maintenance. By the mid-sixteenth century many *zimmi* labor obligations were commuted to cash payments as reimbursement for their elimination. Certain groups of peasants continued to provide the Ottoman authorities with various specialized labor services even after such duties had been commuted for the general peasant population, in return for which they received certain tax privileges. Herein lay the basis for differentiating the *zimmi* peasantry between common and privileged *reaya.*

It is estimated that close to a third of the Balkan *zimmi* population enjoyed some sort of privileged status, particularly exemption from the *cizye.* They were grouped into twenty-six corporate categories based on the types of services provided, and they were divided into two basic functional groups: Those with military assistance functions and those whose services mainly were commercial or productive.

Among the military privileged category, the most numerous and important were the *voynuks,* who supplied the Ottoman military with horses and transport drivers, and the *dervencis,* who defended and maintained militarily important mountain passes and roads. Other groups included *martoloses* (local militiamen) and *yamaks* (auxiliary Janissaries). Military privileged *zimmis* could own weapons and wear certain clothes forbidden to non-Muslims under Hanifid law. The commercial category of privileged *reaya* received tax privileges in return for producing materials and goods, primarily ores and foodstuffs, needed by the army or the court. Included in this service classification were metal ore miners and processors (*madancıs*), sheep and other food livestock dealers and breeders (*celeps*), salt producers, falcon raisers, and rice producers.

Other *reaya* categories enjoyed limited tax and service benefits separating them from common peasants. They were listed in Ottoman *cizye* tax registers as "free"—not totally free from state taxation but from *avaris* payments or from the *devşirme*. "Free" status could be acquired either by performing services for the authorities or through residence on particular classes of land. An example of the former was the "reserve" *voynuks,* who paid common *cizye* but, because they constituted a reserve pool for active-duty *voynuks,* were exempt from paying *avaris.* Examples of the latter were peasants living on *has* lands or on *vakıfs.*

Has lands owned outright by the sultan, members of his family, or high-ranking officials bestowed "free" status on the peasants inhabiting them as a benefit for working capitalistic estates. *Vakıfs* were tax-exempt properties owned outright (*mülk*), usually by Muslims in the military-administrative or religious sectors, from which their incomes were inalienable endowments for Islamic religious establishments. In the legal donative document establishing a *vakıf,* the benefactor usually assigned the administration of the endowment to himself and his family in perpetuity, with much of the revenues set aside for the administrators' use, thus guaranteeing an inalienable income for the donor and his heirs. Similar to *has* land, the *vakıf* primarily was a capitalistic enterprise. Both sought to attract and retain laborers by granting tax breaks.

Almost all Balkan peasants enjoyed local self-government, usually through village communes. The village commune was a closed collective organization comprising a particular village's inhabitants and administered by their clan elders and religious leader, who usually came from the village's most important families and often were its wealthiest and best-educated residents. The commune ordered the mundane affairs of its members and oversaw work on the villagers' assorted family plots and common lands. Dealings with neighboring villages and with local authorities, both Ottoman and *millet,* also were its responsibilities. The Ottomans legalized the commune, its functions, and the lands it administered through *kanuns* that usually preserved pre-Ottoman agrarian statutes, thus freeing them from intimate involvement in mundane local affairs.

The usual absolute religious distinction between Muslims and non-Muslims often was absent in the villages. Communal obligations were fixed by the authorities without regard to religious affiliation. The commune was considered the economic, political, and legal representative of all its members, whether the village was religiously homogeneous or mixed. In mixed Christian and Muslim villages, religious differences resulted in a certain differentiation in work functions, living quarters, and cultural activities. Otherwise, the villagers usually shared common experiences, traditions, songs, and often languages.

The Balkan *reaya* population's urban segment—between 3 and 5 percent of the total—was small. Nearly all Balkan urban centers existed prior to the Ottoman conquest and they served primarily as headquarters for civil-military and *millet* administration as well as centers for the handicrafts and mining industries. Some, especially the coastal and Danubian centers, conducted important commercial activities. Ottoman Balkan urban centers generally retained their pre-Ottoman functions as local artisan and trade centers. What changed after the conquest was the ethnic composition of the urban population. During the conquest some of the native inhabitants were displaced to make room for Ottoman officials, garrisons, artisans, and agents. The conquerors brought the remaining native residents thoroughly into the Ottoman urban social organization. During the fifteenth and sixteenth centuries, the Muslim urban element steadily increased as additional administrative personnel, Janissaries, artisans, and local *sipahi* fief-holders settled in.

Towns in the Ottoman Balkans acquired a distinctly Islamic physical and social character. Hanifid law forbade Christian *zimmis* to possess large houses or buildings performing social functions. With the presence of the Muslim authorities constant and direct, *zimmi* urban residents were forced to accept Turkish material standards of urban development. Skylines became characterized by minarets and mosques. Many large, well-built Orthodox churches were transformed into Islamic religious buildings over time. Town centers were renovated with new, Islamic structures, such as mosques and their satellite buildings, *imarets,* baths, fountains, and caravanserais. While buildings devoted to the Muslims' administrative, cultural, and private well-being usually were large and constructed of stone, those of the subject *zimmis* often were small and poorly built.

Urban populations commonly were ethnically mixed and either evenly divided between Christians and Muslims or divided slightly in favor of the latter. Most Muslims lived in or near the town center, where administrative, defensive, and commercial activities were concentrated. Residential quarters (*mahalles*) ringed the center, where the general population lived in low dwellings along meandering and narrow streets. *Mahalles* frequently were separated from each other by gardens, which tended to make towns appear larger than their actual populations warranted. While Muslim quarters most often were in the oldest, most prominent sections of the town, the *zimmis'* commonly were in less attractive or more peripheral locations.

Mahalles frequently served to segregate the urban population in terms of religion and profession. Most were named after some known structural landmark within their confines or after some local town notable who resided in the quarter. In those possessing an exclusively Christian population, they often acquired the names of churches or noted priests who lived there. Frequently *mahalles* were named after the profession or trade pursued by the majority of their residents. Such named *mahalles* often were of a mixed Christian and Muslim population. For urban *zimmis, mahalles* resembled rural village communes in administrative and functional terms. The Ottoman authorities considered the *mahalle* the corporate representative of its residents and used it as the basic mechanism for urban tax collection. *Mahalles* were administered by elders possessing functions similar to those of their village counterparts.

Artisans owning their own shops comprised an important part of the urban population. Their lives were bound closely to the workings of the Ottoman guilds (*esnafs*). Unlike the Western European system, Ottoman guilds were controlled, regulated, and regimented by the central authorities through local *kadıs*. The state set all prices, authorized all sources of supply and material, decided product quotas, and determined the types of products that could be legally manufactured and sold. The system was structured to eliminate competition and to ensure social and economic harmony, thus maintaining a stable source of materials and tax revenues for the central government.

The *esnaf* system was largely antiprofit in nature and subject to the Muslim principle of *hisba,* which protected the interests of the population against profiteering, fraud, and speculation under the *Şeriat.* The application of this principle was an obligation of the Islamic state that the Ottomans took seriously. All types of speculation in the area of the craft industries were punished as criminal offenses. *Kadıs* set the "just" price for craft goods and determined the "just" profit allowed the artisan producers.

Each *esnaf* organized the artisans engaged in a particular craft into a social "brotherhood." It collectively represented its membership and their professional interests to the authorities, and it regulated all economic relations among its members. Each was granted judicial powers over its membership and complete autonomy with regard to its operations. Guild treasuries were used as a primitive form of workman's compensation for injured or disabled members, as funding for public festivals sponsored by *esnafs* (usually on religious holidays), or as principal for interest-bearing loans to their memberships.

Guild membership could be religiously homogeneous or mixed. Often the religious composition of an *esnaf* depended on the type of craft it represented. For example, Muslims predominated in the fur and leather craft industries, while metalsmithing and most textile-related industries were performed chiefly by Christians. Such endeavors as money-changing, tinsmithing, and glassmaking usually were conducted by Jews and Armenians. Many of the Balkan craft *esnafs* exclusively were Christian. In those with mixed *zimmi* and Muslim membership, the latter displayed tolerance of the religious and cultural manifestations of their non-Muslim "brothers," even when those manifestations entailed a considerable outlay of *esnaf* funds, such as on certain *zimmi* religious holidays.

Merchants (individuals intensively involved in international or interregional trade) were a small but important element in Balkan urban populations. Craftsmen who sold the products of their own labor and tradesmen who sold goods secondhand were not considered merchants by the Ottoman authorities. There were colonies of foreign merchants in the leading centers of international trade, but the majority were

Ottoman *zimmi* subjects. Ottoman merchants enjoyed a certain amount of economic freedom permitting them to conduct truly capitalistic operations.

Similar to artisans, merchants were organized into *esnafs* representing types of goods traded. Unlike artisans, they were not subject to *hisba* and thus not regulated in terms of pricing and profits. Merchants were free to accumulate and increase capital and to engage in all sorts of trading activity. They fit neatly into the concept of putting money to work that served as a fundamental premise of traditional Islamic society. For this reason, merchants were granted social privileges. In return, the state used merchants as a source of steady revenues through customs duties and loan funds. Merchants also served the state as mediators between rulers and ruled in tax matters, as a pool for agents and ambassadors, and as a supply source for goods unavailable within the empire.

The Ottoman Empire provided merchants with ready access to foreign international traders and a unified market for interregional trade. Through their international and regional trading activity, merchants maintained the economic foundations of urban society by providing the larger towns with essential food products and the raw materials most artisans needed. They also were the chief agents in distributing finished craft products to distant markets. Despite the merchants' crucial role in urban economic life, the artisans often despised them as being morally corrupted by their wealth and privilege. Merchants played little or no active part in local markets or in retail sales. Only a few merchant families maintained retail shops in their urban home bases.

Ottoman international commerce mostly was concentrated in the hands of Dalmatian Dubrovnik merchants, Greeks, or Jews, who possessed the capital for long-distance maritime operations. Together they serviced the important markets of the Black Sea, the Mediterranean, and the Levant. Merchants hailing from other Balkan subject peoples were small traders with relatively limited capital, such as the Bulgarians and Serbs. They might participate in international trading as partners or clients of the Dalmatians, Greeks, or Jews, but they primarily operated as independent agents in interregional trade.

A significant portion of urban inhabitants engaged in low-paying, day-laboring activities either in town or on land outside of town in the immediate vicinity of their *mahalles*.

Except for some Jewish and Greek merchants, *zimmis* did not constitute an affluent element in Balkan urban populations relative to the wealthy Ottoman dignitaries and absentee landlords. Nor did they equal in economic standing a great many Muslim artisans, resident Orthodox *millet* leaders, or the wealthier foreign merchants. There did exist some wealthy *zimmi* artisan guilds and a few individual *zimmi* master craftsmen within each of the *esnafs* who were economically better situated than the majority of the guild membership and who furnished *zimmi* guilds with administrative leadership. A smattering of relatively well-to-do *zimmi* merchant families also existed. In the main, however, *zimmis* were either poor or only moderately wealthy members of Ottoman urban society.

The socioeconomic environment that the Ottomans imposed on their conquered Balkan non-Muslim subjects ultimately reflected one fundamental purpose: To ensure a stable source of revenues for the empire's rulers. So long as the *zimmis* paid their taxes, they generally were free to conduct their mundane affairs as they saw fit. Rather than suffering oppression, the Balkan non-Muslims led relatively autonomous lives. Since the empire's crucial military-administrative sector was predicated on the *sipahilık* system, the economic well-being and productivity of the rural and urban subjects had to be nurtured and protected to ensure stable and constant tax revenues. One of the state's most important duties was to protect its *reaya* against provincial military-administrative abuse that might unfavorably affect the tax base. Some scholars have argued that the Ottoman conquest had little effect on the Balkan populations' daily lives other than replacing one ruling class with another and that the non-Muslims' overall situation even may have improved as a result.

CHAPTER SEVEN

The Balkan Peoples under the Ottomans

The traditional approach taken by past Western and Balkan historians toward examining the Ottomans' conquered Balkan populations was grounded in ethnicity. Yet their ethnic focus reflected more Western nationalistic influences than Ottoman human realities. Pre-Ottoman medieval tradition, Islamic theocracy, and the Ottoman *millet* system ingrained religion—not ethnicity—as fundamental in shaping individual and group self-identities. With certain exceptions, there existed among the Ottoman Balkan populations only the most rudimentary sense of ethnic awareness based on vernacular language: All other factors being relatively equal, if one person could understand another's speech, then that other person was recognized as a fellow in some indefinite group sense; if not, that other person was a foreigner. Such "ethnic" group awareness played only a minor role in the daily lives of most Ottoman Balkan subjects before the close of the eighteenth century. Until that time, one can speak of Albanians, Bosnians, Bulgarians, Macedonians, Montenegrins, Romanians, Serbs, and most Greeks in terms of regional habitation rather than ethnicity. The Ottomans' Balkan subject peoples were far more conscious of their identities within the "Ottoman System" as *zimmis,* converts to Islam, or Ottoman vassals.

Zimmis

The *millet* was the most important Ottoman institution in the lives of the empire's non-Muslim Balkan subjects, permitting them to preserve their own religious beliefs and secular traditions in relative security, separate from those of their Muslim overlords and of all others. It provided them with both representation before the Muslim authorities through their own leaders and a large measure of local autonomy. *Millet* identity was paramount in the minds of the Balkan *zimmis*. Such identity, however, was not uniform since all of the *millets* represented culturally diverse memberships.

The Orthodox *millet* essentially was divided along linguistic lines between Greek- and Slavic-rite members—those who conducted the liturgy in Byzantine Greek and those who did so in Church Slavic. From the time of its inception, the Orthodox *millet* was dominated by Greek speakers favored by the Ottomans. During their Balkan conquests prior to capturing Constantinople, the Ottomans placed the Bulgarians' and Serbs' independent, Slavic-rite Orthodox churches into the hands of the Greek Patriarchate of Constantinople. When Mehmed II devised the *millet* system in 1454, he unhesitatingly installed the Greek patriarch as head of the Orthodox *millet,* which effectively placed the *millet*'s administration into the hands of Greeks appointed by the patriarch. Not only did the high Greek clergy continue to enjoy their pre-Ottoman social and political prestige, but their actual power under the *millet* exceeded what they had enjoyed during Byzantine times.

Mehmed sought to maintain the world-state of God on earth by substituting his Islamic empire for the Byzantine. He wholeheartedly embraced Byzantium's autocratic imperial traditions and viewed his Islamic state as that predecessor's logical continuation. Mehmed leaned heavily on Byzantine bureaucratic, military, and ceremonial precedent. In devising the Orthodox *millet,* Mehmed's pragmatic proclivity for adapting Byzantine models determined that it be administered by the Greek Patriarchate of Constantinople.

The office of patriarch was vacant immediately after the fall of Constantinople. In the past, the patriarch was chosen by God's viceroy, the Byzantine emperor. With Byzantium destroyed, Mehmed, leader of the Islamic faithful and successor of the Prophet, appointed Gennadios Scholarios (1454-57, 1464), a renowned anti-unionist bishop, the new Orthodox patriarch, publicly demonstrating the sultan's claim to imperial succession. Mehmed scrupulously followed Byzantine tradition by ceremoniously investing Scholarios with his symbols of office and issuing him an official diploma of investiture, setting the example followed by all of the sultan's successors. From 1454 until the Ottoman Empire's end, the Muslim sultans served as surrogate Christian emperors in determining who held the highest post in Orthodox Christendom and leadership of the crucial Orthodox *millet.*

Because its membership outnumbered all other *zimmis,* the Orthodox *millet* ranked first in Ottoman imperial interests. Within the *millet,* the Greek church of Constantinople held secular administrative jurisdiction over the empire's entire Orthodox population, including the Slavic-rite Bulgarians and Serbs, who possessed their own autonomous churches prior to the Ottoman conquest. Regarding the two Bulgarian churches, that of Ohrid was reduced to an autocephalous archbishopric, officially retaining the label "Bulgarian" but headed predominantly by Greek prelates under patriarchal influence. The Patriarchate of Tŭrnovo was abolished outright by the Greek patriarchate following the Ottoman conquest of Bulgaria, with its ecclesiastical jurisdiction transformed into a metropolitanate under the Greek patriarch's direct control and its administration staffed by patriarchal appointees.

As for the Serbian Patriarchate of Peć, its seat fell vacant sometime prior to Serbia's fall in 1459. Most of Peć's territorial jurisdiction was taken over by the Ohrid archbishopric until the influential Ottoman grand *vezir* Mehmed Sokollu convinced Süleyman I to reinstate the autocephalous Serbian patriarchate in 1557. (Sokollu was born Sokolović, an Orthodox Christian from Bosnia-Hercegovina collected in the *devşirme* who became the most powerful Ottoman grand *vezir* in the second half of the sixteenth century.) Because of favor in high Ottoman quarters, the Peć patriarchate was staffed by Slavic-speaking clergy, although the Greek patriarchate continuously pressed the Ottoman authorities to reduce its autonomy.

Throughout the Ottoman Balkans, towns serving as seats for Orthodox Greek patriarch-appointed church prelates/*millet* leaders served as Greek cultural centers. In lands outside of Peć's jurisdiction, Greeks monopolized the high church offices, with significant cultural consequences for non-Greek-speaking Orthodox Christians, most of whom adhered to the Slavic-rite liturgy. In regions where they predominated, non-Greek speakers were relegated to the Orthodox hierarchy's lower echelons—mostly parish priests and local monks. The Greek hierarchs principally supported Greek cultural activity conducted in ecclesiastical centers, thus stifling Slavic-rite cultural activity in the towns, while activities undertaken in the villages and monasteries were forced to depend on whatever local support that they could garner.

Without recourse to significant church funds, the non-Greek Orthodox believers outside of Peć's jurisdiction found financial support for Slavic-rite cultural activity mostly from local peasants and city dwellers, who generally were among the poorer elements in Ottoman society, possessing limited funds for cultural activity after meeting state and ecclesiastical tax obligations and their own mundane expenses. Such circumstances limited the quantity and quality of Slavic-rite Orthodox cultural endeavors. The Slavic-rite faithful administered by the reestablished Patriarchate of Peć were better situated since church funds were available for supporting cultural activity.

Fortunately for Balkan Slavic-rite culture, the Ottoman social sector unintentionally created new social elements able to lend local religious cultural efforts financial support. Patrons came from the ranks of the privileged rural corporate service groups and the urban artisan and merchant guilds, who funded Slavic-rite schools, literary production, and artistic activities in local parish churches or nearby monasteries. By doing so, they kept Balkan Slavic-rite Orthodox culture alive despite Greek domination of the Orthodox *millet*.

The suppressed urban and predominantly rural situation of Slavic-rite Orthodox cultural life proved somewhat detrimental for its adherents. So overwhelming was the Greek presence in the Orthodox *millet* that a perceptual association generally linking "Greek" and "Orthodox" became common among the Ottoman authorities, who dealt regularly with the *millet*'s leaders, and among Europeans traveling in the Balkans on military, economic, or political business, whose contacts with Orthodox Ottoman subjects came largely in towns located along the major highways. Until well into the eighteenth century, all Balkan Orthodox believers were identified as "Greeks" by European observers.

The Armenian Christian *millet* theoretically represented the Gregorian Monophysite Christian subjects of the empire, who were concentrated mostly outside of the Balkans in eastern Anatolia. Most ethnic Armenians in the Balkans resided in Istanbul, where they were active as commercial agents and merchants. A relatively small number of Armenian merchants were settled in various Balkan urban centers. When Mehmed established the *millet* in 1461, the head of the Armenian church, the *Katholikos,* was seated outside of the empire's borders in the Caucasus. Mehmed brought the Armenian archbishop of Bursa to Istanbul, declared him Armenian patriarch, and bestowed on him *millet* authority similar to that of the Greek patriarch. Even after Selim I's early sixteenth-century conquests in the Caucasus brought the Armenian *Katholikos*'s seat within the empire, the sultan-appointed Armenian patriarchs of Istanbul continued to administer the *millet.*

The Armenian *millet* was given administrative responsibility for all non-Orthodox Christian *zimmis.* Included within the *millet* in the Balkans were scattered settlements of Christian heretics (Bogomils and Paulicians), Gypsies, and Roman Catholics, all of whom enjoyed considerable autonomy. The *millet*'s Balkan Roman Catholics outnumbered the Armenians. Catholic *zimmis* predominated in the western Balkans' Adriatic regions, primarily in Bosnia and Albania, but small Catholic enclaves also were scattered throughout the peninsula's interior in Serbia, Bulgaria, and southern Greece. Additional Catholics inhabited regions bordering the Ottomans' northern frontier with Western states, especially in Ottoman Croatia, Slavonia, Vojvodina, and Banat.

The most important non-Christian component of the Ottomans' Balkan *zimmi* population was the Jewish *millet.* Although not granted official *millet* status until 1839, the empire's Jews enjoyed de facto *millet* administration dating to shortly after the fall of Constantinople. Perhaps Mehmed and his successors saw no need for formally instituting the *millet* because Islam already recognized Jews as a separate "People of the Book" and possessed centuries-old traditional dealings with Jewish subjects. Additionally, in pre-Ottoman Balkan Christian states, anti-Semitic discriminatory practices had forced Jews to exist in separate, self-governing communities. Recognizing the empire's need for its numerous Jewish merchants, and cognizant of the Jews' established traditions of self-government, Mehmed II chose the grand rabbi of Istanbul's rabbinical council to head the administration of his Jewish subjects and granted him similar administrative powers to those given the Orthodox and Armenian patriarchs.

The Muslim Ottomans extended a tolerance toward Jews found nowhere else in Europe. Jewish colonies were scattered throughout the empire's eastern Mediterranean possessions, and, in the Balkans, sizable Jewish colonies were located in Istanbul and Thessaloniki, the two largest commercial port cities. The autonomy granted Jews by the Ottoman authorities, combined with frequent anti-Semitic pogroms conducted in Western Europe during the late fifteenth and sixteenth centuries, brought increasing numbers of Jewish immigrants into the empire. Some 90,000 Jews fled Spain and Portugal following the late fifteenth-century *Reconquista* by the Catholic Spanish rulers Ferdinand and Isabella and the imposition of the Inquisition. Their long-standing association with the Islamic Spanish Moors, and their acknowledged commercial and intellectual skills, made them welcome. The immigrants preserved their language (Ladino) and customs and acquired a distinct identity as Sephardic (southern) Jews. So populous was their colony in Thessaloniki that it became known as the "Jewish" city.

Because of the massive immigration, Sephardic Jews made up the majority of the Jewish *millet*'s membership. Other immigrants fleeing anti-Semitic pogroms in Western Europe's northern states, particularly in the Holy Roman Empire's German states, Bohemia, and Poland, acquired a separate group identity as Ashkenazi (northern) Jews. The division between Sephardic and Ashkenazi Jews had some doctrinal and social manifestations. Doctrinally, the *millet* was split between Karaites (adopted by the Sephardic majority), who were less strict in their religious observances, and Rabbinites (generally adhered to by the Ashkenazi minority), who accepted Talmudic precepts. Socially, the Sephardic Jews' highly developed commercial and intellectual skills and sheer numbers endowed them with the economic and administrative edge over their Ashkenazi coreligionists. They dominated the considerable Jewish involvement in interregional and international trade, and their merchant colonies were found in towns throughout the Balkans. As a result, Sephardic Jews enjoyed considerable influence and favor at the sultans' palace.

The only non-Jewish Balkan *zimmis* who possessed a self-identity transcending strictly *millet* lines were the Greek merchants residing in Istanbul and Thessaloniki. In repopulating Istanbul, Mehmed II enticed back to the city large numbers of Greeks with useful expertise in maritime, military, and commercial activities. Mehmed handed them a living quarter of their own, the *Fener* (lighthouse) district, which lay along the city's thriving Golden Horn commercial harbor. Many of the Greek residents of the Phanar (the Hellenized name for the district), collectively known as Phanariotes, were scions of old Byzantine aristocratic and merchant families who turned their attentions to building lucrative mercantile operations with Ottoman blessings.

The Phanariotes soon acquired a dominant hold over Ottoman commercial and military maritime activities. Ottoman military naval forces were manned predominantly by Greek sailors, and the Ottoman fleet's admiral nearly always was a Phanariote. Greeks also predominated in the Ottoman merchant marine, and they eventually extended their commercial activities to land-based international endeavors, easily weathering competition from Jewish and Armenian traders. The Phanariotes came to control the Ottoman Empire's domestic and international economic life, and, since high Orthodox prelates consistently were drawn from their ranks, they ran the Orthodox *millet* as well. They constituted the single wealthiest and most powerful group of *zimmi* subjects in the empire, and they were well aware of their status within the state.

Unlike the Phanariotes, the mass of Greek peasants and artisans inhabiting mainland Greece resembled their non-Greek *millet* compatriots in possessing a self-identity little beyond that shaped by their *millet* membership and mundane occupations. For all *zimmis,* a vague sense of linguistic identity was preserved by a rich oral folk tradition and, to a limited extent, local education. The majority of *zimmis* were illiterate peasants who existed on the lower rungs of the Ottoman social ladder. The oral tales, festive songs, music, and agrarian instructions preserved their languages and often were expressions of local community pride. Education, on the other hand, frequently was not recognized as necessary. Access to education was sought by the minority of *zimmis* whose occupations—-clergy, artisans, and merchants—demanded a certain level of literacy.

In an Islamic state, all education was religious. Muslims seeking education first studied at elementary schools operated by mosques, where students were taught to memorize prayers and Koranic scriptures. Higher mosque schools, known as *medreses,* operated in larger urban centers and offered literary instruction and in-depth study of the *Şeriat.* They were structured in an ascending order of sophistication spread over a series of schools, starting at the lowest level in small provincial towns and ending in Istanbul's renowned *medreses.*

Balkan *zimmi* schools also were attached to religious establishments, such as local parish churches, monasteries, or synagogues, and used religious texts for instruction. There was no set system of elementary and higher education; the level offered depended on the capabilities and availability of educators as well as on the financial resources of the local community. Elementary education was most rudimentary while secondary studies delved into more sophisticated religious literary and artistic subjects.

The strictly religious curriculum offered to Balkan *zimmi* students primarily served as training for the clergy, although basic literacy provided skills applicable to secular occupations. Both Sephardic and Ashkenazi Jewish schools offered instruction in Hebrew. Latin was the language used in Roman Catholic schools. Greek-rite Orthodox schools taught in Byzantine Greek and used Greek-language materials, while those of the Slavic-rite employed Church Slavic. There was little linguistic ambiguity involved with Hebrew, Latin, and Greek education. Church Slavic, however, was another matter.

Church Slavic denoted any Slavic language written in Cyrillic and used in the Orthodox liturgy. The original Church Slavic was the liturgical language created in medieval Bulgaria and based on the spoken Bulgarian of that time. As other Slavic-speaking states adopted Orthodox Christianity, they imported Bulgaria's ready-made Slavic liturgical language. Over time, those states' literary languages were modified by native usages, and Bulgarian linguistic forms gradually disappeared. By the mid-sixteenth century three variants of Church Slavic were current in the Balkans: A "Bulgarian" form reflecting the original tenth-century language devised in Bulgaria; a "Serbian" form (also called "Resava") developed in Serbia under the patronage of Stefan Lazarović during the early fifteenth century; and a "Russian" form, which modern scholars commonly designate "Church Slavonic," that gradually emerged in Kievan and Muscovite Russian monasteries.

One or more of those variants could be found at any given time in any given region of the Slavic-speaking Balkans. Although apparently identified ethnically, the designations apply more to their place of origin than to the actual ethnicity of their users. The Russian variant, which possessed the least currency, was used because some monasteries and churches acquired liturgical books written in it from Russian monasteries on Mount Athos or directly from Russia. The Bulgarian variant was employed only slightly more than the Russian because of the diaspora of Bulgarian literati outside of Bulgaria after the collapse of the state in the late fourteenth century and the imposition of Greek ecclesiastical and cultural control over the dismantled Tŭrnovo Patriarchate. Most Slavic-speaking Balkan Orthodox populations used the Serbian variant. Its popularity probably stemmed from the Serbian state's longevity during the Ottoman conquest and the reestablishment of the autonomous Slavic-rite Patriarchate of Peć in the mid-sixteenth century.

By the mid-sixteenth century Church Slavic in any variant was so far removed from the Balkan vernaculars as to be virtually unintelligible to the average Slavic-rite Orthodox believer. Its use in the liturgy and in schools reflected its role as an official ecclesiastical language, akin to Latin in Roman Catholicism. For the majority of the Slavic-rite faithful, Church Slavic was a magical and mystical language expressing the spirituality and emotions of their beliefs. It did not need to be understood. The same situation held true for Greek-rite Orthodox believers: The liturgical Byzantine Greek used in their churches and schools was so far removed from *koine* (vernacular) Greek that it too was incomprehensible to the common Greek speaker. All members of the Orthodox *millet*, no matter which rite they followed, recognized the difference between Church Slavic and liturgical Greek; few noticed the differences among the Bulgarian, Serbian, and Russian Church Slavic variants or thought them to be of any great consequence.

Converts to Islam

Significant numbers of the Ottomans' Balkan non-Muslim subjects converted to Islam. Given Ottoman society's theocratic nature, such a step entailed serious consequences. Conversion obviously bestowed certain benefits: Converts joined the state's dominant religious element and were freed of the social restrictions and discriminatory taxes imposed on *zimmis*. On the other hand, conversion carried with it a certain amount of social tension. Converts legally were removed completely from their former *millet*, acquiring an entirely new set of laws, obligations, and rights. Often families were split by conversion, resulting in members of two legally and culturally separate communities living together under a single roof. While domiciles, languages, occupations, and even mundane customs may not have changed, converts immediately became "foreigners" to their former coreligionists. Unless conversion occurred on a mass local scale, converts stood to face social stigmatization. They frequently were branded traitors to their former faiths or collaborators with the foreign ruling authorities. Ultimately, *zimmis* classified converts, along with born Muslims, under the common designation of "Turks."

That large numbers of Balkan Christians converted to Islam under the Ottomans has proven unsettling for many modern European scholars. Some European Balkan specialists have advanced two related approaches toward rationalizing the conversions. One holds that the majority of conversions took place under the threat of force exerted by the Ottoman authorities. The other asserts that most conversions were acts of expediency made under duress and that the converts hoped to both preserve their way of life and escape the Muslim rulers' ire by publicly accepting Islam but secretly maintaining their Christian faith—becoming, in effect, "crypto-Christians."

Neither assertion is borne out by the historical evidence. Regarding "crypto-Christianity," much of the supporting evidence was produced by Roman Catholic high clergymen possibly attempting to rationalize the widespread conversions to Islam among their western Balkan followers. While initially there may well have been some true "crypto-Christians" among the converts, apparently their numbers were few. Most descendants of converts displayed little interest in renouncing their Muslim "cover" and reappropriating their "Christianity" when given later opportunities to do so freely. As for the claim of forced conversions, cultural misconceptions and nationalist agendas have helped it persist despite compelling evidence of its general fallacy.

Contrary to modern nationalist portrayals and past Western cultural perceptions, an officially concerted policy of forced conversions to Islam never accompanied the Ottomans' conquest and control of the Balkans. It was not in the interests of the Islamic state to eliminate the most lucrative source of revenues from its subject population. In fact, the Ottomans went to great lengths to preserve *zimmis* against extinction, as the *millet* system's creation aptly illustrated. Those non-Muslim conversions that did occur were matters of regional circumstances or individual decisions. Whether mass or individual, most conversions appear to have been voluntary. While cases have been made for Ottoman provincial administrators conducting strategic forced mass conversions, the supporting evidence often has proven questionable. There may well have been such religiously motivated coercion in the Balkans on the part of some Ottoman provincial officials, but, if so, it was scattered, sporadic, motivated by local and personal circumstances, and not sanctioned as official policy by the central authorities.

One factor influencing Balkan Christian conversions to Islam was the Islamic *sufi* movement represented by various *derviş* sects, which were active everywhere within the empire. Organized in a way that outwardly resembled Christian monastic orders, *dervişes* commonly accompanied Ottoman military forces on campaign and were given free rein by the sultans to operate in newly acquired territories. Although *derviş* orders technically were considered *sunni,* their attachment to Islamic mysticism often spawned a syncretistic approach in religious matters. The flexibility, eclecticism, and pragmatism exhibited by the *derviş* sects in their beliefs virtually were boundless, and a place often was found for the most un-Islamic rituals and practices. Some *derviş* orders incorporated Christian elements of popular belief into their governing ideologies, such as the veneration of saints and holy shrines, the concept of confession, and, in more extreme cases, the sacrament of holy communion. One *derviş* order—the Bektaşi—not only adopted Christian confession and communion but took to making the sign of the cross as a gesture of respect.

On entering a newly conquered region, *dervişes* confiscated Christian churches, adopted Christian saints held as patrons by local inhabitants, and frequently blended their brand of folk Islam with the similar folk Christianity flourishing among the generally illiterate rural population. Often no discernible overt differences in religious expression existed between *derviş* Muslims and poor Christian villagers. As a result, the *dervişes* won numerous converts to their particular form of Islamic belief among Balkan rural populations. *Derviş* religious syncretism led many Christian church leaders to claim that the converts were "crypto-Christians" hiding their true faith behind a Muslim facade.

Ottoman military formations worked hand in hand with the *dervişes* in facilitating Balkan Christian conversions. A direct correlation often existed between the locations of such units and the areas of intensive *derviş* activity.

Besides the obvious role of the *devşirme* in the conversion process, the empire's *sipahi* cavalry forces played a part. Many local Balkan Christian nobles joined the Ottoman ranks as vassals in the early years of the conquest, fighting alongside their mounted Muslim counterparts. Those *timar*-holding Christian *sipahis* gradually melted into the military's Muslim element as they found membership in the dominant faith less taxing (in every sense of the word). By the end of the fifteenth century, all members of the landed cavalry in Europe were Muslims.

Auxiliary military formations traditionally played an important role in absorbing Christians into the Muslim population. Because of attrition over time, irregular Ottoman units, such as the *yayas* (infantry), *müsellems* (cavalry), and *akıncıs* (raiders), became ethnically mixed, with significant numbers of Balkan Christians filling their ranks. Most of the Christian recruits saw enlistment as a way to escape the taxes and restrictions of *zimmi* peasant life. In time, the Christians in those units converted to Islam.

The *yürük* colonists transplanted from Anatolia to the Balkans by the Ottoman authorities in the fourteenth and fifteenth centuries played a similar role in assimilating Orthodox Christians into Muslim ranks. Organized into military units originally composed exclusively of seminomadic Turks, these tribesmen performed irregular services in conjunction with Ottoman regular forces. Losses in battle over time necessitated new recruitment, and it is likely that the new recruits included enslaved military captives and Balkan Christian locals. Those Christians enlisted into *yürük* formations swiftly underwent conversion to Islam.

Given the constant influences of human self-interest (in preserving property and social standing and in escaping discriminatory taxation and restrictions), the syncretistic activities of *derviş* orders, service in the Muslim-dominated military, and the Islamic concept of "Peoples of the Book" that spared *zimmis* from forced conversion, there is no reason to attribute the majority of conversions among Balkan Christians to premeditated Ottoman coercion.

Zimmi conversions to Islam routinely occurred in every region of the Ottoman Balkans. Most frequently, they were on the scale of individuals or of villages. Less common were mass conversions involving the populations of entire locales or regions. Three regions—Bosnia, Albania, and Bulgaria—were particularly notable for mass conversions during the Ottoman era. In Bosnia and Albania, such conversions indisputably were voluntary. Located in the western Balkans where for centuries Orthodox and Catholic powers vied for local hegemony, those regions had long experience with religion used as a political tool. In Bulgaria, however, the numerous conversions have been attributed primarily to force.

All of the factors facilitating conversion to Islam operated in Bosnia and Albania. After initially resisting the invading Ottomans, the native landowning aristocracy of both regions progressively accepted vassalage under the sultans. When their lands were incorporated outright by the Ottomans, their vassal status was transformed into *sipahilık* tenure. Virtually all of them apostatized their Christianity and turned Muslim, thus retaining their former holdings under the new system. Many common peasants and town dwellers followed their example, perhaps because of economic and social concerns or the influence of *derviş* activities among them, or both.

In mountainous northern Albania, where direct Ottoman control was minimal because of the extremely rugged terrain, a number of Albanian tribes accepted irregular Ottoman military service under their tribal chieftains, many of whom converted to Islam to reinforce their leadership positions and to gain support for their independence from fellow Albanian Catholic and Orthodox neighbors. Again, the tribal chieftains' example often was mimicked by their followers. Less mountainous central and southern Albania experienced a more direct and continuous Ottoman presence, which helped foster the conversion process among urban and lowland Albanians.

After Bosnia fell to Mehmed II in 1463, nearly all of the former Bosnian landed aristocracy gradually converted to Islam. Their mass conversion traditionally has been attributed to their preconquest Bogomil faith. According to the traditional argument, their conversion to Islam stifled centuries-long Catholic and Orthodox assaults, forestalled potential Ottoman persecutions, and guaranteed the retention of their social status and properties. While the above aims attributed to the Bosnian aristocracy's conversion generally can be accepted with reservations, the premise— that the Bosnian church was Bogomil, popular, and widespread among the Bosnians—is open to serious question.

Recent research, focused primarily on Bosnian rather than on hostile Vatican, Hungarian, and Serbian sources, has advanced a different perspective on the heretical nature of the Bosnian church. It finds no concrete evidence for the existence of widespread Bogomilism among the Bosnians. On the contrary, it paints the picture of an originally Catholic-spawned church centered almost exclusively on monasteries, possessing no secular clergy (thus enjoying no mass popular base), and exerting only a sporadic political influence on Bosnian domestic affairs. For all intents and purposes, the Bosnian church ceased to exist in the final years before the Ottoman conquest. The only basis for considering it Bogomil lies in the consistent claims of "heresy" made by Bosnia's enemies.

If the revisionist interpretation is accepted, then the pre-Ottoman factor of significant import for Bosnian mass conversions was the aristocracy's traditional proclivity for placing its members' self-interests before all else. The medieval Bosnian king-*bans* never managed to consolidate central authority over their powerful regional aristocracy. Moreover, the regional lords kept Bosnia in a state of endemic instability through their frequent family rivalries and civil wars, in which they used religious affiliation as a political tool to gain support from Bosnia's powerful foreign neighbors—Catholic Hungarians and Croats or Orthodox Serbs. The Bosnian lords were more concerned with their individual wealth and power than with maintaining a united Bosnian state. When faced with the fact of certain Ottoman domination, it took no major break with tradition for them to accept Islam.

The population of Bosnia, of all those in the Ottomans' conquered Balkan lands, demonstrated the most extensive conversions to Islam. The region was transformed into a stronghold of Islamic culture. The urban landscape became dotted with the material expressions of a flourishing Islamic society—mosques, caravansaries, fountains, baths, *derviş* lodges, and *medreses*, among others—supported by *vakıfs* established by the recently converted Bosnian landholders, who acquired the title of *bey*. In the sixteenth century the towns of Sarajevo and Mostar literally were transformed from small villages into the two most economically and culturally important urban centers in Bosnia and Hercegovina, respectively. Both became the administrative, cultural, and social hubs for the converted-Muslim *beys*, who eventually monopolized the Ottoman provincial administrations.

The Bosnian converts won important concessions from the Ottoman central authorities that endowed them with a unique position within both Muslim society and the military-administrative sector. They also won near-total control of the military-administrative system in the region, despite the general Ottoman policy of not stationing convert-officials in their native lands.

Sarajevo, which rapidly grew from a small village stopping-place on the overland trade route linking Istanbul to Italy by way of Dubrovnik into a large, flourishing mercantile center, served as the focal point for the Bosnian *beys'* activities. They built luxurious residences in and around the thriving center and lavished on it rich endowment monies supporting numerous Islamic institutions and foundations. Sarajevo grew so renowned that the sultans took to adopting it as one of their more important provincial residences (hence its Turkish name, Sarayı). Mid-sixteenth-century Ottoman registers list the city's population as completely Muslim, although large numbers of Catholic Dubrovnik and Jewish merchants were present, either on a permanent or semipermanent basis. So firmly was Sarajevo under the local Bosnian *beys'* control that Ottoman military forces were banned from entering the city and the official Ottoman governor was forced to reside in Travnik.

Mass conversions of *zimmis* to Islam in Bosnia and Albania apparently were linked to the presence of large Roman Catholic populations. One possible factor in that linkage was that Catholicism was the official religion of the Ottomans' Central European and papal enemies. Most Catholic *zimmis* lived close to the frontiers with those enemies. The Muslim conquerors may have made life in those regions more difficult for Catholics, who were viewed as potential fifth columnists by suspicious local authorities. No such danger was posed by the Orthodox or Jewish *zimmis* of those regions. Another possible factor was the structure of the *millet* system. Catholics were placed within the Armenian *millet* headed by the Gregorian Monophysite patriarch. Those who wished to remain Christian thus were forced to accept official administration by an ecclesiastical organization that they viewed as heretical. Rather than submit to the authority of heretics, many Catholics may have preferred conversion to Islam as the more morally correct course of action.

Significant numbers of conversions to Islam occurred among the Orthodox Bulgarians, especially in the Rhodope and Thracian regions. Bulgarian historians traditionally attribute them to Ottoman coercion resulting in mass conversions. According to their view, the early sixteenth-century regime of the fanatically devout Muslim Selim I forced numerous Bulgarians to convert or suffer dire consequences. Likewise, in the mid-seventeenth century thousands of Bulgarians inhabiting the Rhodope Mountain region were forced violently to accept Islam by an Ottoman army commander as he marched his forces through the region on his way south to join in a war with Venice. In his wake he left a region inhabited predominantly by Pomaks, Bulgarian-speaking Muslims.

Recent scholarship casts grave doubt on the validity of the traditional arguments for mass forced conversions among the Bulgarians. The sources used for supporting coercive conversions under Selim I demonstrate little beyond the general factors for such action commonly operating throughout the Balkans. While some violence against Christians is documented, such cases are few. Regarding the Rhodope mass conversions, all of the supporting evidence is suspect. None exists in the original, and internal analysis of the extant copies proves them to be nineteenth-century forgeries. Again, the Rhodope Pomak conversions apparently resulted from the general factors contributing to gradual conversion that operated throughout the Balkans and not from official Ottoman coercion.

Ottoman Vassals

Any state that paid tribute to the sultan was considered a vassal by the Ottomans. The degree of vassalage varied widely. For most Balkan states, Ottoman vassalage was the first step on the road to destruction. For others, mostly the Ottomans' Western European enemies, vassalage was nominal since it accompanied payments made in accordance with treaty or armistice agreements. By the mid-sixteenth century three Balkan states survived as client vassals of the Ottomans—Wallachia, Moldavia, and the Republic of Dubrovnik.

Wallachian Voievod Mircea the Old was the first Romanian prince to pay the Ottomans tribute in 1391, but Wallachia was not reduced to permanent vassal status until after the death of Voievod Dracula in 1376. Likewise, Moldavian Voievod Peter Aron first accepted Ottoman vassalage in 1456, but that status did not become permanent until 1512. The conditions of vassalage imposed on the two principalities were similar. In return for paying annual tribute, cash "gifts" (paid by the *voievods* when ascending the throne), taxes, and other duties (mainly "exports" of foodstuffs targeted for Istanbul), for permitting Ottoman forces to man strategic fortresses on their territories, and for harmonizing their foreign affairs with Ottoman policies, the two Romanian vassal states were granted a great deal of domestic and foreign independence. That situation held unchanged until 1714, when the Ottomans eliminated the principalities' rights to elect their own rulers.

Prior to to the early eighteenth century Romanian *voievods* were elected by their aristocracies but required the sultan's approval before actually taking power. The Ottomans played no direct role in the domestic administrations of the states. Except for strategically important fortresses garrisoned by Ottoman troops, the Muslim presence within the states technically was minimal. Those fortresses, however, brought small colonies of Muslims into the principalities. Some *voievods* (such as the Moldavian Petru Rareş [1527-38, 1541-46]) were forced to accept Janissary "bodyguards" intended to guarantee their loyalty, and a smattering of Ottoman terminology for mundane institutions and items was adopted. Direct Ottoman influences, however, never were significant enough to exert a lasting impact on the principalities.

The Romanian *voievods* theoretically were absolute autocrats in the Orthodox Byzantine mold. Their position, however, was limited in practice by the elective nature of the office. Assemblies of landowning aristocrats (*boiers*) and high Orthodox church officials chose and acclaimed the rulers. Once on the throne, they governed through advisory councils comprised of leading members of aristocratic families. Only *voievods* controlled admission to the noble ranks and grants of land. The electoral process often forced the rulers to use those rights as bribes to win support for their princely tenures from the land-hungry aristocracy. Only a few *voievods* proved strong enough to retain their thrones for long.

Ştefan the Great was one of the last Romanian rulers to enjoy a lengthy reign. Succeeding *voievods,* with rare exceptions, were weak nonentities faced with a number of foreign and domestic problems. Not only had they to deal with their Ottoman vassal lords, but they had to parry combined threats from their imperialist Habsburg and Polish neighbors and fend off disruptive Muscovite Russian, Crimean Tatar, and Ukrainian Cossack incursions. Although the terms of Ottoman vassalage granted them significant latitude in conducting foreign affairs, the corollaries to that freedom were the total lack of any Ottoman obligation to defend them against foreign threats and the possibility of Ottoman punitive invasions for perceived "treasonous" defensive foreign policy decisions.

The necessity of maintaining the loyalty and support of the *boiers* who controlled the noble assemblies and Orthodox church hierarchies was paramount for the Romanian *voievods.* To ensure their crucial backing, every *voievod* was forced to "buy" them. The only steady source of income available was derived through land ownership and the tithes paid by resident peasants. Throughout the sixteenth century the *voievods* turned increasing amounts of state land over to *boier* and church control until there was little left for further dispersal. Consequently, the actual power of the princely thrones declined relative to that of the *boiers,* and the situation of the Romanian peasantry progressively worsened.

There were two categories of Romanian peasants: *Călăraşi* (free), who lived and worked on state land or on their own small plots, and *dorobanţi,* who worked estates owned by the *boiers* and the church. The latter were not technically enserfed since they initially possessed the rights to own small plots and to change their residences. Both groups paid tithes either to the state or to the landowners. As state land passed into *boier* and church hands, the number of free peasants steadily declined. When, in the seventeenth century, the *voievods* had little land left to distribute, they permitted the magnates to increase the *dorobanţis'* tithes. That development coincided with Ottoman demands for expanded tribute, in-kind tax, and "export" payments, and the Romanian peasants' lot deteriorated into one of abject exploitation by their state, *boier,* and church overlords.

The reign of Wallachian Voievod Mihai the Brave (1593-1601) proved the last of strong princely leadership in the Romanian Principalities. When Mihai, a wealthy and ambitious *boier* who bribed his way into office, came to the throne, Wallachia faced total encirclement and possible assimilation by one of the surrounding Polish, Habsburg, or Ottoman foreign powers. His only military resource was the Wallachian army composed of the rural gentry created by state land distribution, who hoped to maintain Wallachia's independence to ensure their own continued benefits. To tie the gentry closer to his authority, Mihai passed laws binding the peasants to the land.

Mihai negotiated a series of alliances with the Holy League—the Habsburg Empire, Venice, the Papal States, and Spain—to strengthen Wallachia's international position. In 1593 the league initiated the Long War (1593-1606) against the Ottomans, during which Mihai led the two Romanian and Transylvanian vassal principalities in a revolt against continued Ottoman suzerainty. After Transylvanian Prince-Cardinal András Báthory (1599) recognized Ottoman suzerainty in the name of Transylvania and the two Romanian Principalities, Mihai swore allegiance to Habsburg Emperor Rudolf II (1576-1608), invaded Transylvania, defeated András, and was hailed as the Transylvanian prince. In 1600 Mihai acquired the throne of Moldavia, becoming the first Romanian ruler to unite under his authority the principalities of Wallachia, Moldavia, and Transylvania.

Mihai's achievement was short-lived. While some Transylvanian nobles were loyal, others resented his ethnic ties to the impoverished Romanian peasant majority in Transylvania, and still others preferred Habsburg rule. Transylvanian noble intrigues led to a Habsburg invasion of Transylvania in 1600 and Mihai's expulsion. Thereupon, the Poles assaulted Moldavia and installed a puppet *voievod* of their own. Undaunted, Mihai reached an amicable agreement with Rudolf and returned to Transylvania in 1601, where he ultimately was double-crossed and murdered by a pro-Habsburg general. Mihai's death opened the door for increasing *boier* control in the Romanian Principalities.

The seventeenth century often is labeled the "the *boiers'* century" in Romanian history. By that period's end, all state lands formerly controlled by the *voievods* was firmly in the proliferating nobility's hands. Most free peasants were transformed into dependent *dorobanţis,* who suffered unrelenting landowner demands for tithes and services. The *boiers* were responsible for paying the duties due the Ottomans and grew increasingly market-oriented, expanding "exports" to the empire for transactions on international markets. Lacking knowledge of advanced agricultural techniques, they maximized profits from the land by placing increased demands on the peasantry, who sank to the level of serfs. Those who worked church monastic lands shared a similar fate.

During the century, a certain social differentiation appeared within the *boiers'* ranks. A class of exceedingly rich magnate families emerged, some of whom were more powerful than the rulers. The magnates monopolized the important offices of state and made up the true ruling element in both principalities. The remaining *boiers* were members of the lesser nobility, or gentry. They held the lower posts in the principalities' governments and formed the bulk of the military forces. The nobility, joined by the Orthodox clergy, easily threw off all tax and service obligations, transferring them to the subservient peasantry.

The only threat to the *boiers'* dominance came toward the middle of the seventeenth century when, for an unusually lengthy period of two decades, Wallachia and Moldavia both enjoyed the leadership of able rulers: Matei Basarab (1632-58) in Wallachia and Vasile Lupu (1634-53) in Moldavia. Unfortunately, the potential both rulers displayed for checking the growing power of the *boiers* was squandered by their concentration on foreign rather than domestic matters.

The two rulers were inveterate rivals. Lupu, an ambitious man who dreamed of reinstating the traditional Byzantine-like autocratic authority of his office, coveted wealthy Wallachia and initiated three military campaigns against Basarab in 1637, 1639, and 1652. The Ottomans, happy to keep their strong and independent-minded vassals at each others' throats, encouraged him. In defense, Basarab consolidated *boier* support by cementing their power over the Wallachian peasantry. Lupu's pretensions to Byzantine autocracy, however, alienated the Moldavian nobles, who overthrew him in 1653. In the end, the reigns of both rulers only served to entrench further their *boiers'* power.

Increased *boier* political control decreased the principalities' autonomy. The Ottoman authorities played on the greed and self-interest of the Romanian nobility to manipulate princely elections so that they occurred as frequently as possible (to maximize the amount of "gifts" paid to the sultan by new rulers) and produced suitably malleable vassals. In addition, the economic terms of vassalage helped the Ottomans to undermine Romanian autonomy further. In purchasing the required "exports"—in reality, tribute—targeted for Istanbul, the Ottomans reserved the right of preemption in Romanian markets. They paid the *boiers* for the sheep and grain involved at rates set well below current market prices and bought them only through Romanian agents directly appointed by the Ottoman government, creating an Ottoman economic monopoly within the principalities lying outside the authority and control of the native rulers.

The decline of princely authority and Ottoman economic encroachment provided the opening for Phanariote Greeks to enter the Romanian Principalities. They appeared in the mid-seventeenth century, assisted by the Greek Orthodox Patriarchate and the Ottoman authorities. Their wealth won them patriarchal appointments to high offices in the principalities' church hierarchies and Ottoman commissions to lucrative positions in the principalities' "export" monopolies. In the early eighteenth century the Phanariotes displaced the native *boiers* in ruling both Wallachia and Moldavia, and the populations were reduced to *zimmi* status.

Unlike the Romanian Principalities, the vassal city-state of Dubrovnik experienced no Ottoman interference of any kind in its internal affairs. Its small Adriatic coastal possessions were never invaded by the Ottomans, and its approximately 30,000 citizens were not considered officially *zimmis* by the Ottoman authorities. Vassal status for Dubrovnik strictly was a matter of cementing mutual economic benefit for both parties.

The Venetians acquired Dubrovnik in 1205 as part of their spoils from the Fourth Crusade. At the time, the city was the seat of a Roman Catholic archbishopric and enjoyed lucrative trade agreements with Bosnia, Serbia, and the recently collapsed Byzantine Empire. Venice's overlordship lasted until 1358, when it was defeated by the Hungarians. A treaty between Hungarian King Louis I and Dubrovnik granted the city complete independence under nominal Hungarian suzerainty.

Dubrovnik's republican institutions were shaped during the period of Venetian rule. Its government was headed by a *comes/knez,* who ruled in partnership with the local nobles and was assisted by a Minor Council, which served as a judicial body with police powers. Both the Minor Council and the *comes/knez* were elected by the three hundred-strong Major Council, which wielded legislative authority and possessed the final voice in all policy decisions. A senate comprised of lifetime-appointed members, which prepared the bills brought before the Major Council, ratified treaties, and conducted all diplomatic activities, was controlled exclusively by a small group of landowning patrician families.

Dubrovnik's middle-class merchants, artisan guild members, and ship captains, who by and large were able to govern their own affairs and cooperate with the patricians, also enjoyed considerable political and economic influence. The central role played by trade in the city's economy ensured that the merchants' interests were taken seriously by the government, and the valuable manufacturing industries guaranteed that artisan and craft guilds were granted a voice in determining the city's affairs. The interests of all groups essentially were similar, and the patricians' dominance stemmed from their noble titles and from wealth, which made them the respected financiers for the population in general.

The majority of Dubrovnik's population were peasants working the lands owned by the patricians and church. They constituted the city's lowest class. Some peasants owned small plots, but most were landless. All successfully resisted the landowners' efforts to enserf them and remained free in status, working the land under terms fixed by contracts and subject only to state judicial authority. The thriving economy, which had great need of manpower, guaranteed relatively benign state and landowner treatment.

By the time of the Ottomans' Balkan conquests, Dubrovnik was active in trade, manufacturing, and mining in Bosnia, Serbia, and Bulgaria. Self-governing colonies of Dubrovnik merchants and miners were scattered throughout the Balkans, particularly in major trading centers, and the colonies owned a number of Bosnian and Serbian mines outright. In the late fourteenth century the city-state negotiated the retention of its citizens' existing rights in areas conquered by the Ottomans.

A 1458 treaty placed Dubrovnik under Ottoman protection and guaranteed the city's rights to trade and freely settle colonies throughout the Ottoman Balkans in exchange for payment of annual tribute. The pragmatic Ottomans saw no reason to displace Dubrovnik's well-established trade network by conquering the city outright. For its part, the republic understood the advantages offered by the unified trade zone created by the Ottomans, which swept away the numerous customs barriers that former Balkan states had erected and imposed a simple payment that opened free access to all Balkan lands. In addition, the Ottomans offered the city "most-favored-nation" status through exclusively low export and import duties. Despite repeated Western European requests that it renounce the treaty, as well as a rapid twelvefold increase in the annual tribute, Dubrovnik steadfastly embraced Ottoman vassalage. It remained the most independent Ottoman vassal until the early nineteenth century and Napoleon's acquisition of all Dalmatia, including Dubrovnik.

As a nominal Ottoman vassal, Dubrovnik governed itself as a sovereign state. One reason why it was able to do so was that the Ottomans had no experience in dealing with a state governed by corporate institutions. There was no single ruler for them to manipulate and control as there had been in the other Balkan states. Another factor in Dubrovnik's independent status was the Ottoman need for the city's commercial role; reducing the republic's colonists inside of the empire to *zimmi* status would have had deadening effects on their trading activities. Dubrovnik's Balkan colonists retained their status as "citizens" of the city, free of *zimmi* taxes and fees and subject to their own authorities and laws. Moreover, the republic maintained consuls in a few Ottoman cities and dealt with the central government through special envoys who acted under specific instructions issued by the city-state's governing authorities, which included set limits on bribes paid to officials.

The Ottomans were so desirous of keeping their Dubrovnik vassal satisfied that they permitted it complete freedom in conducting foreign affairs with other European states and militarily defended the city against its European enemies, especially Venice and the Dalmatian Uskok pirates of Senj. Consequently, after establishing its vassal relationship with the empire, Dubrovnik was never seriously threatened by outsiders. Its ships sailed the Adriatic and Mediterranean under its own flag, trading with European states under treaty terms negotiated by the city's senate. Dubrovnik became the partner of choice for most Europeans wishing to trade in the Ottomans' Balkan markets.

Dubrovnik's unique position in the Ottoman Balkans had implications beyond the political and economic. The city was a model of Italian city-state reality, yet its population mostly was Slavic-speaking. They maintained Western European values and traditions but remained aware of their Balkan Slav roots. Many Italians lived and worked in the city, and just as many Dubrovnik students studied at Italian universities. Dubrovnik was the Balkans' "opening to the West" during the Ottoman era.

Italian models predominated in Dubrovnik's cultural life, but they often were modified by local Slavic elements. The city's professionals and intellectuals operated in the educational, artistic, architectural, artisan, and scientific mainstream of Western Europe. Masterpieces of architecture and painting dotted the city, and one of its natives, Marin Getaldić, played an important role in furthering the Western European Scientific Revolution. The greatest contribution to Balkan cultural life made by Dubrovnik, however, lay in the field of literature.

Although the city's writers worked in three languages—Latin, Italian, and Slavic—those who used the latter were significant for later Balkan (Serbo-Croat) cultural history. Virtually all writers came from the ranks of the highly educated clergy, merchants, and patricians. Because of the commercial nature of Dubrovnik's existence, literacy was widespread among the city's population, and there was a public library as well as numerous private book collections. Initially literary production was in Latin, but by the late fifteenth century Slavic-language works, modeled on Italian originals and using the Latin alphabet, appeared. These included poetry, plays, and assorted works of folklore.

The most influential Ottoman-era Dubrovnik Slavic writer was Ivan Gundulić. His greatest work was the epic poem *Osman,* named after Ottoman Sultan Osman II (1618-22) and chronicling Balkan events during that ruler's reign. Gundulić glorified Dubrovnik and anticipated the liberation and unification of all Balkan Slavs. *Osman* ranks as one of the truly great works of Balkan Slavic epic literature. Gundulić's language and style became the archetypes for West Balkan poets throughout the remaining years of the Ottoman era.

Also significant was Dubrovnik's role as center for Balkan historical writing during the Ottoman era and for translations of Western and Greek works into Slavic. In no other Balkan center was historical writing pursued so persistently. Although none of the histories produced were written in Slavic, the Latin-language works were important records of Balkan events supplementing the official documents. As for translation efforts, the Latin, Greek, and Italian literary and scientific works made available to Slavic speakers in the western Balkans through works produced in the city significantly fostered their continued cultural development.

Dubrovnik's influence on the Balkans' Slavic populations far exceeded its size. Its privileged position kept its population abreast of economic, scientific, and intellectual developments in the West. Its network of merchant and mining colonies throughout the Balkans made such developments accessible to those in daily contact with the colonists as well as to those who visited the city on business. A great deal of the modernization experienced by Greek, Bosnian, Albanian, and Bulgarian merchants in their trading endeavors during the Ottoman era resulted from the example and influence of Dubrovnik practices. Such economic transfers often were accompanied by cultural influences as well.

CHAPTER EIGHT

Ottoman Destabilization

Historians traditionally characterize the period beginning with the death of Süleyman I in 1566 and extending through the eighteenth century as one of Ottoman decline. The word "decline" implies that factors inherent to the Ottomans' society led to its gradual deterioration, with deleterious effects on the empire's internal administration, its international position, and the condition of its assorted subjects. Ottoman society's institutions, which for the previous two and a half centuries proved strong enough to win and uphold a large and powerful empire and flexible enough to integrate a vast, multicultural subject population, did slowly begin to unravel following the mid-sixteenth century. Little evidence exists, however, to suggest that they did so on their own account and of their own accord. Compounding forces exerted by the Ottomans' Western European antagonists primarily were responsible for that development. Rather than "decline," it is more accurate to speak of Ottoman internal "destabilization," a result of consistent external, Western European economic and military-technological pressures. Either way, the period left a lasting negative legacy on the empire's Balkan subjects.

Economic Destabilization

The Western European Age of Discovery struck a damaging blow to the Ottoman economy by both shifting the primary Asian-European trade routes and opening the Americas to Western European exploitation. The former effectively removed the Ottomans as middlemen in the lucrative spice and luxury trade, from which the empire derived tremendous revenues. The latter brought a flood of silver into Europe from Spain's mines in South America, which swiftly spread into Ottoman markets, causing monetary inflation in the traditionally fixed economy. Taken in combination, falling trade revenues and rising inflation sparked a financial crisis within the empire that sent state expenditures soaring, undermined the traditional *sipahılık* landholding system on which the empire's stability depended, and weakened the internal economy.

For Europeans to acquire the Asian spices necessary to preserve their foods in the days before refrigeration, as well as the Asian luxury items desired by their rulers and elites, they were forced to pay handsomely in the Ottomans' eastern Mediterranean markets. By the mid-seventeenth century, however, the West had developed all-water routes bypassing the Ottoman markets and had swept the Ottoman naval presence from the Indian Ocean and Red Sea. With the Ottoman Empire's only maritime carrying trade lost and its Mediterranean commercial markets declining, its role in international commerce increasingly declined and trade revenues suffered.

Problems inherent in reduced trade revenues were exacerbated by the monetary inflation resulting from the influx of Spanish silver into Europe. While Western European economies eventually stabilized after the initial economic disruption caused by the silver flood, the Ottomans were not as fortunate. In the Ottoman economic system, virtually all prices were fixed. The official currency (the *akçe*) was silver-based, and, by the latter decades of the sixteenth century, the inflationary effects of foreign silver in the empire's Mediterranean markets were noticeable.

The Ottomans' initial response to falling trade revenues and inflationary expenditures was to reduce the amount of currency in circulation and devalue the silver *akçe*, but to little avail. Inflation only accelerated. In response, the authorities further degraded their coins' silver content, which led to economic confusion since the nominal face value of the currency ceased to correspond with its actual silver value. Prices soared, speculation became rampant, and counterfeiting proliferated. Monetary devaluation efforts resulted only in compounding inflation further, disrupting normal business transactions, and fomenting distrust of the government among the empire's subjects.

The Ottoman authorities also set about maximizing state revenues. All taxes were raised dramatically. Temporary taxes were made permanent and collected annually. The *cizye* not only was increased in rate but, by the end of the seventeenth century, was collected on an individual rather than a household basis. Tax farms, the preferred mechanism for raising taxes, were auctioned off to the highest bidders, and vacant military fiefs often were not redistributed to other *sipahis* but were transformed into new tax farms. Since tax farmers also sought extensive profits from their investments, tax rates throughout the empire became higher than those mandated by the state, and official enforcement of laws designed to curb the tax farmers' rapaciousness grew infrequent.

A growing desire for increased cash income emerged during the seventeenth century in every sector of Ottoman society. The example set by the central government in buying substitutes for important administrative functions through widespread tax farming filtered down to all administrative levels. Provincial officials and *kadıs* leased their courts to substitutes, and bribery within the governing system became rife. Holding state administrative positions became a means for increasing personal wealth. Positions were sold by the state or their authority was delegated to the bidder who provided the authorities with the most cash. In such a situation, corruption became commonplace.

Continuing needs for more revenues led the central authorities to begin confiscating private (*mülk*) and state (*miri*) lands formerly distributed in the *sipahilık* system. *Sipahilık* lands were amassed in the name of the sultan; a large percentage first was rented out to moneyed dignitaries and palace favorites, who then sublet their rentals to tenants. As a result, the lands involved passed out of direct government control. The new nonmilitary landholders viewed their holdings purely as sources of personal enrichment and bent every rule at every opportunity to convert their leases into hereditary property free of government supervision. Their ultimate goal was to transform their holdings into privately owned, market-oriented estates (*çiftliks*) worked by peasants tied to the soil.

Rich or influential individuals also could acquire great *çiftlik* estates by buying outright from the central authorities land not officially listed in tax registers. Since Ottoman tax records commonly were confused and out of date, the purchase of state lands through bribery or forcing *reaya* to sell their land and enter estate service was not difficult. A capitalistic *çiftlik* also could be established through transforming private holdings into *vakıfs,* with the owners and their heirs ensconced as the inalienable administrators. By the late seventeenth century *vakıfs* developed into plantationlike *çiftlik* estates free of government interference because of their intimate ties to the Muslim religious sector.

The Ottoman government's interference in the traditional landholding system was negative. The amount of land directly supporting the military sector declined. The *sipahi* fief-holders, concerned about declining fixed incomes tied to the old values assigned to their holdings, began following the lead of the nonmilitary newcomers. A competition for land developed between the rich, nonmilitary landholders and the *sipahi* fief-holders, which tended to concentrate landholding in fewer hands and resulted in the ruination of the lessor fief-holders. No matter which side won, the central government lost, since direct control over a great deal of the empire's land progressively slipped from its hands. Loss of control meant loss of revenues and the expansion of the abusive tax farming system.

The ultimate losers in the inflationary situation were the empire's subject *reaya,* whose taxes, duties, and tithes constituted the revenues for the state, landholders, and tax farmers. Taxes continuously rose. In the Balkan countryside, the peasants faced ruinous levels of taxation. By the late seventeenth century taxes often reached over 80 percent of the peasant land's productive value; in some cases they exceeded the total value. To meet the crushing tax burden, peasant households or villages often resorted to borrowing cash from local landholders using their lands as collateral. When they defaulted (as they often did), they lost their lands and found themselves tied to the lenders' *çiftliks*.

Peasants increasingly found themselves working on land transformed from old military fiefs into capitalistic *çiftlik* estates. Whereas under the previous conditions many labor services and tithes had been converted to cash payments, the new *çiftlik* landowners reimposed many services and tithes at a rate higher than formerly levied. By the latter decades of the eighteenth century the formerly positive situation of the Ottoman Balkan peasantry relative to their Western European counterparts was largely reversed and their lot was one of crushing taxation and economic exploitation.

Numerous peasants took advantage of lax Ottoman tax registration to move off their land and settle either in urban centers or on *vakıf* or imperial (*has*) estates. In most instances of the two latter alternatives, they found that they moved from the frying pan into the fire: The administrators of autonomous *vakıf*s and the leasers of most *has* lands both frequently used slave labor without questions from local authorities. Once fugitive *reaya* settled on them, they were tightly bound to the estate and subject to treatment akin to that dealt the slave labor force (or, at the very least, were reduced to near-serf conditions).

Those peasants who fled to Balkan urban centers found some improvement in their situation. Balkan cities and towns were integral parts of the Ottoman *sipahilik* system. They generally constituted *has* or more lucrative *zeamet* lands held by the sultan or *beylerbeyis*. Incomes derived from urban *has* and *vakıf* properties rarely were invested directly into urban productive sectors. Instead, they were used as sources for high-yield interest-bearing loans to merchants, artisans, local peasants, and provincial administrators. Urban revenues were derived from such sources as the common *cizye;* market and custom duties; *avaris;* tithes on land; vineyards; beehives; gardens and meadows; judicial fines; and yields from neighboring fields. Revenues also were extracted from specialized urban industries, such as metalworking, in which case taxes were levied on forges, mines, and furnaces. Compounding the ordinary taxes for which urban inhabitants were liable were special state levies of considerable size (*mukataas*) that were collected through tax farmers.

On average, the tax burden for an urban household was double that of the village household. This, however, did not mean that the financial plight of urban dwellers was twice that of their rural counterparts. The economic opportunities offered by cities and towns provided townspeople with more access to more currency than was possible in rural areas, and the economic condition of urban inhabitants deteriorated far less drastically than did that of village peasants. Moreover, the status of urban centers as mostly important *has* holdings and primary government administrative seats precluded the deleterious landholding developments that wreaked anarchy in the countryside.

Comparatively stable economic and social conditions prevailing in Balkan urban centers attracted a growing number of fugitive peasants, many of whom were village artisans who took advantage of an Ottoman law permitting them to leave their land on payment of an annual fee. They then could take up residence in a city or town, set up shop, and, if successful, eventually would be registered in the artisan records. The numbers of nonspecialized, land-working peasants who fled the countryside for urban centers far outstripped those of village artisans. By the late seventeenth century migrants from the villages began to include significant numbers of privileged peasants, especially *celeps* and *voynuks,* whose dealings in livestock commodities brought them substantial monetary returns. They actively entered the urban merchant class, later developing into an important component of the rising native Balkan regional middle classes.

The peasants' flight to urban centers was facilitated by the landholding system itself. Since the Ottoman authorities primarily were concerned with guaranteeing revenue income and not land ownership, peasants were not bound legally to the land. The purchase and sale of land among peasants was widespread, so long as the revenues owed the state and the landholder did not diminish as a result. The land involved was encumbered by tax, tithe, and service obligations no matter the owner. Most peasants who wished to set up farming near a city or town legally, or to find urban wage-work, needed only to pay an annual fee for leaving the land (similar to that paid by the artisans) or to find a buyer for their land and its encumbrances. The Ottoman legal system proved powerless to prevent large-scale migration from the countryside to urban centers.

The migrants initially faced problems common in all cases of rapid urban expansion: Poor housing, underemployment, low wages, and resistance from the already resident population. Their assimilation was a long, somewhat disruptive process. Artisan and merchant guilds made unsuccessful attempts to prevent the newcomers from joining their ranks or from setting up their own operations. The glut of new labor placed pressure on employment opportunities and wages. Crime rates rose. Eventually conditions stabilized and most migrants were integrated successfully into the urban population.

During the seventeenth and eighteenth centuries the Ottoman domestic economy remained largely self-sufficient, although expensive goods from Western Europe were slowly making inroads. The most fundamental product—food—was grown locally in amounts sufficient to meet the population's demands. All other necessities were produced inside of the empire as well. When the government needed to purchase materials for military purposes from foreign suppliers (such as tin to make bronze artillery), the expenses were financed through normal export trade. Most production and consumption in the empire remained local, and few items imported from the West ever penetrated far inland from their initial ports of entry because of transportation costs caused by the empire's size and generally difficult interior terrain.

The real problems for the Ottoman economy stemmed from a lack of growth built into the traditional emphasis on economic stability and from the low prices of export products. At a time when Western European governments were investing large sums into state-controlled mercantile development, which stressed direct government economic intervention and infrastructural development, the Ottoman domestic economy continued to stress traditional production for traditional consumption levels. While Western European governments fostered domestic industrial, transportation, financial, and educational improvements, expanded their maritime resources, and conducted foreign policies to advance their export trade, the Ottomans continued to sink their funds into the military and its wars at the expense of infrastructural improvements, nonmilitary manufacturing, secularizing education, and maritime development.

Ottoman Islamic tradition did not favor large-scale government intervention in the economy; nor did it include a sophisticated sense of investment. Neither the government nor the wealthy in Ottoman society thought to undertake Western European-style mercantilistic development. Profits were either reinvested in the businesses that produced them or spent on personal pleasures rather than invested in others' businesses or new production methods. Commercial loans were minimal, short-term, and transacted among individuals rather than through banking houses, which practically were nonexistent. The "recycling" of money that fed the transformation from mercantile to industrial capitalist economies in Western Europe totally was lacking.

Western Europe's early Industrial Revolution spelled ultimate economic disaster for the Ottoman Empire's self-sufficient economy. Machine technology in the empire was rudimentary and, because of local self-sufficiency, remained unchanged for centuries. Most labor was performed manually. Never having experienced the Renaissance and its by-products of Humanism and the Scientific Revolution, which opened the door in the West to capitalistic thinking and, subsequently, to mercantilism and industrialization, the Ottoman government and population did not view as outmoded the traditional production methods within the empire. Gradually the westerners' cheap, factory-made import goods progressively displaced native handicraft items, causing unemployment, economic dependency, and commercial deterioration.

Throughout the seventeenth and eighteenth centuries real incomes in the Ottoman Empire experienced a decline because of no-growth conditions, coupled with the impact of rampant inflation. The low prices for goods desired by the West (primarily foodstuffs and basic raw materials) tended to suck them out of the empire at the expense of the domestic economy. A few benefited from the situation, especially some *zimmi* merchants and Muslim *çiftlik* owners, who evolved into a growing middle class, but the merchants were oriented toward commerce with westerners and not production while the landowners concentrated only on their own enrichment and ignored that of others. Most Ottoman subjects experienced only increased financial and labor hardships compounded by rising official bribery, extortion, and corruption. The deteriorating situation fostered a growing discontent among the empire's Balkan *zimmis* toward the Ottoman authorities.

Military-Administrative Disruption

Technological, mercantile, and industrial developments provided Western Europe with the upper hand over the Ottomans in the economic and military fields. Until the late sixteenth century the Ottoman Empire enjoyed the military edge over its disunited European enemies. Territorial conquests constituted an important element in the empire's continued military and financial well-being. Western developments during the late sixteenth through eighteenth centuries reversed the military situation, with dire consequences for the Ottoman Empire's military-administrative stability.

By the mid-seventeenth century in Western Europe statism had supplanted religion as the governing ideology of monarchs, who sought to cement their interests through professionalized state centralization. As was true for the Ottomans, the military ranked high on their list of priorities, since military strength was considered the barometer of a monarch's (state's) worldly position. Some of the earliest Western mercantilistic efforts were aimed at strengthening the monarchs' military capabilities on the battlefield.

So long as Western European armies primarily were comprised of lumbering, heavily armored, and essentially undisciplined mounted feudal warriors supported by a ragtag infantry of impressed peasants, urban militias, and freebooters, the Ottomans' lightly armored, highly mobile horse-archers and professional standing Janissary infantry units were unmatched in combat, especially since both sides essentially used similar traditional weaponry. The Western trend toward military professionalism, which placed paramount emphasis on gunpowder weapons technology and its effective deployment on the battlefield, tilted the scales of combat with the Ottomans in the westerners' favor. The Ottomans, whose Islamic culture held tradition in high regard, saw no reason to change the weapons and tactics that had brought them spectacular successes in the past.

Despite their role as early pioneers of gunpowder weapons during the mid-fifteenth century, the Ottomans held fast to firearms of fifteenth- and sixteenth-century type long after Western technological improvements made them obsolete. More effective firearms transformed Western European military tactics and organizations. Western armies increasingly were composed of professional soldiers paid and maintained by the monarchs. Infantry became the primary combat force, trained to fight in disciplined unit formations that brought maximum firepower to bear on the enemy. Artillery grew smaller, lighter, and more mobile on the battlefield. Cavalry was reduced to secondary combat roles guarding the infantry's flanks or exploiting holes in the enemies' lines caused by gunfire. Sophisticated army organizations guaranteed effective control and deployment of their constituent units. The Western scientific mentality produced commanders who designed and studied battlefield tactics aimed at combining the use of infantry, artillery, and cavalry to greatest effect, and troops were rigorously trained and disciplined to implement those tactics.

The Ottomans, on the other hand, depended on mounted warriors to disrupt enemies with swift cavalry stabs and clouds of arrows that left them vulnerable to a decisive rush by the Janissaries. Cavalry often was used to draw the enemy into traps or ambushes sprung by Janissaries and the heavy artillery. Although Ottoman forces displayed some unit organization, the structure was designed to implement such traditional tactics. Cavalry received no formal tactical training beyond honing traditional warrior skills, and the Janissaries, although organized into units, generally fought in mass formations that required little specialized training. The large artillery pieces, while manned by skilled professionals, were immobile in battle and remained stationary once placed. Commanders functioned as traditional warrior leaders and gave little thought to scientific tactical study.

A similar disparity between Western European and Ottoman military capabilities evolved in the naval sphere. So long as all Mediterranean fleets were comprised of traditional galleys, the Ottomans enjoyed parity with the Europeans, and until defeated in the Battle of Lepanto (1571), which was fought with traditional galleys on both sides, the Ottoman navy dominated the eastern Mediterranean. Even after Lepanto, the Ottomans continued to hold their own for a time. When by the seventeenth century large, oceangoing ships displaced the smaller, slower, less heavily armed galleys in the West, the military scales tipped against the Ottomans. They never created a Western-style fleet of their own, and the westerners came to dominate both the military and commercial sea routes.

By the end of the seventeenth century the Europeans' battlefield edge over the Ottomans was pronounced. Cavalry armies proved disadvantaged in combat against trained enemies armed with deadly effective firearms. In the wars with Europeans during the second half of the seventeenth century, battlefield defeats grew more frequent than victories. In 1676 the Ottomans gained their last territorial conquest in Europe, winning Western Ukraine at the expense of Poland but losing it soon after (1681) to a new enemy—Russia. The Ottoman military collapse before Vienna in 1683 heralded the beginning of the empire's territorial contraction. During the next two decades, Habsburg forces swept the Ottomans out of Hungary and Transylvania. Venice captured most of Morea, besieged Athens (during which action the Parthenon, used as an Ottoman powder magazine, was blown up by Venetian artillery), and took a large slice of Dalmatia. The 1699 Treaty of Sremski Karlovci

(Karlowitz), which ended the conflict begun at Vienna, largely confined the Ottomans to their Balkan possessions south of the Danube, except for Banat, and turned Morea and Dalmatia over to Venetian control. (See Map 6.)

War with Russia continued north of the Black Sea, ending in 1702 with further Ottoman territorial losses. These were regained in 1711 when Tsar Peter I the Great (1682-1725) unsuccessfully invaded Moldavia, found himself encircled by Ottoman forces, and was forced to return past acquisitions to save his army and reputation. In 1715 most of Morea was recovered from the Venetians. Such Ottoman successes, however, proved transitory. The Habsburgs reopened military operations along the Danube in 1716, and, led by Prince Eugene of Savoy, captured Belgrade (1717). By the terms of the Treaty of Požarevac (Passarowitz) signed in 1718, the Ottomans lost Banat and relinquished areas of northern Serbia and western Wallachia (Oltenia) to Habsburg control. (See Map 6.)

The Ottoman military, however, had not collapsed completely. In a renewed war with both the Habsburgs and Russia begun in 1736, the Ottomans managed successful campaigns against both. By the 1739 Treaty of Belgrade terminating hostilities, the Ottomans regained that city as well as northern Serbia and Oltenia from the Habsburgs.

In 1768 Catherine II the Great (1762-96) sent Russian troops into Moldavia and Wallachia to hunt down defeated Polish rebels who had fled to the Ottoman Empire. Sultan Mustafa III (1757-74) declared war in support of his vassal principalities but was unable to prevent the Russians from overrunning them or from taking the Crimea. Only the need to concentrate military resources to crush Emeliyan Pugachev's great Cossack revolt (1773) diverted the Russian empress from her goal of capturing Istanbul and resurrecting an Orthodox *imperium* in the Balkans.

The Treaty of Kyuchuk Kainardzha ending the conflict in 1774 reflected the Ottomans' diminished status as a European Great Power. Russia gained extensive territories along the Black Sea and free commercial navigation of its waters. A controversial clause also gave Russia representation at the Ottoman court on behalf of the empire's Orthodox subjects. Catherine, however, was not satisfied. She forged an agreement with Habsburg Emperor Joseph II (1780-90) to partition the Ottoman Empire's Balkan provinces between them, with the proposed Russian half becoming a Greek client-state ruled from Istanbul by Russian Grand Prince Constantine. The two rulers then provoked a war with the Ottomans in 1787 in an attempt to put their agreement into practice.

Russian forces occupied the Romanian Principalities and Dobrudzha. While Habsburg forces made inroads into Bosnia and Serbia, capturing Belgrade in 1789, Joseph's death brought Leopold II (1790-92) to the throne. Faced with impending problems stemming from the French Revolution (1789) and possible war with Prussia, Leopold signed a peace with the Ottomans in 1791 at Svishtov recognizing the status quo ante. Catherine, with problems of her own in Poland, did the same early in 1792 at Iaşi, returning the Romanian Principalities and Dobrudzha to the Ottomans.

Only the preoccupation of the European Great Powers with affairs among themselves during the eighteenth century spared the Ottomans more drastic territorial losses. In return for retaining most of its Balkan possessions, the empire relinquished a good deal of its freedom of action. Russia gained a voice in the sultan's decision-making process while Britain and France transformed their old economic capitulations into strangleholds on maritime trade in the eastern Mediterranean. Two centuries of near-constant warfare consumed an enormous amount of money, and, as the empire's frontiers contracted, shortfalls in revenues directly correlated to both lands lost and lack of new lands won.

The Ottomans' disadvantaged military situation wrought profound changes in the empire's crucial military-administrative sector. The westerners' firepower rendered the traditional Ottoman *sipahi* warriors irrelevant as combat troops. Growing numbers of *sipahis* refused active service, preferring to stay safely at home in wartime to concentrate on establishing *çifliks*. The central authorities were forced to rely more on an expanded professional infantry force, which meant increasing the numbers of Janissaries and finding the additional revenues to pay them. The resulting shift from landed to professional forces was disruptive. The *sipahilık* landholding system collapsed, thus undermining the traditional military-administrative sector. By the late seventeenth century the old provincial military-administrative units ceased to function and a new system, based on regionally centered infantry forces under the command of *valis,* was improvised.

The heart of the old standing military forces was the Janissary slave infantry recruited through the *devşirme*. When their numbers were rigidly controlled and draconian discipline maintained, they proved effective elite troops. With inflation making the rural population ever more important as a source of revenues, the *devşirme* no longer was a viable means of Janissary recruitment. The last child levy of any consequence took place in the late seventeenth century.

Sons of Janissaries and native-born Muslims were entered illegally into the ranks of the technically slave force, leading to the breakdown of the central government's iron-fisted control. As the Janissaries' numbers grew through nonslave recruitment, so did their unruliness. Units were stationed in major urban centers throughout the provinces, where they showed more interest in marrying and joining the resident artisan class than in performing their military duties. They did, however, relish their roles as local officials' personal guards, tax collectors, and policemen, all of which offered the prospect for monetary gain. Their expanded numbers required increased salaries, and, when salaries fell into arrears, they rebelled, causing considerable disruption until they were paid. Provincial Janissaries also actively participated in the rampant land speculation in the countryside. The end result was a rapid decline in the Janissaries' military value and dependability. They tended to become a law unto themselves, with their loyalties directed more to the regions in which they lived and owned property and to their regional *valis* than to the sultans.

To counterbalance the questionable reliability of the Janissary forces, Balkan regional *valis* were forced to enlist local *martolos* militia units. That practice was particularly widespread in the empire's Albanian and Serbian regions, which were most exposed to direct Western attack. While *martolos* units often proved loyal, their combat value roughly equaled that of the Janissaries. Neither approached the effectiveness of the professional Western infantry that they faced in battle. In the long run, the *martolos* units served more to spread the possession of weapons among the increasingly disgruntled Balkan *zimmi* populations than to protect the empire from its Western enemies.

The stopgap military-administrative reorganization was partially effective, staving off a total collapse but producing only marginally useful combat troops. Unfortunately, in the context of the empire's economic destabilization, the new system proved administratively disruptive. With the passing of the *sipahılık* system, the central authorities lost whatever mechanism that they possessed for controlling provincial administration. Just as the government's crushing need for revenues resulted in its loss of direct control over leased or sold *sipahılık* lands, the sale of official positions in the *vali*-led provincial military-administrative system ultimately led to a similar loss of governmental control over the Balkan provinces. Provincial offices became concentrated in the hands of wealthy individuals who enjoyed strong regional power bases grounded in landownership and influence among the local *kadıs,* fellow landowners, and Janissaries. Although the *valis* and their subordinates nominally recognized the sultans' authority, they increasingly grew strong enough to exert a large measure of regional independence.

The progressive degeneration of the sultan's office that began in the late sixteenth century may have been the only case in which innate Ottoman institutional conditions played a direct role in destabilizing the empire. The sultan was the linchpin of the traditional imperial system. So long as the office was held by individuals of ability, talent, and skill who were dedicated to conducting their duties and shouldering their responsibilities, the system worked. Beginning with the reign of Süleyman I's son Selim II the Sot (1566-74), however, such rulers grew fewer in number.

The capital's *devşirme* slave administration, often acting in collusion with the women of the sultan's harem, was mostly to blame for weakening the sultan's office. Their monopoly on the most important government posts brought the slave administrators immense wealth and power, checked only by the sultan's mastery over their lives and livelihoods. Selim the Sot's (whose sobriquet aptly described his character) acquisition of the throne provided them with their first real opportunity to loosen the sultan's constraints on their activities. Following his death, their efforts accelerated.

The slave administrators took advantage of a growing moral repugnance for the policy of fratricide that new sultans used to cement their successions. Beginning with Mehmed III (1595-1603), and continuing through the eighteenth century, a *devşirme*-harem alliance induced the sultans to confine their sons to the palace from birth, where they could be watched and prevented from organizing provincial power bases that might prove dangerous for the rulers. The practice of palace confinement became known as the "cage" system. Although it prevented threats to the throne and eliminated the possibilities of civil war on a sultan's death, it also stifled all practical training in governance among the pool of possible successors and reduced them to pawns of the powerful slave officials and harem denizens.

In their palace "cage," the sultans' sons were accessible only to their fathers, their mothers, and other female residents of the harem. They were far closer to their harem mothers and educators, with whom they associated daily, than to their fathers. This situation exerted a negative influence on a new ruler drawn from the "cage." By nature an institution of worldly isolation, the harem was ill fitted to prepare future sultans for their crucial role in Ottoman society. Its inhabitants knew little, if anything, about the realities of practical governance. Once on the throne, the products of the "cage" remained heavily under the influence of their harem mothers and cronies, who often served as mouthpieces for influential parties among the slave administrators. Some "cage" sultans were so crippled by their harem upbringing that they were mentally deficient.

During the seventeenth and eighteenth centuries the palace slave administrators co-opted the sultans' authority as much as possible. Riven by parties based on powerful individual officials and their lackeys, the slave administration passed laws and conducted policies designed to reward or punish those parties that happened to be ascendant or otherwise at any given time. Unjust taxes and unrealistic directives grew common. Bribery and corruption proliferated. Alliances were forged between the administrators and the Janissary units stationed in the capital to prevent the sultans from restraining their self-interested antics. Those who tried, such as Osman II (1618-22) and Murad IV (1623-40), either were deposed by Janissary revolts (Osman) or had their attempted reforms undone by administrators who chose an extremely weak successor (Murad). Through manipulating the women of the harem, the slave administration and its Janissary allies bent their collective efforts to keep the sultans weak and thus consolidate their positions of power.

Old tensions between the *devşirme* and warrior classes reemerged with damaging consequences. With the *devşirme* class in control, most Turkish notables and warriors fled the capital for the provinces, where they settled into the ranks of the regional military-administrative system. Many of them consolidated local power bases, taking advantage of the economic instability and the unraveling of the *sipahilik* system to amass extensive *çiftlik* estates, money, and influence with local officials. Their inveterate animosity toward the slave administration and disgust with the "cage" sultans abetted their moves to throw off direct central control. Although still professing loyalty to the sultan, the provincial leaders increasingly refused to forward collected taxes to the capital, ignored the central government's directives, and imposed their own will on the regional populations.

Over the course of the eighteenth century, autonomous *vali* governors, local warrior notables, and even regional tribal groups (as in Albania) vied with one another for control of what essentially became independent provinces. The resulting anarchy was intensified by depredations perpetrated on local populations by destitute *sipahis* and rapacious Janissaries seeking to augment their devalued fixed incomes. Eventually, strongmen (known as *ayans* ["notables"], although they often were freebooting local officials, mutinous soldiers, or bandits) commanding large contingents of armed followers gained control over various Balkan regions, making official provincial delineations moot and rendering Ottoman central authority over most of the Balkans nominal.

Effects on the Balkans

Oppressive taxation, heavy tithes and labor services, high prices, and indebtedness came to characterize the lot of the Ottomans' Balkan peasant population by the late eighteenth century. Things were worse for peasants in Bosnia and the Romanian Principalities, where they were tied securely to estates and mercilessly exploited. Further economic hardship was imposed on Orthodox believers, who were required to pay ecclesiastical taxes and fees to their religious authorities over and above those paid to the state, the local landholders, and the tax farmers.

The monetary crisis had repercussions within the Orthodox *millet*. It was customary for each newly appointed Greek patriarch to pay a sum of money to the sultan in return for official legitimization. By the end of the seventeenth century that custom became a requirement and the sum involved was exorbitant. A candidate for the patriarchal throne had to be personally wealthy or enjoy a stable source of credit, usually from Ottoman administrators or notables, to pay the investiture fee as well as the "gifts" (*bakşiş*) to high government dignitaries necessary even for consideration.

The patriarchal throne represented a lucrative source of income for the Ottoman treasury. Patriarchs were appointed and removed in rapid succession to collect the fees and bribes as frequently as possible. The expenses incurred in gaining the patriarchal throne were passed along to the church administration with interest. It also became customary for all provincial prelates (metropolitans) to pay fees to the patriarch before being confirmed in their offices by the Ottoman authorities. In addition, every newly installed metropolitan paid an ecclesiastical tax to the patriarchate as well as *bakşiş*. The situation, which mirrored that of the patriarch's vis-à-vis the sultan, resulted in the patriarch changing his provincial prelates to collect the investiture fees and taxes as often as possible. Provincial church seats were thrown open to the highest bidders, and frequently total incompetents were elevated to high church offices. Akin to the situation in Istanbul, acquiring high provincial church offices entailed incurring huge debts, with the hierarchy as a whole usually responsible for their repayment.

In all cases, the ultimate bearers of the monetary burdens involved were local Orthodox parishioners, who were responsible for supplying the money to repay their prelates' loans as well as all extraordinary payments and taxes levied on the church by the state. Fixed ecclesiastical taxes, due both the patriarch and the local prelate, were raised through collections and imposts on the general Orthodox population, for which the lower clergy were held responsible. If the payments were not met, those unfortunate clerics were accountable to the prelate at the price of having their church or monastery valuables pawned. Since a prelate's debts were transferred to his successor if he was replaced or died before satisfying his creditors, the financial plight of the lower clergy, local churches and monasteries, and parishioners often grew heavy.

Provincial prelates enjoyed the right to collect ecclesiastical taxes and fees. Church income was derived from contributions made by monasteries, duties charged by priests for certain rituals (such as baptisms and marriages), special donations on religious holidays, devotional tributes imposed at holy shrines, donations made at pilgrimage sites, taxes levied on certain divine services, and the sale of religious trinkets. On ordination, priests had to make a cash payment to the prelate. Upon elevation, a new prelate was granted a cash gift from all of the parishes and monasteries under his authority.

Normally, the monies owed to the prelate were dispatched to his seat. If the prelate was in desperate need of funds, however, or if a new prelate desired that both his and the patriarch's cash gifts be paid promptly, he or his personal representative toured the districts under his authority. Such tours were apt demonstrations of the Greek Orthodox church's position as a pseudo-official branch of Ottoman state administration. The touring prelate often was accompanied by a detachment of Janissaries who acted as the church's henchmen. Legitimate ecclesiastical taxes frequently were coerced from the faithful by violence. Since church taxes constantly increased, only the limitations on amounts that legally could be demanded in Ottoman investiture warrants prevented totally unbridled extortion on the part of the church authorities.

The vast sums of money involved in maintaining the Orthodox *millet*'s ecclesiastical administration, and the Greek Orthodox Patriarchate's growing need to expand its revenue base, undermined the continued autocephaly of the Ohrid and Peć Slavic-rite patriarchates. The Greek Patriarchate increasingly encroached on their positions by raising its financial demands on payments that they technically owed as part of their official relationship. The Ottoman central authorities, whose interests were bound to the Greek Patriarchate and its *millet* functions, generally supported those efforts. Both Peć and Ohrid resisted paying and persistently complained to the capital, while the Greek Patriarchate ratcheted up pressure on the government to terminate their autocephalous status. Evidence of the Peć Patriarchate's collusion with the Habsburgs and the importance of the Greek Patriarchate's continued cooperation eventually led the government to place all Orthodox *zimmis* under the sole ecclesiastical authority of its *millet* partner. The Peć Patriarchate was abolished in 1766 and direct jurisdiction over its territories was transferred to the Greek Patriarchate. A year later (1767), the Ohrid Patriarchate suffered the same fate.

In addition to crushing state and ecclesiastical financial exploitation, most Balkan peasants suffered personal, property, and crop depredations inflicted on them by both military operations and the endemic provincial anarchy.

As the *sipahılık* system collapsed and territories were lost to European enemies, landless *sipahis* outstripped the land available for distribution. Frustrated in their hopes of gaining lucrative incomes from landholding, growing numbers of destitute *sipahis* turned to extortion or to outright banditry. They frequently were joined by provincial officials and Janissaries in periodically roaming the countryside, extorting cash, crops, and maintenance from the local peasantry. Even regular tax collections became occasions for violence, with peasants beaten mercilessly by the collectors' guards if they could not pay what was demanded. Urban Janissary garrisons were leading exponents of rural terrorism, using their police authority to intimidate and exploit local villagers. Because of the central government's weakness, such actions largely went unchecked.

Summary violence against Christian *zimmi* peasants intensified in times of war. Regions associated with the fighting not only experienced the normal devastation of military operations, but, as victories dried up, Ottoman troops and their commanders frequently vented their frustrations by making local Christian *zimmis* the scapegoats for their military woes. Churches or even entire villages might be looted and burned, priests and village elders tortured or humiliated, crops destroyed or confiscated, village women raped, or villagers' cash extorted. Degenerating rural conditions forced increasing numbers of peasants to flee their villages for urban centers, for other regions within the empire, for havens outside of the empire, or for a life of banditry.

Banditry was endemic in the Balkans. It had been a problem for the Byzantine Empire and for the various pre-Ottoman regional states, and it remained so after the Ottoman conquest. Its impact historically was marginal, constituting more of a nuisance than a serious threat, until the onset of Ottoman destabilization. Generally known as *haiduks* among Slavic speakers and as *klephts* among Greeks, bandits mostly were renegade locals who preyed on villages and highways in their regions. By the late seventeenth century, however, banditry took on graver overtones.

With conditions in the countryside worsening, the bandits' numbers increased and their activities grew more audacious and widespread. Besides raiding local villages, large bandit gangs started attacking marketplaces in small towns and, less frequently, cities. Sometimes bandit leaders were enlisted by Western agents to provide military support during campaigns south of the Danube, enticed with the prospects of substantial loot. The bandits then expanded their operations to prey on the Ottomans' lines of communication and supply depots while the westerners attacked their front. Although such activity earned bandits lasting immortality in regional folk songs and legends (and acclaim as national heroes by later Balkan nationalists), their operations generally were motivated by self-interested greed and the thirst for notoriety or revenge. The military value of their wartime raiding operations was marginal, at best, but they certainly contributed to the suffering of the local populations affected by the campaigns.

During the seventeenth and eighteenth centuries a number of outright uprisings, fueled by economic hardship and persistent anarchy, erupted in various Balkan regions—especially Albania, Bulgaria, Greece, Kosovo, and Serbia. These usually occurred during wars in regions close to the military fronts and sometimes were inspired by enemy agitators attempting to foment fifth column–like activities in the Ottomans' rear. In most cases the Ottoman provincial authorities brutally crushed the rebels and inflicted terrible and indiscriminate reprisals on the populations inhabiting the rebellious regions. Villages and towns were destroyed, thousands were killed or physically abused, and thousands more took flight, some joining *haiduk* bands.

Although armies of the Ottomans' enemies frequently penetrated into the empire's Balkan territories, they rarely remained for long, and uprisings counting on their permanent presence were doomed. In fear of Ottoman retribution, inhabitants of regions that did rise often fled north in significant numbers, attempting to join the retreating European forces for protection. Such was the case with Orthodox Serbs from Serbia and Kosovo who in 1689 and 1690, with the active encouragement of Peć Patriarch Arsenije III Črnojević, staged rebellions and *haiduk* actions in support of a Habsburg drive into their regions. When Ottoman forces expelled the invaders and reestablished their control amid a welter of atrocities, some 40,000 Serbs, Patriarch Arsenije among them, fled across the Danube, ultimately settling in Vojvodina, a newly established Habsburg military border region north of the Sava and Danube rivers. Although later Serb nationalist historians claimed that the number of refugees involved reached as many as 500,000 and that Arsenije heroically led them, recent scholarship discredits those contentions.

Amid the regional anarchy in the Balkan provinces there arose a group of strongmen who succeeded in carving out virtually independent realms for themselves. These *ayans,* usually local landholders, rebellious local officials, or bandit leaders with large armed followings, acted as autonomous regional rulers, jealous of their local independence but too weak to throw off entirely Ottoman suzerainty. By the late eighteenth century ten such lords operated in the Balkans, controlling eastern and western Thrace, all of northern Bulgaria, Dobrudzha, Didymoteichon

(Dimotika), Silistra, northern Albania, and Epiros. (See Map 6.) Two of them proved particularly influential in late eighteenth-century Balkan affairs—Pasvano-ğlu Osman Paşa (1799-1807), who controlled northwestern Bulgaria, and Tepedenli Ali Paşa (1788-1822), who ruled southern Epiros.

Pasvanoğlu, originally a minor landholder from Vidin in northwestern Bulgaria, became a successful bandit leader, taking control of Vidin and amassing an army of brigands and renegade ex-soldiers attracted by the possibilities of rich plunder under his command. Pasvanoğlu openly rebelled against the Ottoman government in 1795, overran much of northwestern Bulgaria, and raided into Serbia, Wallachia, and the rest of Bulgaria. Although Pasvanoğlu was defeated in battle by the Ottomans in 1797 and besieged in Vidin, the need to concentrate his troops against Napoleon's invasion of Ottoman Egypt in 1798 forced Sultan Selim III (1789-1807) to pardon him and name him official governor of Vidin province (1799). The Vidin *ayan* then continued his raiding. In 1800 Pasvanoğlu briefly captured Belgrade, and in the following year his allies seized control of Serbia. The Ottoman forces sent to expel them, many of whom were unpaid or bandit recruits themselves, did more looting than fighting. The misery caused the Serb population by the powerful *ayan,* his allies, and his enemies helped spark the Serbian rebellion of 1804.

Similar to Pasvanoğlu, Tepedenli Ali was a cruel and treacherous bandit leader who took advantage of provincial anarchy to gain control of southern Epiros. Born in Tepelenë in southern Albania, Ali turned to banditry and then to Ottoman service, eventually winning appointment as *paşa* in Ioannina (1788). He used his office's power and the threat of his followers to win the local notables' and financiers' support. His forces raided neighboring regions and extorted cash and "vassalage" agreements from their populations and officials. Ultimately Ali forged his own state-within-a-state, which included most of Macedonia and mainland Greece (except for Attica, Bœtia, and the island of Euboea), all of Morea, the Ionian Islands, and southern Albania—the single largest *ayan* province in the Balkans. So powerful was Ali that, during the Napoleonic Wars, he dealt with the French, British, and Russians directly. He declared his complete independence from Ottoman authority in 1819 and was a factor in igniting the Greek Revolution in 1821. In 1822 Sultan Mahmud II (1808-39) finally crushed Ali and had him decapitated, thus releasing the Ottoman army for concentrated operations against the Greek rebels.

Neither Ali's possessions nor any of the other *ayan* creations rivaled that of Bosnia in longevity and stability. The Bosnian Muslim *beys* were active and enthusiastic contributors to the sultan's imperial administration, but they fiercely remained attached to their local and regional loyalties. When destabilization set in, the Bosnian *beys* banded together to maintain order in their land. The grateful central government officially granted them a monopoly on local regional power, appointing only native Bosnians to posts below that of provincial governor, who thereafter functioned as a figurehead. By the end of the eighteenth century the *beys* ran Bosnia as they pleased—taxes collected were not sent to Istanbul but remained in the *beys'* hands, the disruptive Janissaries were not permitted on Bosnian soil, and Ottoman provincial governors were confined to the small town of Travnik rather than residing in Sarajevo, the provincial capital.

Bosnia did not escape the socioeconomic changes surrounding the breakdown in central authority. The Muslim *beys* wholeheartedly transformed their conditional military fiefs into private *çiftliks* and reduced the Bosnian *zimmi* peasantry to serflike status. Nouveau riche tax farmers and land speculators, adventurers, and *sipahis* expelled from lands lost to the Habsburgs in the late seventeenth century appeared among the ranks of the traditional *beys* and took a leading role in oppressing the non-Muslim peasants. With the expansion of privately owned estates, the peasantry lost its former security and protection, taxes and tithes continuously rose, and confiscations of peasant holdings grew commonplace. No serious challenge to the rule of the *beys* was raised because they enjoyed the support of the Muslim free peasantry, who comprised about a third of Bosnia's peasant population, and *millet* differences between Orthodox and Catholic kept the remaining two-thirds divided.

One segment of the Ottomans' Balkan *zimmi* population actually benefited from the empire's destabilization—the Phanariote Greeks of Istanbul and Thessaloniki. Their hold over Ottoman maritime commercial and military activities brought them immense wealth and influence within the empire. The growing presence of Western Europeans in the eastern Mediterranean and of Russians in the Black Sea during the late seventeenth and eighteenth centuries solidified and expanded their privileged position. Fertilized by a revival of neoclassical interest in the West, which idealized the ancient Greek past and glorified perceived cultural linkages with it, westerners readily adopted Phanariote merchants as their preferred Ottoman trading partners. Likewise, the Phanariotes' Orthodox faith served the same purpose with the Russians in the Black Sea trade. The Phanariotes came to enjoy direct and continuous relations with Western Europe and Russia. They established trading colonies throughout Central-Eastern and Western Europe, and, by the end of the eighteenth century, similar colonies flourished in Russian Black Sea coastal ports, particularly Odessa. Whether dealing directly with their foreign trading partners in the Ottoman markets or in the colonies located on foreign soil, the Phanariotes earned both lucrative profits and skills useful for feathering their position within the Ottoman Empire.

Phanariote wealth and worldly knowledge brought immense influence and power. They came to monopolize most of the high offices within the Greek Patriarchate and thus to dominate the Orthodox *millet,* since they of all the Orthodox *zimmis* alone had the money needed to acquire the patriarchal and regional prelate offices in the church hierarchy. Their wealth made them the empire's premier bankers, the source of loan money for government administrators, church officials, and vassal rulers. Their foreign language skills and familiarity with foreign cultures and customs made them increasingly indispensable to the Ottoman authorities as the empire's continued existence grew tied to the interests of those foreigners. Phanariotes represented an invaluable source of intelligence regarding Western European and Russian developments, and they predominated in the Ottomans' crucial diplomatic relations with those powers as diplomats, advisors, and interpreters.

The apex of Phanariote power and influence came in 1711, when they acquired the princely thrones in the Ottoman vassal principalities of Wallachia and Moldavia. After Peter the Great's unsuccessful invasion of Moldavia in 1711, during which the Moldavian *voievod* defected to the Russians, the Ottomans placed on the throne a reliable Phanariote from the capital, Nicholae Mavrocordat (1711-15). When the Ottomans discovered that Wallachian Voievod Constantine Brancoveanu (1688-1714) was in contact with the Habsburgs, he was arrested and executed. His brief successor was ousted in favor of Nicholae Mavrocordat (1715-16), who desired control of more lucrative Wallachia rather than Moldavia. The vacant Moldavian seat was given to another Phanariote, Mihai Racoviţa (1715-26). Thereafter, until the early decades of the nineteenth century, Phanariotes enjoyed monopoly control of both Romanian thrones.

Phanariote rule in the vassal Romanian Principalities was initiated for two reasons. First, Habsburg control of Transylvania made Wallachia vulnerable to their influence, and Russia had emerged as a new, threatening force on Moldavia's borders. The self-interested native Romanian *boiers* no longer could be depended on to defend the empire's frontier in the northeastern Balkans. The Phanariotes, whose interests mirrored the Ottomans' own, were far more reliable in that role. Second, the central government's perennial need for cash revenues led it to place a high price on the thrones, which guaranteed that only dependable Phanariotes could qualify. Just as was the case in the Greek Orthodox church, the Ottomans replaced the Phanariote Romanian princes (now called *hospodars,* meaning governors rather than rulers) as frequently as possible to maximize profits.

Greeks who bought the Romanian thrones often took up residence in the principalities accompanied by large retinues of fellow Phanariote followers, who were granted *boier* titles and lands. Many of the older Phanariote Greek "export" merchant families in the principalities had become Romanianized prior to 1711, while numerous Romanian *boier* families had been Hellenized. The fate of the *hospodars'* most important dignitaries always remained tied to that of their masters, but the interests of the merchants, old *boiers,* and "new" *boiers* lay in preserving their positions and wealth within the principalities, resulting in the rise of parties that either supported or opposed any particular prince at any given time. They all spoke Greek but their actual ethnic composition grew mixed. The term "Phanariote" took on a new meaning, implying identity with the established regimes and total subservience to the Ottoman authorities rather than a class of ethnic Greeks.

Just as was the case prior to 1711, the principalities' peasant populations played no role whatsoever in the new "Phanariote" system beyond providing the tithes and taxes for its support. Their lot remained as miserable as before, if not more so.

FURTHER READINGS

General

Atiya, Aziz S. *The Crusade of Nicopolis*. London: Methuen, 1934.

Barker, Thomas M. *Double Eagle and Crescent: Vienna's Second Turkish Siege and Its Historical Setting*. Albany: State University of New York Press, 1967.

Halecki, Oskar. *The Crusade of Varna: A Discussion of Controversial Problems*. New York: Polish Institute of Arts and Sciences, 1943.

Petkov, Kiril. *Infidels, Turks, and Women: The South Slavs in the German Mind, ca. 1400-1600*. New York: Peter Lang, 1997.

Roider, Karl A., Jr. *Austria's Eastern Question, 1700-1790*. Princeton, NJ: Princeton University Press, 1982.

Setton, Kenneth M. *Venice, Austria, and the Turks in the Seventeenth Century*. Philadelphia, PA: American Philosophical Society, 1991.

Sugar, Peter F. *Southeastern Europe under Ottoman Rule, 1354-1804*. Seattle: University of Washington Press, 1977.

Albania

Noli, Fan S., [Bishop]. *George Castrioti Scanderbeg (1405-1468)*. New York: International Universities Press, 1947.

Bosnia

Andrić, Ivo. *The Development of Spiritual Life in Bosnia under the Influence of Turkish Rule*. Durham, NC: Duke University Press, 1990.

Hickok, Michael R. *Ottoman Administration of Eighteenth-Century Bosnia*. Leiden: E. J. Brill, 1997.

Bulgaria

Gandev, Hristo. *The Bulgarian People during the 15th Century: A Demographic and Ethnographic Study*. Sofia: Sofia Press, 1987.

Hupchick, Dennis P. *The Bulgarians in the Seventeenth Century: Slavic Orthodox Society and Culture under Ottoman Rule*. Jefferson, NC: McFarland, 1993.

Kiel, Machiel. *Art and Society of Bulgaria in the Turkish Period: A New Interpretation*. Maastricht: Van Gorcum, 1985.

MacDermott, Mercia. *A History of Bulgaria, 1393-1885*. New York: Praeger, 1962.

Todorova, Maria. *Balkan Family Structure and the European Pattern: Demographic Developments in Ottoman Bulgaria*. Washington, DC: American University Press, 1993.

Byzantine Empire

Dereksen, David. *The Crescent and the Cross: The Fall of Byzantium, May, 1453*. New York: Putnam, 1964.

Mijatović, Čedomilj. *Constantine XI, the Last Emperor of the Greeks, or the Conquest of Constantinople by the Turks*. Reprint ed. Chicago, IL: Argonaut, 1968.

Runciman, Steven. *The Fall of Constantinople, 1453*. Cambridge: Cambridge University Press, 1965.

Sphrantzes, George. *The Fall of the Byzantine Empire: A Chronicle*. Amherst: University of Massachusetts Press, 1980.

Croatia

Bracewell, Catherine W. *The Uskoks of Senj: Piracy, Banditry, and the Holy War in the 16th Century Adriatic.* Ithaca, NY: Cornell University Press, 1992.

Guldescu, Stanko. *The Croatian-Slavonian Kingdom, 1526-1792.* The Hague: Mouton, 1970.

Rothenberg, Gunther E. *The Austrian Military Border in Croatia, 1522-1747.* Urbana: University of Illinois Press, 1960.

Zlatar, Zdenko. *Our Kingdom Come: The Counter-Reformation, the Republic of Dubrovnik, and the Liberation of the Balkan Slavs.* Boulder, CO: East European Monographs, 1992.

Greece

Henderson, G. P. *The Revival of Greek Thought, 1620-1830.* Albany: State University of New York Press, 1970.

Papadopoullos, Theodore H. *Studies and Documents Relating to the History of the Greek Church and People under Turkish Domination.* Brussels: Wetteren, 1952.

Runciman, Steven. *The Great Church in Captivity: A Study of the Patriarchate of Constantinople from the Eve of the Turkish Conquest to the Greek War of Independence.* London: Cambridge University Press, 1968.

Spiridonakis, B. G. *Essays on the Historical Geography of the Greek World in the Balkans during the Turkokratia.* Thessaloniki: Institute for Balkan Studies, 1977.

Vakalopoulos, Apostolos E. *The Greek Nation, 1453-1669: The Cultural and Economic Background of Modern Greek Society.* Translated by Ian Moles and Phania Moles. New Brunswick, NJ: Rutgers University Press, 1976.

Zakythinos, Dionysios A. *The Making of Modern Greece: From Byzantium to Independence.* Totowa, NJ: Rowman and Littlefield, 1976.

Macedonia

Vakalopoulos, Apostolos E. *History of Macedonia, 1354-1833.* Translated by Peter Megann. Thessaloniki: Institute for Balkan Studies, 1973.

Ottoman Empire

Babinger, Franz. *Mehmed the Conqueror and His Time.* Translated by Ralph Manheim. Princeton, NJ: Princeton University Press, 1978.

Barkey, Karen. *Bandits and Bureaucrats: The Ottoman Route to State Centralization.* Ithaca, NY: Cornell University Press, 1994.

Bashan, Eliezer. *Economic Life of the Jews in the Balkans and Anatolia, 1453-1600.* Oxford: Oxford University Press, 1989.

Bridge, Anthony. *Suleiman the Magnificent: The Scourge of Heaven.* New York: Dorsey, 1988.

Busbecq, Ogier Ghiselin de. *The Turkish Letters of . . . , Imperial Ambassador at Constantinople, 1554-1562.* Translated by Edward S. Forster. Oxford: Clarendon, 1968.

Cassels, Lavender. *The Struggle for the Ottoman Empire, 1717-1740.* New York: Crowell, 1967.

Clot, André. *Suleiman the Magnificent.* Translated by Matthew J. Reisz. New York: New Amsterdam, 1992.

Darling, Linda T. *Revenue-Raising and Legitimacy: Tax Collection and Finance Administration in the Ottoman Empire, 1560-1660.* Leiden: E. J. Brill, 1996.

Faroqhi, Suraiya. *Making a Living in the Ottoman Lands, 1480 to 1820.* Istanbul: Isis, 1995.

Fisher, Sydney N. *The Foreign Relations of Turkey, 1481-1512.* Urbana: University of Illinois Press, 1948.

Fleet, Kate. *European and Islamic Trade in the Early Ottoman State: The Merchants of Genoa and Turkey.* Cambridge: Cambridge University Press, 1999.

Gibbons, H. A. *The Foundation of the Ottoman Empire: A History of the Osmanlis up to the Death of Bayezid I (1300-1403).* New York: Century, 1916.

Inalcik, Halil. *The Ottoman Empire: The Classical Age, 1300-1600.* London: Weidenfeld and Nicolson, 1973.

Kafadar, Cemal. *Between Two Worlds: The Construction of the Ottoman State.* Berkeley: University of California Press, 1995.

Köprülü, M. Fuad. *The Origins of the Ottoman Empire.* Translated and edited by Gary Leiser. Albany: State University of New York Press, 1992.

Kritovoulos. *History of Mehmed the Conqueror.* Edited and translated by Charles T. Riggs. Reprint ed. Westport, CT: Greenwood, 1970.

Lybyer, Albert H. *The Government of the Ottoman Empire in the Time of Suleiman the Magnificent.* Cambridge, MA: Harvard University Press, 1913.

McGowan, Bruce. *Economic Life in Ottoman Europe: Taxation, Trade, and the Struggle for Land, 1600-1800.* Cambridge: Cambridge University Press, 1981.

Merriman, Roger B. *Suleiman the Magnificent, 1520-1566.* New York: Cooper Square, 1966.

Mihailović, Konstantin. *Memoirs of a Janissary.* Translated by Benjamin Stolz. Ann Arbor: University of Michigan Press, 1975.

Mutafchieva, Vera P. *Agrarian Relations in the Ottoman Empire in the 15th and 16th Centuries.* Boulder, CO: East European Monographs, 1988.

Pantazopoulos, N. J. *Church and Law in the Balkan Peninsula During the Ottoman Rule.* Thessaloniki: Institute for Balkan Studies, 1967.

Parry, V. A., et al. *A History of the Ottoman Empire to 1730: Chapters from the Cambridge History of Islam and the New Cambridge Modern History.* Cambridge: Cambridge University Press, 1976.

Parvev, Ivan. *Habsburgs and Ottomans Between Vienna and Belgrade, 1683-1789.* Boulder, CO: East European Monographs, 1995.

Peirce, Leslie P. *The Imperial Harem: Women and Sovereignty in the Ottoman Empire.* New York: Oxford University Press, 1993.

Pitcher, D. E. *An Historical Geography of the Ottoman Empire from Earliest Times to the End of the Sixteenth Century.* Leiden: E. J. Brill, 1972.

Rycaut, Paul. *The Present State of the Ottoman Empire.* Reprint ed. New York: Arno, 1971.

Vaughan, Dorothy M. *Europe and the Turk: A Pattern of Alliances, 1350-1700.* Reprint ed. New York: AMS, 1976.

Wittek, Paul. *The Rise of the Ottoman Empire.* London: Royal Asiatic Society, 1938.

Romania

Florescu, Radu, and Raymond T. McNally. *Dracula, Prince of Many Faces: His Life and His Times.* Boston, MA: Little, Brown, 1989.

Treptow, Kurt W. *Vlad III Dracula: The Life and Times of the Historical Dracula.* Iaşi: Center for Romanian Studies, 2000.

Serbia

Emmert, Thomas A. *Serbian Golgotha: Kosovo, 1389.* Boulder, CO: East European Monographs, 1990.

Popović, Tatjana. *Prince Marko: The Hero of South Slavic Epics.* Syracuse, NY: Syracuse University Press, 1988.

PART THREE

Era of Romantic Nationalism

1804–1878

By the first half of the nineteenth century the Western European concept of Romantic nationalism appeared among the non-Muslim Balkan peoples. As a sense of ethnic group awareness, based on recognition of a common language and shared history, grew and spread among the various Balkan populations (a process termed "national revival" or "renascence"), so too did the idea of group self-governance. Rebellions by Serbs and Greeks during the early decades of the century resulted in the establishment of autonomous, ethnic-based states that set the example for others. The Revolutions of 1848-49 intensified Croat and Romanian national efforts. The Ottomans, realizing that the spread of nationalism among their non-Muslim subjects spelled doom for the empire, made efforts by midcentury to stabilize their situation and adapt to Western pressures. Both the nationalist movements and Ottoman reforms, however, became pawns in the imperialist policies of the Western European Great Powers and Russia, in which control of the Balkan Peninsula played a strategically important role. The Congress of Berlin (1878) imposed the Western European concept of the nation-state on the small states of Serbia, Greece, Romania, Montenegro, and

Bulgaria carved from a reduced Ottoman Empire; brought Habsburg Austria-Hungary deeper into the Balkans; and sowed the seeds of future nationalist conflicts among them all.

CHAPTER NINE

The Rise of Romantic Nationalism

The Western European concept of nationalism—the supposition that a unique group of people (a self-identified "nation") possesses the right to sovereign, independent political existence (a state and government of its own)—was rooted in two forms of group consciousness. One constituted identities originating in the traditional, increasingly secularized monarchical states that were modified by the rationalistic principles of science, the Enlightenment, and liberalism. It was state and civic oriented and emphasized the militant support of the state's collective citizenry and the sanctity of the state's territorial sovereignty. The other form sprang from the late eighteenth- and nineteenth-century Romantic Movement, which rejected the predominance in Western European realities of rationalism rooted in Renaissance, scientific, and Enlightenment traditions. Instead, it emphasized identities based on irrational and emotional ethnic and religious factors. For the Romantics, human group identity fundamentally was a function of the group's unique culture and history within a specific territory rather than of generic scientific, political, social, or economic development. The Western form of national group identity that found initial acceptance among the Balkan populations was the Romantic.

Development and Forms of National Identity

To comprehend fully Balkan history during the nineteenth and twentieth centuries, an understanding of nationalism is needed, since national issues dominated the region's developments throughout most of that period. Nationalism is complex. Although a number of varying definitions enjoy current usage among the assorted social sciences, one singular fact is certain: Use of the suffix "-ism" in any instance denotes a faith (or belief) in the validity of the term to which it is attached. In this case, it expresses conviction in the notion of "nation" as defining a unique group of people. Determining what group constitutes a "nation" leads to nationalism's complexity.

Human group identities existed long before the rise of nationalism in Western Europe. Families, clans, tribes, settlements, regions, social standings, professions, languages, and religions served as bases for collective identities since earliest times. Group identities always have been created to satisfy human social drives. They are manufactured and exist in the minds and emotions of their members, anchored in perceptions of selective shared traits and usually reinforced by myth and invention— in essence, abstractions "believed" to be concrete realities and acted on as such. Group identity, therefore, is always a function of the culture in which it operates. The emergence of the "nation" as a unique group, and its sanctification in nationalism, was a singularly Western European cultural phenomenon.

In Western Europe the term "nation" first appeared in the thirteenth century as a collective label for the numerically small privileged elite in feudal society—the nobility. It originally did not denote the state or its general population. A state at that time represented the lands technically held by a particular monarch, who governed through the privileged military and landholding feudal nobles. Only the rulers and their nobilities had any real concept of, or attachment to, their states. The majority of the populations counted for little beyond serving as the primary source of royal and aristocratic revenues.

The Western European concept of nationalism germinated in the successes of the regional monarchs in throwing off papal restrictions on their temporal power and gradually consolidating their central authority over all of their subjects. The threat to the nobility's privileged position inherent in monarchical centralization further cemented that class's self-image as a "nation"—an exclusive group possessing the right to determine how it was governed to protect and further its members' collective interests. In most thirteenth-century Western European states, the aristocratic "nations" succeeded in wringing from their monarchs royal decrees guaranteeing their privileged positions. Until the late eighteenth century the word "nation" denoted a state's nobility and not its general population.

Centralized secular authority was abetted by the sixteenth-century Protestant Reformation, which entrenched temporal monarchical authority against the claims of the weakened papacy and its champion, the Holy Roman emperor, and by the close political alliances that most Western European monarchs forged with their urban subjects.

In return for granting urban dwellers local self-government, freedom from feudal entanglements, and protection from rapacious feudal nobles, the monarchs received cash tax revenues that they used to hire, equip, and maintain professional military forces to counterbalance, and ultimately replace, the feudal levies of their independent-minded nobles. Urban revenues also permitted the monarchs to throw off dependency on church clerics in government administration and to create professional bureaucracies staffed by salaried literate laymen. Recruitment for both the military and the bureaucracy drew heavily on urban populations, since, in otherwise rural feudal societies, they alone fundamentally valued money and education. As Western European monarchical states expanded in size, so too did the role of the urban middle class. Its commercial economy generated the taxes needed to pay the salaries of the increasingly numerous soldiers and functionaries, and its membership supplied the manpower, skills, and materials for both professions. By the seventeenth century urban participation in the military and government of Western European states largely made possible the emergence of absolutist, divine-right monarchies.

The leading role assumed by the urban sector embedded secular middle-class values in monarchical state government. State interests were tied to the monetary economy, which led first to state-sponsored mercantilism in the seventeenth century and then to state-encouraged industrialization by the late eighteenth. The secular, humanistic outlook of urban-centered universities, grounded in Renaissance mentality, permeated the middle classes and, through them, state institutions. Educated urbanites brought to state service crucial middle-class attributes—rational organization, hard work, efficiency, enterprise, and loyalty to the employer—and they embraced new ideas considered useful in furthering those qualities, such as the late seventeenth-century precepts of the Scientific Revolution.

In similar fashion, the concepts of the Enlightenment gradually infiltrated Western European political culture during the eighteenth century. Essentially a middle-class intellectual movement inspired by the scientific precepts of rationally discoverable and definable universal laws governing the physical universe, the Enlightenment sought to popularize scientific laws, to apply them in everyday life, and to use them as models for uncovering hitherto unknown universal "natural" laws controlling all aspects of human social existence in the belief that the results would bring human "progress" toward the "natural rights" of human "happiness" and "freedom."

Because the monarchs were well educated, middle-class workers predominated in state bureaucracies, and the leading exponents of the movement proved talented and erudite in advancing their arguments, Enlightenment ideas found their way into official government circles in many Western European states. Those monarchs who in some measure embraced them were labeled "enlightened despots," who often undertook such practical initiatives as administrative reorganization, educational expansion, agrarian reform, serf emancipation, legal reform, technological development, and infrastructural improvement.

The aristocratic "nation" stood as an obstacle to the full implementation of Enlightenment principles. Despite their general success in forging centralized state organizations, the Western European monarchs, scions of the aristocracies, did not disenfranchise their nobles, who constituted the dominant landowning class and thus were important in the states' crucial agricultural sectors. The nobles' militant self-image and willingness to fight for their legal privileges constrained monarchs to purchase their support by guaranteeing them a monopoly on the highest military, government, and religious offices. Thus the aristocratic "nations" maintained their privileged positions in the centralized monarchical states.

In Enlightenment terms, a state structured and governed in the interests of a numerically small, privileged, and mostly unproductive elite was "unnatural." There emerged in Western Europe two new political philosophies addressing that issue. Although neither was a direct product of the Enlightenment per se, both won support among its middle-class adherents because they made practical political sense.

Liberalism, formulated in the late seventeenth century by the Scotsman John Locke, advanced such concepts as government by the consent of the governed, the separation of governmental powers to ensure against despotic rule, and the right of the governed to revolt against a despotic government, all of which were defined in a legal political instrument called a constitution. In the liberal scheme, all individuals were considered born with certain "inalienable ('natural')" rights: Life, liberty, and property ownership. Liberalism defined happiness as a function of owning property and liberty as its unfettered acquisition and defense. It assumed that all individuals acted out of self-interest, expressed through owning property (or acquiring money), and that protecting property was a primary political obligation. It followed that the liberal precept of government by the consent of the governed actually meant by the consent of the property owners.

Democracy followed liberalism's lead in espousing a constitutional basis for government. Grounded in the political thought of the mid-eighteenth-century French intellectual Jean-Jacques Rousseau, it envisioned a state structure in which all persons were active "citizens" obligated to participate in shaping the laws that governed their society. All citizens helped make the laws, and all agreed to obey them once they were formulated through majority consensus (majority rule). This active agreement constituted human liberty. To be workable, there could be no autocratic monarchs or privileged nobility, but only a society of loyal and active political equals who willingly suppressed many of their personal self-interests for the collective good. A constitution guaranteed the citizens' individual freedoms and delineated their collective responsibilities to the state.

Both liberalism and democracy required expanding the "nation" beyond membership in the aristocratic elite. While liberalism consciously included the landowning nobility, its emphasis on property and money encompassed the middle class as well. Democracy rejected the idea of privilege derived from birth and extended political rights and obligations to all in society on the basis of equality, including the lower (peasant and laboring) classes, whom neither the nobility nor the middle class traditionally held in esteem.

Of the two political models, liberalism appealed to the Western European middle class, who over time grew more aware of their crucial role in upholding their states. Although opposite in their fundamental political emphases—liberalism stressed individual rights while democracy asserted the ultimate precedence of society as a whole—the two were wedded together and put into practice by the American Revolution (1775-83) (with its Declaration of Independence [1776], Constitution [1787], and Bill of Rights [1789]), and the more decisive political upheavals of the French Revolution (1789-99) (with its Declaration of the Rights of Man and the Citizen [1789]) and the Napoleonic Wars (1799-1815) (which spread French revolutionary concepts throughout Europe).

The French revolutionary creed expressed a mixture of liberal and democratic ideals in a tone more universal and radical than the American example. Beyond embracing constitutional government, abolishing hereditary privileges, protecting "inalienable rights," and asserting the citizens' sovereignty, "patriotic" obligations to the state were demanded, state borders were declared inviolate, and all citizens within those borders were proclaimed members of the "nation." The state was transformed from a political structure serving a restricted elite's interests into the "father-/motherland" of all of its citizens; thus the identities and interests of the state and its citizens became synonymous.

The Revolutionary and Napoleonic wars spread French political ideals and militant nationalism over the length and breadth of Western Europe. By declaring the "fatherland in danger," the revolutionary French government tapped its new nation-alist ideology to mobilize all of the state's human and material forces and create the first "nation in arms"—mass armies steeped in patriotism and political commitment. During two decades of war, French armies successfully carried their nationalist and political convictions to their enemies' populations throughout Europe.

In the process of disseminating their revolutionary ideologies, the success of the French ultimately led to military and political defeat. Non-French populations introduced to national ideals by lengthy French occupations eventually acquired anti-French sentiments as their own national identities developed. In addition, France's enemies—primarily England, Russia, Prussia, and the Habsburg Empire—eventually were forced to make expedient official adaptations of French ideals. To mobilize their own mass armies to vanquish those of France, the monarchies resorted to tapping the budding sense of patriotism among their general populations, encouraging them with promises of political reforms and expanded political participation following the successful close of the fighting.

Immediately following France's decisive defeat at Waterloo (1815), the victorious monarchies bent all of their efforts to suppress the nationalist and liberal-democratic genies that had been unbottled. Led by Habsburg Chancellor Prince Klemens von Metternich at the Congress of Vienna (1814-15), they made their last attempts to retain the traditional elite-dominated political order. They tried to turn back the political clock by autocratic force, aiming to stamp out all vestiges of liberal-democratic and nationalist thought (including those they themselves had fostered during the wars) and to prevent their future recurrence. Although England generally opted out, the Habsburg Empire, Russia, Prussia, and defeated France (once again a monarchy) instituted systems of legislative and judicial repression, increased police enforcement and surveillance, and applied strict media and educational censorship. Such measures were of scant use. In post-Vienna reactionary Western Europe, liberal, democratic, and nationalist concepts continued to spread among the populations despite the repressive efforts of the monarchical governments. That phenomenon was abetted greatly by the rise of the generally popular Romantic Movement.

Romanticism was a reaction against the French wars' devastation and post-Vienna repression. Among its consequences was the creation of a new sense of group awareness that eventually became integrated with the concept of "nation." Participants in the Romantic Movement blamed the Enlightenment's rationalism and the Industrial Revolution's rampant materialism for the repressive postwar atmosphere. They rejected them in favor of emotionalism and escapism—primarily into a fictionalized medieval past dominated by human emotion (mythology and religion)—which they believed permitted various groups of people to express their "native" cultural realities without corruption by "foreign" (classical Greco-Roman) elements "artificially" imposed by the Renaissance.

The Romantics demanded that idealized "native" cultures be known, understood, and nurtured, spawning the concept of "ethnicity" and its corollary, ethnic group awareness. In Romantic human reality, every ethnic group carried within itself a collective consciousness of its cultural uniqueness that lent intrinsic meaning and value to the group as a whole. Ethnic uniqueness fundamentally was expressed through common religious belief and, most important, common language. For the Romantics, religion was the emotional expression of civilization, but language was the key to human group identity. The "true" nature of any ethnic group lay in its language and its historical (and mythical) past.

In their quest to validate the unique worth of various Western European ethnic groups by tracing and documenting their pasts, the Romantics gave birth to modern historical study. History became focused on "peoples" as specific language groups developing over time rather than on states and their leaders alone. In their emphasis on peasant folk songs, tales, legends, customs, and mores as the "purest" forms of ethnic cultural expression, the Romantics also created a new field of intellectual inquiry—ethnography. The tales collected and published by the Grimm brothers, Hans Christian Andersen, and others were more than mere children's stories, they were intended to convey the very soul of ethnic identity.

Because the Romantics routinely couched their ideas in broadly popular, readily accessible works innocuous enough to pass the usually obtuse official censors, it did not take long for the Romantic sense of ethnic group consciousness to find a large audience and to be integrated with the civic-based sense of nationalism created by the French Revolution. In Romantic terms, each ethnic group possessed a history and culture that bestowed on it a character, aspirations, interests, and homeland uniquely its own. Each possessed collective "inalienable rights" and deserved the opportunity to determine its own fate. By logical extension, each constituted an ethnic "nation" rightfully entitled to its own state to represent and defend its cultural uniqueness politically, socially, economically, and territorially.

Romantic ethnic awareness added a powerful new ingredient to Western Europe's already revolutionary nationalist mix. It provided an emotional dimension to the concept of "nation" transcending purely political, social, and economic parameters, and it forcefully validated such liberal-democratic national tenets as inalienable rights, popular sovereignty, consensual government, and territorial inviolability. Bolstered by the new sense of ethnicity, liberal-democratic and nationalist ideas not only weathered post-Vienna monarchical repression but expanded their social appeal.

For those inhabiting existing large regional states encompassing relatively homogeneous ethnic "homelands" (such as France and Spain), national aspirations tended to stress political ideals. In large multiregional and multiethnic states (such as the Habsburg Empire and Russia), or in small, territorially contiguous subregional states sharing common ethnic populations (such as the German Confederation and the Italian states), ethnicity tended to predominate in national priorities. While in the former case an existing state could be politically transformed to satisfy an assumed ethnic reality, in the latter ethnic realities first had to be established before completely new states were created.

Mounting national and political pressures within post-Vienna society exploded in the revolutions of 1830 and, most important, 1848, which assured the ultimate victory in Western Europe's political culture of nationalism and its fundamental expression through liberal-democratic and ethnic forms. Monarchism was swept away in France by the upheavals of 1848 (the brief later imperial interlude of Louis Napoleon [1852-70] was a hollow exception), and in most other states the monarchs subsequently found it expedient to compromise with the new political forces by accepting liberal constitutional forms along English lines to preserve their thrones. Some monarchies, such as the multiethnic Habsburg Empire, could not do so because the attempt would have entailed their utter demise. In the end, those that resisted survived the revolutions' initial threats but were doomed to protracted internal national disorders and eventual dissolution.

In the new national-based Western Europe of the mid-nineteenth century, the ethnic and political concepts of "nation" appeared harmoniously compatible. That perception, although ubiquitous, proved mistaken. The Revolution of 1848-49 in the Habsburg Empire provided a grim glimpse of that ill-conceived notion. During that upheaval two negative aspects of ethnic-based nationalism were revealed. One was its inherent divisiveness. The diverse ethnonational makeup of the empire's population permitted the Habsburgs to defeat the revolution in detail by playing off one national group against another. The second negative manifestation involved the ephemeral Hungarian Republic (1848-49) proclaimed by liberal-minded, ethnically Hungarian noble and middle-class revolutionaries. Although the state was grounded in liberal-democratic principles, these were valid only for ethnic Hungarians, who constituted a minority in the total population. The non-Hungarian ethnic groups comprising the majority essentially were disenfranchised and subjected to cultural discrimination as nonmembers of the Hungarian ethnic "nation." The Hungarian episode demonstrated that ethnic-based nationalism was not liberal-democratic. Ethnic nationalists had little inclination to guarantee the "inalienable rights" of others not part of their "nation." In a truly ethnonational world, those not belonging to ruling "nations" could expect oppression, persecution, and even aggression.

In the final analysis, an individual's awareness of group "belonging" was key to national and ethnic identity. Both civic and Romantic patriots generally assumed that nationality and ethnicity were inalienable human traits and frequently considered the two synonymous. Often overlooked, however, was the fact that both were emotional and mental constructs shaped by a process of socialization. An individual identified with a particular national or ethnic group for emotional and rational reasons. Should those attachments be questioned or severed, an individual could transfer membership (either voluntarily or involuntarily) to a new group. Likewise, members of a national or ethnic group could chose to accept into their ranks a person who originally "belonged" to a different group.

Thus individuals could change their nationality or ethnicity. Both civic and ethnic national programs implicitly recognized that reality in their efforts to cement group consciousness by means of sacrosanct rituals, symbols, and myths. To instill patriotism, civic nationalism wrapped itself in elaborate state ceremonies, secular icons (flags and official emblems), and neoclassical allusions (official architecture, art, and institutional rhetoric). To uphold ethnic pride, Romantic nationalists glorified culture (primarily language and religion) and history (either verifiable or fictionalized), sanctified ethnography, and stressed intrinsic ethnic uniqueness (often to the point of chauvinism).

Early National Awareness on the Northern Balkan Periphery

Among the earliest Balkan populations to develop a sense of ethnic national consciousness were those inhabiting the Habsburg Empire's lengthy border with the

Ottoman Empire on the peninsula's northern periphery. Living within a Western European state, they were directly exposed to the West's process of ethnonational development, and they all maintained contacts with Ottoman Balkan populations across the border.

Since accepting union with Hungary in 1102, the Croats were immersed in Western Europe. The Croat nobility enjoyed "nation" status within the Hungarian Kingdom. The partnership with Hungary was not always harmonious, but, until the early nineteenth century, neither was it especially antagonistic. Croat nobles enjoyed regional autonomy and many played roles of importance within Hungary itself.

In a disputed royal election after Hungary's defeat by the Ottomans in the Battle of Mohács (1526), the Croat nobles supported the Habsburg candidate Ferdinand I (1526-64) on condition that he protect Croatia against the Ottomans and recognize the Croat nobility's continued rights and privileges. Thereafter, they ranked among the Habsburgs' most loyal supporters in rump Royal Hungary, which primarily consisted of Croatia, a strip of northern Hungary, and Slovakia— all that remained of the former Hungarian Kingdom following Süleyman I's conquests in the 1540s.

Repeated Ottoman incursions into Royal Hungary from Bosnia resulted in the Habsburgs' establishing the Croatian Military Border in 1538. Manned by settled military colonists commanded by the local Croat aristocracy, the border zone (*Krajina*) was placed directly under the authority of Habsburg military headquarters in Vienna. Only the northern Croatian region of Zagreb officially remained bound to Hungary. The military border freed the Croat nobility from direct Hungarian control through the seventeenth century. There followed, however, a period of disappointment and growing discontent in the eighteenth, during which time the Habsburgs courted the Hungarians' support against threats from Prussia and other European rivals by gradually permitting them to reassert some authority in the Croatian Military Border.

The Napoleonic wars fanned Croat discontent into a nascent national movement. France won possession of Dalmatia, Istria, much of the Croatian Military Border, and most of Slovenia from the Habsburgs in 1809, organized them into the Illyrian Provinces, and then annexed them (1809-13). French administration, law, and language were imposed, public works projects (road and bridge building, reforestation, land reclamation) and social reforms (serf emancipation, land redistribution) were initiated, and, most important, the tenets of liberal democracy and nationalism were put into actual practice. Although the French interlude lasted only a few years and its thrust essentially was imperialist (Napoleon wanted the military skills of the border troops [*grenzers*] and material resources for his forces), the Croats and Slovenes gained an awareness of their own ethnonational identities and briefly experienced firsthand the benefits of liberal, nationalist political culture.

While the Croats did not regret the end of France's direct rule in 1813—taxes had been heavy and conscription into the French army odious—the national self-identity that they developed as a result of the French interlude left them unhappy over Croatia being reincorporated into the Habsburg Empire as an appendage of Hungary, where Hungarian ethnonationalism was rearing its head.

The Croats enjoyed a strong position regarding newly emerging Romantic nationalism. They possessed both a recognized history grounded in a medieval state and a literary language traceable to the thirteenth century and the Slavic literary traditions of Dubrovnik. Yet in the early nineteenth century, just as in Hungary, Latin was Croatia's official administrative language. Although Latin usage helped emphasize the Croats' and Hungarians' Western European cultural affinities, it was growing anachronistic in a world rapidly being permeated by ethnonational consciousness. The Croats realized that they must modernize their native literary language and abandon the administrative use of Latin. Their opportunity to do so came in the 1820s when, in reaction to the Hungarians' use of their vernacular in the Hungarian Diet, the Croats did the same in theirs.

The "Illyrian Movement," as the Croats' national program was called, was fomented by the Croat nobility, who sought to create and lead a great South Slav ("Yugoslav") state in the Balkans. It arose soon after 1815 and reached full maturity in the 1830s and 1840s. Despairing of renewed Hungarian control, the early Croat nationalists idealized the Illyrian Provinces experience. Instead of crediting the freedom, prosperity, and creativity that had characterized that episode to enlightened, liberal French rule, however, the Croat nationalists claimed that the unification of Slavs from Croatia Proper, Dalmatia, and Slovenia was primarily responsible for those achievements. Their perspective spawned the belief that the Balkan Slavs' future depended on their unification within a greater Balkan South Slavic state (an idea first broached two hundred years earlier by the Dubrovnik monk Juraj Križanić), which the movement's members Romantically labeled Illyria.

Count Janko Drašković provided the movement with its initial national program: The creation of a greater Illyria (comprised of Croatia Proper, Dalmatia, Slavonia, Bosnia, and Slovenia) under Croat leadership; its political autonomy within the Habsburg Empire; use of Croatian as the administrative language; and economic and educational modernization. The movement's definitive philosophical framework was expressed in the publications of Ljudevit Gaj, a prolific Zagreb journalist and publisher who was influenced by Czech Panslav ideas proclaiming the brotherhood of all Slavs and calling for the creation of a single Great Slavic state. From the 1830s through the 1850s Gaj agitated for South Slav unity, proposed the reform of Croatian orthography along lines closer to Serbian to serve as the basis for a common "South Slav" literary language, and expanded Drašković's "Illyrian" program into one envisioning the political unification of all South Slavs.

The Croatian nationalists bolstered their program by creating a specious historical foundation for proposed Illyria, which maintained that the ancient Illyrians who inhabited the Balkans' Adriatic coastline and its hinterlands actually were Slavs. Furthermore, since the Croats culturally were Western European and possessed unbroken medieval political and literary traditions, they claimed superiority over all other Balkan Slavic peoples and the right to lead the future greater South Slavic state.

When the Hungarians precipitated the Revolution of 1848-49 in the Habsburg Empire, the Croat nationalists in the Zagreb Diet declared independence from Hungary but continued loyalty to the Habsburgs. Croatian troops under the command of Habsburg-appointed Croat Ban Josip Jelačić (1848-59) actively helped defeat Austrian German liberal revolutionaries in Vienna and, especially, the radical Hungarian nationalists. Instead of being rewarded for their loyal efforts in the Habsburgs' cause by receiving expected national independence once the revolution was crushed, the Croats found themselves still tied to Hungary and burdened with the official postrevolution system of repression that the Habsburgs imposed throughout the empire. In the revolution's aftermath, "Illyrian" ideas fell out of favor in Croatia and the Croatian national movement fragmented.

In 1867 the Habsburgs' power-sharing Compromise (*Ausgleich*) with the Hungarians, which handed over to them direct control of more than half of the empire's territories, including Croatia, weakened Croat faith in the Habsburg monarchy. Even after the compromise, however, many Croat nationalists continued to envision a Croat-led greater South Slav state under some sort of Habsburg aegis. Among the most influential of these nationalists was Catholic Bishop Josip Strossmayer. He strove to create an autonomous Croatia within post-Compromise Austria-Hungary that would serve as the core for a future "Yugoslav" (Strossmayer popularized the term) state encompassing all South Slavs, no matter their religious cultures. (He believed that an Orthodox-Roman Catholic Slav religious union would eliminate any differences.) Beginning in the 1860s and continuing until his death in 1896, Strossmayer patronized South Slavic intellectual and cultural efforts by building schools, subsidizing scholars, and founding important institutions, including a national university, in Zagreb. Through his efforts, Zagreb became a leading Balkan Slavic cultural center.

A side effect of the Croatian national movement was the faint spark given to Slovene national consciousness. Ruled by Germans since the ninth century, divided among numerous small Austrian provinces, and long submerged under German and Italian cultural influences, the Slovenes were the least ethnically visible Balkan Slav population. Some Slovene intellectuals and Catholic clergymen, however, sympathized with the "Illyrian" national program, and during the Revolution of 1848-49 they first made public their own modest national aspirations: The creation of a unified, autonomous Slovene province within the

Habsburg Empire that used Slovene as its official administrative and educational language. A few more radical nationalists sought the political unification of Slovenia and Croatia into a Habsburg-ruled "South Slav" political entity, and fewer still wished to include Vojvodina as well. The Slovene national program enjoyed little popular support among the general population, and, following the collapse of the revolution, the Slovenes remained relatively quiet regarding national issues until the early twentieth century.

While the Habsburg military border system played an indirect role in shaping Croatian national awareness, it was more important in the rise of Serbian Romantic nationalism. When the Habsburgs acquired Slavonia from the Ottomans in the late seventeenth century, like Croatia, it was designated a military border region. The border system was extended into Vojvodina by Emperor Leopold I following the Treaty of Sremski Karlovci (1699). To maintain the numerical strength of the frontier troops, the Habsburgs settled any available and willing peoples as military colonists, who came to represent a hodgepodge of ethnicity—Croats, Germans, Serbs, Hungarians, Czechs, Slovaks, Italians, and others. Among the most numerous were Orthodox Serb refugees who fled the Ottoman Empire in the late seventeenth century. Large enclaves of Serb émigrés were settled in the newly designated Slavonian and Vojvodinan military border zones.

The border Serbs of Vojvodina and Slavonia were able to pursue their native Orthodox culture within the Habsburg Western European state while they also enjoyed exposure to the intellectual movements current in the West and, through their Orthodox church connections, Russia. Despite periodic frictions with their Austrian German and Hungarian hosts, the border Serbs developed an East-West European intellectual alloy that eventually spawned modern Serbian nationalism. The two cultural streams merged primarily within the ranks of the Serbian Orthodox church and spread to the lay believers, first in the border zones and then southward across the Danube among Serbs in the Ottoman Empire.

To ensure the numerous border Serbs' faithful service, Leopold granted them a variety of privileges, including landowning rights and assorted economic incentives. The most significant was autonomy for the Serbs' Orthodox church within the Habsburg Empire. In 1713 an independent Serbian archbishopric was established in Sremski Karlovci with jurisdiction over all Slavic-rite Orthodox believers in Vojvodina, Slavonia, and Pannonian Hungary. Its first primate was the refugee Peć Patriarch Arsenije Črnojević.

The border Serbs' religious autonomy harmonized well with their former Ottoman *millet* traditions and reinforced their old *millet* sense of group identity. Direct exposure to emerging Western European national and ethnic concepts linked their autonomous Orthodox church organization to a growing sense of ethnic awareness. By the opening of the nineteenth century the Orthodox border Serbs viewed the Sremski Karlovci church as their quasipolitical collective voice.

In the Orthodox world the church traditionally played a leading role in its followers' cultural, intellectual, and educational lives. Under the patronage of the Sremski Karlovci archbishopric, schools, printing presses, and reading rooms were established in the local parishes and monasteries under its jurisdiction. Close cultural ties were forged with the Russian Orthodox church and, through it, the Russian government, whose growing imperialist interests in the Balkans made patronage of the Serbs potentially valuable. Throughout the eighteenth century the border Serb communities were inundated with Russian funds, books, and schoolteachers, and many Serb youths were granted scholarships for study in Russia. A lasting consequence of the Serbs' Russian connections during this period was their staunchly ingrained Russophilism.

In Serbian monasteries founded in eastern Slavonia's Fruška Gora hills, monks discovered the Serbs' pre-Ottoman history in Russian and Western European books. They passed their awakened sense of the Serbian past to the Serb border community through their own writings and teachings and subsequently disseminated it to the Ottoman Serbs, either directly across the Danube or through the renowned, multiethnic monastic communities of Mount Athos in the southern Balkans, with which all Orthodox churches maintained close and continuous contact. The pioneer in such activity was the monk Jovan Rajić. In 1794 he produced the first modern history written in Serbian Church Slavic, based on his research in monastic libraries and extensive travels, particularly in Russia. Although his work purported to cover the various European Slav groups, it concentrated on the South Slavs, especially the Serbs. Hints of Croat influence were found in Rajić's acceptance of South Slav kinship, even between Orthodox and Catholic communities.

Following in Rajić's footsteps came another Serb Fruška Gora monk, Dositej (Dimitrije) Obradović, who grew discontented with the Serbs' artificial Church Slavic literary language and the limited intellectual scope of the few available Church Slavic books. Obradović's outspoken dismay over the Serbs' church-led cultural position resulted in heated disputes with church authorities and in his voluntary defrocking (1760). During the 1760s and 1770s he traveled extensively throughout Western Europe, where he imbibed Enlightenment and rationalist ideas. Obradović created an exclusively Serbian (but artificial) literary language, in which he produced works expounding anticlerical, rational, and Enlightened concepts for the elucidation of the few Serbs who could read them.

At the turn of the eighteenth century, Obradović's efforts to propagate a Serbian ethnonational awareness were taken up inside the Ottoman Empire by Vuk Karadžić, a Hercegovinian Serb goatherd who received a monastic education. The Habsburg border Serbs' century of exposure to Western and Russian ideas, culminating in Obradović's Westernizing efforts, had sparked in them a growing sense of ethnonational self-identity. In 1804 an uprising of Ottoman Serbs, swiftly supported by the border Serbs, erupted in reaction to the arbitrary and anarchistic rule of the local Ottoman governor of Belgrade and his Janissary garrison. Karadžić joined one of the rebel bands as a secretary to its commander, but, when in 1813 the uprising was stifled temporarily by the Ottomans, he fled the empire for safety among the Habsburg border Serb community.

Karadžić eventually made his way to Vienna, where he fell in with Jernej Kopitar, a young Slovene scholar working to awaken ethnonational sentiments among his fellow Slovenes. Both men became heavily influenced by early Romantic ideas, especially by the work of the German Johann von Herder, who predicted that ethnic Slavs would enjoy a leading role in future European affairs. Embracing Romantic ethnographic tenets, Karadžić collected and published (1814) an immediately popular and successful collection of Serbian folk songs and tales. He was so impressed by the simplicity and directness of the Serb peasant vernacular that he turned his full attention to philology. By the time he produced an expanded, four-volume edition of his original collection in 1824, Karadžić had devised a refined and accurate Serbian Cyrillic literary language reflecting vernacular realities. Because he used as linguistic foundation his native Hercegovinian dialect, which represented a transitional bridge between spoken Serb and Croat, Karadžić's reforms ultimately became the basis for the modern conception that there existed a common "Serbo-Croatian" language, with all of the nationalist connotations that this later entailed. Despite violent opposition from the Serbian Orthodox church, which defended the linguistic priority of traditional Church Slavic, Karadžić's language reform had won acceptance among all Serb literati by the time of his death in 1864.

Unlike the Croats and border Serbs, the Transylvanian Romanians in the Hungarian Kingdom lacked political recognition because they had neither an aristocratic "nation" nor a specialized military usefulness. Even though they constituted the majority in Transylvania's population, the principality's Romanians essentially were a community of peasants and pastoralists dominated by three non-Romanian elites who enjoyed official "nation" status—Hungarian nobles, Székelys (a group ethnically related to Hungarians), and Saxon Germans. Beginning in the fifteenth century the three "nations" cemented their collective monopoly on political power in the principality and, during the Protestant Reformation, when Transylvania was an autonomous Ottoman vassal state, further solidified their dominance by officially recognizing only the four religions that held currency among themselves: Catholicism, Calvinism, Lutheranism, and Unitarianism. Both politically and religiously, therefore, the Orthodox Romanian majority was disenfranchised.

After gaining control of Transylvania in 1691, Habsburg Emperor Leopold I sought to use the region's numerous Romanians as a counterweight against the militantly proud Hungarian nobles in both Hungary and Transylvania. He attempted to win the Orthodox Romanians' loyalty by extending to them circumspect official religious recognition through their union with the Roman Catholic church. Given their lowly situation under the existing governing arrangement in

Transylvania, a successful church union among the Transylvanian Romanians portended their looking to Leopold as a friend and benefactor.

The Jesuit-led unionist efforts focused on the Orthodox Romanian upper clergy, who enjoyed a higher standard of living than did the Romanian parish priests and general population and were more resentful of the inequitable sociopolitical situation in Transylvania because of their elevated community standing. The disgruntled Orthodox officials assumed that union automatically would bring them religious recognition by the Transylvanian authorities; they were led to believe that it also would bestow on them the privileges enjoyed by the other recognized "nations" in the principality.

The union was accepted formally by the Transylvanian Orthodox hierarchy in 1700. The Uniates (as the unionist clergy were called) soon were disappointed in their hopes for Romanian sociopolitical elevation. Their new church was placed under the authority of a Hungarian archbishop, and the three official "nations" refused to grant them equal political status. Leopold declined to elevate the Romanians politically for fear of civil war with the Hungarian nobility. Many Uniates then recanted their decision and returned to the Orthodox fold. Those who held to the union worked hard at winning imperial support for the Romanians' political recognition and used what privileges the union bestowed on them to improve the educational and cultural conditions of the general Romanian population.

Roman Catholic schools and colleges throughout Transylvania were opened to Uniate Romanian students, the most talented of whom were eligible for scholarships to study in Italy. Participants in Uniate study-abroad programs emerged as the vanguard of Transylvanian Romanian ethnonational consciousness. None was more influential than the eighteenth-century Uniate Bishop Ion Inocenţiu Micu (Klain). A talented product of Jesuit education, Micu viewed the Uniate church as a vehicle for socially emancipating the Transylvanian Romanian peasantry and gaining their political recognition as a "nation." Micu transformed his seat at Blaj into a Romanian cultural center and actively pleaded the case for Romanian "nationhood" before both the Transylvanian Diet and the imperial court in Vienna. When his efforts failed, Micu left the empire for Rome, resigned his bishop's office, and entered a Roman monastery, where he died in 1768.

Micu later was credited with "discovering" the Latin origins of Romanian ethnicity. While in Rome, he purportedly noticed that the bas-reliefs on Trajan's Column, erected by Emperor Trajan to commemorate his conquest of Dacia, portrayed the ancient Dacians wearing hats similar to those worn by Romanian peasants in Micu's time. Although the story probably was apocryphal, Romanian Uniate Latin scholars studying in the West developed an ethnonational doctrine based on their philological studies. They traced the Romanian vernacular to roots in the form of Latin current during Dacia's second- and third-century period of Roman occupation, ultimately concluding that the Romanians actually were the indigenous inhabitants of Transylvania and the Romanian Principalities, directly descended from the Romanized Dacians.

By the end of the eighteenth century Habsburg support for the Uniate church waned and increasing numbers of its adherents returned to the Orthodox ranks. Among the remaining Uniates were a group of Romanian intellectuals who sent a list of proposals to Habsburg Emperor Leopold II (1790-92) known as the *Supplex libellus Valachorum.* The *Supplex* expounded a broad political program for both the Uniate and Orthodox Transylvanian Romanians, demanding their official equality with the other three "nations." It included proposals aimed at gradually incorporating the Romanians into the political oligarchy controlling the principality, and it called for the end of anti-Romanian sociopolitical discriminatory practices. Although a failure, the *Supplex* marked the initial public emergence of Romanian political national consciousness.

By the outbreak of the Revolution of 1848-49, the originally Uniate ethnonational consciousness had gained popularity among all Transylvanian Romanian intellectuals. After the Hungarian revolutionaries reunited Transylvania with Hungary in 1848, the principality's Romanians demanded recognized political rights. As the Hungarian nationalists grew more radicalized, the Transylvanian Romanians were forced to devise a strong national program of their own or risk losing completely any possible recognition. Romanian intellectuals and church officials devised a national program that included: Recognition of the Romanians as a separate "nation"; the use of the national name "Romanian"; the official use of the Romanian language in matters pertaining to Romanians; the equality of the two Romanian churches with those already officially recognized; and all of the standard liberal-democratic rights granting self-determination.

The Hungarians rejected the Romanian national program, and the Hungarians' subsequent declaration of independence from the Habsburgs in 1849 sparked a civil war between them and the Transylvanian Romanian nationalists. The Romanians established contacts with the Habsburgs and aided them in defeating the Hungarians. But, just like the pro-Habsburg Croats after the revolution's suppression, the Romanians found their efforts unrewarded. They were subjected to Habsburg repression and eventual national abandonment to the mercies of the Hungarians following the 1867 Compromise.

Early National Awareness in the Ottoman Balkans

The overriding factor affecting Ottoman Balkan non-Muslims was the degeneration of mundane life caused by two centuries of destabilization. Maladministration, political anarchy, rampant monetary inflation, crushing taxes, coercion, and rising levels of violence led many to overcome their traditional cultural prejudices and consider the new Western European ethnonational concepts as alternatives to the "Ottoman System."

For most of the empire's non-Muslims, Romantic ethnonational awareness was a foreign import and not a matter of native cultural development—theocratic Islamic Ottoman society precluded such a process. When national consciousness was spreading across Western Europe, the Ottoman Balkans exhibited none of the preconditions for similar evolution. Except for the Romanian *boiers,* there existed no privileged *zimmi* noble elites with claims to "nation" status. Nor did the Balkan *zimmi* urban middle class enjoy the sort of political, intellectual, and educational development experienced by its Western European counterpart—no political partnership was forged with the Ottoman sultans; no Renaissance leading to sociopolitical secularization occurred; and no secular education of any kind arose. Lacking such indigenous developmental factors, ethnonational awareness needed to be "awakened" among the Ottoman *zimmi* populations from outside.

Centuries of *millet* existence cemented religion as the Ottoman *zimmis'* primary criterion for group identity. Free to practice their faiths and cultivate their religious cultures, they identified with their religions and devotional languages. Other criteria—family, village, local region, and language among the rural populations; family, *mahalle,* occupation, town, and language for urban dwellers—remained rudimentary and localized. Any sense of group "belonging" beyond the local and immediate lay in the *millet.*

The Ottoman sultans built a political partnership with the ecclesiastical *millet* leaders and not, as did Western European monarchs, with the urban middle class. While superficial similarities existed between the Ottoman and Western European situations, they differed in nature. Instead of using the partnership to consolidate central monarchical control against internal opposition, the Ottoman sultans imposed the *millet* system from a position of central, autocratic political strength. They set all of the terms and regulated all of the functions in the relationship. Any collective voice enjoyed by the *zimmis* was funneled narrowly through their *millet* leaderships, which operated within strictly confined official bounds.

Because the *millets* took no intrinsic account of ethnicity, only the Phanariote Greeks controlling the Orthodox *millet* hierarchy had any potential advantage stemming from *millet* identity within the context of Romantic ethnonational awareness. They were positioned to serve as the privileged elite in shaping ethnonational group identities. The Greek Orthodox *millet* hierarchs held a sense of continuity with their pre-Ottoman, Byzantine past that no other group within the empire possessed. That the Ottomans turned to former Byzantine institutional and social elements for *millet* and commercial leadership guaranteed that a self-consciously Greek elite was preserved. Through the Orthodox *millet,* the Greek language became the lingua franca of the non-Muslim Ottoman Balkans, and Greek religious culture was fostered in virtually every Orthodox ecclesiastical center under

Greek patriarchal control. After the autocephalous Slavic-rite Peć and Ohrid patriarchates were eliminated in the 1760s, Greek cultural hegemony within the Orthodox *millet* went unchallenged until the middle of the nineteenth century.

Through the Orthodox *millet,* the Phanariote Greek partnership with the ruling Muslim authorities granted them the most prestige and privilege available to non-Muslim Ottoman subjects. That position, however, tended to retard the evolution of an anti-Ottoman Greek national movement once Western European ethnonational concepts appeared among the Phanariotes. The Ottoman authorities and the Phanariote *millet* leaders enjoyed a relationship of mutual self-interest, in which actual sociopolitical differences grew blurred. The Phanariotes had a vested interest in preserving Ottoman society as it stood. They controlled the Orthodox *millet,* dominated the empire's economic and foreign affairs, and monopolized the rulership in both Romanian Principalities. All important *millet* administrative positions were in their hands. Their language reigned supreme throughout the Orthodox Balkans, to the point that Greek threatened the Church Slavic literary languages of the Bulgarians and Serbs and the Latin-based tongue of the principality Romanians.

The Phanariotes' diverse commercial and political functions within the empire also offered them direct and near-continuous relations with Western Europe and Russia. By the middle of the eighteenth century Greek merchant colonies operated in Central European trade centers, in Western Mediterranean commercial ports, and in a number of Russian Black Sea port cities. Those Greek trading colonies served as channels through which Western European and Russian ideas entered the empire and spread among the Greek merchant class. By the turn of the eighteenth century such ideas increasingly included Western national concepts. Fertilized by Western and Russian neoclassical interests (which idealized an ancient Greek heritage and fed widespread publishing of Greek-language texts), and abetted by Napoleon's continental blockade against England (which expanded the Greeks' Western European commercial volume and income), the merchant colonists evolved into the nationalist vanguard for Greeks within the Ottoman Empire.

Many Greek colonial merchants took advantage of their situation to study and travel throughout Western Europe and Russia, where they imbibed secular attitudes fed by the Scientific Revolution and the Enlightenment. A split evolved within Phanariote ranks between those adhering to traditional Orthodox mentality (focused on preserving *millet* leadership and commercial dominance within the Ottoman Empire) and those giving secular interests their highest priority (espousing ethnonational political aspirations that increasingly rejected continued Ottoman sovereignty).

The Greek national movement began among the secularized merchant colonists and expatriates. Evgenios Voulgaris, born in Corfu, educated in Padua, and a renowned teacher, was its early precursor. During the second half of the eighteenth century his secular teaching led to conflicts with the traditional *millet* leadership and his ultimate self-imposed exile to Russia, where he actively propagandized for Greek liberation from the Ottomans by means of Russian military intervention. In his efforts, Voulgaris made current Western European and Russian political and scientific thought accessible to his fellow Greeks through Greek-language translations and political pamphlets.

More directly responsible in shaping an emerging Greek ethnonational consciousness was Adamantios Koraïs. Scion of a wealthy İzmir (Smyrna) merchant family, Koraïs was educated in France and spent most of his life in Paris, where he embraced liberal concepts and classical ideals. He bent his intellectual skills toward Greek philology and classical Greek scholarship, publishing multivolume collections of ancient Greek authors between 1789 and his death in 1833. He also wrote numerous political pamphlets addressed to his fellow Ottoman Greeks extolling French revolutionary ideals. Following Napoleon's defeat, Koraïs continued writing on such issues as liberal politics, secular education, the significance of linguistic study, and the importance of printing presses for preserving and disseminating knowledge and culture. His prolific publications collectively resulted in creating and standardizing the modern Greek literary language.

While Koraïs was an intellectual, Rhigas Pherraios (Velestinlis) was an activist. Son of wealthy Thessalian parents and a teacher, Pherraios turned fugitive after killing a Turkish notable, hiding out with bandits before fleeing to Mount Athos, Istanbul, Moldavia, and ultimately Vienna. After the outbreak of the French Revolution, Pherraios became an ardent revolutionary and pioneer for a Greek nationalist uprising. He published a number of books in Greek, which circulated widely within the Ottoman Empire and the Romanian Principalities, attacking traditional Phanariote values and calling for a Greek revolution that would establish a Greek-led Balkan federation. In 1797 Pherraios set out from Vienna to join Pasvanoğlu's Vidin uprising, intent on starting his own revolt in the Peloponnese aimed at liberating all of what he considered "Greece" (present-day Greece, Macedonia, and Albania). He was arrested en route by Habsburg police, extradited to the Ottoman Empire, and beheaded as a rebel in 1798, becoming the first Greek national martyr.

Under the influence of Napoleonic France, the Greek nationalists in the trading colonies stepped up their revolutionary activity. Beginning with the founding of the Society of Friends (*Philike hetairia*) in the Ukrainian Black Sea port of Odessa by Greek traders in 1814, secret revolutionary societies sprang up in Greek merchant colonies throughout Europe. With the defeat of Napoleon, the revolutionaries turned to Orthodox Russia for support, especially since one of their number from Corfu, John Capodistrias, had been appointed Russia's foreign minister by Tsar Alexander I (1801-25).

Although the Phanariote *millet* leadership was susceptible to the ethnocultural aspects of Romantic nationalist ideas filtering into it from the merchant colonies abroad, it naturally viewed their anti-Ottoman political thrust as threatening its dominance within non-Muslim Ottoman society. The *millet* leaders consistently resisted the spread of such political concepts among their multiethnic flock in a futile effort to sustain the traditional Ottoman structure, in which they played such an important role. Rejecting nationalism's revolutionary aspects, traditional Phanariotes embraced the cultural-linguistic ones, which reinforced their existing sense of Greek cultural superiority over the non-Greek—mostly Slav—members of the Orthodox *millet.* This act, in turn, fed a deeply rooted anti-Greek ethnic reaction among many non-Greek Orthodox believers, which evolved into outright national hostility once they espoused ethnonationalist concepts themselves.

For two centuries the Slavic-rite Ottoman Serbs had enjoyed near-separate *millet* status under the autocephalous Patriarchate of Peć. Led and staffed by Serb-speaking clerics, that organization provided Serb *zimmis* with a modicum of independent representative administration, grounded in pre-Ottoman medieval religious traditions and rudimentary folk democracy, unavailable to other Slavic-rite Orthodox believers in the empire. Peć patriarchs pursued direct diplomatic relations with foreign powers (Russia, the Habsburg Empire, Venice, and Rome) independent of the Ottoman authorities, a practice that ultimately led to the patriarchate's demise in 1766 and its takeover by Greek clerics. The Serb lower clergy thereafter were reduced to playing the role that other Slavic-rite clerics long had been forced to adopt—grassroots cultural leaders among local villagers and townspeople. Leadership in developing an elevated Serbian ethnonational consciousness then fell to the Habsburg border Serbs and their Sremski Karlovci archbishopric.

The Bulgarians shared the sociopolitical and socioeconomic fate of the Serbs—membership in an Orthodox *millet* controlled by ethnically foreign Greeks, the lack of a traditional native leadership class, and incorporation into the Ottoman *reaya* peasant and urban classes—but they faced additional challenges to their ethnic self-identity. For the most part, they essentially were cut off from the world outside of the Ottoman Empire. Located in the very heart of the Ottoman Balkans, far from the empire's borders and in close geographical proximity to the Ottoman capital at Istanbul, astride all the vital overland military, administrative, and commercial lines of communication between the capital and its outlying European provinces, the Bulgarians were one of the most completely subjugated non-Muslim populations in the empire.

Because of their strategic geographical situation, the Bulgarian lands were heavily colonized by Muslim Anatolian Turks, who were settled by the Ottoman central authorities to secure the important highways and to repopulate the war-ravaged Bulgarian territories during and after the fourteenth century. Mundane familiarity with Turks provided the Bulgarians with a comparative yardstick for measuring their own social situation against that of their Muslim neighbors. Over time, hundreds of Bulgarians found the comparison unacceptable and took to local banditry and rebellion, while thousands of others weighed the differences and opted for the advantages offered by conversion to Islam, despite the fact that such an act removed them from the Orthodox *millet,* with which Bulgarian self-identity, like that of all other non-Muslims, was linked.

Although the medieval Bulgarian Archbishopric-Patriarchate of Ohrid retained its autocephalous status after the Ottoman conquest and the title "Bulgarian" remained attached to it until its abolishment in 1767, nearly all of the clergy staffing its upper hierarchy were Greeks. Unlike the Serbs, from the beginning of Ottoman rule the Bulgarians found themselves relegated to the lowest ecclesiastical positions in the religious institution that represented their interests to the Ottoman government through the Orthodox *millet.* By the seventeenth century a noticeable animosity had developed between Orthodox Bulgarians and Greeks, which soon spilled over into the cultural realm.

Any cultural reinforcement of Bulgarian ethnic self-awareness rested in the grassroots efforts of Bulgarian monks and priests to preserve a sense of Slavic identity among their faithful through Orthodox literary and educational endeavors. In church literature, they shaped a new Bulgarian literary language that reflected the vernacular more closely than did the fossilized Church Slavic, in which a number of secularly tinged but still religious works were produced. Beginning in the seventeenth century, church schools were opened in Bulgarian towns and villages teaching literacy in the new language to a growing number of artisans, local merchants, miners, and livestock traders who were evolving into a Bulgarian middle class. The efforts of the Bulgarian lower clergy prepared the way for a ready readership for the first highly fictionalized modern Bulgarian history, produced by the Bulgarian monk Paisii at Hilandar Monastery on Mount Athos in 1762.

Paisii Hilendarski produced his history in the new Bulgarian literary language to combat the threat to Bulgarian identity posed by the combination of Greek domination of the Orthodox *millet* and increasing Greek pretensions to cultural superiority. In his effort to provide Bulgarians with a glorious history of their own, Paisii mined Byzantine and Russian source materials available on Mount Athos as well as Croat, Western, and Russian sources that he found in the Fruška Gora border Serb monasteries. Afterward, he wandered throughout the central Balkans discussing his manuscript with fellow Bulgarian monks and having copies made for dissemination. A humble man completely dedicated to his ethnonational mission, Paisii did not mind that his name rarely appeared on the many copies of his manuscript. (It was not until the late nineteenth century that the Bulgarians generally recognized him as the father of their national movement.)

One Bulgarian cleric whom Paisii deeply affected was Sofronii Vrachanski. Born Stoiko Vladislavov, he took the ecclesiastical name Sofronii on becoming bishop of Vratsa. He was Paisii's student and disciple and made two of the earliest copies of his history. Sofronii tirelessly promoted anti-Greek sentiment and literacy in the Bulgarian vernacular, for which he constantly was harassed by Greek ecclesiastical and Ottoman civil authorities. He fled to Wallachia to escape Pasvanoğlu's activities in the Vratsa region and took up residence in Bucharest, where he remained until his death in 1813, conducting Bulgarian literary and nationalist activity. During his exile, Sofronii compiled a Bulgarian-language anthology (which included his autobiography), published the first printed book in modern Bulgarian (1806), and undertook translations of Western European political tracts.

In the early nineteenth century, aided by Sofronii's efforts, Paisii's history made an impact on some Bulgarian artisans and merchants, many of whom were associated with Greek domestic and foreign commercial enterprises. Vasil Aprilov, an expatriated Bulgarian Odessa merchant, invested in secular education for the Bulgarians and supported book printing in the new Bulgarian literary language aimed at disseminating Western European political and national concepts. The first modern Bulgarian secular school was founded with merchant support in 1835, and its example quickly spread throughout the Bulgarian regions. The school curricula were filled with current Western European publications in translation. By the middle of the nineteenth century a large segment of the Bulgarian middle class was committed to a nationalist agenda aimed at both religious independence from the Greeks and political independence from the Ottomans.

In the vassal Romanian Principalities, anti-Phanariote sentiment among the native Romanian *boiers* first sparked a sense of Romanian ethnonational awareness. Originally the *boiers* exhibited no true ethnic group identity, only a class consciousness. Although ethnonational developments among the Transylvanian Romanians were known in the principalities through the Wallachian Orthodox church (which held jurisdiction over the Orthodox in Transylvania), the wealthy landowning *boiers* had no intention of linking their own interests to those of their enserfed peasants. They constructed an anti-Ottoman/anti-Phanariote ideology based on French Enlightenment concepts introduced into the principalities during the late eighteenth century by their Phanariote masters. The *boiers* showed no concern for Romanian history, language, or ethnicity. Rather, they claimed exclusive "inalienable rights" for themselves as an aristocratic "nation."

Not until the 1820s and 1830s, when Transylvanian Romanian refugees from post-Vienna Habsburg repression appeared in the principalities (which at the time were occupied by Russia), did the *boiers* take up the Transylvanian-spawned ethnonational cause of the Romanians' Latin origins. In the principalities, however, the *boiers* linked Latin-based ethnicity with an affinity toward France (then the leading Latin state in Europe) and French political philosophy, whose constitutional model appeared best suited for advancing their political interests. The elitist national ideology that emerged in Wallachia and Moldavia during the early nineteenth century retained the old class exclusivity in calling for independence from the Phanariote Greeks, from the Muslim Ottomans, and from the encroaching Slavic Russians under the guidance and protection of France.

Regarding other Ottoman *zimmi* populations, little or no evidence exists for their developing any mature ethnonational awareness beyond *millet* identity by the opening of the nineteenth century. Ethnonational concepts remained completely alien and unattractive to the Ottomans' Muslim subjects, despite the sad state of mundane living conditions within the destabilized empire.

CHAPTER TEN

Revolutions
and Resurrected States

Once the Balkan populations were exposed to ethnonational concepts, it was only a matter of time before they actively attempted to attain some measure of group self-governance within the multiethnic empires that they inhabited. While autonomy initially was acceptable to many of the new nationalists, outright ethnonational independence was the ideal goal of most. Neither the Ottomans nor the Habsburgs could hope to satisfy such aspirations and still escape the likely internal dissolution and ultimate collapse of their respective states. Given that situation, revolutionary action was seen as the only alternative by most Balkan nationalists. National revolutionary activity began among the Serbs and the Greeks during the opening decades of the nineteenth century amid chaotic conditions in the Ottoman Empire's provinces. The Revolution of 1848-49 in the Habsburg Empire offered the principality Romanians an opportunity to break free of titular Ottoman vassalage and Russian occupation. All three revolutionary movements eventually succeeded in establishing new states grounded in Western European ethnonational principles.

The Serbian Insurrections and Autonomous Serbia

Throughout the eighteenth century the Serb-inhabited Ottoman regions were perennial battlegrounds, causing significant demographic changes. Large numbers of Serb émigrés fled to the Habsburg Empire, and their abandoned lands were resettled by more militant, independent-minded migrant mountain Serbs. Conversely, the numbers of Turk inhabitants steadily declined as many fled southward to avoid the conflicts. In effect, the eighteenth-century wars created a compactly Serb-inhabited Ottoman province of Belgrade.

Although a brief Habsburg occupation of Ottoman Serbia (1718-39) was oppressive and exploitative, it also benefited the Serbs. The Habsburg authorities permitted them a measure of local self-government; organized, trained, and armed autonomous auxiliary Serbian militias for the Habsburg military; and forged economic ties with local Serb merchants and livestock breeders. After the Ottomans regained control of Belgrade province in 1739, the authorities encouraged continued Serbian local autonomy to ensure some semblance of order in the region against growing provincial anarchy caused by local *ayans,* renegade warriors and Janissaries, and bandits. The Ottomans' efforts proved in vain. The renegades increasingly harried and coerced the Serb population. During the Ottoman-Habsburg War of 1788 to 1791 the Serbs in Belgrade province, led by Koča Andjelković, fought as the Habsburgs' allies only to be abandoned by them in the Treaty of Svishtov (1791) that ended the conflict. "Koča's War" (as the Serbs labeled it) convinced them that they could not depend on foreign support in resisting continued Ottoman anarchy.

Sultan Selim III tried to appease the Serbs and use them as a counterweight to the renegades by forbidding the Janissaries, who had fled Belgrade province during the fighting, to return and by granting the Serbs more extensive local self-government. Those measures were nullified by Pasvanoğlu's activities in the region. In self-defense, the Serbs organized their own militia with Selim's blessings and funding. Napoleon's Egyptian campaign, however, frightened Selim into making peace with the rebel *ayan* in 1798 as a hedge against a possible empire-wide, French-supported Christian uprising. The sultan also feared the Serbs' growing power—they were heavily armed, largely self-governing, collecting their own taxes, and aware of the central authorities' weakness.

In late 1798 Selim executed many local Serb leaders, imprisoned others as hostages, raised the Serbs' taxes, confiscated their weapons, and reinstalled the Janissaries in Belgrade. The returning Janissaries took control of the province, beheaded the legitimate governor (1801), and eradicated all vestiges of Serbian autonomy. In 1802 local *sipahi* landowners revolted against the Janissary regime, and a number of rural Serbs, led by Djordje Petrović, a prosperous pig dealer whose large size and swarthy complexion earned him the nickname Karadjordje ("Black Djordje") and whose profession and former bandit experience won him support among the Serbian middle and renegade classes, armed themselves with weapons purchased from Habsburg Vojvodina. To avert a Serb uprising, in February 1804 the Belgrade Janissaries systematically tried to massacre Serb village commune leaders, but the move only precipitated the act that they hoped to squelch.

Karadjordje escaped assassination and raised a rebellion. His reputation as a militia commander during Koča's War, and widespread popular disaffection with the Janissary regime, attracted numerous recruits to his banner and ensured the rebellion's broad popular support. Within months the rebels successfully confined the Janissaries to a few fortresses, and the Janissary commanders sought to end the conflict through Habsburg mediation. Although a meeting of leaders from both sides took place in Zemun, a Habsburg border town near Belgrade, no agreement was reached.

Initially, neither Karadjordje nor his followers sought Serbian national independence. Rather, they fought to overthrow the oppressive local Janissary regime and reinstate stable Ottoman provincial administration as it had functioned before the sultan's compromise with Pasvanoğlu. It was the Habsburg border Serbs who transformed the uprising into a revolutionary struggle for Serbian independence, sending armaments, volunteers, and supplies to Karadjordje's rebels. In late 1804 they contacted Russia requesting intervention on behalf of the rebels, but Tsar Alexander, concerned about French ambitions in the Balkans, declined, offering them arms and diplomatic support instead.

The Serbs' Russian contacts hardened Sultan Selim against Karadjordje's professions of continued loyalty, and the border Serbs' growing vocal demands for Serbian autonomy led him to declare war on the rebels. Karadjordje repeatedly defeated the Ottoman forces sent against him, and by the end of 1806 he captured Belgrade. In that same year Selim allied himself with Napoleon, which caused Russia and Britain to attack the Ottoman Empire. Selim offered to meet the Serbs' demands for autonomy to free forces for use against the invaders, but Russia kept the rebellion alive by promising the Serbs more money and arms. By mid-1807 Karadjordje controlled all Ottoman fortresses in Belgrade province and signed a formal alliance with Russia.

Karadjordje's act transformed the rebellion into a war for Serbian national independence. Unfortunately, the alliance also subjected the rebellion to the whims of European Great Power politics. At Tilsit (1807), Napoleon imposed a treaty ending the Franco-Russian war. Russia then halted hostilities against the Ottomans, leaving the Serbs in the lurch. Reprieved by a renewed Russo-Turkish war (1809-12), the Serbs again were abandoned when Russia was compelled to sign the Treaty of Bucharest (1812) to meet Napoleon's impending invasion. Despite clauses requiring the Ottomans to grant the Serbs autonomy and full amnesty, the Russians could not ensure their enforcement. The Serbs then fell into disarray. Karadjordje and a number of Serb leaders fled to the Habsburg Empire, and the Ottomans reoccupied all of the rebellious Serb territories (1813).

In 1815 the Serbs, now committed to throwing off direct Ottoman control, again rose in revolt. Karadjordje and most of the former rebel commanders still were in exile. The renewed rising was led by Miloš Obrenović, a middle-class individual with an abiding personal hatred of Karadjordje, whom he accused of poisoning his half brother. Miloš had remained in Serbia following 1813 and had been appointed an Ottoman agent for keeping the Serbs in line. Unlike Karadjordje, who was a straightforward military leader, Miloš was cunning and complex, capable of both crafty diplomacy and competent military command. He initially made efforts to win the Serbs' gainful collaboration with the Ottoman authorities, but continued arbitrary treatment of himself and the local population finally convinced him to raise the second rebellion.

Through dogged military leadership, astute diplomacy, and highly refined bribery of Ottoman officials, Obrenović won Sultan Mahmud II's recognition of a virtually autonomous Ottoman Serbian province (1816). He was appointed supreme leader in Belgrade province, and the Serbs were permitted to retain their arms and establish a local self-governing assembly of notables (*skupština*). As part of the arrangement, Ottoman officials and military garrisons remained on the province's soil and taxes continued to be paid to Istanbul. When Karadjordje returned to Belgrade from exile in 1817, he voiced opposition to Miloš's seemingly pro-Ottoman stance. The two leaders were inveterate rivals, and a decisive clash was inevitable. Miloš moved first. Karadjordje was axed to death in his sleep by Miloš's supporters, sparking a blood feud between the two future Serbian royal families that plagued Serbian politics into the mid-twentieth century.

Although the Ottomans maintained garrisons in the province, Miloš commanded numerous heavily armed men whose presence prevented the garrisons from acting arbitrarily. A standoff ensued, during which Obrenović's skillful diplomacy, using the potential threat of Russian intervention to full advantage, led to de facto enforcement of autonomy within Belgrade province. The outbreak of the Greek national revolution in 1821 gave Miloš further opportunity to expand his independent authority by once again threatening the Ottomans with a possible Russian alliance openly sympathetic to the Greek cause, while he scrupulously avoided any actual pro-Greek activities.

In 1828 Russia declared war on the Ottomans and invaded the Balkans by way of the Romanian Principalities. Russian forces penetrated deep into the empire's Bulgarian provinces and captured Edirne (1829), forcing Sultan Mahmud to sue for peace. By the terms of the Treaty of Edirne (Adrianople), Belgrade province was declared an autonomous Serbian principality within the Ottoman Empire governed by Obrenović as hereditary prince. Formal Ottoman recognition of the terms came in 1830, but boundary disputes persisted for another three years. (See Map 7.)

In no way did autonomous Serbia resemble any contemporary Western European state. Its infrastructure almost was nonexistent, hampered by extensive dense forests and only a few primitive roads. Except for a very small urban middle class, Serbian society essentially was egalitarian. The predominantly illiterate majority peasant population mostly lived at subsistence level, eking out a living using rudimentary, centuries-old agricultural techniques. Their life continued as it had under the Ottomans: Villagers worked lands or tended livestock under village communal elder supervision, and collective social activities centered on local Orthodox churches and monasteries.

After winning autonomy, little changed for Miloš's government, except that it acquired a Serbian ethnic identity. As prince (*veliki knez*), Miloš Obrenović (1830-

39; 1858-60) wielded full executive power, controlling all government appointments and intervening in local affairs at will. As a consciously Orthodox ruler, he concerned himself with church matters, and, although his religious policies were autocratic, arbitrary, and inconsistent, he drove out the Greek bishops who ran the Serbian church since 1766 and won recognition of the Serbian church's autonomy from the Greek Patriarchate (1831). Although an assembly of notables existed, Miloš controlled it by executive authority—the *skupština* met only when he summoned it. He ruled as an autocratic Serb *ayan*.

Miloš acted autocratically, partly out of powerful Orthodox and Ottoman political traditions and partly out of necessity. Both Byzantine and Islamic political cultures, which in combination influenced the Serbs for seven centuries, considered centralized, autocratic authority "natural." Miloš, a product of Ottoman Serbian society, acted within those traditions. On the practical side, since the former rebel forces were composed of bands led by strong local chieftains, Miloš was forced to act ruthlessly and arbitrarily against them or risk internal political anarchy. Additionally, he sought to break the village communes' influence over the peasantry, who traditionally possessed only a local political perspective, and to impress on them obligations to the state. Thus tradition and suppression of internal centrifugal forces demanded that autonomous Serbia be strongly centralized.

Opposition to Miloš's autocratic ways emerged early among military and village leaderships and continually grew thereafter. In 1835 he accepted a constitution to appease his opponents but found it too democratic for his liking, so with Ottoman and Russian backing Miloš abrogated it and continued his autocracy. Opposition intensified and Serbian politics split into two contentious factions—pro- and anti-Miloš. Serbia's political situation had implications beyond the principality's borders, however, since by the 1830s the Balkans were becoming an important factor in Great Power relations, particularly in the so-called "Eastern Question" that pitted the imperialist interests of Britain against those of Russia.

As part of a policy to forestall Russia's penetration into the eastern Mediterranean by way of the Bosphorus-Dardanelles straits, Britain sought to bolster the Ottoman Empire as an ally. Russia, on the other hand, strove to weaken the Ottomans by fostering pro-Russian sentiments among the Balkans' Orthodox and Slav populations in hopes of forging future Russian dependencies that would loosen Ottoman control of the straits. Autonomous Serbia was a primary Russian candidate for such a role. Neither the Ottomans nor Britain could afford to have the Russophile Serbs move firmly into Russia's orbit. Britain expediently supported Miloš's autocracy against the Russian-supported opposition that sought a more liberal-democratic constitutional government.

Sultan Mahmud decided the issue in late 1838. Fearing an impending uprising of radically nationalist Serb oppositionists, and learning that Britain would not risk conflict with Russia over Serbia, he proclaimed a Serbian constitution and forced

Miloš to accept a senate with extensive political powers. By that time the majority of the principality's leadership was hostile to the prince and most of the general population was alienated. In June 1839 the senate demanded Miloš's abdication. Lacking any support, Miloš complied and fled in exile to the Habsburg Empire. His son and successor Mihajlo Obrenović (1839-42; 1860-68) was a minor heavily under the thumb of senate-appointed regents, who all were hostile to his family and enjoyed Ottoman and Russian support. He too fled the principality after making an abortive attempt to oust them.

Symbolically demonstrating anti-Obrenović sentiment, the *skupština* elected as prince Aleksandr Karadjordjević (1842-58), the son of the revolutionary hero whom Miloš had butchered. Aleksandr, although personally upright and committed, proved weak. He failed to assert his authority against the powerful senators, who controlled the government during his reign. That, however, was not altogether a negative development. Aleksandr's weakness permitted a certain amount of authentic liberal-democratic governance in Serbia that effected a measure of modernization by Western European standards.

The Serb senators mostly were middle-class merchants and functionaries who encouraged increased foreign trade, especially with the nearby Habsburg Empire, and valued secular education. During Aleksandr's reign over three hundred primary schools were founded, whose curricula were shaped by the Western European concepts rapidly spreading among the politicians and expanding middle class as a result of increased commercial foreign contacts. An Academy of Sciences (1841) and a university (1844) were founded in Belgrade, laying the groundwork for gradually transforming Serbian society into a more Western-like modern, middle-class-dominated community.

In the rapid effort to create a Western European-style state, the gap between ideal goals and the population's actual developmental level often had unfortunate consequences. A sophisticated, Habsburg-like judicial system was instituted, but the lack of adequately trained personnel rendered it ineffective. Old traditions of bribery died hard. So too did those of arbitrary, Janissary-like brutality in the police force. Traditional local communal authorities were replaced by officials appointed from the capital at Belgrade, and numerous government appointees were drawn from the Habsburg border Serbs, who possessed the skills needed for their positions but who also generally acted in a superior fashion toward the former Ottoman Serbs. Tensions between border and principality Serbs led to the latter's rising discontent over the new, more "European" conditions within the state.

Given Ottoman sovereignty and Great Power interests in the Balkans, Aleksandr's government was limited in conducting independent foreign affairs, as was apparent during the Revolution of 1848-49 in the Habsburg Empire. The border Serbs took up arms and joined the Croat nationalists against the radical Hungarian revolutionaries who claimed their territories as part of the ephemeral Hungarian

Republic. Croat-inspired South Slav confederative ideas became popular among the border Serbs and, through them, filtered into Serbia. When the Habsburg upheavals began, Aleksandr's chief minister was Ilija Garašanin, whose foreign policy concepts already envisioned unifying all Balkan Slavs under Serbian auspices. Aleksandr sympathized with those views.

A Panslav club was formed in Belgrade and issued a call for a general rising of all Ottoman South Slavs aimed at establishing a "Yugoslav" state headed by Aleksandr. Adamant Ottoman and Russian objections forced Aleksandr to curb the club's activities and adopt official neutrality toward events in the Habsburg Empire. Unofficially, however, arms and volunteers from Serbia poured into the empire's border regions for the Serb insurgents. After the revolution's suppression, Aleksandr was decorated for his neutrality by the Habsburg and Russian governments. While his official actions earned him elevated respect from his neighbors and benefactors, they won him little popularity among his Serbian subjects, who resented his lack of support for their ethnic "brothers."

During the Crimean War (1853-56) Aleksandr again was forced to adopt official neutrality regarding the conflict, which cost him a further loss of credibility among his subjects. Although the Serbs overwhelmingly favored entering the war on the side of Slavic Orthodox Russia, Ottoman and Habsburg forces stationed on Serbia's borders convinced Aleksandr to refrain from such action. Despite a clause in the Treaty of Paris (1856) requiring the Ottomans to first gain Great Power approval for any decisions regarding their autonomous Serbian principality, Aleksandr suffered greatly in Serbian public opinion for his neutrality during the war. In late 1858 the *skupština* called for his abdication. Aleksandr complied after some initial resistance and was replaced by the "Old Lord," Miloš Obrenović, who was recalled from exile by popular demand.

Then in his late seventies, Miloš had not mellowed with age. He immediately imprisoned those responsible for his earlier abdication and then demanded that the Ottomans recognize his hereditary princely title and keep their garrison forces confined to fortresses. When Sultan Abdülmecid I (1839-61) delayed his response, Miloš, with the wholehearted approval of the *skupština,* officially pronounced (1860) that the Serbs' will within the principality held precedence over the sultan's legal sovereignty. Within a month of that success, Miloš died and was succeeded by his exiled son Mihajlo.

Mihajlo's second reign proved successful. Unlike his father, Mihajlo was well educated and well traveled. He returned from exile convinced that the patriarchal system of personal government must give way to constitutional rule. He also was dedicated to implementing the principles of nationalism as the Serbian state's foundation. Mihajlo held two fundamental policy goals: The acquisition of total sovereignty within the principality by removing all Ottoman troops and the restoration of the medieval Serbian state by uniting under his authority all Serbs and the lands that they inhabited.

A new constitution was promulgated (1861) granting Mihajlo extensive powers at the expense of both the senate and the *skupština*, thus freeing him to make decisive decisions in both domestic and foreign affairs. He then constructed a modern army based on the French model, which provided him with over 50,000 well-equipped, trained, and disciplined troops to replace the old local chieftains and their bands of followers. A military academy, conscription, and an income tax were instituted to support the new force.

When the Belgrade Ottoman garrison commander stupidly bombarded the city after a clash between Ottoman troops and the city's inhabitants (1862), Mihajlo demanded a Great Power conference to address the "intolerable" situation of Ottoman garrisons in Serbia. At the ensuing meeting in Istanbul, the Ottomans agreed to withdraw from Serbia most of their garrisons (except for that in Belgrade) and all Turkish civilians. During the tensions surrounding the Cretan Rebellion (1866), with the Ottomans on the brink of war with Greece, Mihajlo requested that Sultan Abdülaziz (1861-76) remove all remaining Ottoman garrisons from Serbia. Under Great Power pressure, the sultan consented in early 1867.

While achieving the removal of Ottoman troops from Serbia, Mihajlo also moved toward gaining his second goal of creating a larger, completely independent Serbian state. He sought to forge a military league composed of neighboring Christian states to drive the Ottomans completely out of the Balkans. Between 1865 and 1868 he organized the first such alliance system, concluding agreements with Romania (1865 and 1868), Montenegro (1866), Greece (1867), and a Bulgarian revolutionary organization (1867). The times appeared propitious for concerted action since the Habsburg Empire, the Great Power upholding the status quo in the Balkans, was handcuffed by defeats in Italy by France (1859) and in Central Europe by Prussia (1866). The Ottoman suppression of the Cretan uprising, Greece's growing anti-Slav nationalist sentiments, and, most important, Mihajlo's assassination in June 1868, however, ended the alliance efforts.

Ultimate responsibility for Mihajlo's murder remains a mystery to this day. His assassins were known and a number were brought to trial. Their motives ranged from personal vengeance grounded in pro-Karadjordjević sympathies, through liberal reaction against the prince's autocratic (although "constitutional") regime, and frustrated militant nationalism, to fear of a possible devastating war. In any event, Serbia lost an effective ruler whose successor fell short of his standards.

The Greek Revolution and Independent Greece

Throughout the eighteenth century the Greek middle-class merchant colonists increasingly grew discontented over the contrast between Western European and Russian living standards and conditions in the Ottoman Empire. The Enlightenment principles imbibed by Greek communities in Western Europe and Russia filtered back to the Ottoman Greeks through their extensive trade networks. By the beginning of the nineteenth century secular schools were opened in numerous Balkan Greek urban centers, and some secular intellectual activity flourished in Greek merchant circles. Also appearing among the imported influences were the new civic- and ethnic-based national ideals.

Ottoman Greek society was divided between Phanariotes and peasants and between traditionalists and secularists. Most *millet* hierarchs, large shipowners, and government functionaries (the traditionalist Phanariotes) opposed overthrowing the Ottoman state and society as they stood, while less wealthy secularist merchants longed for the benefits and stability of liberal constitutional rule, technological development, and infrastructural improvement along Western European lines. The secularists were joined by numerous illiterate peasants, who proved highly receptive to ethnonational revolutionary calls for throwing off oppressive landowners and acquiring their own land.

Beginning during the Napoleonic wars, Greek émigré nationalists conducted an intensive ethnonational propaganda campaign among their Ottoman conationals through publications, correspondence, and direct conversations. After 1817 members of the revolutionary *Philike hetairia* took the lead both in nationalist agitation among the Ottoman Greeks and in organizing a national revolution aimed at creating an independent Greek state.

Orthodox cultural affinities led the Greek émigré nationalists to view Russia as the most promising source of Great Power support for their cause. They initially put far more store in the Orthodox Byzantine cultural traditions that they shared with the Russians than in the intellectual philhellenism exhibited by some Western Christian Europeans. Initially the Russians' sense of cultural affinity with the Greeks was mutual. Successive Russian governments welcomed resident Greek merchant colonists as useful agents for furthering Russia's Balkan interests. Many of their number were recruited into the Russian government and military. The revolutionary *Philike hetairia* was established in Odessa, site of the largest Greek merchant colony in Russia.

Founded by secularist merchants, the *hetairia* gained widespread support among like-minded émigrés in the various commercial colonies. Much of the society's popularity rested on its members' assurances of Russian support. Those assertions, however, proved false. After the Napoleonic wars ended, Russian Tsar Alexander I increasingly grew suspicious of all revolutionary activity. Capodistrias, his Greek foreign minister (who had been offered the *hetairia*'s leadership), was forced to resign and accept exile in Switzerland, where he continued working for the national movement.

Alexander Ypsilantis, scion of a wealthy Phanariote family and a major general in the Russian army, then was chosen *hetairia* leader. Ypsilantis's military ties did not reflect official Russian support for the revolutionaries, but that did not stop *hetairia* propaganda from claiming Russian backing. Such unjustified claims won over to their cause numerous Greek Orthodox church primates, whose prestige and influence among the Greek peasantry were crucial in gaining a broad popular base for future revolutionary action.

While building support among the Ottoman Greeks, the *hetairia*'s leadership struggled to devise a workable revolutionary policy. Conservative elements cautioned delay and careful preparation. The radicals called for immediate action in 1821, since the Ottomans were distracted by problems in Anatolia and, more directly, by the rebellion of the Balkan *ayan* Tepedenli Ali Paşa of Ioannina. Ypsilantis sided with the radicals and hastily devised a plan for a national uprising involving a diversionary action in the Romanian Principalities coupled with a rebellion in the Peloponnese and the Greek-inhabited Mediterranean islands.

In early March 1821 Ypsilantis, at the head of a *hetairia* contingent called the Sacred Battalion, invaded Moldavia. He hoped for Russian assistance but Tsar Alexander repudiated him. The attempted takeover of the Principalities, which the Greek nationalists mistakenly considered Hellenized by a century of Phanariote rule, was unsuccessful. The Romanians, who suffered greatly under their Phanariote rulers, considered the Greeks greater enemies than the distant Ottomans. Armed Romanian peasants resisted the invaders and turned against the local Phanariotes and Romanian *boiers*. Beyond massacring numerous Muslim inhabitants, the invading Greeks accomplished little. The Ottomans quickly concentrated enough troops to annihilate Ypsilantis's forces. Ypsilantis fled to the Habsburg Empire, and his surviving followers retreated to Russia.

Although a failure, news of the Ypsilantis episode sparked a rebellion among local Orthodox *millet* primates and Greek peasants in the Peloponnese. Tensions ran high in the region because of Ali Paşa's rebellion and its accompanying atrocities. When the Ottoman authorities summoned some primates sympathetic to the *hetairia*'s plans to a meeting after receiving the initial reports of Ypsilantis's actions, the primates feared a trap and took their own action. In early April 1821 Bishop Germanos proclaimed a rebellion in Patras.

The Greek uprising initially was more a widespread bandit movement than an authentic national revolution. Its leaders fought only when it suited them, and their forces were uncoordinated and often mutually antagonistic. Most had no concept of nationalist ideals and acted simply in the time-honored fashion of brigands, seeking freedom from local Ottoman authority and booty from Muslim civilians, thousands of whom they slaughtered or drove out. The Aegean island rebel leaders operated as a freewheeling pirate fraternity, wreaking havoc on the Ottomans' sea communications. Old regional and class rivalries pitted Peloponnesians against continentals, islanders against mainlanders, Phanariotes against bandit leaders, upper against lower clergy, landowning prelates against peasants, and shipowners against sailors. Despite the intense differences, the chaotic activity initially amounted to a successful guerilla war against weak Ottoman regional forces.

The Ottomans' first reaction to events was to hang Patriarch Gregory V from the gate to his cathedral in the Phanar, despite the fact that he had issued an encyclical condemning the uprising. Early efforts to quell the rebels were hampered by Greece's mountainous terrain and severe winter weather, which made successful operations in a single campaigning season virtually impossible. The rebels' anarchistic tactics let them hold their own but precluded decisive strategic operations, so the military situation soon became deadlocked. The Ottomans cleared northern Greece and most of the islands of rebels, but the Peloponnese, Attica, Bœotia, and Mesolongion remained in rebel hands.

In the midst of the fighting, the rebels fell deeper into internal disarray. A Greek republic was proclaimed (1822) at Epidavros with the Phanariote Alexander Mavrokordatos as president, but his power was illusory. Real power lay with the guerilla leaders, the Orthodox primates, and the wealthy shipowners. The Peloponnesian rebel leader Theodore Kolokotronis controlled Navplion, the state's assumed capital. He forced Mavrokordatos's government out of the Peloponnese to the island of Hydra, where a new government was formed, headed by George Koundouriotis. Civil war then erupted between Kolokotronis and Koundouriotis, providing the Ottomans with an opening to defeat the rebellion.

In 1825 Sultan Mahmud II called in Egyptian troops, the only effective military forces in the empire. As Egyptian successes mounted, Western Europeans, imbued with philhellenic and Romantic sympathies, grew fed up with "infidel" Muslims killing fellow Christians in Greece. Western volunteers streamed into the region to join the rebels, whom they mistakenly considered direct descendants of the classical Greeks. Britain and Russia tried to mediate the conflict on the basis of gaining Greek autonomy under Ottoman suzerainty similar to the Serbian model. Their efforts resulted only in the Convention of Ackerman (1826) between Russia and the Ottomans, which did not affect Greece directly but required the Ottomans to evacuate the Romanian Principalities. Meanwhile, Britain, Russia, and France dispatched fleets to the eastern Mediterranean. In 1827 their combined intervention (made by their respective admirals without their governments' authority) destroyed the Egyptian-Ottoman fleet in Navarino (Pilos) Bay.

The Battle of Navarino decisively turned the Greek revolution in the rebels' favor. Britain officially condemned the actions of its fleet's admiral in the affair, which emboldened Mahmud to renounce the Ackerman Convention and continue suppressing the rebellion. Russia then declared war on the Ottomans (1828) and forced the sultan to sign the Treaty of Edirne (1829), by which Russia gave up its conquests in the Balkans but won the right to occupy the Romanian Principalities. Greek matters were relegated to a conference in London, the decisions of which would be binding. The London Protocol issued early in the following year (1830) declared Greece an independent monarchical state under the guaranteed protection of Britain, Russia, and France. Because Britain demanded that Ottoman territorial integrity be upheld as much as possible, the new Greek state's borders included little more than the Peloponnese, Attica, and the Cyclades Islands.

In Greece, the protocol's territorial and monarchical provisions were rejected. Less than 1 million Greeks lived within the new state's borders. Far more remained Ottoman subjects, and they soon found themselves disadvantaged—held suspect by the Ottoman authorities and stripped of their privileged commercial and administrative positions. In the Romanian Principalities, the sultan briefly turned to native *boiers* for *hospodar* candidates rather than Phanariotes. Armenians took the Phanariotes' administrative and commercial places, while Bulgarian merchants acquired the formerly Greek-dominated lucrative government trade and military supply contracts.

In contradiction of the London Protocol, John Capodistrias, returning from exile, was elected president (1830-31) of a proclaimed Greek Republic. He took swift measures to stabilize his state's condition: Imposing an administrative system, creating the beginnings of a public education system, suppressing banditry and piracy, calling for land distribution to rebel veterans, and curbing the independence of local church primates. Although needed, his policies, coupled with his ascerbic attitude toward opponents, earned Capodistrias widespread enmity among those threatened by his reforms or insulted by his acrimonies, and his pro-Russian leanings alienated Britain and France. In 1831 Capodistrias was assassinated and Greece fell into anarchy.

The European Powers were skeptical of the abilities of any native Balkan people to govern competently or in accordance with Great Power interests. They had little say regarding Serbia, where Obrenović had ensured native control. Beginning with Greece, however, the Great Powers instituted a policy of imposing foreign, Western European monarchs on Balkan national states carved out of the reeling Ottoman Empire. In 1832 the three protector Great Powers convinced Bavarian Wittelsbach Prince Otto, the Roman Catholic, underage son of Bavaria's king, to accept the Greek crown (1832-62). Sultan Mahmud then recognized Greece's independence in return for a hefty cash indemnity. King Otto (Othon), accompanied by his Bavarian regents, arrived in Greece (1833) and established his capital at Athens. (See Map 7.)

Otto's Greece faced grave national and economic problems. In size, the state was less than that envisioned by Greek nationalists, and, in population, three times as many Greeks lay outside of the state as within. National irredentism became an overriding political factor in Greek affairs. The nationalists' launched a powerful irredentist movement known as the "Great Idea" (*Megale idaia*). In its more temperate form, the "Great Idea" demanded the incorporation of all Greek-inhabited islands as well as mainland territories (Epiros, Thessaly, and Macedonia) north of the 1833 border. In its more radical form, the "Great Idea" sought the Byzantine Empire's restoration as the "natural" Greek state, with borders defined by Greek linguistic dominance within the Ottoman Orthodox *millet.*

The imposition of a foreign monarch intensified Greece's national problems. Otto's presence insulted the Greeks' traditional oligarchical leadership. With no constitution in force, Otto considered himself a divine-right prince. His Bavarian-staffed government, ignorant of Greek conditions, devised educational, judicial, and bureaucratic systems far too complex for traditional Greek society. The Bavarians' high-handed attitude alienated the Greeks, whom they considered too primitive to be trusted with important administrative responsibilities. Well-paid Bavarian volunteers replaced the revolutionary military forces, and the police became almost exclusively non-Greek. Many demobilized Greek fighters turned to banditry for a living, and their activities plagued Greece for decades.

In 1833 Otto's government, in collaboration with those religious leaders who sympathized with the Russian model for a government-dependent Orthodox church, founded an autocephalous national Greek Orthodox church independent of the Istanbul Greek Patriarchate and nationalized some large monastic properties. The new church fell under the authority of a synod headed by the archbishop of Athens, who was responsible to the government through a procurator. The action aroused the ire of the Greek patriarch and the enmity of the dispossessed monks, all of whom despised the young ruler and his associates as Catholics. The split within Greece's Orthodox ranks between pro-synod and pro-patriarchal factions was resolved only in 1850, when the Russians convinced the patriarchate to recognize the Greek national church's autocephaly.

Native Greek political leaders were divided into three camps—pro-British, pro-Russian, and pro-French—yet all were united in their distrust and resentment of Otto. After attaining his majority in 1835, Otto attempted to appease Greek public opinion by ridding his governing cabinet of most Bavarians. Unfortunately, he relished the role of autocratic ruler and acted as his own prime minister. Greek distrust and resentment turned to animosity. In 1843 the pro-British and pro-Russian parties revolted against Otto's domination, but the two pursued different agendas—the pro-British faction sought a constitutional monarchy while the pro-Russians demanded an Orthodox ruler. Neither could impose its program because the army, acting on its own initiative, intervened in Athens and forced Otto to accept a constitution (1844).

The 1844 constitution called for a popularly elected assembly, an appointed senate, and an Orthodox successor to the throne. Otto turned to the pro-French party for support and organized a government-controlled political machine—the "System"—that imposed a French-style administration which ensured that Otto's nominated candidates were returned in all elections. Because the pro-French party enjoyed the support of the majority of Greeks and professed allegiance to the "Great

Idea," Otto's corrupt "System" elicited little opposition. Fear of unleashing a radical social revolution prevented the pro-British and pro-Russian parties from actively moving against the government.

Otto's irredentist foreign policy regarding Ottoman territories north of Greece's border earned him Great Britain's displeasure but much popularity among his subjects. During the Crimean War, with pro-Russian popular sympathies running high, Otto permitted Greek guerrilla bands to operate in Ottoman Thessaly and Epiros. In retaliation, a combined British-French fleet occupied Athens' port of Piraias (1854-57), forcing the government to recall the insurgent bands and muffle its territorial claims.

In the economic arena, Greece was devastated by the rebellion's effects. Great swaths of olive groves and vineyards, which constituted the staples of Greek agriculture but required years of intensive effort for market fruition, lay destroyed. Most buildings were either damaged or ruined. Otto's Bavarian administration did little to relieve the peasants' plight. The state's mountainous terrain made agricultural land a premium. Although former Turkish-owned lands were confiscated as state lands, some of which initially were distributed to peasants, much passed into the hands of local church primates. A gradual process of uncoordinated and unplanned land distribution emerged, but, when peasants did acquire land, their cultivation techniques remained primitive and underproductive. The lack of adequate infrastructure, especially roads, kept markets undersupplied. The situation on the land was so bad that many peasants actually emigrated to Ottoman territories for escape.

The backwardness of Greek handicraft industries relative to Western European industrialized manufacturing doomed them in the competitive marketplace. Only the shipping industry portended a viable economic future. The Greek merchant marine rapidly recovered its wartime losses and regained its dominant position in Black Sea and eastern Mediterranean trade. That predominance held until foreign competitors introduced steamships at the end of the nineteenth century, after which the Greek merchant marine was forced to buy discarded steamships from the foreigners, since no industrial base for producing such vessels existed in Greece.

Although Otto's nationalist policies during the Crimean War earned him popularity, he lost that support within six years of the war's end. During the Franco-Habsburg War of 1859 fought in northern Italy, Otto espoused the Habsburg cause while most Greeks sympathized with the Italians and their French patrons. His monarchist views were unwelcome to a new generation of Greek politicians schooled at the national University of Athens. Having learned through the Western-style curriculum of the Greeks' classical past (most Greek peasants were ignorant of ancient Greek history, while many middle-class Greeks retained their consciously Byzantine heritage), the young leaders were inspired by images of Athenian democracy as well as by Rousseau's and Locke's concepts. To make matters worse for Otto, he was childless, which constitutionally disqualified any other Catholic

Wittelsbach prince from succeeding him, and he enjoyed no active support among the three protecting Great Powers.

In October 1862 Otto was toppled by his political opponents and fled back to Bavaria. A provisional government immediately declared the Wittelsbachs deposed. Forced by the Great Powers to find an acceptable new Western ruler, a member of the obscure Danish Glücksburg family, Prince William George, was enticed to mount the vacant Greek throne (1863). King George I (1863-1913) brought with him the formerly British Ionian Islands, which were turned over in return for promises to refrain from anti-Ottoman irredentism. In 1864 George swore allegiance to a new constitution issued by the national assembly that imposed a democratic constitutional monarchy. The ruler's prerogatives were strictly limited by shared authority with a parliament elected by adult male suffrage. King George won popularity and longevity by his willingness to abide by the constitution's provisions.

The Revolution of 1848 and a Unified Romanian State

When Ypsilantis invaded Moldavia in 1821, he counted on the armed support of one Tudor Vladimirescu, an exceptionally wealthy Romanian peasant who, at the head of a small band of followers, sought social and political reform in the Romanian Principalities. After the Russians repudiated Ypsilantis, Vladimirescu turned on him and helped the Ottomans drive the Greek *hetairia* nationalists out of Moldavia. When he called for allegiance to a briefly constituted *boier*-led government in Bucharest, however, Vladimirescu lost his peasant following and was turned over to the Phanariote authorities for execution as a rebel.

Vladimirescu's activities marked the beginning of the end for Phanariote rule in the Romanian principalities. After 1821 the Ottomans appointed native Romanian *boiers,* rather than Phanariotes, as *hospodars,* whose class-oriented sense of Romanian self-identity now was reinforced by Transylvanian-fostered Latinism. The post-1821 *boier* leadership began replacing Greek with Romanian (written in Latin letters) as the administrative and educational language in the principalities. French ideas formerly imported into Wallachia and Moldavia by the Phanariotes were turned against them by the newly empowered *boier* leaders, who looked to France for models of all things "Latin."

Under the terms of the Edirne Treaty, Russia occupied Wallachia and Moldavia in 1829. To appear "(Western) European," Tsar Nicholas I's (1825-55) military officers were decidedly Francophil in their conscious cultural affectations—speaking French, mimicking French manners and etiquette, and indulging in French entertainments. Thus the Russian occupation served to intensify the Romanian *boiers'* pro-French Latinist proclivities. Students from *boier* families were sent to study at French universities and returned ardent Francophiles. The *boier* leadership grew so deeply enamored of all things French that their native Romanian language nearly disappeared from their homes. The appearance of the principalities' larger cities, where the *boiers* resided, was transformed by adopted French-style architecture. In Bucharest, Wallachia's capital, French-style structures grew so numerous that the *boiers* proudly dubbed it the "Paris of the Balkans."

In 1833 *boier* intellectuals founded the Philharmonic Society, which served as a front to mask young Romantic nationalists' activities. The society called for Wallachia's and Moldavia's unification into a single, liberal-democratic Romanian state. Throughout the 1830s the Philharmonic Society's example was followed by a number of cultural organizations, each espousing an activist national agenda. The most radical was the secret *Frăția* (Brotherhood), formed in 1843, which embraced a national and social revolutionary platform. Romanian students in Paris particularly were active in the national movement, forming a Society of Romanian Students that openly called for a liberal-democratic, united Romania. The student society established close ties with the French liberal opposition to King Louis Philippe's monarchy (1830-48) and with leaders of the Polish nationalist emigration in Paris, including Adam Czartoryski and Adam Mickiewicz.

Russian occupation proved both beneficial and detrimental to Romanian national interests. The Edirne Treaty returned the principalities to native rule for the first time in over a century, abolished the annual tribute paid to the Ottomans, and assured commercial freedoms. Such benefits were counterbalanced by the fact that they were granted by Russian fiat. To cement Russia's standing as the principalities' protector Great Power, Russian-created governing statutes—"Organic Regulations"—were imposed in both.

The regulations for Wallachia and Moldavia virtually were identical and explicitly recognized the ethnonational commonality of the two principalities. Each was to be ruled by a prince elected by a national assembly and advised by an administrative council. New judicial, financial, military, and economic systems were introduced, and Russia's pervasive protecting role was confirmed. The regulations concentrated power in the *boiers'* hands and marginalized the peasantry, who lost land under the new property laws and found their pastoral and common usage rights severely restricted, leading to increasingly endemic rural unrest. The Organic Regulations ironically proved both modernizing and reactionary.

The dependent nature of the principalities was inescapable. Rather than being elected by the Romanian *boiers,* the new princes were chosen by foreign Great Powers. Russia imposed Alexandru Ghica as Wallachian prince (1834-42) while the Ottomans turned Moldavia over to Mihai Sturdza (1834-49). Both faced constant Russian interference in their affairs, difficult economic conditions caused by six years of Russian military occupation, and domestic problems associated with the traditionally inequitable sociopolitical system cemented by the governing regulations that they were constrained to follow.

In Wallachia, Ghica was amenable to national and reform ideas, but his strict enforcement of the regulations, over which he recognized Russian and Ottoman veto authority, earned him a great deal of animosity from Wallachian politicians. Fearful of irking the Russians in any way, Ghica rescinded the Philharmonic Society's government subsidy, repressed radical émigré Bulgarian nationalists who had established themselves in Bucharest, and unsuccessfully attempted to enact agrarian reforms. By 1840 Ghica had lost all native Romanian political support, and two years later (1842) he was dismissed as prince by the Russians, who had become convinced that he was incapable of ruling effectively. Ghica's successor, Gheorghe Bibescu (1842-49), was so conscious of the Russian presence that he essentially continued Ghica's unfavorable policies. Despite his real achievements—expanding the army, forging a customs union with Moldavia, stabilizing finances, and improving Bucharest's urban planning—he too earned the enmity of the native radical nationalists by enacting other overtly pro-Russian and antirevolutionary policies.

In Moldavia, Sturdza, a Russian sycophant, also proved a shrewd, skilled, and firm ruler. He easily imposed his will by having the authorization for Russian and Ottoman veto powers on the regulations accepted without acrimony. The cooperation of native politicians permitted Sturdza to implement tighter fiscal controls, create a postal service, undertake infrastructural improvements, develop the Danube port city of Galaţi for expanded commercial purposes, and found the University of Iaşi in his capital. Sturdza, however, proved increasingly despotic and rapaciously avaricious, using the throne to enhance his immense personal wealth. When revolutionary activity erupted within Moldavia in 1848, Sturdza nipped it in the bud, but he survived only a year longer because his lurid personal dealings lost him any continued Moldavian and Russian support.

During the 1848 Revolution in Paris, resident Romanian students actively participated—the Romanian flag proudly flew over the Hôtel de Ville, along with the flags of France, Poland, and Italy. Full of Romantic nationalist and liberal notions, many student revolutionaries returned to Wallachia and Moldavia and set in motion plans for establishing an independent and united Romania. Their Western European-oriented outlook was decidedly anti-Russian, portraying Tsar Nicholas as the "policeman" of Europe. While in France, many had published writings intended to convince Western Europeans that an independent, united Romania could act as a barrier against Russian western encroachment.

The radical student nationalists' first revolutionary effort—a poorly organized uprising in Iaşi, the Moldavian capital—was crushed handily by Sturdza. In Wallachia, the revolutionaries' efforts enjoyed more success. After Prince Bibescu, at Russian insistence, rejected petitions for national reforms, riots erupted in

Bucharest. Bibescu then lost his nerve. In June 1848 he accepted a revolutionary constitution and resigned. The ensuing revolutionary provisional government promptly decreed reforms abolishing class ranks and implementing liberal freedoms. The new government also declared its willingness to unite Wallachia with Moldavia into a single Romanian state.

Wallachia's revolutionary success was short-lived. The rebels counted on Ottoman support to prevent Russian intervention. Indeed, the Wallachian developments pleased the Ottomans, who resented and feared Russia's proximity to their Balkan border—Sultan Abdülmecid personally would have welcomed the unification of the principalities to serve as a buffer between his empire and Russia. Britain and France were unwilling, however, to forcefully oppose Russia's demand that Wallachia's revolutionary regime be eradicated. Abdülmecid then had no other recourse than to invade the principality and overthrow the provisional government, whose leaders fled the state.

Without active Great Power support, the principalities' revolutions were doomed from the start. Furthermore, the young revolutionaries' outlook was flawed. Products of middle-class and *boier* families, they failed to consider the peasants in their programs. Only a few grasped the perilousness of the peasant situation, and fewer still desired a social revolution. Most sought *boier* support for their national reforms. By ignoring the peasantry's problems, the revolutionary provisional government ultimately forestalled any possible mass support, and, to the end, the nationalists remained numerically few and isolated from the general population. After the revolution collapsed, they continued on in the same fashion, with radicals dreaming of a liberal-democratic, united Romanian state and conservatives seeking a unified Romania free of Russian control.

The united Romania of the nationalists' dreams ultimately was granted them as a gift by French Emperor Napoleon III (President Louis Napoleon, 1848-52; emperor, 1852-70), a self-proclaimed champion of ethnonational rights. Napoleon III became involved in Ottoman affairs as an outgrowth of his personal domestic political agenda. In building support for his bid to be crowned French emperor, President Louis Napoleon courted the Catholic party, which led him to make a show of defending Catholic interests in a trivial quarrel with the Greek Orthodox Patriarchate over control of certain Christian shrines in the Ottoman-controlled Holy Lands. With France distracted by the revolutionary and Napoleonic episodes during the late eighteenth and early nineteenth centuries, the traditionally shared control of the shrines had fallen exclusively into Orthodox hands. In 1850 Napoleon began pressuring Sultan Abdülmecid on the Catholics' behalf, and, by 1852, the sultan made a number of pro-Catholic concessions regarding the shrines.

Orthodox Russia backed the patriarchate in the matter of the shrines, and Napoleon's activities sparked anti-French opinion among the Russians, who became incensed that the Catholics had won concessions from the sultan. The resurgence of old Catholic-Orthodox cultural animosities led to the breakdown of French-Russian negotiations over the matter. Britain became involved after Tsar Nicholas, using as an excuse an ambiguous article regarding Russia's right to "protect" Orthodox Ottoman subjects contained in the 1774 Kyuchuk Kainardzha Treaty, threatened the Ottomans with military action. Confident of British and French support, the Ottoman government's stance against the Russian pressures grew strident. Two years of intense diplomatic efforts failed to stem the situation's deterioration. In October 1853 Russian-Ottoman warfare broke out along the Danube, and, in March 1854, Britain and France declared war on Russia to protect the Ottoman Empire from threatened invasion and forced dissolution.

The Romanian Principalities played a marginally important role in the resulting Crimean War. In the early days of the war, Russian forces were concentrated in the principalities for an invasion of Ottoman territory. Tsar Nicholas counted on the traditional support of the Habsburgs, who shared Russia's anti-Ottoman interests, to protect his flank and rear during the planned Balkan campaign. Nicholas miscalculated. Habsburg Emperor Francis Joseph (1848-1916) had no wish to participate actively in the conflict. Prussia gradually was muscling the Habsburgs out of German Central Europe, and the only area where they could hope to demonstrate their continuing Great Power imperial status was the Balkans. Circumstances thus transformed the former allies into competitors regarding Balkan expansion. As war erupted, Francis Joseph had no wish to see Russia move deeper into the peninsula or even remain in the Romanian Principalities.

In June 1854 the Habsburgs issued an ultimatum demanding that Russia cancel its planned Balkan invasion and evacuate the principalities. The "Four Points" agreement (August 1854) among the Habsburgs, Britain, and France transferred protection of Serbia and the Romanian Principalities from Russia to the "European" Great Powers, guaranteed the open passage of the Danube Delta, abolished Russia's "protectorate" of Ottoman Orthodox subjects, and restricted Russia's access to the Dardanelles-Bosphorus straits. Nicholas evacuated the Romanian Principalities for fear of bringing the Habsburgs into the war against him. As Russian troops withdrew, Habsburg forces took their places for the duration of the war. A Habsburg general military mobilization in October constrained Nicholas to accept the "Four Points."

Nicholas died in 1855 while the war still raged in the Crimea, and his successor, Alexander II (1855-81), sought a way to end the fighting. The fall of the Russian stronghold of Sebastopol in September 1855 led to extended diplomatic peace efforts. At Napoleon's insistence, the peace conference that convened in February 1856 met in Paris with all of the European Great Powers in attendance.

Napoleon urged the unification of the Romanian Principalities into a single autonomous state under a foreign prince. The Habsburgs, fearful of the proposal's impact on their Transylvanian Romanian subjects, stood in strong opposition. So too did the Ottomans, who saw unification as the last stage before the principalities' outright independence. Britain, which considered the principalities too strategically important to be removed permanently from Ottoman suzerainty, sided with the Ottomans. Prussia, which sought to weaken the Habsburgs by any means, backed Napoleon, who also surprisingly found support from the Russians because they saw his proposal as a way to continue Russian influence among the Romanians while driving a wedge between Britain and France.

No final settlement of the Romanian question was reached at Paris. It was decided to put off a decision until the wishes of the Romanians themselves could be ascertained through democratically elected assemblies representing all classes in the principalities' populations. Although the plan appeared workable in theory, it was unrealistic in practice. Autocratic and aristocratic traditions, combined with mass illiteracy and social inequity, led to electoral fraud and intimidation. The elections in Moldavia (1857), conducted under blatant intimidation by Ottoman-appointed officials, produced an anti-unionist assembly, causing a serious rift among the Great Powers. Over Britain's opposition, France, Russia, and Prussia demanded that the results be annulled. Abdülmecid refused, diplomatic relations with him were broken, and war threatened. Personal conversations between Napoleon and British Queen Victoria (1819-1901) led to a compromise that defused the hostile atmosphere. In return for annulling the first election, Napoleon agreed that the Romanian Principalities remain divided but endowed with identical civil and military institutions.

When new elections were held in both principalities and the representative assemblies met in Bucharest and Iaşi in October 1857, they both voted overwhelmingly to unite into a single Romanian state, an autonomous constitutional principality under Ottoman suzerainty and ruled by a foreign prince. The Romanians' fait accompli placed the Great Powers in an awkward position. After lengthy deliberations, they issued the Paris Convention (1858), declaring that Wallachia and Moldavia were to remain separate and ruled by native princes. Each was to elect its own representative assembly, but affairs common to both were to be handled by a joint Central Commission with equal representation from the two. The convention's clumsy, artificial arrangement lasted less than six months. With war clouds looming between France and the Habsburgs in Italy (1859), the Wallachian and Moldavian assemblies met separately, and each unanimously elected as prince the same individual, Romanian *boier* and military officer Alexandru Cuza (1859-66).

Cuza's joint election, although symbolic of Romanian unity, did little to overcome the cumbersome administrations imposed on the two principalities by the Paris Convention. Dual administrations, which ensured massive duplication of effort, mired the two states in bureaucratic gridlock. Cuza faced repeated internal crises and political instability. He was a poor administrator and speaker, unable to push policies through to their conclusion. Most of the politically sophisticated *boiers* opposed his regime, and his distaste for public ceremonies or speeches lost him the chance to win mass popular support. In spite of his handicaps, however, Cuza did achieve some important political and economic successes.

Tired of the wasted personal time and effort in dealing with two separate administrations, Cuza lobbied hard in Istanbul for a true personal union of the principalities. In December 1861 his efforts were rewarded. With French support, Cuza won the Great Powers' assent for the formal unification of Wallachia and Moldavia into a single, autonomous Romanian state. Cuza designated Bucharest his capital, to the disappointment of the Moldavians, who desired that honor for Iaşi (See Map 7.)

Cuza followed unification with a flood of reform efforts. First, he solidified his ruling position by carrying out a bloodless coup d'état against the powerful *boier* opposition. He conducted an overwhelmingly successful mass plebiscite (1864) regarding a new constitution granting increased authority to the prince and a new voting law with universal suffrage. Cuza then rapidly instituted a series of reforms: Obligatory public education (and new universities in Bucharest and Iaşi); a civil code like that of France; judicial improvements (including limited trial by jury); tax reforms; and selected government monopolies.

Cuza's most important and controversial reform was the 1864 Agrarian Law. As a *boier,* he differed in one important way from most others of his class: He possessed a sense of social responsibility. Cuza recognized the peasants' miserable plight and sincerely wished to improve their situation. Serfdom was a thing of the past in Western Europe and Russia, but Romanian *boier* and church landowners adamantly clung to their stranglehold on peasant labor. This fact was the underlying motivation for Cuza's coup.

Assisted by his chief minister, the Moldavian reformer Mihail Kogălniceanu, Cuza's rural reforms started in late 1863 with the expropriation of lands owned by Greek-dominated monasteries, an act that threatened no native landowner. When a bill giving peasants clear title to the land that they tilled was killed in the national assembly by solid *boier* opposition, Cuza dissolved the assembly, called for the plebiscite, and carried out his coup. The agrarian law that followed abolished all restrictions on peasant movement, eliminated all labor and kind dues to landlords, granted peasants land in an amount totaling up to two-thirds of any given landowner's holdings, and compensated the *boiers* for their losses with state bonds.

Despite good intentions, however, the law failed to solve the peasantry's problems. Enforcement was the responsibility of *boier*-dominated local authorities. The two-thirds provision permitted the *boiers* to retain immense amounts of land in regions with low populations, while in densely inhabited regions state lands were swallowed up to provide peasants with adequate plots. What land the peasants received was soon fragmented into ever smaller plots by the traditional process of equal inheritance among a growing population. Rather than creating the intended small peasant proprietor class, the 1864 reform actually spawned a peasantry possessed of increasingly inadequate landholdings, reducing them to near-total economic dependence on the still-large landowning *boier* class. The peasants remained land-hungry, depressed, poor, and dissatisfied.

Although a benevolent autocrat, Cuza earned the irreconcilable hatred of fellow *boiers* though his coup and the agrarian reform. His personal failings ultimately played into his enemies' hands. He flagrantly cheated on his wife, who hailed from the powerful Rosetti *boier* family. His aversion to public appearances left the peasants, confused and uncertain because of the problems surrounding the agrarian reform, without assurance from their ruler and lukewarm toward his fate. By early 1866 these shortcomings, combined with his fiscal laxities that left the treasury bankrupt and many government and military officials unpaid for months on end, undermined Cuza's governing ability.

In February 1866 Cuza was forced to abdicate by disgruntled military officers, and he fled to Vienna. The choice for his successor fell on Prince Karl of Hohenzollern-Sigmaringen, a cousin of the Prussian king. Encouraged to accept the Romanian crown by Prussian Chancellor Otto von Bismarck (1862-90), who was about to initiate war against the Habsburgs and saw a Hohenzollern-ruled Romania as strategically advantageous, Karl agreed. A young man of regal bearing, Prince Karl (Carol) I (1866-81; King Carol I, 1881-1914) impressed his new subjects. He accepted existing Romanian institutions as they stood and earned the support of the *boier* class.

CHAPTER ELEVEN

Ottoman "Reform" Efforts

Centuries of continuous competitive interaction with Western Europe and Russia left traditional Ottoman society destabilized and fragmenting. Western Europe's unique secular and scientific development proved almost invincible in direct competition with that of non-Western societies. From the late seventeenth century, Orthodox Eastern European Russia, beginning with Tsar Peter I the Great, recognized that fact and adapted Western European models as best it could, eventually ensuring its position as a "European" Great Power. During the eighteenth and nineteenth centuries, only one other non-Western society managed to preserve its independent cultural existence in the face of overwhelming pressures on its native institutions exerted by direct contact with the West: The Ottoman Empire. It did so by making adaptations—euphemistically termed "reforms" by westerners—in response to mounting Western imperialist and nationalist pressures during the nineteenth century. Although those adaptations often were halfhearted and only partially effective—earning the Ottoman Empire the cynical title of "Sick Man of Europe" bestowed by Russian Tsar Nicholas I—they succeeded in preserving the empire into the early twentieth century, despite its losing half of its Balkan possessions.

Early Adaptive Efforts

The Ottomans were among the first non-European civilized societies to face the problem of direct competition with Western European scientific-technological, economic, and political-national development. Beginning with the defeat before

Vienna in 1683, and continuing through the eighteenth century, Ottoman imperial fortunes in Europe obviously were on the wane. As history has repeatedly demonstrated, however, it was safer for the government to rationalize that situation than to undertake disruptive changes in society's traditional structure. Even minor attempts along those lines could be dangerous for a sultan. When Ahmed III imported a few European military advisors to help improve Ottoman military effectiveness (1718), he was deposed by members of the military and religious elite for being too pro-Western European. Those who eventually came to realize that changes were necessary for the empire's continued survival had no desire to be "westernized" in the process—they sought to both adapt *and* retain their Islamic cultural identity.

Ottoman "adaptive" reform efforts began after Sultan Selim III ascended to the throne (1789). Selim, whose education prior to his reign included some tutelage in Western European mores and thought, realized that something needed to be done to reverse his empire's fortunes. The most obvious problem lay with the military, so he addressed that issue by gathering a small group of officials who shared his views and charging them with devising a way to improve the empire's forces. He and his associates assumed that upgrading the military along European lines alone would suffice to save their state.

Selim convinced some of the high military-administrative officials and *ulema* members of the necessity for emulating Western ways. European instructors and weapons were imported and a Western-style army regiment—the *Nazami Cedid* ("Newly Ordered" troops)—was created. Dressed in modified European-style uniforms, the new troops were drilled in Western European military techniques, given a Western command structure, and paid from a special treasury account created expressly for them. The *Nazami Cedid* played a leading role in repelling Napoleon's invasion of Palestine (1799), demonstrating that the new military approach might be fruitful. It also appeared to provide the sultan with an effective force against domestic political opponents.

Those opponents, mostly conservative military-administrative and Islamic religious leaders, understood the implications of Selim's military reform. Fearful that the military changes represented the first step toward dismantling the traditional system, and led by the Janissaries, who had most to lose by reforms, Selim's opponents revolted (1807). For reasons still unclear, Selim balked at using the *Nazami Cedid* against the rebels. (Perhaps he detested the thought of sparking civil war too much to offer resistance.) He acquiesced to the rebels' demands for disbanding the new force and eliminating reformers in the government. The Western-style military reform experiment was ended. Many of the disbanded *Nazami* soldiers and deposed reformist government officials fled the capital and found refuge with various Balkan *ayans*.

Shortly after the coup, Selim was replaced by Mustafa IV. In reaction, an army of Balkan *ayan* forces descended on Istanbul (1808), entered the capital, killed

Mustafa, and replaced him with Mahmud II. When most of the *ayans,* smug with victory, then returned to their lands, however, the conservatives staged another uprising, murdering Selim but sparing Mahmud because he was the last remaining male of the ruling Ottoman house.

Mahmud proved a patient and cunning ruler. He spent the next eighteen years cultivating friends among the military-administrative and religious leadership, carefully and progressively staffing important government posts with those he trusted and found personally loyal. He bought the support of others, especially of religious leaders, through enticing financial arrangements. So successful was Mahmud in forging a broad-based personal constituency that even many conservatives found themselves supporting his reign. Outwardly Mahmud acted the traditional sultan, upholding traditional values and institutions. Secretly he harbored the same reforming ideas as the unfortunate Selim.

The stupidity of the militantly radical conservative Janissaries abetted Mahmud's covert plans for changing the Ottoman military. The actions of the Janissaries (more an unruly praetorian guard than an effective military force) during the years Mahmud spent currying favor earned them ill-repute among the general population. They often refused to fight the empire's foreign enemies, and their proclivities for widespread extortion were hated by all and sundry. While the Janissaries' disrepute grew, Mahmud managed by various means to restore much of his authority over many independent-minded Balkan *ayans.* Gradually the obstreperous Janissaries were isolated within Ottoman society, with even traditional conservatives unwilling to support or justify their actions.

In 1826 Mahmud moved against the Janissaries and the conservatives. All the while he had publicly played the traditional sultan, he inconspicuously had made moderate changes in some traditional army units, notably in the artillery corps. When in June he announced the formation of a Western-style military unit composed of the best Janissary troops and the demobilization of the rest, the Istanbul Janissaries rebelled. Mahmud unleashed his upgraded artillery units against them and called on the city's population for support. The Janissaries, caught off guard, holed up in their barracks, where Mahmud's artillery pounded them into submission. Provincial Janissary garrisons experienced a similar fate. In the end, thousands of Janissaries were killed, while equal numbers deserted. Mahmud disbanded the Janissary corps and reestablished the central government's control over its military, depriving the conservative opposition of their traditional armed support. Thereafter, the Ottoman military played a leading role in all reform efforts.

Having disposed of the Janissaries, Mahmud enacted a moderate military and governmental reform program. He permitted the publication of the first Ottoman newspaper, but its circulation was limited almost exclusively to government officials. He opened new secondary schools to train young military officers and government officials in Western European techniques, but they were few in number and posed no threat to traditional religious education. Lacking any real knowledge of modern Western-style economics, nonmilitary technologies, and politics, Mahmud did not consider changes in those areas of Ottoman society.

After the Janissaries' demise, thousands of men remained under arms in the Ottoman military, fragmented into a number of regional forces without any real centralized structure. To make matters worse, the Greek Revolution was in full swing and Russia threatened military intervention over both Greece and Serbia. The divided forces were proving unable to cope even with the anarchistic and uncoordinated Greek rebels, let alone the possibility of facing the Russian military machine. Mahmud needed immediate military reform but circumstances worked against him. Unable to quell the Greek Revolution, Mahmud called upon the westernized troops of his independent-minded Egyptian governor Mehmed Ali (1805-48). The Battle of Navarino, however, prevented the Egyptians from suppressing the Greek rebellion and led to the Greeks' ultimate victory.

Thanks to Great Power imperial interests in maintaining the Ottoman Empire's existence, Mahmud survived the military defeats of the Greek Revolution, the subsequent war with Russia (1828-29), and the rebellious actions of Mehmed Ali in Syria and Palestine throughout the 1830s. Slowed by the frictions of military traditionalism, ignorance of Western European concepts and techniques, and the reluctance of most Ottoman officers (and many soldiers) to adopt the ways of their traditional cultural enemies, Mahmud managed to initiate his Western-style military reforms. He dealt harshly with those who opposed him. A hotbed of conservative opposition was Bosnia, where the local Muslim *beys* dominated the region's administration on a par with the *ayans*. Mahmud imposed a modicum of central control over Bosnia in the 1830s, forcing the *beys* to relinquish their monopoly on the region's internal affairs. The government's ultimate success in imposing its authority in Bosnia, however, required a lengthy military suppression of the *beys'* resistance, ending only in 1850, long after Mahmud's death.

While dealing with his rebellious Bosnian *beys,* Mahmud's military reforms progressed. A Western-style pyramidical command structure and unit organization was instituted, and the army was divided into standing and reserve forces. Supreme command was removed from the provincial governors and assumed by the central government. Conscription was enacted (but volunteers were accepted), and recruits were furnished with European-style training and weapons (when possible). Western military advisors (mostly Prussians) assisted in the process. Although the government's military expenditures soared, slow but steady progress was made. At Mahmud's death, the new army remained a work in progress, but the ground was laid for future military efficiency.

In the area of administratively restructuring the government, Mahmud proceeded along European lines, instituting departments headed by ministers, each assigned specific duties and responsibilities. In an effort to stifle corruption and *bakşiş*, functionaries were paid regular salaries rather than fees for services rendered. A new postal system was created, and a regular census system was developed to regulate taxation and military conscription. The *Divan* was replaced by a pseudo-cabinet, composed of the new ministers and officials representing administrative departments, and legislative bodies were appointed to enact new laws. The reforms were intended to centralize the sultan's authority through Western-style institutions. Again, by the time of Mahmud's death, the administrative reforms only were in progress—not all of them functioned effectively or were fully implemented.

Implementation was key to adaptive reform and proved a major problem early on. Ignorance, inefficiency, lack of enthusiasm, cultural repugnance, and personal reluctance or uncertainty on the part of those responsible for carrying out reform orders all played a role in hindering change. Centuries of conflict with Christian Europeans bred prejudice, disdain, and fear regarding all things Western. These attitudes had to be overcome before adaptive reforms could take hold. Mahmud understood this. He realized that ignorance of European languages prevented the knowledge of European ways that was necessary for the reforms to work. Language training for Ottoman government functionaries was shifted from Persian and Arabic to French (especially), German, and English, and each government department was required to offer such schooling. Those who excelled in the new languages quickly rose to the most important offices in Mahmud's government.

Mahmud made a start toward successful adaptive changes in official Ottoman society, but progress was slow. Reforms were supported more enthusiastically by younger members of the military and government, but the older ones, who held the superior positions, were far less committed. It took years before those younger enthusiasts rose to the top leadership positions and for Mahmud's reform vision to take secure hold.

The *Tanzimat* Period

Abdülmecid I, Mahmud's son and successor, was committed to continuing his father's adaptive reform policy. He was assisted in his efforts by Mustafa Reşid Paşa, past Ottoman ambassador to France and Britain and Mahmud's former foreign minister. There gathered around Reşid a group of like-minded "reformers" dedicated to preserving the empire through Western European-like political, military, economic, and educational adaptations while retaining Ottoman government, Islamic beliefs and practices, and most traditional customs and mores. Reşid and his followers acquired the name "Men of the *Tanzimat*" (from *tanzimatçılar,* meaning "those who give order to things"). Because they were responsible for the more radical Ottoman reform efforts made during the middle half of the nineteenth century, that period came to be known as the *Tanzimat*.

Two unsettling facts stemming from the empire's destabilized condition were apparent to the *Tanzimat* group: The Ottoman state was becoming a helpless pawn in the imperialist policies of the European Great Powers; and Western-inspired nationalism threatened to strip the empire of its Balkan territories and resources. It was clear that Britain, France, and Russia permitted the empire's survival only so long as it served their interests in the eastern Mediterranean. If their objectives were attainable through alternative means, the empire could do little to defend its continued existence. The spread of nationalism among the empire's non-Muslim Balkan subjects potentially offered the Great Powers that alternative by creating Christian European client states carved from the Ottomans' Balkan territories. The Serbian and Greek ethnonational revolutions demonstrated the fatal consequences of such a development for the empire and its Islamic society—well over 35,000 Muslim inhabitants of those regions had been either killed or driven out by the Christian rebels.

Under such grave circumstances, the *Tanzimat* group's aim of maintaining the Ottoman Empire through adaptations of Western European models while preserving the essence of traditional Islamic society was well neigh impossible. Its members had no choice, however, but to try. That their efforts ultimately succeeded in preserving the empire into the 1920s is a testament to their determination and dedication, but their success proved relative. The Ottoman Empire survived only at the expense of many of its Islamic traditions.

According to the *Tanzimat* group's assessment of the situation, an elemental change in the state's nature was necessary. In November 1839 Abdülmecid issued a decree framed by the group—the *Hatti Hümayun* (imperial edict) of Gülhane—outlining plans for radical changes aimed at bringing efficiency to the central government and stability to the provinces. He proclaimed that all of his subjects possessed government-guaranteed "rights" to life, honor, and wealth (and thus were not merely taxpayers). To that end, he decreed a new penal code and created a new judicial council charged with framing laws protecting those rights. Tax farming was abolished and replaced by a regular system for assessing and levying taxes. Personal property was declared inviolate. Codes of conduct for government officials and bureaucrats were enacted. A military council was created to head the army, and equitable conscription (restricted to Muslim subjects) was mandated.

Abdülmecid's proclamation modified the role of the traditional Islamic state, which no longer would be concerned exclusively with defense, protecting religious belief, and maintaining civil order while leaving such social activities as education and economic life to *millets* or individuals. Western European–like state activism was adopted, and, for the first time, the Ottomans planned to implement civil laws and schools free of the Islamic religious leadership, to stimulate the economy, and to upgrade the state's infrastructure.

The 1839 *Hatti Hümayun* proved difficult to implement. Most successes were scored in government administration. Actual ministries, headed by ministers, slowly were created. Each was staffed by officials given specialized training in their areas of responsibility. (Formerly, all functionaries conducted whatever tasks any given situation demanded.) A Council of Ministers advised the sultan and regulated the ministries' activities. While administrative changes aped Western European models, there were significant differences. Ministers were responsible directly to the sultan and not to any representative assembly, political party, or the grand *vezir* (whose newly defined position resembled that of a European prime minister). There were no political parties to speak of, other than those that formed around particularly influential individuals. The sultan and his grand *vezirs* constantly were forced to play politics with the various ministers, many of whom were not reformers and actively tried to block or slow the reforms. Fear of a conservative backlash that might end their efforts completely kept the pace of reforms slow.

The *Tanzimat* group's reforms also achieved gradual success in the area of infrastructural improvements. Abdülmecid's government repaired and improved existing roads and constructed numerous new ones. A small amount of railroad track was laid with Western European assistance. Telegraph lines were erected connecting the major provincial centers with the capital. A postal system was established that took full advantage of the new means of travel and communication. Although progress was excruciatingly slow, its benefits were substantial. Infrastructural improvements eventually resulted in more efficient central administration and new markets for the empire's commercial classes.

Slow but steady progress also was made in reforming education. Religious *medreses* did not provide the technical training required by the transformed government and military. During the *Tanzimat* period the number of government departmental technical schools was expanded and new nongovernment schools were established, including teacher training schools and a system of middle schools to prepare religiously trained students for study in advanced technical institutions. It took time to develop the number of teachers needed for widespread Western-style technical education, and, by the late 1860s, less than 3 percent of the population actually attended any of the new schools. Educational successes lay predominantly in training students for the military and bureaucracy, from which there emerged a small educated elite who embraced the *Tanzimat* group's reform efforts.

The failures of the 1839 *Hatti Hümayun* equaled its successes. In the areas of finance and economics, the reforms proved ineffective. Despite improvement in the reorganized central government's effectiveness, it never ensured that the population fully paid its taxes. There were not enough qualified government functionaries and financial resources to replace the tax farmers speedily or compile the extensive assessment data necessary for crucial large-scale taxation. Few government officials possessed firsthand expertise in commerce or manufacturing. Ignorant of Western-style industrialism, unfamiliar with market mechanics, and totally lacking factories, machinery, managers, and trained workers, the Ottomans could not compete realistically with the Europeans in the economic sphere. Moreover, the old "capitulations" system with the Europeans had degenerated by the nineteenth century into a European stranglehold on Ottoman foreign trade.

The reforms also failed to live up to the 1839 proclamation's spirit of equality for all of the empire's subjects. Although equal rights in matters of taxation, justice, education, social respect, and public office-holding were decreed for all of the empire's subjects, these often were ignored or poorly implemented in the provinces. A major problem of inequality lay in the realm of military service, for which only Muslims originally were eligible. Since the military enjoyed extensive police powers and frequently served as a stepping-stone for advancement within the governing administration, the inability of non-Muslims to enter its ranks was disadvantageous. They were left at the penal and judicial mercy of local authorities (who might or might not act as the reformers planned) and were effectively barred from entering local or central government service.

Abdülmecid and the *Tanzimat* group recognized the snaillike pace and many failings of the reforms. Facing the real possibility of serious conservative reaction, they bided their time, hoping that a propitious opportunity for more decisive action would arise. The 1856 Paris Peace Conference provided them with such an opening. One week prior to the conference, Abdülmecid issued a new *Hatti Hümayun* reaffirming the 1839 proclamation's principles, asserting the full equality of non-Muslim and Muslim subjects, and requiring the use of Turkish (cleansed of archaic Persian and Arabic terms) as the empire's official administrative language. One aspect of the new decree particularly was important for the Balkans: Realizing that the *millet* administrations suffered liabilities similar to traditional Islamic institutions—graft, corruption, bribery, blind adherence to tradition—Abdülmecid declared a reorganization of the empire's *millets*.

The new proclamation was primarily a political vehicle for firmly cementing Great Power support in Paris for the Ottoman reform regime. Armed with its terms, the Ottoman delegation to Paris won the Great Powers' official guarantees of the empire's territorial integrity and formal admission into the European Great Power fraternity (for the first and last time), opening European financial institutions for loans to support the reforms.

The *Tanzimat* and the Ottoman Balkans, 1856-71

The 1856 *Hatti Hümayun* marked the beginning of the *Tanzimat*'s direct impact on the Ottoman Balkans. Ambiguities regarding non-Muslim equality contained in the 1839 Gülhane decree, the slow pace of provincial administrative restructuring, continued tax farming, the predominance of conservatives among local authorities, and the abuse and corruption of *millet* religious officials kept life relatively unchanged for the empire's Balkan non-Muslims during the first two decades of *Tanzimat* reforms. Abdülmecid's 1856 decree, however, made addressing his non-Muslim subjects' situation a priority.

The first initiative specifically aimed at improving the Balkan non-Muslims' situation involved enforcing existing reform legislation in the provinces. In 1858 a new penal code based on the French Napoleonic model was promulgated. Other, primarily commercial regulatory codes also were instituted. All were intended to lessen or eradicate inequities experienced by non-Muslims. To ensure that the reform laws were implemented in the Balkan provinces, periodic inspection tours were made by reform officials from the capital.

An example of such a tour was that conducted (1860) in the empire's Macedonian and Bulgarian territories by Grand Vezir Mehmed Kıbrıslı Paşa. Kıbrıslı spent four months traveling in the regions and compiled a report on local conditions. Although he concluded that Muslims were not systematically oppressing non-Muslims, he determined that old inequities grounded in traditional Islamic religious discrimination still generally prevailed, that tax farming continued at extortionate levels, and that local Orthodox Greek *millet* officials were corrupt and tyrannical, especially in dealings with their Slavic-rite charges. Other tours followed, and, although none resulted in effecting fundamental reforms, they did stop some local abuses, inspired local authorities to initiate improvements, and provided the central government with data for enacting additional measures.

The second post-1856 reform targeting Balkan non-Muslims was *millet* reorganization. By 1860 the number of non-Muslim *millets* had increased, because of Great Power pressure, from the original three to six: The Orthodox, Jewish, and Gregorian Armenian were joined by the Roman Armenian, Roman Catholic, and Protestant. Only the original three were ordered to be reorganized since, as the 1856 *Hatti Hümayun* declared, they were deemed unable to function effectively under their outdated original organizations. The provincial inspection tours revealed the rife corruption within the Greek-dominated Orthodox *millet,* particularly when operating in predominantly Slavic-inhabited regions. In addition, lay elements within the *millets* actively agitated for the end of the religious hierarches' exclusive hold on *millet* administration. In 1857 Abdülmecid ordered the Orthodox church to hold a general council for the purpose of reorganizing the *millet.* Despite the Greek patriarch's reticence, such a council convened in Istanbul (1860-62).

An unexpected consequence of the call for Orthodox *millet* reorganization was the rapid emergence of a Bulgarian ethnonational movement couched in *millet* terms. When the council convened with Greeks constituting the majority of attendees, the underrepresented Bulgarian clergy failed to win the right to elect their own native bishops. Wealthy Bulgarian merchants in the capital, realizing that the council would not produce a Bulgarian church free of Greek control, announced in 1860 that the Bulgarians no longer would recognize the authority of the Greek patriarch or his Greek subordinates. The method of their pronouncement was instructive regarding the nature of their national program—during Easter services at their church, they substituted the sultan's name for the Greek patriarch's in the liturgy's petitionary prayers. That ceremonial notice launched the opening phase of a mature Bulgarian ethnonational movement—the "Bulgarian Church Question."

Ethnonational awareness had spread slowly among the Bulgarians since the efforts of Paisii and Sofronii Vrachanski in the early nineteenth century. Predominantly a peasant society at that time, the Bulgarians possessed only a nascent middle class to serve as harbingers of ethnic consciousness. Literacy and the financial wherewithal to propagate it were crucial for actively generating ethnonational awareness, and the Greek Revolution's repercussions within the Ottoman Empire offered the Bulgarians an opportunity to acquire them. Bulgarians long served as junior associates in numerous Greek commercial enterprises, and, for centuries, Bulgarian livestock breeders and textile makers were the preferred suppliers for the Ottoman military, capital, and palace. With Greek subjects held in suspicion because of the revolution, the Ottomans turned to the Bulgarians as their economic replacements. Much of the trade and many of the commercial contracts formerly held by Greeks were granted to Bulgarian merchants and suppliers, sparking the rise of a relatively numerous and wealthy Bulgarian middle class.

Beginning with the first Western-style Bulgarian-language school in 1835, the new Bulgarian middle class increasingly undertook a concerted effort to spread Slavic Bulgarian literacy and Western secular-scientific concepts (learned through long associations with Greek *millet* leaders and merchants) by supporting literary, linguistic, and translation activities, new schools, reading rooms, and literary societies throughout the empire's Bulgarian-inhabited territories. The resulting educational and literary network gradually produced a Bulgarian intelligentsia. Just like their Greek former associates and mentors, many middle-class Bulgarians also embraced Romantic nationalist ideals. In a classic example of "what is good for the goose is good for the gander," the Bulgarians' rising sense of ethnonational awareness was turned on the Greek *millet* leadership.

The Bulgarians felt the cultural ramifications of rising Greek nationalism as early as the late eighteenth century through the Greek Patriarchate's increasing efforts to entrench Greek cultural superiority within the Orthodox *millet*. After the successes of the Serbian and Greek revolutions, Greek-language schools were founded in all Balkan regional Orthodox *millet* administrative centers, and the Greek high clergy exerted pressure on the *millet*'s members to attend. Non-Greek clergy were forced to become Hellenized if they hoped for *millet* administrative advancement. Bulgarians constituted the single largest non-Greek ethnic component in the Orthodox *millet* by the mid-nineteenth century, and growing Hellenization increasingly affected the influential Bulgarian middle class. So closely associated were the Ottoman ruling elite and the Orthodox *millet* that Hellenization came to signify political, cultural, and economic prestige in Ottoman society. Ironically, Hellenization was so pervasive in early nineteenth-century Bulgarian society that many leading nationalists often spoke and wrote Greek in their personal lives while they called for elevating and expanding Bulgarian language and education in public.

In rejecting the Greek Patriarchate's authority in the early stages of *millet* reorganization, and then calling for the creation of a separate Bulgarian Orthodox church organization, the Bulgarian middle-class leaders were demanding that the Ottoman government officially recognize a new and ethnically unique *millet*. The mass of Bulgarian peasants remained politically inactive but sympathetic to the idea of having their own Orthodox church. Most middle-class nationalists were comfortable with their newfound prosperity and favored an evolutionary religious approach to national satisfaction because it entailed the least amount of economic and social disruption.

The caution of most middle-class Bulgarians was reinforced by post-1856 *Tanzimat* reforms, which proved especially beneficial to the Bulgarians in the 1860s, when they were governed by Ahmed Şefik Midhat Paşa (1864-68), a Bulgarian Pomak by birth and a dynamic, pro-Western, and enlightened reformer who transformed the region under his authority into a model province. As governor of a newly organized, experimental Danube *vilayet* (province) encompassing all of the empire's Bulgarian lands, he built bridges, roads, and schools. An agrarian bank was founded, banditry was suppressed (as was any manifestation of Bulgarian nationalist revolutionary activity), and, to facilitate administrative effectiveness, provincial laws and regulations were published in both Turkish and Bulgarian (for which purpose the first official Bulgarian-language printing press inside the Bulgarian territories was established in Ruse, the provincial capital).

A bitter decade-long conflict between Bulgarians and Greeks began within the Orthodox *millet* following the Bulgarian Istanbul merchants' rejection of Greek patriarchal authority. From the start, it was a nationalist dispute—no doctrinal positions were involved. The Bulgarians demanded a church of their own that would define, in *millet* terms, the geographic extent of a Bulgarian ethnonational territory, while the Greeks viewed that demand as a threat to Hellenism and the future of an enlarged Greece based on the "Great Idea" and centered on a re-Christianized Constantinople. Over the course of the church struggle, the Bulgarians toyed with French Catholic and American Protestant missionaries, who entered the Ottoman Empire under the *Tanzimat* umbrella in hopes of gaining Bulgarian converts. Despite the assistance of American Protestants in developing a reformed modern Bulgarian literary language, the Bulgarian nationalists viewed all of the missionaries as pawns in their attempt to force Russia into influencing the sultan in their favor by playing to Russia's Orthodox and imperialist fears.

The ploy worked. Concerned that the Bulgarians might renounce Orthodoxy in favor of "foreign" Catholic or Protestant faiths (and remove themselves from

Russian influence), in 1870 Count Nicholas Ignatiev, Russian ambassador to Istanbul, forged a compromise solution to the church issue. When that effort failed because of the Greek patriarch's intransigence over a minor technicality, Sultan Abdülaziz, Abdülmecid's successor, issued an imperial decree recognizing an independent Bulgarian church headed by an exarch seated in Istanbul. The new Bulgarian Exarchate was granted jurisdiction over large tracts of three regions within the empire (Bulgaria, Thrace, and Macedonia) and the sanctioned ability to acquire further territories should two-thirds of their inhabitants vote to join. Official Ottoman recognition of the new Bulgarian church came two years later (1872). The Greek Patriarchate then declared the existence of a schism within Orthodoxy on canonical grounds (the illegality of ecclesiastical jurisdiction based solely on ethnicity). The Bulgarians, of course, were little disposed to tremble at the patriarchate's action. In 1872 the Bulgarian Bishop Antim of Vidin was elected first exarch and took up his duties in the capital.

The implications of the Exarchate's creation were far-reaching. A new *millet* was created within the empire that, while overtly retaining a religious identity, primarily represented the interests of a particular ethnic group within a specific territory, which handed the Bulgarians a concrete territorial definition for a Bulgarian national heartland. Moreover, Bulgarian nationalists viewed the ability to extend the Exarchate's territorial jurisdiction as an Ottoman-sanctioned opportunity for future state expansion. From the Greek perspective, the Exarchate was both a blow to Greek nationalism (it removed from Greek cultural influence regions claimed, according to the "Great Idea," by right of the Orthodox *millet*, such as Macedonia and Thrace) and an asset (it eliminated the perceived threat of Slavic mongrelization to Greek culture and ethnicity in territories marginal to the "Great Idea"—those north of Macedonia and Thrace). The Exarchate guaranteed that future national conflicts would occur in regions where the two sides' claims coincided. Furthermore, as events related to the Bulgarian national movement played themselves out, the Serbs were forced to deal with the Exarchate's national implications as well.

The *Tanzimat* group's third initiative principally directed toward the empire's Balkan non-Muslims was a sweeping reorganization of provincial administration begun in 1864. The *Vilayet* Law of that year divided the empire into *vilayets* that, in turn, were subdivided into *sancaks*. Unlike former provinces (*eyalets*), however, the new *vilayets* were to enjoy greater administrative decentralization and increased local participation in their governance. Larger than previous provincial units, their governors wielded expanded authority, assisted by advisory boards composed of both appointed and elected members. Midhat's Danube *vilayet* was the first of its kind, and its success led the government to apply the *vilayet* system universally throughout the empire.

Once the *vilayet* system became standard, its flaws swiftly came to the fore. The greatest shortcoming was the *vilayet* governor's crucial role. Given increased responsibilities and authority, the governor vitally determined the administration's efficiency and effectiveness. It quickly became obvious that not all (or many) *vilayet* governors were as talented or dedicated as Midhat. The lack of sufficiently qualified and trained governors plagued the new administration, and the problem was compounded by a similar situation among subordinate officials. Without able or committed governors, and with subordinates frequently drawn from more conservative ranks, *vilayets* generally functioned as badly as the old provinces, if not worse.

One Ottoman Balkan province was an exception to the general mediocrity of the *vilayet* system. Blessed with a talented governor nearly Midhat's equal during the 1860s, Bosnia experienced cultural efflorescence and political development. Topal Osman Paşa, both a military man and an intellectual, was a reform party ally and implemented the *Vilayet* Law in 1866. He expanded education in Bosnia by building new Muslim and Christian schools, founded a library and the first public hospital, created new courts, established a printing press, and started a weekly newspaper written in both Slavic and Turkish. A joint Muslim-Christian governor's advisory board met once a year, and a standing executive council (also with a joint membership) consulted with Topal on a weekly basis.

Bosnia's worst problem was the abject domination of the peasantry by the large landowning Muslim *beys,* which the *Tanzimat* reforms did little to alleviate. Topal enforced new codes aimed at regulating peasant dues to landlords. Even when the codes were implemented, however, those dues, combined with various state taxes, claimed over 40 percent of the peasants' crops. Moreover, taxes generally were collected in an arbitrary and unjust fashion, whether by tax farmers or government functionaries. Despite Topal's enlightened leadership, animosities simmered between the Muslim administration and landowners and the mostly Christian peasantry. They intensified after Topal's death (1869) through the infiltration into Bosnia of ethnonational agitation among the Christians from across the province's borders with Habsburg Croatia and Serbia.

At the death (1871) of Ali Paşa, Reşid's last heir as *Tanzimat* leader, Sultan Abdülaziz reasserted the supreme authority of his office over the remaining *Tanzimat* group. The reforms had not decentralized the top level of Ottoman government, and, with no strong reform party leadership at hand, central power rested completely with the sultan. Abdülaziz was not an enemy of reform, he simply was not as committed as had been his predecessors. Reforms still were enacted, but their pace was slowed. His propensity for contracting huge loans from European banks to finance both needed programs and lavish personal expenditures ran the state into increasing indebtedness. The economic ineptness of the *Tanzimat* programs never produced the expected revenues to cover the debts, so Abdülaziz continually defaulted on repayments. With bankruptcy looming, he had little incentive to invest resources in additional, possibly risky reform measures.

CHAPTER TWELVE

The "Eastern Question"

The "Eastern Question" lends general meaning to a complex web of nineteenth-century European Great Power relationships that dealt with the balance of power established at the Congress of Vienna among Britain, France, Russia, and the Habsburg Empire. The congress accorded that each was free to pursue its own essential interests so long as the others' were not threatened. Generally, Britain, supported by France, upheld the balance system while Russia and the Habsburgs threatened its stability, but circumstances in any given situation often determined on which side a particular Great Power stood. Ottoman destabilization, the rise of Romantic nationalism among that empire's non-Muslim subjects, and the possible specter of total Ottoman demise focused the issue of Great Power balance on the eastern Mediterranean and the strategically important Dardanelles and Bosphorus straits. Because of the Balkan Peninsula's geographic location relative to the eastern Mediterranean in general and the Straits in particular, its control became a crucial issue in the Great Powers' imperial interests, and any major event in the region became a matter of their concern.

The Balkans in European Imperial Interests

While both the Serbian and the Greek revolutions served as models regarding the fulfillment of ethnonational aspirations for other Ottoman Balkan non-Muslims, they also demonstrated that the fate of any national success ultimately lay in the hands of the European Great Powers and not in their own. That message also applied to the Ottomans, whose *Tanzimat* reforms were enacted to secure their empire on their own terms through placating the Great Powers by compromise modernization. For the Balkan non-Muslims and Ottomans alike, successfully playing to the Great

Powers' interests was a complicated and risky game, since each of the Great Powers involved in the region followed its own agenda.

The conflicting interests of two European Great Powers—Britain and Russia—lay at the heart of the "Eastern Question." Although the states acted in concert at times, Russia's desire to end its essentially landlocked international military and economic situation by breaking through to the Mediterranean via the Bosphorus and Dardanelles straits and, from there, into the open oceans was viewed by the British as an intrinsic threat to the maritime routes linking them to their most important colony, India. British fear of Russia severing those sea links was fed and intensified throughout the nineteenth century by growing diplomatic and military skirmishes between the two in Afghanistan and Iran, as the Russians pushed their borders ever deeper into Central Asia, bringing them closer to British-controlled India.

Britain's involvement with the Ottoman eastern Mediterranean began with its late-sixteenth-century trade capitulation in the Ottomans' Levantine markets. Maritime superiority gave Britain preeminence in the Levant over its traditional European competitor, France. Napoleon's Egyptian Campaign (1798-1801) demonstrated the vulnerability of Britain's primary sea route to India. The shortest, most direct maritime line of communication between England and India lay through the Mediterranean to Egypt's narrow Suez Isthmus, where goods headed for India were unloaded and transported overland to the Red Sea and then reembarked and shipped on by way of the Indian Ocean. Napoleon's brief occupation of Egypt demonstrated the threat that the presence of another Great Power in the eastern Mediterranean could pose for that vital British lifeline. Although originally Britain viewed France as its primary enemy in the region, France's defeat in the Napoleonic wars diminished its threat to the Indian route.

Relations between Britain and Russia historically were friendly. Sixteenth-century Britain forged lasting trade agreements with Russia and, by the late eighteenth century, controlled over half of Russia's foreign trade, becoming highly dependent on imported Russian timber for building its ships. In partial return for such economic advantages, Britain supported the Russian Black Sea fleet's right to enter the Mediterranean.

British policy regarding Russia changed after the Napoleonic wars because of a series of disagreements with Russia over such issues as the fate of Poland and interpretations of Vienna's "Concert of Europe" concept. Powerful British imperialist political factions enacted laws restricting Russian imports and requiring ship construction to use only British colonial timber. Despite Britain's growing suspicion of Russia's intentions concerning maintaining the balance system during the 1820s, the two acted to ensure the victory of the Greek nationalist rebels in the Balkans at the decade's end.

By the 1830s Britain was convinced that upholding the Ottoman Empire as a strategic buffer in the eastern Mediterranean was the only practical way to protect its vital Indian sea route against a growing potential Russian threat. Britain therefore needed to ensure that the Ottomans were strong enough to accomplish their assigned mission while remaining too weak to close the trade route themselves. Economic means were used to reduce the Ottomans to a desirable level of dependency. British merchants operating in Ottoman markets accounted for 20 percent of Britain's exports and 10 percent of its imports. In return for Ottoman cereals, raw materials (especially cotton), silk, dyes, and opium, Britain provided the Ottomans with finished textiles, machinery, and iron. The economic ties with the Ottomans furnished Britain with the means to bend them to British will.

Britain transformed its long-standing Ottoman trade capitulation into a tool for forcing the Ottomans into dependency. While Ottoman markets were flooded with cheap British-manufactured textiles, undercutting native Ottoman production, in 1838 Britain (followed by other Western European states) used the capitulation's discounted import tariffs to force an unusually low fixed rate on the Ottoman government. Likewise, the *millet*-like autonomy granted foreign merchant colonies by the capitulations was extended, under British diplomatic pressure, to the non-Muslim agents (*dragomans*), through whom all foreign merchants transacted their business. By then selling their *dragomans* British passports, ethnic and religious tensions within the empire were exacerbated while the British gained inordinate influence in Ottoman mercantile and governmental circles.

The simplest way to prevent Russia from threatening British maritime traffic in the eastern Mediterranean was to bottle the Russian fleet in the Black Sea, and that was best accomplished by restricting its access to the Bosphorus and Dardanelles straits through preserving the Ottoman Empire, which controlled them. From the British perspective, the Ottoman buffer state faced two potentially fatal threats to its continued existence: Outright utter military defeat by Russia and loss of control over its Balkan territories to new national states serving as Russian clients. Britain proved its seriousness about protecting the Ottomans from Russian aggression by fighting the Crimean War. It also strongly backed Ottoman *Tanzimat* adaptive reforms and consistently intervened on its buffer client's behalf to forestall or minimize Balkan national developments.

Preventing Russia from gaining control or dominant influence in the Ottomans' eastern Balkan possessions was crucial to British interests. The fact that the majority of non-Muslims in those territories consciously shared an Orthodox European culture and Slavic ethnicity with the Russians posed a difficult problem for Britain. Although powerful philhellenic public opinion in Britain prevented it from actively opposing the Greek Revolution, the government managed to keep the Greek state as small as possible and to impose on it a non-Greek, non-Orthodox, European monarchy by having the international meeting for settling the Greek issue held in London, where British influence proved decisive.

Britain sought to stifle future Balkan nationalist movements by supporting the *Tanzimat* group's reform efforts. In hopes of reducing ethnonational tensions within the Ottoman Empire, British ambassador to Istanbul Stratford Canning pressed Abdülmecid to issue the 1839 *Tanzimat* decree. Thereafter, Canning and other British officials and merchants in the empire continuously acted as advisors to the *Tanzimat* group. During the Crimean War, British diplomatic pressure to advance the *Tanzimat* program by specifically targeting Balkan non-Muslims intensified, playing a role in the promulgation of the 1856 *Tanzimat* decree. In the end, however, the *Tanzimat* failed to win the continued loyalty of the Balkan non-Muslims, and, as national concepts spread and grew among them, most Orthodox Slavic Balkan nationalists viewed Britain as an unfriendly Great Power.

Orthodox and Slavic Russia used its shared religious and ethnic cultural ties with the Ottoman Balkan non-Muslims to its imperialist advantage in the eastern Mediterranean.

The Russians had converted to Orthodox Christianity in the late tenth century through Byzantium, just as the Bulgarians had before them and the Serbs afterward. Conversion to Orthodoxy entailed embracing the Byzantine concepts of reality expressed through autocratic political and mystical religious ideologies. Those cultural traditions were intensified by nearly two centuries of subsequent subjugation to the Islamic Mongol-Tatar state. Cut off from direct contact with their Orthodox cultural fountainhead in the Balkans, treated arbitrarily by their Muslim Mongol-Tatar overlords, and constantly in conflict with non-Orthodox Europeans on the plains to their west, the isolated Russians consolidated their self-identity by reinforcing their Byzantine-style Orthodox culture. The net result was a general distrust of non-Orthodox, Western Europeans (following the 1054 Great Schism and the horrors of the Fourth Crusade) and an abiding cultural animosity toward Islam.

From its beginnings, post-Mongol-Tatar Muscovite Russia was an empire, and its rulers espoused traditional Orthodox imperial ideals, although its political model—the Byzantine Empire—had ceased to exist. Of all the European Orthodox states, Russia alone survived by the late fifteenth century. That fact was not lost on the Byzantinized Russian rulers and the Russian Orthodox church. Together, in the early sixteenth century, they devised a divinely ordained imperial ideology known as the "Third Rome Theory." "Third Rome" thinkers claimed that, since the God-ordained Christian Roman empires of Rome and Constantinople had fallen because they had strayed from correct divine will, only the Muscovite Orthodox Russian imperial state rightly could lay claim to the divine mantle of political leadership within the general Orthodox world. Despite the overt Westernizing adaptations of the Russian ruling classes since the late seventeenth century, the idea persisted that Russia possessed a (sacred) mission to reconstitute a (Orthodox) world-state that would include the Balkan heartland of Orthodoxy. While those aims mostly became couched in secular, rather than religious, terms, "Third Rome" concepts provided an underlying impetus to Russian foreign policy.

Western European-like military and economic adaptations helped advance Russia's abilities to attain "Third Rome" goals. Russia progressively gained control of all Orthodox-inhabited European territories to its west and south. In pushing southward, the Russians came into antagonistic contact with the Ottoman Empire, which obstructed their reaching the Black Sea, the direct route to Byzantium. Access to the Bosphorus and Dardanelles straits at the southwestern corner of the sea would open to Russia important year-round ice-free maritime routes, possession of which determined a Great Power's position relative to others' in Western European political thinking.

All of the other European Great Powers considered Russia a fellow member of their exclusive group. Russia's incorporation of Ukraine and Belarus during the seventeenth and eighteenth centuries brought it into direct and continuous contact with the continental Western European Great Powers and involved it in the general European wars of the eighteenth century. In the early nineteenth, Russia played a decisive role in defeating Napoleon, fielding the largest army on the continent, and at the Congress of Vienna it was instrumental in shaping the reactionary postwar European political system. Britain's role throughout the wars essentially as a banker for anti-French forces, fighting only when and where it chose, demonstrated that a maritime-based, global Great Power wielded more actual power than those that primarily remained landlocked (Prussia and the Habsburg Empire). Of the land-based Great Powers, Russia's geographic size rendered it unique.

Although Russia territorially was huge, its very size mitigated the full exploitation of its numerous resources, since existing overland routes were few, lengthy, and vulnerable to the vagaries of humans and climate. Russia's only useable sea ports lay in the extreme northwest on the Baltic, White, and Barents seas, which were closed by ice for extended periods during the year. For military, economic, and prestige purposes, Russia needed warm-water ports open year-round, and the only ones available were located on the coast of the Black Sea. To exploit those ports, Russia required free access to the crucial Straits controlled by the Ottomans.

Traditional anti-Islamic sentiment, "Third Rome" pretensions, and concerns over maritime routes conspired to make Russia the Ottoman Empire's most inveterate European enemy. Beginning with Peter the Great's late seventeenth-century invasion of Moldavia, a series of Russo-Turkish wars took place during the eighteenth and early nineteenth centuries, which won the Russians possession of the Ukrainian and Caucasian coasts of the Black Sea and naval access to its waters. By the mid-eighteenth century the Russians realized that the subject Orthodox Balkan populations might serve as useful fifth columns in their struggles against the Ottomans, and propaganda efforts stressing Orthodox solidarity and shared cultural values were undertaken among émigré Greeks in the Black Sea port cities and border Serbs in Habsburg Vojvodina and Slavonia.

Once ethnonational concepts appeared in the Ottoman Balkans during the early nineteenth century, the primary stress of Russian propaganda among the peninsula's non-Muslims broadened from Orthodoxy alone to include Slavic ethnicity, a development that first became apparent during the Serbian uprisings and was concretely expressed in the Edirne Treaty. The Russian Orthodox church served as an agent of Russian interests through its direct religious contacts with Balkan Slavic-rite clerics and monasteries. Slav merchants operating in Black Sea commercial centers, particularly Bulgarians, followed in their Greek mentors' footsteps and functioned as pro-Russian agents among their Balkan conationals in return for vague promises of Russian assistance for their national aspirations. Young Russian intellectuals, energized by Romantic nationalist notions and convinced of Russia's mission to bring national liberation to the Balkan Slavs, reinforced those hopes.

By the 1840s Russian intellectuals were in the throes of a deep philosophical division between Westernizers and Slavophiles over the nature of Russia's cultural identity. Principally an outgrowth of serious domestic social, economic, and nationalist problems, the cultural debate partially was stoked by anti-Russian sentiment among the Western European Great Powers after the Napoleonic wars. Led by Britain, westerners were uncomfortable over Russia's strong presence in European affairs. Western publications often portrayed Russia in unfavorable terms and insinuated that the "non-European" Russians posed a threat to the Western way of life. The French, massively defeated by Russia and highly sympathetic to Polish nationalist efforts, needed little prompting to think the worst. Neither did the Prussian Germans, who experienced two centuries of contention with Russia along Western Europe's eastern frontiers. After 1848-49 even the Habsburgs, Russia's dependable allies in previous anti-Ottoman wars, came to view the Russians as dangerous rivals in the Balkan arena.

In simplified terms, the Russian Westernizers called for totally rejecting Russia's Orthodox and Slavic cultural traditions and for completely embracing Western European secular and scientific concepts, thus carrying the westernization begun by Peter the Great to its logical conclusion. The Slavophiles, Romantic nationalists heavily influenced by Panslavic concepts originating in the Habsburg Empire, idealized Orthodox and Slavic traditions as lending the Russians unique and superior qualities among Europeans, but believed that these were being undermined and corrupted by the foreign, Western adaptations made since Peter. Both sides sincerely were patriotic, convinced that their views ultimately would bring Russia supremacy among the Great Powers: The Westernizers believed that Russia could undertake modernization from a clean slate because it was the Great Power least corrupted by decadent materialism, while the Slavophiles, echoing old "Third Rome" concepts, held that remaining true to Orthodox and Slavic cultural traditions would confer on Russia universally acknowledged moral leadership in the European Slavic world. Although neither party earned official Russian state policy acceptance, both won adherents among government and military officials, and both were used unofficially (depending on circumstances) to further Russia's foreign policy interests.

In 1851 Nicholas I adopted the Slavophile position that Russia was the rightful leader and protector of all Orthodox Slavs in instigating the crisis over the sacred Christian shrines in the Ottoman-held Holy Lands. Bolstered by terms in the Kyuchuk Kainardzha Treaty that seemingly granted Russia such a role within the Ottoman Empire, Nicholas manipulated Slavophile opinion to cement support for his belligerent stance toward the Ottomans, France, and Britain and for his declaration of war against the Ottomans in late 1853 in the face of certain French and British military involvement. Defeat in the Crimean War dampened the Russian government's reliance on Slavophile support but did not render it entirely useless. Throughout the 1860s and 1870s Slavophiles in the Russian diplomatic corps operated in the Ottoman and Habsburg empires as consuls, consular agents, and ambassadors (Nicholas Ignatiev). Their duties included fostering the national aspirations of various Balkan Slav populations and gaining their sympathy for and gratitude to Russia. The Slavophiles most dramatic foreign policy achievement was the creation of the Bulgarian Exarchate through Ignatiev's efforts.

Important secondary players in the "Eastern Question" were France and the Habsburgs.

France's eastern Mediterranean interests began as early as the Crusades but were solidified in 1536, when it became the first Western European Great Power to sign an alliance and conclude a commercial capitulation agreement with the Ottomans. For the following two centuries the French enjoyed preeminence among Europeans in Ottoman Levantine trade, in return for which France consistently supported the Ottomans as useful allies in its various wars with the Habsburgs. Napoleon's invasion of Ottoman Syria (1799) near the end of his Egyptian Campaign, however, undermined French credibility in Istanbul. The loss of the Ionian Islands, off of the Balkans' Adriatic coast, and Malta to Britain during the Napoleonic wars crippled France's presence in the eastern Mediterranean.

In the late 1820s and 1830s France attempted to improve its eastern Mediter-ranean position by forging ties with the Egyptian governor Mehmed Ali. After helping crush Mehmed Ali's fleet at Navarino, France assisted him in westernizing the Egyptian military and generally supported his insurgency against his nominal Ottoman suzerains during the 1830s in hopes of regaining commercial advantage in the Syrian lands that fell to his control and acquiring leverage against Britain with a presence in Egypt. Combined British and Russian pressures led to the collapse of the French scheme by 1841. Thereafter, France generally supported Britain regarding the eastern Mediterranean and Russia, joining the British in manipulating capitulation terms with the Ottomans, diplomatically pressuring the Ottoman government in support of *Tanzimat* reforms, and fighting Russia in the Crimean War. France cooperated with Britain in barring free Russian access to the Straits to protect its own eastern Mediterranean commercial routes. As part of that policy, the French supported Catholic missionary activity among the Ottomans' Balkan subjects and successfully pressured the sultan to recognize a separate Catholic *millet*.

Since the late seventeenth century the Habsburgs shared Russia's anti-Ottoman stance and, throughout the eighteenth century, conducted a series of wars against the Islamic empire in the Balkans, often in alliance with Russia. Despite the two Great Powers' seemingly common interests, the Habsburgs did not relish the idea of Russian territorial conquests in the peninsula, which they considered their own sphere of interest based on historical right. After the Napoleonic wars the Habsburgs acquired all of Venetian Dalmatia, giving them dominance in the Adriatic and the western Balkans. Habsburg Balkan interests were intensified after the Revolution of 1848-49, which demonstrated that ethnonationalism exerted a powerful force on the empire's subjects and that those who were Balkan (such as the Serbs and Croats) possessed an alternative to continued Habsburg loyalty in autonomous Serbia lying just south of the empire's border. To nullify Serbia's potential attraction on their Balkan subjects, the Habsburgs moved to gain influence over the Serbian government by reducing the principality to economic dependency.

After being expelled from German affairs by Prussia in 1866, the Habsburgs concluded the 1867 Compromise with the Hungarians to ensure their empire's continued survival (as Austria-Hungary [or the Dual Monarchy]). Defeat by Prussia also negatively affected the Habsburgs' Great Power standing. Lacking an oceangoing navy, and permanently barred from meaningful influence in Central Europe by the creation of a united Germany (1871), the Habsburgs could demonstrate continued Great Power status only by expanding their territories and influence in the Balkans, despite the fact that such a policy would increase the number of their Balkan subjects and magnify the risks of internal nationalist unrest.

Given their situation, the Habsburgs had no choice but to view as undesirable Russia's pretensions in the Balkans. It was in Habsburg interests, therefore, to bar Russia from the peninsula and minimize, or prevent completely, the spread of Russian-influenced nationalist movements among the Ottomans' Balkan subjects. The Habsburgs' new anti-Russian stance regarding the Balkans became apparent as early as the Crimean War. Thereafter, they stood with Britain and France in preserving the status quo concerning Ottoman control of the Straits while attempting to extend their dominant influence over Serbia and the various western Balkan Ottoman populations.

To the Europeans, the Ottoman Empire, whose territories and very existence lay at the heart of the "Eastern Question," counted for little beyond being their pawn or target. Only for one brief moment—at the 1856 Paris Peace Conference—did the Ottomans win fleeting acknowledgment of Great Power status, but that proved both self-serving and condescending on the part of the other Great Powers. Despite official declarations to the contrary, the Europeans' traditional anti-Islamic cultural prejudices simmered barely below the public surface. All of the Europeans, including the Ottomans' allies, demonstrated their subliminal unwillingness to accept the Ottoman Empire's permanence in Europe—half of a millennium after 1453, they all persisted in referring to Istanbul as "Constantinople."

The Balkan Crisis of 1875-76

In 1875 a series of Balkan events brought Europe to the brink of war. The uprising of Christian peasants in Bosnia and Hercegovina that sparked the crisis was far more portentous than the squabble over sacred shrines that led to the Crimean War because Serbia's and Montenegro's involvement threatened the Ottomans' continued hold on the Balkans, imperiling the balance of Great Power interests. Russia stood to gain should the Orthodox Slav nationalists tear Balkan territories from Ottoman control. Conversely, Austria-Hungary stood to lose and was prepared to prevent such a development by force. Britain wanted no war at the time and exerted strong diplomatic pressure to that end. France, recovering from defeat in the Franco-Prussian War (1870-71), concentrated on domestic rebuilding and was not interested in becoming involved. The Ottomans were the designated losers; they faced the question of how to limit their losses.

In a Bosnian and Hercegovinian population numbering a bit over 1 million, Muslims (the vast majority of them peasants) accounted for 40 percent, Orthodox (peasants) 42 percent, and Catholics (also mostly peasants) 18 percent. Despite Topal's reforms, the condition of the peasantry remained abject. The numerically small landholding Muslim *beys* controlled the provincial administration and were not interested in reforms. Tax and tithe rates on the peasants were inordinately high and collected by corrupt tax farmers. Tenant peasants paid exorbitant rents, undertook unpaid corvées, and submitted to a mandatory military exemption poll tax. The judicial process, also controlled by the Muslim *beys,* offered the peasants no effective protection or recourse for righting grievances. What made the situation in the two provinces during the 1870s explosively different from previous times, however, was a charged political atmosphere permeated by Serbian nationalism, Russian Panslavism, and Habsburg predilections for Balkan expansion.

In neighboring Serbia during the 1860s, Prince Mihajlo Obrenović actively fostered expansionist, "Greater Serbia" nationalist pretensions aimed at territorially re-creating Car Dušan's medieval Serbian Empire. Although Bosnia never fell under medieval Serb control, the "Greater Serbia" party sought to rectify Dušan's "national failure." A number of Orthodox religious academies were founded by Serbs in Bosnia and Hercegovina to disseminate Serbian nationalist propaganda among the disgruntled Orthodox peasants. Even though Mihajlo's successor, Milan Obrenović (1869-89), was less disposed to promote militant national expansion, he could not rein in the "Greater Serbia" nationalists led by Jovan Ristić, and nationalist agitation continued within Bosnia and Hercegovina.

By the time that Russian Slavophile influences seeped into Bosnia and Hercegovina during the early 1870s, their pro-Russian message was more political than cultural. The demise of the original Habsburg Panslavs during the Revolution of 1848-49, and the discredit inflicted on Slavophile idealism by the Crimean War, transformed the Romantic Slavophiles into Panslavs dedicated to uniting European Orthodox Slavs under Russia's aegis. A network of Panslav societies in major Russian cities propagated their views by directly contacting émigré nationalists and disseminating Panslavic political publications. The Balkan Slavs were targeted expressly through members of Russia's diplomatic corps working in the Ottoman and Habsburg empires and through agitation among expatriate nationalists in Russia. Little concrete evidence, however, exists for accurately gauging the actual impact of the Russian Panslavs on the Bosnian and Hercegovinian Orthodox Slavs.

Habsburg Austria-Hungary's policy toward the Ottoman Balkans was divided. The Hungarian half of the Dual Monarchy contained numerous groups of contentious non-Hungarian ethnic minorities, many of whom possessed ethnic ties to Ottoman Balkan populations. The Hungarian administration had no wish to increase the number of non-Hungarians through state expansion deeper into the Balkans. Hungarians serving in the Habsburgs' imperial cabinet (such as Foreign Minister Gyula Andrássy in the 1870s) curbed expansionist policies at that level as much as possible but were willing to consider limited interventions in the Balkans to prevent the rise or spread of dangerous nationalist movements along the empire's borders, including the expansion of Serbia.

Hungarian reticence regarding Balkan expansion was countered by Habsburg concerns over Great Power status. Having been displaced in Central Europe by Germany, Habsburg Austria-Hungary sought compensation through Balkan expansion. Otherwise, the Habsburgs faced a fate similar to that of the unfortunate Ottomans.

The Habsburgs' imperialist Balkan policy aims were supported by certain factions within the empire. One such group was the Croat-led Yugoslav nationalists headed by Zagreb's Bishop Strossmayer. They believed that the Habsburgs were duty-bound to unite the Balkan South Slavs into a single entity within the Dual Monarchy, which then would be transformed into a triune Austro-Hungarian-Yugoslav state, with the Croats heading the Slavic component. A more forceful Balkan expansionist proponent was the Austro-Hungarian officer corps. For strategic military reasons, the army's leaders, among whom ranked many Croat Strossmayer "Yugoslav" adherents, considered possession of Bosnia and Hercegovina essential for the defense of Habsburg Dalmatia. In 1875 the officers successfully urged Emperor Francis Joseph to conduct a tour of Dalmatia. By the time his tour ended, the emperor was convinced that Austro-Hungarian forces had to occupy Bosnia and Hercegovina for both humanitarian and military reasons.

Centuries of social and fiscal exploitation of the Bosnian and Hercegovinian non-Muslim peasantry by the landowning Muslim *beys* came to a head in July 1875, when the Christians in the two regions rebelled. Croat Habsburg officials in Dalmatia aided the rebels as best they could short of direct intervention. So too did the Russians through their consular representatives in Dubrovnik. While both the Habsburgs and Russia worked behind the scenes to assist the rebellion, they outwardly called for a mediated settlement. The Ottoman authorities promised further reform, but the rebels countered with demands for either political autonomy under a Christian prince or foreign occupation until all of their grievances were redressed. With the breakdown of mediation efforts, the fighting grew more widespread and vicious. By early 1876 over 150,000 refugees had fled the carnage in the two provinces, flooding into the surrounding states.

While both Austria-Hungary and Russia were anxious to avoid openly inter-vening in the Bosnian situation, the Serbs held no such reservations. Despite Prince Milan's unwillingness to become involved, nationalist Serbian public opinion demanding intervention ultimately prevailed. In August 1875 Ristić and his Liberal opposition party, which advocated Serbian national expansion at any cost, won a resounding election victory, and Milan, pressured by mass nationalist public demonstrations in Belgrade, was forced to give way. In June 1876 Serbia declared war on the Ottomans in support of the rebellion and Serbian troops invaded Bosnia. The following month Prince Nikola (Nikita) I Petrović (1860-1918) of Montene-gro, not to be outdone by Milan in a growing rivalry to lead a Serb-dominated "Greater South Slav" movement, followed suit and invaded Hercegovina.

Montenegro enjoyed a history unique in the Ottoman Balkans. When the Ottomans overran much of Montenegro's lower-lying territories in the late fifteenth century, many Orthodox Slav Montenegrins sought refuge in the upper reaches of the rugged, inhospitable Black Mountains (from which the name "Montenegro" is derived) of the Dinaric Alps. While they eventually accepted Ottoman suzerainty, since their habitation was so forbidding and their living conditions so primitive and poor, the Ottomans concluded that maintaining direct control over them was not worth the cost. The mountain Montenegrins were left to their own devices under nominal Ottoman authority.

The Orthodox Montenegrins benefited from the *millet* system. The Greek *millet* authorities also were intimidated by Montenegro's terrain and poverty, so the Montenegrins were represented within the Orthodox *millet* by native prelates, who stood as the region's actual political leaders. By the second decade of the sixteenth century the bishops of Cetinje, Montenegro's major mountain town, established a governing Orthodox theocracy headed by a prince-bishop (*vladika*) elected by the clergy and populace from among the monks of Cetinje Monastery. Under Vladika Danilo Petrović (ca. 1696-1735) the office was made hereditary in the Petrović family. Montenegro's religious leaders proved to be skilled military commanders and politicians, creating a strong patriarchal government and expanding Montenegrin territory at the expense of neighboring Ottoman regions. Ottoman punitive efforts against them were ineffectual, and, in 1799, Vladika Petr I Petrović (1781-1830) finally convinced Sultan Selim III to grant Montenegro full independence.

Petr's successor, Petr II Petrović-Njegoš (1830-52), was both an effective military commander and a talented poet, writing the highly nationalistic *Mountain Wreath,* a renowned work of South Slavic literature. He exerted great effort in subjugating neighboring, independent-minded mountain tribes. Despite the appearances of political sophistication, of diplomatic relations with the Ottomans, Russia, and Epiros, and of literary achievement, however, Montenegro remained a loose confederation of warlike, relatively primitive mountain tribes totaling less than 100,000 people, held together only by their willingness to accept the prince-bishop's authority. Little agricultural land was available, and pastoral livestock breeding was the population's primary economic activity.

In 1851 Vladika Danilo I Petrović (1852-60) secularized the state and conducted military operations against neighboring Ottoman regions. When Nikola I took the throne in 1860, he continued the conflicts with the Ottomans in hopes of expanding his state into areas of Bosnia, Hercegovina, and Albania and of winning control of an Adriatic port.

Small, poor, inaccessible Montenegro played a role in Serbian national affairs disproportionate to its size and resources. To the lowland Serbs, it represented a beacon of Serbian independence and anti-Ottoman resistance. Autonomous Serbia's relations with Montenegro were close—the two shared a Slavic language, Orthodox faith, and anti-Ottoman interests. Closeness also fed an undercurrent of rivalry over leadership in Serbian and South Slav affairs. In Romantic nationalist terms, Montenegro owned the more valid historical claim: It had been one of the earliest components of medieval Serbia and had never truly fallen under foreign domination; therefore, it preserved direct linguistic, religious, and political links to Serbia's medieval past. Montenegro's leaders were cognizant of the Romantic argument and often subtly exerted the validity of their claim to preeminence by meddling in Serbia's dynastic feud between the Karadjordjević and Obrenović factions.

Ristić and the nationalists counted on Russian Panslav aid and direct Russian military intervention against the Ottomans in going to war over the rebellious provinces. Panslav assistance slowly arrived in the form of money, weapons, and volunteers, but the expected Russian intervention did not materialize. Despite mass mobilization and military command by "on-leave" Russian Slavophile officers, the war did not fare well for the Serbs.

Morale was high among the Serbian troops, who viewed the war as one between Christian South Slavs and Muslim Turks. To their surprise, the Ottoman forces in Bosnia were just as highly motivated by religious and ethnic emotions. The war efforts of both Serbia and Montenegro were uncoordinated. Each fought for its own nationalist aims: Serbia to acquire both Bosnia and Hercegovina; Montenegro for Hercegovina and continued parity in the rivalry for South Slav leadership. Montenegrin operations were confined to Hercegovina, where Ottoman troops were few, leaving the Serbs to face the concentrated Ottoman forces in Bosnia. While Montenegrin troops advanced deep into Hercegovina and overran parts of northern Albania, on the decisive Bosnian front the Serbs were soundly defeated. Ottoman forces then invaded the territory of their stunned enemy.

Tensions among the Great Powers increased. A crushing Serb defeat raised the specter of direct Russian military intervention in the Balkans that, in turn, would force Austria-Hungary to take preventive action in kind. In desperation, the Serbs begged the Great Powers for a mediated armistice, but the Ottomans were intransigent. Only a Russian ultimatum in October 1876 forced them to agree to a six-week cease-fire.

Two developments permitted the Russians to issue their ultimatum without risking war with either Austria-Hungary or Britain. The first occurred in July, when Habsburg Foreign Minister Andrássy met with his Russian counterpart, Prince Alexander Gorchakov, at Reichstadt to discuss the Balkan situation. An arrangement was reached that essentially divided the Balkans between them, with Austria-Hungary dominant in the western and Russia in the eastern halves of the peninsula. It was agreed that, should Serbia and Montenegro be defeated, the prewar situation would be restored. If they emerged as victors, however, Austria-Hungary and Russia would determine any resulting territorial changes in close cooperation. In no case would a large, unitary South Slavic state be established. Unfortunately, both Andrássy and Gorchakov negotiated from positions of mutual misunderstanding. Andrássy understood that, in the matter of territorial changes, Austria-Hungary would acquire most of Bosnia and Hercegovina, while Gorchakov believed that they would be divided between Serbia and Montenegro.

While the Reichstadt talks were taking place, news of Ottoman massacres of Bulgarians involved in a separate uprising (May 1876) filtered into Britain from missionaries, journalists, and diplomatic agents in the Balkans. The opposition to Conservative Prime Minister Benjamin Disraeli, led by the Liberal Party's William Gladstone, manipulated the rumors and field reports in newspaper articles and pamphlets to attack Disraeli's pro-Ottoman policy, portraying it as abetting the barbarous treatment of Christians by infidel Muslims. So effective were the Liberals in swaying British public opinion in their favor that Queen Victoria (1837-1901) publicly questioned the moral righteousness of Britain's pro-Ottoman stance. His hands tied by the situation, Disraeli informed the Ottomans that Britain could not defend them against possible Russian attack. When the Russians issued their cease-fire ultimatum, the Ottomans thus had no recourse but to comply.

The break in the fighting permitted British and Russian representatives to meet in Istanbul—at Britain's insistence—to hammer out an acceptable joint plan for ending the crisis that could be imposed on the government of Sultan Abdülhamid II (1876-1909).

The Istanbul Conference opened in December 1876, attended by British plenipotentiary Lord Robert of Salisbury and Russian ambassador to the Ottoman Empire Count Ignatiev. Together they devised a compromise agreement that united Bosnia and Hercegovina into a single province and created two provinces out of the Ottomans' Bulgarian territories. All were to be autonomous. Montenegro retained its war gains in Hercegovina and Albania, and Serbia regained its prewar borders. Although Salisbury and Ignatiev liked and respected each other and worked well together, their efforts came to naught.

With the encouragement of British Ambassador Sir Henry Eliot, who purposely undermined Salisbury to preserve traditional anti-Russian British policy, the Ottomans publicly rejected the conference's terms. Instead, Abdülhamid proclaimed a new liberal constitution, ostensibly rendering the Great Powers' plans for the disturbed provinces unnecessary. The Ottoman Constitution of 1876 was not simply a matter of expedient Ottoman duplicity (as it later was painted by some Western diplomats and historians). Although the Istanbul Conference did force the issue of the timing of its promulgation, the constitution was the creation of forces within Ottoman society that sincerely sought to broaden the *Tanzimat* reforms along highly westernized political lines.

By the mid-1860s a young generation of Ottoman officers and functionaries, schooled in the empire's new technical institutions and respectful of Western European political and economic thought, had emerged. Unlike the *Tanzimat* group, they were convinced that the empire's future depended on adopting Western liberal-democratic institutions, including a governing constitution. In 1865 they founded the Young Ottoman Society. When more conservative reformers among the *Tanzimat* group, joined by Sultan Abdülaziz, cracked down on their propagandizing activities, many Young Ottomans fled to the West, where they continued their activities, publishing a radical newspaper that clandestinely circulated inside the empire among reform-minded officers and bureaucrats. Abdülaziz's profligate monetary policies won them support among the newspaper's readership, who feared economic and political disaster if dramatic and speedy changes were not made.

The Young Ottomans were political philosophers and idealists, not practical politicians. Their program was a mixture of Western liberal-democratic concepts, Islamic idealism, and Romantic ethnonational naïveté. They interpreted Islam as being fundamentally democratic and believed that universally applied liberalism would obliterate diverse *millet* and ethnic identities and create a new common

Ottoman nationality. The Young Ottomans were out of touch with Ottoman society's human realities. Traditional Islam presupposed the dominance of Muslims within an Islamic state, in which the *millet* system was the non-Muslims' only option for self-administration. Centuries of legal discrimination and *millet* self-identity rendered the empire's non-Muslims more attracted to European Romantic ethnonational concepts than to the simple political concessions granted by the Young Ottomans' liberal program. To implement their agenda, the Young Ottomans would have to impose it from above, thus contradicting the liberal ideals that they avowedly embraced.

The reform plans of the Young Ottoman exiles required the help of Ottoman officials at the highest levels of government. They found their champion in Midhat Paşa, the powerful former governor of the Danube *vilayet*, who espoused the idea of constitutional government because of Abdülaziz's financial incompetence and autocratic disposition, the government's inability to quell rebellion in the provinces, and the Great Powers' increasing intervention in the empire's affairs. After deposing the financially profligate Abdülaziz (1875) and then the alcoholic and paranoid Murad V (1875-76), Midhat and his followers installed Abdülhamid. Appointed grand *vizir*, Midhat pressed the sultan for a constitution, and many Young Ottomans returned from exile to assist Midhat in his effort. Young Ottoman idealism joined with Midhat's practicality, and, by mid-December, only days after the Istanbul Conference convened, the two produced their desired constitution.

The document contained all the trappings of Western European representative government, including: A parliament, a cabinet administratively controlling the bureaucracy, an independent judiciary, freedom of religion, a graduated income tax, and the usual liberal guaranteed personal liberties. Voting for the parliament was to be conducted along religious lines, and, to placate the Balkan non-Muslims' national aspirations, Christians were granted more electoral power than their numbers merited. Midhat incorporated significant divergences from Western constitutional examples, however, to placate conservative Muslims. The sultan retained considerable power independent of government institutions: He could declare war, make treaties, coin money, and issue legally binding decrees without parliamentary approval; all laws required his official promulgation before taking legal effect; and he alone could declare a state emergency and convene or dissolve parliament. Thus Ottoman political realities compromised the Young Ottomans' liberal-democratic ideals.

It is doubtful that the 1876 constitution would have achieved its goals even without Midhat's compromise provisions. Almost no one in the empire possessed any experience with liberal democracy, and the vast majority of Muslim and non-Muslim subjects completely were ignorant of such concepts. Before the constitution's new system could operate effectively, the administrators needed training and the population required education in the necessary precepts, and both had to be convinced that liberal democracy was beneficial. That would require a great deal of time and experimentation, and during the ongoing Balkan crisis, time for the empire was at a premium.

Since the constitution's Western-like liberal-democratic provisions appeared to address the issues firing unrest among the empire's Balkan non-Muslims, the Great Powers had no recourse but to shelve their plans for forcing a solution on the Ottomans and support the proclaimed reforms. Both Britain and Russia, however, knowing that Abdülhamid had no personal interest in abiding by liberal-democratic restraints on his authority, realized that the constitution was worthless, and they doubted that the Ottoman government could actually implement its terms.

In January 1877 Russia brokered the Budapest Convention with Austria-Hungary that stipulated the latter's neutrality in case of hostilities with the Ottomans (avoiding in advance a repetition of the Crimean War's strategic fiasco). The convention implied the Habsburgs' acceptance of a Russian presence in the eastern Balkans in return for their right to occupy Ottoman Bosnia-Hercegovina. With Habsburg neutrality secured and British resistance muzzled by public opinion, the way was cleared for another Russo-Turkish war.

Russo-Turkish War, San Stefano, and Berlin

Beginning with the Bosnian and Hercegovinian rebellion, Russia incrementally moved toward war with the Ottoman Empire. Unofficial Panslav support of the rebels evolved into blatant assistance for Serbian and Montenegrin involvement. Reichstadt neutralized the Habsburgs in case of hostilities with the Ottomans and permitted Russia to issue its October ultimatum. That act heralded a change in the attitude of Tsar Alexander II, who up to that point resisted the militant Russian Panslavs' cries for military intervention in the Balkans out of concern for preserving pacific relations with Britain. When the Istanbul Conference collapsed, Alexander was convinced that war was inevitable. The Balkan development that tipped the scales in the *tsar*'s mind in favor of war and made such action possible by neutralizing British opposition was the failed Bulgarian 1876 uprising.

The Bulgarian national movement had proceeded along two tracks since its inception. The majority of middle-class Bulgarian nationalists favored an evolutionary approach, seeking an ethnically Bulgarian state by first winning official Ottoman recognition of a Bulgarian *millet* that could be parleyed into an autonomous political entity. Most Bulgarian nationalists considered their goals assured once the Bulgarian Exarchate was established.

Since most middle-class Bulgarians were not anxious to overthrow the Ottomans by force, a small band of revolutionary nationalists who rose from their ranks was a minority from the start. They placed no stock in evolutionary hopes but, rather, sought swift and complete independence for a Bulgarian state won through armed rebellion modeled after the uprising of the Serbs and Greeks, and they looked to Orthodox Russia and Serbia for support. Once the evolutionaries' struggle for an independent Bulgarian church was won, nationalist momentum swung to the revolutionaries' approach. This was not a natural development of victory in the Bulgarian Church Question but a shift forced by the radicals themselves.

After a series of ill-fated, poorly conceived, and unsupported uprisings in the 1840s and 1850s, the revolutionaries, led mostly by a group of writers, were forced either outside of the empire or underground. They eventually won support from a community of wealthy Bulgarian merchants residing in Romania's capital, Bucharest, just north of the Ottoman Bulgarian lands. The first Bulgarian nationalist revolutionary committee founded in Bucharest essentially was composed of conservative middle-class merchants who conceived "safe" plans that depended for success on outside support or intervention, thus minimizing actual Bulgarian participation and blame for failure. The fiery authentic revolutionaries—Lyuben Karavelov, Vasil Levski, and Hristo Botev—bore little truck with such schemes. They founded their own revolutionary organization (1871) and constructed a secret network of revolutionary cells among the Ottoman Bulgarians. Their plans for an uprising were stifled when Levski was captured and executed (1872) while conducting a clandestine trip in Ottoman territory.

The revolt in Bosnia and Hercegovina spurred the Bucharest-based Bulgarian revolutionaries into action. A Bulgarian uprising was hastily prepared to take advantage of Ottoman preoccupation, but it fizzled before it started. In the spring of 1876 another uprising erupted in the south-central Bulgarian lands. That sad affair was even more haphazardly planned than the previous one. The ill-armed and disorganized rebels did little more than publicly rally, sing newly written patriotic songs, and butcher their mostly pacific Muslim neighbors. Because few elementary security precautions were taken by the rebels, the Ottomans were able to organize swift retaliation. Within a month they crushed the uprising and reestablished control over the rebellious territories.

Had the Ottomans merely quashed the affair, the Bulgarians' 1876 "April" uprising would have passed virtually unnoticed by a Europe preoccupied with the looming international crisis sparked by the revolt in Bosnia and Hercegovina and the subsequent Serbo-Ottoman War. Unfortunately, the Ottomans, lacking adequate regular troops because of the problems in the northwest, were compelled to use irregular *başıbazuks* to quell the Bulgarians. Those irregulars mostly were drawn from Muslim inhabitants in the Bulgarian regions, many of whom had suffered at the rebels' hands or had heard horror stories of rebel maltreatment of local Muslims. Their blood hot with revenge, the *başıbazuks* inflicted an orgy of destruction, pillage, rape, and enslavement on the Bulgarians in the regions that had risen, making little distinction between rebels and passive peasants. The number of Bulgarians who perished before the irregulars' wrath burned itself out was at least 15,000. (Later Bulgarian nationalists exaggerated the toll to as high as 100,000.)

Word of the *başıbazuks'* atrocities filtered to the outside world by way of American-run Robert College (the first American foreign institution of its kind), located just north of Istanbul. The majority of the students were Bulgarian, and many received news of the grisly events from their families back home. Soon the Western diplomatic community in Istanbul was abuzz with rumors, which eventually found their way into newspapers in the West. Rumor-mongering news stories about Ottoman Muslim atrocities against Christians were particularly unwelcome in Britain, where Disraeli's government was committed to supporting the Ottomans in a situation already tense because of the ongoing Balkan crisis. A renowned American journalist from Ohio, Januarius A. MacGahan, who happened to be in London at the time, was hired by the Liberal opposition's newspaper *Daily News* to report on the massacre stories firsthand.

MacGahan toured the stricken regions of the Bulgarian uprising, accompanied unofficially by Eugene Schuyler, a member of the American legation in Istanbul and a seasoned diplomat and Russian scholar, and officially by Walter Baring of the British legation, who was sent along by his superiors to whitewash any unpleasantness that might be uncovered. While the reports of both Americans confirmed the savagery of the Ottoman retribution, MacGahan's purple descriptive prose, splashed across the *Daily News*'s front pages, galvanized British public opinion against Disraeli's pro-Ottoman policy. Most public support for the Ottomans melted when Gladstone published his *The Bulgarian Horrors* (based more on Schuyler's objective report on the situation than on MacGahan's emotionally charged yellow journalism). Hands tied by public pressure, Disraeli was forced to stand aside when Russia (where MacGahan's reports had been circulated in translation to St. Petersburg newspapers) declared war on the Ottoman Empire in 1877 with the publicly avowed goal of winning independence for the Bulgarians.

Bolstered by the Budapest Convention, Russia went through the motions of making a last effort to maintain peace by convincing the Great Powers to sign the London Convention (March 1877). Although that agreement requested that the Ottomans carry out measures already announced in the 1876 Constitution, it stipulated that the signatory Great Powers reserved the right to intervene within the empire if the Ottomans failed to do so in timely fashion. When the Ottomans rejected the convention, Tsar Alexander considered Russia free to implement the document's interventionist clause and declared war in April 1877.

Russia was in a favorable diplomatic position for initiating hostilities: France was noncommittal; Austria-Hungary was neutral; and Britain was hamstrung by anti-Ottoman public opinion and able only to warn Russia against attacking or occupying Istanbul and the Straits. To invade the Balkans, however, Russia would have to pass through Romania, which was still technically an Ottoman vassal state.

Just days before Alexander declared war, Russia signed an anti-Ottoman military convention with Romania, which permitted the Russians free passage through the principality's territory in return for recognition of Romanian sovereignty and territorial integrity. Romania then mobilized its forces, declared war on the Ottomans, and proclaimed its complete independence (May 1877).

Eschewing direct Romanian, Serbian, and Montenegrin military participation, Russian forces confidently crossed the Ottomans' Danube border in late June and penetrated southward to the Balkan Mountains. Units of Bulgarian volunteers joined the Russian ranks. Fearing a total Ottoman collapse, Britain prepared for war in the event that Istanbul fell, placing its eastern Mediterranean fleet on alert for possible intervention in the Straits. Just as international tensions rose over their initial advances, however, the Russians suffered an unexpected military reversal.

At the strategically located fortress city of Pleven (Plevna), Ottoman resistance stiffened. Fumbling leadership and poor tactics resulted in the Russians' failure to take the city quickly and free their communications for a deeper advance. A siege ensued and the humiliated Russians requested military assistance from Romania, Serbia, and Montenegro. Despite the intervention of those allies, Pleven held out until December, when starvation finally exacted its toll. The Russians resumed their advance and Ottoman resistance collapsed. As Russian forces pushed south in January 1878, the troops, the Bulgarian volunteers, and the emboldened local Bulgarian villagers inflicted a welter of atrocities on the local Muslim population. Some 260,000 Muslims perished in the war's carnage, and over 500,000 refugees fled with the retreating Ottoman forces.

In the midst of the military and human chaos, the Ottomans opened armistice talks with the Russians and Britain ordered its eastern Mediterranean fleet to Istanbul. By the end of February the Russians were in sight of the Ottoman capital. It seemed that Russia would realize its imperialist dream of acquiring the "Second Rome" and validating its Panslav claim to Orthodox European Slavic leadership. The English fleet then demonstrated in the Straits, and the Russians, taking the less-than-subtle hint, forced the Ottomans to sign the Treaty of San Stefano (3 March 1878), ending the war.

By the treaty's terms, Serbia, Montenegro, and Romania were granted complete independence, and the former two retained some (not all) territories occupied by their troops during the war. Russia received territories in eastern Anatolia, but the most important provisions involved the creation of an autonomous Bulgarian Principality.

The new Bulgarian state included virtually all of the central Balkans except for small regions around Istanbul, Edirne, and Thessaloniki. At the stroke of a pen, the Russians handed the Bulgarians possession of Bulgaria Proper (less Dobrudzha, which was given to Romania in compensation for Russia's annexation of Bessarabia), Thrace (less the three cities noted above), and all of Macedonia, making Bulgaria the single largest Balkan state. This was intentionally so. By rewarding the Bulgarians' national aspirations with borders exceeding even those of the Exarchate, Russia expected a rich return. Unable to control the strategic Straits directly, Russia believed that Bulgarian gratitude would accomplish that for them—new Bulgaria was intended to be a Russian puppet. (See Map 8.)

All of the European Great Powers and Balkan states raised a howl when San Stefano's terms became public. No Western European Power could accept a settlement that handed Russia virtual control of the crucial Straits. In Britain, anti-Ottoman public opinion quickly turned into intensely belligerent anti-Russian sentiment. (The lyrics of a popular song at the time—"We don't want to fight, but, by jingo, if we do, we've got the ships, we've got the men, we've got the money, too"—spawned a new term for bellicosely aggressive nationalist foreign policy: "Jingoism.") Romania chafed over Russia's annexation of Bessarabia, which Romanian nationalists claimed. Neither Serbia nor Montenegro was satisfied with its winnings, desiring all of the territories occupied during the war. Greece had been kept out of the war by a British blockade and so received nothing, while new Bulgaria was given Macedonian territories claimed by Greek nationalists. It was obvious that San Stefano's terms needed modification to safeguard Europe's continued peace.

German Chancellor Bismarck, eager to demonstrate the international weight of young Germany, invited all concerned to a June congress in Berlin to work out an acceptable final treaty. Only the concerns of the Great Powers were addressed there. Realizing that the Western Great Powers essentially were united in opposing a Russian-dominated eastern Balkans, Russia hoped to retain as many gains as possible without causing a major European war. The Balkan states' interests were listened to politely but carried little weight in the deliberations. The Ottomans were reduced to spectators at their own funeral, ignored and insulted by all. On 13 July 1878 the Balkan states received the final treaty's dictate.

Berlin upheld most of San Stefano's non-Bulgarian provisions. The independence of Serbia, Montenegro, and Romania was recognized; Russia retained its Anatolian acquisitions and Bessarabia; Romania received its slice of Dobrudzha. Greece again received nothing and actually lost territory, since Cyprus was handed over to Britain. To the Serbs' and Montenegrins' utter dismay, in a development completely unrelated to San Stefano but in accordance with the Reichstadt and Budapest conventions (as well as with a prevalent undercurrent of Western European anti-Russian and anti-Orthodox sentiment), Habsburg Austria-Hungary was permitted to occupy Bosnia-Hercegovina and the Sandjak of Novi Pazar, an Ottoman territory separating Serbia from Montenegro (a development that would hinder their future unification into a single Serbian state).

San Stefano's Bulgarian provisions underwent drastic modification. The large Russian-created principality was sliced into four parts. Bulgaria Proper, lying north and northwest of the Balkan Mountains, emerged as an autonomous Bulgarian Principality ruled by an elected prince governing under technical Ottoman suzerainty. The region directly south and southeast of Bulgaria was designated the Ottoman province of Eastern Rumelia, with its governor a Christian appointed by the sultan and approved by the Great Powers. Western Thrace, lying along the Aegean coast south of Eastern Rumelia, was returned to direct Ottoman control to cut off any Bulgarian access to that sea. Also returned to the Ottomans was all of Macedonia. (See Map 8.)

While the Berlin settlement may have headed off the immediate war crisis by satisfying the imperialist concerns of the Western European Great Powers, it created deep-seated dissatisfaction among all of the small Balkan states. The dismemberment of San Stefano Bulgaria struck the Bulgarians' short-lived national jubilation like a hammer blow. Euphoria swiftly changed to disillusionment and then to stubborn resolution to win back that which had been lost. Their faith in brother Orthodox Russia was shaken, even though the new liberal-democratic Bulgarian government was shaped with Russian encouragement and Russians held most of the prominent ministry and military offices in the principality.

The Serbs, forced to accept Habsburg occupation of territories that they considered their national preserve, felt betrayed by their longtime Russian allies, who had been willing to give away to Bulgarians Macedonian regions just as important to Serbian national aspirations. They made expedient accommodation with the Habsburgs to free themselves to deal with their new Bulgarian national rivals. The Greeks, their national territorial ambitions having been totally neglected at Berlin, resolved to bend every effort to win what they considered their rightful borders in the north.

The nationalist ambitions of all Balkan peoples would collide violently in the decades following the Berlin Congress, the Western European-imposed terms of which became the fundamental motivation for the peninsula's subsequent divisive events. (The same Western Europeans came to label those events disparagingly as "balkanization.") Nor would Europe in general be spared the consequences of the radicalized Balkan nationalisms generated by the Berlin settlement. Berlin became the first step taken down the road to the horrors of World War I.

FURTHER READINGS

General

Anderson, Matthew S. *The Eastern Question, 1774-1923.* New York: Macmillan, 1966.

Duggan, Stephen P. H. *The Eastern Question: A Study in Diplomacy.* Reprint ed. New York: AMS, 1970.

Gewehr, Wesley M. *The Rise of Nationalism in the Balkans, 1800-1930.* Reprint ed. Hamden, CT: Archon, 1967.

Harris, David. *A Diplomatic History of the Balkan Crisis of 1875-1878: The First Year.* Reprint ed. Chicago, IL: Archon, 1969.

Hutchinson, John, and Anthony D. Smith, eds. *Ethnicity.* Oxford: Oxford University Press, 1996.

Hutchinson, John, and Anthony D. Smith, eds. *Nationalism.* Oxford: Oxford University Press, 1994.

Jelavich, Barbara. *Russia's Balkan Entanglements, 1806-1914.* Cambridge: Cambridge University Press, 1991.

Jelavich, Charles, and Barbara Jelavich. *The Establishment of the Balkan National States, 1804-1920.* Seattle: University of Washington Press, 1977.

Macfie, A. L. *The Eastern Question, 1774-1923.* Revised ed. London: Longman, 1996.

Marriott, John A. R. *The Eastern Question: A Study in European Diplomacy.* 4th ed. Oxford: Clarendon, 1940.

Medlicott, W. N. *The Congress of Berlin and After: A Diplomatic History of the Near Eastern Settlement, 1878-1880.* London: Methuen, 1938.

Milkman, Richard. *Britain and the Eastern Question, 1875-1878.* Oxford: Clarendon, 1979.

Miller, William. *The Ottoman Empire and Its Successors, 1801-1927.* 4th ed. Cambridge: Cambridge University Press, 1936.

Milojković-Djurić, Jelena. *Panslavism and National Identity in Russia and in the Balkans, 1830-1880: Images of the Self and Others.* Boulder, CO: East European Monographs, 1994.

Petrovich, Michael B. *The Emergence of Russian Panslavism, 1856-1870.* New York: Columbia University Press, 1966.

Rupp, George H. *A Wavering Friendship: Russia and Austria, 1876-1878.* Reprint ed. Philadelphia, PA: Porcupine, 1976.

Seton-Watson, Robert W. *The Rise of Nationality in the Balkans.* Reprint ed. New York: H. Fertig, 1966.

Stojanović, Mihajlo D. *The Great Powers and the Balkans, 1875-1878.* Cambridge: Cambridge University Press, 1939.

Sugar, Peter F. *Nationalism and Religion in the Balkans Since the 19th Century.* Seattle: University of Washington, Donald W. Treadway Papers, July 1996.

Sumner, B. H. *Russia and the Balkans, 1870-1880.* Oxford: Oxford University Press, 1937.

White, George W. *Nationalism and Territory: Constructing Group Identity in Southeastern Europe.* Lanham, MD: Rowman and Littlefield, 1999.

Albania

Fleming, K. E. *The Muslim Bonaparte: Diplomacy and Orientalism in Ali Pasha's Greece.* Princeton, NJ: Princeton University Press, 1999.

Plomer, William C. F. *Ali the Lion: Ali of Tebeleni, Pasha of Yanina, 1741-1822.* London: J. Cape, 1936.

Bulgaria

Clarke, James F. *Bible Societies, American Missionaries and the National Revival of Bulgaria.* Reprint ed. New York: Arno, 1971.

Firkatian, Mari. *The Forest Traveler: Georgi Stoikov Rakovski and Bulgarian Nationalism.* New York: Peter Lang, 1995.

Gavrilova, Raina. *Bulgarian Urban Culture in the Eighteenth and Nineteenth Centuries.* Selinsgrove, PA: Susquehanna University Press, 2000.

Genchev, Nikolai. *The Bulgarian National Revival Period.* Sofia: Sofia Press, 1977.

Greene, Francis V. *The Campaign in Bulgaria, 1877-1878.* London: Hugh Rees, 1903.

Harris, David. *Britain and the Bulgarian Horrors of 1876.* Chicago, IL: University of Chicago Press, 1939.

MacDermott, Mercia. *The Apostle of Freedom: A Portrait of Vasil Levsky Against a Background of Nineteenth Century Bulgaria.* Sofia: Sofia Press, 1979.

MacGahan, Januarius A. *The Turkish Atrocities in Bulgaria* [with parallel Bulgarian translation by Theodore D. Dimitrov]. Geneva: published by the compiler and translator, 1966.

Mach, Richard von. *The Bulgarian Exarchate: Its History and the Extent of Its Authority in Turkey.* London: T. F. Unwin, 1907.

Meininger, Thomas A. *The Formation of a Nationalist Bulgarian Intelligentsia, 1835-1878.* New York: Garland, 1987.

———. *Ignatiev and the Establishment of the Bulgarian Exarchate, 1864-1872: A Study in Personal Diplomacy.* Madison: State Historical Society of Wisconsin, 1970.

Croatia

Bjelovučić, Harriet. *The Ragusan Republic: Victim of Napoleon and Its Own Conservatism.* Leiden: E. J. Brill, 1970.

Despalatović, Elinor M. *Ljudevit Gaj and the Illyrian Movement.* Boulder, CO: East European Monographs, 1975.

Prpić, George J. *French Rule in Croatia: 1806-1813.* Thessaloniki: Institute for Balkan Studies, 1964.

Rothenberg, Gunther E. *The Military Border in Croatia, 1740-1881: A Study of an Imperial Institution.* Chicago, IL: University of Chicago Press, 1966.

Voinovitch, Louis. *Dalmatia and the Jugoslav Movement.* London: Allen and Unwin, 1920.

Greece

Chaconas, Stephen G. *Adamantios Korais: A Study in Greek Nationalism.* New York: Columbia University Press, 1941.

Crawley, C. W. *The Question of Greek Independence: A Study of British Policy in the Near East, 1821-1833.* Cambridge: Cambridge University Press, 1930.

Dakin, Douglas. *The Greek Struggle for Independence, 1821-1833.* London: Batsford, 1973.

Dontas, Domna N. *Greece and the Great Powers, 1863-1875.* Thessaloniki: Institute for Balkan Studies, 1966.

———. *The Last Phase of the War of Independence in Western Greece (December 1827 to May 1829).* Thessaloniki: Institute for Balkan Studies, 1966.

Finlay, George. *History of the Greek Revolution and of the Reign of King Otho.* 2 vols. in 1. Reprint ed. London: Zeno, 1971.

Frazee, Charles A. *The Orthodox Church and Independent Greece, 1821-1852.* Cambridge: Cambridge University Press, 1969.

Herzfeld, Michael. *Ours Once More: Folklore, Ideology, and the Making of Modern Greece.* Austin: University of Texas Press, 1982.

Jelavich, Barbara. *Russia and Greece during the Regency of King Othon, 1832-1835.* Thessaloniki: Institute for Balkan Studies, 1962.

———. *Russia and the Greek Revolution of 1843.* Munich: R. Oldenbourg, 1966.

Kaldis, William P. *John Capodistrias and the Modern Greek State.* Madison: State Historical Society of Wisconsin, 1963.

Kofos, Evangelos. *Greece and the Eastern Crisis, 1875-1878.* Thessaloniki: Institute for Balkan Studies, 1975.
McGrew, William W. *Land and Revolution in Modern Greece, 1800-1881: The Transition in the Tenure and Exploitation of Land from Ottoman Rule to Independence.* Kent, OH: Kent State University Press, 1985.
Pappas, Nicholas C. *Greeks in Russian Military Service in the Late Eighteenth and Early Nineteenth Centuries.* Thessaloniki: Institute for Balkan Studies, 1991.
Petropulos, Anthony. *Politics and Statecraft in the Kingdom of Greece, 1833-1843.* Princeton, NJ: Princeton University Press, 1968.
St. Clair, William. *That Greece Might Still Be Free: The Philhellenes in the War of Greek Independence.* London: Oxford University Press, 1972.
Todorov, Varban. *Greek Federalism During the Nineteenth Century: Ideas and Projects.* Boulder, CO: East European Monographs, 1995.
Woodhouse, Christopher M. *The Battle of Navarino.* London: Hodder and Stoughton, 1965.
———. *Capodistria: The Founder of Greek Independence.* London: Oxford University Press, 1973.
———. *The Greek War of Independence: Its Historical Setting.* London: Hutchinson University Library, 1952.

Macedonia

Pandevski, Manol. *Macedonia and the Macedonians in the Eastern Crisis.* Translated by Alexandra R. Gjuzelova. Skopje: Macedonian Review Editions, 1978.
Tachiaos, Anthony-Emil N. *The Bulgarian National Awakening and Its Spread into Macedonia.* Thessaloniki : Society for Macedonian Studies, 1990.

Montenegro

Djilas, Milovan. *Njegoš: Poet, Prince, Bishop.* Translated by Michael B. Petrovich. New York: Harcourt, Brace and World, 1966.

Ottoman Empire

Bailey, F. E. *British Policy and the Turkish Reform Movement: A Study in Anglo-Turkish Relations, 1826-1853.* Cambridge, MA: Harvard University Press, 1942.
Berkes, Niyazi. *The Development of Secularism in Turkey.* Montreal: McGill University Press, 1964.
Davison, Roderic H. *Reform in the Ottoman Empire, 1856-1876.* Princeton, NJ: Princeton University Press, 1963.
Devereux, Robert. *The First Ottoman Constitutional Period: A Study of the Midhat Constitution and Parliament.* Baltimore, MD: Johns Hopkins University Press, 1963.
Göçek, Fatma Müge. *Rise of Bourgeoisie, Demise of Empire: Ottoman Westernization and Social Change.* New York: Oxford University Press, 1995.
Jelavich, Barbara. *The Ottoman Empire, the Great Powers, and the Straits Question.* Bloomington: Indiana University Press, 1973.
Karpat, Kemal. *An Inquiry into the Social Foundations of Nationalism in the Ottoman State: From Social Estates to Classes, From Millet to Nationalism.* Princeton, NJ: Princeton Center for International Studies, 1973.
Mardin, Serif. *The Genesis of Young Ottoman Thought: A Study in the Modernization of Turkish Political Ideas.* Princeton, NJ: Princeton University Press, 1962.
McCarthy, Justin. *Death and Exile: The Ethnic Cleansing of Ottoman Muslims, 1821-1922.* Princeton, NJ: Darwin Press, 1995.
———. *The Ottoman Peoples and the End of Empire.* Oxford: Oxford University Press, 2000.

Palmer, Alan. *The Decline and Fall of the Ottoman Empire.* New York: M. Evans, 1992.
Shaw, Stanford J. *Between Old and New: The Ottoman Empire under Sultan Selim III, 1789-1807.* Cambridge: Cambridge University Press, 1971.

Romania

Bobango, Gerald. *The Emergence of the Romanian National State.* Boulder, CO: East European Monographs, 1979.
Bodea, Cornelia. *The Romanians' Struggle for Unification, 1834-1849.* Translated by Liliana Teodoreanu. Bucharest: The Academy, 1970.
Campbell, John C. *French Influence and the Rise of Roumanian Nationalism.* Reprint ed. New York: Arno, 1971.
East, William G. *The Union of Moldavia and Wallachia, 1859: An Episode in Diplomatic History.* Reprint ed. New York: Octagon, 1973.
Florescu, Radu R. *The Struggle against Russia in the Roumanian Principalities, 1821-1854.* Munich: Societas Academica Dacoromana, 1962.
Georgescu, Vlad. *Political Ideas and the Enlightenment in the Romanian Principalities, 1750-1831.* Boulder, CO: East European Monographs, 1971.
Hitchins, Keith. *The Rumanians, 1774-1866.* Oxford: Clarendon, 1996.
Jelavich, Barbara. *Russia and the Formation of the Romanian National State, 1821-1878.* Cambridge: Cambridge University Press, 1983.
Kellogg, Frederick. *The Road to Romanian Independence.* West Lafayette, IN: Purdue University Press, 1995.
Michelson, Paul E. *Conflict and Crisis: Romanian Political Development, 1861-1871.* New York: Garland, 1987.
Oldson, William O. *A Providential Anti-Semitism: Nationalism and Polity in Nineteenth Century Romania.* Philadelphia, PA: American Philosophical Society, 1991.
Riker, Thad W. *The Making of Roumania: A Study of an International Problem, 1856-1866.* London: Oxford University Press, 1931.

Serbia

Karanovich, Milenko. *The Development of Education in Serbia and the Emergence of Its Intelligentsia, 1838-1858.* Boulder, CO: East European Monographs, 1995.
MacKenzie, David. *The Serbs and Russian Pan-Slavism, 1875-1878.* Ithaca, NY: Cornell University Press, 1967.
———. *Serbs and Russians: Some Historical Relationships.* Boulder, CO: East European Monographs, 1996.
Meriage, Lawrence P. *Russia and the First Serbian Insurrection, 1804-1813.* New York: Garland, 1987.
Obradović, Dimitrije. *The Life and Adventures of . . .* Translated and edited by George R. Noyes. Berkeley: University of California Press, 1953.
Ranke, Leopold von. *The History of Servia and the Servian Revolution, with a Sketch of the Insurrection in Bosnia.* Translated by Louisa A. Kerr. London: H. G. Bohn, 1853.
Stokes, Gale. *Politics as Development: The Emergence of Political Parties in Nineteenth Century Serbia.* Durham, NC: Duke University Press, 1990.
Wilson, Duncan. *The Life and Times of Vuk Stefanoviş Karadžić, 1787-1864: Literacy, Literature, and National Independence in Serbia.* Oxford: Clarendon, 1970.

PART FOUR

Era of Nation-State Nationalism

1878–1945

Romantic nationalism turned to nation-state nationalism in the Balkan states of Serbia, Montenegro, Greece, Romania, and Bulgaria after 1878. Each structured domestic affairs in support of nationalist territorial expansion at the expense of the contracting Ottoman Empire, often in mutually exclusive competition with one another. Particularly contentious was the rivalry for Macedonia. For self-defense, the Ottoman Albanians and Macedonians were forced to develop their own national agendas. During 1908 Austro-Hungarian annexation of Bosnia-Hercegovina and the Young Turk Revolution in the Ottoman Empire exacerbated the nationalist tensions. The Balkan states grudgingly united against the Ottomans in the Balkan Wars of 1912-13 but swiftly fell out over dividing the resulting territorial spoils. With the Sarajevo assassination of 1914, Serbian nationalism ignited World War I, and the Balkan states aligned themselves in the struggle so as to advance their nationalist goals. After the war, the treaties of Versailles rewarded the victorious Great Powers' Balkan allies with large nation-states—the nationally artificial Yugoslavia and Greater Romania. Bulgaria, ally of the defeated Central Powers, was truncated, and Albania was relegated to Italian dependency. During the interwar years, national and economic problems in the Balkan states ultimately led to Nazi domination during World War II and, except for Greece, the Communist takeover of them all by war's end.

CHAPTER THIRTEEN

Early Nation-States

Noone of the Balkan states was satisfied nationalistically by the results of the Berlin Congress. Fired by Romantic ideals of ethnic unity regarding the "nation" concept, their leaders considered the borders drawn in Berlin unacceptable—their respective boundaries encompassed too little of their historically claimed ethnic "homelands" and too few of their conationals. The political reality demonstrated by Berlin, however, initially precluded any major unilateral action on their part to satisfy their nationalist territorial interests. It was obvious that the nature and extent of the Balkan states' existence depended on the European Great Powers' will and not on that of their own. Thus their leaderships made every effort to shape their states as springboards for national territorial state expansion should future international circumstances permit them to present the Great Powers with faits accomplis.

From Romantic to Nation-State Nationalism

Because the Balkan Peninsula was controlled by two large imperial states—the Ottoman and Habsburg—when its non-Muslim populations were exposed to Western-type nationalist precepts, they initially embraced Romantic ethnonationalism, grounded in language, history, religion, and ethnography. Among most of the Orthodox Balkan populations, their earliest national leaders rose from the ranks of either the clergy or the nascent middle class; among the Catholic Balkan peoples in the Habsburg Empire (such as the Croats) and the Orthodox Principality Romanians, an existing aristocratic class provided additional, and predominant, national leadership.

The Balkan national "Enlighteners" (as they later were labeled) were traditional Romantics, researching, collecting, and writing ethnic-oriented history, ethnography, and literature, leavened with heavy doses of contemporary Western rationalist and scientific ideals, and propagating their efforts among the middle classes through education and publishing. Often working outside of the Balkans in Western Europe or Russia, where they directly imbibed scientific rationalist, nationalist, and Romantic currents, the Ottoman and Habsburg Balkan Enlighteners imbued their activities with near-messianic zeal, producing voluminous collections of folk tales, epics, and songs, ethnonational histories (much of which often consisted of myths or specious interpretations of the available sources), and translations of Western European and Russian secular literature with introductions extolling Western concepts. Clerical Enlighteners continued publishing religious texts, but they frequently appended to them prefaces with similar content.

In the heady days of Panslavism during the 1830s and 1840s, the efforts of the Ottoman Balkan Enlighteners were augmented by those of noted Panslav advocates, such as the Slovak Pavel Šafařík, the Slovene Bartolomej (Jerej) Kopitar, the Ruthenian Iuri Venelin, and the immigrant American Therese Albertine Louise von Talvj (often considered the first American Slavist). Through their ethnic-oriented linguistic and historical efforts, coupled with their idealization of Western scientific rationalism, the nationalist Enlighteners succeeded in shaping national identities and engendering a desire for political self-determination independent of continued Ottoman suzerainty among the educated elements in the various Ottoman Balkan non-Muslim populations.

The Enlighteners' Ottoman non-Muslim devotees succeeded in winning their initial national goals of separate ethnically identified states by 1878 (some four decades before the Western European Habsburgs' Balkan populations did so). Whether achieved through revolution, religious restructuring, or administrative defiance, the process was emotionally charged. That emotionalism, fed by the impassioned tocsin of ethnonationalism and the heat of the struggle for statehood, was carried over into the national policy making of the new states by their political leaders, the former Romantic nationalist vanguards.

Just as the Balkan Romantic nationalists found their inspiration and models in Western Europe, the leaders of the post-Berlin Balkan states also looked to the West in shaping their new nation-states.

The goals of nineteenth-century Romantic nationalism were to transform an ethnic group into a culturally, historically, and geographically unique "nation" and then provide it with a state representing and defending its sovereign uniqueness politically, socially, and economically, with borders delineating a homogeneous national "homeland"—a "nation-state." In Western Europe the nation-state concept evolved from the merging of French revolutionary civic and Romantic ethnic national ideals that occurred in the years preceding the Revolution of 1848.

Following that event, which signaled the failure of post-Vienna repression, even monarchist societies adopted the nation-state as the ultimate, most "natural" (in Enlightenment terms) form of political organization, since its structure ideally encompassed all aspects of human social existence. By the third quarter of the nineteenth century the leaders of most European societies believed that the nation-state truly represented, in Voltaire's words, the "best of all possible worlds." Those who did not—in the Habsburg Empire and Russia—ultimately were doomed to political extinction.

The ideal nation-state envisioned by Western European nationalist leaders rarely was attained in reality. Virtually all of the ethnic-oriented Western European nation-states were not ethnonationally homogeneous (nor are they today), and many had conationals left beyond their borders in neighboring foreign nation-states. That they all eventually were accepted as nation-states testified to the innate force of nationalist ideals and to the ability of the leaders of various national groups to indoctrinate the masses in those ideals.

The road from civic, through Romantic, to nation-state nationalism was paved by small nationalist elites who successfully forged increasingly expanding popular bases among various regional and ethnic populations through widened education and literacy. While mass education undoubtedly served an economic purpose in creating a more literate (and thus productive) workforce for the states' industrial sectors, it also cemented national ideals and pride, identity with the state, and support for the leaders' nationalist policies among the general citizenry. So forceful was this indoctrinating process that those Western European nation-states that did not quite fit the overt ethnic-oriented model (such as Belgium and Switzerland) were created by the willingness of assorted ethnonational groups to cooperate to avoid incorporation into neighboring ethnic-oriented nation-states. That cooperation was cemented by successfully inculcating regional ethnic identities and liberal-democratic ideals through education.

While Western Europeans came to view the nation-state as the definitive political expression of their cultural evolution, it certainly also was inherently divisive and potentially violent. This became apparent by the mid-nineteenth century, when the intellectual stimulus of Charles Darwin's theory of natural selection, as first applied to nation-state politics by Napoleon III and Bismarck, fed a series of inter-Western European national wars: The Franco-Austrian War (1859), the Schleswig-Holstein War (1864), the Austro-Prussian War (1866), and the Franco-Prussian War (1870-71).

The Romantic notion of a nation's cultural uniqueness implied a sense of group self-superiority. Although beneficial to the process of creating strong ethnonational group bonds where none previously existed, once nation-statehood was achieved, such national self-perceptions easily took on more belligerent overtones, expressed as xenophobia (the "we're-number-one" syndrome), messianism (America's "Manifest Destiny," Britain's "Rule the Waves," or the Soviet's "Vanguard of the World Proletariat"), or even outright racism (Nazi Germany). Hand in hand with national self-superiority was an innate suspicion of all other national groups, which posed potential threats to any nation's national political, economic, or territorial interests. From its inception, modern nation-state nationalism spawned an "us-against-them" group mentality that ensured relations among states would be highly competitive and often antagonistic.

The highest expression of national self-superiority was possession of a sovereign nation-state, whose borders definitively delineated the nation's "homeland." Borders meant lines drawn on maps that reflected inviolable barriers on the earth's surface ideally separating distinct nations. At no time in modern history, however, have lines on a map neatly and definitively separated any two neighboring ethnically defined nations on the actual ground. The utter inability of borders to represent such an ideal frequently created bitter territorial disputes among neighboring nations, which claimed conational persons and lands inevitably left on the "wrong side" of virtually every nation-state border. This fact, the so-called national minorities problem, combined with nationalism's innate senses of self-superiority and suspicion of others, rendered national conflict endemic in the political culture of the modern Western European nation-state.

Despite the numerous nationalist-motivated conflicts among Western European nation-states during the second half of the nineteenth and first half of the twentieth centuries, certain elements in the West's cultural makeup, although never completely effective, tended to dampen the frequency (but not the intensity) of such conflicts. Liberal-democratic principles often restrained the rash use of military force and helped reconcile national minorities with the majority nation in some nation-states. Industrial capitalism, despite its underlying motivation for a number of national conflicts, also could inhibit conflicts because of its need for markets and raw materials beyond the confines of nation-state borders, thus creating mutually important international commercial networks among separate nation-states that stood to lose economically should they be disrupted. With a few exceptions, Western Europe's freedom from multiethnic imperial states made nation-state building a process of either civic transformation (transforming an existing state) or national unification (combining a number of existing ethnically similar and geographically contiguous states into a single whole), rather than one of national liberation. While both the civic and unification processes often entailed revolution and warfare, that of national liberation demanded such actions and engendered the most intense and extreme attributes of national animosity (as in the Habsburg Empire during 1848-49).

Western Europe's rise to global preeminence by the nineteenth century resulted in the export of its nationalist, nation-state political culture to non-Western European populations, many of whom lay within large multiethnic empires ruled by ethnically foreign masters and whose own cultural traditions did not include liberal democracy or industrial capitalism to mitigate its potentially explosive effects. For them, adopting Western European political culture meant undertaking national liberation. As the nonwesterners in closest proximity to Western Europe, the Ottoman Balkan non-Muslims were the first to adopt the West's nationalist and nation-state models, becoming the first to demonstrate the divisive and violent extremities to which they could be taken in non-Western societies.

Among the Ottoman Balkan non-Muslims, Ottoman theocracy and its *millet* traditions, which provided an Orthodox group identity to the illiterate masses, made religious affiliation an inescapably crucial component of their ethnonational identities. Imported Romantic ideals not only laid the foundation for their ethnic national identities but fired the intensity of national emotions in their liberation struggles against an empire perceived as completely "alien" in culture because of its different religion. By the time Berlin confirmed the existence of Balkan national states, the "nations" in all of them were consciously self-identified as Orthodox Christian as well as ethnic.

The majority of those involved in Balkan national liberation movements (including some of the leaders) understood their struggle essentially in terms of ethnically identified Orthodox Christians versus Muslims (most often inaccurately amalgamated into religiously defined "Turks")—a civilizational conflict with heightened emotional enmities. The endemic national animosities of Western European nation-state nationalism proved downright vicious in the Balkans, where Orthodox Christian nationalists initially characterized Ottoman Islamic society as the completely foreign and threatening enemy par excellence. Whereas in Western Europe national struggles involved parties sharing common civilizational values, in the Balkans such was not the case, and, during the national liberation struggles leading to Berlin, human atrocities abounded. (Tens of thousands of Christians were killed by Ottoman forces and well over a million Muslims perished or were driven out by the Christians in the regions of 1878 Greece, Serbia, and Bulgaria.)

The fiery nationalist emotionalism continued in the national policy making of the post-1878 Balkan states, which, once again following Western European models, were recognized as nation-states. Theoretically, they should have included within their borders all of their respective conationals and claimed historic "homelands." Great Power interests at Berlin, however, determined otherwise. Great Britain, to bolster its Ottoman buffer as much as possible, prevented the mass transfer of Ottoman territories claimed by the nationalists to the Balkan states. Austria-Hungary, eager to exert renewed Great Power status, blocked Serbian nationalist territorial goals by occupying Bosnia-Hercegovina and the Sandjak; and Russia, desperate to maintain a Balkan foothold, annexed mostly Romanian-inhabited Bessarabia. All of the Great Powers completely ignored the national territorial ambitions of the Greek nationalists.

After Berlin, the national leaderships of the Balkan states were frustrated but determined to win control of every territory that they considered vital for validating "true" nation-state existence. Radicalized by the emotional intensities of their various ethnonational liberation struggles, each became obsessed with the idea of state "national unification." For Serbia, that meant incorporating Bosnia-Hercegovina, Kosovo, Macedonia, and parts of northern Albania with an outlet on the Adriatic Sea. The Greeks demanded that their nation-state encompass Ottoman Thessaly, Epiros, southern Albania, and much of Macedonia (as well as assorted Aegean, Adriatic, and Mediterranean islands). The Bulgarian nationalists in the autonomous Bulgarian Principality burned to win back those San Stefano territories (Eastern Rumelia, Macedonia, Western Thrace, and part of Dobrudzha) stripped away by Berlin. The Romanian nationalists demanded Bessarabia and all of Dobrudzha. Leaders in Montenegro laid claim to Hercegovina, northern Albania, and the Sandjak of Novi Pazar.

All of the leaders of the post-Berlin Balkan states bent every effort to develop the wherewithal for achieving their nationalist goals. Again, they enjoyed Western European models for such efforts. Bismarck's wars of German unification and the localized warfare of the Italians' unification provided clear examples of successfully using military force for such ends. The political leaders of the Balkan states subordinated political structures, economic development, and nationalist-oriented education to their overriding national objective: To advance their states' military capabilities for winning ethnonational nation-state unification when circumstances permitting their use arose. Whether the national enemy was the Ottoman Empire or another Balkan nation-state territorial competitor made little difference in the nationalists' schemes. The consequences of the militant ethnonational nation-state unification approach taken by the Balkan states after Berlin truly were unfortunate: Ingrained state divisiveness; heightened ethnonational animosities and violence; and unhealthy, inequitable, and stunted social and economic development.

The Balkan States' National Imperative and the Great Powers

Prior to 1878 the Serbs, Greeks, and Romanians possessed small, ethnically identified states in which some nation-state nationalism already was present. Constraints imposed by the "Eastern Question" largely prevented them from actively pursuing expansion. The Berlin Congress changed the situation. Although Berlin was convened to determine Great Power relationships, that determination was couched almost exclusively in terms of Balkan national development. By officially recognizing the national independence of the four existing states, by sanctioning the creation of a fifth (autonomous Bulgaria) at the Ottoman Empire's expense, and by giving highest priority to matters of those states' territories and borders, the Great Powers unwittingly signaled that the Balkans' future lay with the Ottoman Empire's Christian European inhabitants by bestowing their imprimatur on nation-statehood for them. In validating the creation of Balkan nation-states but then obstructing their implementation in practice through the treaty's territorial terms, the Great Powers virtually assured future national unrest and conflict in the Balkans.

All of the post-Berlin Balkan nation-states shared a common national imperative: To satisfy their "rightful" territorial ambitions within the context of existing Great Power relationships. Of primary consideration was the new but adamant antagonism between Habsburg Austria-Hungary and Russia for dominant control over the Balkans.

In essentially rewarding the Habsburgs and punishing the Russians regarding Balkan expansion, Berlin intensified the two rivals' animosities. In response to the heightened tensions, German Chancellor Bismarck forged an alliance with Austria-Hungary (1879). After his attempt to dampen German-Russian stresses through the Three Emperors' League collapsed (1881), he concluded the anti-Russian Central Alliance among Germany, Austria-Hungary, and Italy (1882). When Kaiser William II (1888-1918) expelled Bismarck from office (1890), German-Russian relations deteriorated further, and Russia, needing outside investment for its tardy industrialization, moved closer to France, which was willing to provide large loans in return for support against Germany. French loans to Russia led to a military alliance (1894), which finalized the web of international treaties that came to divide the European Great Powers into two opposing camps: The Central Powers (Austro-German) and the Entente (Franco-Russian). Italy and England, on the peripheries of the alliances, were drawn into the system on opposite sides—Italy unsteadily with the Central Powers, England with the Entente.

The Balkan states' leaders, except in Greece, felt somewhat betrayed by Russia at Berlin. Serb nationalists were incensed that their Russian allies accepted Bosnia-Hercegovina's Habsburg occupation. The Romanians were infuriated that Russia annexed Bessarabia. To Bulgarian nationalists, genuinely grateful to Russia for their national liberation, Russia appeared too ready to accept San Stefano Bulgaria's dismemberment; although willing to receive Russian assistance in maintaining their new state, they had no intentions of serving merely as Russia's pawns.

No other Balkan nationalists were as disillusioned over Berlin's results as the Serbs. Prince Milan Obrenović, an intelligent but dissolute man personally not enamored of the state he ruled (calling it "that damned country"), correctly realized that the Berlin Congress represented a major Russian diplomatic defeat that crippled its Great Power standing. Milan never enjoyed good relations with Russia because his acquisition of the Serbian throne had spoiled Tsar Alexander II's hopes of uniting Serbia and Montenegro into a single state under the Montenegrin prince's rule. For both policy and personal reasons, therefore, Milan saw no alternative for Serbia but to establish closer ties to Austria-Hungary, despite the fact that, at Berlin, the

Habsburgs frustrated Serbian expansion into Bosnia-Hercegovina and enabled the Ottomans to retain the Sandjak of Novi Pazar. (See Map 8.)

With the support of Premier Jovan Ristić, and to the dismay of pro-Russian Serbian nationalists, Milan built an understanding with Austria-Hungary. In the post-Berlin atmosphere of Russian betrayal prevailing among the nationalists, however, the diehard pro-Russians were in no position to counter Milan's foreign policy reorientation. His efforts were aided by the rise of educated middle-class, Western-leaning Progressive and Radical political parties espousing liberal-democratic ideals. The highly liberal Progressives viewed Russia as backward and primitive relative to the West, while the more democratic Radicals, led by Nikola Pašić, lived up to their name with some of the near-socialist types of institutions that they espoused.

With pro-Western sentiment in the ascendant, Milan brought his state into the Habsburg orbit through a series of railroad, commercial, and political agreements, all of which were weighted in Austria-Hungary's favor. A railroad construction agreement (1880) extended Serbian rail lines southward from Belgrade but tied them directly to the Austro-Hungarian network in the north. After difficult negotiations, a commercial treaty with the Habsburgs was signed (1881), by which Austria-Hungary became the near-exclusive market for Serbian products while its goods received privileged tariff status in Serbia. A political agreement (also 1881) promised Habsburg support for Serbian southward expansion into Macedonia should future developments permit, approved kingdom status for Serbia, and stipulated that, should either state find itself at war, the other would remain neutral. In return for Habsburg concessions, Milan was obliged to squash all anti-Habsburg agitation on Serbian soil and actively combat such activity in both Bosnia-Hercegovina and the Sandjak. Also, Serbia agreed not to negotiate with any foreign state or permit foreign military forces on Serbian territory without the Habsburgs' express prior approval.

As a result of these agreements, Serbia was transformed into a dependent Habsburg satellite. Milan had no other choice. Prevented from expanding into Bosnia-Hercegovina, Serbia could seek national expansion only in Macedonia, and Austria-Hungary was willing to back such an effort so long as Serbian attention was deflected from the occupied provinces. Thus the Habsburgs tolerated Milan's self-elevation to king (1882) and saved Serbia from serious military defeat after Milan unwisely declared war on Bulgaria (1885) hoping to gain new territory in the southeast. Within Serbia, however, Milan's misstep regarding Bulgaria and his pro-Habsburg policies spawned unrest among the nationalists. Public quarrels with his Russian-Romanian wife over personal issues and foreign policy quickly became reflected within Serbia's governing factions, eventually forcing Milan to accept a new, more democratic constitution (1888) and then to abdicate in favor of his young son Aleksandr Obrenović (1889-1903).

Less skilled than his father and a capricious individual, Aleksandr's personal qualities played a role in shifting Serbia's foreign ties from Austria-Hungary back to

Russia. He caused national humiliation by insisting on marrying his mistress, Draga Mašina, a widow, a commoner, and a women of ill moral repute, who also was thought infertile. Disgusted by public scandals surrounding the reigning family that made the Serbs European high society's laughingstock, and fearful that the Obrenović line was in danger of dying out, in 1903 a group of young nationalist military officers broke into the royal palace in Belgrade and butchered Aleksandr, his wife, the premier and war minister, and two of Draga's brothers, earning the Serbs the abhorrence of Western European public opinion. The conspirators installed as king the only possible royal candidate, Petr Karadjordjević (1904-21), a staunch traditional Serbian nationalist with decidedly pro-Russian sentiments.

Under Petr's rule, the Obrenović links to Austria-Hungary were broken and Serbia's foreign policy was realigned in favor of Russia and France. The process began with the so-called "Pig War" (1906-11), in which the Habsburgs attempted to punish Petr's attempts to expand Serbia's commercial contacts beyond the Austro-Hungarian monopoly to neighboring Bulgaria by closing their border to Serbian pork products (the single most lucrative commodity in Serbia's export trade with Austria-Hungary). The Habsburgs' tariff war backfired, since it freed Serbia to seek commercial relations with other states and acquire new markets for its products. The situation also permitted Serbia to acquire military armaments outside of Austria-Hungary, so Serbia signed a new weapons contract with France, severing dependence on Austro-Hungarian manufactured arms and opening an armaments trade relationship with the Entente Powers. By the time that the "Pig War" came to a negotiated end (1911), Serbia was firmly entrenched in the Entente camp, a fact that freed the Serbian nationalists to intensify efforts at national expansion into Bosnia-Hercegovina as well as into Ottoman lands.

Unlike the attitude in Serbia and the other Balkan Slavic states, non-Slav Romanian nationalists did not view Russia as a "brotherly" Great Power. Outside of a shared Orthodox tradition, they held little in common with the Russians. Unhappy memories of the early nineteenth-century Russian protectorate were still fresh in their minds, and, in light of the Romanian military assistance given Russia during the recent war under treaty terms guaranteeing Romanian territorial integrity, Russia's acquisition of Bessarabia rankled. Although Romania received "compensation" of sorts—conditional international recognition as an independent state and a large portion of Dobrudzha—Russia had blocked the inclusion of the important Danubian port city of Silistra in Romania's grant to preserve it for Bulgaria. On the whole, the Romanian nationalists considered themselves ill-served by the Russians at Berlin. (See Map 8.)

Fearful that Russia planned to reestablish a protectorate over Romania, and wary of the Russian presence in Bulgaria, Prince Carol turned to Austria-Hungary for support. After having himself crowned Romanian king (1881), Carol, a German Hohenzollern, first tried to secure an alliance with Germany but was instructed by

Bismarck to negotiate with his Habsburg allies instead. An alliance with Austria-Hungary was not the most desirable for the Romanians. The position of "brother" Transylvanian Romanians following the 1867 Compromise, which placed them under direct Hungarian rule, progressively deteriorated, and the Habsburgs threatened to cripple Romania's economic situation by seeking to extend their control over all river traffic on the Danube. The perceived Russian threat, however, overcame the Romanians' concerns with those issues.

In 1883 Romania signed a secret anti-Russian defensive military treaty with Austria-Hungary, which was immediately joined by Germany and later (1888) by Italy, thus associating Romania officially with the Central Alliance. Although the treaty was periodically renewed until 1914, for reasons of foreign policy with regard to Russia and Bulgaria as well as domestic concern over reaction from the more vocal nationalists who viewed the Habsburgs as a threat equal to the Russians, Carol kept the alliance secret from all but a few handpicked government ministers.

Disappointment over San Stefano Bulgaria's dismemberment at Berlin was immense among the Bulgarian nationalists. Although forced to accept a state that was only one-third the size of the Russian-created Greater Bulgaria, they became galvanized in their determination to win back all of the territories lost. The Berlin losses provided them with a well-defined blueprint for national territorial expansion and an abiding distrust of the European Great Powers, including, in some measure, Russia.

By the Treaty of Berlin's terms, the new Bulgarian Principality existed under loose Ottoman suzerainty but it was ruled directly by an elected prince governing through a constitution and a representative assembly. It maintained its own military but, as an Ottoman vassal, was obliged to honor all international conventions with the Great Powers in effect within the Ottoman Empire. In early 1879 an assembly of elected and nominated nationalist delegates from the various Bulgarian-inhabited regions (including those outside of the principality's borders) met in Bulgaria's medieval capital of Tŭrnovo with Russian encouragement to devise the new state's political system. Among the delegates were representatives of the Jewish, Greek, and Muslim minority communities.

The primary agenda items at the Tŭrnovo assembly were the question of "national unity" and the drafting of a governing constitution. Regarding the former, it was decided that the highest priority in the state's foreign policy would be reacquiring all lands stripped from San Stefano Bulgaria. To that end, Sofia was designated the capital because of its proximity to Macedonia and its position as a major crossroad on overland communication routes. As for the latter item, a draft constitution was presented to the assembly by Prince Dondukov-Korsakov, head of the Russian provisional administration installed at the close of the Russo-Turkish War. The heated debates that followed produced a highly liberal-democratic constitution that placed executive power in the hands of a Christian (Orthodox, except for the first) prince governing through a cabinet chosen from member parties in a legislative national assembly (*sŭbranie*).

An important section of the constitution dealt with the Bulgarian Orthodox church. To preserve Bulgaria's national claims to territories beyond its Berlin borders, the traditional Orthodox church-state partnership was modified. Since the Bulgarian Exarchate's jurisdiction included most of those territories, the exarch's seat remained in Istanbul rather than being moved to Sofia, where his authority automatically would be reduced to only the principality's lands. The church inside of Bulgaria was declared an inseparable part of the Exarchate, governed by a Holy Synod in Sofia but subordinate to the exarch in Istanbul.

As first Bulgarian prince, the Tŭrnovo assembly chose young Alexander (Aleksandŭr) I of Battenberg (1879-86), a German acceptable both to the Bulgarians, because he had served in the Russian forces during the recent war, and to the Great Powers, because he was related to the English royal family through marriage and was a favorite nephew of Tsar Alexander II. Aleksandŭr's reign was riven by domestic conflict. His constant efforts to entrench princely dominance spawned resistance from Bulgaria's political leadership, who were intent on preserving liberal-democratic constitutional rule. Since the important government ministries, especially that overseeing the military, were controlled by Russians, Aleksandŭr's drive to exert direct authority over all administrative matters caused friction with Tsar Alexander (dubbed by Bulgarian nationalists the "Tsar-Liberator"), who consistently restrained Battenberg from tampering with the constitutional constraints on his office. After the more reactionary Alexander III (1881-94) came to the Russian throne, Aleksandŭr's attempts to gain authority over the Russian-run Bulgarian Ministry of War, which controlled the army, heightened tensions between the two states.

A series of blatantly self-interested Russian foreign policy demands on the Bulgarians (such as railroad construction programs aimed at benefiting Russia's possible future military intervention in the Balkans and attempts to gain control of the newly established Bulgarian National Bank) won Aleksandŭr growing support among disgruntled Bulgarian nationalists, who could not accept direct Russian interference in Bulgarian internal affairs. By 1884 a constitutional modus vivendi was effected, and Aleksandŭr was free to cement his position within the state by pursuing Bulgarian nationalist territorial expansion. The opportunity arose in the post-Berlin Ottoman province of Eastern Rumelia. (See Map 8.)

Eastern Rumelia was inhabited predominantly by ethnic Bulgarians, although its population included significant numbers of Greeks and Turks. While at Berlin great pains had been taken to construct a provincial government representing all of the population's elements by mandating a Christian governor who ruled through a proportionally representative assembly, Bulgarian nationalists in the province succeeded in their electoral efforts to gain control of the crucially important permanent governing council, which served as a cabinet comprised of elected officials drawn from the assembly. They then enacted programs creating Rumelian institutions (schools, literary alphabet, and military training) mirroring those in the Bulgarian Principality. Since Rumelia was more politically and economically stable than the principality, the Rumelian Bulgarian nationalists' goal of union with Bulgaria was postponed until Bulgaria's constitutional situation was resolved and the Western European Great Powers' perception of the principality as a Russian puppet was dispelled. After Bulgaria rejected Russia's railroad and banking demands and Aleksandŭr's accommodation with the principality's leadership, the Rumelian Bulgarians, assisted by radical nationalists from Bulgaria, acted.

In 1885 the Bulgarian-dominated Rumelian militia overthrew the province's government and proclaimed unity with the Bulgarian Principality. Fearful of Great Power reaction, Aleksandŭr at first hesitated to accept the union. Challenged by the fiery former revolutionary and ardent nationalist speaker of the *sŭbranie* Stefan Stambolov to go either to Plovdiv (Rumelia's capital) or back to Germany, Aleksandŭr ordered the Bulgarian army into the province and journeyed to Plovdiv, where he embraced the union.

An international diplomatic crisis erupted immediately. The union of Eastern Rumelia with Bulgaria was accomplished over the vehement protests of Russia, which, not wishing to upset the international apple cart at the time, withdrew all of its advisors, ministers, and military officers from Bulgaria. Russia's actions prompted Serbia, fearing that the Bulgarians' nationalist momentum from the unification would carry them over into Macedonia and thwart Serbia's future expansion there, to chasten the Bulgarians further. Serbia declared war on Bulgaria in late 1885 in hopes of an easy victory (because of Bulgaria's loss of its Russian military commanders) and territorial acquisitions. Instead, the Bulgarians repulsed the Serbian invasion at the Battle of Slivnitsa and then invaded Serbia itself. Only Habsburg threats to intervene on the Serbs' behalf stopped the victorious Bulgarians. A peace treaty, urged by both the Habsburgs and Russia, was signed in Bucharest in March 1886 (symbolically, on San Stefano's eighth anniversary) securing the unification of Bulgaria and Eastern Rumelia.

The unification's aftermath proved unfortunate for Aleksandŭr. His proclivities for exerting dominant authority led him to grant military promotions only to those whom he considered politically reliable, while many who demonstrated outstanding efforts in the war with Serbia were passed over. That foolish policy cost him the support of the army. Additionally, the nationalists were disappointed by the Bucharest Treaty's terms, which recognized the union only as a personal one—the Bulgarian prince served as Rumelian governor-general and was required to seek periodic Ottoman and Great Power reapproval for that office. The Russians ensured that Aleksandŭr was not mentioned by name in the document, thereby keeping open the possibility for his removal at some later date. They did not need to wait long for the opportunity.

Political turmoil over government mismanagement of railroad contracts soon after the unification, coupled with nationalist unrest over the Bucharest Treaty terms, led a group of disgruntled army officers, serving as Russian agents, to depose Aleksandŭr (1886) and "escort" him out of the state. Stambolov, unwilling to tolerate Russia's or the military's intervention in Bulgarian internal political affairs, took control of the capital with the aid of some loyal army units and returned Aleksandŭr to Sofia. Shaken by his kidnapping, the prince was unwilling to continue ruling without promises of Russian support. When Tsar Alexander refused to furnish such assurances, Aleksandŭr abdicated and fled, leaving Bulgaria ruled by a regency under Stambolov until a new prince was found.

The process of finding a new ruler was complicated by the obvious interference of Russia in Bulgarian affairs, which intensified after Aleksandŭr's abdication. Few Western European candidates were attracted to a state exhibiting political instability and vulnerability to Russian pressures. The search delegation sent to Western Europe found no takers until, reportedly in desperation, in Vienna they stumbled on a minor prince from the German aristocratic Saxe-Coburg-Gotha family who personally was anxious to make something of himself and willing to risk being Bulgarian prince, Ferdinand I (1887-1908; *tsar,* 1908-18). No Great Power officially recognized Ferdinand's election to the Bulgarian throne, and only Stambolov's adept political leadership as prime minister kept him in power during the crucial early years of his reign. Gradually, economic agreements were forged with the various Great Powers and assorted other European states until, by the 1890s, most came to treat Bulgaria as if it were an independent and recognized sovereign state in its own right.

Although Bulgarian-Russian relations remained frigid after Ferdinand came to power, a thaw set in following the succession of Russian Tsar Nicholas II (1894-1917), who realized that the two states must cooperate if they were to gain their maximum national goals in the Balkans should the Ottoman Empire collapse. Despite Nicholas's personal repugnance for Ferdinand, Russian-Bulgarian relations improved. In 1896 Russia finally recognized Ferdinand as Bulgarian prince and governor-general of Rumelia, and all of the Great Powers quickly followed Russia's lead. In consequence, Bulgaria essentially remained aligned with Russia until 1913 and the aftermath of the Balkan Wars.

At Berlin, the Great Powers had ignored Greece. In return for their "inviting" the Ottomans to turn parts of Thessaly and Epiros over to Greece, the Greek nationalists had been forced to accept Great Britain's occupation of Cyprus, which they considered Greek. Such perfunctory treatment demonstrated that Greece was considered of little account in the predominantly Habsburg-Russian contention for Balkan hegemony. Because of its location at the extreme southern tip of the peninsula, Greece fell more within Great Britain's sphere of interests and its concerns over eastern Mediterranean maritime routes. Britain, however, remained committed to the Ottomans and focused its immediate concerns on securing Egypt and Cyprus.

In 1881 the Great Powers convinced the Ottomans to accept the Berlin "invitation" and grant Greece nearly the whole of Thessaly. Despite British efforts, most of Epiros was not included in the territorial transfer because of Great Power interest in an emerging Albanian national movement in the region. When Greece mobilized its military forces (1886) to invade Ottoman Epiros and take it as "compensation" for Bulgaria's unification, the Great Powers, led by Britain, blockaded the state until the Greek troops were stood down. Later (1897), Greece, although militarily unprepared, declared war on the Ottomans in support of an ethnic Greek uprising (1896-97) on Ottoman Crete. Great Power objections to the war prevented any other Balkan state from joining Greece, which then suffered an ignominious defeat. Last-minute Great Power intervention spared the Greeks the full measure of Ottoman retaliation for their action, but Greece was prevented from acquiring Crete outright.

Until the outbreak of the Balkan Wars (1912), Greece held no concrete foreign policy orientation toward either of the two Great Power camps. Greek nationalists were wary of all the Great Powers, given their sorry record concerning Greece's expansionist efforts. Great Britain was the leading Great Power sympathetic to Greek national aims but it more often blunted the Greeks' rash nationalist actions than furthered their territorial ambitions. Only with Greek Premier Elevtherios Venizelos were steps taken toward the Entente (1910) by negotiating military missions from Great Britain and France to reorganize the Greek navy and army, steps that were undertaken despite the personal misgivings of Greek king George I, whose sympathies, as a member of the Danish Glücksburg family, lay with the German Central Powers. Although Venizelos's moves signaled tentative attraction to the Entente, Greece officially remained neutral toward the fundamental split among the Great Powers.

Domestic Affairs

The domestic situations of the post-Berlin Balkan states were strikingly similar. All were constitutional monarchies with constitutions either mandated for them by the Great Powers or produced by Western-leaning native nationalists. Their rulers (mostly foreigners imposed by the Great Powers) chafed at their constitutional limitations. In each, Western-style constitutional government suffered because paternalistic, authoritarian Orthodox European and Islamic Ottoman political traditions persisted, and party politics were little more than struggles among influential individuals and their followers for the spoils of administrative offices. All the states were primarily agrarian and vulnerable to Great Power economic exploitation. Their populations were composed mostly of illiterate peasants, while their political leaderships (except for the landholding aristocracy in Romania) sprang from small but educated middle classes.

Only Serbia and Montenegro sported native ruling princes, because they acquired a measure of statehood before the "Eastern Question's" maturation focused Great Power interest on the Balkans. After the 1828-29 Russo-Turkish War, the strategic importance of the Balkans precluded the Great Powers' acceptance of native ruling houses in any new Balkan state. Great Britain and France could not countenance Balkan rulers whose Orthodox religion, Slavic ethnicity, or both might render them Russia's allies, so they ensured that Greece, Romania, and Bulgaria accepted Western European rulers in return for international recognition. Since the Germans geographically were closest to the Balkans and, until the rise of the alliance system, were considered "neutral" in the "Eastern Question," they were the imposed Western rulers of choice for the Balkan states.

Once the Great Powers became divided by the system of grand alliances, the intricate web of European dynastic family interrelationships and the necessity of embracing their states' national interests to remain in office mitigated the potential of the Balkan Germanic rulers for serving as Central Powers lackeys. Whether of native or foreign stock, however, all Balkan rulers shared a common domestic political ambition: To concentrate as much central authority as possible in their hands at the expense of constitutional constraints.

The Balkan rulers' efforts in that regard drew on both Orthodox and Islamic political traditions, coupled with Western European nation-state nationalism. The states' often mixed Orthodox, Muslim, and Jewish populations were conditioned by centuries of tradition, whether Ottoman (by sultans and local *ayans*) or *millet* (which preserved the political traditions of the Byzantine era), to accept, often fatalistically, paternalistic, authoritarian rule. The native Serbian and Montenegrin Obrenović, Karadjordjević, and Petrović houses were bound to those traditions from the start. The foreign Greek Wittelsbachs and Glücksburgs, Romanian Hohenzollern-Sigmaringens, and Bulgarian Battenburgs and Saxe-Coberg-Gothas embraced their subjects' pro-authoritarian tendencies, which were reinforced by the states' official Orthodox church institutions.

Constitutions generally enjoyed shallow support among the populations of the Balkan states. In each state, peasants and pastoralists predominated, and initially their level of educational and political literacy was low. Most possessed little functional understanding of constitutions and their political and legal significance. Traditional peasant distrust of urban centers (the "natural habitats" for overbearing absentee landlords, greedy tax collectors, rapacious policemen, and cheating traders) persisted, obstructing close ties between the rural populations and their political leaders, who usually were middle-class, educated urbanites.

The mostly Orthodox Christian rural majority followed tradition by accepting their local clergy's immediate leadership. Monks and priests in the villages, who differed from their lay followers only in vocational calling and in possessing a modicum of religious education, shared the peasants' mundane conditions and perceptions. Their leadership principles rested in Orthodox church traditions. Since in every Balkan state Orthodox Christianity enjoyed official status as the state religion, the church's traditional conception of political authority—originating in God and administered on earth through divinely ordained central authority personified by the ruler—retained widespread acceptance. Thus the rulers' efforts to consolidate power in their own hands enjoyed potential, although frequently passive, natural sympathy among the peasant majorities.

Also favoring the rulers was the situation of the native political leaderships, who were composed of numerically small minorities that, to some degree, were disconnected from their states' rural majorities. In Romania, where a landowning aristocracy held the political reins, the disconnect was fundamental. In all of the other states, where an amorphous middle class (into which peasants might rise out of desire or happenstance) held political leadership, the disconnect was more a matter of perception on the part of both sides—the peasants' traditional suspicions of the city acting in conjunction with the city dwellers' commonplace sense of self-superiority relative to rural folk.

Economic and cultural factors—the concentration of moneymaking pursuits and secular literacy within the politically dominant middle class—further separated political leaderships from the masses. Those factors originally created the leaderships by opening to them direct contacts with Western Europeans, exposing them to Western cultural realities, and providing them with the models and means for transplanting those realities to the Balkans. The native middle classes acted as vanguards in the westernizing process by establishing commercial ties to the West, espousing Western ideals, and leading the efforts to win independent states shaped in the West's image. They attempted to put that image into practice by formulating their new states' governing constitutions and consolidating their role as Western-style political leaderships.

Despite their conscious westernizing ideals, their inexperience in practical Western-style politics and their unconscious propensities for non-Western practices frequently betrayed the leaders' efforts to make image reality. Once statehood was gained, their activities, although couched in terms of Western-like political party systems, resembled more the approach taken by Ottoman *Tanzimat* reformers than Western politicians.

While the Balkan states' political parties publicly espoused particular political viewpoints (conservative, liberal, democratic, agrarian, or some other), in practice they commonly represented the interests of groups coalesced around influential or charismatic individuals, whose personal qualities and ambitions set party policy. Politics frequently slid into strident factional conflicts among party bosses and their followers. The rulers participated in the personal political approach as well and, depending on their individual qualities and abilities to influence, helped determine the consequences of party infighting for the balance of authority within their respective states. Strong rulers (Milan and Mihajlo Obrenović or Petr Karadjordjević in Serbia, George I in Greece, Carol I in Romania, and Ferdinand I in Bulgaria), who attracted supporters within the political leaderships and played on the peasantry's traditional sympathies, manipulated party conflicts to their own advantage. Weak ones (Aleksandr Obrenović in Serbia and Aleksandŭr I in Bulgaria) exerted little control over factional struggles and were overshadowed by forceful premiers or prime ministers (Stambolov in Bulgaria and Venizelos in Greece), who then laid claim to the pro-autocratic sympathies of the masses for support.

Personal partisan politics rendered the governing regimes inherently weak and unstable. Those who controlled administrative offices generally treated their positions as prizes to be exploited for personal benefit, which motivated their drive to attain—and their Machiavellian efforts to retain—office. Although democratic political forms overtly were followed, democracy in practice suffered. While their extent and intensity varied among and within states, nepotism, cronyism, patronage, rigged elections, coercion, and repression characterized gaining and holding political power and shaping and conducting policies.

In every Balkan state, governing constitutions frequently came and went. Whether constitutions were more or less liberal-democratic mostly concerned the rulers and the political elites competing for dominance within the states. The constitution in force might minimize constraints on a ruler's executive authority or impose liberal-democratic freedoms at the ruler's expense. In the latter case, the political emphasis fell on liberal concepts favoring middle-class interests. In all cases, democracy was paid merely lip service since, by definition, it involved the whole population, including the rural majority. For both the rulers and political elites, that majority was deemed useful only in lending democratic appearances to their personal political machinations. Political authority went to those who proved themselves the strongest at any given time and involved little constitutional or democratic validity.

The overall economic situation of the post-Berlin Balkan states was as muddled as the political. All of the states essentially were agrarian. Subsistence-level agriculture that used techniques and implements unchanged in any significant way for centuries was the norm. What did change for most Balkan peasants as a result of statehood (with the exception of the Romanian) was legal land ownership. Except in Romania, ownership of former Ottoman-era plots was transferred legally to the peasants who worked them, although the pace of the transfers varied among the states. The Orthodox church's former *vakıf* holdings, especially its extensive and widespread monastic properties, posed problems because the politically important state churches claimed their outright ownership at the resident peasants' expense. In Greece, where Orthodox prelates who played an important role in the national revolutionary movement also were large landowners, the problem was especially difficult and took longer to sort out than in the other states (except in Romania, where Orthodox prelates were partners with the aristocracy in landowning).

Although land transfers were based on legal equality for all peasants, such did not guarantee economic equality. Gaps reflecting holding sizes existed, with those who successfully claimed larger plots benefiting more than those who obtained less. Both, however, remained poorer than the urban commercial and manufacturing sectors, and both suffered economically from the effects of a general population increase in the Balkans during the second half of the nineteenth and early twentieth centuries. Because population density was low when the increase began and the land's productivity generally high, growth did not reduce available food supplies. Food staples often changed (shifting the diet from meats to grains) but gradually, through direct and frequent Western contacts, improvements in farming techniques and implements appeared, compensating for the increasing number of mouths to feed by expanding productivity.

The essential economic problem caused by population growth for Balkan peasants was its impact on landholding. Rising demographic pressures brought new land into cultivation, but the mountainous terrain limited its extent and the accompanying deforestation had unfortunate environmental consequences. More important in human terms, most peasant families followed the traditional inheritance practice of dividing estate property equally among surviving sons. As family sizes grew, landholdings fragmented into ever smaller plots, reducing their economic returns. While the situation eventually led to the collapse of the traditional inheritance system and, in some cases, the resurgence of centuries-old extended family institutions (such as the Serbian *zadruga*), it also created an increasing number of landless peasants no longer needed on family lands, who fled the countryside in large numbers for urban centers in hopes of finding new livelihoods. After Berlin, every Balkan state experienced rapid urban population expansion, but traditional practices and international constraints stunted urban economic growth.

Although all of the middle-class leaders of the Balkan states were determined to westernize their economies rapidly to demonstrate their "Europeanness" and gain shares of Western prosperity, their efforts were hobbled by inherited Ottoman-era economic legacies. Manufacturing initially resembled the Ottoman model, in which manpower, craftsmanship, low productivity, and high prices, rather than machinery, mass production, high productivity, and cheap prices, were the norm. The Europeans' manipulation of Ottoman capitulations had reduced most Balkan commerce dependent on foreign interests. The underdeveloped Ottoman banking sector limited the availability of investment capital for the Balkan successor states, while the Ottomans' failure to undertake infrastructural improvements made transportation and communication difficult, slow, and expensive. The parochial nature of education precluded the new states launching sophisticated industries that required high technical skills. Such handicaps prevented the states from reaping the full benefit for independent industrial development from cheap labor and available raw materials. (Romania proved a limited exception; by 1914 it had developed the world's fifth largest petroleum industry.)

Additional obstacles to Balkan economic development were imposed by the Great Powers at Berlin, who wrote into the treaty articles restricting the new states' ability to levy assorted tariffs and dues on Western imports that retarded native industrial growth and undermined internal markets. The Balkan states' subsequent trade agreements with the European Great Powers tended to obstruct their domestic industrial development. Since most such treaties gave the Great Powers near monopolies over particular exports from the various states (such as Austria-Hungary's exclusive hold on Serbia's pork exports), their independent industrial development was restrained out of fears that, by trying to compete directly with their trading partners, they would lose their export markets.

Given the political leaderships' pro-Western proclivities and the limitations imposed by existing domestic economic realities, the Balkan states turned to the West for "help" in developing their economies. Western assistance came in the form of loans for industrial and infrastructural development, trade agreements that usually established a narrow range of exclusive export products, and joint stock companies highly favorable to Western investors. Since every Balkan state's top priority was nation-state expansion, an inordinate amount of foreign assistance was devoted to the military, at the expense of nonmilitary economic development. Industries and infrastructural improvements servicing military needs—especially railroads—became preponderant political and economic priorities.

Direct foreign involvement, particularly in railroad-related, banking, and export endeavors, permeated the westernizing economic efforts of most Balkan states, while the foreigners' primary motivation was furthering their own interests. Investments were concentrated in industries demanding low levels of technological development (such as food and tobacco processing, textiles, and raw materials extraction). Railroads, the primary means of overland transportation and communication and symbols of national economic and military maturity, were constructed with heavy foreign investment. While the rail networks could help further the expansionary military goals of the Balkan governments, preponderant foreign involvement insured that they were built as southeastward extensions of existing European systems for opening West Asia to Great Power economic and military interests. (The "Orient Express" line, generally following the millennia-old route of the Diagonal Highway, was built through Serbia and Bulgaria expressly for that purpose.)

An obvious result of the post-Berlin Balkan states' general economic situation was their status as Great Power dependencies. Another was the reinforcement of traditional acceptance of strong, central, paternalistic authority within the state. Without a broad-based middle class and a strong native private financial sector, the state governments, which controlled most available capital either directly (through their treasuries) or indirectly (as funnels for foreign investment), served as the ultimate economic "patrons." That reality, more than any constitutional or democratic underpinning, lent them practical validity. The states owned all public utilities and mines and almost all munitions and manufacturing plants, forests, and foundries. The private sector depended on state patronage and "favors" for the capital that it needed, which it received through government contracts, subsidies, franchises, monopolies, tax exemptions, and selective protectionism. The states' economies were as dependent on their governments as were the governments themselves on their European patrons, which led to yet another disadvantage. Just as the foreigners took advantage of their dominance to squeeze maximum benefit from their dependent Balkan partners, the Balkan governments did the same to their native capitalists, perpetuating the harmful legacy of Ottoman destabilization in the form of official corruption and reinforcing the personal nature of politics.

An expansion of Western-style secular education accompanied the governments' economic westernization efforts. The Western premise that an educated workforce was a productive one was accepted by all of the Balkan states, and the fact that it harmonized well with the governments' goal of indoctrinating their citizens in official nationalist ideologies led to the creation of secular-oriented public education systems. Although actual levels varied among the states, by 1910 some 35 to 40 percent of all children between the ages of five and fourteen attended primary schools, and secondary schools were thriving.

The Balkan peasant majorities generally embraced education because of the expansion of the monetary economy into the countryside. Market agriculture had been important under the Ottomans for earning money to pay taxes and became more so following the Balkan states' establishment and their official efforts to westernize. As assorted domestic enterprises slowly evolved along Western lines, and as imports of foreign goods multiplied, villagers increasingly grew tied to the broader commercial economy as both suppliers and consumers. Food, household, and tool items once considered luxuries in the countryside became more readily available to those with the cash for their purchase. Earning money gradually displaced self-sufficient subsistence as the primary economic goal of agrarian life. Over time, peasants sensed that education was essential for benefiting from the new economic situation and welcomed the new public school systems.

Expanding education had socioeconomic consequences. A generational gap was created between the older, more tradition-bound peasants, who essentially remained illiterate, and the younger, increasingly educated peasants, whose secular schooling led them to question the closed provincial, often passive, introverted, and superstitious realities of traditional peasant existence. Among the educated younger generation, a sense of individualism and a desire for self-advancement displaced the traditional communal approach to rural life. Many educated peasants also developed an acute and knowledgeable awareness of economic inequalities and social differentiation. All Balkan states spawned intelligentsias (educated elites who felt deserving of political and economic positions commensurate with their education level), whose efforts to assert themselves either complicated the partisan political systems further by proliferating the number of political parties or inflamed unrest in the countryside about social and economic inequalities, class differentiation (the 1907 Romanian peasant revolt was the most violent), and "foreign" ethnic minorities (viewed as dual national and economic threats).

Post-Berlin Balkan societies were dominated by political and economic elites comprised of government officials, military officers, party politicians, professionals, businessmen, and entrepreneurs, whose roots lay in the small middle class or in the peasantry. (The Romanian elite included all of these but was dominated by the aristocracy and Orthodox prelates.) Membership in these elites was open to any combination of talent, money, and good fortune. With the exception of Romania, the lack of aristocratic traditions of deference and deportment made the elites approachable and practical in their dealings but also may have opened the door to unrestrained struggles for authority and its attendant spoils, misuse of authority, and corrupt, self-serving practices. The political and economic gap between "haves" and "have-nots," although fluid, remained wide. A perceptible sense of peasant alienation from their political and economic leaderships emerged. Rigged elections, changing laws, and fluctuating and inequitable economic relationships caused many peasants to lose faith in their new states and to distrust their governments. Partly to counter that trend, the leadership elites of each state continuously stressed the one factor that possessed the innate potential for uniting the masses behind them: Nation-state nationalism.

CHAPTER FOURTEEN

National Conflicts

Between 1878 and 1914 the Balkan states' conflicting aspirations for national expansion, and intensified nationalist movements among Balkan populations lacking states of their own, produced a period of incessant turmoil. So tumultuous was the time that Western Europeans came to characterize the Balkan nations as inherently belligerent, irreconcilable mutual antagonists set on gaining their individual national goals no matter the costs. Although the term "balkanization," which was coined in the West to describe the turmoil, has retained currency into the present, it reflects more its creators' perceptions than those of the Balkan nations themselves. The national divisiveness manifested in the Balkans during the period operated within the framework of adopted Western European nation-state nationalism. It was the European Great Powers themselves who legitimized the Ottoman Empire's fragmentation at Berlin by recognizing new nation-states carved from its lands while, at the same time, they blocked them from acquiring territories claimed on the basis of nation-state imperatives. In adopting the term, Western Europeans, who historically demonstrated a near messianic impulse to spread their cultural values to non-westerners, proved unable to fathom accurately the Frankenstein monsters that they created.

The "Macedonian Question"

After Berlin, inter-Balkan state relations largely focused on Macedonia's possession or division. Bulgarian nationalists claimed the region on historical grounds as an integral part of medieval Bulgaria, the seat of the first independent Slavic-rite (Bulgarian) Orthodox patriarchate (Ohrid), and the birthplace of the Bulgarian-created Slavic Cyrillic literary language. Serbian nationalists considered it the heartland of Stefan Dušan's medieval empire and the location of Serb-oriented principalities destroyed by the Ottomans. Greeks used classical historical arguments (Philip II [356-37 B.C.E.] and Alexander III the Great [337-23 B.C.E.] of Macedon) to buttress their "Great Idea" claims to the region, which otherwise were grounded in reestablishing Byzantium's territories as the rightful Greek nation-state, validated by Greek control of the Orthodox *millet*. The vitriolic national antagonisms and mutually exclusive territorial claims involved in the so-called "Macedonian Question" poisoned relations among Bulgaria, Serbia, and Greece until well into the twentieth century (and, to some extent, they continue to do so).

Nineteenth-century Macedonia, encompassing the Ottoman territories of Thessaloniki, Bitola (Monastir), and Kosovo, was an ethnic meeting ground where disparate peoples—primarily Albanians, Bulgarians, Greeks, Serbs, and Turks—lived in close, often intermingled proximity. Along its northwestern and western borders were large numbers of Albanians. Serbs were found in the north. In the south were Greeks, who also mixed with Albanians in the region's southwest. Turks inhabited scattered central and south-central towns and villages. Also present were seminomadic Vlahs and Gypsies, who migrated among seasonal residences throughout the region. A populous Jewish merchant community resided in Thessaloniki, and some Jews lived in most towns of any note, frequently along with Armenian merchants. Bulgarians populated the eastern frontiers, extending southward to the Aegean and mixing with Greeks in and around Thessaloniki. That much of Macedonia's ethnodemographic picture relatively was certain. Less so was the ethnic composition of the region's majority population in its core territories, whose ethnicity became the main bone of contention in the "Macedonian Question."

Macedonia was an isolated and backward region. Its inhabitants were predominantly Slavic at the time of the Ottoman conquest, and largely for that reason they were left ignorant and illiterate—as lowly Slav peasants of little account in the Greek-dominated Orthodox *millet*. After the Slavic-rite churches were abolished in the 1760s, they came completely under the Greek patriarchate's jurisdiction and experienced a concerted Hellenization effort. Their general illiteracy, however, insulated all but a few against the full brunt of Greek cultural assimilation. The overwhelming majority remained Slavs.

Until the 1870s and the advent of Bulgarian, Greek, and Serbian nationalist agitation, Macedonia's inhabitants held *millet* religious identities. Specific linguistically defined ethnicity meant little to them. That most spoke Slavic sufficed. Their loyalties lay in their local villages and Orthodox faith, which differentiated them from Muslim neighbors. Things changed once the issue of the Bulgarian Exarchate exploded in their midst.

What disconcerted Greek and Serbian nationalists about the Bulgarian Exarchate was its official right to acquire religious jurisdiction over any Ottoman territory in which two-thirds of the Orthodox population voted for membership. While few

consciously ethnic Greeks or Serbs would join the Exarchate, Macedonia's Orthodox majority lacked any such concrete ethnic self-identity. Greeks were aware that
the majority Macedonian Slavs likely would join a culturally Slavic Orthodox church
whose literary-liturgical language closely resembled their own native vernacular. The
Serbs, preoccupied with Bosnia-Hercegovina in the 1870s, initially ignored the
Exarchate's potential threat to Serbia's future expansion.

The Bulgarians were quick to propagandize for the Exarchate in Macedonia.
Early on Bulgarian nationalists actively forged connections with Macedonia's small,
new Slav middle class. While the Bulgarians' national revival had been late to bloom,
the Macedonian Slavs lagged even further behind. Bulgarian teachers and books
circulated among Macedonia's Slav communities, where they warmly were welcomed, partly because the Macedonian Slavs were "starving" for understandable
education and literature and partly because of the close linguistic affinity between
the Bulgarians' and their native tongues. The early Bulgarian cultural efforts in
Macedonia were so well received that a number of leading figures in the pre-1870s
Bulgarian national movement (such as the brothers Dimitŭr and Konstantin
Miladinov) were, in fact, Macedonian Slavs.

Representatives from all of the Macedonian Orthodox dioceses expressed their
desire to join the Exarchate. The Greek patriarch responded by declaring the
Exarchate schismatic. The Macedonians' wishes, however, needed validation by
actual vote counts. Pro-Exarchate Bulgarians traversed Macedonia proselytizing
among the Slavs. Pro-patriarchate Greeks, unwilling to lose their *millet* monopoly,
countered with similar efforts. The heated religious-national campaigning soon
degenerated into terrorism and bloodshed. Organized gangs of exarchatists and
patriarchatists intimidated the Slav villagers and frequently came to blows. Deaths
mounted. Voting often was conducted under the threat of mortal danger from one
or both sides. By the time that Berlin Bulgaria appeared, most Orthodox Macedonian Slavs had joined the Exarchate, but the price had been heavy.

After being humiliated by the Bulgarians in 1886, the Serbs realized the full
national implications of the Exarchate's victory in Macedonia. Since Bulgaria had
expanded into Eastern Rumelia and acquired a new prince publicly ambitious to
annex Macedonia, the Serbs needed to act in Macedonia to keep alive their own
expansionary national aspirations. During the late 1880s Serb teachers, priests, and
gangs joined in the religious "campaigning" on behalf of the Serbian Orthodox
church but scored few victories over the more popular Bulgarian effort. They did,
however, intensify the terror of the Macedonian Slavs, large numbers of whom fled
eastward into Bulgaria seeking asylum and expecting aid. Once there, they quickly
developed into a separate and powerful force in Bulgarian politics that demanded
state intervention in Macedonia.

While the church question boiled, Macedonia lay under direct Ottoman
control. This reality was key during the 1880s, when the outwardly religious facet

of the Macedonian struggle perceptibly gave way to blatant nationalism once the Serbs entered the fray. The Bulgarian may have won out over the Greek and Serbian churches, but Ottoman administration and garrisons remained, as did armed Christian bands. Sporadic fighting among the Christian contenders continued, but, as the church issue stabilized in the Exarchate's favor, its Macedonian followers, supported by Macedonian immigrants inside of Bulgaria, increasingly turned to guerilla attacks on the Ottoman authorities.

The Bulgarian government's official position regarding Macedonia was touchy. Although nationalist sympathies lay with the exarchatist guerillas, Bulgaria technically remained an autonomous Ottoman state. Prince Ferdinand may have dreamed of annexing Macedonia, but his prime minister Stefan Stambulov realized that Bulgaria needed time to develop economic strength and diplomatic support before engaging in expansionist policies, and time could be bought only by placating the Ottomans (and Britain). Stambulov conducted peaceful intervention in Macedonia, often cooperating with the Ottoman authorities by tightening Bulgaria's borders with the troublesome province. In return, the Ottomans rewarded his moderation with concessions in Macedonia, such as appointing Bulgarian bishops to Macedonian exarchatist dioceses (1890).

Although proving effective, Stambulov's policy seemed far too timid and slow to the Macedonian immigrants in Bulgaria, and they cried out for vigorous anti-Ottoman government action to support the exarchatists in Macedonia. They brought the tactics of intimidation learned in their homeland during the church "campaigns" to the streets of Sofia. Placing himself at the head of the nationalist movement, and signaling a policy shift away from the Ottomans and Britain and toward Russia, Ferdinand dismissed Stambulov (1894), who shortly thereafter was assassinated by Macedonian revolutionaries. (It was rumored that Ferdinand had a hand in arranging the deed.)

In 1893 a small band of anti-Ottoman Macedonian Slav revolutionaries secretly met in the town of Resna and founded the Internal Macedonian Revolutionary Organization (IMRO) with a militant program for creating an autonomous Macedonian state completely independent from the Ottoman Empire, Bulgaria, Greece, and Serbia. They considered Macedonia an indivisible territory and all of its inhabitants "Macedonians," no matter their religion or ethnicity, thus signaling the beginning of a new, strictly Macedonian national movement. The IMRO nationalists essentially embraced a modified version of the Bulgarian historical argument for justifying Macedonia's right to independent national existence, substituting the term "Macedonian" for "Bulgarian" in its descriptive details. In its espousal of unceasing militant anti-Ottoman activities and intimidation of neighboring states' governments (especially Bulgaria's), IMRO represented Europe's first consciously created political terrorist organization. It spread rapidly throughout Macedonia, training men and gathering arms in preparation for a great mass anti-Ottoman uprising.

(In an interesting sidebar to IMRO's story, the United States was the first non-Balkan Great Power victimized by the first European political terrorist organization. In 1901 Jane Sandanski, a local IMRO leader, kidnapped and held for ransom Ellen Stone, an American Protestant missionary working in eastern Macedonia, for the purpose of extorting money from the American government to purchase weapons for the revolutionaries. Stone's political abduction—the first time an American was so treated abroad—proved a successful publicity stunt for IMRO. Newspaper correspondents hounded the trail of the American hostage negotiators, making the kidnapping front-page news at home and throughout Europe. The $66,000 ransom eventually paid was raised through a highly publicized subscription campaign in America. By the time she was released and returned to the United States, Stone had been converted to her IMRO captors' cause. She gave public lectures and wrote popular articles for *McClure's Magazine* on Macedonia and the righteousness of IMRO's aims. Her pregnant companion in the abduction, Ekaterina Tsilka, had given birth during her captivity, and she too stumped America after her release, offering even more popularly attended lecture appearances, in which baby Elena played a starring role. Thus the Americans came to accept their earliest concession to terrorist intimidation!)

IMRO's "Macedonia for the Macedonians" revolutionary program was a logical outgrowth of two decades of turmoil, in which the region's native population was cynically manipulated and brutally abused solely for outsiders' national interests. The natives had been reduced to little more than statistics supporting the various contenders' nationalist claims (all of which were massaged by nationalist biases). Although the Macedonian Slav majority still retained Bulgarian affinities, those were worn thin by the domineering attitude often taken by Bulgarian-born exarchatist clergy toward their Macedonian-born flocks and by the self-superior airs assumed by many Bulgarian educators and intellectuals operating in Macedonia. As for the Greeks, only a fraction of the Macedonian Slavs had been Hellenized; for most Macedonians, the Greeks were foreigners who threatened their native Slavic culture. Although the Serbs were Slavs, their language was noticeably different from the Macedonians', and they proved themselves just as brutish as Greeks in their treatment of native Macedonian inhabitants. No Greeks or Serbs were enrolled in IMRO's ranks.

Originally IMRO was decentralized, composed of loosely connected regional groups. In 1894 Goce Delčev, a young Sofia-trained revolutionary, transformed it into a highly effective underground rebel network controlled by a central committee. He also extended IMRO's operations outside of Macedonia into Ottoman-controlled Thrace. IMRO headquarters were established in Thessaloniki, and representatives were sent to Sofia, Athens, and Istanbul. Along with the network of revolutionary regions, districts, and communes, IMRO established its own internal civil administration, postal and courier services, police forces, courts, and newspapers. Each district maintained armed units for conducting guerrilla operations in the countryside. In towns, IMRO maintained terrorist cells for use if and when needed.

Soon after Delčev's reorganization, IMRO split into two factions over the issue of future Macedonian autonomy. Delčev, supported by Sandanski and others, held to the original goal of an independent autonomous Macedonia and adamantly opposed Macedonia's incorporation into Bulgaria, which a number of his colleagues advocated. Viewing the anti-Ottoman struggle as necessary for Macedonia's eventual unification with Bulgaria, Delčev's opponents moved to Sofia (1895) and, with Bulgarian assistance, founded their own organization in competition with IMRO—the External Macedonian Revolutionary Organization (EMRO). Supported by the Bulgarian state and backed by the Macedonian immigrants, pro-Bulgarian EMRO members soon gained majority representation in IMRO's governing central committee.

The two organizations not only held opposing views concerning Macedonia's future, but also espoused different tactical approaches in the revolutionary struggle. IMRO focused on organizing a mass uprising and tried to avoid armed activities as much as possible, but preparation for the great revolutionary event remained its uppermost priority. EMRO embraced armed activities from the start. From its Bulgarian home base, it carried out political assassinations of opponents inside Bulgaria and organized raiding parties into Macedonia, which frequently included former or inactive Bulgarian army officers. (The first such raid occurred in 1895.)

While Macedonian revolutionary activity fomented, Serbs and Greeks were not idle. In Serbia, the Society of Saint Sava was founded (1886) with the express purpose of whipping up Serbian nationalism in Serb-claimed regions, especially in Macedonia. By 1889 the society came under the direct authority of Serbia's foreign ministry. The Ottoman administration in Macedonia welcomed the Serbs' activities, hoping to use them to counterbalance rising Bulgarian efforts. As for the Greeks, a secret National Society was founded in Athens (1894) with the goal of liberating all Greeks under Ottoman control, but it primarily aimed at combatting Bulgarian activities in Macedonia. With its leadership staffed mostly by Greek army officers, and supported by wealthy Greek merchants and consuls in Macedonia, the society propagandized heavily and sponsored raids into Macedonia to fight the Ottomans and Bulgarians.

A seemingly unlikely contestant in the Macedonian entanglement was Romania, which in the late 1870s began supporting educational efforts for the many seminomadic Vlahs roaming the Macedonian countryside. Claiming the Latin-speaking Vlahs as kindred nationals, the Romanians staked out a minor role in the Macedonian fracas to own leverage in future nationalist dealings with the main contenders, especially with Bulgaria over conflicting territorial claims in Dobrudzha.

The heated nationalist animosities over Macedonia's possession tended to obscure the fundamental factor in the "Macedonian Question." The Ottomans first had to be expelled before any nationalist solution could be reached. In the emotionally charged nationalist atmosphere of the late 1880s and early 1890s, Serbia and Greece unsuccessfully tried to bring Bulgaria into anti-Ottoman alliances, the terms of which would delineate peaceably their respective Macedonian claims. Both Stambulov and Ferdinand rejected the proposals, although for different political reasons. Serbia and Greece themselves discovered that their own conflicting claims in Macedonia made cooperation at the time impossible.

While the contending Balkan states failed to address the problem of evicting the Ottomans from Macedonia, the Macedonian revolutionaries acted. In early 1903 the Bulgarian-dominated IMRO leadership decided to raise a concerted uprising, even though many of its district units were unprepared. Delčev, Sandanski, and other original leaders stood opposed but, after Delčev was killed by Ottoman police in the spring, they accepted the plan. On 2 August 1903 the Ilinden Uprising (named after the day on the Orthodox calendar dedicated to St. Iliya [Elijah]) was proclaimed. The rebels briefly gained control of the Bitola region, and a short-lived "republic" was established around Kruševo by a group of IMRO socialists. Bulgaria, uninformed of IMRO's plans and unprepared for war against the Ottomans, was caught off guard and did little more than keep its border with Macedonia open to appease the Macedonian immigrants and assuage the Bulgarian populace's national sympathies. The Ottomans took nearly three months to quash the rebellion with their usual indiscriminate devastation and violence. Hundreds of villages were destroyed and a new flood of immigrants poured into Bulgaria.

The Ilinden debacle stirred the European Great Powers into action. Austria-Hungary and Russia, the two most directly concerned with the Balkans, hammered out the so-called Mürzsteg reform program for the stricken province and had it approved by the others. Inspectors from both Great Powers were attached to the Ottomans' Macedonian administration, and a reformed Ottoman Macedonian gendarmerie was placed under foreign command. The reform also required the Ottomans to enact judicial reorganization and provide financial assistance for returning refugees and rebuilding programs. The Ottomans accepted the provisions to retain support among the Great Powers. Far from dampening Macedonian unrest, the Mürzsteg program stoked it, since one of its provisions called for a future administrative reorganization of the province along ethnic lines. That provision caused Bulgaria, Serbia, and Greece to intensify their propaganda efforts in Macedonia to improve their positions in that reorganization, which resulted in heightened violence but deadlock.

The Rise of Albanian Nationalism and "Yugoslavism"

Compounding the divisive turmoil surrounding Macedonia were two additional national factors not addressed at Berlin. One—the Albanian national movement—arose as a self-defensive response by a traditional Balkan society to its neighbors' nation-state nationalism. The other—"Yugoslavism"—was a broader, more politically sophisticated expression of the original Croatian idea with significant ramifications for the Balkan states and Habsburg Austria-Hungary alike.

Without the very real threat of Greek, Serbian, Montenegrin, and Bulgarian territorial encroachment into their lands, Albanians most likely would not have adopted Western-style nationalism—at least not when they did. A set of factors conspired against their evolving such a consciousness. One such factor was the Albanians' religious diversity. As the Albanians were dispersed among three Ottoman *millets*, religion could not serve as a unifying element in national formation. After the Ottoman conquest, 70 percent of Albanians converted to Islam, and many played important roles in Ottoman society: One-fifth of all Ottoman grand *vizirs* were Albanians; they constituted the backbone of the empire's European military forces; and most Albanian Muslims were deeply conservative regarding religious and social traditions. Among non-Muslim Albanians, 20 percent were Orthodox and 10 percent Catholic.

Islamic traditions of religious toleration and the strong presence of the syncretistic Bektaşı sect (which co-opted many Christian rituals and beliefs) among the Albanian Muslims mitigated many Muslim-Christian differences, creating as near an ideal living environment as the Ottoman Empire could offer. There was no perceived official oppression; there was extensive local autonomy; and military-administrative positions generally were open to both Muslim and Christian Albanians. During the periods of destabilization and the *Tanzimat*, Albanians experienced less disruption than did other Balkan subjects and, if anything, grew more important in Ottoman internal affairs. The Albanians had little cause for general unrest or antigovernment revolts. Rebellions that did occur were motivated largely by local economic, military, or administrative conditions sparked by destabilization or were local conservative reactions against *Tanzimat* reforms.

A factor dividing Albanians was the linguistic split between the northern Gheg dialect and the Tosk dialect used by southerners, despite the fact that their shared mother tongue was unique among all other Balkan languages. North-south communication was minimal, and the pronounced dialectic differences prevented the common language from unifying an ethnic Albanian self-identity. Linguistic ethnonational identity was inhibited further by the lack of a standard literary alphabet, and the few attempts to produce writings in Albanian employed either modified Latin- or Arabic-based vernacular transcriptions.

Until the Ottomans founded government-run schools in 1860, the Albanians' education remained traditionally religious, with instruction in Islamic schools emphasizing an Arabic Koranic curriculum and Greek used in Orthodox schools (since Orthodox Albanians lay under the Greek Patriarchate's direct jurisdiction). Albanian was the language of a few Catholic-run schools. Both the Ottoman government and the Greek Patriarchate were aware of the danger that language-based ethnonationalism posed to their continued authority, so they moved to prevent the Albanians from acquiring a literary language: The Ottomans mandated Turkish as the instructional language in their Albanian state schools and forbade the publication of works in Albanian, while the Patriarchate used its church schools to foment pro-Greek sympathies among their Albanian students.

Zealously guarded traditional clan and tribal identities within the Albanians' generally pastoral and agricultural society, along with fervent adherence to age-old customary laws (codified in the fifteenth-century "Law of Lek Dukagjin") by most, reinforced their disinclination to pursue Western-style national formation.

The Albanians, however, were not completely immune to formative ethnona-tional development. Numerous Albanians had fled their lands for Greece, southern Italy, and Sicily in the face of medieval Serbian and Ottoman encroachments, where they founded communities whose members eventually absorbed Western national concepts and developed an Albanian ethnonational identity. Albanian émigré nationalists participated in the Greek Revolution and the Revolutions of 1848 in France, Italy, and Romania.

Particularly active in forging a Western-style Albanian national consciousness were the émigrés in Italy, where they enjoyed recognized local political and cultural autonomy. Heavily influenced by the Italian *Risorgimento,* which dealt with a north-south split in vernacular dialect similar to their own, the Albanians in Italy set about creating a unifying Albanian literary language using a modified Latin-based alphabet. By the 1870s they produced a number of works defining the Albanians as an ancient and unique ethnonational group and extolling the achievements of past Albanians, especially of Skanderbeg. Notably active were the philologist Demetrio Camarda and the poet Girolamo De Rada.

Until the Crimean War, the nationalist efforts of the Albanian émigrés made little impact on their Ottoman conationals. Although a few southern Ottoman Albanians were exposed to the émigrés' works and proved susceptible to their national message, most remained satisfied with their comfortable position in the empire and unwilling to disturb the status quo. The Ottomans' dependency on European Great Powers made obvious by the war, Greece's effort to capture Albanian-inhabited northern Epiros during the war, and increasing nationalist propaganda in Albanian-inhabited territories by Greece, Montenegro, and Serbia after the war raised questions regarding the Ottomans' continued retention of their Balkan possessions. For the Albanians, tied intimately to Ottoman society as it stood, such questions carried with them crucial consequences for their future.

When the Albanians learned that the San Stefano Treaty granted extensive swaths of Albanian-inhabited lands in Macedonia to Bulgaria and in the Shkodër region to Montenegro, they immediately realized that the treatment of Muslim Albanians placed under highly nationalist Slavic Orthodox control would be less than benevolent. The mostly traditionalist and conservative northern Albanian Muslim landlords and notables in the Kosovo and Shkodër regions, and the few authentic nationalists concentrated in the south, joined together in organizing antitreaty protests.

In June 1878 the protest leaders banded together in the Albanian League (or the League of Prizren, after the Kosovar town in which they met). Led by Abdul Frashëri, the foremost southern Albanian nationalist, the league demanded recognized territorial integrity for all Albanian-inhabited lands. It founded committees to fend off Montenegrin attempts to enact San Stefano's terms, organized armed units, supported Ottoman territorial integrity at Berlin, and petitioned the Ottomans to unite all Albanian-inhabited provinces into a single autonomous political-administrative unit. Although the league's declared aims and organizational actions outwardly resembled Western-style nationalist efforts, its purpose was to guarantee the continued preservation of the Albanians' traditional way of life rather than to embrace Western European sociopolitical development.

Great Power interests at Berlin, not Albanian protests, determined that the Ottomans lost less land than stipulated by San Stefano and that the Albanian territories mostly escaped untouched, except for areas in the north granted Montenegro (1880) despite two years of armed resistance by the Albanian League. Armed Albanian opposition kept Greece's acquisitions in southern Epiros confined to the Arta region when the Great Powers forced the Ottomans to make some territorial concessions in that direction (1881).

While the Ottoman authorities and the Albanian League found common cause in resisting the new Balkan states' initial post-Berlin nationalist territorial pressures, they soon parted ways. The Albanians pressed their demand for an autonomous province, but, fearing that Albanian autonomy would lead to outright independence, the Ottomans refused. After the Albanians forced a number of provincial Ottoman officials out of office (1881), Sultan Abdülhamid II crushed the league's forces in Kosovo and disbanded its organization.

The Albanian League's demise did not stifle further Albanian national development. Because of the league, the Albanian leaders recognized that their future could not be tied to the Ottomans', the northern Ghegs and southern Tosks were brought into a concerted working partnership for the first time, and the Albanians possessed a program for achieving political unity. Although essentially concerned with political matters, the league's very existence opened the door to Albanian ethnocultural development since a concrete ethnic identity was required for the newly spawned national program's success.

Building on growing interests of Western European philologists in the Albanian language—which they proclaimed an ancient Indo-European language (Illyrian) and for which they produced grammars, vocabularies, and folklore collections—Ottoman Albanian intellectuals, led by the nationalist Frashëri family, founded the Society for the Development of the Albanian Language (1879). After much bickering between conservative northerners (who wanted Arabic script) and Italian-influenced southerners (who supported Latin), the society successfully created a standardized Latin-based Albanian alphabet (1908). No agreement on a standard literary language was reached regarding the Gheg and Tosk dialects.

In the early 1900s an attempt to establish independent Albanian secular schools was made, but the Ottomans and the Patriarchate stood adamantly opposed to further Albanian cultural development. The Ottomans reimposed their ban on Albanian publications and schools, making possession of books written in Albanian or using that language in correspondence a crime, while the Patriarchate threatened any Albanian who attended the new schools with excommunication. In response, Albanians staged sporadic rebellions to win political and cultural autonomy. Although usually ignored by the major contenders, they eventually joined in Macedonia's endemic anarchy, militantly opposing both the local Ottoman authorities and the nationalist protagonists' armed gangs.

Just as the participants in Berlin took little account of rising Albanian nationalism, neither did they pay significant attention to the "Yugoslav" nationalists among the Croats and Serbs of Habsburg Austria-Hungary. While Albanian nationalism came to complicate already contentious Balkan nation-state expansionary efforts, "Yugoslavism" ultimately proved dangerously explosive for both the Balkan states and the European Great Powers.

The "Yugoslav" national movement emerged after the Croats' "Illyrian" program was crippled by the aftermath of the 1848-49 Revolution and was rooted in the work of Bishop Strossmayer, who expanded Croat "Illyrianism" into a concept embracing all South Slavs and coined the term "Yugoslav" to express their "authentic" nationality. Although he envisioned the Balkan Slavs' national unification under the umbrella of a reconfigured Habsburg Empire, Strossmayer's concept influenced Habsburg Croat and Serb intellectuals who, given their national situation within the Dual Monarchy and the rise of independent Balkan Slavic states (especially Serbia), did not share his pro-Habsburg affinities.

Strossmayer attempted to bridge the gaps separating the Balkan Slav peoples. His assertion that all Balkan Slavic languages were closely related was grounded in Panslav and "Illyrianist" philological studies that came to embrace Vuk Karadžić's Serbian literary language as the benchmark for all South Slavic linguistic relationships. By using as its base a Hercegovinian dialect, a median in the range of Serbian and Croatian dialects, Karadžić's creation gave the impression that the two tongues constituted a single language—Serbo-Croatian. The dissimilarities between standard Serbo-Croatian and other Balkan Slavic languages—Bulgarian (later, Macedonian) and Slovene—were attributed to differences in historical development. Strossmayer's message stressed the necessity of cultural unity for South Slav political unity. Few Slovenes, Bulgarians, and Macedonians heeded its call. Nor was it accepted by all Croatian and Serbian nationalists.

Among the Croats, Strossmayer's "Yugoslav" approach was not the only alternative open to the nationalists. A radical nationalist movement rejecting Strossmayer's moderate concepts emerged after the 1867 Habsburg-Hungarian compromise. Founded by Ante Starčević, the Party of Right sought an independent "Greater Croatia" nation-state, which would include all of Croatia proper, Dalmatia (with Istria), Slavonia, and Bosnia, rather than a Strossmayer-inspired confederative "Yugoslavia." Within its borders Serbian nationalist aspirations would be little tolerated. Starčević later gravitated toward a Trialist position, seeking a reshuffling of Habsburg Dualism in favor of making the Croats a third ruling partner on a par with the Hungarians. At his death, Starčević's party fragmented. The largest offshoot—the Party of Pure Right (in terms of "righteousness")—led by Josip Frank advanced an extreme "Greater Croatia" program emphasizing Croatian Catholicism and denigrating the Serbs as degenerated Croats who had sold out to Orthodoxy and Byzantine culture in the medieval past.

In Serbia, the "Greater Serbia" concept of the nationalist Nikola Pašić and his Radical political party envisioned a Serbian nation-state that included all ethnic Serb-inhabited territories cemented together culturally by Orthodox Christianity and the Serbian language. Bosnia-Hercegovina was particularly important for "Greater Serbia" since it offered an Adriatic opening to an otherwise landlocked state. Non-Serb-inhabited Slavic territories—Croatia, Slovenia, Dalmatia, Vojvodina—might be acquired but were not considered essential. No matter the state's ultimate extent, the Serbian nationalists demanded that it be centralized under the Karadjordjevićes and that Serbs dominate politically and culturally.

The Habsburg Croatian "Yugoslav" nationalists opposed Pašić's "Greater Serbia" program. They sought an all-inclusive South Slavic state fundamentally organized along federalist lines and structured to preserve all of the individual political, religious, and ethnic identities of its member peoples. The Karadjordjevićes were acceptable as rulers only if they renounced exclusive Serbian identity and reigned as "Yugoslav" monarchs.

While some Habsburg Serbian nationalists expressed interest in "Yugoslav" ideals, few intended to foreswear their Orthodox cultural identity for the Uniate-based solution initially entailed by the "Yugoslav" concept. The Hungarian governors of Croatia, understanding the religious cultural divide separating Croats and Serbs, played Serbs living in Croatian regions against the Croat nationalists. The ostensible favor they showed to the Serbs in educational, religious, and employment matters riled the native Croats' sensibilities. In the late nineteenth century Croatian and Serbian nationalists frequently came to blows throughout Croatia. Eventually, however, the Hungarian authorities' pro-Serb actions became transparently specious to the Serbs, who increasingly grew enamored of joining the independent Orthodox Serbian state just across Austria-Hungary's southern border.

The Habsburg Serbs' realignment toward Serbia was aided by the murder of Serbia's pro-Habsburg King Aleksandr I in 1903. The anti-Habsburg Serbian nationalist Petr I Karadjordjević, who succeeded Aleksandr, sought the loyalty of all Habsburg Slavs by linking "Yugoslav" aspirations to "Greater Serbia" nationalism. Modified to replace Croatian with Serbian leadership, "Yugoslavism" became the unofficial state ideology of Petr's Serbia and was used to justify Serbian nationalist activities in Macedonia, Bosnia-Hercegovina, and Habsburg Croatia itself, where both the Serbs and Croats were encouraged to look to Belgrade for their national future in a Serb-created "Yugoslav" state.

From 1908 through the Balkan Wars

The year 1908 was momentous for the course of Balkan affairs. If Berlin represented the first step taken by the Europeans on the road to World War I, with the events of 1908 they broke into a jog. The acceleration began in July, with the Young Turk Revolution.

The revolution's roots lay in the ideals of the Young Ottoman movement, expressed in Midhat Paşa's 1876 constitution, which was never implemented effectively after its proclamation by Sultan Abdülhamid II. Although a true heir of the *Tanzimat* in sincerely believing that preserving his empire required reforms, the sultan was not a liberal democrat in the Western sense. (Neither was the majority of his subjects.) He used his "constitutional" powers to abolish the short-lived Ottoman parliament (early 1878) while the disastrous Russo-Turkish War still raged, eliciting strong protests from the Young Ottomans but passive acceptance by most of his subjects, who in traditional fashion looked to the ruler for strength and protection in the face of foreign (in this case, Russian) danger. The sultan then proceeded to rule in traditional Ottoman autocratic manner.

Abdülhamid's autocracy was not reactionary. He carried out a number of modernizing reforms advancing the *Tanzimat* goals of government centralization and increased administrative efficiency, including new ministries to oversee the police and new postal and telegraph services. Beyond governmental reforms, existing secular schools were improved and their numbers increased; old roads and bridges were repaired and new ones, along with extensive rail and telegraph lines, were built; local industries were fostered; and state-run businesses (such as agricultural exporting and mining) thrived. Moreover, Abdülhamid stabilized the empire's woeful financial situation through an expedient deal struck with European financiers and governments (1881): All government finances were placed under the control of a European-run Public Debt Administration in return for access to additional loan money needed to keep the empire functioning. By the opening of the twentieth century Abdülhamid's autocracy had preserved his empire, despite conditions that many believed fatal.

To westernized Young Ottoman politicians, military officers, and bureaucrats, Abdülhamid's reform ends did not justify his autocratic means. Many of them fled the empire, mostly settling in Paris, where they eventually were joined by a small but steady stream of like-minded émigrés throughout Abdülhamid's reign. Within the empire, the sultan's success in westernizing and expanding education had the ironic effect of increasing the opposition to his rule. The schools made Western ideas accessible to their students. By the close of the nineteenth century both the Ottoman political émigrés and many educated younger individuals in the empire (mostly military officers, since the primary goal of Ottoman education was staffing the army with a westernized leadership) embraced the Western European nationalist concepts of the nation-state and were determined to apply them to the Ottoman Empire.

By 1902, when an Ottoman political émigré congress met in Paris to organize action against Abdülhamid, the westernized radical reformers were known as Young Turks (because they generally espoused a Western-style "Turkish" ethnonational rather than an "Ottoman" identity). The attendees at the congress, although representing a new Turkish national movement, soon discovered that they shared only a few basic political perceptions in common: A dislike of the sultan's autocracy, a resentment of European interference in the empire's internal affairs, and varying degrees of Turkish ethnonationalism. On the latter, and on most other points, they disagreed among themselves. Some, convinced that Abdülhamid favored the empire's Christians and the Great Powers at the expense of ethnic Turks, stood for centralizing the existing Ottoman Empire under ethnic Turkish predominance. Others called for decentralizing the empire and granting full ethnic autonomy to all subjects.

While the Young Turks argued in Paris, officers of the Ottoman military units stationed in Macedonia and sympathetic to Turkish nationalist ideals acted. Many officers, educated in the Western-type schools, were disaffected with Abdülhamid's autocracy. In 1889 students in the military medical school founded a Turkish nationalist revolutionary organization known as the Committee of Union and Progress (CUP). The group's revolutionary cells spread throughout the advanced education system, producing a core of Turkish nationalist partisans among the younger military officers and government bureaucrats. One such officer was Mustafa Kemal, who founded a Turkish nationalist revolutionary organization while stationed in Damascus (1905). His group swiftly was absorbed into an empire-wide secret military officers' nationalist organization—the Society of Liberty—which espoused the Turkish ultra-nationalist, centralizing program of the more extreme Young Turk émigrés and was headquartered in Thessaloniki, Ottoman Macedonia's largest city.

Macedonia, a hotbed of bloody nationalist guerilla and terrorist war, provided a ready environment for activist Turkish nationalist sentiment among the officers stationed there. Continuously assaulted by IMRO terrorists and Balkan nationalist gangs (often joined by native Slav and Albanian sympathizers), while lacking the military resources to eliminate those threats completely and secure the region, the officers grew disgruntled with Abdülhamid's policies. They believed that the central government was stingy in providing support for their efforts and that the Mürzsteg program was an ominous portent of approaching Ottoman dissolution.

Well organized, and having nourished strong rank-and-file support in the units under their command, in July 1908 the officers in Macedonia, led by Enver Paşa, revolted in response to a planned new Great Power Macedonian intervention. Fearing a possible partition of the empire, they put their well-considered plans into operation. An ultimatum demanding implementation of Midhat's 1876 constitution was telegraphed to the sultan in Istanbul. The Third Army Corps in Macedonia demonstrated its support for the ultimatum by assassinating government agents, staging urban riots, and sending its own guerrilla bands into the countryside. Facing a genuine revolution that might spread from Macedonia to other regions, Abdülhamid complied and called for parliamentary elections.

The revolution's swift success caught the Young Turk politicians off guard, and political tumult erupted. A majority of the officers and CUP members favored the hard-line Young Turk nationalist approach to state reorganization, while a majority of *Tanzimat*-influenced bureaucrats and many returning émigrés espoused the moderate Young Turk policies of state decentralization and political autonomy for Christian minorities. In elections held late in the year, the CUP-led radical nationalists won a majority and began implementing their program. Their efforts at Western-style centralization and cost-cutting measures alienated the conservatives, the traditionalists, and the moderates in the government and the military, who staged a counterrevolutionary uprising in Istanbul (April 1909) with Abdülhamid's tacit approval. Units from Macedonia, commanded by Mahmud Şekvet Paşa, arrived in the capital, crushed the rebellion, and deposed the sultan. Although a new sultan—Mehmed V (1909-18)—was installed, actual power thereafter lay with the nationalist Macedonian officers and the CUP, who were committed to transforming the Ottoman Empire into a Western-style Turkish nation-state.

The revolutionary change in Ottoman government threw Europe into turmoil. The Great Powers hastily convened policy meetings with one another in a flurried attempt to reshuffle the balance of power in the Balkans should the Ottoman state completely disintegrate amid conflicting nationalisms. In September 1908 such a meeting between the foreign ministers of Austria-Hungary and Russia took place at Buchlau in Austria. There the Habsburg representative, Count Alois Aehrenthal, finessed Russian Foreign Minister Alexander Isvolsky into accepting the Habsburgs' outright annexation of Bosnia-Hercegovina in exchange for essentially nothing— empty words regarding future Habsburg support for Russia's claim to free access to the Straits. In October 1908 Austria-Hungary publicly announced its intention to annex Bosnia-Hercegovina.

The announcement was met by frenzy and rage among the Serbs, who considered the region a rightful nationalist legacy. Serbia and Montenegro prepared for war, hoping for Ottoman and Greek assistance. The Russians protested loudly that they had been duped. Germany supported its ally Austria-Hungary, while France and Britain stood by their Russian ally. Although all strongly voiced concerns over the Habsburgs' territorial coup, none acted, since, given the existing alliance system, all feared that a general European war would result. In early 1909 the CUP-led Ottoman government accepted the annexation in return for compensation from Austria-Hungary. The crisis ended, and the annexation of Bosnia-Hercegovina was implemented.

Reaction to the annexation among Croatian and Serbian nationalists in both Croatia and Bosnia-Hercegovina was strong. The moderate, traditional Croat "Yugoslavs" saw it as opening a bright future, in which their trialist dreams would be fulfilled. Emperor Francis Joseph's heir, Archduke Francis Ferdinand, made it known that he was considering restructuring the empire once he attained power. The radical Croat nationalist Party of Pure Right considered the annexation the first step on the road toward creating "Greater Croatia." A recently founded, powerful Serbo-Croat coalition considered the event a catastrophe, for the same reasons that the others found it so promising. In the coalition's eyes, Francis Ferdinand's trialistic sympathies marked him as the personification of the Habsburg threat to a future Serbian-led "Yugoslavia." Nurtured by Belgrade, the Serbo-Croats bewailed the annexation as an insulting blow to "Yugoslavism" (by which they meant, whether the Croat partners realized it or not, Serbian nationalism).

In October 1908 Bulgarian Prince Ferdinand I took advantage of the Great Powers' preoccupation with the annexation to declare Bulgaria completely independent of Ottoman suzerainty, thus freeing him to pursue Bulgarian national expansionist ambitions in Macedonia unfettered by Ottoman restraint. Pre-1908 events in Serbia already opened a new potential avenue for attaining that goal. Following the bloody 1903 coup in Belgrade that brought the pro-Russian Petr I Karadjordjević to the Serbian throne, Russia's preoccupation with Japan in the Far East forced the new Serbian ruler to attempt an accommodation with Bulgaria for resisting mounting Habsburg hostility, an effort that sparked the "Pig War." Unfortunately, the rapprochement between the two Slavic Balkan states was short-lived, floundering over the issue of Macedonia. Rather than resurrecting cooperation, however, Ferdinand's declaration of Bulgarian independence appeared to doom any chances for future Bulgarian-Serbian joint action.

Adding to the Ottoman territorial losses of Bosnia-Hercegovina and Bulgaria entailed by the aftermath of the Young Turk Revolution, Ottoman Crete, which had been granted autonomy at Berlin, declared its unification with Greece in October 1908. Ranking second only to Macedonia in the Greek nationalists' expansionary plans following Berlin, Crete's Greek inhabitants were adamant nationalists since the days of the Greek Revolution, staging recurring but unsuccessful insurrections against the island's Ottoman authorities the entire time. In 1897 Greece foolishly had gone to war with the Ottoman Empire in support of a Cretan Greek uprising, only to be ignominiously defeated by the German-trained Ottoman forces. Despite the Greeks' defeat, Great Power intervention at the peace table gave Greece control of the autonomous regime established on Crete. The 1908 unification of Crete with Greece caused increased international tensions, an effective economic boycott of Greece by the Young Turks, and a military coup d'état in Athens by a group of officers calling themselves the Military League, who took control of the Greek government.

Lacking experience in practical political affairs, the Military League turned to renowned Cretan Greek politician Elevtherios Venizelos for advice (1910), paving the way for his rise to the Greek premiership within a year. Gaining King George's trust by staunchly opposing a swelling antidynastic tide among Greek nationalists because of past failures to acquire claimed national territories, Venizelos pushed through a revised constitution (1911) that strengthened the state's governing institutions, expanded public education, mandated economic reforms, and modernized the military. An ardent nationalist, Venizelos did little to dampen national efforts to win claimed territories in Ottoman Macedonia and Epiros.

In yet another example of history's ironies, the Young Turk Revolution, intended to preserve the Ottoman Empire through westernization, resulted in the Balkan states briefly overcoming their national differences and the loss of most Ottoman Balkan possessions.

News of Abdülhamid's overthrow and the ascendancy of the Western-oriented CUP was greeted with jubilation by many westerners and by the Ottoman Empire's non-Muslim subjects, all of whom initially thought that the change could only be for the better. Their joy soon turned to anger and fear as it became apparent that the new military-CUP power brokers were intent on preserving the empire as a Turkish nation-state. The Young Turk revolutionaries initiated a policy of centralization and Turkish hegemony formerly unknown in the empire and counter to the spirit of the constitution that they ostensibly espoused. With the new policy stressing Turkish national identity, virtually every non-Turkish population in the empire, whether Muslim or not, was forced to react against the regime. The situation intensified the Albanians' national development and spawned national awakenings among the Armenians and Arabs. The Young Turks' pseudo-Western ultranationalist program accelerated centrifugal national forces within the empire and galvanized the Balkan states' resolve to acquire quickly their desired national expansionary goals at Ottoman expense.

The Young Turks' repressive Turkish nationalist policies played into the hands of the Balkan states' nationalists, permitting them to overcome, for a time, their mutual national animosities and form an anti-Ottoman military alliance in 1912.

That development was encouraged by Russia, now free of its commitments in the Far East and again eager to stymie Austro-Hungarian Balkan ambitions by forging an anti-Habsburg coalition of Balkan states. Knowing that Russia was supportive of a Serbian-Bulgarian alliance, and taking advantage of the Young Turks' involvement in a war with Italy over Tripoli (1911), Bulgaria and Serbia hammered out a mutual assistance military treaty in early 1912 aimed at both Austria-Hungary and the Ottomans. A secret annex dealt with the future of Balkan regions lying under Ottoman control: The Sandjak of Novi Pazar, Kosovo, and a large strip of northern Macedonia (called "Old Serbia" by the Serbian nationalists) went to Serbia; western Thrace, with its Aegean coastline, was ceded to Bulgaria. The bulk of Macedonia was to comprise an autonomous province, which the Bulgarians, through their control of EMRO and influence within IMRO, viewed as a future puppet state (until its future incorporation). Should the autonomous province prove unworkable, Macedonia would be divided further, with Bulgaria and Serbia each receiving additional strips of territory and the final allotment of remaining areas subject to Russian arbitration.

Later in 1912 a Greek-Bulgarian anti-Ottoman military alliance was signed; no territorial issues were defined in it, since both states desired important Thessaloniki. In the fall, by which time all of the Balkan states were intent on attacking the Ottoman Empire, Montenegro signed alliances with both Serbia and Bulgaria that committed it to initiating the hostilities against the Ottomans. Thus the Balkan League attained its final composition. All of its members were heavily armed and united in their determination to pursue unrelenting offensive warfare against their common Islamic enemy.

Meanwhile, the Ottoman Empire was harried by Italian attacks and in internal disarray. In May 1912 the Albanians rebelled against the Young Turks' policies and briefly succeeded in gaining control of the core Albanian lands. The Ottoman military's morale and strength were collapsing under pressure from external and internal defeats. Furthermore, the Bismarckian alliance system made it difficult for the Great Powers to take any effective action to defuse local crises without their first consulting both allies and enemies as to the extent of acceptable action. By October 1912 conditions were right for the Balkan League to commence its war on the Ottomans.

Ignoring Russian pleas to wait, Montenegro declared war on 7 October. Ten days later the other Balkan allies followed suit. There was no doubt that the First Balkan War was fought primarily to decide Macedonia's ultimate fate. When viewed in such terms, it is obvious that the Balkan League's formation and its military nature was a deft piece of nationalist strategy on the part of the underdogs in the Macedonian struggle—the Serbs and Greeks—to nullify the advantages of the natural front-runner—Bulgaria. Simple military geography forced the Bulgarians, the easternmost of the allies, to concentrate their military efforts in the wrong direction, against the main Ottoman forces in Thrace, while their three allies faced mostly demoralized and understrength enemy units in the west, in and around Macedonia itself. Serbian forces easily overran Kosovo and occupied two-thirds of Macedonia while the Montenegrins invaded Albanian lands. Greek troops pushed into northern Epiros and into southern Macedonia, occupying Thessaloniki over loud Bulgarian protests. Meanwhile, the Bulgarians faced a bloody contest over possession of Edirne and received a gruesome foretaste of trench warfare in their assaults on successive Ottoman fortified defensive positions. (Interestingly, the Bulgarians were the first to use an airplane in actual combat during those battles.) When Edirne fell to a Bulgarian siege (March 1913), only Istanbul itself and Shkodër, in Albania, remained of "Turkey-in-Europe." In May the Treaty of London, imposed by Great Power demand, ended hostilities.

The treaty had barely been signed before dissention arose among the victorious Balkan allies over the conquered territories' disposition. At London, the European Great Powers decided that an autonomous Albania should be created. Their planned Albanian state included areas ceded to Serbia in the original alliance treaty with Bulgaria. In compensation, the Serbs demanded a larger share of Macedonia, to which the Bulgarians adamantly objected. Both the Bulgarians and the Greeks soon were at loggerheads over the possession of Thessaloniki. Smelling nationalist blood, the Romanians, who were neutral during the war, placed a bid for a part of Dobrudzha that had been held by Bulgaria since the Berlin Congress. Russia attempted to smooth the frictions among the allies, but relations between Bulgaria and the others steadily worsened. In June 1913 Serbia and Greece concluded an anti-Bulgarian alliance to defend their occupation zones in Macedonia against possible Bulgarian encroachment and then proceeded to win Montenegrin support. Both Romania and the Ottomans also were approached by Serbia and Greece, but they gave no concrete assurances of support. As tensions mounted, Russia offered to mediate the crisis, but its initiative was ignored.

While diplomats argued and schemed, the contentious former allies transferred troops to lines established in and around Macedonia, and border clashes multiplied. Bulgarian nationalist emotion built to fever pitch. The army grew restless, demanding either action or demobilization. Bulgarian public opinion, whipped up by the agitation of Macedonian immigrants who threatened to assassinate Prince Ferdinand and important members of his government if they failed to act, clamored for war against the Greeks and Serbs. The Bulgarian military high command, which hurriedly redeployed the bulk of the army from the east facing the Ottomans to the west facing the Serbs and Greeks in Macedonia, assured Ferdinand that all was ready for decisive action. In late June 1913 the Bulgarians attacked the Serbian and Greek positions in Macedonia. It was a naïve and foolish move.

Serbia and Greece immediately declared war on Bulgaria. Montenegro followed suit, and in July both Romania and the Ottoman Empire did likewise.

The Bulgarians found themselves in an untenable military position, assaulted simultaneously on three fronts—from the west, east, and north—and unable to offer effective resistance to their enemies' concerted attacks. They were swiftly defeated by the Serbs and Greeks in Macedonia; the Ottomans regained Thrace up to and including Edirne; and the Romanians captured Bulgarian Dobrudzha. In little over a month the Second Balkan War ended disastrously for Bulgaria. Again, deft diplomatic efforts by the anti-Bulgarian allies succeeded in maneuvering Bulgaria into a disadvantageous position, this time forcing it to play the role of aggressor and thus forfeiting any sympathetic support within the international diplomatic community.

Bulgaria was stripped of most gains won in the first war, including western Thrace and the port city of Kavala (which was given to Greece), Edirne and most of eastern Thrace (returned to the Ottomans), and most acquisitions in Macedonia, except for a slice of the region in the Pirin Mountain-Struma River areas. Romania retained much of Dobrudzha, while Greece and Serbia divided the rest of Macedonia between themselves—the Greeks retaining Thessaloniki and the southern portions of the region, the Serbs acquiring the lion's share of the central and northern portions, including Bitola. (See Map 9.)

The net result of the two Balkan wars was a huge national humiliation for the Bulgarians. From the founding of the Exarchate until the First Balkan War, there had been little doubt in their collective mind that Macedonia eventually would be joined to the Bulgarian nation-state. History and culture appeared to validate that certainty. Western observers, such as American Protestant missionaries working in the region, had concurred. So too had Russia, which had given them the region at San Stefano. As the Ottoman Empire had slipped deeper into internal chaos, making its dismemberment seemingly imminent, impatience over acquiring Macedonia had lit an increasingly fervent nationalist fire among the Bulgarians that, by 1913, exploded. But in little over a month in that year, all of their national hopes and dreams were dashed. A national depression, followed by frustration and then deep rumblings calling for revenge, descended on the Bulgarians.

More immediate for Balkan and world developments than Bulgaria's loss, however, was the aftermath of Serbia's gain. When the Serbs' overconfident sense of nationalism, stoked by success against the Bulgarians in Macedonia during the Balkan Wars, led them to intensify their dangerous nationalist revolutionary activities in Bosnia-Hercegovina, the cataclysmic result was World War I.

CHAPTER FIFTEEN

World War I and Versailles

Serbian nation-state nationalism, under the guise of a reoriented "Yugoslavism," ultimately struck the spark that ignited the Bismarckian alliance system powder keg, which exploded as World War I. What began as a Habsburg punitive action against Serbia for supposed complicity in a political assassination rapidly spread into a global cataclysm, the consequences of which—finalized in the Versailles Peace Conference (1919-20)—profoundly influenced the course of Balkan, European, and world history into the present.

Sarajevo, 1914

The road to the 1914 assassination of Habsburg Austro-Hungarian Archduke Francis Ferdinand in Sarajevo began at the 1878 Berlin Congress, when Austria-Hungary was permitted to occupy Ottoman Bosnia and Hercegovina. The Habsburgs implemented the occupation almost immediately and united the regions into the single province of Bosnia-Hercegovina. An efficient administration was imposed that initiated a civic works regime not seen in the Balkans since the Napoleonic Illyrian Province episode: Railroads and bridges were constructed; industries (primarily mining, chemical, and timber) were developed; reforestation projects and agricultural research were undertaken. By all Western European standards, Habsburg occupation should have been a boon for the inhabitants. Unfortunately, it was not the case.

The province's population was divided among three civilizational cultures. The largest was the East European Orthodox (43 percent), followed by the Islamic (39 percent), and the Western European Catholic (18 percent). Both Christian components had developed ethnonational self-identities under influences from Bosnia's neighbors—the Orthodox espoused a Serbian identity and the Catholics a Croatian one. Given Islam's theocratic culture, the Muslims, although ethnically Slavic and speaking the same language as the Christians, held no ethnonational affiliation, maintaining an Islamic *millet* self-identity alone.

Despite their modernizing efforts, the Habsburgs did not dismantle Bosnia's preoccupation landholding regime, and a relatively few Muslim *beys* owning large estates wielded immense local power over thousands of Christian peasants. The estates were run in age-old fashion using outdated land-use methods, equipment, and techniques. Agriculture, the primary economic activity, remained backward and the peasants poor (in Western European terms). The majority of the population—Christians of both stripes—remained downtrodden and grew increasingly discontented.

The Habsburgs' annexation of the regions was hailed by Croatian nationalists but excoriated by Serbia and the Belgrade-influenced Habsburg Serbo-Croats. In Bosnia-Hercegovina itself, similar-minded nationalist groups demonstrated similar reactions.

Serbia's nationalists were irate over the annexation. Their emotional response, shared by King Petr and most government officials, was an implacable determination to remove the Habsburg presence from the province and secure Serbian control in its place. In 1908 the *Narodna Odbrana* (National Defense Society) was founded in Serbia to promote revolutionary anti-Habsburg Serbian nationalist activities. It recruited Serbs in the kingdom, in Bosnia-Hercegovina, and in Habsburg Croatia.

Until the twentieth century, the number of consciously Serbian intellectuals in Bosnia-Hercegovina was small and limited to the middle class. In 1902 they established a cultural society called *Posveta* (Enlightenment), funded in part by Serbia, to educate peasant and lower-class Serb children. It became a prime recipient of *Narodna Odbrana* attention after 1908, spawning a new type of Bosnian Serb intellectual—poor, often jobless, with no vested interest in the Habsburg-imposed establishment (which hired Croats over Serbs), and with a chip-on-the-shoulder attitude because of the inequitable social system. After 1908 a nationalist movement known as Young Bosnia emerged from *Posveta*'s ranks. The movement was an amorphous but widespread association that sought independence from the Habsburgs and social reforms within a Serb-led "Yugoslav" nation-state. Its members disagreed over tactics, but their general affinity for Russian revolutionary literature bred thinking along radical lines. The Young Bosnians embraced terrorism, which they elevated into a cult.

By 1912 Young Bosnia members were in direct contact with a secret Serbian ultranationalist revolutionary organization commonly known as the Black Hand (more correctly, "Union or Death" *[Ujedinjenje ili Smrt]*), founded in Belgrade (1911) by Serbian military officers (those who had killed King Aleksandr) holding high positions in Serbia's government and led by Colonel Dragutin Dimitrijević (known as "Apis"), a former ringleader of the regicides and chief of Serbian army intelligence. While King Petr personally disliked the Black Hand's leaders, who operated beyond his control and often at variance with his policies, he tolerated the organization because of its anti-Habsburg and Serb-oriented "Yugoslav" stance. Through *Narodna Odbrana,* which it successfully infiltrated, and its own Young Bosnia contacts, the Black Hand engineered and armed terrorist activities inside Bosnia-Hercegovina.

The Habsburg authorities in Bosnia-Hercegovina came down hard on Young Bosnian agitation, but the pro-Serb Bosnian revolutionaries intensified their actions, aided after the Balkan Wars by *Narodna Odbrana* and the Black Hand, which, having won their goals in Macedonia, were eager to maintain their victorious momentum.

When in the early summer of 1914 it was announced that Archduke Francis Ferdinand would make an inspection tour of Bosnia-Hercegovina and visit Sarajevo on 28 June—*Vidovdan* (St. Vitus's Day)—the anniversary of the Serbian national-ists' morbidly "sacred" Battle of Kosovo Polje (1389), a small group of Young Bosnians decided to murder that personification of the Habsburg threat to pro-Serbian "Yugoslav" national aspirations. In Serbia, two of their student leaders studying in Belgrade—Gavril Princip and Nedeljko Čabrinović—acquired pistols, bombs, and a border pass permitting them to cross over into Bosnia-Hercegovina and implement their assassination plan.

Debates continue among scholars as to the complicity of the Black Hand and the Serbian government in the plot. The conspirators' weapons came from the Serbian state arsenal and were issued by Black Hand operatives. Although Dimi-trijević certainly was aware of the young Bosnians' intentions, no evidence exists clearly demonstrating his direct role in the plan. Likewise, Serbian Premier Nikola Pašić was informed of the conspiracy and knew of the Black Hand's dealings with the Bosnian revolutionaries. At the time, Pašić and his Radical party were at odds with the Black Hand over nationalist ideology (the Black Hand espoused a Serb-oriented "Yugoslavism" while the Radicals adhered to the "Greater Serbia" approach) and over the administration of newly won Macedonia (the Black Hand favored military control). Fearing a possible war with Austria-Hungary, Pašić tried to stop the Bosnian conspirators at the border and notified the Habsburg authorities of the plot through Serbia's ambassador in Vienna. Both attempts failed—the border guards were Black Hand members, and the Serbian ambassador was so vague and facetious that no word of the plot was forwarded to Francis Ferdinand or the Habsburg military authorities in Bosnia-Hercegovina.

Archduke and Crown Prince Francis Ferdinand was intelligent and talented but emotionally volatile, stubborn, and suspected of being mentally unstable by many, including Emperor Francis Joseph. His morganatic marriage had shocked Viennese society, and he and the emperor so disliked each other that they barely spoke. The heir publicly considered his uncle's dualist system innately flawed, and he certainly was aware that his Trialist ideas, intended to rectify dualism, were feared and hated by both Habsburg Serbo-Croat "Yugoslavs" and Serbian "Greater Serbia" nationalists.

As Habsburg military inspector general, he ordered maneuvers in Bosnia-Hercegovina for June 1914 to warn Serbia against pressing its victory in Macedonia further by targeting the province. The archduke decided to attend them personally in the company of his wife, scheduling a visit to the province's capital, Sarajevo, on 28 June, their wedding anniversary. The Habsburg authorities were aware that the Balkan Wars had heightened Serbian nationalist sentiment in Serbia and among pro-Serbian Bosnians, and that the archduke's presence in Sarajevo on the anniversary of the medieval battle posed an insult to them. That the court agreed to his visitation was a policy decision of the highest folly.

All arrangements for the tour were made through military, rather than civil, authorities, which partly accounts for the unbelievably lax security in place when the archduke entered Sarajevo on the fatal day. Even so, the assassination was more a matter of accident than of the conspirators' prowess. After bungling an initial bomb attempt, a dejected Gavril Princip was making his way home when Francis Ferdinand's automobile stopped in front of him while its driver tried to correct a wrong turn on the way out of town. In that brief instant, Princip collected himself and fired two shots at the stationary vehicle's passengers before being subdued by police, killing both the archduke and (unintentionally) his wife.

At the swiftly constituted trial of the five youthful conspirators, all were found guilty. The *Narodna Odbrana* (the Black Hand's existence was secret) and certain active Serbian military officers were judged responsible for the assassination. Habsburg Foreign Minister Count Leopold Berchtold and the army chiefs pushed Francis Joseph for war against Serbia, but the emperor and his Austrian and Hungarian premiers were reluctant to initiate hostilities before a complete investigation of the event was concluded. An expression of unconditional support for any Habsburg punitive measure against Serbia soon arrived from their Central Alliance ally German Kaiser William II. Although still a matter of scholarly debate as to its motivations, William's "blank check" tilted the scales in favor of the war hawks in Vienna.

A drastic ultimatum essentially demanding the veritable loss of Serbia's national sovereignty (intentionally crafted to be rejected and thus be the excuse for war) was sent to Belgrade (23 July). The Serbian authorities accepted all but one point and suggested that the entire matter be settled by the Great Powers. Unfortunately, the Serbian reply was worded in an evasively qualified fashion and was accompanied by Serbian military mobilization. Austria-Hungary broke off diplomatic relations and began its own mobilization, secure in the delusion that the war it was beginning would remain localized.

In 1914, however, Russia was not hamstrung as it had been in 1908. The Russian army had recovered from its 1905 defeat by Japan in the Far East, and Russia's Entente ally France, unwilling to risk war over Bosnia-Hercegovina in 1908, now viewed the Balkan situation as a test of Entente solidarity in the face of Central Alliance threats and considered the Habsburg-Serbia crisis a European, rather than strictly a local, matter. Russia initiated its military mobilization even before the Serbs officially replied to the Habsburg ultimatum. A flurry of hectic European-wide diplomatic activity erupted, and, afraid that diplomacy would forestall Austria-Hungary's effort to settle the Serbian threat definitively, Habsburg Foreign Minister Berchtold pushed through a declaration of war on 28 July.

The weblike alliance system stymied all efforts to halt the war's proliferation once Habsburg guns opened fire on Belgrade (29 July). Russia could support Serbia only by threatening Austria-Hungary with full mobilization. Once Russia mobilized, Germany was obliged to do the same in support of its Central Alliance ally, which, in turn, forced France to follow suit according to its treaty with Russia. Since all of the mobilizations were conducted according to predetermined military plans drawn up years in advance, and since the human, materiel, and logistical expenses incurred by the process were astronomical, full military mobilization meant that combat could not be averted without grave political, social, and economic repercussions, no matter the frantic efforts of rulers and diplomats.

War: Balkan Alignments and Fronts

The conflict begun by Austria-Hungary never was confined to the Balkans and achieved no swift victory. Once fighting became general in Europe, the quick knockout blows sought by all of the participants never materialized. The war rapidly settled into a grueling, horrendously costly conflict, in which ultimate victory went to the side best able to survive the astronomical price. After only a few months, it became obvious that the war would be long, so both sides set about enlisting new allies from initially neutral or uncommitted states. The Balkan states, other than Montenegro (which had joined Serbia), constituted a ripe recruiting ground for the warring alliances.

The Ottoman Empire was the first neutral Balkan state to enter the fray. When war erupted, opinion within the Young Turk CUP ruling party was divided. Traditional sentiment for Britain and France was reinforced by political, economic, and cultural ties, but both states stood allied with Russia, the empire's ancestral enemy. Great Britain's support appeared waning because a unified Germany had replaced Russia as its perceived primary Great Power menace, and growing pro-Russian British foreign policy was worrying. German support, on the other hand, had increased prior to 1914. German sponsorship of a Berlin-to-Bagdad railroad expanded Germany's military and economic influence in the empire. After the First Balkan War, German advisors rebuilt the Ottoman army, and German officers gained positions in the empire's military high command. As a "new" Great Power, Germany was free of associations with both the capitulations agreements, which France and Britain had turned to their own economic advantage at Ottoman expense, and the "Straits Question," which threatened the empire's very existence.

Young Turk political realism won out over traditional sentiment. It appeared obvious that, should Russia win the war, the Ottomans faced certain catastrophe: Russian control of the Straits would cripple the empire economically, strategically, and perhaps fatally. Britain's protectorship was uncertain; hence a new Great Power guardian was needed. Germany was the only available choice. That realization, combined with the fact that the empire witnessed the death of nearly 1.5 million Muslims and accepted over 400,000 Muslim refugees during the Balkan Wars, led the pro-German Young Turk faction, headed by Enver Paşa, to a secret alliance with Germany (2 August 1914). Secrecy was dropped after the British confiscated two battleships being built for the Ottoman navy in Britain. When two German battle cruisers—the Breslau and the Goeben—thereafter were "sold" to the Ottomans (both retained German officers and crews) and Germany provided them with a trove of gold, the Entente allies declared war on the Ottoman Empire (2-5 November).

Bulgaria, still smarting from its defeat in the Balkan Wars, remained neutral when the new conflict erupted, savoring the harsh price about to be charged Serbia for its nationalist pretensions. Once the war grew general and the initial Habsburg offensive in Serbia failed, both the Central Powers and the Entente attempted to woo Bulgaria for its large, well-equipped army and its strategic location. As an Entente ally, Bulgaria would cut off the Ottomans from their German allies and divide the Central Powers at their weakest link—the Ottoman Empire. Bulgaria in the Central Powers' ranks, however, would establish a solid and well-connected military bloc extending from the Baltic to the Aegean and Black seas.

Bulgarian Tsar Ferdinand and his premier, Vasil Radoslavov, having learned the lesson of haste in 1913, played neutrality to the hilt, soliciting territorial concessions from both sides in return for Bulgarian allegiance. The Entente offered the eastern half of Serbian Macedonia and a chunk of Ottoman eastern Thrace. Ferdinand countered with demands for all of Macedonia, part of eastern Thrace, most of western Thrace (including the Greek port of Kavala), and that portion of Dobrudzha lost to Romania in 1913. The Entente's negotiating position was restricted by the fact that Serbia was an ally over whom they ostensibly had gone to war, Greece was almost an ally, and neutral Romania also was being wooed. Meeting Bulgaria's demands entailed forcing concessions from allies and friends alike. The Central Powers had no such concerns. They freely granted Ferdinand all that he desired since it cost them virtually nothing.

Bulgarian negotiations with the warring sides dragged on for months. In early 1915 Pašić made it clear that Serbia would not cede any territory to win Bulgaria's support. As the Entente allies worked to overcome that stumbling block, their early military advantages in the war evaporated by the beginning of summer: The Russians suffered huge losses on the Eastern Front; the Serbs, upset that, in the London Treaty (26 April 1915), the Italians were promised Habsburg Istria and Dalmatia in return for their entry into the war as Entente allies, grew more intractable regarding Macedonia; and a fierce Ottoman defense had Anglo-Australian troops pinned desperately to beaches at Gallipoli. By autumn the Entente seemed to be losing the war and unwilling to pay the territorial price for Bulgarian assistance. On 11 October 1915 Bulgaria entered the war as a Central Powers ally, intent on winning back the lands lost in 1913 and gaining complete control of Macedonia.

By the terms of its secret treaty with Austria-Hungary, Romania should have entered the war as a Central Powers ally. It, however, did not. The treaty had remained secret because most Romanians held marked anti-Habsburg sentiments over the treatment of the Transylvanian Romanians in Austria-Hungary. Following the 1867 Compromise, the controlling Hungarian nationalists in their half of the Dual Monarchy essentially reduced Transylvania's Romanian ethnic majority to second-class status and subjected them to Magyarization. Although the Transylvanian Romanians mostly looked to the Habsburg imperial authorities for redress of their ethnic political and cultural grievances rather than to Romania and its *boier*-controlled government, the nationalists in Romania adopted their cause for themselves, developing a "Greater Romania" nationalist program that called for the unification of Transylvania with the Romanian nation-state.

Before World War I, King Carol I and his government frequently played to the "Greater Romania" nationalist sentiment prevalent among Romania's upper and middle classes by agitating among the Transylvanian Romanians for union with the kingdom. The secret treaty was signed partially in hopes that Romania would gain Transylvania in return for the alliance with the Central Powers. Although the Hungarians actively suppressed Romanian nationalist agitation in the principality, Francis Ferdinand, who despised and distrusted the Hungarians, made secret promises to Carol that involved ceding Transylvania to Romania if Carol joined his state to the Habsburg Empire. By 1914, however, "Greater Romania" agitation among the Transylvanian Romanians was largely unsuccessful—they mostly remained committed to securing full political recognition within a reformed Habsburg monarchy.

The Treaty of Bucharest (1913) ending the Second Balkan War accelerated Romania's alienation from its Central Powers partners and heightened both its prestige among the Balkan states and the self-confidence of its national leadership. Under pro-French Prime Minister Ionel Brătianu, head of the Liberal party and leading "Greater Romania" nationalist, Romania moved away from the Central

Powers, despite King Carol's personal sympathies for his German relatives and Austria-Hungary's dominant role as Romania's trading partner. While not officially abandoning the secret treaty, Brătianu undertook a rapprochement with France without committing Romania to a formal Entente alliance.

Carol died in October 1914, and although his successor, Ferdinand I (1914-27), was pro-Entente, Romania maintained its neutrality into 1916, during which time the Brătianu government blatantly touted its Entente sympathies and overtly prepared to enter the war on advantageous national terms. The treaty with Austria-Hungary was declared void, and, at French and British insistence, Russia was approached diplomatically. While the Central Powers offered Romania Russian-held Bessarabia, the Entente countered with offers of a free hand in acquiring Habsburg Romanian-inhabited territories (Transylvania, Banat, and Bukovina). Declaring that Austria-Hungary had not given Romania national satisfaction regarding Transylvania, King Ferdinand declared war on the Habsburgs (27 August 1916).

An independent Albanian nation-state principality was created at the London Conference ending the First Balkan War. It was placed under joint Great Power protection and ruled by German Prince William of Wied (1914). An International Commission was formed to delineate the new state's borders and provide it with a working organic administrative statute. Albania's unfixed borders, which failed to include all territories claimed by Albanian nationalists (particularly Kosovo and northwestern Macedonia); the continued presence of foreign (Montenegrin and Greek) troops from the First Balkan War; the Albanians' endemic tribal, social, and linguistic disunity; and the Albanians' general distrust of outsiders made William's reign brief (six months).

When World War I began, Albania lay in political shambles. It was in the throes of a peasant uprising. The International Commission was split by an Italian and Austro-Hungarian rivalry that spilled over into the rebellion. William's government was dominated by landlords, and Greece continuously interfered in Albania's southern regions. William refused to enter the war as the Habsburgs' ally, so their support, which kept him in power, was withdrawn. He fled Albania (September 1914), and Esat Toptani, a powerful landowner, installed himself as president with Serbian and Italian backing.

Toptani (1914-20) did little to stabilize Albania's situation. A pro-Ottoman movement among traditionalist Albanians demanded either the state's reincorpora-tion into the Ottoman Empire or the election of an Ottoman prince. The Italians occupied the Adriatic port city of Vlorë, Greek forces pushed into Albanian Epiros, and Serbian and Montenegrin troops swept through northern Albania (June 1915). Under pressure from Serbia, Toptani joined the Entente and declared war on Austria-Hungary, only to be swept up in the Serbs' defeat and retreat (winter 1915-16). He fled Albania and eventually established an ineffectual government-in-exile in Thessaloniki. Most of Albania was occupied by Austria-Hungary.

Greece was the last Balkan state to enter the war officially but was involved unofficially from the opening months. Greece's road to war was paved with the political leadership's divided sympathies and veritable civil war between factions headed by King Constantine (1913-17), who sympathized with the Central Powers (he was German Kaiser William II's brother-in-law) and upheld Greek neutrality, and Premier Venizelos, pro-Entente and desirous of Greek intervention on that side. Constantine feared British and French naval supremacy in the Mediterranean, while Venizelos, a proponent of "Great Idea" Greek nationalism, was optimistic that the Entente would win the war and that Greece, if its ally, could acquire all of its claimed national territories.

In the war's earliest days, Venizelos unsuccessfully offered to join the Entente; Britain and France, however, had no desire to give Greece's national antagonists— the Ottomans and Bulgaria—an excuse to enter the war on the Central Powers' side. During the negotiations with Bulgaria, the Entente urged Greece to cede sections of Greek-held Thrace in return for vague promises of compensation in Albanian-held northern Epiros. Constantine rejected the offer and then refused to assist in the Entente's Gallipoli landings. After Bulgaria attacked Serbia (October 1915), Venizelos invited Britain and France to land a large expeditionary force at Thessaloniki to support the Serbs. The arrival of Entente troops on Greek soil sparked an overt political break between King Constantine and his premier. Venizelos resigned and then embraced revolutionary opposition to the monarchy.

Constantine's continued refusals to cooperate with the Entente allies led them to make extraordinary, and nationalistically insulting, demands on the king (June 1916): That he dissolve his parliament, replace his government, reduce his army to peacetime status, and purge his police officials. There followed a German-Bulgarian occupation of Kavala (September) and the internment of its Greek garrison in Germany. Venizelos, then on Crete, proclaimed a revolution against Constantine, won enthusiastic followers from the Greek islands and among the army's officers, and landed at Thessaloniki (October), where he established a revolutionary provisional government with its own army. France and Britain officially recognized Venizelos as Greece's legal head and blockaded those mainland regions remaining loyal to Constantine.

Greece's outright political division continued into 1917. Once the United States entered the war on the Entente's side (6 April 1917), Britain and France felt free to remove the Greek king without causing an uproar among Greek Americans. In June they demanded Constantine's abdication. The king complied and fled to Switzerland, leaving behind his son Alexander (1917-20) as successor. Venizelos thereupon reassumed the premiership and brought Greece formally into the war as an Entente ally (2 July 1917).

While the various Balkan states aligned themselves in the struggle, World War I in the peninsula played out on four military fronts. The first was the Serbian.

World War I opened with an ineffectual bombardment of Belgrade by Austro-Hungarian artillery, followed by two unsuccessful Habsburg invasions of Serbia from Bosnia. Because of Belgrade's exposed position on the border with the enemy, Serbia's government moved to Niš, where, in the December Niš Declaration, it officially called for the unification of all Serbs, Croats, and Slovenes into an ill-defined "Yugoslav" state. Intended to weaken the Habsburg war effort from within, Serbia's "Yugoslav" proclamation made little initial impact on the Catholic Croats and Slovenes, who dutifully supported the war against Serbia, or on the Serbo-Croat coalition in Habsburg Croatia, which proved distinctly nonsubversive at the war's start. Only a few, mostly Dalmatian Croat Serbo-Croat leaders, headed by Ante Trumbić, responded favorably, fled Austria-Hungary, and founded the Yugoslav Committee in London for advancing the union of Habsburg South Slavs with Serbia and Montenegro.

Operations on the Serbian front briefly died down during the first half of 1915 since Austria-Hungary was forced to deal with the Italians in northern Italy. During that time, Britain opened a new, short-lived Balkan front against the Ottoman Empire on the Gallipoli Peninsula, which formed the upper lip of the Mediterranean mouth of the Dardanelles. The campaign was intended to capture Istanbul swiftly, thereby opening the Straits for direct communication with Russia and perhaps knocking the Ottomans completely out of the war. Expecting weak Ottoman resistance, British and Australian forces carried out an amphibious landing (April 1915). Their expectations proved wrong. Under the inspired leadership of Mustafa Kemal, German commander-in-chief Liman von Sanders's deputy, and assisted by inept British command, the Ottoman forces kept the invaders confined to narrow beachheads, where they spent the next seven months exposed to continuous artillery bombardment. A second flanking landing attempt met a similar fate (August). Unwilling to admit defeat, the Entente forces held on until late November, when the operation was called off and the troops evacuated (early January 1916).

As the Gallipoli operations ground to a close, the Central Powers reopened the Serbian front (October 1915). This time the combined Austro-Hungarian, German, and Bulgarian armies overwhelmed the outnumbered Serbian troops. Assaulted in front and flank by superior forces, the Serbs escaped envelopment by retreating southwestward into Albania. British and French attempts to support the Serbs from their base in Thessaloniki were uncoordinated and repulsed by the Bulgarians, after which they entrenched against possible Bulgarian assaults on the city.

By late November the Serbian army was in full retreat through Montenegro and Albania. Accompanied by a horde of civilian refugees, and carrying along a physically debilitated King Petr, the army's remnants experienced the ghastly ordeal of withdrawing through the Albanian Alps in winter under constant harassment from Albanian guerilla bands intent on winning revenge for the ravages inflicted on Kosovar Albanians by Serbs during the First Balkan War. After suffering some

100,000 casualties, an additional 160,000 men taken prisoner, and the loss of some 900 guns and all heavy equipment, the 70,000 survivors of the retreat reached the Adriatic coast and were transferred by French and Italian ships to Corfu for reorganization and refitting. Montenegrin King Nikola fled to Italy after Serbia's collapse (January 1916), and a rump government quickly tendered Montenegro's surrender to Austria-Hungary.

After inflicting a telling blow on the Serbs and bottling up the French and British forces in Thessaloniki, the Bulgarians occupied most of Macedonia. In January 1916 the government officially defined its war aims as the unification of all Balkan territories claimed by the nationalists—in essence, San Stefano Bulgaria—and partially successful efforts were made to break the population's traditional pro-Russian sentiment. If there was general national joy, however, there also were rumblings of dissatisfaction with Bulgaria's role in the war. Not everyone desired the officially expressed maximalist territorial goals, and many resented the exploitation of Bulgaria's resources by the Central Powers. In Macedonia, the Bulgarians' heavy-handed administration and self-superior cultural policies alienated the Macedonian Slavs. Moreover, food shortages in Bulgarian towns and throughout Macedonia affected both the populations' and the troops' morale.

The third Balkan front, called the "Bird Cage" by Entente troops, opened around Thessaloniki and in southern Macedonia on the heels of Serbia's defeat. With the addition of reconstituted Serbian forces, Entente strength reached 250,000 men under titular French overall command. (British troops took orders only from their home government.) The Central Powers' strategy was one of containment, but Entente assaults managed to push the front lines as far north as Bitola in southern Macedonia by November 1916.

While the fighting in southern Macedonia flared, the fourth Balkan front opened in the northeast when, immediately after declaring war in August, Romanian armies invaded coveted Transylvania but were thrown back by German and Habsburg forces (September). Bulgarian troops then drove north through Dobrudzha into Romania (November). The Romanians were crushed by the united Central Powers forces (December) and their army and government driven northeastward into Moldavia, where they tenuously retained a foothold around Iaşi thanks to timely Russian military intervention. Bucharest was occupied by the Central Powers, and the bulk of Romania's oil- and grain-producing regions was captured. The failed attempt to win Transylvania by force cost the Romanians 350,000 casualties and the loss of over half of their state.

By the end of 1916 the Habsburgs began to question their continued participation in the war. Emperor Francis Joseph died in November, and his successor, Charles I (1916-22), was far less determined to carry on as Germany's subservient partner after defeats by Russia on the Eastern Front reduced Austria-Hungary to satellite status. During 1917, when the March Revolution crippled

Russia's war efforts and the Bolshevik star was on the rise, Charles, aware that a Central Powers defeat would spell disaster for his empire and fearful of a potential social revolution, attempted to take Austria-Hungary out of the war before it was too late. His endeavors came to naught.

Initially France and Britain were susceptible to schemes for detaching Austria-Hungary from Germany intact. Should the Habsburgs collapse completely, they feared a possible vacuum in Central-Eastern Europe that would open the door to radical social revolution. Inside Austria-Hungary itself, Serbo-Croat and "Yugoslav" Croat members of parliament, led by the Slovene Anton Korošec, called for the unification of all Habsburg South Slav lands into a single Slavic state under Habsburg rule (May 1917). Fearful that the Habsburg "Yugoslav Group" might gain dominant influence with the Entente leadership, the Serbian government on Corfu and the Yugoslav Committee in London joined forces and produced a common program for South Slav unification without a Habsburg role. In July 1917 they issued the Corfu Declaration calling for the creation of a united Serb, Croat, and Slovene state.

With the entry of the United States into the war, at which time President Woodrow Wilson (1913-21) stated that America fought to uphold the principle of "national self-determination" (subsequently proclaimed formally as America's war aim in his 8 January 1918 address to congress known as the Fourteen Points), the case for a separate Entente peace with the Habsburgs was weakened. German pressures on Emperor Charles ultimately killed it outright.

Operations on the main Balkan front around Thessaloniki remained stalemated throughout 1917 and well into 1918, with disease taking a greater toll of troops than combat. As the impasse dragged on, the Serbian forces increasingly grew distrustful of their allies, the Germans maintained air superiority over the front, causing the Entente added woes, and the civil strife in Greece posed a serious distraction until Venizelos emerged triumphant. Problems, however, were not confined to the Entente. Bulgarian morale, both at the front and at home, plummeted because of increasing food and supply shortages caused by Germany's massive exploitation of Bulgaria's resources. The Bulgarian army's military effectiveness declined; only the Entente's failure to mount any concerted effort during the period spared it from military collapse.

The 1917 revolutions in Russia had an impact on the war in the Balkans. Following the first Menshevik coup in March, Romanian King Ferdinand promised sweeping agrarian and democratic political reforms once the war was won to bolster his population's morale. Only Russian military support kept his forces in the field, but after the Bolshevik November Revolution, Russian aid ceased and Russian troops on Romanian soil ran amuck. When Vladimir Lenin (1917-24) opened peace negotiations with the Central Powers, Romania was forced to do so as well (January 1918). Amid the anarchy sweeping over Russia, Romania annexed Bessarabia (March 1918).

In May Romania signed the Treaty of Bucharest with the Central Powers, sealing its defeat: Romania was forced to demobilize, hand much of Dobrudzha to Bulgaria, and accept German occupation of 70 percent of the prewar state.

In Austria-Hungary, the Russian Bolshevik Revolution led to increased socialist propaganda that, along with shortages and war weariness, stoked rising discontent among its various ethnic populations. Desertions from the ranks dramatically increased among Slavs who considered the war lost and sought to return home. The Russian revolutions also freed thousands of Habsburg Slavs taken prisoner by the Russians on the Eastern Front, many of whom were recruited by the Serbian government-in-exile and the London Committee for a "Yugoslav" force stationed in the Russian Black Sea port city of Odessa.

In Bulgaria, the Russian revolutions revived pro-Russian sentiments in hopes that a separate peace would end the fighting. Discontent with Tsar Ferdinand and Premier Radoslavov swelled. An Agrarian Union party, led by Aleksandŭr Stamboli-iski, agitated for peace without territorial annexations before it became too late. Inflation, Agrarian Union propaganda, food shortages, and German exploitation brought down Radoslavov, and his successor, Aleksandŭr Malinov, could not overcome the Bulgarians' rising war weariness.

Exhausted Bulgaria was the first Balkan Central Powers ally to collapse. In mid-September 1918 the Entente forces at Thessaloniki finally ironed out their command problems and, taking advantage of German defeats on the Western Front, launched a major offensive against the Bulgarian lines in southern Macedonia. In fifteen days the Bulgarian army disintegrated and Entente troops raced deep into the Balkans' interior. A Bulgarian military mutiny and an Agrarian republican governmental coup were suppressed only with German aid. On 29 September Bulgaria signed an armistice while Serbian and French forces pushed into Kosovo and Serbia. (Armistices also were signed with the Ottoman Empire [30 October] and Austria-Hungary [3 November].) By the time that the 11 November armistice ended the general fighting, Entente forces were across the Danube and poised to move into Hungary. Tsar Ferdinand abdicated (3 October) and left Bulgaria, leaving behind his son Boris III (1918-43) as successor. Much of Bulgaria was occupied by Entente forces, and the Serbs recovered their prewar portion of Macedonia.

With Bulgaria's collapse, Austria-Hungary evacuated Albania, which then was occupied by Italian and French forces. By October the Habsburg state had totally disintegrated. Realizing that the old empire would not survive the war, the various nationalities that made up the state proclaimed their national independence and established new states, hoping for recognition from the victorious Entente Powers. As Austria-Hungary died, Romania broke the recent Bucharest Treaty and reentered the war (10 November), invading Transylvania, secure in the knowledge that it faced little or no resistance. Transylvanian Romanian nationalists thereupon established a Romanian National Council and, after failing to reach an accommodation over

Transylvania with a newly established republican Hungarian government, proclaimed their union with Romania (1 December) at a national assembly convened in Alba Iulia. Romanian forces pushed through Transylvania and into Hungary to ensure the union's finality; thus the "Greater Romania" desired by Brătianu and the Romanian nationalists was achieved.

Confusion reigned among the various South Slav political factions at Austria-Hungary's disintegration. The "loyal" Habsburg South Slav parties haggled over the extent and terms of a future Slavic state until Bulgaria's collapse made a definitive decision imperative. Korešec's group of Slovenes, Croats, and Dalmatians met in Zagreb (October) and demanded the unification of all South Slavs into one state that could resist Italian claims to the Adriatic coast. Korešec was elected president of a Yugoslav National Council, which then (28 October) repudiated all ties to the Habsburgs; proclaimed the union of Slovenes, Croats, and Serbs in an independent South Slav state; and placed itself at the new state government's head. Most "Greater Croatia" nationalists, and nearly all of the Muslims inhabiting lands claimed by the state, rejected the council's actions.

Korešec's state received expedient recognition from Pašić and the London Committee, which agreed to its coexistence with Serbia until some future union took place, but Serbian Prince Aleksandr II, regent for the disabled King Petr, and most of the Serbian government did not accept the decision. Italy attempted to implement its claims to the Adriatic lands granted it by the London Treaty (1915), and revenge clashes between local Serbs and non-Serbs (primarily Bosnian Muslims and Kosovar Albanians) proliferated. In the end, the chaos prevailing in most territories claimed by both Serbia and the Korešec state led to Serbian military intervention and Serbia's dominant presence. One by one, the Slavs in the regions claimed by "Yugoslavs" of all stripes proclaimed union with Serbia (late November-early December). The Montenegrins deposed the Petrović dynasty and declared unification with Serbia (28 November). As the crowning touch, on 1 December a delegation sent to Belgrade by Korešec's National Council in Zagreb formally accepted unification, following which Serbian Prince-Regent Aleksandr announced the founding of a Serbian-led Kingdom of Serbs, Croats, and Slovenes, comprised of Serbia, Kosovo, Vojvodina, Montenegro, Croatia, Dalmatia, Slavonia, Slovenia, Bosnia-Hercegovina, and Macedonia. The new state encompassed the maximalist dreams of both the "Greater Serbia" and Serb-oriented "Yugoslav" nationalists.

Peace: The Versailles Settlements

The Versailles (or Paris) Peace Conference was one of the seminal events of the twentieth century. As a result of the deliberations at Versailles and other sites around Paris, much of the world's political cartography literally was created and fixed for the following seven decades (acquiring the mystique of some near-immutable standard order). The victorious British, French, and Americans (Italy and Japan, though allies, were marginalized at the conference) decided the political borders for the European, Western Eurasian, and West Asian postwar states. No matter that those decisions were based on the victors' political and economic self-interests, the borders drawn became political reality because of their creators' military and technological muscle. The world's Western-imposed Versailles configuration was institutionalized in the League of Nations founded by the victors (minus the participation of the United States), an organization legitimizing the settlement through a set of international laws created in the nation-state image. The Versailles peace settlements publicly demonstrated Western Europe's global predominance and the imposition of its nationalistic nation-state political and capitalist economic culture on most of the world.

Only Bolshevik Russia, with its Marxist political and economic ideology, potentially posed a serious threat to the Western Great Powers' claims of global hegemony at Versailles. Because Lenin took Russia out of the war and advocated international socialist revolution, Russia was excluded from the Versailles delibera-tions and lay beyond the imposition of their determinations. Bolshevik Russia repudiated Western European political culture—self-interested liberalism and democracy, industrial capitalism, the nation-state, and inviolate state borders—and looked to replace them by a universal Marxist utopian society based on political, social, and economic egalitarianism. Its absence from Versailles portended the onset of the twentieth century's most fundamental global rivalry, pitting the upholders of the Versailles order (Western European-style capitalist nation-states) against those who rejected its premises (Soviet-style Communist states).

That new Western order was shaped by five treaties signed with the defeated Central Powers allies: Versailles (28 June 1919—symbolically, the Sarajevo assassi-nation's anniversary) with Germany; Saint-Germain-en-Laye (10 September 1919) with Austria (an independent republic); Neuilly-sur-Seine (27 November 1919) with Bulgaria; Trianon (4 June 1920) with Hungary (also an independent republic); and Sèvres (10 August 1920) with the Ottoman Empire (later modified by the Cairo Conference [1921] and the Treaty of Lausanne [24 July 1923]). All except that of Versailles itself affected the Balkans.

Ostensibly, the guiding principle of the victorious Entente allies when they gathered in January 1919 was the creation of a new international order based on Wilson's Fourteen Points that would prevent future regional or global wars by providing all "nations" with states of their own—"national self-determination." Britain and France, however, had entered the war to defend their national imperialist interests but were forced to adopt Wilsonian ideals publicly to guarantee the American economic and military resources that decisively tipped the war's scales in their favor. Having won because of American participation, and with Wilson personally heading the U.S. delegation to the conference, Britain and France, represented by British Prime Minister David Lloyd George (1916-22) and French Premier Georges Clemenceau (1917-20), overtly agreed with the Americans' stated goals but gave priority to their own national interests.

In the end, British and French priorities prevailed. Wilson, like most Americans at the time, was inexperienced and naïve when it came to high-level international politics and readily was circumvented by his more seasoned and pragmatic colleagues, who did not share his idealistic scruples regarding the self-determinant nature of the nation-states created or modified in the final treaties. The old anational Habsburg and Ottoman empires were dismantled, but the new "national" states created in their place were constructed more to ensure the defeated Central Powers' prolonged punishment, to reward allies and formerly stateless friendly "nations," and to advance British and French political and economic interests than to uphold Wilsonian ideals.

It was obvious from the start that the peace settlements would be the victors' dictates rather than actual expressions of national self-determination. Representatives from the defeated Central Powers were banned from the treaties' negotiations, which took place only among the delegations from the Entente Powers. The resulting treaties, while couched in self-deterministic terms, were intended to preclude any future challenges to the victorious Entente Powers' dominance in European or global affairs by the defeated states. Besides levying crushing war reparations and restrictive military limitations on Germany, Austria, Hungary, Bulgaria, and the Ottoman Empire, the treaties, under the guise of satisfying national self-determination, also redrew their borders to cripple their economic and demographic bases.

State borders drawn at Versailles generally followed the victors' shortsighted policy of rewarding those peoples regarded as allies and punishing those who were defeated. The victors played loose with the publicly proclaimed ideal of national self-determination as the framework for nation-state cartography. Nowhere in the states addressed by the treaties did the national territorial claims of any one people go uncontested by those of another. The Versailles political mapmakers resorted to public polls (plebiscites) to adjudicate border disputes among "friends" in a seemingly equitable fashion, but similar conflicts between allied and "enemy" peoples almost always were judged in favor of the former, often with their most grandiose nationalistic territorial pretensions completely satisfied. The borders of nation-state "winners" were determined at the direct expense of equally valid, but disregarded, nationalist claims of nation-state "losers." (See Map 10.)

That there could be "winners" and "losers" in drawing European state borders pointed to an innate but unrecognized fallacy in Western European nation-state nationalism. History, whether in Europe or elsewhere, militated against neat territorial divisions in terms of exclusive human habitat among neighboring groups of people. Within the Habsburg and Ottoman empires, there were few internal boundaries confining such neighbors, which resulted in widespread territorial intermixing of different societies and ethnic cultures. By the time that Western nation-state precepts were applied to them at Versailles, no truly national borders could have been drawn had the mapmakers been objective in their determinations. The mapmakers, however, consciously were subjective, and they openly admitted as much when they inserted protective minority clauses (which proved ineffective in fact) in every treaty and established a League of Nations commission in Geneva to arbitrate the disregarded claims of the many national minorities created by their decisions.

By adopting a policy of punishment and reward, the Versailles settlements contradicted not only the ideals of national self-determination but also one of the important components in Western European nation-state political culture: The complete rejection of artificial and arbitrary monarchical states. In replacing monarchism by nationalism as the "natural" basis for state building, the West declared "unnatural" the combination of different nationalities within common borders merely for the benefit of an elite governing class, whose only loyalties were to itself. The Versailles mapmakers violated their own political culture's precepts by creating states artificially encompassing disparate nationalities, often possessing different historical experiences and cultural realities, but actually dominated by one of them alone (Czechoslovakia, Romania, and the Serb-Croat-Slovene Kingdom). In placing their own political interests in the forefront of their mapmaking, the victorious Entente Powers willfully sanctioned new states just as arbitrary in national makeup as the former enemy empires that they dismantled in the name of the nation-state principle.

In the Balkans, where national emotions sparked by the 1878 Berlin Congress continued to run hot and nation-state border issues were paramount among all nationalists, the Versailles settlements exerted a deep and lasting impact.

In terms of the Versailles definition of "national self-determination" (actually meaning British and French determination), Serbia, Romania, and Greece were "winners" while Bulgaria, the Ottoman Empire, and, indirectly (since it lay under Italian occupation), Albania were "losers." Among the prewar "stateless" nations (those that lived in the dismantled empires), the Croats and Slovenes joined the ranks of the "winners," while the "losers" included the Macedonians, Balkan Muslims of all ethnic stripes, and the Hungarians, Székelys, and Saxon Germans of Transylvania (who, with a brief seventeenth-century exception, found themselves tied to the Balkans for the first time).

No single treaty recognized the new Kingdom of the Serbs, Croats, and Slovenes. The United States was the first Great Power to recognize it officially (February 1919), and the other victorious mapmakers pragmatically followed suit by stamping their approval into the four treaties (all except that with Germany) that dealt with territories held by the kingdom. As the bases for bestowing their recognition, the victors used the 1917 Corfu Declaration and Prince Aleksandr's 1918 Belgrade pronouncement. Until Wilson began encouraging it in mid-1918, there had been little enthusiasm among the Entente Powers for establishing a "Yugoslav" state after the war. At Versailles, the self-proclaimed kingdom was represented by the Serbs alone because the victors technically considered the former Habsburg Slavs who formed part of the new state as "enemies."

Settling the Versailles borders of the Serb-Croat-Slovene Kingdom proved complicated and lengthy. When the conference met, only the kingdom's border with Greece was fixed and undisputed, since the Serbian army reclaimed Macedonia and Kosovo for the Serbian state in the war's final campaign. A rancorous quarrel erupted between the kingdom and Italy over possession of Adriatic coastal regions. The kingdom adamantly opposed Italy's efforts to acquire the Dalmatian, Istrian, and Albanian territories promised it in 1915. The clash of the two states dragged on into 1920, when the Treaty of Rapallo (12 November) finally granted the kingdom most of the disputed territories. Italy acquired Istria (with a large Slav population), the Dalmatian port of Zadar, most of Albania as a protectorate (less northern portions, which went to the kingdom, and part of Epiros, turned over to Greece), and a few islands off the Dalmatian coast. The disputed Istrian port city of Rijeka (Fiume) was declared an independent city-state but remained closely tied to Italy.

In the kingdom's Slovenian lands, many of the Catholic and highly Germanized Slovenes inhabiting the old Austrian province of Carinthia expressed mixed feelings about being linked to the heavily Orthodox, Serb-led kingdom. They successfully petitioned the peace conference for a plebiscite to decide the issue, which duly was held (the only instance of such a national referendum taking place in the Balkans) in October 1920. Over half of the Carinthian Slovenes chose to remain with the new Austrian Republic rather than join their South Slav relatives, and Carinthia, with its capital of Klagenfurt, was lost to the kingdom. That part of Slovenia centered on Ljubljana, however, made no such request and remained within the new South Slav kingdom.

Finally, the portion of the former Habsburg military border lying across the Danube north of Serbia was apportioned among the kingdom, Romania, and Hungary in the 1920 Trianon Treaty. A northern strip was retained by the new Republic of Hungary; Romania gained its eastern portion (Banat); and the western part (Vojvodina), housing a mixed population but a large percentage of Serbs, was turned over to the kingdom.

Banat represented a minor portion of Romania's territorial acquisitions legitimized by the Trianon Treaty with Hungary. More significant were Bessarabia and Transylvania. Conditions prevailing in the rump Hungarian republic after the November 1918 armistice delayed finalizing a peace settlement until mid-1920. Hoping to maximize its territorial gains, Romania had pushed its army beyond

Transylvania into Pannonia against mixed resistance offered by the newly formed Hungarian republic. When in March 1919 it became obvious that the former Kingdom of Hungary would be dismantled at Versailles, the republican government was overthrown in a Bolshevik coup led by Béla Kun (1919). Kun's regime instituted disruptive revolutionary reforms and invaded Slovakia and Ruthenia to win back Hungarian-inhabited lands apportioned to newly created Czechoslovakia. Amid fears that Kun's coup portended the spread of revolutionary international communism, Hungary's fall into political anarchy, and continued warfare between Hungarians and Romanians, the Bolsheviks were forced out (August) and Romanian troops occupied Budapest, Hungary's capital. Entente pressure persuaded the Romanians to evacuate Budapest and resume their positions along Transylvania's frontier. Not until March 1920 did the Hungarians establish a relatively stable government, headed by former Habsburg Admiral Miklós Horthy, that was reluctantly willing to sign the final peace treaty. Although they signed, the Hungarians never accepted Trianon's terms as final.

The Romanian delegation at Versailles was surprised to learn that, because Romania had signed a separate peace with the Central Powers in 1918, the Entente victors initially felt little obligation to honor the 1916 alliance agreement's terms promising recognition of all Romanian territorial winnings. The Entente allies also largely blamed Romania for Hungary's chaos in 1919. Only after the intractable nationalist Brătianu resigned were the problems between Romania and the allies resolved: Romania was required to sign the Trianon Treaty with Hungary before its annexation of Bessarabia was recognized.

Bulgaria received the punishment dealt all of the "losers" at Versailles. Following the elevation of Tsar Boris III, elections returned an Agrarian Union-led coalition government headed by Stamboliiski as premier (August 1919). Boris and Stamboliiski had no option but to sign the Neuilly Treaty and accept its punitive terms imposing a large war indemnity and severe military limitations. More nationalistically repugnant were the territorial terms, which stripped the state of all lands acquired since 1912. Southern Dobrudzha (won in 1916) was restored to Romania, the Serb-Croat-Slovene Kingdom received four small but strategic plots of land on Bulgaria's western border, and Bulgaria's portion of western Thrace won in the Balkan Wars (with access to the Aegean Sea) was given to Greece. Bulgarian requests for plebiscites to determine the involved territories' ethnic composition fell on deaf ears at Versailles. National resentment over the treaty's terms was widespread throughout Bulgaria, and the Bulgarians refused to consider it final.

Greece wanted far more than western Thrace from the Versailles settlements. Venizelos and the "Great Idea" nationalists sought northern Epiros from Albania and all Greek-inhabited territories, including Istanbul if possible, from the defeated Ottoman Empire. Greek nationalist aspirations, along with internal Ottoman conditions and conflicting Entente wartime secret agreements, made the treaty with the Ottoman Empire the most complicated and longest to finalize at Versailles.

The war utterly discredited the Young Turk CUP Ottoman government. After Sultan Mehmed V's death (July 1918), his successor Mehmed VI (1918-22) cleaned house of the CUP and signed the October armistice with the Entente. To eradicate all Young Turk political influence, the new government fully cooperated with the victors by permitting Entente forces to operate freely inside the empire. A secret treaty handing Russia Istanbul and the Straits was not implemented because of the Bolshevik Revolution. Lenin not only repudiated the treaty but published the texts of all wartime secret Entente treaties regarding the Ottoman Empire's dismemberment, raising distrust among many westernized, nationalist-leaning Ottoman officers and politicians and friction within the Entente's ranks. The Italians briefly occupied the southeastern corner of Anatolia promised them in the 1915 London Treaty, but the hubbub created by the publication of the secret treaties prevented them from occupying the portions of Western Anatolia, including the important port city of İzmir (Smyrna), granted them in the 1917 Saint-Jean-de-Maurienne Treaty. The United States raised strong objections over the blatant contradiction between the secret treaties and the Fourteen Points. The general atmosphere among the other Entente allies of feigned shame over being caught in a lie, combined with an Italian boycott of the peace conference over not receiving Rijeka outright, allowed Venizelos to gain permission for a Greek landing in Western Anatolia and the occupation of İzmir.

Atrocities perpetrated on the local Turkish population accompanied the May 1919 Greek landing, sparking the outbreak of a militant Turkish nationalist movement headed by the war hero Mustafa Kemal, who operated outside the control of both the Entente allies and the Ottoman government. Ottoman elections (October 1919) produced a new parliament with a nationalist majority, which voted to uphold the empire's territorial integrity, much to the displeasure of the British and French, who already had agreed on draft treaty terms dismembering it in favor of newly created Christian and Arab states. Greece was to receive all of eastern Thrace to the gates of Istanbul, islands off of the Anatolian coast (except for the Dodecanese, which went to Italy), and the right to occupy the İzmir region for five years (pending a plebiscite through the League of Nations before possible outright annexation).

In response to the Ottomans' opposition to territorial dismemberment, Entente troops occupied Istanbul and forced Mehmed VI to dissolve parliament and sign the Sèvres Treaty as written (August 1920). Those actions discredited the sultan's authority among most Anatolian Turks, who viewed him as an Entente puppet, and reinforced Kemal's Turkish national resistance against the outsiders' presence in Anatolia, particularly the Greeks ensconced at İzmir. The Sèvres Treaty was never ratified, and actual political authority slipped from the sultan in occupied Istanbul to Kemal's opposition government sitting in the central Anatolian city of Ankara.

Deft Turkish military action repulsed a Greek push into Anatolia's interior, and outright war erupted between Turkish nationalists and Greece, the latter technically acting as the Entente's agent to suppress Kemal's national movement.

In October 1920 Greek King Alexander died from a monkey bite, and, in a surprise move in the following month, Venizelos was voted out of office by a Greek electorate growing weary of war. Viewing the election as a referendum, formerly deposed King Constantine returned to the throne (1920-22) with enthusiastic popular support. Because of his known pro-German sympathies, the Entente Powers withdrew their support for Greece's presence in Anatolia, but Constantine decided to continue anti-Turkish nationalist military operations to gain full control of Western Anatolia and Thrace.

In mid-March 1921 Kemal negotiated the withdrawal of Italian forces from Anatolia and came to a tentative understanding with the Soviet Union regarding border issues in the Caucasus, thus freeing troops to parry the Greeks in Western Anatolia. A major Greek offensive (March) was blunted, and King Constantine assumed personal field command of his Anatolian forces, who drove Kemal's troops back on Ankara but were stalled (September) by fierce Turkish resistance and the king's reluctance to extend already lengthy communication lines. The ensuing lull in the fighting (September 1921-August 1922) permitted Kemal to concentrate military reserves and mend diplomatic fences with France, which agreed to withdraw its troops. While the overextended Greek army steadily grew weaker, the Turkish nationalists' internal and international positions constantly improved.

In August 1922 Kemal launched a massive counteroffensive that drove the Greeks back toward the coast in confusion. The defeated but enraged Greek troops, reduced to a veritable rabble, exacted revenge on Turkish civilians in their path, engaging in a frenzy of atrocity as they fled toward İzmir. Thousands were captured or massacred by Kemal's forces, who sought retribution for the atrocities, before the remaining Greek troops finally were evacuated to islands lying off of the coast. When İzmir fell to the Turks (September), the city's Greek-inhabited quarters were sacked and burned, and many Greek civilians received the same treatment that the routed Greek troops had inflicted on Turks.

The military catastrophe in Anatolia staggered Constantine's government. In late September a group of military officers forced the king to abdicate in favor of his son, George II (1922-23; 1935-47), after which they tried and executed six of the deposed king's advisors and then set off for Lausanne, Switzerland, to attend negotiations for a peace with Kemal's nationalist government.

Having dispensed with the Greek invasion, in October Kemal marched on Istanbul and its small Entente occupation force. A diplomatic deal struck with them promised the restoration of eastern Thrace (including Edirne) to the Turks and provided for the demilitarization of the Straits. Kemal then abolished the Ottoman sultanate (Mehmed VI fled Istanbul in a British warship in November), thus ending the Ottoman Empire, and opened peace negotiations with the Entente allies, including Greece, at Lausanne.

The July 1923 Treaty of Lausanne superseded that of the dead Sèvres. It formally recognized Kemal's nation-state Republic of Turkey and officially brought the Ottoman Empire to an end. Eastern Thrace (up to the Maritsa River, including Edirne) and a few Aegean islands close to Turkey's coast were restored to Turkish control. Unlike other Central Powers "losers," Turkey was not required to pay war reparations. Free passage of the demilitarized Straits was stipulated (except for warships in wartime and in the case of Turkey being involved directly in a war). A final action at Lausanne that proved important for future Balkan ethnographic affairs was a separate agreement providing for the compulsory exchange of respective Greek and Turkish minority populations.

Lausanne completed the peace settlements ending World War I. While the settlements were intended to preclude a similar future war, and the victors said they intended to use national self-determination as their guiding principle in reshaping the European world, their cynical system of rewards and punishments ultimately manufactured the very threat that they sought to avoid. All of the punished "losers"—Germany (especially), Hungary, and Bulgaria—considered the treaties unacceptable national insults imposed on them by force and demanded their revision. When such was not forthcoming through the international legal processes set in place at Versailles (primarily the League of Nations), all grew susceptible to more radical means for gaining their revisionist goals. Thus the Versailles settlements sowed the seeds of World War II.

CHAPTER SIXTEEN

The Interwar Years and World War II

The Versailles dictates of the Entente Powers regarding the new nation-states of "friends" and "enemies" came with both strings attached and scant consideration for the collateral difficulties that they caused. Whether "winners" or "losers" at Versailles, the postwar Balkan states suffered almost equally in terms of national, political, and economic problems stemming from the settlements. Nationally, the problems of the "losers" were blatant, while the "winners" paid for their favored status with subsequent intense internal national problems. Politically, all reverted from outwardly Western-like liberal-democracy toward more overt traditional Eastern-like (Orthodox and Islamic) authoritarian rule. Economically, all primarily remained agrarian and commercially dependent on the West, leaving them highly vulnerable to Western market changes—especially the Great Depression—and ultimately susceptible to Nazi Germany's influence through economic assistance.

Continuing National Problems: The "Winners"

The Kingdom of Serbs, Croats, and Slovenes was the most artificial European nation-state to emerge from Versailles. Contrary to the ideal of national self-determination, the kingdom recognized by the Entente Powers was considered somehow a single nation-state representative of numerous disparate groups—Albanians, Bosnian Muslims ("Bosniaks"), Croats, Hungarians, Macedonians, Montenegrins, Serbs, Slovenes, and a smattering of others—not all of whom were South Slavs or willing participants. Recognition overtly was based on the Corfu

Declaration and the Belgrade Proclamation, but it actually was a reward to the Serbs under the guise of Serbia's wartime espousal of "Yugoslavism."

Disparities in nationalist ideology among the three "Yugoslav" movements during the war—the Pašić government, the London Committee, and the "Yugoslav Group"—were evident, but expedient compromises in response to wartime situations led to both the Corfu and Belgrade pronouncements. The emergence of the Slovene-led pro-Habsburg "Yugoslav Group" (1917) forced the Pašić government and the London Committee to unite in defense of an independent postwar South Slav state. That unity, expressed in the July 1917 Corfu Declaration outlining a future Yugoslav state, was no easy matter.

Neither the London Committee's Ante Trumbić, a Dalmatian Croat, nor the few Slovenes in attendance were certain that they spoke for the majority of their respective conationals—most Croats and Slovenes were wary of Serb intentions. In the Strossmayer tradition, they envisioned the future "Yugoslav" state as a decentralized confederation of separate nations and were aware that Pašić advocated "Greater Serbia" nationalism. The specter of possible continued Habsburg rule, however, led them to the table with the Serbian government-in-exile on Corfu in hopes of finding a workable compromise.

Pašić accepted Trumbić's demands for a constitutional monarchy responsible to a democratically elected national assembly as the governing framework for the proposed postwar state, which was to encompass all of prewar Serbia (including Kosovo and Macedonia), Montenegro, Croatia (including Slavonia and Dalmatia), Slovenia, Bosnia-Hercegovina, and Vojvodina. He did so, however, only because at the time of the meeting Serbia lacked Russian support since the March Revolution had thrown it into internal turmoil, the Americans (crucial to Entente war efforts) favored the London Committee's "Yugoslav" ideas, and continued Entente support was needed to regain occupied Serbia.

Just as the London Committee was constrained to cut a deal with the Pašić government, so was the "Yugoslav Group" when Austria-Hungary disintegrated. Without a Habsburg-led option, the group's Slovene and Croat members first tried establishing a South Slav state on their own under the guise of the Zagreb Yugoslav National Council. Lacking a military force, the council became dependent on the Serbs, who fielded the only effective troops in the region, and ultimately was obliged to acknowledge Serbia's right to postwar South Slav leadership under the Belgrade Proclamation (December 1918).

Given the circumstances leading to the Belgrade Proclamation, the Serbian government felt no obligation to honor the Corfu Declaration's terms calling for a confederation providing each national component with an authentic voice in the state through liberal-democratic constitutional means. Its intentions first were displayed when, shortly after the proclamation, it declared Serbian Prince Aleksandr Karadjordjević king-regent (1921-34).

From the start, Stjepan Radić's Croatian Peasant party opposed Aleksandr I's acceptance until a liberal-democratic constitution was created. Croat fears were justified. Pašić and the Serbian nationalists refused to relinquish their centralizing program and delayed elections for a constitutional assembly. The Serb-dominated interim government passed a land reform program that they used to win support from Bosnian and Macedonian Muslim landowners controlling a number of seats in the national assembly, who received overly generous compensation for lands confiscated by the reforms. Even though elections for the constitutional assembly (1921) demonstrated widespread opposition to the Serbs' centralism, the Serbian nationalists passed a strongly centralized state constitution that essentially copied Serbia's prewar monarchical document. A solidified national breech between Serbs and Croats resulted.

Serbian nationalists dominated the state in every way, controlling the top government ministries and offices, the military's officer corps, and the police. King Aleksandr's complete control over the army guaranteed that situation. Before World War I ended, he crushed the Black Hand, which contested royal authority over the military, by trying and executing its leaders on trumped-up treason charges. He then installed a group of trusted, loyal officers (whom he called the "White Hand") in its place, who placed the military unquestioningly behind Aleksandr during his subsequent reign.

The Serbs also counted on the many ethnonational differences fragmenting the state's non-Serb population to preclude effective unified majority opposition. Radić's Croatian nationalists, the only cohesive opposition, committed numerous political mistakes (ill-timed boycotts of the national assembly, erratic "waffling" in political tactics) that hampered their effectiveness. The Serbs bought off lesser national groups with minor political concessions and frequently resorted to traditional extralegal political tactics—bribery, police coercion, election rigging, patronage, and legal manipulation—when necessary. Such tactics commonly were used on the Macedonian Slavs, whom the Serbs refused to recognize as ethnically different (officially calling them "Southern [or 'Vardar'] Serbs").

The Croats responded with blatant and continuous opposition. After Radić was murdered in the national assembly by a radical Serb nationalist (1928), they declared all-out political war on the Serbs. A Croatian ultranationalist revolutionary terrorist organization—the *Ustaše*—was formed by the expatriate Ante Pavelić. Basically an outgrowth of the Party of Pure Right, the *Ustaše* established ties with the similarly terroristic Bulgaro-Macedonian IMRO, with revisionist Hungary, and with fascist Italy. A separate Croatian "parliament" was set up in Zagreb, and King Aleksandr, raised in the Orthodox authoritarian culture of the Russian tsarist court, declared a royal dictatorship to stave off the kingdom's dissolution. To mollify the Croats and unite the various non-Serbs under his rule, Aleksandr changed the state's name to Yugoslavia (1929), but the Croats (joined by the

Bulgaro-Macedonians) remained adamantly opposed and the royal dictatorship acquired noticeable anti-Croat overtones. To weaken regional power bases, the kingdom was reorganized administratively, with ahistorical *banovinas* (administrative regions) replacing historical provinces.

Aleksandr's heavy-handed methods eventually discredited his dictatorship. Most non-Serbs considered the term "Yugoslav" synonymous with "Serb." By eliminating all party politics, Aleksandr lost even Serbian nationalist support. He issued a new constitution (1931) that superficially lent political respectability and representative government to what remained a centralized, authoritarian, monarchical state. By 1934 the king realized that his dictatorship had failed to solve the national-political conflict, but before he could end it he was assassinated during a state visit to France by an *Ustaše*-connected Macedonian revolutionary in the pay of Italian fascists.

Fear of Italian ambitions in Dalmatia briefly united some level-headed Croats and Serbs behind the regency of Prince Pavel, who, in the name of young King Petr II (1934-41), governed in continued dictatorial fashion. The honeymoon was brief, with the Croats again boycotting the national assembly after receiving no concessions from the Serbs regarding their federalist demands (1935). The Serb-dominated government tried cultural bribery to placate them—a concordat with the Vatican giving Roman Catholics wider privileges in Yugoslavia (the Orthodox and Muslims already enjoyed legal official standing) was signed (1937). Swift and widespread Orthodox opposition, however, forced the government to treat the deal as a dead letter, reinforcing the Croats' displeasure.

Another Balkan "winner"—Romania—emerged from Versailles as the "Greater Romania" of the nationalists' goals, having acquired coveted Transylvania, Banat, and Bukovina from postwar Hungary and Austria and Bessarabia from collapsed Russia. Romanian ethnic majorities in all of these regions superficially justified their acquisition on national self-determinant grounds. In reality, however, Romania's national situation resulting from their possession closely resembled that of the Yugoslav Kingdom: Transylvania contained large Hungarian, Székely, and German minorities; Banat's former military border population was an ethnic hodgepodge; Bukovina included numerous Poles, Ruthenians, and Slovaks; and Bessarabia housed Ukrainian, Russian, Bulgarian, and Turkish minorities.

A Romanian-Hungarian dispute over Transylvania's possession that erupted with the Trianon Treaty's signing—the "Transylvanian Question"—dominated Romania's national stage through the outbreak of World War II. Romania's Transylvanian national problem was complex, involving both domestic and foreign components.

Until the 1918 Alba Iulia Union, which was an act of last-resort expediency in the face of Habsburg collapse and the presence of Romanian troops in Transylvania, Transylvanian Romanian nationalism aimed at gaining status equal to the Hungarians, Székelys, and Germans within both the principality and the Habsburg Empire as a whole. Egalitarian social reform essentially lay at its core. Even as their national situation worsened after the 1867 Compromise, only a handful of Transylvanian Romanians sought closer relations with Romania. Most wanted a national partition deal from the Habsburgs similar to the Hungarians' rather than unification with Romania, whose Byzantine-like Phanariote and Ottoman cultural ties seemed foreign. On the other hand, the Principality Romanians mainly were concerned with blotting out their Greek Phanariote legacy while preserving their highly aristocratic and essentially feudal sociopolitical traditions within a "Greater Romania." In the charged atmosphere prevailing at Alba Iulia, few Romanians from either side of the Carpathians gave much thought to the real differences existing between their two nationalist traditions. Romania's military occupation of Transylvania rendered such consideration moot and ensured the Trianon Treaty's implementation.

After Trianon, Romania's non-Romanian minorities, especially the Transylvanian Hungarians, initially hoped that the historical and cultural differences between the Transylvanian and Principality Romanians would preserve them from Romanian ultranationalist discrimination. Their hopes quickly were dispelled. Some minorities were stronger socially and economically than the Romanians, who viewed that situation as a threat to their national superiority within the Romanian nation-state. The government reacted by implementing programs intended to weaken the minorities' position.

King Ferdinand I's government, intent on centralizing its control, eliminated pre-Trianon governing institutions in the newly acquired territories and installed administrators from the Regat (prewar Romania). Minority officials were weeded out of their posts, and numerous minority church and private schools were closed. Schools became tools for Romanianizing the minorities, with Romanian-language classes made mandatory. Systematic personal attacks on minority individuals and local communities followed.

Romania's oppression of minorities, particularly in Transylvania, often escaped outside notice because of its legal facade. The 1923 constitution was a model of liberal-democratic ideals: It guaranteed minority rights, proportional representation in government, and freedom of religion, education, and national organization for all. As frequently was the case in the Balkan states, the law itself was good but its enforcement was poor. Romanian officials bullied the minorities and showed utter contempt for the laws that they were sworn to uphold. At first, the corruption permeating the Romanian administration proved useful for the minorities, who found that bribery helped have the laws enforced. As time went on and the older political generation died out, their "Westernized" younger, more efficient and chauvinistically nationalist replacements reduced corruption but increased the injustices.

The Agrarian Reform (1920) also was an outwardly progressive program used to attack minorities. The reform was needed in the Regat, where aristocratic great landowners literally lorded it over the abjectly poor peasant masses. In Transylvania and other former Habsburg territories, it was used to divest minorities of their land. Nationalistically important minority religious denominations supported themselves and their schools through profits derived from landownership. By expropriating church lands and handing them over to Romanians, the government weakened the minorities' national aspirations and gained direct control of minority education. The Agrarian Reform was a financial, spiritual, and cultural blow to the non-Romanian minorities in Transylvania, Banat, and Bukovina.

Romania's discriminatory policies helped keep alive the "Transylvanian Question" as an international issue throughout the interwar years by providing the Hungarians with ammunition for diplomatic efforts to have Trianon revised. The Hungarians made continuous and vociferous detailed complaints to the League of Nations' Minorities Question Section at Geneva and in the national and international media. Hungary's unwillingness to drop its Transylvanian cause forced the Romanians to respond in kind, and the two states' incessant public dispute became an open diplomatic and media sore. Both produced mountains of statistical data to support their respective nationalist historical claims on Transylvania. The Versailles victors, however, were uninterested in such historical arguments. They were predisposed toward their Romanian allies because of war-related commitments, and that factor decisively overrode all others. Having favored Romania in the Trianon Treaty, Britain and France stubbornly refused to modify it later in any major way. Although other European states proved a more susceptible audience for Hungary's revisionist pleas, their hands were tied without the two Great Powers' consent.

The increasing belligerency of frustrated Hungary over its inability to win Trianon's revision led all "winner" states that benefited territorially from the treaty to band together for protection against possible Hungarian aggression. In a series of agreements signed in 1920 and 1921, Romania, the Yugoslav Kingdom, and Czechoslovakia formed an anti-Hungarian political-military alliance—the "Little Entente." Although taken seriously by Britain and France as a guarantor of regional stability, the alliance produced little practical results and only further poisoned relations between Hungary and its allied neighbors.

Greece technically was a Versailles "winner" but actually emerged a "loser." The nationalistically favorable Sèvres Treaty with the Ottomans proved a dead letter. Although Italy handed Greece the Dodecanese Islands (except for Rhodes) in 1920, Kemal's Turkish nationalist movement foiled Greek nationalist claims in Anatolia and Thrace. After much fruitless military effort and domestic political turmoil, Greece was obliged to sign the Lausanne Treaty recognizing the new Turkish nation-state. Greek "Great Idea" nationalist aspirations in Anatolia were ended and heightened anti-Turk national sentiment became cemented among Greeks in general. Moreover, Greece faced problems with Italy over occupation zones in Albania. (Greece held most of northern Epiros, Italy the rest.)

A significant national development for postwar Greece was the compulsory exchange of minorities with Bulgaria called for in the Neuilly Treaty and the separate agreement with Turkey struck at Lausanne. These exchanges represented the culmination of Balkan population shifts that began with the Balkan Wars and continued through World War I, during which time some 216,000 Greeks, 410,000 Muslims, and 60,000 Bulgarians moved, either voluntarily or by force, from their home regions to locations within newly established states. As a result of Neuilly, an additional 53,000 Bulgarians voluntarily emigrated from Greek-held Macedonia, while 30,000 Greeks left Bulgaria. The magnitude of the Lausanne population transfers dwarfed most others: Some 1.3 million Greeks were expelled from Turkey (except for those residing in Istanbul, including the Greek Orthodox patriarch, who were exempted) and 480,000 Muslims were removed from Greece (excluding those in Greek Western Thrace, who remained as a quid pro quo for the Istanbul Greeks).

The population exchanges were a mixed blessing for Greece. Greece's control over its Macedonian territories was strengthened ethnically—numerous non-Greeks left, and most Greeks repatriated from Turkey and Bulgaria were settled there to reinforce the Greek presence. Remaining non-Greeks were subjected to forced Hellenization. Successive Greek governments attempted to eradicate permanently any non-Greek ethnocultural presence in Greek Macedonia, singling out Slav inhabitants—officially termed "Slavophone Greeks"—for particular attention. The Slavic vernacular was suppressed, police intimidation became commonplace, Slav villages were destroyed, recalcitrant Slavs were expelled by force, and other systematic acts of anti-Slav violence were carried out.

The "Slavophone" policy had some negative repercussions. The Greek government never felt completely certain that its Hellenization policy succeeded, and a sense of paranoia regarding the national situation in Greece's northern territories persisted. Greek nationalists feared the Slavs living north of their borders, and relations with Greece's Slavic neighbors suffered. It took six years (1923-29) to finalize an official friendship pact with the Yugoslav Kingdom. As for Bulgaria, which refused to recognize Greece's hold on Macedonian lands as final, relations were strained. Greece suffered continuous incursions into its Macedonian holdings by Bulgarian-based IMRO terrorists, and a Greek invasion of southwestern Bulgaria to crush IMRO in its lair (1925) was stopped by the League of Nations, after which IMRO attacks persisted.

The population exchanges also raised serious socioeconomic issues for Greece. The influx of over a million immigrants into an already overcrowded state was costly and socially explosive. The supply of habitable, arable land was limited by mountainous terrain. The expulsions of non-Greeks from Greek Macedonia freed some plots for resettlement, but fell short of satisfying the immigrants' overall needs. It became necessary to redistribute all available land, which reduced average private landholdings, further impoverished the majority agrarian population, and intensified general discontent. Both native mainland Greeks and Anatolian immigrants experienced a sense of culture shock, and mutual prejudices emerged. Many immigrants spoke only Turkish, Anatolian Greek dialects, or scholastic Greek learned in schools. Former urban immigrants often found their new society "provincial," offering fewer opportunities and diminished livelihoods, making them susceptible to radical political and social ideas.

National frustration over the postwar Anatolian adventure and the domestic and foreign relations impact of the immigrants were reflected in Greece's political sphere. A sense of national defeat and abandonment permeated politics, resulting in a succession of governments exhibiting varying institutional forms—the military junta and puppet monarchy of George II (1923-24), a constitutional republic (1924-35), and the constitutional monarchy of a restored George II (1935-36)—and ultimately culminating in General John Metaxas's military dictatorship (1936-41) with the blessing of King George. Western-style liberal-democratic institutions proved unable to cope with the interwar period's national, social, and economic pressures, and the Greeks resorted to the authoritarianism rooted in their Orthodox cultural traditions.

Even during the republic's eleven-year existence, one individual—Elevtherios Venizelos—dominated affairs. He returned to power following the failed military dictatorship of General Theodore Pangalos (1925-26). As the premier for a series of presidential nonentities (1928-33), Venizelos manipulated electoral laws to ensure republican parliamentary majorities against royalist opposition. To his credit, Venizelos used his power to address Greece's domestic and foreign problems. He conducted the largest land redistribution program undertaken in the Balkans, made credit available to peasants, fostered industrial development, and expanded Greece's merchant marine. Venizelos forged friendship pacts with Italy (1928) and the Yugoslav Kingdom (1929), ending Greece's international isolation caused by King Constantine's return (1920), and called the First Balkan Conference (Athens, October 1930) to improve mutual political and economic relations among the Balkan states. Convinced that Greek-Turkish relations needed mending, Venizelos visited Turkey, where he signed the Treaty of Ankara (October 1930) settling outstanding population exchange issues and recognizing the territorial status quo. Venizelos no longer held office when a Balkan Entente was signed by Greece, Yugoslavia, Romania, and Turkey in February 1934, but his earlier diplomatic efforts laid much of the preparatory groundwork for that alliance.

After being voted out of office (1933), Venizelos led a failed uprising (1934) and fled to France. The victorious royalists then restored King George II to the throne (1935). George appointed as premier retired General John Metaxas (1936), who convinced the king that "strong government" was necessary. Using the threat of a national labor strike as his excuse, Metaxas staged a coup (August 1936) with George's acquiescence. Metaxas declared martial law, closed parliament, reorganized the government (gaining direct control over the military, foreign affairs, and education), banned political parties, and muzzled the press. With the army aligned completely behind him, Metaxas assumed the premiership for life (1938) and all liberal-democratic pretense ended.

Metaxas's dictatorship was both nationalist and populist—he called his governing ideology the "Third Hellenic Civilization," theoretically linking classical and Byzantine Greece to that of the 1930s. It emphasized conservative Orthodox values mixed with a populist preference for, among other things, the vernacular (demotic) Greek language, for which the first grammar was published. Metaxas attempted to inculcate his ideals through mass indoctrination that resembled similar tactics taken in the rising European fascist states. In Metaxas's case, dictatorship was paternalism with a few fascist trappings—he saw himself as a benevolent father figure (an aspect of Byzantine emperors) and not as "Big Brother."

Although his dictatorship rested squarely on the army's backing, Metaxas made efforts to win popular support. He exerted control over the state's industrial sector, permitting him to initiate social benefits, including a minimum wage, pay increases, social security, and artificially low food prices. Numerous agricultural debts were cancelled, and low-interest agrarian loans made available. The merchant marine again was expanded, and a huge public works program emphasizing military rearmament was implemented. (Despite the jobs it created, the program led to higher taxes and general public discontent.)

In foreign affairs, Metaxas maintained close relations with Turkey and adhered to the Balkan Entente. In the late 1930s, however, he laid Greece open to German economic penetration. By 1938 German products accounted for 30 percent of Greece's imports, while Germany bought 40 percent of the state's exports. Yet Germany's importance in Greece's foreign trade did not eclipse the British and French roles as primary Great Power partners and supporters. Britain especially was an important friendly Great Power: The British had encouraged the king's restoration and bestowed on him their traditional support. As a new world war threatened in 1938, Metaxas proposed a formal alliance with Britain but received no response. (The British feared that it would cause British-German relations to deteriorate further than they were at the time.) In April 1939, after the Italian Fascist ruler Benito Mussolini (1922-43) occupied Albania, Metaxas accepted a British and French guarantee of Greece's territorial integrity in return for resisting Italian aggression.

Continuing National Problems: The "Losers"

Bulgaria was the chief Balkan state "loser" at Versailles. The Neuilly Treaty's imposed territorial losses (in Macedonia, Thrace, and Dobrudzha), reparations payments, and military restrictions hobbled the government and inflamed Bulgarian nationalist emotions. To make matters worse, some 250,000 refugees from Macedonia and Thrace flooded into Bulgaria, causing overcrowding and concomitant political and social pressures.

Following Bulgaria's wartime collapse, Agrarian Union party head Aleksandŭr Stamboliiski came to power as premier (1919-23) for the politically weak and uncertain Tsar Boris III. Leader of the first peasant-oriented government in the Balkans (and in Europe), Stamboliiski represented a symbolic alternative to Lenin's Bolshevism for many postwar-era European statesmen, holding out the possibility that his "Orange" movement (the Agrarian Union's official color)—although radical in traditionalists' eyes because of its egalitarian ideology, it adhered to traditional liberal-democratic parameters—might stymie the spread of the anti–liberal-democratic "Reds" (Bolshevik Communists).

Stamboliiski espoused a radical policy of peasant empowerment: All state lands and larger private estates (there were no great ones because there were no aristocratic landowners) were redistributed; a heavy progressive income tax was levied on all but the peasants; compulsory labor service replaced military service for youths; the governmental role of the middle class was reduced; rural education was expanded and curricula modified to include increased vocational and technical training. He aimed to build an egalitarian society enjoying such modern benefits as clean habitations, paved streets, good water, proper sanitation, universal primary and secondary education, and cheap, abundant necessities.

The Agrarians alienated the commercial and professional classes, who often were targeted officially as threats to their government's egalitarian goals. The Bulgarian Communists, founded in the 1880s by Dimitŭr Blagoev, considered the Agrarian Union their sociopolitical enemy, while traditional political parties chafed over being discredited for past political ineffectiveness. Unfortunately for the Agrarian movement in general, Stamboliiski's governing approach was embedded in the authoritarian traditions of the Orthodox and Ottoman Balkans. He ruthlessly cemented near-autocratic power in his own hands.

On assuming office, Stamboliiski cleaned house in the government—most previous ministers were fired and some were tried. He replaced them with inexperienced peasant leaders who often were vulnerable to power's corrupting impulses. When the Communists threatened his government with a general strike, Stamboliiski unhesitatingly declared martial law, using the army and "Orange Guard" peasant gangs to break the opposition. He arbitrarily manipulated elections to retain a popular mandate and muzzled political opposition through rigid press censorship and police crackdowns.

His efforts in foreign policy, which was intimately linked to domestic national issues, ultimately proved fatal for Stamboliiski, who personally was uninterested in national territorial expansion. His stance so pleased the Entente victors that Bulgaria was the first defeated state admitted to the League of Nations (1920), and reparations were reduced (1923). Stamboliiski realized that continued ferment over Macedonia's possession weakened Bulgaria's international position and threatened any further advances opened by League membership. He tried to dampen the Macedonian issue by developing friendly relations with the Yugoslav Kingdom and clamping down on IMRO. His efforts stirred up intense hatred among IMRO's leaders and nationalistic army officers, who staged a concerted coup (June 1923), in which Stamboliiski brutally was murdered. Effective central authority then evaporated for a time: A reactionary government was installed; political parties proliferated; and winning parties in elections considered government a source of personal enrichment rather than a responsibility. Nationalist agitation increased to dangerously anarchistic levels, and IMRO stepped up terrorist raids into Yugoslav and Greek Macedonia.

For a decade following the coup, IMRO played a leading role in Bulgarian national life, abetted by general national frustration over the Neuilly Treaty and, particularly, the bitterness of the large Macedonian immigrant population over the postwar loss of Macedonia. IMRO's influence was magnified by reports of the sad treatment of Macedonian Slavs in Yugoslavia and Greece.

Following the war, both the Serb-dominated Yugoslav and the Greek governments initiated ethnonational policies in their Macedonian territories to erase pro-Bulgarian sentiment among their inhabitants permanently. In neither state were Macedonian Slavs granted nationality status. They were forced to use either Serbian or Greek as their official and educational languages, and they rarely attained high government or church offices. In the Yugoslav Kingdom, the government called them "Serbs" and the region "South Serbia"; in Greece, they were "Slavophone Greeks" (the regional name "Macedonia" was retained). Faced with such ethnonational discrimination, the Macedonian Slavs not only clandestinely supported IMRO but formed similar secret organizations of their own to combat the overweening Serbs and Greeks. In the Yugoslav Kingdom, they established contacts with the Croatian *Ustaše* and frequently conducted joint actions with them.

In the 1920s IMRO was entrenched in southwestern Bulgaria's Pirin region, over which it exerted veritable total governing control. For all practical purposes, the region became a small Macedonian state within Bulgaria. IMRO's increasing terrorist incursions led the Yugoslav and Greek authorities to fortify heavily their borders with Bulgaria.

Although IMRO appeared formidable, it was wracked by internal dissention. The persistent division between annexationists and autonomists was multiplied when Communists seeking to create an autonomous socialist Macedonian republic appeared in its ranks. A short-lived coalition of all three parties in the early 1920s gave way to internal civil war. Between 1924 and 1934 (when IMRO finally was outlawed in Bulgaria), some 400 persons died in the intraterrorist fighting that degenerated into gangsterism. The streets of Bulgaria's capital, Sofia, were like those in Chicago during the Capone years. The pro-Bulgarian annexationists, led by Ivan Mihailov, briefly enjoyed the protection of the king and the government. Their non-Communist opponents, who sought an autonomous Macedonia within a Bulgarian-Yugoslav federation, did not and suffered accordingly.

Calmer heads within Bulgaria eventually tired of the violence. Realizing that normalizing relations with Yugoslavia and Greece was necessary for future Balkan peace, a group of reserve officers and progressive intellectuals staged a coup (1934) that established a one-year dictatorship. As one of their first acts, IMRO was suppressed. By the time of its demise, IMRO no longer was a true revolutionary organization but a racketeering-gangster operation extorting money from the Macedonian immigrants in southwestern Bulgaria. It was heavily involved in illegal drug manufacturing and smuggling and operated numerous opium refineries. Blackmail, extortion, "protection," forced "contributions," and "taxes" were its primary games, providing it with extremely lucrative property assets. In the end, IMRO espoused no concrete program other than the retention of its wealth and power through using empty slogans and naked violence.

While IMRO terrorized both Bulgaria and neighboring states during the 1920s and early 1930s, Boris's successive governments dealt with ballooning problems caused by the Neuilly-imposed reparations, an agrarian economy that increased the state's debt and dependency on the world market, a flood of Macedonian and Thracian refugees, and continuing border incidents with Greece and Yugoslavia. Communist activity rose, resulting in an unsuccessful uprising following the anti-Stamboliiski coup (1923) and culminating in a failed bombing attack on Boris at an Orthodox cathedral in Sofia (1925), after which the Communist party was declared illegal. To cure the anarchistic domestic political situation and reassert central royal authority, Boris disbanded the military dictatorship (1935) and inaugurated an unpopular royal dictatorship (1936).

The 1934 Balkan Entente was an effort by Bulgaria's neighbors (who benefited territorially at Bulgaria's expense in the Neuilly Treaty) to stymie Bulgarian revisionism. Boris, however, managed to conclude formal agreements with Yugoslavia (1937) and Greece (1938) that somewhat lessened Balkan tensions. Bulgaria was permitted to rearm, but that process already had started with German support. German influence on the state was growing, although Bulgaria was not wholly committed to Nazi Germany. A Bulgarian National Socialist organization set up by Germany was disbanded (1938), and Boris readily accepted a large Anglo-French loan to support his rearmament program. As world war loomed in 1939, efforts were made to bring Bulgaria into the pro–Anglo-French Balkan Entente, but they were frustrated by Boris's demand to negotiate a revision of Neuilly's territorial terms. Thereafter, Bulgaria moved closer to Germany.

Postwar Albania was in poor shape. Prior to the war, it suffered from ill-defined borders and political factionalism. During the war, it experienced successive occupation by six foreign armies. In 1917 Italy claimed Albania as a protectorate; it relinquished that assertion (1920) only to focus its efforts on gaining Dalmatia and Istria. Endemic Albanian political anarchy continued following the war: The exiled Toptani persistently claimed leadership until his assassination (1920); an Italian-supported national assembly sat in Durrës (1919); and anti-Italian Albanian nationalists attacked the occupying Italians and created a government in Tiranë (1920), headed by local clan chieftain Ahmed Zogolli.

The Entente victors at Versailles, although ostensibly committed to preserving independent Albania, also sympathized with Italian and Greek claims to Albanian territory and permitted the Yugoslav Kingdom to build a railway to the Adriatic through northern Albania. The specter of an Italian protectorate, and the growing harshness of Italian military occupation, discredited the pro-Italian Durrës assembly and reinforced Albanian nationalist support for Zogolli's Tiranë movement. A Tiranë-inspired anti-Italian uprising pushed out the Italians (September 1920), solidified Zogolli's leadership of the nationalists, and earned international recognition for an independent Albania within its 1913 borders.

True to form, the new government was rent by factionalism, which coalesced roughly along two lines: The rich central and northern landowners wanted to retain existing Ottoman legislation and opposed land reform, while southern middle-class reformers, led by Zogolli and Bishop Fan Noli (a former emigrant to the United States and founder of an Albanian Orthodox church organization in Boston), favored land reform. Although the government theoretically was a regency serving under a national assembly, Zogolli, a traditional authoritarian centralist who consistently controlled important ministries and adeptly maneuvered among the various political factions, dominated its affairs.

Albania was the only European state with a Muslim majority population (approximately 70 percent, with 20 percent Orthodox and 10 percent Catholic), and its governing institutions leaned heavily on Ottoman traditions. Zogolli exerted authority through local clan elders and landowners in the north and the urban middle class in the south. Arbitrary police tactics suppressed political opponents. His preference for consolidating central authority before pursuing irredentist nationalist claims to Kosovo and western Macedonia in the Yugoslav Kingdom earned him the wrath of Albanian ultranationalists. Zogolli's predilection for dictatorial methods sparked a powerful reformist-nationalist opposition movement, led by Noli and the Kosovar National Committee of émigrés.

To allay public opinion while he dealt harshly with his opponents, Zogolli established a constitutional assembly and an interim government. He assumed the premiership, changed his name to Zogu (because "Zogolli" seemed too Turkish), and overtly aligned with the conservative landowners. His continued friendly dealings with the Yugoslav Kingdom intensified the ire of the Kosovar Albanian immigrants, who conducted guerrilla actions against his authority and staged periodic local uprisings.

Kosovo, with its Albanian ethnic majority (at least 80 percent), was conquered by the Serbs in the First Balkan War (1912). Serbian nationalists mythologized the region as the "cradle" of medieval Orthodox Serbia—home of the first Serbian Orthodox Peć Patriarchate and numerous monasteries sporting the best extant works of medieval art and literature and site of the 1389 battle representing medieval Serbia's martyrdom. Serbs considered it unthinkable that such a nationalistically important region should be an Albanian ethnic preserve. After acquiring the region, the Serbs consistently conducted anti-Albanian policies in Kosovo—language discrimination, land confiscations, police brutality, and Serb colonization—to either Serbianize the Albanians or make their lives so unbearable that they would leave. Over 100,000 Kosovar Albanians fled to northern Albania, while others carried out persistent anti-Serb guerrilla attacks. The Serb-dominated Yugoslav government created a Prizren Republic (1921) comprised of Albanian collaborators to lend overt legitimacy to the discrimination. In the early 1930s the government drew up an official policy paper (supported by numerous Serbian nationalists, including Nobel laureate Ivo Andrić) calling for the mass removal of most Kosovar Albanians and their replacement by Serb colonists. Only World War II prevented the plan's implementation.

In early 1924 Noli led an anti-Zogu uprising that forced the premier to flee to the Yugoslav Kingdom. Noli soon discovered that governing was no easy task. The population remained divided along tribal, clan, social, and linguistic lines. The state was isolated economically from the rest of the Balkans by the rugged Albanian Alps. Most Albanians were illiterate. There were no real state finances and corruption ran rampant. Political power lay with those who exerted the most brute force. While Noli talked of creating a modern, democratic, sound state, he lacked the means to achieve his goals. Albania's instability precluded foreign loans. When lack of resources forced him to abandon irredentism, he lost the nationalists' support. His flirtation with obtaining the Soviet Union's aid so frightened everyone that he lost his domestic base. With Yugoslav assistance and promises of economic concessions to Italy and Britain, Zogu gathered an army in the Yugoslav Kingdom, invaded Albania (December 1924), and drove Noli out.

In January 1925 Albania became a republic with Zogu as its first president. Despite outward constitutional trappings, he governed in dictatorial fashion from his hometown of Tiranë. Bribes won the allegiance of tribal chiefs, clan elders, and large landowners. Realizing that the Kosovo situation made overt reliance on the Yugoslav Kingdom's support impractical, Zogu opened closer relations with Italy, which was eager to remain involved with Albania because it was Albania's primary export market and housed numerous Albanian émigrés. A new Italian-controlled Albanian National Bank (1925) attracted foreign investment. An international conference fixed Albania's borders as they stood (1926), and Zogu signed the Treaty of Tiranë with Italy (November 1926) recognizing the territorial status quo and minimizing Italian interference in Albanian affairs.

A 1927 French-Yugoslav alliance worried both Albania and Italy. They signed a second Tiranë Treaty to counter that pact, establishing an Albanian-Italian defensive alliance, as a result of which Albania became a veritable Italian protectorate. Zogu's government grew dependent on Italian loans made in return for extensive mineral concessions. Secret supplements to the second treaty gave Italy control of Albania's military, while overt legislation granted it rights to build roads, bridges, port facilities, and schools. With Mussolini's approval, in September 1928 Zogu was proclaimed King Zog I (1928-39), and a new constitution cementing royal authority was promulgated.

Zog attempted to modernize his kingdom by enacting language reform to standardize Albanian, recognizing religious independence, and updating the education system. With his head turned by the royal title, however, Zog broke with his Italian benefactors. He rejected an Italian-proposed customs union (1932), tried some Italians in Albania for alleged antigovernment plots, and closed Italian schools (1933). Zog was intimidated into reversing his anti-Italian policies by an Italian naval demonstration along the Adriatic coast (1934). There followed increased Italian control of Albania's military, expanded Italian trading and financial investments, and an influx of Italian colonists.

Not content with Zog, who continuously resisted Italian interference, Italy invaded Albania in the midst of the international furor surrounding Germany's takeover of Czechoslovakia (1939). Zog, whose dictatorial ways had alienated all elements in Albanian society, enjoyed scant support and was pushed out. Italian forces overran the state, and a rump Albanian government was forced to accept Albania's personal union with Italy and recognize as ruler Italian King Victor Emmanuel III (1900-46). The king, who never set foot in his new acquisition, exerted his authority through a Superior Fascist Corporative Council. In June 1939, Albania disappeared as an independent state.

Balkan Developments into World War II

Certain socioeconomic and political interwar trends were noticeable in every Balkan state: Their mainly agrarian economies, supplemented by small industrial sectors, lay at the mercies of overpopulation and the international market; agrarian and socialist movements arose; and governments grew highly centralized and authoritarian. These trends, combined with continuing national issues and the Great Depression's economic impact, drew the Balkan states into the orbit of the Axis Powers and eventually into World War II.

The economies of all Balkan states were overwhelmingly agricultural. Interwar-era land reforms were carried out by all of the governments, which wished to eradicate all vestiges of "foreign" landownership (in Romania, Transylvanian Hungarians and

Bessarabian Russians), settle large numbers of immigrants (Greece and Bulgaria), and forestall possible social revolution. Redistribution varied from some 6 percent of available arable land in Bulgaria to 38 percent in Greece. Land reform was more a matter of political necessity than economic policy: The Romanian peasants' abject situation threatened a social explosion; Greece needed to cement a Greek Macedonian ethnonational presence; the Yugoslav Kingdom's Serb-controlled government sought to weaken non-Serb nationalist opposition; Albania's Zogu targeted it to further his political dominance; and Stamboliiski's Bulgarian reforms aimed to punish the political opposition of the Agrarian Union government.

Despite widespread land redistribution, Balkan agriculture remained at or a bit above subsistence level. Ironically, westernization contributed to that situation. Although healthcare, hygiene, and nutrition were abysmal compared to the West, death rates declined but birth rates were high, creating rural overpopulation. A rising "surplus" labor force (generally over 50 percent of the rural populations)—those not needed to work the land—led to ever smaller family plots and more mouths to feed. Technological advances were implemented slowly, and agricultural productivity remained low. With little possibility of finding work in urban centers (the existing industries could not absorb the surplus labor) or emigrating to the West (where immigration was restricted in the 1920s and 1930s), permanent pools of poor, largely illiterate, and disgruntled "unemployed" rural workers became susceptible to ultranationalist or socialist agitation.

Increased industrialization was a priority for all Balkan states, who hoped that it would solve looming social problems and open lucrative markets. Industry expanded to some degree in most Balkan states but did not address the desired goals. Foreign investment drove all industrial expansion, but at the price of siphoning most capital generated out of the states. Since foreigners sought only profits, the enterprises that they supported (raw materials extraction and semifinished products) paid scant attention to the local populations' needs (finished products). The economic relationships of the Balkan states with Western partners reduced them to semicolonial status. The few native capitalists concentrated on gaining monopolies through state support or favorable tariff and import laws, and the governments' presence in the industrial sectors remained inordinately strong.

Balkan state governments did not relieve the plights of their peasant majority populations. They generally failed to provide them with adequate access to credit, technological and instructional services for updating their agricultural methods, or a proper return for their taxes. Governments concentrated on expanding and modernizing their militaries and feathering their functionaries' nests. In time-honored, pre-westernized fashion, government offices were considered sources of personal benefit rather than positions of civic responsibility. Corruption at all government levels abounded. The outward forms of Western-type institutions meant little.

Within months of World War I's end, small Communist and agrarian movements openly operated in many Balkan states. Whereas by the early 1920s, fearful of the Russian and Hungarian examples, Communists everywhere were declared illegal and forced underground, the agrarians enjoyed a modicum of success. Their calls for an egalitarian society, agricultural cooperatives, public ownership of restricted industry, true democratic government, universal suffrage, and pacifistic foreign policy won them popularity among the states' peasant majorities. Bulgaria's Stamboliiski dreamed of a "Green International"—a peasant organization countering the Communist "Red International," the reactionary monarchists and landowners, and traditional ultranationalists.

Only the Bulgarian agrarians attained political power immediately after the war, but traditional political forces ended their rule within four years. Elsewhere, agrarian movements either were suppressed (that of Romanian Premier Iuliu Maniu [1928-30]) or forced to espouse more nationalist than agrarian programs to survive (Radić's Croatian Peasant party). Agrarianism declined as a viable movement because its ideology was flawed fatally: By opposing industrialization, it attacked the only option for creating a workable state economy in the face of growing "surplus" rural populations, reduced Western agricultural markets (because of protectionism), and depressed agricultural prices.

All of the Balkan states sought solutions in traditional autocratic political authority grounded in military power. The military dictatorships took advantage of the failed peasant movements and economic hardships inflicted by the Great Depression to gain absolute political control while maintaining a thin veneer of Western-style liberal democracy. For the largely illiterate peasant majorities, the overt reemergence of authoritarian rule almost was taken for granted as "natural"— it harmonized with their accepted traditional notions of government. Their acceptance of (if not outright loyalty to) the authoritarian regimes was encouraged by the dictators' use of emotional nationalist propaganda.

Nationalism remained a potent force in the interwar Balkans. The Serbs and Romanians attained their "Greater" goals at Versailles, but success brought them grave domestic national problems. All of the others either lost "national" territories or failed to gain them. Four semiofficial "Balkan Conferences" (Athens [1930], Istanbul [1931], Bucharest [1932], and Thessaloniki [1933]) did not overcome the states' burning national tensions. The Balkans' interwar situation somewhat resembled Western Europe's, in that similar national stresses led to similar dictatorial results in Germany and Italy. Unlike the Balkan states, Italy and Germany (especially the latter) transformed their post-Versailles national grievances into explosive extremist movements capable of threatening the Versailles order.

General European war weariness and dread of the past war's unparalleled devastation aided the rise to power of Benito Mussolini's Fascists (1922) in nationalistically unrequited Italy (where failure to secure the Balkan Adriatic territories promised by the Entente during the past war rankled) and Adolf Hitler's Nazis (National Socialists) in defeated Germany (1933). Those two revisionist states—wedded together as the Axis Powers (1936)—highlighted the weaknesses of the Versailles order. Both demonstrated to the "loser" states that ultranationalist authoritarian (totalitarian) military dictatorships could break Versailles's restrictions. Their apparent early economic and political successes, achieved through militant mass mobilizations of their human and material resources in the name of national rights, initially won admiration and partial imitation throughout Europe (even in the United States). The Balkan states—all national "losers" in some fashion—paid close attention.

Throughout the Balkans, nationalists of all stripes adopted fascist trappings— military dress, youthful uniformed paramilitary units, mass public demonstrations, authoritarian-tinged slogans and chants. Both the Croatian *Ustaše* and the Bulgaro-Macedonian IMRO established contacts with the Italian Fascists and German Nazis. In most states, pseudofascist, ultranationalist expression became the norm.

Romania spawned a true fascist movement. Founded by Corneliu Codreanu (1927), the Legion of the Archangel Michael (known as the Iron Guard) displayed a xenophobic fear of "foreigners" (domestic minorities, outside investors, and Communists), a Romantic espousal of traditional Orthodox values, and a rabid anti-Semitism grounded in disgruntled peasants' perceptions (holding post–World War I Polish and Russian Jewish immigrant land managers responsible for the continuing abject sociopolitical situation). The Iron Guard distrusted the government and traditional politics, but King Carol II (1930-40) patronized the movement and used it for his own political advantage until its growing power and influence threatened his authority. In 1938 Carol declared a royal dictatorship, abolished all political parties, and had Codreanu tried and executed on trumped-up treason charges. The next year (1939) he ordered the Guard's leadership murdered. Thereafter, the Guard came under the influence of Hitler's Nazis.

In the wake of the Great Depression, which struck the Balkans in the early 1930s, the Axis Powers became the Balkan states' primary trading partners—they purchased Balkan cereals and tobacco products when no one else would. While Italy monopolized Albania, the rest of the Balkan market lay open to Germany. Eager to acquire cheap foodstuffs for his population and raw materials for his military, Hitler paid the Balkan states well and bought in large quantities. His trade agreements tied payments to credits against their purchases of German products set at competitive prices and without product restrictions. By 1939 Germany dominated the Balkan economies (except Albania's), and, when war erupted in that year, its economic position translated into political influence.

The kings of Bulgaria, Romania, and Greece ethnically were German and held pro-German sympathies. Bulgaria's Tsar Boris had personal reasons for favoring the Axis—he was German by birth and married to the daughter of Italy's King Victor

Emmanuel. With war imminent in 1939, the Ribbentrop-Molotov Agreement partitioning Eastern Europe between Germany and Russia opened the possibility of Bulgaria aligning with Germany without offending its traditional Russian ally. Although not a fascist by nature or inclination, Boris drew closer to Nazi Germany hoping to gain Macedonia and Dobrudzha. In the Treaty of Craiova (September 1940) Hitler forced his Romanian ally to return southern Dobrudzha to Bulgaria, and in December, Mussolini having started an unsuccessful war with Greece, he infiltrated German troops into Bulgaria for an attack on Greece in support of the Italians. In March 1941 Bulgaria officially joined the Axis pact.

After Hitler's 1939 annihilation of Czechoslovakia, Romania signed a trade agreement with Germany, tying it closely to Hitler. The need to bail out a faltering economy overcame the fact that Hungary, Romania's national enemy, already was Hitler's satellite. Hitler needed both Hungary and Romania to dominate Eastern Europe. A faithful Hungary, itching to revise Trianon by force and kept at bay only by Hitler's power, ensured that its neighbors remained subservient to his will. Romania was a source of much-needed petroleum (which Germany lacked) and a potential source of manpower when Hitler initiated a planned invasion of the Soviet Union ("Operation Barbarossa").

Hitler forced Romania to relinquish Bessarabia and northern Bukovina to the Soviets (as stipulated in the Ribbentrop-Molotov Pact) and headed off an impending war over Transylvania between Hungary and Romania by imposing a compromise solution to the "Transylvanian Question." Without discussions with either state, he dictated to them the Second Vienna Award (August 1940), giving the northern two-fifths of Transylvania to Hungary. The region's partition made no geographic, economic, or political sense, and both Hungary and Romania considered the award a temporary settlement until Germany won the war. Its immediate result was the disaffection of both states.

Romanian nationalists found it difficult to accept the state's territorial losses. Carol was overthrown by a nationalist military coup (September 1940) and his son Mihai I (1940-47) installed as successor. True power rested with Premier-Marshal Ion Antonescu, who was forced to accept the Craiova Treaty granting Bulgaria southern Dobrudzha and a German "protective" occupation of the Ploieşti oil fields (October) in return for Hitler's recognition of his dictatorship. As nationalist public outrage swelled, Antonescu expediently called on the Iron Guard, whose reign of terror on Jews and other political opponents brought Romania to the brink of economic collapse and political anarchy. Finally Antonescu crushed the Guard by military force (January 1941) with Hitler's blessings. Hitler preferred a subservient Romanian dictator (whom he personally admired) to anarchistic fascists as he prepared to intervene against Greece before turning on the Soviet Union.

By keeping Mussolini in the dark concerning his planned invasion of the Soviet Union and demanding that Italy make no move in the Balkans that might disrupt his secret preparations, Hitler's dispatch of troops to Romania in October 1940 convinced Mussolini that Germany intended to take the Balkans for itself and leave Italy only Albania. Without informing Hitler, Mussolini invaded Greece from Albania (late October) to ensure a significant share of Balkan spoils. Hitler's annoyance with his ally's move turned to anger when the incompetently led Italian forces were routed by the Greeks.

Despite his growing prewar ties to Germany, Metaxas retained traditional British support. Britain rushed troops and planes to Greece. Reinforced, the Greeks counterattacked into Albania, and the Italians barely managed to hold a tenuous defensive front in northern Epiros. Desperate to bail out his bumbling ally while continuing his invasion preparations against the Soviets, Hitler forced Romania and Hungary to join the Axis alliance officially (late November). Bulgaria's March 1941 Axis membership permitted Hitler to mass German troops on Greece's northern border. In a final effort to ensure a swift, conclusive assault on Greece (and simultaneously secure his southern flank for the planned Soviet invasion), Hitler turned his attention to Yugoslavia.

Yugoslavia was in internal turmoil. The rift between Serbian and Croatian nationalists remained wide following the concordat fiasco. Fearful of Hitler's record of swallowing Versailles-created East European states, Regent Pavel drew closer to the Nazi strongman and tried to settle the internal divisions lest he take a hankering for Yugoslavia. Pavel granted the Croats an autonomous territory (the *Sporazum*) within the state (August 1939) and offered their leader, Peasant party chief Vladko Maček, a vice-premiership. Extremists on both sides remained unhappy, and the two other politically powerful groups in the state—the Slovenes and the Bosnian Muslims—immediately demanded similar autonomy. Despite Pavel's efforts, the internal turmoil continued into early 1941.

Serbian nationalists had no affinity for Germans, whom they traditionally equated with their former Habsburg nemesis. Already unhappy with Pavel's compromise, they were in no mood to accept the regent's reluctant agreement to join Yugoslavia to the Axis alliance (25 March 1941). Nationalist anti-German army officers ousted Pavel (27 March), recognized King Petr II, and renounced the Axis pact. Infuriated, Hitler ordered an immediate assault on Yugoslavia and Greece. After a devastating terror bombing of Belgrade (6 April), German, Italian, and Hungarian forces poured into Yugoslavia from Austria, Hungary, Romania, and Bulgaria. Overrun before its army was mobilized, Yugoslavia collapsed in eleven days and surrendered unconditionally (17 April). King Petr fled to London.

Greece underwent simultaneous invasion. Pushing out of Bulgaria, German forces swiftly took Thessaloniki and drove back the defending British troops. Threatened by encirclement from Macedonia, the Greek forces retreated from Albania. On 23 April Greece surrendered. The British troops fought their way to the Peloponnese, where they were evacuated to Crete (27 April). A month later

German airborne assaults conquered that island as well. In under two months, Hitler was master of the Balkans: Yugoslavia, Greece, and Albania were conquered outright; Bulgaria and Romania were allies.

Conquered Yugoslavia was dismantled. Slovenia was divided between Germany and Italy. Vojvodina was shared between Hungary and local Germans. Most of Macedonia went to Bulgaria. The Italians acquired a slice of western Macedonia, Kosovo, Montenegro, most of Dalmatia, and portions of Bosnia-Hercegovina. Croatia Proper, Slavonia, most of Bosnia-Hercegovina, and the remainder of Dalmatia were turned over to a neofascist Croatian puppet state ruled by the *Ustaše's* Ante Pavelić, who ostensibly was the Italian king's viceroy. What was left of Serbia came under direct German military control, with Serb General Milan Nedić serving as puppet chief. (See Map 11.)

Although not dismembered, conquered Greece was forced to cede most of southern Epiros to Italian-dominated Albania (which also received Kosovo from its masters), while Bulgaria acquired Western Thrace and part of Greek Macedonia, including the Aegean port of Kavala. Italy annexed the Ionian Islands. The rest of Greece fell under direct German or Italian occupation, operating through a Greek puppet government in Athens.

All of the conquered states were exploited rapaciously by their Axis masters. Arbitrary governance and police intimidation were the rule. The conquerors manipulated existing ethnonational rivalries and antagonisms to ensure their own domination and ignored the resulting pervasive atrocities. That especially was so in dismembered Yugoslavia, where such discord was diverse, deep-seated, and widespread.

The ethnonational situation within the divided state rapidly degenerated. Albanians, Hungarians, and Vojvodina Germans indiscriminately massacred Serbs in the regions under their control. Bulgarians pressured Macedonian Slavs to adopt Bulgarian identities. Pavelić's Croatia was the worst culprit. His *Ustaše* regime set out to either exterminate all Serbs and Jews in Croatia or forcibly convert them to Catholicism. A litany of massacres occurred, and gruesome prison camps filled to overflowing. In Bosnia, the Muslims turned on the Serbs with a vengeance and joined in the bloodletting once political power shifted to the Croats. The situation in Bosnia came to resemble a veritable religious-cultural war, with Catholics and Muslims pitted against the Orthodox and Jews. The Serbs retaliated as best they could, and former Yugoslavia became a cultural battleground.

Although Hitler's allies Romania and Bulgaria suffered economic exploitation, the presence of German troops, and internal ethnonational problems, at least they preserved native self-rule and made national territorial gains. Romania, lying on the Soviet Union's border, could not avoid involvement in Hitler's assault on that state (began 22 June 1941). In return for direct participation, Romania received Bessarabia and occupied additional territory to its east beyond the Dniester River ("Transnistria"). The fruits of Romania's pro-German involvement proved short-lived. In November 1942 the collapse of Romanian forces on the Eastern Front led to decisive German defeat in the Battle of Stalingrad, initiating a gradual Axis retreat. In 1943 the Ploieşti oil fields were destroyed by American and British air bombardment. By August 1944 the Soviets retook "Transnistria" and Bessarabia and lay ready to invade Romania.

The price Hitler paid for Bulgaria's participation in the 1941 Balkan Campaign was Macedonia. The second Bulgarian foray into the region in as many world wars proved even less happy than the first. The Bulgarians comported themselves as occupiers and earned little gratitude from the natives for freeing them of Serbian control. Unlike Romania, Bulgarian King Boris refused an active role in Hitler's war against the Soviets, contenting himself with meeting the minimum demands of his treaty obligations and attempting to consolidate control over Macedonia. Boris also somewhat undeservedly earned the distinction of saving Bulgaria's Jews from extermination in Nazi death camps. More through his minister Bogdan Filov's efforts and his wife's compassion than through Boris's own decision, trains loaded with some 15,000 Jews set to depart for the camps in 1943 never left Sofia. (Jews in Bulgarian-controlled Macedonia, however, were not as fortunate.) Because Boris refused to declare war on the Soviets, Hitler summoned him to Berlin (1943). Soon after returning, he died under mysterious circumstances and the leaderless Bulgarian government lapsed into ineffectiveness.

The turn of the Eastern Front's military tide against Hitler in 1943 sparked anti-Axis resistance movements throughout the Balkans. Although they shared a common general enemy, they were divided ideologically. Traditional nationalists (such as the Serbs led by the Hercegovinian Serb Colonel Dragoljub [Draža] Mihailović and the Greeks under Colonel Napoleon Zervas) sought to restore prewar governing institutions and conditions. More radical movements—Communists, agrarians, and assorted socialists—espoused wide-ranging reforms or revolutionary changes. Radical anti-Axis guerillas, dominated by Communist partisans (particularly the Yugoslav Communist partisans led by Josip [Broz] Tito), were the most active and consistently effective. The anti-Axis Allies (Britain, the Soviet Union, and the United States), eager to assist those who inflicted the most damage on the enemy and initially willing to postpone ideological problems until after the war, concentrated support on the radical guerrillas. (Tito's Communist partisans received more allied military assistance than Mihailović's Serbian nationalists.)

The decision to support Communist partisans had repercussions for the postwar Balkans. In August 1944 Romanian King Mihai ousted Antonescu, ended military dictatorship, and joined the anti-Axis Allies. Romania's about-face opened the Balkans to the Soviet Red Army, which poured through Romania into Bulgaria and Yugoslavia. Axis resistance collapsed and, in its wake, the various heavily armed Communist partisans, relying on immediate Soviet military support, swiftly gained control of the political situations on the ground everywhere except in Greece.

FURTHER READINGS

General

Aspinall-Oglander, C. F. *Military Operations Gallipoli*. 2 vols. London: Heinemann, 1932.

Blau, George E. *Invasion of the Balkans: The German Campaign in the Balkans, Spring 1941*. Shippensburg, PA: Burd Street Press, 1997.

Butler, Nicholas M. *Report of the International Commission to Inquire into the Causes and Conduct of the Balkan Wars*. Washington, DC: Carnegie Endowment for International Peace, 1914.

Cassels, Lavender. *The Archduke and the Assassin: Sarajevo, June 28th 1914*. London: F. Muller, 1984.

Crane, John O. *The Little Entente*. New York: Macmillan, 1931.

David, Wade D. *European Diplomacy in the Near Eastern Question, 1906-1909*. Urbana: University of Illinois Press, 1940.

Duffy, Thomas G. *Russia's Balkan Policy, 1894-1905*. New York: Carlton, 1975.

Durham, Mary E. *Twenty Years of Balkan Tangle*. London: Allen and Unwin, 1920.

Dutton, David. *Politics of Diplomacy: Britain, France and the Balkans in the First World War*. London: I. B. Tauris, 1997.

Falls, Cyril B. *Military Operations, Macedonia . . .* 2 vols. London: H. M. Stationery Office, 1933-35.

Feuerlicht, Roberta S. *The Desperate Act: The Assassination of Franz Ferdinand at Sarajevo*. New York: McGraw-Hill, 1968.

Geshkoff, Theodore I. *Balkan Union: A Road to Peace in Southeastern Europe*. New York: Columbia University Press, 1940.

Geshov, Ivan E. *The Balkan League*. Translated by Constantine C. Mincoff. London: Murray, 1915.

Hall, Richard C. *The Balkan Wars, 1912-1913: Prelude to the First World War*. New York: Routledge, 2000.

Helmreich, Ernst C. *The Diplomacy of the Balkan Wars, 1912-1913*. New York: Russell and Russell, 1969.

Jelavich, Charles. *South Slav Nationalisms: Textbooks and Yugoslav Union before 1914*. Columbus: Ohio State University Press, 1990.

———. *Tsarist Russia and Balkan Nationalism: Russian Influence in the Internal Affairs of Bulgaria and Serbia, 1879-1886*. Berkeley: University of California Press, 1958.

Kerner, Robert J., and Harry N. Howard. *The Balkan Conferences and the Balkan Entente, 1930-1935: A Study in the Recent History of the Balkan and Near Eastern Peoples*. Berkeley: University of California Press, 1936.

Ladas, Stephen P. *The Exchange of Minorities: Bulgaria, Greece, and Turkey*. New York: Macmillan, 1932.

Macartney, C. A., and A. W. Palmer. *Independent Eastern Europe: A History*. London: Macmillan, 1966.

Machray, Robert. *The Little Entente*. Reprint ed. New York: H. Fertig, 1970.

Mann, Arthur J. *The Salonika Front*. London: A. and C. Black, 1920.

Mitrany, David. *The Effect of the War in Southeastern Europe*. New Haven, CT: Yale University Press, 1936.

Moorehead, Alan. *Gallipoli*. New York: Harper and Row, 1956.

Nagy-Talavera, Nicholas M. *The Green Shirts and the Others*. Stanford, CA: Hoover Institution, 1970.

Newman, Bernard. *Balkan Background*. New York: Macmillan, 1935.

Orlow, Dietrich. *The Nazis in the Balkans: A Case Study of Totalitarian Politics*. Pittsburgh, PA: University of Pittsburgh Press, 1968.

Paikert, G. C. *The Danube Swabians: German Populations in Hungary, Rumania and Yugoslavia and Hitler's Impact on Their Patterns*. The Hague: Nijhoff, 1967.

Palmer, Alan. *The Gardeners of Salonika.* New York: Simon and Schuster, 1965.

Pasvolsky, Leo. *Economic Nationalism of the Danubian States.* New York: Macmillan, 1928.

Pribichevich, Stoyan. *World without End: The Saga of Southeastern Europe.* New York: Reynal and Hitchcock, 1939.

Remak, Joachim. *Sarajevo: The Origins of a Political Murder.* New York: Criterion, 1959.

Rossos, Andrew. *Russia and the Balkans: Inter-Balkan Rivalries and Russian Foreign Policy, 1908-1914.* Toronto: University of Toronto Press, 1981.

Rouček, Joseph S. *Balkan Politics: International Relations in No Man's Land.* Stanford, CA: Stanford University Press, 1948.

Schurman, Jacob G. *The Balkan Wars, 1912-1913.* Princeton, NJ: Princeton University Press, 1914.

Seton-Watson, Hugh. *Eastern Europe Between the Wars, 1918-1941.* 3rd ed., reprint. New York: Harper and Row, 1967.

———. *The "Sick Heart" of Modern Europe: The Problem of the Danubian Lands.* Seattle: University of Washington Press, 1975.

Seton-Watson, Robert W. *The Southern Slav Question and the Habsburg Monarchy.* London: Constable, 1911.

Stavrianos, L. S. *Balkan Federation: A History of the Movement toward Balkan Unity in Modern Times.* Reprint ed. Hamden, CT: Archon, 1964.

Sukiennicki, Wiktor. *East Central Europe during World War I: From Foreign Domination to National Independence.* 2 vols. Boulder, CO: East European Monographs, 1984.

Thaden, Edward C. *Russia and the Balkan Alliance of 1912.* University Park: Pennsylvania State University Press, 1965.

Van Creveld, Martin L. *Hitler's Strategy, 1940-1941: The Balkan Clue.* Cambridge: Cambridge University Press, 1973.

Vukmanović, Svetozar. *Struggle for the Balkans.* Translated by Charles Bartlett. London: Merlin, 1990.

Williamson, Samuel R., Jr. *Austria-Hungary and the Origins of the First World War.* London: Macmillan, 1991.

Wynot, Edward D. *Caldron of Conflict: Eastern Europe, 1918-1945.* Wheeling, IL: Harlan Davison, 1999.

Albania

Fischer, Bernd J. *Albania at War, 1939-1945.* West Lafayette, IN: Purdue University Press, 1999.

———. *King Zog and the Struggle for Stability in Albania.* Boulder, CO: East European Monographs, 1984.

Peacock, Wadham. *Albania: The Foundling State of Europe.* New York: D. Appleton, 1914.

Robinson, Vandeleur. *Albania's Road to Freedom.* London: Allen and Unwin, 1941.

Skendi, Stavro. *The Albanian National Awakening, 1878-1912.* Princeton, NJ: Princeton University Press, 1967.

———. *The Political Evolution of Albania, 1912-1944.* New York: Mid-European Studies Center of the National Committee for a Free Europe, 1954.

Stickney, E. P. *Southern Albania or Northern Epirus in European International Affairs, 1912-1923.* Stanford, CA: Stanford University Press, 1926.

Swire, Joseph. *Albania: The Rise of a Kingdom.* Reprint ed. New York: Arno, 1971.

———. *King Zog's Albania.* London: Robert Hale, 1937.

Bosnia-Hercegovina

Dedijer, Vladimir. *The Road to Sarajevo.* New York: Simon and Schuster, 1966.

Donia, Robert J. *Islam under the Double Eagle: The Muslims of Bosnia and Hercegovina, 1878-1914.* Boulder, CO: East European Monographs, 1981.

Schmitt, Bernadotte E. *The Annexation of Bosnia, 1908-1909.* Cambridge: Cambridge University Press, 1937.
Seton-Watson, R. W. *The Role of Bosnia in International Politics, 1875-1914.* London: H. Milford, 1932.
Sugar, Peter F. *Industrialization of Bosnia-Hercegovina, 1878-1918.* Seattle: University of Washington Press, 1963.

Bulgaria

Bell, John D. *Peasants in Power: Alexander Stamboliski and the Bulgarian Agrarian National Union, 1899-1923.* Princeton, NJ: Princeton University Press, 1977.
Black, Cyril E. *The Establishment of Constitutional Government in Bulgaria.* Princeton, NJ: Princeton University Press, 1943.
Chary, Frederick B. *The Bulgarian Jews and the Final Solution, 1940-1944.* Pittsburgh, PA: University of Pittsburgh Press, 1972.
Constant, Stephan. *Foxy Ferdinand, 1861-1948, Tsar of Bulgaria.* London: Sidgwick and Jackson, 1979.
Corti, Egon C. *Alexander von Battenberg.* Translated by E. M. Hodgson. London: Cassell, 1954.
Crampton, Richard J. *Bulgaria, 1878-1918: A History.* Boulder, CO: East European Monographs, 1983.
Durman, Karel. *Lost Illusions: Russian Policies towards Bulgaria in 1877-1887.* Stockholm: Acta Universitatis Upsaliensis, 1988.
Genov, Georgi P. *Bulgaria and the Treaty of Neuilly.* Sofia: Danov, 1935.
Groueff, Stephane. *Crown of Thorns: The Reign of King Boris III of Bulgaria, 1918-1943.* Lanham, MD: Madison, 1987.
Hall, Richard C. *Bulgaria's Road to the First World War.* Boulder, CO: East European Monographs, 1996.
Hall, William W., Jr. *Puritans in the Balkans: The American Board Mission in Bulgaria, 1878-1918.* Sofia: Studia Historico-Philologica Serdicensia, 1938.
Kostadinova, Tatiana. *Bulgaria, 1879-1946: The Challenge of Choice.* Boulder, CO: East European Monographs, 1995.
Lampe, John R. *The Bulgarian Economy in the Twentieth Century.* London: Croom Helm, 1986.
Macdonald, John. *Czar Ferdinand and His People.* Reprint ed. New York: Arno, 1971.
Madol, Hans R. *Ferdinand of Bulgaria: The Dream of Byzantium.* Translated by Kenneth Kirkness. London: Hurst and Blackett, 1933.
Miller, Marshall L. *Bulgaria during the Second World War.* Stanford, CA: Stanford University Press, 1975.
Nestorova, Tatyana. *American Missionaries among the Bulgarians, 1858-1912.* Boulder, CO: East European Monographs, 1987.
Oren, Nissan. *Bulgarian Communism: The Road to Power, 1934-1944.* New York: Columbia University Press, 1971.
Perry, Duncan M. *Stefan Stambulov and the Emergence of Modern Bulgaria, 1870-1895.* Durham, NC: Duke University Press, 1993.
Rothschild, Joseph. *The Communist Party of Bulgaria: Origins and Development, 1883-1936.* New York: Columbia University Press, 1959.
Şimşir, Bilâl N. *The Turks of Bulgaria (1878-1985).* London: K. Rustem, 1988.

Croatia

Miller, Nicholas J. *Between Nation and State: Serbian Politics in Croatia before the First World War.* Pittsburgh, PA: University of Pittsburgh Press, 1998.

Omrčanin, Ivo. *Croatia, 1941-1945: Before and After.* Washington, DC: Samizdat, 1988.

Greece

Augustinos, Gerasimos. *Consciousness and History: Nationalist Critics of Greek Society, 1897-1914.* Boulder, CO: East European Monographs, 1977.

Cruickshank, Charles G. *Greece, 1940-1941.* Newark: University of Delaware Press, 1979.

Koliopoulos, John S. *Greece and the British Connection, 1935-1941.* Oxford: Clarendon, 1991.

Kondis, Basil. *Greece and Albania, 1908-1914.* Thessaloniki: Institute for Balkan Studies, 1976.

Leon, George B. *Greece and the Great Powers, 1914-1917.* Thessaloniki: Institute for Balkan Studies, 1974.

Llewellyn-Smith, Michael. *Ionian Vision: Greece in Asia Minor, 1919-22.* London: A. Lane, 1973.

Mavrocordatos, George. *Stillborn Republic: Social Conditions and Party Strategies in Greece, 1922-1936.* Berkeley: University of California Press, 1983.

Mazower, Mark. *Greece and the Inter-War Economic Crisis.* Oxford: Clarendon, 1991.

Pallis, Alexander A. *Greece's Anatolian Venture and After: A Survey of the Diplomatic and Political Aspects of the Greek Expedition to Asia Minor, 1915-1922.* London: Methuen, 1937.

Pentzopoulos, Dimitri. *The Balkan Exchange of Minorities and Its Impact upon Greece.* Paris: Mouton, 1962.

Petsalis-Diomidis, N. *Greece at the Paris Peace Conference, 1919.* Thessaloniki: Institute for Balkan Studies, 1978.

Tatsios, Theodore G. *The Megali Idea and the Greek-Turkish War of 1897: The Impact of the Cretan Problem on Greek Irredentism, 1866-1897.* Boulder, CO: East European Monographs, 1984.

Theodoulou, Christos. *Greece and the Entente, August 1, 1914-September 25, 1916.* Thessaloniki: Institute for Balkan Studies, 1971.

Toynbee, Arnold J. *The Western Question in Greece and Turkey.* London: Constable, 1922.

Vatikiotis, P. J. *Popular Autocracy in Greece, 1936-41: A Political Biography of General Ioannis Metaxas.* London: Cass, 1998.

Vlastos, Doros. *Venizelos: Patriot, Statesman, Revolutionary.* London: Lund Humphries, 1942.

Macedonia

Anastasoff, Christ. *The Tragic Peninsula: A History of the Macedonian Movement for Independence since 1878.* St. Louis, MO: Blackwell Wielandy, 1938.

Barker, Elisabeth. *Macedonia: Its Place in Balkan Power Politics.* London: Royal Institute of International Affairs, 1950.

Dakin, Douglas. *The Greek Struggle in Macedonia, 1897-1913.* Thessaloniki: Institute for Balkan Studies, 1966.

Hristov, Alexander. *The Creation of Macedonian Statehood, 1893-1945.* Translated by Bernard Meares. Skopje: Kultura, 1972.

Londres, Albert. *Terror in the Balkans.* London: Constable, 1935.

MacDermott, Mercia. *For Freedom and Perfection: The Life of Yane Sandansky.* London: Journeyman, 1988.

———. *Freedom or Death: The Life of Gotsé Delchev.* London: Journeyman, 1978.

Perry, Duncan M. *The Politics of Terror: The Macedonian Revolutionary Movements, 1893-1903.* Durham, NC: Duke University Press, 1988.

Radin, A. Michael. *IMRO and the Macedonian Question.* Skopje: Kultura, 1993.

Sherman, Laura B. *Fires on the Mountain: The Macedonian Revolutionary Movement and the Kidnapping of Ellen Stone.* Boulder, CO: East European Monographs, 1980.

Sowards, Steven W. *Austria's Policy of Macedonian Reform.* Boulder, CO: East European Monographs, 1989.

Swire, Joseph. *Bulgarian Conspiracy.* London: Hale, 1939.
Zotiades, George B. *The Macedonian Controversy.* Thessaloniki: Institute for Balkan Studies, 1954.

Montenegro

Devine, Alexander. *The Martyred Nation.* London: St. Clement's, 1924.
Treadway, John D. *The Falcon and the Eagle: Montenegro and Austria-Hungary, 1908-1914.* West Lafayette, IN: Purdue University Press, 1983.

Ottoman Empire

Ahmad, Feroz. *The Young Turks: The Committee of Union and Progress in Turkish Politics, 1908-1914.* Oxford: Clarendon, 1969.
Deringil, Selim. *The Well-Protected Domain: Ideology and the Legitimation of Power in the Ottoman Empire, 1876-1909.* London: I. B. Tauris, 1998.
Hanioglu, M. Sükrü. *Preparation for a Revolution: The Young Turks, 1902-1908.* Oxford: Oxford University Press, 2000.
———. *The Young Turks in Opposition.* New York: Oxford University Press, 1995.
Kinross, [John P. D. B.] Lord. *Ataturk: The Rebirth of a Nation.* London: Weidenfeld and Nicolson, 1964.
Lewis, Bernard. *The Emergence of Modern Turkey.* London: Oxford University Press, 1967.
Macfie, A. L. *The End of the Ottoman Empire, 1908-1923.* London: Longman, 1998.
Mardin, Serif. *The Genesis of Young Ottoman Thought: A Study in the Modernization of Turkish Political Ideas.* Princeton, NJ: Princeton University Press, 1962.
McCarthy, Justin. *The Ottoman Peoples and the End of Empire.* London: Arnold, 2001.
Ramsaur, Ernest E. *The Young Turks: Prelude to the Revolution of 1908.* Princeton, NJ: Princeton University Press, 1957.
Sonyel, Salâhi R. *Minorities and the Destruction of the Ottoman Empire.* Ankara: Turkish Historical Society, 1993.
Trumpener, Ulrich. *Germany and the Ottoman Empire, 1914-1918.* Princeton, NJ: Princeton University Press, 1968.
Zürcher, Erik J. *Socialism and Nationalism in the Ottoman Empire.* London: I. B. Tauris, 1994.

Romania

Bolitho, Hector. *Roumania under King Carol.* London: Eyre and Spottiswoode, 1939.
Clark, Charles U. *Greater Roumania.* London: Dodd, Mead, 1922.
Dima, Nicholas. *From Moldavia to Moldova: The Soviet-Romanian Territorial Dispute.* Boulder, CO: East European Monographs, 1991.
Frucht, Richard C. *Dunărea Noastră: Romania, the Great Powers, and the Danube Question, 1914-1921.* Boulder, CO: East European Monographs, 1982.
Giurescu, Dinu C. *Romania in World War II, 1939-1945.* Boulder, CO: East European Monographs, 2000.
Hitchins, Keith. *Rumania, 1866-1947.* Oxford: Clarendon, 1994.
Ioanid, Radu. *The Sword of the Archangel: Fascist Ideology in Romania.* Translated by Peter Heinegg. Boulder, CO: East European Monographs, 1990.
Livezeanu, Irina. *Cultural Politics in Greater Romania: Regionalism, Nation Building, and Ethnic Struggle, 1918-1930.* Ithaca, NY: Cornell University Press, 1994.
Lungu, Dov B. *Romania and the Great Powers, 1933-1940.* Durham, NC: Duke University Press, 1989.
Mitrany, David. *The Land and the Peasant in Rumania: The War and Agrarian Reform, 1917-1921.* London: H. Milford, 1930.
Pearton, Maurice. *Oil and the Roumanian State, 1895-1948.* Oxford: Clarendon, 1971.

Roberts, Henry L. *Rumania: Political Problems of an Agrarian State.* New Haven, CT: Yale University Press, 1951.

Spector, Sherman D. *Rumania at the Paris Peace Conference: A Study of the Diplomacy of Ioan I. C. Brătianu.* New York: Bookman, 1962.

Turdeanu, Emil. *Modern Romania: The Achievement of National Unity, 1914-1920.* Los Angeles, CA: Mircea Eliade Research Institute, 1988.

Watts, Larry L. *Romanian Cassandra: Ion Antonescu and the Struggle for Reform, 1916-41.* Boulder, CO: East European Monographs, 1993.

Webster, Alexander F. C. *The Romanian Legionary Movement: An Orthodox Christian Assessment of Anti-Semitism.* Pittsburgh, PA: University of Pittsburgh Center for Russian and East European Studies, 1986.

Serbia

Cohen, Philip J. *Serbia's Secret War: Propaganda and the Deceit of History.* College Station: Texas A&M University Press, 1996.

Dragnich, Alex N. *Serbia, Nikola Pašić, and Yugoslavia.* New Brunswick, NJ: Rutgers University Press, 1974.

Dragnich, Alex N., and Slavko Todorović. *The Saga of Kosovo.* Boulder, CO: East European Monographs, 1984.

MacKenzie, David. *Apis, the Congenital Conspirator: The Life of Colonel Dragutin T. Dimitrijević.* Boulder, CO: East European Monographs, 1989.

———. *The "Black Hand" on Trial: Salonika, 1917.* Boulder, CO: East European Monographs, 1995.

McClellan, Woodford D. *Svetozar Marković and the Origins of Balkan Socialism.* Princeton, NJ: Princeton University Press, 1964.

Stokes, Gale. *Legitimacy through Liberalism: Vladimir Jovanović and the Transformation of Serbian Politics.* Seattle: University of Washington Press, 1975.

Vucinich, Wayne S. *Serbia Between East and West: The Events of 1903-1908.* Reprint ed. New York: AMS, 1968.

Slovenia

Grafenauer, Bogo. *The National Development of the Carinthian Slovenes.* Ljubljana: Research Institute, 1946.

Harriman, Helga H. *Slovenia under Nazi Occupation, 1941-1945.* New York: Studia Slovenica, 1977.

Rogel, Carole. *The Slovenes and Yugoslavism, 1890-1918.* Boulder, CO: East European Monographs, 1977.

Yugoslavia

Banac, Ivo. *The National Question in Yugoslavia: Origins, History, Politics.* Ithaca, NY: Cornell University Press, 1993.

Beard, Charles A., and George Radin. *The Balkan Pivot: Yugoslavia. A Study in Government and Administration.* New York: Macmillan, 1929.

Djilas, Aleksa. *The Contested Country: Yugoslav Unity and Communist Revolution, 1919-1953.* Cambridge, MA: Harvard University Press, 1991.

Djordjević, Dimitrije, and Stephen Fischer-Galati, eds. *The Creation of Yugoslavia, 1914-1918.* Santa Barbara, CA: ABC-Clio, 1980.

Dragnich, Alex N. *The First Yugoslavia: The Search for a Viable Political System.* Stanford, CA: Hoover Institution Press, 1983.

Hoptner, Jacob B. *Yugoslavia in Crisis, 1934-1941.* New York: Columbia University Press, 1962.

Lederer, Ivo J. *Yugoslavia at the Paris Peace Conference: A Study in Frontiermaking*. New Haven, CT: Yale University Press, 1963.

Lodge, Olive. *Peasant Life in Jugoslavia*. London: Seeley, Service, 1941.

Ristić, Dragisa N. *Yugoslavia's Revolution of 1941*. University Park: Pennsylvania State University Press, 1966.

Roberts, Allen. *The Turning Point: The Assassination of Louis Barthou and King Alexander I of Yugoslavia*. New York: St. Martin's, 1970.

Sforza, Carlo. *Fifty Years of War and Diplomacy in the Balkans: Pashich and the Union of the Yugoslavs*. New York: Columbia University Press, 1940.

West, Rebecca. *Black Lamb and Grey Falcon: A Journey Through Yugoslavia*. 2 vols. in 1. New York: Viking, 1943.

Živojinović, Dragan R. *America, Italy and the Birth of Yugoslavia, 1917-1919*. Boulder, CO: East European Monographs, 1972.

PART FIVE

Era of Communist Domination

1945 – 1991

Communist partisan movements and the Soviet Red Army ensured that prewar sociopolitical systems would not return to most of the Balkan states after World War II. The Soviet Union imposed Stalinist governments on all of them except Greece, which escaped by defeating a Communist-inspired civil war (1947-50) with Western assistance. In every Balkan state, including Greece, authoritarianism triumphed. Assorted cold war–era Soviet sociopolitical models were followed scrupulously in all of the Communist states, except for Tito's Yugoslavia, which broke with Stalin (1948) and attempted a hybrid form of independent socialism, and Hoxha's Albania, which broke with Khrushchev (1960) over his anti-Stalinist policies. Despite the political defections from the Soviet bloc, all Balkan Communist states officially adhered to socialist precepts of authoritarian government, planned economies, and controlled sociocultural expression. Prewar nationalist issues, although publicly suppressed in the Communist states, persisted: Discrimination against ethnonational minorities and conflicting territorial nationalist claims simmered below the surface in the Communist states and openly erupted between Greece and Turkey. By the late 1980s

European Marxism everywhere was proved fatally flawed. The collapse of Soviet communism under Gorbachev (1989-92) opened the door to a similar result in the Balkans, after which pressurized national issues once again exploded.

CHAPTER SEVENTEEN

Communist Takeover

On 20 August 1944, the Soviet Red Army crossed the Prut River into Romania in an assault on retreating German and Romanian forces. Within three days, Romanian King Mihai capitulated and Romania joined the Soviets in their drive into the Balkans. Like dominoes, each Balkan Axis-allied state fell before the onslaught. Communist partisan forces swiftly moved to gain political control while their overt partnership with the Soviet military eased the way. Many Slavs inhabiting the states through which the Red Army pushed considered the Soviets "Russians" (rather than "Soviets"), and "Russia" possessed a certain popularity because of historical Orthodox religious and Slavic ethnocultural associations. Traditional nationalist images of Russia as friend and Great Power protector enjoyed widespread resonance. Many romantically believed that, just as Russia once helped free the Balkans from Ottoman rule, it now was resuming its "national liberator" role by saving them from fascist Axis domination. A good deal of such Romanticism rubbed off on the native Communist partisans, who operated in obvious coordination with the Soviet Red Army.

Initial Coups

The strengths of the various Balkan Communist partisan movements varied from the insignificant Romanian to Tito's powerful "Yugoslav" following. Size had little to do with their political victories, since their alliance with the Red Army gave them the edge in most of the Balkan states.

Such was blatantly the case in Romania, which sported the smallest partisan movement. Nationalist bad blood existed between the Romanians and Russians, stemming from the past Russian occupation of the Principalities and conflicts over Bessarabia. The ethnically Latin Romanians did not share the sense of brotherhood with Russians so common among other Balkan populations south of the Danube, and they feared Slavic encirclement. Direct Soviet intervention was required to ensure a Communist political victory in Romania.

When it first appeared that the tide was turning against the Axis on the Eastern Front (1943), Marshal Antonescu tentatively considered taking Romania out of the war, but nothing came of it because he feared being caught between a Nazi-supported, rejuvenated Iron Guard coup and a Soviet occupation. As the Red Army closed on Romania, agrarian and other traditional leftist parties joined with the few Communists in opposing both the war and Antonescu's dictatorship. Some opportunistic rightist nationalists, led by Gheorghe Tătărescu, encouraged by Soviet propaganda, aligned with the leftist coalition. After King Mihai overthrew Antonescu (August 1944), Romania joined the anti-Axis alliance, an armistice was concluded, and the Red Army occupied the state. Romania was forced to pay the Soviets reparations, provide material support for the continuing war against Germany, and participate in the Soviet invasion of the Balkans and Central Europe.

Taking advantage of the army's absence in the ongoing Soviet campaigns, Romanian Communists, many of whom returned from exile in the Soviet Union with the Red Army, were installed as the Soviet military's local officials, virtually limiting King Mihai's actual governing authority to Bucharest alone. Buoyed by the Soviet military presence, the Communists dropped all pretense of nominal allegiance to Mihai and openly campaigned for a "National Democratic Front" government. The Front staged demonstrations in the capital (February 1945), in which pro-Front demonstrators were killed (probably on Front orders to discredit the government), which led to direct Soviet intervention. The Soviets installed a Front government, headed by the pro-Communist peasant leader Petru Groza (1945-52). Although the nationalist Tătărescu was retained as vice-premier and foreign minister, Communists held all important government ministries, especially those controlling the military and police. Mihai had no choice but to accept the Soviets' dictate.

Groza swiftly enacted agrarian reform, expropriating large amounts of land without compensation and redistributing it to nearly 1 million peasants. When the war ended in Europe (7 May 1945), a Soviet-Romanian trade company, Sovrom, was founded to camouflage the Soviets' systematic stripping of Romania's wealth. King Mihai attempted to ruin the Groza government by refusing to sign new governmental decrees into law (late 1945), but his efforts failed in the face of American and British attempts to preserve Allied unity with the Soviets. Their February 1946 recognition of the Groza government, on condition that non-Communist parties be included and that parliamentary elections be held, forced Mihai to continue a tense working partnership with the Front.

Elections duly were held (November 1946). Through standard Balkan election manipulation—falsified vote counts, threats, and polling intimidation—the Communists, operating under cover of a new coalition called the Bloc of

Democratic Parties, won 80 percent of the vote and 91 percent of parliament. Groza's Communist-dominated government signed the Paris Treaty (10 February 1947), in which Romania lost Bessarabia and Bukovina to the Soviet Union in return for prewar Transylvania. The Communists eliminated agrarian competition through massive arrests and outlawing the Agrarian Union party, and all traditional party representatives were forced out of the government and replaced by Communists or their collaborators. Blackmailed by the Communist authorities, King Mihai abdicated (December 1947) and fled to Switzerland, where he ineffectually repudiated that action. The Groza government then proclaimed Romania a people's republic.

After Romania fell to the Soviets, Bulgaria was laid open to Red Army assault. Until it was outlawed in 1925, Bulgaria's Communist party had been the largest in the Balkans. Bulgaria's Axis alliance, its refusal to furnish combat troops for the Eastern Front, and its population's consequent lack of human and material suffering during the war hampered partisan efforts of the relatively few and clandestine Bulgarian Communists. Moreover, Axis-allied Bulgaria acquired Macedonia, Dobrudzha, and Thrace during the war's early years, acquisitions that even many Bulgarian Communists considered nationalistically justified.

The war came directly to Bulgaria when Sofia first experienced an anti-Axis Allied air raid (November 1943). The regency governing for six-year-old King Simeon II (1943-46) considered defecting from the Axis but balked at losing the territories gained earlier as the price for such action. Inconclusive secret talks with the Allies dragged on until the Red Army appeared on Bulgaria's Danube border (late August 1944). Desperate to avoid invasion, the regency appointed as premier the pro-Western Agrarian party leader, Konstantin Muraviev. He immediately proclaimed Bulgaria's neutrality, abolished all fascist institutions, and returned Bulgaria to liberal-democratic constitutional rule. It was too late. Encouraged by the proximity of the Red Army, Bulgarian Communists denounced Muraviev as a Nazi agent and staged strikes and demonstrations. The Soviet Union declared war on Bulgaria (5 September), despite Muraviev's declaration of war on Germany.

The Soviets acted to aid the few armed Bulgarian Communist partisans in overthrowing the government. After the Red Army entered Bulgaria (8 September 1944), the Communists and their allies (the *Zveno* [Link] group of radical intelligentsia authoritarians, agrarians, and social democrats), operating under the guise of the "Fatherland Front," staged a coup in Sofia early the next morning (9 September). Muraviev was removed and a Communist-led regency council was installed. Although a *Zveno*ist (Kimon Georgiev, premier [1944-46]) served as the new government's titular head, Communists controlled the judiciary and police. An armistice was declared as the Red Army occupied most of the state, and the Bulgarian army was required to join the Soviets in their push into former Yugoslavia and Central Europe.

Under the rubric of the Fatherland Front, the Communists cemented their control over Bulgaria. The occupying Soviet forces provided them with assistance, and they won popular support by including traditional political parties in their government and tapping the population's genuine pro-Russian sentiments. The Agrarians, however, enjoyed more popularity. To eliminate the Agrarians and other opponents, the Communists instituted a policy of terror, conducted through local committees, industrial workers' councils, a new militia (the "People's Guard," which included a secret service), and "people's" courts. By February 1945 all post-1941 government and national assembly officials had been tried, and many were executed. The government bureaucracy was purged, and Soviet concerns over military efficiency were all that prevented similar drastic action in the army.

The brutality of the Communists' terror eroded their popularity, but, secure in their Soviet ally, they intensified their efforts once the war in Europe ended. Their Agrarian party partner was split and its anti-Communist leader, Nikola Petkov, forced out of the government. When the Communists called for obviously rigged parliamentary elections, American and British objections forced their postponement until November 1945. Petkov's Agrarians boycotted the polls and the Communists won an easy victory, which placed the government into the hands of their leader, Georgi Dimitrov, a political exile since the 1930s newly returned from the Soviet Union, associate of Joseph Stalin, and renowned (undeservedly so, as it now is known) Communist hero for defying Hitler at his trial as one of those unjustly accused of setting the 1933 Reichstag fire in Germany.

From behind the scenes, Dimitrov orchestrated the total elimination of all opposition to the Communists. Trials of opponents—army officers, remaining IMRO leaders, other party heads—on trumped-up charges continued into 1947, and many were executed (a fate dealt Petkov in 1947). A rigged referendum abolished the monarchy (September 1946), sending King Simeon and his family into exile, after which a people's republic was proclaimed. By the time Dimitrov took over the premiership himself (1946-49), the government, national assembly, army, and media securely were in Communist hands. Bulgaria signed the Paris Treaty, which permitted it to retain only southern Dobrudzha of its wartime territorial spoils and required it to indemnify Greece and Yugoslavia for war damages.

When the Red Army entered dismembered Yugoslavia (October 1944), it found actual military support from the large Communist partisan force commanded by Josip Tito.

The first organized antifascist Yugoslav resistance was formed in Serbia in 1941, soon after the state's fall, among former Yugoslav soldiers led by Serbian nationalist Colonel Draža Mihailović. His followers were called "*četniks*," the name for Ottoman-era Serbian guerrilla bands. Mihailović supported King Petr II's government-in-exile and avidly espoused traditional "Greater Serbia" nationalism. The movement's nationalist exclusivity and lack of organization won it limited popular appeal. Communist resistance forces also were fielded, led by party boss Tito, a Croat. Instead of cooperating against their common fascist foes, the two camps fought a civil war between themselves, and resisting the enemy often was a secondary concern. Tito's Communists, with their superior organization and unified purpose, won out over Mihailović's loosely organized, essentially regional forces. The more effective Communists earned the bulk of support from the anti-Axis Allies and represented the dominant Yugoslav resistance force by late 1944.

Tito's pragmatism and unflinching dedication to achieving undisputed control of postwar Yugoslavia contributed to the supremacy of the Communist partisans. He used nationalist sentiments of all stripes to create a unified force. By overtly embracing every nationalist program, his partisans enjoyed continual popular recruitment. Unlike any other Balkan political movement, whether Communist or not (especially Mihailović's), Tito publicly proclaimed national toleration and self-determination. He deftly tied the antifascist struggle to the old "Yugoslav" national problem by considering the two as one. His partisans fought not only to expel the fascists but to create a truly federal Yugoslavia. Tito thus won significant success among Croatia's and Bosnia's inhabitants.

Ideological flexibility regarding nationalism, reinforced by a strong grassroots political organization, guaranteed Tito's Communist partisans political victory. His transfer of main partisan headquarters to mountainous Bosnia-Hercegovina and Montenegro helped him win militarily. Within his mountain strongholds, Tito began planning and organizing future Communist Yugoslavia by holding congresses of partisan representatives from every region of the former state at Bihać (1942) and Jajce (1943). At the latter, a National Committee was established as an alternative Yugoslav government under Tito (1943-80), who received the title of marshal, and the outlines of his planned federated state stressed his effective slogan regarding nationality—"Brotherhood and Unity."

Soviet troops entered Serbia and, with Communist partisan assistance, took Belgrade (20 October) before pushing on into Hungary. Tito's now heavily supplied partisans were left to liberate the rest of Yugoslavia and finish their civil war with Mihailović's *četniks*. The fighting to crush fanatical *Ustaše* forces in Croatia was vicious and lengthy (concluding on 15 May 1945, a week after the Germans surrendered in Berlin). The civil war with Mihailović ended much sooner—exiled King Petr, accepting the reality on the ground, disowned the *četnik* leader, and his movement quickly collapsed.

After the last *Ustaše* and German troops laid down their arms, they and all other armed anti-Communist factions (*četniks,* Slovenian White Guards, Croatian Home Guards, and German *Volksdeutsche*) were rounded up by Tito's forces and executed. (Estimates of the number of those killed range from 30,000 to 200,000.) Although during the war Soviet Premier Joseph Stalin (1928-53) warned Tito to moderate public Communist ideological expressions for the benefit of the Western Allies' goodwill, he steadfastly refused to comply. His partisans brazenly displayed Communist symbols and made no secret of their revolutionary aims. Victorious, Tito and his followers brooked little compromise and no opposition.

Tito bent a bit by agreeing to a new regency council for exiled King Petr and a provisional government under his own authority, which was to include a few token non-Communist ministers. That thin liberal-democratic facade swiftly ended with the founding of "people's courts" for dealing with "enemies of the people" and "collaborators." Able to rely on a true popular majority earned as a successful antifascist leader, Tito passed a universal suffrage law, giving all those over the age of eighteen voting privileges, and then called for elections to a constituent assembly from a single-party list—that of his People's Front. As intended, the elections (November 1945) returned an assembly that abolished the Yugoslav monarchy and proclaimed the Federal People's Republic of Yugoslavia.

The new constitution (January 1946), modeled on the 1936 Soviet document, organized Communist-controlled Yugoslavia as a federation of Serbian, Montenegrin, Croatian, Slovenian, Bosnia-Hercegovinian, and Macedonian republics, centrally controlled from the capital at Belgrade by the Communist party. Kosovo and Vojvodina were recognized as autonomous provinces of Serbia. No pretense of liberal-democracy was made. The Communists ruled the state and Tito ruled the Communists. He pursued his interests at will, which meant crushing all remnants of the prewar sociopolitical situation and any postwar opposition within Communist ranks. Mihailović was captured and executed (July 1946). Croatian Communists who opposed Tito's centralizing policies were arrested, and the Croatian Catholic church was attacked when Zagreb Archbishop Alois Štepinac was sentenced to years of hard labor as a fascist collaborator. By the end of 1946, all important industries in Yugoslavia were nationalized.

In 1947 Tito implemented the first Soviet-style industrial five-year plan, negotiated a customs union with Bulgaria, and embraced the new Soviet-controlled Cominform (Communist Information Bureau), founded to replace the former Comintern (Communist International) dismantled by Stalin. So pro-Soviet were Tito and his close associates (particularly Milovan Djilas) that Belgrade was designated Cominform's headquarters. This close association with the Soviet Union frequently resulted in strained relations for Yugoslavia with Western states. In the 1947 Paris Treaty, Yugoslavia gained most of Istria, while against Tito's wishes a Free Territory of Trieste was established under United Nations supervision. The resulting conflict with Italy over the Free Territory's possession persisted until 1954, when an agreement between them granted Trieste itself to Italy while Yugoslavia retained the outlying districts and guaranteed access to the city's port.

An offshoot of the Yugoslav partisans' political triumph was the partisan victory in Albania. Throughout much of the war, Albanian antifascist resistance was fragmented. Italy and its puppet Albanian government tried to convince the Albanians that only pro-Axis sympathy could keep Kosovo and the southern Epiros (acquired in 1941) part of Albania, but their attempt largely failed. An Albanian Communist party was founded in Tiranë (November 1941) among a small number of intellectuals holding disparate socialist beliefs. They immediately contacted Tito, who assigned Yugoslav party emissaries from Kosovo to organize their new party. The schoolteacher Enver Hoxha was chosen head of the governing central committee. From their inception, the Albanian Communists essentially formed a branch of the Yugoslav party, and Tito's representatives held the actual power within Hoxha's Communist National Liberation Front.

A year later (November 1942), a secret non-Communist National Front resistance movement, led by the democratic nationalist Midhat Frashëri, formed in Albania's north. Essentially dedicated to forming a republican, ethnic-based Albanian state, the National Front was open to everyone except Communists. A year later still (November 1943), Abaz Kupi broke with the Communists and formed the royalist Legality Organization, which sought to reinstate King Zog after the war. By late 1943 Albania lay divided among the three resistance forces: The Communists dominated the south; Kupi's royalists controlled the center; and Frashëri held sway in the north. Over the winter of 1943-44, Germany (having taken Albania over from faltering Italy) tried to smash all antifascist opposition by recruiting Albanians into the SS "Skanderbeg" Division to terrorize Kosovar Serbs, round up Jews, and eradicate guerrillas. That effort proved ineffective. By mid-1944 the Tiranë fascist puppet government exercised control only over the main towns and coastal regions.

With the Soviet invasion of the Balkans, civil war broke out among the various resistance groups. Hoxha's Communists held clear advantages over their opponents. They adamantly were committed to liquidating their opposition and taking total control of the state. Both Tito and the Soviets furnished them with arms and other supplies, as did the British, since Hoxha's partisans effectively combated the Germans while fighting their Albanian political rivals. Effective propaganda won popular support for the Communists, who staged a congress in the southern town of Përmet (May 1944), where a countergovernment based on the Yugoslav model was declared, headed by Hoxha (1944-85).

His forces swelling, Hoxha defeated the Germans and royalists (Summer 1944) and turned on Frashëri and the clan opposition in the north. By the time the Germans evacuated Albania (November 1944), Hoxha's Communist partisans were the dominant resistance force in the field. They occupied Tiranë and controlled most of the state by the end of the year. They were, however, unable to acquire Kosovo, which Yugoslav partisans, in conjunction with local Albanian Communists, held for Tito's Yugoslavia.

Trials of "war criminals" and other "enemies of the people" were opened throughout the regions under Hoxha's control (January 1945), lasting over a year and resulting in hundreds of executions and thousands of imprisonments. All serious opposition to Hoxha's regime was eliminated. Middle-class merchants were eradicated as a class through the imposition of enormously high tax rates, followed by confiscation of their property when they failed to pay. Existing industries and all transportation were nationalized. In a ploy to win Western recognition, Hoxha changed his movement's name to the Democratic Front, but the United States and Britain demanded that elections be held for a constitutional assembly. Since all organized anti-Communist opposition was destroyed, the Democratic Front won 93 percent of the vote (December 1945).

The assembly officially abolished the monarchy and declared Albania a people's republic (January 1946). A constitution patterned after that of Tito's Yugoslavia was promulgated, giving the Communist party an undisputed monopoly on political authority. By concentrating numerous party and government offices in his own hands, Hoxha ensured his absolute personal power. Mass arrests of opponents both within and outside of the party crushed all opposition. He played the national card by vehemently denouncing American efforts to turn northern Epiros over to Greece at the Paris Peace Conference and continued to harp on the issue (even after the Americans dropped the matter at Paris) to maintain a pronounced anti-American foreign policy. The major item affecting Albania in the final Paris Treaty was Italy's requirement to pay Albania a relatively small reparation.

Factors in the Communists' Successes

A combination of domestic and foreign factors aided the successful Communist takeover of four of the five postwar Balkan states. Some have been noted above: The Red Army's presence; the Communist partisans' unflinching pursuit of their political objectives; the anti-Axis Allies' policy of overriding military concerns in supporting resistance movements; and widespread traditional pro-Russian popular sentiment. There also were others.

A development assisting the Communists' successes was the appearance during World War II of what some historians call a "new spirit" among the Balkan populations—a popular rejection of the traditional sociopolitical order. In Axis-conquered and occupied states, prewar political, economic, and social institutions systematically were demolished and replaced by fascist totalitarian conventions. In Axis-allied states, prewar institutions were discredited because of their regimes' fascist associations. The popular resentment created by those situations fed a desire for radical change, resulting in heightened receptivity for Communist revolutionary propaganda, a willingness to support partisan efforts (particularly in regions under direct Axis occupation), and an initial disposition to accept the Communists' new regimes in hopes that they would prove for the better.

The widespread desire for radical change at the war's end, which largely was an outgrowth of the resistance movements, was manifested in various ways. The peasant class for the first time became a dominant political and social force. Peasants predominated in the partisan resistance forces, and their victory made an indelible mark on their self-image. They—not the city folk—endured guerrilla warfare's hardships in the countryside, existed off of the land, and ultimately triumphed. Victory lent them an air of sociopolitical indispensability. All Balkan Communist regimes leaned heavily on peasant support, and programs addressing peasant grievances were their first priority once they took power.

The new peasant mentality toppled age as a qualification for leadership. Traditionally, older individuals were considered naturally qualified for positions of authority, since it was assumed that age conveyed experience bestowing knowledge. Partisan movements tapped youth's propensities for rejecting the status quo and embracing new ideas and change. Teens frequently fought in their ranks, young officers were common, and partisan youth organizations overflowed with eager and devoted members. In the postwar Communist states, the parties' cadres were generally younger, more committed, and backed by more indoctrinated youthful reserves than any of the traditional parties, whose attempts to persist in prewar fashion left them bereft of broad popular support and doomed to failure.

The war also transformed gender relationships. Prewar traditions subordinated women to men in society's pecking order and strictly limited women's activities and interests. With men commonly absent from home during the war, either off fighting or in labor-internment camps, women frequently assumed the responsibilities traditionally held by men as well as performed their traditional roles. Many young girls joined the fighters and were active at all levels in resistance organizations. During the war, gender equality became a fact throughout the Balkans before it became a law. Since communism ideologically espoused such equality, the Communist partisans won broad-based female support and officially legitimized gender equality in their postwar governments.

The new peasant and youth sociopolitical presence in the Balkans discredited the traditional leadership for many in the general population. Unlike the Communists, whose prewar illegality conditioned them to clandestine operations, traditional political leaders found such activity unattractive and difficult. They mostly refrained from active anti-Axis resistance and considered (rightfully) the resistance leaders threats to their authority. By isolating themselves both mentally and politically from the newly emerging social forces, they retained little popular support at war's end. Their incomprehension of the changed situation resulted in their rejection by the new forces, creating a political vacuum into which the Communists swiftly stepped. The Communists not only recognized and exploited the new sociopolitical situation, they deftly harnessed traditional nationalist sentiments by specifically linking national anti-Axis resistance to their revolutionary programs.

Interrelationships among the three anti-Axis Allies—Great Britain, the Soviet Union, and the United States—also were crucial for the Balkan Communists' successes. Of the three, only Britain consistently considered Balkan affairs throughout the war because of its traditional imperialist concerns with the eastern Mediterranean. British Prime Minister Winston Churchill (1940-45) repeatedly called for an Anglo-American invasion of the Balkans ("the soft underbelly of Europe," as he characterized the peninsula) to gain control of its numerous harbors and islands (particularly those in Greece). Until the Red Army invaded the Balkans (1944), Britain was the main military supplier for all Balkan resistance movements and expended great effort to ensure that non-Communist Greek resistance forces held their own against the Communists. When the Red Army arrived on Romania's borders, the Soviets began to take an active, sustained interest in Balkan military matters.

After the 1943 Allied Tehran Conference definitely ruled out a Balkan invasion, Churchill tried to reach an understanding with Stalin regarding the postwar Balkans acceptable to Britain, but a tentative agreement (1944) creating respective Balkan "spheres of interest" was shelved because the Americans rejected the concept on principle. In October 1944 Churchill met Stalin in Moscow hoping to forge new political arrangements in line with the rapidly developing military situation: Germany was collapsing and Red Armies were sweeping through Poland and the Balkans headed for Central Europe. During their talks, Churchill cavalierly scribbled out an outline proposal sketching the two Allies' shares of postwar political "predominance" in the Balkans by state and "percentage:" Romania—90 percent Soviet, 10 percent British; Greece—90 percent British (with American accord), 10 percent Soviet; Yugoslavia—50-50 percent; Bulgaria—75 percent Soviet, 25 percent Anglo-American. (Albania was not mentioned.) Stalin signaled his approval. Although Churchill, struck by the cynicism of his act, suggested that the proposal be "burned," Stalin refused. Churchill considered the matter dead, since the Red Army then was sweeping through the Balkans and no British forces were on the ground.

When Churchill, Stalin, and American President Franklin D. Roosevelt (1933-45) met in Yalta (February 1945) to finalize postwar settlement plans, Britain had just secured Greece against immediate Communist control and the Soviets were de facto military masters of Eastern Europe. Stalin scrupulously adhered to the arrangements in Churchill's infamous "Moscow Note." He raised no objections to British actions in Greece (accepting Britain's "90 percent predominance") and won his allies' agreement to Tito's arrangement with Yugoslavia's government-in-exile establishing a new regency until a referendum on the monarchy was held (preserving the 50-50 percent predominance).

The signature product of the Yalta Conference was the joint Declaration on Liberated Europe, which laid out postwar Europe's restructuring process. It called for the formation of interim democratic governments in the former Axis and Axis-occupied states to organize "free elections" for permanent governments "responsive to the will of the people" according to Wilsonian national self-determination. In pressing Churchill and Stalin to sign the declaration, Roosevelt reasserted American opposition to "spheres of interest," especially as expressed in Churchill's Moscow Note. Roosevelt, only a bit less naïve than Wilson at Versailles, thought that the allies' signatures on the declaration would ensure free elections and prevent such "spheres of influence." Although Britain and the Soviets signed, the note's terms continued to underlay their basic diplomatic positions.

Britain was ambivalent about the declaration. The Moscow Note's percentage agreements aided its efforts to secure Greece for itself without Soviet objection, and, if the declaration's terms were enforced, it stood to gain the specified positions in Romania and Bulgaria. The Soviets considered their interpretation of the note's terms sacrosanct and the declaration's of little account. The Red Army ensured their predominance in Romania and Bulgaria. Stalin felt certain that his hands-off approach to Britain's Greek intervention assured that the note, not the American-inspired declaration, remained the operating agreement. He was surprised and outraged when Churchill joined Roosevelt in insisting that the declaration's terms be fulfilled.

Stalin attended Yalta convinced that the Soviet Union required a buffer zone of "friendly" (that is, Communist) states along its western border as security against possible future attack by the "capitalist" Western states. With victory in the war assured, he had no intention of jeopardizing his state's perceived security needs by permitting "free" democratic elections in the border states that might return anti-Communist governments.

Soviet-Western political-ideological differences came to the fore at the Potsdam Conference (July-August 1945), making it the most contentious of all Allied wartime meetings. The Communists' initial repressive actions in Romania, Bulgaria, and Yugoslavia blatantly violated the Yalta Declaration's terms and obviously enjoyed Soviet support. Churchill (who attended only the opening sessions because he was voted out of office and replaced by the new Prime Minister Clement Attlee [1945-51]) was angered that Tito's total takeover of Yugoslavia excluded Britain from its "50 percent" influence. With Roosevelt having died before the conference convened, President Harry S. Truman (1945-53) was in no mood to tolerate deviations from the Yalta Declaration.

Stalin held the strongest negotiating position, being Eastern Europe's military master and able to pursue a precise, single policy. Britain and the United States suffered from changed leaderships and divergent policy positions. Stalin made no secret of his chief priority—guaranteeing "friendly" Communist buffer states on the Soviet Union's borders. He considered the Yalta Declaration a dead letter and branded any possible "freely elected" non-Communist government in the border states as "anti-Soviet." Soviet "predominance" in the Balkans expressed in the Moscow Note remained Stalin's adamant position.

Heated arguments over the Balkans' political situation erupted among the three allies. Britain and the United States issued a joint memorandum condemning Soviet-supported Communist actions. Stalin responded by charging Britain with gross misbehavior in Greece. Truman followed traditional American Anglophile tendencies and generally sided with Britain, although he rejected Britain's percentage policy. His advocacy of free elections eventually won the grudging acceptance of Stalin, who consented to setting up Allied Control Commissions for assisting and observing the elections only after Soviet military officers were permitted to head them in states under Red Army occupation. Those officers, using the army's presence, ultimately guaranteed that any "elections" held produced pro-Soviet Communist governments.

The two diplomatic positions holding at Potsdam—the Moscow Note and the Yalta Declaration—decisively divided the wartime allies. The cold war's lines were drawn, and the four postwar Balkan Communist states were planted squarely on the Soviets' side.

Despite the allies' division, Potsdam created an official mechanism for ending the war and recognizing the postwar Eastern and Central European states. A Council of Foreign Ministers drawn from the three allies was established to construct the treaty process and oversee elections and the control commissions. Although the council was powerless to intervene in those Balkan elections held between 1945 and 1947, its existence somewhat dampened overt Communist terrorism and temporarily slowed the Communist takeovers. Compromise was common in the council: The Soviets granted the United States certain latitudes in its dealings with defeated Japan in return for reciprocal considerations in Eastern Europe.

The council produced the final Paris Treaty (February 1947). By the time that it was signed, faits accomplis had forced the reluctant United States and Britain to recognize the new Balkan Communist states, but the ill will on both sides could not be hidden. Later in 1947, Churchill delivered his "Iron Curtain" speech and Truman proclaimed the "Truman Doctrine," protecting Greece and Turkey from Communist threat.

The United States and Britain viewed Stalin's Communist satellite buffer zone in East-Central Europe and the Balkans as an expression of Lenin's original Bolshevik call for global socialist revolution. Stalin's rhetoric, labeling Britain and the United States "capitalist enemies," reinforced that perception. With Britain's empire unraveling and France still recovering from the war, the United States assumed leadership in resisting the perceived global Soviet threat to Western liberal-democratic, industrial-capitalist civilized society. It initiated the Marshall Plan (1948), offering economic assistance to the war-wracked European states. Overtly humanitarian, the plan had political purposes: Acceptance of American assistance entailed acceptance of American liberal-democratic and capitalist principles, American market penetration, and an American military alliance—thus rejection of communism. Stalin understood the Marshall Plan's implications and forbade his European satellites to participate. Through a series of bilateral agreements with each European Communist buffer state, the Soviets established the Council of Mutual Economic Assistance (Comecon) as the plan's Communist counterweight (1949).

Stalin's blockade of West Berlin (1948-49) and Mao Zedong's Communist victory in China (1949) convinced the United States and its European allies that Western military unity was needed to counter communism's global spread, and so the North Atlantic Treaty Organization (NATO), consisting of the United States, Britain, France, and eight other allied states, was founded (1949). Greece and Turkey joined in 1952. In response, the Soviet-bloc states formed a similar organization, the Warsaw Pact military alliance (1955), which included all of the European Communist states except Yugoslavia.

The Soviet Communist Model

By 1948 the Red Army's presence and the imposition of the Comecon network guaranteed that Stalin's "friendly" Communist states were established firmly along the Soviet Union's European borders. Those states were authentic Soviet satellites, obliged to adopt Moscow's sociopolitical system and accept economic dependency in their international trade. The Soviet Communist bloc thus created stood in stark contrast and opposition to the Western states led by the United States, which responded to the situation with increased ideological politicization of liberal democracy and capitalism. All-out warfare between the two opposing ideological blocs was prevented by the advent of nuclear weapons in the arsenals of both sides shortly after World War II. There evolved the so-called cold war, in which the sides battled each other on a global scale through propaganda, diplomatic oneupsmanship, covert operations, and localized warfare primarily fought by surrogates.

The cold war commonly was characterized as an West-East conflict, with "West" alluding to Western European liberal-democratic and industrial-capitalist precepts and "East" denoting an autocratic ("Asiatic" or "Eastern") sociopolitical command system. Opposition or adherence to Marxism was its defining feature. While the conflict was real enough, the simplistic delineation of Marxism as its definitive basis was flawed culturally.

Marxism was a Western European creation, spawned by a German philosopher as the alternative to the Industrial Revolution's negative impacts and firmly planted in Western Enlightenment ideals of human progress and happiness stemming from structuring society in harmony with "scientifically" discovered "natural laws" governing human existence. Karl Marx claimed to have "discovered" such laws in his economic-philosophical analysis of history: The fundamental role of "economic determinism" in shaping societies, and the dialectical workings of property-defined "class struggle" in furthering progressive human development. He concluded that the inevitable goal of human progress was a classless egalitarian ("Communist") society, without private property, in which all members shared equally the benefits of communal self-government and economic effort.

Marx outlined his views in the *Communist Manifesto* (1848), coauthored with German historian Frederick Engels, in which he devised a revolutionary program for hastening the class conflict that would push industrialized society further along the historically preordained road toward an egalitarian future. In his view, it was his followers' duty, through an international Communist party representing industrialized society's working class (the proletariat), to lead the struggle against capitalists and industrialists (the bourgeoisie), overthrow their rule, and structure the postrevolutionary society in accordance with the egalitarian historical imperative. That duty demanded temporary party authoritarian rule—the "dictatorship of the proletariat." Once the party's task was fulfilled, authoritarianism would "whither away" and true egalitarianism emerge. (Exactly how this would occur was never defined.) Marx devoted his life to critiquing capitalism and organizing an international revolutionary movement—the First Communist International (founded 1864).

Although rightly viewed by the West's traditional establishment as radical and dangerous, Marxism was not considered "Eastern" until Vladimir Lenin's Marxist Bolsheviks took control of Russia. Thereafter it acquired an overriding "foreignness" and "Easternness" for westerners, partly because they traditionally considered Orthodox Russia as such and partly because Lenin (and his successor Stalin) modified Marxism to fit Russian cultural realities, thus giving Soviet communism its lasting European order.

Marxism was a foreign ideology imposed by force on an Orthodox European society. Lenin and Stalin made it acceptable by expropriating many of the overthrown state's imperial forms and much of its political ideology, pragmatically modifying both them and Marxism (termed "Marxism-Leninism [-Stalinism]") to achieve outward compatibility. While official ideology and terminology changed, Soviet communism exhibited a striking cultural continuity with Orthodox European Russian society.

The old empire, which Russians viewed as their rightful and historic state, was retained as the Soviet Union. The Communist party replaced the Russian aristocracy as society's new elite and displaced the Orthodox church as the institution lending validity to absolute political authority, with a trinity of Marx, Lenin, and Stalin as the new nonreligious deity. Supreme authority lay with the party leader, considered Marx's (Marx-Lenin-Stalin's) leading disciple and direct representative. Soviet political ideology thus mirrored the traditional Byzantine and Russian Orthodox construct: One God (Marx-Lenin-Stalin), one emperor (the head of the Soviet Communist party), one empire (the Soviet Union).

Soviet Communist political ideology, in conformity with Russia's Orthodox-Byzantine traditions, left no room for democracy. The party general secretary ruled in much the same autocratic and absolutist fashion as did the former *tsars*—only now such rule was described as the necessary "dictatorship of the proletariat." Much of the Soviet governing body's organization was modeled directly on its *tsarist* counterpart, including the Supreme Soviet, an assembly resembling the last *tsar*'s ill-fated *Duma,* which had little authentic power and served to rubber-stamp the party leader's dictates, and the infamous NKVD (later, the KGB), which paralleled the nineteenth-century *Okhrana* secret police that, in turn, had its roots in Ivan IV's *Oprichnina* (founded 1564).

Soviet Communists made use of the emotional ambiguities in Russian self-identity earlier expressed in the Westernizer and Slavophile movements. Their domestic policies—rapid industrialization and forced agricultural collectivization to swiftly "modernize" the Soviet Union in Western terms by transforming it into a predominantly urban industrialized society through a complete break with past agrarian economic traditions—reflected Westernizer concepts in action. Communal institutional structures and collective governance imposed on the process supposedly were grounded in old Slavic traditions, such as the village communes (*mirs*), idealized by Slavophiles.

In foreign policy, Westernizer claims that Russia was destined to correct a flawed and corrupted Western Europe and Slavophile assertions of Russia's Slavic primacy harmonized well with the Soviet Communists' Marxist concepts of international socialist revolution. As Europe's first practicing Marxist society, the Soviets assumed the right to lead the historically ordained global Communist movement. When it became obvious that the anticipated spread of Communist revolution throughout Europe would not occur, Stalin pragmatically settled for imposing communism on the Soviet Union's immediate European neighbors to create his desired "friendly" state security buffer zone. Since the populations of most of those neighboring states were predominantly Slavic, the Soviets used former Slavophile arguments and past Slavophile affiliations with them to bolster their presence.

Despite the Orthodox Balkan states' serious past half-century stabs (never totally successful) at functioning liberal democracy (compared to Russia's prerevolution record, which spanned eleven years), the Soviets' expropriation of traditional Orthodox cultural legacies and deft associations with Slavophilism earned them sympathy among the populations of most Balkan states. Those factors, combined with the Balkan populations' postwar "new spirit," eased the way for the Soviet model's acceptance once Communist regimes were established.

Communist parties assumed supreme political authority in Albania, Bulgaria, Romania, and Yugoslavia. Traditional political parties were suppressed, with the exception of small, subordinate, radical agrarian splinter movements retained to lend token "democratic" appearances. Nearly all postwar elections involved candidates from a single list of Communists or their subordinate allies. Media censorship prevented public criticism of the regimes. A combination of intimidation and indoctrination—purges, "show" trials, and ubiquitous domestic propaganda—eliminated political opposition. Traditional political leadership was replaced by a Communist party elite composed of officials, military officers, bureaucrats, and experts, and government institutions became ancillary surrogates of the party's. Heading both the party and the government was an autocratic leader: Dimitrov (later Todor Zhivkov [1954-89]) in Bulgaria; Groza (later Gheorghe Gheorghiu-Dej [1952-65] and Nicolae Ceauşescu [1965-89]) in Romania; Hoxha (later Ramiz Alia [1985-92]) in Albania; and Tito (later Slobodan Milošević [1989-2000]) in Yugoslavia.

The Balkan states' economies primarily were agrarian when the Communists took over. The Communists followed the Soviets' lead and concentrated on initiating rapid industrialization to shed the impression of backwardness and create a widespread proletariat (whom they ideologically claimed to represent). Party governments nationalized all economic sectors and moved against private ownership and management. The states' resources were mobilized to develop industries that, in Soviet fashion, focused on basic heavy production (steel manufacturing, ore extraction and refining, energy generation) at the expense of consumer goods. The states attempted to develop Soviet-style independent industrial units, despite their lack of many natural resources (specific ores and chemicals) to do so. That handicap was overcome early on by importing necessary raw materials through Comecon. Rigid party-state control and long-term planning (à la the Soviets' Five-year Plans) brought high industrial capacity.

Central economic planning lay at the heart of the imported Stalinist model. Since Marxism-Leninism rejected market transactions in determining economic value and replaced them with nonmarket concepts of labor and social need, a central plan based on economic calculus encompassing those factors was required. To ensure that planning worked, industrial and financial institutions were nationalized and assigned set specializations. Early plans relatively were simple: Communist planners issued all industries compulsory global output targets over a set period (commonly five years), each having a predetermined optimum balance of perceived demand and known resources. Domestic and foreign trade were isolated from one another by price equalization. The goal of each state's plan was economic self-dependency while building toward the universal socialist future.

Communist planners always ideologically stressed industrial development, since they supposedly governed in the name and interests of the "workers." Collectivization became an ideologically driven means to transform the predominant agricultural sector into one more closely akin to the industrial. Industrialization affected all aspects of life in the Communist Balkan states. New factories and mills addressed the old problem of rural overpopulation by opening new job opportunities. Concomitantly, urbanization grew rapidly until, by the 1970s, urban dwellers constituted population majorities (attaining 75 percent levels in some cases). All urban centers were embellished with new architectural structures expressing the party's power, glorifying its achievements, and reinforcing ideological loyalty. As urban populations grew, so too did the need for consumer goods. Since native industries generally concentrated on heavy materials, most consumer products were imported from the Soviet Union or other Comecon states with mature industries (East Germany, Czechoslovakia, and Poland).

Total control of the economic planning process bestowed validity on the Stalinist Communist party system. Marxism theoretically demanded that, once in undisputed political control, the Communist party initiate central planning to create the historically inevitable socialist future as rapidly as possible. While Marx thought in democratic centrist terms, Lenin created the actual model, which was centrist but undemocratic. Lenin's (and Stalin's) party retained its prerevolutionary hierarchical and conspiratorial aspects after gaining power in Russia, and it became the model adopted by the Communist satellite states.

A pyramidical chain of command operated within Communist party organization, and orders passed through the levels from the top down. Only the party's leadership elite was privy to all available political and economic data. The lower one stood in the organization, the less such information was available. That situation permitted the leaders to hide flaws and failings in the planning process, while maintaining the devotion of the lower party echelons to planning goals through factual ignorance. Committed to communism's avowed goals, and kept preoccupied with their planning tasks, the rank-and-file members had little reason to question the party's official propaganda and dictatorial authority.

For mathematical comprehensiveness, Communist planners needed to possess all ideological and concrete economic facts. Through trial and error, they expanded the originally small number of factors specifically integrated into the planning formulas. Product groups were refined into more precise type categories. Nonmaterial factors, such as the value-added aspect of labor, needed quantifying. As each new factor requiring the planners' attention was plugged into the planning process, an administrative structure was created, dedicated to keeping tabs on it alone in hopes of refining the process further. The protozoalike bureaucracy that resulted continuously expanded through the fission of existing departments into ever-multiplying subdivisions or entirely new departments.

The demand for technically trained and skilled personnel to staff the new industries and bureaucracies, and the need of rapid urbanization for expanded economic service sectors, led to the swift growth of state-controlled compulsory public education and technical and trade schools to augment existing universities.

Curricula emphasized technical subjects (math, sciences, engineering, mechanics) as well as social and humane subjects (history, literature, art, Marxist philosophy) as tools for ideological (and often nationalist) indoctrination. By the late 1970s every Balkan Communist state boasted of high literacy levels—as much as 99 percent. Though the reality was lower (averaging 70 to 80 percent), it certainly was the highest in the Balkans' history.

Health and municipal services, public utilities and housing, urban renewal, communications, infrastructural development, and all of the other "modern" European social necessities were developed and controlled by the Communist governments. Their funding came from taxes on the expanding industrial and urban workforces.

The agricultural programs of the Balkan Communist regimes were far less effective than their industrial and urban efforts. Again aping the Soviets, agricultural collectivization was imposed on peasants who initially (except for Romania) owned the small plots that they tilled, many of which were acquired in the land redistributions carried out immediately after Communist partisans took power. In theory, abolishing private landownership and consolidating large state-run collective farms permitted organizing agriculture along industrial lines, transforming peasants into factorylike "workers," and making mechanized, high-yield farming possible. In practice, however, collectivization in the Balkans never lived up to Communist expectations.

Balkan party leaders were more concerned with industrialization than with agriculture, so they expended few resources and little effort on collective farms. Equipment, materials, and managerial expertise on the collectives often were substandard or insufficiently upgraded. Moreover, the peasants, who generally remained emotionally attached to the traditional concept of landowning, passively resisted collectivization and were distinctly uninterested in becoming rural land "workers." They performed their collective farm duties perfunctorily, giving more effort and care to small garden plots at their homes. Collectivization did so poorly that agriculture, once the Balkan states' economic backbone, became their weakness. Eventually collectivization lost its ideological appeal. While most Communist governments halfheartedly tinkered with marginal improvements, Yugoslavia ultimately abandoned it entirely.

The centralized autocratic governments, domestic ideological unity, rapid industrial and urban growth, mass education, extensive public and social services, and improved infrastructures provided Balkan Communist states by the Soviet model were achieved at a price. These states existed as subservient Soviet satellites and relinquished most domestic and virtually all international freedom of action. Their populations were forced to accept a living standard perceptibly lower than in non-Communist European states. Until the 1980s most consumer goods were periodically in short supply, mediocre to substandard in quality, and expensive relative to average incomes. Public utilities, public housing, and infrastructure experienced quality, obsolescence, and maintenance problems. Balkan Communist societies survived with what they had because those conditions typically defining "modern" quality of life—food, work, housing, education, communications, social services—were more readily available than ever before.

CHAPTER EIGHTEEN

The Greek Exception

Greece escaped Communist takeover at the end of World War II because of direct Western intervention. Thereafter, the Greeks consciously cultivated a self-image as "Western" (rather than Balkan "Eastern") Europeans by playing to classical Greek culture's historical importance for Western European civilization and aligning themselves directly with the non-Communist West by joining NATO (1952) and the European Community/Union (EC/U, 1981). Despite those memberships, Greece persisted as a historically traditional Balkan state. Continuing domestic political discord and nationalist ferment with Turkey led to a decade of military authoritarian rule, followed by the monarchy's abolition and the installation of a republic. No matter Greece's form of government, nationalist territorial disputes with Turkey and ethnonational concerns over Macedonia continued.

Liberation and Civil War

The wartime situation of Axis-occupied Greece somewhat resembled that in occupied Yugoslavia. Axis satellite Bulgaria held parts of Greek Macedonia and Thrace; Italian puppet Albania controlled Greek Epiros; Italy occupied the bulk of mainland Greece and most Aegean islands; while Germany dominated strategically important Athens, Thessaloniki, Crete, and the crucial border with neutral Turkey. An Axis puppet government in Athens replaced that of King George II and Colonel Metaxas, who fled to London and won official British recognition as Greece's legitimate government. (See Map 11.)

Occupied Greece suffered massive exploitation and repression. Hitler stripped the state of food and resources to supply his forces, and Britain's anti-Axis Mediterranean blockade included Greece. Since Greece's terrain greatly limited food production, and close to 50 percent of its population's food depended on imports, German policies and British blockade brought on widespread famine. An estimated 7 percent of the Greek population and 30 percent of the state's national wealth were lost during the occupation. Food shortages, rampant inflation, and black-marketeering were the post-1941 wartime norm, and arrests, executions, and deportations (of Jews and slave laborers) were commonplace.

Anti-Axis resistance movements spawned by such adverse conditions spanned the political gamut from royalists, through republicans, to Communists. The Greek National Democratic League (EDES), led by Colonel Napoleon Zervas, represented the royal government-in-exile. The most powerful movement was the National Liberation Front (EAM), which included Communists, socialists, agrarians, and center-leaning traditional parties. EAM's military organization— the National Popular Party of Liberation (ELAS)—was the strongest and most active guerrilla force and received the lion's share of anti-Axis Allied assistance. Tightly organized EAM/ELAS, though politically left leaning and brutally intolerant of other Greek resistance movements, recognized the government-in-exile's legitimacy and hoped to play an important political role once it was restored. When the Axis evacuated Greece during the Soviet Balkan invasion, EAM/ELAS controlled most of the state.

With British sponsorship, an interim coalition government, which included all active political parties and factions, was established in Lebanon under George Papandreou (1944-46), a staunch anti-Communist and former Venizelos disciple. When it was formed, left-leaning EAM/ELAS enjoyed a four-to-one military edge over Zervas's royalist forces. Papandreou's government arrived in Athens (October 1944) protected by a small British force and immediately decided to hold a referendum on the king's return and place all armed resistance fighters under its authority. An attempt was made to disarm EAM/ELAS.

Metaxas's dictatorship had grown unpopular by the time of the Axis invasion, and much discontent rubbed off on King George, which contributed to EAM/ELAS's wartime popularity. Only British assistance had kept Zervas's royalists in the field. With Greece liberated, EAM/ELAS suspected the motives of the anti-Communist Papandreou government regarding their disarmament. It pulled out of the government (December 1944) and declared a general strike, during which government police in Athens fired on demonstrators and a full-blown EAM/ELAS-royalist conflict erupted. Only British military intervention saved the royalists from defeat. The Soviets, adhering to the Moscow Note, warned EAM/ELAS leaders to make accommodations with the British-backed authorities, so an agreement was reached to end the fighting (February 1945). That agreement called for an interim regency and a plebiscite to determine the monarchy's fate, followed by parliamentary elections. Although EAM/ELAS was required to disarm, many of its weapons were hidden away for possible future use.

Bolstered by British support and aware of the Soviets' hands-off policy, government ultrarightists terrorized Communists and socialists. The government's repression progressively drove EAM/ELAS partisans into Greece's north-central and Macedonian mountains, and militant extremism erupted on both sides.

Britain, under heavy international pressure from friends and foes alike to fix what its meddling had wrought, forced the Greek authorities to reverse the order of the recent political settlement: Elections were called before the referendum on the monarchy. Circumstances for the elections (March 1946) were terrible. EAM/ELAS refused to participate. Centrist republican parties were in disarray, and rural unrest was endemic. Only those prepared to accept the monarchy were listed on the ballot.

The elections returned a rightist government under Constantine Tsaldaris (1946-52). King George II was restored by the subsequent plebiscite (September 1946), signaling the total political victory of the royalist-rightists. Communists in EAM/ELAS refused to accept the defeat and decided on civil war. A (Communist) Democratic Army commanded by former ELAS leader Markos (Vafiadis) commenced antigovernment military operations from its northern mountain strongholds, inflicting a string of defeats on the government's forces. Frustrated, Britain washed its hands of the deteriorating situation and handed it over to the United States (March 1947). President Truman, determined to combat communism's spread wherever possible, dispatched emergency military and economic aid to the Greek government, bringing America into direct Balkan involvement for the first time. His action was the first in an official foreign policy of supporting "free" (non-Communist) governments against domestic Communist threats known as the Truman Doctrine. It appeared at the time that, if Athens fell, all of the Balkans would lie under Soviet control.

As the United States emerged as the royal national government's benefactor in the name of saving the Balkans from total Communist domination, Tito became the Liberation Army's sponsor to spread communism to the peninsula's last bastion of "capitalism." The Communist rebels' strongholds along the border with Yugoslavia facilitated easy support from Tito. Proximity, however, proved both a short-lived boon and a long-term liability. Yugoslav Communist assistance of all kinds streamed across the border to such an extent and in such quantities that Tito and his Communist Macedonian Slav forces became the dominant players in the Greek Communists' movement. Furthermore, within the Greek Communists' own ranks, Macedonian Slavs came to constitute the majority, and the ethnic shift in the balance of power within the ranks of the Communist rebels was unsettling for Greek participants.

During World War II Tito nurtured Greece's Communist movement. The Greek Communist party, however, toed the traditional nationalist line regarding Macedonia. It refused to cede control over the "Slavophone Greeks" to Yugoslavia's Macedonian Slav Communists and intended to keep all of Greece's territory under ethnic Greek control. After instigating the Greek Civil War and seeking Tito's support, it was forced to accept help from the Yugoslav Macedonian Slav Communists, which produced new internal tensions between the party's ethnic Greeks and Slavs over the political future of Greek Macedonia.

During the civil war's first year (1947), the Communist rebels' guerrilla military approach gained them much of mainland Greece, and they proclaimed a Provisional Democratic Government. Their inability to capture a major town to serve as capital, however, led to a change in tactics. Party leader Nikos Zakhariadis demanded that the army forgo guerrilla activities and fight as a regular military force. The decision coincided with a transformation in the royalist government forces accomplished through American assistance and retraining. Most important, the new American-supplied and trained government air force enjoyed total air supremacy. Changed rebel tactics and royalist air superiority turned the military tide against the Communists (late 1947).

In growing desperation, the Communists resorted to forced general conscription in regions under their control. They evacuated children to Soviet-bloc states, for either their "protection" (as they declared) or their "indoctrination" (as the royalist government claimed). Although intended to strengthen their positions, such actions worked against the Communists. The conscriptions and evacuations eroded their popular support, while the new draftees increased the numbers of ethnic Slavs in their ranks (to 40 percent of the total) since Greek Macedonia most firmly was in Communist hands, heightening tensions between Greek and Slav Communists over Macedonia's future.

In 1948 international developments dealt a blow to the Greek Communists' fortunes that doomed them to failure. Tito and Stalin fell out over Soviet interference in Yugoslav Communist affairs, and Yugoslavia was expelled from the Cominform Soviet bloc. The break immediately strained relations between the Yugoslav and Greek Communists and split the Greek Communist leadership. The majority, convinced that the Soviet Union was global communism's bastion, sided with Moscow. Unfortunately for their cause, they faced a Faustian choice when it came to embracing either Tito or Stalin. Preoccupied with defending his position against the Soviets and their Balkan allies and maintaining control over all of Yugoslavia, including Yugoslav Macedonia, Tito became unwilling to assist the Greek Communists. Stalin, hoping to undermine Tito's position within Yugoslavia and convinced that the Greek Communists' cause was not worth a risky direct confrontation with the United States, endorsed the idea of creating an independent Communist Macedonian state that would include Greek Macedonia. If the Greek Communists retained their ties with Tito, they were doomed to defeat through lack of support. If they sided with the Soviets, they would be forced to accept Greece's future dismemberment.

The Greek Communists decided against continued reliance on Tito (early 1949). In July Tito closed his border with Greece, after which, alone and poorly equipped, the Greek Communists faced the modernized Greek army commanded by General Alexander Papagos. Papagos defeated the Communist forces in a series of decisive battles in northwestern Greece and drove the remnants of the Democratic Army into Albania (late Summer 1949). The defeated Greek Communist leaders declared a temporary cease-fire (October), and, although their exiled fighters were kept on a war footing for some years, the civil war ended.

Authoritarian Legacy and the "Cyprus Problem"

As the 1940s closed, the battered and bruised Greeks were determined to rebuild their state and restore their national pride. The savage fighting and atrocities committed by both sides during the civil war left an emotionally intense psychological legacy.

Important in the national restoration process was the Greeks' awareness that they were the only Balkan people to successfully reject communism. Although that benefited national pride, it also lent negative qualities to post–civil war Greek society. Anti-Communist domestic and foreign policies characterized succeeding Greek governments, which successfully gained NATO membership (officially, 1952). Resources that should have been devoted to economic reconstruction often were funneled into the military, whose civil war experiences made it radically anti-Communist and devoutly royalist. The large military and security forces had little toleration for socialist or left-leaning political factions. Since most of Greece's Communist neighbors were Slavs, and Macedonian Slavs predominated in the Communists' ranks during the civil war, Greek nationalist paranoia over the "Slav danger" to Greek Macedonia was reinforced. The same held true regarding Communist Albania and Greek Epiros. Anticommunism and Greek nationalism merged, intensifying the Greeks' traditionally divisive and confrontational Balkan nation-state perceptions.

Greece's anti-Communist stance virtually reduced it to United States client status. America poured military and economic aid into Greece to prevent a Communist takeover. Most assistance was channeled into the war effort, but some filtered into civil projects and helped preserve Greece's traditional social order. Both the government and the private sector grew dependent on their American partners. Major political, military, or economic decisions rarely were made without first consulting the Americans. The British never achieved such a dominant voice in Greek affairs as did the Americans by the 1950s.

Greece was tied securely to the West during the cold war, despite millennium-old Orthodox Eastern cultural and historical traditions central to Greek national identity. Given the cold war situation, anti-Western aspects of those traditions (shared by Balkan and Soviet Communists) were incongruous. Unlike those of their

Communist Balkan neighbors, however, the traditions of the Greeks possessed a classical component, providing them with a cultural bridge to the West without requiring outright rejection of their non-Western, Orthodox heritage.

Western European awareness of the impact of the classical Hellenic heritage on the Renaissance and Enlightenment benefited Greek nationalism from its inception. While the majority of prenationalist-era Greeks had no idea of their classical past, and most of the nationalists looked to their Byzantine heritage, the few early expatriate nationalists used Western awareness of classical Greece to further their national agenda. That awareness provided them with ready-made tools for propagandizing (such as the existence of typefaces for publishing their ideas and works of classical Greek literature) and a natural reservoir of Western philhellenic assistance for their revolutionary activities. No other Balkan national movement enjoyed such culturally ingrained Western support. (The Cyrillic typeface was nearly nonexistent and most non-Greek medieval Balkan literature was unknown in the West.)

After Greece acquired independence from the Ottomans, its governments tapped persistent Western philhellenism for international support and broadened domestic popular awareness of classical Greek achievements. The British and Germans assisted the latter effort, but their help came at a price—neither had qualms about raping Greece of the monuments of its classical heritage to benefit their renowned museum collections. Greece's classical past helped further the Greeks' national cause through sympathetic Western assistance, while it also served as a frictional flash point with the West. The American patrons of post–civil war Greece were no less sympathetically philhellenic than other westerners.

The governments of King Paul (1947-64), George II's successor, nourished the classical Greek cultural heritage to reinforce Greece's pro-Western, anti-Communist position. Educational and cultural programs stressed classical topics, institutes of classical studies (often American-supported and run) were founded, and laws protecting classical works from foreign pillage were rigidly enforced. The stress on the classical intentionally differentiated Greece from its Communist Balkan neighbors, whose heritage lay in medieval and Ottoman "Eastern" traditions. Greece's Byzantine traditions were portrayed as natural continuations of the classical in Orthodox Christian form, providing a pretext for separating Greeks from their Slav neighbors, who were characterized as "interlopers" into that tradition. Most post–civil war Greeks came to believe that they were a "non-Balkan" people. Within the context of cold war polarization, most westerners and Communists agreed—"the Balkans" became equated with the peninsula's Communist states.

Athenian democracy played a central role in the Greek classical heritage. To most westerners, classical Greece was synonymous with democratic politics. In that view, however, mythology overshadowed historical realities. Of the numerous classical Greek city-states, only Athens developed democracy because of its unique commercial middle-class society. Athenian democracy lasted only for a relatively short time and resembled more an oligarchy than a popular government. Many classical Athenians—including Socrates and Plato—despised democracy and yearned for more authoritarian rule. The operations of most post-Ottoman Greek governments did little justice to Western democratic precepts, being more continuations of Byzantine-Ottoman authoritarian traditions than the idealized classical. Post–civil war Greek governments, for all their stress on classicism, long did the same.

In the first post–civil war election, the Greeks rejected Tsaldaris's extreme rightists and returned a centrist coalition government claiming adherence to Venizelos traditions. The surrogate party of the illegal Communists, the United Democratic Left (EDA), earned measurable popular support, which worried the American diplomats in Athens. At their insistence, Greek electoral laws were changed for the next election (1952) to permit General Papagos's rightist party to benefit from overwhelming army support. Although most traditional party leaders protested American interference, Papagos won a landslide victory.

A new constitution (1952) guaranteed standard liberal-democratic freedoms, but a number of emergency laws enacted under martial law during the civil war remained in effect. The state security police maintained political files on individuals; surveillance of leftists was widespread; revolutionary ideas were subject to punishment; and police clearance was required for state employment, passports, or driver's licenses. The rightist Greek governments exerted as much regulation as their American patrons would tolerate and kept themselves in power by employing traditionally coercive Balkan electoral techniques.

While the rightist Papagos (1952-55) and Constantine Karamanlis (1955-63) governments cracked down on leftists, they rebuilt Greece's economy. Rapid urban renewal and housing construction projects were initiated. (By 1971 Greece's population was 53 percent urban and 35 percent rural, with the remaining 12 percent classified as "semiurban.") Industry remained small and concentrated in low-technology sectors (textiles, food, drink, and tobacco), but service sectors thrived. Tourism exploded into the leading service sector because of higher standards of living in the West, better global communications (air travel), improved domestic infrastructure (roads, bridges, and rail lines), and growing tourist-friendly services (restaurants, hotels, shopping). Heavy maritime investments were made. Greek investors purchased foreign-built ships (especially supertankers), and, by the late 1960s, the Greek merchant marine was the largest in the world. By that time as well, most of the civil war's physical ravages were healed and economic recovery, although unevenly distributed socially, brought a slow but steady rise in Greece's standard of living.

In 1955 events on Cyprus lit a Greek national crisis that questioned Greece's American and NATO associations, a crisis that has affected Greek domestic and international affairs into the present.

Britain took over Cyprus from the Ottoman Empire in 1878 at Berlin as compensation for Russia's Bessarabian and Caucasian acquisitions and formally annexed it in 1914. Although the island was 600 miles (960 kilometers) east of the Greek mainland and only 40 miles (64 kilometers) off of Turkey's southern coast, its population ethnically was 80 percent Greek and 20 percent Turkish. A strong Greek nationalist movement arose, demanding unification with Greece. So long as Britain served as Greece's major supporter, Greek governments did not encourage the Greek Cypriots' nationalist hopes. Once Britain was replaced as patron by the traditionally anticolonial Americans, the Papagos government felt free to embrace pre-Berlin Greek nationalist claims to Cyprus.

When Britain granted India independence (1948), it maintained economic ties with the former colony and continued to view a British presence in the eastern Mediterranean as strategically necessary. Britain made it known that Cyprus would remain under British sovereignty. The Greek Cypriots, led by General George Grivas, a ruthless former resistance leader, staged an anti-British uprising with the connivance of local Orthodox Metropolitan Makarios III (April 1955). To counter the revolt, Britain encouraged fellow NATO ally Turkey to intervene. Turkish demands for the protection of Turkish Cypriots led to anti-Greek riots in Istanbul (September) and official Turkish calls for Cyprus's partition.

The Istanbul riots ended a decade of friendly Greek-Turkish relations. Prior to World War II, political necessity led Greece to forge workable diplomatic ties with its national adversary Turkey. After the war, both states shared a common perception of danger from their immediate Communist neighbors—the Communist Balkan states for Greece, and the Soviet Union and Bulgaria for Turkey. Their "front-line" locations in the cold war gained them membership in NATO and facilitated good bilateral relations between them. They negotiated (1953) a formal alliance (which also included Tito's breakaway Communist Yugoslavia) that, although fragile, brought them closer together than before. Greek and Turkish national emotions over Cyprus dealt their friendly ties a fatal blow.

As bloodshed among the Greeks, Turks, and British on Cyprus mounted, there grew in Greece a sense of national disillusionment. Widespread resentment of NATO's seeming failure to support the Cypriot Greeks against Britain and Turkey, and the inability of Greece's center-leaning political parties to voice the national indignation, earned the Communist-front EDA party increased popularity. EDA became the leading opposition to Karamanlis's rightist government. The situation shook both the government and the American legation, who then sought a swift solution to the Cyprus problem to counter rising anti-NATO and pro-leftist popular sentiments. The Suez Canal crisis (1956) convinced Britain to relinquish its direct sovereignty in Cyprus in return for retaining military bases on the island.

Intense negotiations among Greece, Turkey, and Britain constructed a solution to the Cyprus problem (1960): Cyprus became an independent republic within the British Commonwealth under joint British, Greek, and Turkish protection; Britain retained two sovereign military bases; Greece and Turkey could station small military detachments on the island; and a new constitution guaranteed the Turkish minority a 30 percent share of government positions and 40 percent of the police force. Makarios and Grivas were compelled to accept the solution, and Makarios became the new republic's first president.

Popular reaction in Greece was negative. Karamanlis was blamed for betraying the Greek national cause in the interests of NATO and the Americans. In new elections (1963), George Papandreou, head of a centrist political coalition called the Center Union, was elected prime minister. King Paul and the Americans approved the new government hoping that it would keep EDA at bay. Papandreou's adroit political maneuvering replaced EDA's parliamentary majority with a seemingly unassailable one by the Center Union.

Developments on Cyprus (November 1963) changed the political situation in Greece. The power-sharing Cypriot constitution broke down because President Makarios governed in traditional Orthodox fashion, joining together political and religious authority. He demanded that the presence of the Turkish minority in government be reduced. When Turkey refused on behalf of the Turkish Cypriots, fighting erupted between the island's two ethnic groups. Only American President Lyndon Johnson's (1963-68) warnings and the arrival of a UN peacekeeping force on Cyprus (1964) prevented a Turkish invasion. With nationalist tensions rising, the Greek army feared that Papandreou's less rigorous authoritarian stance might open the door to dangerous socialist and Communist influences, and it resented the public leftist political sentiments of his son Andreas Papandreou.

Papandreou's efforts to gain political control over the army were thwarted by newly installed King Constantine II (1964-74), who wished to reassert royal authority. Papandreou was forced to resign (1965), and the subsequent interim government enjoyed little popular support. Before new elections were held, a group of junior military officers—the "Colonels"—staged a successful political coup (April 1967). With virtually no resistance because all political factions, from king to trade unionists, were caught off guard, the ultrarightist-nationalist "Colonels" took full control of the government.

Following Metaxas's precedent (allusions to Metaxas's authoritarian paternalism were numerous), the junta justified its action as necessary to block a possible Communist takeover. Its proclaimed mission was defense of traditional "Helleno-Christian civilization" against communism and increasing Western-style secularization caused by postwar socioeconomic transformations. While overtly idealistic, the motivation of the Colonels was fear that a moderate, center-leaning government would purge the military of ultrarightist officers—themselves. Provincial and of low social origins, they resented the traditional political elites' privileged lifestyle, wallowing in affluence in Athens while they lived in spartan provincial garrisons protecting the state's borders against Communists and Slavs.

The Colonels enjoyed no support from any traditional political faction, including the rightists, and ruled in strict authoritarian fashion, using the police and army to suppress opposition across the political spectrum. Thousands of accused leftists were exiled internally; party leaders were imprisoned, exiled, or placed under house arrest; the officer corps was purged of possible leftists and centrists; and a brutal security apparatus prevented any organized opposition. After King Constantine failed to overthrow the Colonels by an amateurish countercoup (December 1967), he fled to Rome and the junta established a regency headed by their prime minister (later president, 1973) Colonel George Papadopoulos (1967-73). An authoritarian constitution was ratified by a fraudulent referendum (1968). Profligate international borrowing and lavish inducements to foreign and domestic investors kept the economy growing (until the global oil crisis of 1973). Economic growth, combined with effective government repression, prevented concerted political opposition.

The junta's commitment to fulfilling Greece's NATO obligations deflected most international displeasure with their actions. Although vocally condemned by Western states (including the United States), few took concrete action against them. America continued aiding its staunchly anti-Communist client, earning widespread Greek popular approbation as the junta's accomplice (a charge still unsubstantiated at present). One area of international affairs, however, did not favor the Colonels. Relations with Turkey over Cyprus deteriorated. Cypriot President Makarios grew more committed to maintaining the island's independence and less willing to cooperate with the junta.

In 1973 the junta's hold over Greece began to unravel. A global oil crisis increased inflation to double-digit proportions. Students in Athens occupied the university to protest the junta's repressive educational and sociopolitical policies, while antiregime naval officers conducted an abortive mutiny. Papadopoulos declared the exiled Constantine deposed for alleged complicity in the mutiny and proclaimed a "presidential parliamentary republic." He then staged a show election, in which he was the only presidential candidate listed on the ballot. Large-scale student demonstrations erupted in Athens, and Papadopoulos's violent suppression of them led to his ouster by even harder-line fellow junta colleagues. The hard-liners' leader, Dimitrios Ioannidis, head of the military police, became the actual force behind a new puppet president.

Those events coincided with a sharp deterioration in relations with Turkey over oil drilling rights in the Aegean, a situation that spilled over into the Cyprus problem. Ioannidis took a chauvinistic stance to win popular support, seeking a spectacular nationalist victory by uniting Cyprus with Greece. Makarios refused to accept unification and tried to remove all mainland Greek officers from the Cypriot National Guard. Ioannidis launched a coup against the president (July 1974), forcing him into exile. Fearing that the coup was the island's first step toward unification with Greece, Turkey invaded northern Cyprus.

Greece and Turkey mobilized and a war splitting the NATO alliance loomed. Fortunately for NATO, Greece's mobilization was uncoordinated. Many commanders refused to obey the junta's orders, demonstrating that the Colonels' authoritarian policies had alienated the power on which their authority rested. With no support whatsoever, the regime disintegrated. Leading military commanders met with senior members of the traditional parties and agreed to return the state to civilian liberal-democratic government. The exiled Karamanlis was called on to return and to oversee the dictatorship's dismantling.

Karamanlis returned amid widespread popular support, convinced that general elections were necessary to dispel any image of his dependence on the army or the exiled king. His rightist New Democracy party won overwhelmingly (November 1974). As most Greeks believed that the monarchy was imposed by foreign powers in the nineteenth century and caused constant political divisiveness and turmoil, Karamanlis called for a referendum on its retention (December 1974). Seventy percent of the voters desired the monarchy's end. Karamanlis's government proclaimed Greece a liberal-democratic republic.

The Second Republic

The first seven years after the Colonels' demise under Prime Minister Karamanlis's (1974-80) guidance were remarkable for the smooth transition from military dictatorship to democracy. Karamanlis adapted to the state's post-junta political climate. Formerly an ultrarightist and staunch anti-Communist, during his republican stint in office he opened Greece's political system to all factions and legalized the Greek Communist party. His toleration of the left illustrated that the junta repression had blunted extreme civil war–era political animosities. He recognized a post-junta popular temperament less sympathetic to ultrarightist approaches and more willing to consider leftist political programs.

A new republican constitution was passed (1975) granting extensive presidential executive powers. Although the presidential office thereafter possessed potentially dominant state authority, the presidents—Constantine Tsatsos (1975-80), a conservative academic philosopher, Karamanlis himself (1980-85), and his presidential successor Christos Sartzetakis (1985-90), a supreme court judge—never chose to exercise the office's authority in a manner detrimental to other government institutions.

To consolidate democratic authority, former junta collaborators in all public sectors were purged and Karamanlis conducted televised trials of those responsible for the military junta's repressive activities (1975). The fact that the general population watched the proceedings on television and that those convicted were jailed made a lasting—and intended—impact. The trials were public warnings to every political faction that attempts to subvert the republic's liberal-democratic institutions would be punished to the full extent of the law.

Besides democratic consolidation, Karamanlis faced serious economic problems caused by the junta's irresponsible and wasteful financial policies. Efforts were made to exploit the oil discovered off of Greece's Aegean island Thasos, but the production of the government-run field never met expectations. Hopes persisted (and continue today) that Aegean oil would provide Greece with a significant oil reserve. To combat the rampant inflation that was part of the junta's economic legacy, the government, although ostensibly committed to a free market economy, nationalized numerous industries and banks and transformed a significant portion of Greece's population into state employees of one sort or another.

Karamanlis concentrated on winning Greece's fast-track acceptance into the emerging European Community (EC; later, Union [EU]). Greece had signed a treaty of association with that organization (1961) that provided for possible full admission in 1984. Karamanlis wished to accelerate the process, hoping that membership would bring economic benefits and provide much-needed international support for the state's troubled diplomatic position. An unspoken but pervasive motive was the assumption that official membership definitively would legitimize Greece's position as a "Western" European society. Despite EC concerns about Greece's economic abilities to withstand the competitive pressures of the Common Market, Karamanlis won the state's membership (January 1981) by exploiting the West's guilt over having done little to bring down the junta dictatorship.

The domestic attentions of the post-junta government were limited by the continuing national conflict with Turkey and its foreign relations problems. Republican Greece remained intensely nationalistic regarding Cyprus, the Aegean, and domestic ethnonational identity. As the United States and the Soviet Union embraced détente in the 1970s, fears of the common Communist menace lessened in Greece and Turkey and their mutual nationalist distrust reemerged. Their clashes over Aegean control and Cyprus, fueled by historical memories of real or imagined wrongs, proved contentious and long-lived.

Greek-Turkish disputes over oil rights, the extent of home coastal waters along their Aegean border, the (de-)militarization of Aegean islands, and air traffic control boundaries poisoned their relations. All involved military, economic, and ethnic issues perceived as crucial to their respective national well-being. The Cyprus problem, however, remained the most intense point of conflict. The Turkish force on Cyprus advanced from its northern beachhead and occupied 40 percent of the island (August 1974). Greece enjoyed little American support because of the Watergate debacle, while Britain, whose colonial policies originally created the Cyprus problem, refused to become involved.

The Cypriot Greeks fell into nationalist hysteria over the Turkish invasion, the displacement of 200,000 Greeks from the island's north, and the perceived favor of the United States for Turkey over themselves (and Greece). Their violent demonstrations culminated in the assassination of the U.S. ambassador to Cyprus. In Greece, nationalist sentiment held the United States accountable as the former junta's accomplice and for failing to restrain Turkey. In response to the emotional anti-American outbursts, Karamanlis questioned the future of American military bases in Greece and withdrew Greece from NATO's military wing. Although the immediate crisis over the Turkish invasion and occupation eventually was defused, Greek-Turkish antagonisms remained, further souring relations within NATO.

Hoping to gain support for Greece's nationalist position and improve relations with neighbors, Karamanlis reached out to the Balkan Communist states, with whom mutual relations were bad since the civil war. Although détente initiated a certain thaw in former hard-line attitudes on both sides, and a Balkan summit meeting was held in Athens (1976), Karamanlis's efforts had few concrete results. Greeks continued to distrust the "Slavs," and Greece's fortified northern borders with its Communist neighbors remained intact.

The nationalist fervor surrounding the junta, Cyprus, and the Aegean, and its ramifications for relations with the United States and NATO, highlighted the · problematic nature of the Greeks' dual sense of modern identity. On one hand, they made efforts to convince the West that they rightfully were charter members of its cultural tradition—their ancestors laid its foundations and they were its most direct heirs. On the other hand, they were the leaders of Orthodox Christendom's struggle against the Balkans' historical Turkish enemy as well as Byzantium's heirs of the "Slav menace." That the West seemed unwilling to support the Greeks' national cause against the "non-European" Turks and the "Eastern" Slavs raised questions about its reliability, which spawned a gnawing sense of insecurity concerning the "place" of Greece in Western Europe. Relations with the United States, NATO, and the EC acquired symbolic significance for post–World War II Greek national and cultural identity.

A political movement playing to growing national frustrations and insecurities emerged under the tolerant policies of Karamanlis. Andreas Papandreou wedded together leftist and anti-junta resistance groups into the Panhellenic Socialist Movement (PASOK) political party. By tying nationalism to socialist rhetoric, PASOK won increasing membership and a growing presence in parliament during Karamanlis's tenure as prime minister. While touting the party slogan of "National independence, popular sovereignty, social liberation, and democratic structures," Papandreou called for military measures against Turkey, resistance to Greece's entry into the EC, Greece's precipitate withdrawal from NATO, and the closing of American military bases in Greece. PASOK's positions were backed by the first truly statewide, highly organized political structure that was unmatched by any other party. Finally PASOK won outright parliamentary victory (1981), displacing Karamanlis's rightists (he himself now served as president) and installing Papandreou as prime minister (1981-89).

PASOK broadened its general appeal by moderating its original radicalism and moving closer to the center. Papandreou dropped his anti-EC stance and did not oppose Greece's official entry into the EC. Regarding NATO, he declared that withdrawal was a "strategic objective" dependent on future international develop-ments. U.S. military bases in Greece became a matter of negotiation rather than outright unilateral closing. To reassure centrists of PASOK's moderation, the governing cabinet included a noted leader of their party.

Papandreou remained committed to social reforms and guaranteeing Greece's sovereign independence. He issued a "Contract with the People" outlining his proposed reforms, ranging from eliminating urban smog to "objective" instruction of history in schools. "Change" became the new PASOK slogan, which captured significant numbers of young voters. Among the initiatives introduced were: Permitting ethnically Greek Communist civil war émigrés (Macedonian Slavs excluded) to return; ending official ceremonies celebrating the Communists' civil war defeat; simplifying the writing system; instituting civil marriage and divorce by consent (against stiff Orthodox church opposition); decriminalizing adultery; and abolishing wedding dowries. Women gained increased legal rights, universities were reorganized, and provincial cultural life was encouraged. Administrative decentral-ization was attempted but failed because local authorities had no means to raise revenues. A national health service with rural medical facilities was implemented. Fundamental socialist economic reforms, however, were few and made no appre-ciable headway, although EC membership brought significant agricultural subsidies.

PASOK did not moderate its original nationalist approach. Although its rhetoric failed to translate into action, PASOK's style of foreign relations was maverick. Its emphasis on national pride was out of step with other NATO and EC states. Papandreou refused to join the sanctions against the Polish military regime (1980), criticized Israel's invasion of Lebanon (1982), and supported Yasser Arafat's Palestinian movement. He championed a nuclear-free zone in the Balkans and opposed NATO's deployment of cruise and Pershing missiles in Europe. When Greece held the EC presidency (1983), it stifled criticism of the Soviets' downing of a Korean Airlines jet. Greek-U.S. relations were strained further when it was alleged that PASOK tolerated Arab terrorists operating out of Athens and refused to suppress native Greek terrorist activities.

Nationalist antagonisms with Turkey dictated PASOK's foreign relations and defense policies. Papandreou, intransigently anti-Turkish, publicly expressed his confrontational emotions in a visit to Cyprus (1982), the first ever by a Greek prime minister, which contributed to the Turkish Cypriots' declaration of an independent Turkish Republic of Northern Cyprus (1983, formally recognized only by Turkey). PASOK issued a defense doctrine (1984) stating that Turkey, a NATO ally (and *not* the Warsaw Pact), constituted Greece's primary threat. Border incidents in Thrace (late 1986) and a Turkish oil-drilling attempt in disputed Aegean waters

(1987) resulted in a crisis that briefly threatened war, events for which Papandreou held NATO (particularly the United States) responsible.

In January 1988 a "no-war agreement" was signed by Greece and Turkey at Dravos, establishing a "hot line" between their two capitals, scheduling annual talks, calling for expanded tourist and cultural exchanges, and forming joint committees promoting closer relations. Despite a brief rapprochement, Greek-Turkish relations quickly degenerated. Accusations of Turkish violations of Greek airspace arose (late 1988), and the contentious Aegean issues resurfaced. In 1988 and 1989 cases of anti-Turk discrimination in Greek Western Thrace were documented (Greek authorities refused to recognize ethnic Turks, claiming that they were "Greek Muslims"), while the Greeks charged Turkey with supporting a Turkish ethnic political movement in Greek Thrace.

PASOK lost its parliamentary majority in June 1989 elections. The state's economy underwent a downturn, and the formerly disunited right jettisoned most ultrarightists and formed a new, consolidated party led by Constantine Mitsotakis. A temporary conservative-Communist coalition government was followed by an ineffective all-party "ecumenical" government. Finally Mitsotakis's moderate and unified rightist party won an electoral majority (April 1990), and Constantine Karamanlis again was elected president. Greece's central government thus was weak when the events of 1989 to 1991 in the Communist world unfolded. The dissolution of Yugoslavia (1991-92) and the proclamation of an independent Macedonian state (1991) raised the traditional specter of the "Slav" threat to Greek Macedonia and ignited an ongoing emotional nationalist reaction.

CHAPTER NINETEEN

Splits in Socialism

Until the Warsaw Pact's founding (1955), Cominform was the heart of the Soviet "bloc," ensuring conformity with Soviet ideological, political, economic, and social models, and leading the West to view the European Communist states as a monolithic whole. Although the bloc concept provided westerners with a conveniently generalized approach for dealing with their Communist ideological enemies, it was, in fact, oversimplified, particularly with regard to the Balkan Communist states. Over the course of the cold war era, Yugoslavia, Albania, and Romania demonstrated marked divergences from the official Soviet position—the first two through formal breaks in their relationships with the Soviet Union and the latter by noticeable degree. Only Bulgaria consistently remained faithful to its pro-"Russian" traditions and loyally toed the Soviet line throughout.

Yugoslavia's "Different Road to Socialism"

No post–World War II non-Soviet Communist leader was as ideologically strident as Yugoslavia's Josip Tito. As Communists were pushed out of postwar Western European coalition governments and their socialist allies were bought off by American Marshall Plan dollars and investments, Tito was more outspoken than Stalin in attacking the United States and its aid package as threats to communism. He helped organize Cominform as a bulwark against the American-led "bourgeois" West and provided it with one of its most critical policy platforms—Communist control of Soviet-"friendly" states based on strength "from below," meaning Communist armed muscle used to eliminate traditional political parties in postwar front governments. Tito's concept of consolidating Communist authoritarian control through force was embraced by Stalin and became official Cominform policy

(1947). The Soviet leader designated the Yugoslav capital, Belgrade, Cominform's headquarters and gave the Yugoslav Communists responsibility for publishing its official mouthpiece journal.

Flattered by Stalin's overt favor and proud of his own successful partisan achievements, Tito's somewhat inflated self-image rapidly led to misunderstandings with the Soviets. He was convinced that Stalin wished him to lead an active anti-Western revolutionary offensive. Stalin's seeming endorsement of founding a Communist Balkan federation and his permission for Yugoslavia to increase its assistance to the Greek Communists in the Greek Civil War appeared to permit Tito independent action in conducting foreign policy. Tito persuaded his Communist neighbors (late 1947) to follow his lead in structuring their front governments "from below" by mobilizing disciplined, mass Communist organizations. Through a series of treaties with Albania, Bulgaria, and Romania, he created a Balkan Communist customs union as the first step toward an actual federation.

After Tito expanded his commitment to the Greek Communists (January 1948) and stationed Yugoslav support troops in Albania without first requesting Soviet permission, Stalin grew concerned. He had no desire for a Tito-led Balkan federation pursuing an independent foreign policy, and he feared that Tito would undertake adventurous anti-Western foreign initiatives counter to Soviet interests. When Stalin demanded that Tito seek his permission before taking foreign policy initiatives and that a Balkan federation be established in a way that guaranteed Soviet control, Tito, convinced that Stalin was compromising ideology and official Cominform policy for the Soviets' own sake, refused.

Stalin convened a Cominform meeting in Bucharest (June 1948) and had a resolution, symbolically dated 28 June (the anniversary of the medieval Kosovo battle and the Sarajevo assassination), passed condemning Tito and calling on the Yugoslav Communists to change either their policies or their government. In Belgrade, Tito denounced the Soviets.

Soviet reaction to Tito's defiance was swift. The Cominform states severed relations with Yugoslavia and purged all party members suspected of any associations with Tito (as well as all opposition elements, Communist or not, and anyone who voiced anti-Soviet criticisms). In Albania, Enver Hoxha threw off Yugoslav influence and control. Incidents erupted along Yugoslavia's borders with neighboring Cominform states, and border fortifications were erected. Tito and his followers were attacked in the media, while support was given to anti-Tito Yugoslav opposition groups operating abroad. Plans for Yugoslavia's dismemberment into small, independent Communist states were floated. Concerted Cominform pressures on Yugoslavia forced Tito to abandon his support for the Greek Communists and concentrate primarily on defending his independent position.

Isolated within the European Communist world, Tito had no option but to turn to the Western powers that he previously so vehemently reviled. While refusing to compromise his Marxist-Leninist tenets, he pragmatically sought Western assistance and opened diplomatic contacts with Britain and the United States. When Yugoslavia's agriculture was threatened by drought (1950), the Americans furnished millions of dollars in assistance, offered military aid, and opened further financial assistance for Yugoslavia from Western international banks. Tito signed friendship and cooperation pacts with Greece and Turkey (1953), which evolved into a mutual defense agreement (1954), and settled the ongoing dispute over Trieste with Italy (1954). By the 1960s the United States, once a hated ideological enemy, was one of Communist Yugoslavia's largest sources of foreign aid, and Yugoslavia was dependent on non-Communist Western military and economic support.

While shoring up Communist Yugoslavia through Western support, Tito strengthened his domestic position. He attempted to demonstrate that a state could embrace communism without relinquishing its unique national identity and independence by aping Soviet models. Yugoslavia's condemnation by Cominform contained specific allegations of non-Communist developments that Tito immediately sought to refute. Accusations that Tito's party operated "illegally" were addressed by holding a Communist party congress (1948), at which elections were held for all executive offices. To counter charges that Tito had not collectivized agriculture, a statewide collectivization program was initiated (1949). Cominform's claim that Tito exaggerated his partisan movement's importance (a subject with nationalist overtones) was defused by a propaganda blitz glorifying the partisans.

Besides reacting against Cominform's list of "deviations" from the Soviet line, the Yugoslav Communists reconsidered their guiding socialist principles. They concluded that Stalin was the actual "deviationist" while they were the "true" Marxists-Leninists, arguing that the Soviet Union represented "state capitalism" and not communism. The Yugoslav Communists quickly produced a counter-Soviet doctrine (January 1950): Worker self-management in all economic sectors would lead to improved productivity and, ultimately, the Marxist goal of the "withering away" of the authoritarian party-led state.

Yugoslav industrial workers elected councils that were made responsible for running their respective plants, including determining product prices, work hours, and working conditions. Workers' incentives, such as profit sharing, were introduced, and competition among factories was instituted to elevate product quality and help control prices. Declaring that the monstrous Soviet-style central planning bureaucracy stood in the way of socialist development (1951), the Yugoslav Communists progressively decentralized the planning process, granting the workers' councils control of their enterprise funds and freedom to make investment decisions (1952). Worker self-management was officially proclaimed to constitute "true" Marxist socialism, and the party's name was changed to the League of Communists to reflect that truth (late 1952). In 1953 agricultural collectivization was abandoned, permitting peasants to work the land on their own.

A significant shift in the notion of the Communists' role in society occurred. While the party retained its dictatorial political control, it no longer was inseparable from the economic structure. Thus emerged the "mixed" socialist-capitalist system associated with Tito's Yugoslavia. Theoretically, the party's role was to guide and organize society by providing the ideological and educational framework through its continued political authority. Just how that was to be accomplished was a matter of heated debate within the party. Tito and his Foreign Minister Edvard Kardelj wished to preserve the party's voice in economic decisions while party leader Milovan Djilas sought to dismantle totally the party's bureaucracy and ultimately create an elected, worker-run central governing assembly.

Stalin's death (March 1953) and the consequent rise of Nikita Khrushchev (1953-64) influenced Yugoslav developments regarding the nature of Communist party rule. Khrushchev proposed restoring diplomatic relations with Yugoslavia (June 1953). Tito, concerned that the workers' councils might render economic decision making incoherent, used the Soviet opening to brake radical party reform. Djilas rejected Tito's decision and proclaimed the Communist party obsolete, attacking the party bureaucracy and calling for more radical decentralization to eliminate the party and create a workers' assembly. Tito then expelled Djilas from the party (January 1954), protesting that he sympathized with the withering-away concept but was not prepared to dismantle the party until all of socialism's potential "enemies" were eliminated. Thereafter, Communists would not interfere in industrial management but would guarantee that all industries followed general policies laid down by the party's leadership in Belgrade. Thus Yugoslavia's "mixed" economy remained a command one, despite apparent decentralization and flexibility. As for the party's continued authoritarian power, Tito never seriously questioned the issue.

Khrushchev's anti-Stalinism wrought changes in the Soviet Union and in relations among the European Communist states, making a Yugoslav-Soviet rapprochement possible. While he did not repudiate the ideological reasons for Yugoslavia's expulsion from Cominform, Khrushchev admitted that Stalin's treatment of Yugoslavia had been in error. He canceled Yugoslavia's old Soviet debts and granted it aid without the high interest rates charged by the West. As part of Khrushchev's official de-Stalinization policy (introduced at the Soviets' Twentieth Party Congress [1956]), it was announced that "different roads" to socialism were possible and that all Communist states need not blindly follow the Soviet model. Soon afterward Cominform was disbanded. Tito and the Yugoslav Communists felt validated: The Soviets, not they, had been forced to change their policies.

The Soviets' newly proclaimed tolerance for different roads to socialism proved ambiguous and limited. While Khrushchev clearly had Yugoslavia in mind when he announced the new policy, he never intended to permit any other European Communist state to follow its lead literally. In a cold war that showed little sign of ending, the Soviets continued to need their "friendly" anti-West buffer zone.

In October and November 1956 Communist Poland and Hungary were taught the realities of Khrushchev's toleration of any real divergences from Soviet interests à la Yugoslavia among the Warsaw Pact states. In Poland, the mere threat of Soviet military intervention dampened moves by its anti-Stalinist leadership to allow greater internal political and cultural freedoms and open academic exchanges with the United States. In Hungary, however, the Yugoslav example inspired an anti-Soviet revolutionary effort by reform-minded, anti-Stalinist Hungarian Communists to gain national independence. They were crushed violently by Red Army forces after Khrushchev and Tito met and hammered out a joint agreement on ending their attempt to create a completely independent Communist Hungary. Immediate post–World War II circumstances had permitted Yugoslavia to establish its independence from the Soviet Union without Soviet intervention; a decade into the cold war, it was too late for most other European Communist states to be as fortunate.

Despite reestablished Yugoslav-Soviet relations, Yugoslavia remained outside of the Soviet camp, an independent and influential member of the Communist community of states but tied definitively to neither side in the cold war. Tito maintained a delicate balancing act between the West and the Soviet bloc to preserve that position. He had no intentions of relinquishing Communist control within Yugoslavia, but he sought to maintain American military and economic aid, which helped his state retain independent action on the international stage. To strengthen Yugoslavia's international position outside of the cold war alignments, Tito espoused the concept of a third, "nonaligned" bloc of states (1955). Chiefly comprised of Yugoslavia, India, Egypt, Indonesia, and other "third world," "underdeveloped" states, the nonaligned bloc potentially served as a "neutralist" counterweight to the cold war alliances, positioned to accept assistance from both. With Egypt's President Gamal Abdel Nasser (1956-67) and India's Prime Minister Jawaharlal Nehru (1947-64), Tito emerged as a leading figure in the nonaligned movement and spent much time and effort traveling to promote its interests, hoping to enlist new Asian and African state members. The attempt to form a globally united nonaligned front constituting a real alternative force in world affairs never panned out as hoped, but it bestowed much international prestige on Tito and kept assistance from both the "capitalist" West and the Soviet "East" flowing into "neutral" Communist Yugoslavia.

Albania: Stalinism, Maoism, and Isolation

Enver Hoxha's post–World War II Communist Albania existed as a satellite of Tito's Yugoslavia. So completely had Yugoslav partisans dominated the Albanian resistance movement, and so closely was Albania politically and economically tied to Yugoslavia in the immediate postwar years, that Albania initially was not given its own place within Cominform. Hoxha's government essentially served as a regional administration for Tito, and Yugoslav credits accounted for over half of Albania's state income. The Albanian Communists fervently adhered to Tito's anti-Western and authoritarian ideological lines and enthusiastically cooperated with him in supporting the Greek Communists.

While the Albanian Communists embraced Marxist-Leninist internationalist precepts, their relationship with Yugoslavia threatened Albania's continued state sovereignty. Albania faced total absorption into an ethnically Slav state, which raised problems that had little to do with Marxist internationalism but a great deal to do with traditional ethnonational concerns. Aware of Albanian ethnic uniqueness and the Slavs' sorry record regarding Albanian civil and political rights in former Serbian, Montenegrin, and "Yugoslav" nation-states, they feared that foreign Italian domination would be replaced by equally foreign Slavic mastery. The Communist furor caused by the Tito-Stalin split offered a solution to their problem.

Joining the anti-Tito political offensive allowed the Albanians to break the Yugoslav hold. Hoxha became Stalin's most loyal ally and staged the first Cominform "anti-Titoist" political trial (May 1949). Albania's borders with Yugoslavia were closed and fortified. Stalin rewarded the Albanians' anti-Yugoslav stance with Soviet and Cominform aid and declared Albania crucial to his planned anti-Yugoslav Balkan federation. In return, the Albanian party adopted strict Stalinist authoritarian political and economic models.

With the post-Stalin Yugoslav-Soviet rapprochement, the Albanian Communists grew concerned that continued Albanian independence might be in jeopardy. Hoxha feared that Khrushchev might buy Yugoslav support for his new policies at Albania's expense. His apprehension grew as Soviet de-Stalinization progressed, while he resented Soviet plans to relegate Albania to the status of raw materials supplier—the lowest rank in the industrial order—for Comecon.

Prior to the 1956 Polish and Hungarian crises, Comecon accomplished little. Each member state was busy building its own economy and pursuing its own policies. After 1956, Khrushchev decided that Comecon should actively promote economic cooperation and unity among its members. Economic specialization and division of labor was introduced, and the Soviets proposed establishing a supranational agency for coordinating the members' industries (1962). According to the scheme, states already highly industrialized would specialize in existing industries while the others would concentrate on either agricultural or raw material production. A permanent developmental hierarchy would become institutionalized: Highly industrialized Czechoslovakia and East Germany would hold vested positions of superiority; Poland, Hungary, and Bulgaria would become designated breadbasket agricultural states with supplemental industry; and Romania and Albania would be relegated to lowly raw material suppliers to the others.

Ideologically Stalinist, Hoxha correctly viewed the new Soviet line as a direct threat to his authority and the continuation of his regime's control in Albania. It even threatened Albania's continued independent existence. For the first time since the Communists came to power, Albania publicly assumed an anti-Soviet stance. Hoxha, who lost faith in Khrushchev, cast about for an alternative ally. In 1960 he found one in Maoist China.

The Chinese (Sino)-Soviet conflict portended global implications for communism's future since China's leader Mao Zedong, who dominated Communist East Asia, commanded a following that outnumbered any European Communist movement. The Sino-Soviet rivalry was a blatant power struggle for Communist world leadership. Maoists claimed to be "purer" Marxists than the Soviets and, thus, more deserving of preeminence. They attacked Khrushchev's policy of "coexistence" with the West, his failure to militantly advance revolutionary global communism, and his "fear" of using nuclear weapons. Mao maintained that the Soviet Union had forfeited its right to lead the world Communist revolution. By 1960 it was clear that Communist China stood outside of the Soviet camp.

With the apprehension of the Albanian Communists growing over Soviet de-Stalinization, Hoxha won Chinese assistance (1956-57) and openly sided with the Maoists in their mounting attacks on the Soviets. He criticized the Soviets for failing to consult with him regarding their expanded relations with Yugoslavia and publicly adopted the Chinese position in the global Communist power struggle (November 1960). The Soviets immediately reacted by terminating economic aid to Albania and publishing anti-Albanian attacks in the media of all the European Communist states. Hoxha then signed a trade deal with China (February 1961) and publicly reiterated his party's new anti-Soviet, pro-Chinese line. Throughout 1961 the Soviets halted all of their operations in Albania. Khrushchev officially denounced the Albanian Communists and severed all diplomatic relations with Albania (December), leaving it unambiguously alone in the Chinese camp.

China and Albania shared a common attitude regarding Yugoslavia: They condemned its "neutralist" position and refused it recognition as a socialist state. Khrushchev's fall (1964) did nothing to improve Albanian-Soviet relations. Inspired by visits from China's Foreign Minister Chou En-lai, Hoxha launched his own Maoist "cultural revolution," complete with overwhelming propaganda campaigns and mass political and economic mobilizations. Red Guard units were formed. Intellectuals, teachers, and workers were denounced. Religion was attacked, and the few remaining private farms in the state were collectivized. After the Soviets invaded Czechoslovakia (1968), Albania left the Warsaw Pact. Geographically buried behind steadfastly "neutralist" Yugoslavia on the far western Balkan coast, Albania was invulnerable to direct Soviet or Warsaw Pact attack and escaped the fate of Cominform dissidents Hungary and Czechoslovakia.

Although Albania's alliance with China provided it with support against possible Yugoslav threats, China was too poor and too distant to furnish Albania with significant aid. The relationship of the two states essentially was symbolic rather than practical: Albania maintained its political and ideological independence while China won an opportunity to play a role in the Balkans and Europe. Albania, however, needed practical economic support. Somewhat ironically, the state's poverty and low living standard made it less dependent on foreign aid for survival than most other European states. Nevertheless, some outside support was needed. While accepting as much aid as China could spare, Hoxha also sought assistance from the non-Communist West (excluding his American ideological archenemies, whose pro-Greek stance demonstrated their anti-Albanian policy regarding Epiros). Once again, Italy assumed a primary role in Albanian commerce.

Isolated within the European Communist world, Albania's leaders institutionalized their pro-Chinese stance. A new constitution more blatantly authoritarian than the Stalinist document that it replaced was passed (1976): The Communist party gained sole right to political power, and the party's leader (Hoxha) became military commander-in-chief (a unique position in European Communist states). The constitution contained new socioeconomic initiatives, such as the abolition of all remaining private property and individual taxes, and drastic limitations on foreign investment. Economic policies became exaggeratedly Maoist. The existing agricultural household plots of the collective farm workers were reduced to minuscule legal size, and the private sale of produce from such plots was forbidden (1971). During the first half of the 1970s, Maoist-style industrial decentralization was attempted, with a number of plants placed under local rather than central administration, but by 1976 the trend reverted to centralization.

Albania's Chinese attachment came to an unhappy end, with Sino-Albanian relations turning sour soon after Mao's death (1976). China's expanding relations with the United States, the downfall of Mao's "Gang of Four" successors, and the welcome given Tito on a state visit to China (1977) roused the Albanian leadership's bitterness. They accused the Chinese of mimicking Khrushchev's "revisionism" (de-Stalinization) policy, blamed Chinese "experts" in Albania for alleged economic sabotage, and supported Vietnam in its war with Chinese-backed Cambodia. In response, China suspended aid to Albania (1978). Without an economic patron, Albania's economy slipped into decline. Economic output plummeted and Albania was forced to increase its foreign trade with Western partners (minus the United States), Yugoslavia, Greece, and Romania. Those commercial relations mostly consisted of trading surplus electrical power and minerals for items necessary to Albania's industrial sector, but such activities were conducted in deficit and funded by Western loans (despite the constitutional illegality of such actions). None of Albania's trading efforts prevented continued decline in its industrial and agricultural sectors.

European economic openings did not transfer to the international political arena. In 1979 Hoxha proclaimed that Albania was the only existing Communist state still faithful to Marxist-Leninist ideological principles—a stance that guaranteed continued icy relations with the rest of the Communist world. Albania forged no regional or global alliances and stringently controlled access to its borders. French, Greeks, Italians, Yugoslavs, and nationals of some smaller European states were eligible for entry, but those from the United States, the Soviet Union, and China expressly were excluded (except for limited diplomatic purposes). The isolationism of the Hoxha regime was so rigid that, after a major earthquake ravaged northern Albania (April 1979), no appeal was made for international relief.

By the 1980s Albania's isolationism, failing economy, and its leadership's stubborn, dogmatic hold on power had reduced the overall living standard to near-primitive levels. Albanians were permitted to own only a few major household appliances (which could be acquired only incrementally over time) from a government-approved list. Utilities rationing was set in place to ensure maximum foreign trade output. Although the capital Tiranë possessed wide modern boulevards (thanks to government-run urban renewal projects), only high party officials were allowed to own automobiles, and the streets lay mostly deserted. In many ways, Albania came to resemble more an isolated, almost primitive mountain society than a late-twentieth-century European state.

Maverick Romania

In the early days of the Yugoslav-Soviet controversy, Stalin considered Romania the only reliable "friendly" Communist state for initiating the Yugoslavs' formal expulsion from Cominform: Past Balkan federation negotiations with Tito compromised Bulgaria and Albania; Hungary and Czechoslovakia were too recent and untested Cominform members; and Poland expressed some displeasure with certain Cominform policies and overall Soviet control. Stalin turned to Romania's party leader Gheorge Gheorghiu-Dej to pronounce his anathema on the Yugoslavs at the 1948 Cominform meeting in Bucharest, where Cominform's headquarters were relocated. No anti-Tito purge trials commonly used to impose Soviet domination over Cominform member states occurred in Romania. There was no need. Soviet control began in Romania in 1945.

Gheorghiu-Dej replaced the non-Communist Prime Minister Petru Groza when the front government was dissolved (1953). By the end of the 1950s, Romanian society was Sovietized totally: Industries and financial institutions were nationalized; agriculture was collectivized; urbanization exploded; traditional political parties and all opposition were liquidated; and two Soviet-style constitutions were adopted (1948 and 1952). A series of show trials eliminated the remaining traditional political leadership. Forced labor on a Danube-Black Sea canal (begun 1949) further reduced political opposition.

The 1956 events in Poland and Hungary made a significant impact on the Romanian Communists, who used the crises to reassert Romania's national independence by moving toward a foreign policy semi-independent of the Soviets. At first, it appeared that Gheorghiu-Dej might join Tito and the Hungarians in bids to "reform" communism. He was in Belgrade when the Soviets invaded Hungary and issued a communiqué condemning one state "intervening" in another's internal affairs. Romania even provided the Hungarians' revolutionary Communist leader Imre Nagy temporary refuge after he was ousted from Hungary. Gheorghiu-Dej then requested the removal of all Soviet troops stationed in Romania because they no longer were needed to safeguard communications with Soviet forces in Austria (which had gained independence as a neutral state). After lengthy negotiations, the garrisons were withdrawn (1958), in exchange for the Romanians handing Nagy over to the Soviets for execution.

Romania was designated a raw materials supplier for the most industrialized member states of Comecon. The scheme angered the Romanians, who already were committed to developing their own heavy industry. By 1962 Romanian industrial production significantly had increased and Gheorghiu-Dej's industrialization policy appeared destined for success. The Romanian Communists opposed Comecon's planned revamping by making overt trade overtures to the West and adopting independent diplomatic positions. The Soviets accepted Romania's objections to a supranational controlling agency for Comecon, and the scheme was shelved (1963).

To ensure that Romania would not become totally dependent on the Soviet Union, Gheorghiu-Dej resumed diplomatic relations with breakaway Albania (1963) and opened negotiations with China and the West. A strong declaration regarding national independence was issued (1964), asserting that all Communist parties and states were equal in status and could not be ranked in a discriminatory fashion within Comecon. Gheorghiu-Dej cloaked his essentially nationalist stance in Marxist principles, arguing that industrialization was an absolute necessity for building a viable socialist society.

An important part of Soviet de-Stalinization was reform of Stalinist economic controls and political strictures. As the possibility of all-out war with the West receded, Khrushchev decided that the Communist states should concentrate on economic catch-up by making changes in economic policies. Romania, however, was slow to participate, and, when changes finally were initiated (late 1960s), they were merely formal. The Romanian Communists stubbornly refused to relinquish their iron grip on the economy and, more important, their authoritarian political power.

The Sino-Soviet split offered a new opportunity for increasing Romania's independence from the Soviets by developing its own brand of "nationalist communism." Politically and economically, Romania continued in Stalinist fashion, but pro-Soviet Marxist internationalism was displaced by a nationalist ideology that, while remaining socialist, espoused an independent foreign policy. After signifi-cantly reducing the Soviets' share of Romania's foreign trade, the Romanian Communists tried to "de-Russianize" the state, going so far as replacing Russian with Romanian names on city street signs. Opposition to the planned Comecon restructuring helped Romania reorient its foreign trade to such an extent that it largely became independent of the Soviets and Comecon.

By the mid-1960s Romania was disassociated from strict Soviet policy control. The Romanian Communists officially embraced traditional anti-Russian Romanian nationalism, although they could ill afford to do so blatantly. A veiled public expression of that stance was their publication (1964) of Karl Marx's *Notes on the Romanians,* which were highly critical of tsarist Russia's threats to Romania's independence. Romania's long and open Moldavian frontier with the Soviet Union, however, offered few natural lines of defense against Soviet attack, should the Romanian leadership's bent for nationalist independence grow too intemperate. Additionally, continued bad relations with Hungary over Transylvania and close Bulgarian-Soviet associations complicated Romania's nationalist policy efforts and rendered the state vulnerable to potential national enemies on all sides.

On Gheorghiu-Dej's death (1965), Nicolae Ceauşescu assumed control. He continued distancing Romania from the Soviets and reinforcing Communist authoritarian power through nationalism, which he took to the extreme. During his twenty-four-year "reign," Ceauşescu parleyed his position into a veritable Phanariote-like personal, feudal-style autocracy. Party rules were changed to permit him to hold multiple offices in both the party and the state (1967). All potential competitors were purged, and a nepotistic system for holding key government and party posts was instituted. Under the guise of outwardly worthy programs, Ceauşescu installed his wife, son, and numerous other relatives in positions of great power. With all internal opposition eliminated and the state's leadership reduced to sycophantic dependency, Ceauşescu ran Romania as a personal, *boier*-style feudal holding. Romania, overtly touting modern socialist principles, essentially reverted to Ottoman-era sociopolitical conditions. Often labeled "dynastic socialism," Ceauşescu's governing approach can just as well be characterized as "socialist Phanariotism."

Ceauşescu cemented his position by using nationalist symbols and rhetoric. He made a pointed public toast (1965) to the region of Bukovina (which lay in Soviet territory) and delivered a fiery speech against Soviet-bloc policy (1966), raising the nationalist specter of Romanian claims to Bessarabia (then the Soviet Republic of Moldova). A new constitution proclaimed Romania a "unitary (ethnically and territorially Romanian) state," in open contradiction of the Soviets' former description of Romania as a "multinational state." In Nero-esque fashion, Ceauşescu sometimes appeared on stage with actors portraying great Romanian national heroes, with whom he would have "personal encounters." Avant-garde and spiritualist poets formerly banned as "decadent" and "bourgeois" were rehabilitated as spokespersons of the "Romanian spirit." The number of historical publications touting the Romanians' nationalist claim to Daco-Roman origins (demonstrating the Romanians' historical "right" to possess Transylvania and Bessarabia) multiplied.

Ceauşescu applied his version of "nationalist communism" to Romania's administrative and demographic sectors. A provincial reorganization (1968) replaced the Stalinist structure with the traditional pre-Communist system. Non-Romanian ethnonational minorities, especially in Transylvania, came under increasing pressures to Romanianize. Although the Hungarian minority officially received some regional autonomy in 1952, their autonomous region was renamed Mureş Magyar province (1960) and placed under ethnic Romanian administration. Ceauşescu tried to dampen rising Hungarian opposition to Romanianization by creating two officially recognized Hungarian-majority counties (1968), but he ensured that their economic development was suppressed.

In the arena of foreign policy, Ceauşescu established diplomatic relations with West Germany, Israel, and the Vatican (1967), and he publicly supported Czechoslovakia's 1968 "Prague Spring" Communist reform efforts, visiting Prague and renewing a Romanian-Czechoslovakian friendship treaty (early August 1968). He refused to join the other Warsaw Pact states in condemning developments in Prague, declaring that they had no right to interfere in a sovereign state's internal affairs. Ceauşescu denounced the Soviets' invasion of Czechoslovakia (late August 1968) and placed Romania's military on alert against possible attack by the Soviet Union and its Bulgarian ally.

Throughout the 1970s' détente era, Romania bucked the trend taking place in other European Communist states, and the Communist party continually increased its authority, bringing national and local government totally under central control. The party itself grew synonymous with Ceauşescu, his family (especially his wife, Elena), and his dependent minions. While de-Stalinization in the other Warsaw Pact states denounced the "cult of personality," no so-called cult approached that surrounding Ceauşescu by the close of the 1970s. His sycophantic followers proclaimed him the leading Marxist thinker and the living embodiment of Romanian national independence. Monuments were erected to his glory and pretensions, the most grotesque of which was the leveling of entire districts (and numerous historical monuments) in Bucharest to build broad boulevards leading to a massively overblown official residence and government palace—supposedly in the name of socialist "public works." Surrounded by a vast, devoted security force and domestic spy network—the Securitate—Ceauşescu reigned as a Communist hospodar.

Any pretense at economic decentralization ended completely in the 1980s. Although there were institutional name changes in line with contemporary reform trends in other Communist states, they served as window dressing to hide the Ceauşescu-dominated party's increasingly centralized power. Ceauşescu's authoritarian presence permeated all of society. Attempting to stay ethnic Romanian population decline, he made abortion illegal (1984). Aware of religion's role in national consciousness, he intensified attacks on non-Romanian Catholics and Protestants (while squeezing the Orthodox on Marxist principle). The Danube–

Black Sea canal project (begun 1949; restarted 1973) finally was completed after much waste of lives, materials, and finances. (Its actual economic value was minimal.) Ceauşescu's obstruction of Romanians wishing to emigrate earned the ire of the United States, which revoked Romania's "most favored nation" status (1983). (America considered maverick Romania a useful potential cold war tool and encouraged its anti-Soviet stance through favorable trade and financial deals.)

Despite commercial and financial relations with the West, Romania's economy progressively declined under Ceauşescu. His refusal to decentralize, his retention of Stalinist agricultural collectivization, his stringent cost and price controls, and his economic microregulation led to worsening conditions. Ceauşescu resorted to extreme measures for heading off the decline. To maximize agricultural production and expand the industrial workforce, he passed a law (1974) "systematizing" the rural population—razing certain villages and transferring their inhabitants to new regions to concentrate the population. That law was implemented seriously only in 1988, when it was used to weaken the Transylvanian Hungarian minority by eradicating many of their villages and dispersing the inhabitants among ethnic Romanian populations in Moldavia and Wallachia.

By the end of the 1970s, Romania's economic decline had worsened. In 1980 growth was negative, and in late 1981 Romania requested that Western financial creditors reschedule its hard currency debt. Ceauşescu, fearing the prospects of Romania becoming financially dependent on the West, initiated typically extreme measures. In 1982 he announced his determination to settle Romania's foreign debt entirely by 1990. Draconian food, utilities, and fuel rationing was imposed on the general population, and the use of a host of common household appliances was banned. On a daily basis, Bucharest, once the "Paris of the Balkans," lay dark, semideserted, and lifeless by nightfall. Shortages of necessities were widespread and frequent, and unconfirmed rumors of desperate crimes (even of cannibalism) abounded. That such tales circulated widely and gained a certain credibility reflected the misery to which most Romanians were reduced by Ceauşescu's belt-tightening policy. Resentment and anger toward the Ceauşescu regime percolated throughout the 1980s, intensified by the blatant luxury in which Ceauşescu, his family, and their close Communist associates lived.

CHAPTER TWENTY

Communist Decline and Collapse

Communists portrayed their success in acquiring state power as the inevitable victorious outcome of the ultimate class struggle—that of society's worker majority over its bourgeois capitalist elite—which would lead to history's crowning goal: A totally egalitarian workers' society. To construct that "workers' paradise," the Communists (the workers' "true" representatives) asserted the need for their "temporary" dictatorial state authority to eradicate the vestiges of inequitable capitalism and lay the fundamental framework for future egalitarianism. Thus they claimed absolute authoritarian control over all aspects of society to ensure "proper" development. Central to the Communists' totalitarian governing responsibilities was economic planning, since economics determined all of society's institutions. Their eventual failure to "scientifically" plot every aspect of economic activity gave the lie to their pretensions as bearers of absolute historical human "truth." Rather than advance the human condition in their societies, they crippled it, becoming the poster children for Western Europe's flawed cultural pretense of "scientific" superiority. The Balkan Communists' failures facilitated the reemergence of an older, more deeply rooted Western European cultural phenomenon—nation-state nationalism.

Stalinism and De-Stalinization

Prior to Stalin's death, the Balkan Communist states adopted the Soviet Union's Stalinist model: The Communist party held absolute power; state institutions virtually were indistinguishable from the party's (despite a constitutional veneer);

industry, finance, and media were nationalized; agriculture mostly was collectivized; opposition was suppressed; and educational and cultural activities were either ideologized or marginalized. Although Communist society's actual model changed with Soviet de-Stalinization, the ideological foundations did not. De-Stalinization and succeeding Communist reform efforts failed to achieve the economic realities necessary for fulfilling the ideological promise.

No matter whether Soviet, Titoist, or Maoist, Communist regimes emphasized central economic planning as crucial for shaping the Marxist future. Therein lay their Achilles' heel. Although central economic planning aspired to balanced economic growth, the very nature of such planning made balance impossible. The preference for industrial development distorted the overall economy since nonindustrial sectors received fewer resources.

Central planning possessed innate problems. For it to succeed, the planners needed absolute command of all economic factors and immediate access to all information regarding changes in those factors to make timely modifications in the plan. Such omniscience was impossible to attain, resulting in imprecision and product aggregation, at best, and wholesale shortages and wasted production, at worst. Communist leaders were aware of the discrepancy between planning theory and reality. They hid that fact from the party's cadres and general population, hoping that expedient measures would surmount consequent economic drawbacks and prevent questioning of their continued dominance. Communist central planners never mastered every economic factor, and administering the multitudinous details involved in their efforts to do so devolved into a complex bureaucratic quagmire.

Contentions that the Communist party was the workers' sole representative, arbiter of economic value, and architect for the socialist future through totalitarian control intensified the inherent problems of central planning. The party's hierarchical structure engendered among its members a Confucian-like obedience to superiors. Orders issued by the planners at the top percolated down through the multifarious bureaucratic levels, where those involved were concerned only with obeying their immediate superiors. The entire system was predicated on unquestioning subordination, little autonomy, and minimal responsibility.

The multiplicity of bureaucratic divisions and subdivisions resulting from constant micromanaging refinements in the central plan created a disjointed web of isolated administrative command chains. Often one ministry or office had no concrete idea of what the others were doing. New administrations created to handle specific planning refinements commonly assumed responsibilities formerly held by other offices. As bureaucratic administrations multiplied, the lines of authority stretching to the top of the hierarchy grew confused. The lack of administrative integration in Communist central planning, coupled with blind bureaucratic subordination, led to a proliferation of uncoordinated economic efforts and surreal disconnections in practical administration. Commonsense economic relationships that non-Communist societies took for granted frequently were absent in the Communist planned economic structure for ideological or bureaucratic reasons.

A basic aspect of centrally planned economies—shortages of goods—emerged in every Communist state. Because the planners mostly dealt in general product categories (shoes, coats, vegetables, and such) without specifying precise types, those types easiest to produce usually were made, without regard for cost or consumer demand. As a result, some product types were readily available while others of the same category were scarce. The central planners responded to such situations by breaking general product categories into more precisely defined classifications and setting new output targets for each, which made planning more cumbersome and further multiplied bureaucratic administration.

Another factor contributing to inherent shortages and innate economic waste was the emphasis on gross output with no real attention to costs. Their precepts grounded in the Marxist rejection of market value principles, and adhering only to concepts of social need, Communist planners generally ignored cost-effective manufacturing. Moreover, the planners' inability to develop an economic calculus that realistically accounted for production labor time led to resource waste and arbitrary product prices that had no economic relationship to manufacturing costs.

Compounding the inherent factors contributing to shortages were others that came with the Soviet planning model. The emphasis on investment to force rapid economic growth ensured that industry received the lion's share of available resources at the expense of other economic sectors. The Soviet industrialization model emphasized heavy industry, so production of capital goods received precedence over consumer items.

Planning's shortcomings and shortages were readily apparent. Domestically produced products were cheap to buy but of uneven quality and availability. Foreign-made products were limited in availability or completely unavailable and expensive to purchase. Persistent shortages of most mundane items made queueing at stores and markets a way of life. Not surprisingly, many individuals resorted to alternative means for acquiring needed or desired goods. On-the-job thefts became common, bribery and corruption thrived, and the black market flourished as a way to fill the product shortages created by the planning process.

Despite the flawed nature of planning, the Balkan Communist regimes were determined that their supreme sociopolitical positions enjoyed overt legality. They all issued new Soviet-style constitutions referring to the Communist party's "leading role." All except Yugoslavia (which had a federal structure) established a unicameral legislative body dominated by the Communist party. When that body was not in session (which was most of the time), its tasks were undertaken either by a presidium council or a council of state (in Bulgaria and Romania) appointed by the legislature. The councils of state (directly) and the presidiums (indirectly) issued legally binding decrees. In federated Yugoslavia, the government was an executive council appointed by the federal legislature. The heads of state also were selected by the legislatures. Bulgaria and Albania followed the example of the non-Balkan Communist states in having a collective presidency that included the presidium or state council, with that body's leader serving as its personification. In Yugoslavia, special arrangements were made to ensure that Tito alone held the presidency, and in Romania, a special presidential office was created for Ceauşescu (1974).

Judicial authority rested in supreme courts and prosecutors general appointed by the legislatures or the state councils (in Bulgaria and Romania). Constitutional interpretation was left to legislatures or state councils, but Yugoslavia created a constitutional court (1963) to oversee conformity between the laws of its republics and the federal constitution.

The legislatures were elected undemocratically from lists presented by the Communists and subject to few checks and balances. True power resided in the Communist party, whose members controlled the legislatures and whose leaders held all high government posts (in direct coordination with their party positions). Only Bulgaria retained the vestiges of a multiparty political system. The Bulgarian Agrarian Union party served as a Communist electoral and social umbrella, but its actual governing role was slight—helping select legislative candidates to ensure Communist majorities and fronting social organizations to spread Communist indoctrination and propaganda.

The Communists attempted to cement their dominance through ideological cultural efforts, seeking to replace traditional cultural values with those stemming from Marxism-Leninism, particularly internationalism and materialism in place of nationalism and religion. Social relations were reduced to Communist principles holding that the common ownership of the economic "means of production" automatically guaranteed equality. Communist regimes therefore systematically destroyed most pre-Communist social organizations and instituted replacement associations (such as youth groups, women's organizations, and industrial trade unions), which they carefully and fully supervised.

Marxist ideological principles of internationalism were advanced by empha-sizing peace and social harmony. Official peace movements and organizations representing ethnic minority interests were created. Early on, "eternal" friendship with the Soviet Union played a role in the internationalist push, but eventually Yugoslavia, Albania, and Romania dropped that tack. Only Bulgaria continued to include the Soviet Union in its internationalist efforts and promoted friendship with the Soviets.

Marxist materialism was expressed through official atheism and hostility toward religion. Religion was considered "the opiate of the people," embraced by former bourgeois ruling elites as a mechanism to prevent workers from realizing their class subordination. The Communists took a systems approach in attacking religion, believing (mistakenly) that, once the class system served by religion was eradicated and all religious content was removed from education, religious beliefs would die out. Until that occurred, churches officially were nationalized, depoliticized, and, aping the historical example of Russia's Peter the Great, placed under government-run ministries—"synods." Official clergy associations, resembling trade unions, were used to subordinate religious conduct.

Only in Albania (during its Maoist period) and Romania (where Transylvanian Uniates were attacked) were churches banned outright. Churches, however, were forbidden to conduct political activity or offer religious instruction in state schools. The level of religious restrictions depended on relations with the West at any given time, and strictures tightened or loosened with the ebb and flow of cold war events. Instead of suppressing religion completely, the Communists subordinated and marginalized it while actively discouraging the populations' continued religious beliefs. Unless particular churches and monasteries were deemed "culturally" important, the Communists provided few resources for their upkeep. Believers could attend religious services and perform other religious rituals so long as they did not involve proselytizing or political expression.

Marxist materialism also was expressed through dogged conviction that all social inequity was class-based. It was thought that, by eliminating private economic property and instituting programs of state-run, generally universal health and social welfare, inequity would be eradicated. The Communist regimes developed extensive insurance-based health and social welfare schemes, and rights to health and work constitutionally were protected.

The benefits of Communist insurance-based health and welfare systems were distributed unevenly. Their administration was left to official trade unions, since both were viewed as work-related issues, and work was obligatory in Communist society. Peasants working on noncollective farms and artisans working in small handicraft sectors were not members of official trade unions and thus not necessarily covered by the programs. Benefits were higher for industrial workers than for those working on collectives. In Romania, collectivized farmers were forced to pay for health and welfare insurance. In contrast, Bulgaria operated social benefits systems covering the entire population.

The Communist regimes introduced universal free education. Curricula, while providing instruction in most traditional disciplines, was amended to include Marxist history and introduced the new "science" of dialectical materialism. Topics and disciplines that conflicted with either were eliminated.

The Communists assumed that all social problems automatically would be solved as their approaches took hold. No Communist state espoused an "official" social policy, since doing so would have been tantamount to an admission of flawed ideology. It was presumed that problems concerning such issues as women's and minority rights would be corrected by the complete integration of women and minorities into the workforce. No mass organizations founded to represent such interest groups were involved in shaping social policy for their constituencies.

In the end, the populations of the Communist states took the educational, health, and social welfare services offered them for granted, despite their often suboptimal functioning. For decades, they also regarded overall living conditions in much the same way. They grew content to have jobs, housing, public utilities, and other modern social amenities, even though they were forced to tolerate the Communists' overweening presence, political and personal restrictions, consumer goods shortages, and a gamut of social inequalities.

The Yugoslav Communists were the first to see that blind adherence to the Stalinist model might not fit conditions outside of the Soviet Union and to address the innate problems of party domination and central planning. Djilas's realization that ideological rigidity and planning bureaucratic complexity crippled economic performance potentially was revolutionary. His attempts to decentralize the planning process by giving enterprises more production authority and permission to take market values into account provided flexibility and the possibility for improved economic performance, greater product variety and availability, and more realistic prices. If taken to its logical conclusion, however, Djilas's approach questioned the need for the Communist party's continued absolute control. Tito and other party leaders soon realized the implications and halted Djilas's reforms in mid-process. Thereafter, the Yugoslav ("Titoist") Communist system remained a hybrid of continued party domination and central planning with decentralized economic input. All succeeding Yugoslav reforms aimed at refining and preserving the "mixed" approach.

Changes crept into the systems of the other Balkan Communist states in the 1960s. Stalin's death and the Sino-Soviet split created uncertainties about the Stalinist model's validity. Khrushchev's de-Stalinization demonstrated that ideologically acceptable modifications to rigid Stalinist structures were possible.

Decentralization became a catchword of de-Stalinization. Planning priorities were reordered by reducing investments in heavy industry and increasing those in agriculture, consumer goods, and services. An attempt was made to simplify the monstrous planning bureaucracy. Structures resembling the Yugoslav model were created, with formally autonomous enterprises amalgamated into large administrative units ("associations") representing product categories and responsible directly to appropriate governing ministries. The new organization eliminated entire levels of the old bureaucratic pyramid, reduced the number of separate planning bureaucracies, and simplified the planning process. Instituted in the 1960s, associations remained the standard for central planning until the system's demise. All subsequent reforms were attempts to refine it further. Although such reforms tinkered with changes in the associations, the economic structure essentially remained based on ideology and not the market (except in Yugoslavia). While bureaucratic simplification and the limited operational autonomy of the associations reduced the party's overt presence, its lock on sociopolitical control was in no way compromised.

All of the Balkan Communist states initiated economic reforms in the 1960s, but only Bulgaria and Romania followed the Soviet de-Stalinization model. Albania moved firmly into the Maoist Chinese camp, while Yugoslavia dealt with its own Titoist system.

Bulgaria's economy grew rapidly during the Stalinist period and was still expanding when de-Stalinization began. Thus the Bulgarian Communists had few incentives for instituting reforms. Until the inevitable economic decline associated with central planning set in during the 1970s, the Bulgarians spoke a great deal about reform, and went through the outward motions, but did little concrete. As the economy slipped in the 1970s and 1980s, however, some actual reforms were initiated, such as abolishing agricultural collectives (1977) and relaxing controls on banking (1981-82); still, actual change was insignificant.

In the cultural sphere during the 1960s and 1970s, Bulgaria's leader Todor Zhivkov somewhat relaxed ideological restrictions on literature and art (two fields in which he took a paternalistic interest). While officially committed to preserving socialist realism in the arts through the Committee for Culture (headed in the 1970s by his unorthodox, eccentric daughter Lyudmila Zhivkova), Zhivkov permitted a limited number of previously prohibited works to appear. Zhivkova herself encouraged artistic experimentation and the cultural reassertion of Bulgarian national identity.

Romania, leery of copying things Soviet, initiated no meaningful reforms of its Stalinist system during the 1960s. "Associations" were introduced (1969) as mere formalities, serving only to reduce the bloated bureaucratic tangle. Unlike other Balkan states, in which de-Stalinization partially reduced the political and social presence of the Communist party, Ceauşescu's Romania took the opposite tack, increasing overt party domination and tightening security on the population (which helps explain why Romania alone experienced a bloody popular revolution when Balkan communism collapsed in 1989).

In Albania, reform took on a Maoist approach rather than a Soviet one. Albania's Stalinist planning process did not create a well-working economy. Agricultural output and industrial production fell far short of their planned targets by the early 1960s. After siding with the Chinese (1960), the Albanian Communists tried to secure planning fulfillment through Maoist-like mass mobilizations and propaganda. Although "worker control" frequently was touted, it possessed little real substance. Albanian planners, however, reduced the number of their output targets and trimmed the administrative bureaucracy (significantly, one of the offices cut was that of statistical services) during the 1970s.

Only Yugoslavia's Titoist system undertook reforms beyond modifying planning priorities and bureaucracy to address the market's role in the economy. Djilas's reforms eliminated command planning and introduced market considerations at the enterprise levels. While financing, investment, and foreign trade remained in the central authorities' hands, enterprises enjoyed a modicum of self-investment. In the reform environment of the post-Stalin Communist world, Yugoslavia's leaders pushed their unique system further.

In 1965 new reforms expanded economic decentralization. Banks became actual commercial institutions, capable of making investments and extending credits. Workers' councils appointed managers and set wage rates with reduced party influence. Prices were liberalized; a sales tax was introduced; tariffs were reduced; and import restrictions were lifted. Self-managing enterprises enjoyed increased decision making and financial independence, becoming the closest things to authentic worker ownership of the "means of production" in the Communist world.

Communist Yugoslavia, however, had problems. Economic decentralization threatened to lessen the party's supremacy, something that "old guard" Communists could not accept. Student demonstrations in Belgrade (1968), inspired by events in France, united die-hard Communist opponents of further reforms around the Praxis Group, which criticized social and economic reforms throughout the 1960s and into the 1970s. A relaxation of party control over cultural and intellectual affairs accompanied economic reforms, allowing the Praxis conservatives to express their opinions openly and providing similar opportunities for those espousing nationalist views (which, within a multinational state with a strained domestic nationalist past, potentially was dangerous). By the early 1970s Tito was forced to reestablish party "discipline" over intellectual and cultural expression.

Despite its unique economic system, Yugoslavia's economy did not outperform those of more centrally controlled Communist states during the 1970s. In fact, it did worse—rapidly degenerating into inflation, overinvestment, and debt. Enterprise workers, who nominally "owned" their operations, received unrealistic pay raises. Increased labor costs were covered through loans from banks that were assumed permanently solvent because of state ownership. By the 1970s pay increases outstripped gross national income, while enterprise indebtedness mushroomed beyond control. Worker strikes over pay proliferated. The net result was burgeoning inflation and domestic debt, exacerbated by a series of unprofitably large investments in unworkable projects that were funded through foreign loans, which exploded the state's foreign debt to dangerous proportions.

By the mid-1980s the economy of every Balkan Communist state had declined to the point of stagnation. Although outright economic ruin was avoided through de-Stalinization reforms, the Communists rarely moved beyond fiddling with the source of their problems—the ideological commitment to the planning process itself. Only the Yugoslavs made fundamental changes by "mixing" capitalist with Marxist values, and their economic failure was more spectacular for the effort. They ended up with much the same situation as their traditional Marxist neighbors—

stagnant economic growth—but outstripped them in two areas—rampant inflation and enormous debt.

Persistent Nationalism

Marxism theoretically rejected nationalism, branding it a vehicle for preserving the social dominance of bourgeois elites by preventing worker majorities from realizing the "truths" of universal economic class (not ethnic or national) identity and class struggle (not nation-state rivalries). Such "internationalism" was modified by Leninism, which, though touting universal Communist revolution, was forced to deal with establishing Marxism in a single state (Russia/Soviet Union). Stalinism elevated nationalist concepts within Marxism-Leninism by giving priority to "consolidating" communism in the single state over concerns for universal revolution. Stalin himself took the opportunity handed him at World War II's end to spread communism to Eastern European states, but did so for Soviet "national interests." The "friendly" Communist state buffer regimes all adopted his "single-state" approach (they retained their individual national identities and, generally, their pre-Communist national borders), and the institutions founded to coordinate their affairs with Soviet interests (Cominform, Comecon, and the Warsaw Pact) all preserved the separate "state" concept. Thus cold war–era Marxist-Leninist internationalism primarily was expressed through traditional national structures. (See Map 12.)

When Stalin imposed Communist regimes on his "friendly" satellite buffer states, the Communists could draw on only twenty-five years of prior Soviet efforts to completely transform traditional society in line with their ideological views. By that time, however, nationalist precepts were ingrained among those states' populations by over 150 years of direct development. That situation largely accounted for the claim by all Communist state leaders (including the Soviets) that communism was in the "process of building" the inevitable universal egalitarian workers' society, rather than representing that condition as accomplished simply because of their sociopolitical control. Despite their autocratic, totalitarian endeavors, however, they "built" on ideological sand, and their socioeconomic structures collapsed before traditional national concepts were eradicated by their efforts.

Nowhere in the post–World War II Communist world had nationalism played such a powerful and continuous role in prewar political culture than in the Balkans. Nor was there a region within the European Communist world more ethnonationally diverse with such virulently deep-seated national rivalries and animosities. Shortly after the Communists took over Yugoslavia, Bulgaria, Romania, and Albania, they attempted to suppress nationalism's public vestiges, changing the names of numerous public places, buildings, institutions, streets, and monuments from those honoring past national heroes, events, and institutions to ones commemorating native socialist or Soviet exemplars. (Even the official spelling of Romania briefly was changed to "Rominia" to hide its Western, Latin origins.) Traditional national holidays were replaced by socialist or Soviet celebrations. National symbols were modified by adding socialist motifs. Wholesale borrowings of things Soviet were customary, including heroes' names, mass events, and cultural products. Except in Bulgaria, however, such antinational, pro-Soviet policies were short-lived.

Nationalism never was suppressed completely. Within a few years of attaining power, the Communist leaders in Yugoslavia, Albania, and Romania undertook independent political moves with nationalist overtones. Their actions regarding the Yugoslav-Soviet and Sino-Soviet splits essentially were motivated by national concerns, given a veneer of Marxist ideology. Following the Tito-Stalin split, Yugoslavia created a model for communism that emphasized adaptation to national interests rather than blind adherence to Soviet examples. Albania's and Romania's Communist leaders used traditional nationalist sentiment to consolidate their authority, break the Soviets' influence over them, and differentiate themselves from their Communist neighbors. Even Zhivkov's Bulgaria, dutifully pro-Soviet and outwardly internationalist, hid continued nationalist ambitions behind closed doors at its party, academic, and media institutions.

All Balkan Communist regimes encouraged native ethnographic studies and pastimes. Folk music, dancing, and official performance ensembles were nurtured and supported. By the 1960s and 1970s, native artists in all fields received official sanction and often sponsorship (so long as they toed the current ideological line). National histories, couched in Marxist ideological terminology, took pride in many past political, economic, educational, and artistic achievements. Overall, traditional nationalist ideals were suborned to the interests of the ruling Communist leaderships. Although many of traditional nationalism's components (particularly religion) commonly were marginalized (or excluded altogether) in Communist nationalist efforts, their versions essentially aimed at similar purposes—unique nation-state identities enjoying their respective representative populations' mass affiliation.

Despite the pretense of ideological solidarity exhibited by all European Communist states, traditional nation-state rivalries and domestic ethnonational minority problems persisted. These rivalries and problems were particularly characteristic of the Balkan Communist states.

Romania revived its claims to Bessarabia and Bukovina and continued to discriminate against its Transylvanian Hungarians. Hungarian Communist leader János Kádár (1956-89) publicly criticized Romania for their mistreatment (1971), essentially resurrecting the prewar "Transylvanian Question." The Romanian Communists' continued maltreatment of their Hungarian minority erupted into an open media war, with nationalist overtones, between the two Communist states during the

1980s, and each side manipulated fiery public national sentiments through press attacks, new national and regional (Transylvania) histories, and national celebrations. When Ceauşescu revived his "systemization" plan to destroy villages and transfer their populations to agrarian-industrial complexes (1988), Hungary viewed the initiative as a direct attack on Romania's Hungarian minority. Mass anti-Romanian demonstrations occurred in Budapest, and the Romanians closed the Hungarian consulate in Transylvania. National animosities between the two states stood at a post–World War II high on the eve of communism's collapse in Romania.

Albania's former national border problems carried over into the Communist era. National tensions with Greece ran high since no official treaty ending World War II hostilities was signed between them (not officially until 1987). Long-standing Greek claims to Albanian northern Epiros, with its Greek community (60,000 strong, according to Albania; 200,000, according to Greece), were intensified by Albania's role as a Communist staging area during the Greek Civil War, which nationalistically radicalized its Greek minority and made them a continuing source of concern for Hoxha's regime. One of Hoxha's accusations against the Soviets in justifying his pro-Chinese stance was alleged Soviet encouragement of Greek irredentism in Albania. Greek minority Communist party representatives were repressed. During Albania's Maoist "cultural revolution" (1966-69), all religions were attacked as sources of anti-Albanian consciousness, and Albanianization was used to eliminate the Greek minority (with minimal success).

Fearing possible Soviet aggression against Albania, Hoxha reconciled with Greece and signed an agreement resuming bilateral trade relations (1970). Full diplomatic relations were reestablished after the Greek government officially renounced all territorial claims on Albanian Epiros (1971). Thereafter, Greece became one of Albania's few consistent trading partners during its post-Maoist period of isolation. Greek minority problems in Albania, however, were not resolved by the rapprochement. Because the Greek minority population grew rapidly during the early 1970s, Hoxha initiated a policy of Albanianizing the names of all non-Albanian citizens (1975). As Albania grew more dependent on trade relations with Greece, the situation of its Greek minority gradually improved (usually because of stipulations in bilateral Albanian-Greek commercial agreements), but discriminatory pressures on them still existed at the time communism ended in Albania (1990).

Besides Albanianizing the population, Hoxha proclaimed Albania the protector of all Albanians living beyond the state's borders—those inhabiting Kosovo and Macedonia within Yugoslavia. Active pursuit of that "protective" role waxed and waned with the vagaries of Albanian-Yugoslav relations. When national animosities ran high between the two states (1948-late 1960s; the 1970s-1980s periodically), Hoxha vociferously decried Yugoslav discrimination against Kosovar and Macedonian Albanians. When Hoxha viewed Yugoslavia as a buffer against potential Soviet aggression, he was conciliatory.

So long as both states embraced communism, Albania's nationalist influence on Yugoslavia's Albanians was nominal. Kosovar and Macedonian Albanian Communists, directly controlled by Tito at the end of World War II, had little say in determining their homelands' postwar state disposition. That Kosovo, with its Albanian majority, would form part of Yugoslav Serbia never was questioned. Neither was the future of postwar Yugoslav Macedonia. The Tito-Stalin split erected an ideological-national wall between Albania and Yugoslavia that precluded any common development between Albanians living on opposite sides of their border. The Kosovar and Macedonian Albanians were left as ethnonational minorities in Slavic Yugoslav republics. During most of the Communist era, Yugoslav Albanians enjoyed a living standard significantly higher than that of their conationals in Maoist, isolated Albania, which permitted them to tolerate somewhat their minority status. Rising Serbian nationalist emotions during the 1970s and 1980s over Kosovo's mostly Albanian ethnonational makeup, however, strained the Kosovar Albanians' tolerance to the breaking point. Their unrest heralded the Communist era's end in Yugoslavia and played a role in its post-Communist dissolution.

Although Communist Bulgaria officially toed the pro-Soviet internationalist line, it was not free of nationalist concerns that were primarily focused on two issues—its Muslim-Turkish minority and the long-standing "Macedonian Question."

Bulgaria was the most ethnically homogeneous Balkan Communist state. Its only minority of any consequence was religious—Muslim. Approximately 10 percent of the population were Muslim Turkish speakers and Pomaks, who resided in Bulgaria's eastern, southeastern, and southern Rhodope Mountain regions. Bulgaria's failures to win national territorial expansion in the Balkan and world wars resulted in rising pressures for assimilating the Muslim minority and strengthening the domestic national base for anticipated future efforts in Macedonia, to which the new Communist leaders were not immune.

Georgi Dimitrov's regime initially granted the Muslims representation in the legislature, encouraged their participation in local Communist administrations, and founded bilingual media, but such efforts ended after the Communists no longer required the Muslims' support for solidifying their takeover. In the late 1940s the Islamic religion and Turkish-language schools were subjected to state regulation. The 1950 collectivization drive in predominantly Muslim-inhabited tobacco-growing regions was an escalation of official anti-Muslim policy, with Muslims compelled either to emigrate or to have their property confiscated. The situation degenerated into the forced emigration of over 155,000 Turks and Pomaks to Turkey (1950-51). The émigrés arrived at the frontier in such numbers and poverty that Turkey, unable to handle the situation adequately, closed its borders. The miserable refugee camps caused an international scandal, and rising international diplomatic pressures convinced the Communists to ease their collectivization policies.

In the situation's immediate aftermath, the Communists made token efforts to salve Muslim sensibilities to limit the harm done the important Bulgarian tobacco industry by emigration. Assimilation pressures on the Muslims continued: To change Turko-Arabic to Slavic names; to cease attending mosques; to adopt modern dress; and to renounce numerous religious practices. Bulgaria and Turkey worked out a bilateral emigration agreement (1968) permitting a controlled number of Bulgaria's Muslims to leave for Turkey (some 130,000 between 1969 and 1977). Those Muslims who remained (their numbers kept relatively large by a high birth rate) experienced continued discrimination.

With Bulgaria's planned economy stagnating and the population's living standard declining, by the mid-1980s Todor Zhivkov's regime was on the brink of losing governing validity. Zhivkov decided to intensify anti-Muslim assimilation efforts to foment the Slavic majority's traditional anti-Turk nationalist sentiments in his favor. An official "unity of the Bulgarian nation" campaign was enacted (1985). Academics were used to justify forced name changes among the Muslims by claiming that Bulgaria's Turks were not ethnically Turkish but, rather, descendants of "forcibly" converted Ottoman-era Slavs. Through mass intimidation, Slavic (Christian) names replaced Turko-Arabic (Muslim) ones in all official documents, the public and private use of the Turkish language was proscribed, all public Islamic rituals were banned, and numerous mosques were demolished.

In desperate self-defense, many Muslims took up armed resistance, and jailed Muslim leaders staged hunger strikes. Whole Muslim-inhabited regions came under martial law. By 1989 the situation was tense. Zhivkov came under growing diplomatic pressure to resolve the problem. Domestically, the situation crippled economic activity and eroded the regime's credibility even further among a growing number of dissident intellectuals. The Communists tried to end the affair definitively by expelling most of the Muslim minority. Beginning in May 1989, amid organized, neofascist mass public demonstrations in support of "national unity," some 360,000 Muslims were forced to flee to Turkey, under the guise of being granted "tourist" exit visas for "vacations." The "Muslim/Turkish Problem" played an important role in the collapse of Bulgarian communism later that year.

Less overt than the Muslim issue, but simmering just below the public surface, was Bulgaria's continuing nationalist claim on Macedonia. During World War II, Communist partisans controlled by both the Yugoslav and Bulgarian parties operated in Macedonia. A dispute over administrative authority erupted between Tito's movement and the Bulgarian party organization headed in Macedonia by Sharlo Shatorov. The Soviet-controlled Comintern, blistering from Germany's invasion of the Soviet Union, backed Tito. Given past experience, the Macedonian Communists initially were uncomfortable with the idea of continued Yugoslav affiliation. Tito's public rejection (1943) of the "Greater Serbia" approach formerly taken by the Yugoslav Communists, however, won them over by mid-1944. At

St. Prohor Počinjski Monastery (August 1944), Macedonian partisans proclaimed a Macedonian People's Republic that would take an equal place among the other republics in Tito's planned federated Communist Yugoslavia.

That Macedonia lay in Communist Yugoslavia at the war's end complicated Communist Bulgaria's pursuit of blatant nationalist efforts. Immediately following the war, Tito broached a plan for a Communist South Slav federation composed of Yugoslavia and Bulgaria to Bulgarian leader Georgi Dimitrov, who realized that the long-standing Bulgarian-Yugoslav dispute over Macedonia's possession could be resolved only by dealing with Tito. A customs union was signed (1947) that included plans for conducting a common foreign policy. The plan, however, helped spark the Tito-Stalin split. Dimitrov, Stalin's close personal associate, supported his friend and benefactor in the controversy and repudiated the federation plan, accepting Stalin's decision to create a future independent Macedonian state if that would counter Tito. All official relations between Bulgaria and Yugoslavia were severed (until late 1956). In the 1965 Bulgarian census, Macedonians living in Bulgaria's Pirin region lost their official recognition as a separate nationality.

As for relations with Greece regarding Greek Macedonia, Bulgaria supported the Communist rebels in the Greek Civil War but ceased supplying them when so ordered by Stalin. Incidents with Greece along their Macedonian border persisted into the 1950s. Bulgarian-Greek relations remained sour until 1964, when an agreement was reached regarding Bulgarian reparation payments to Greece for World War II damages.

The Tito-Stalin split made overt expressions of Bulgarian nationalism exceedingly difficult. Publicly voicing such sentiment became liable for punishment. Because of Bulgaria's close Soviet ties, whenever Yugoslav-Soviet relations soured, Bulgaria launched anti-Yugoslav propaganda attacks implying Bulgaria's right to Macedonia. Most public disputes over Macedonia during Zhivkov's reign remained academic and under close party ideological control. Zhivkov never permitted the issue to become an international question. In private, continued Bulgarian nationalist aspirations toward Macedonia were fed by closed discussions among academics and party officials. The cultural efflorescence of the 1970s and early 1980s glorifying Bulgaria's long history and cultural "continuity," fostered by Lyudmila Zhivkova, vented public expression of implied nationalist claims.

Macedonia's potential for keeping nationalist antagonisms alive in the Communist Balkans highlighted the fact that Communist Yugoslavia (in which most of Macedonia lay) was the most volatile focus of latent nationalist strife. Much of the reason for that situation was Tito's decision to retain prewar Yugoslavia's territories and borders.

Communist Yugoslavia received a federalist constitution. Each of its six federated, supposedly autonomous and equal, republics was considered territorially representative of a major ethnonational group. Serbs constituted the largest single ethnonational population in the state. The large Serbian Republic included two autonomous regions (later [1963] elevated to autonomous provinces) created to satisfy the national sensibilities of the Vojvodina Hungarians and Kosovar Albanians. Croatia, the second largest Yugoslav republic, encompassed all of the Dalmatian and Slavonian territories traditionally claimed by Croatian nationalists. Slovenia represented a relatively well-off, Germanized, and industrious Slav population. Montenegro preserved the identity of a Serb people who long rivaled their conationals in Serbia for Serbian national leadership. Macedonia appeared as an official national entity for the first time in its tortured history. Bosnia-Hercegovina, ethnically and religiously divided, nevertheless was recognized as a unitary republic.

Tito's first efforts to consolidate pro-Communist national loyalty in the state's republics addressed Macedonia, whose continued participation in Yugoslavia potentially was threatened by Bulgarian nationalism. When World War II ended, Yugoslav Macedonia was in the sticky position of creating a unique national language, history, and culture by any means (real or artificial) to justify its existence separate from neighboring Bulgaria.

Macedonian nationalists, stemming from IMRO's old pro-autonomy faction, essentially plagiarized Bulgarian historical claims to Macedonia by substituting the term "Macedonian" for "Bulgarian" in all of their arguments for a separate Macedonian ethnicity, which could be supported only by linguistic reality. That worked against them until the war. Prior to the Macedonian Communist partisans' mandating a modern Macedonian literary language (1944), most outside observers and linguists agreed with the Bulgarians in considering the Macedonian Slavs' vernacular a western dialect of Bulgarian. In the interwar period, Serbian was imposed as the official Macedonian language and the use of Bulgarian was forbidden. The Macedonian partisans established a commission to create an "official" Macedonian literary language (1945), which became the Macedonian Slavs' legal "first" language (with Serbo-Croatian a recognized "second" and Bulgarian officially proscribed).

The new Macedonian literary language intentionally was based on a dialect spoken in the central Vardar area to remove it geographically as far as possible from Bulgarian and Serbian linguistic "contaminations." A separate Macedonian Cyrillic alphabet (including wholly new letters and a few Serbian characters) was devised to make the language different from Bulgarian. "Bulgarianisms" were replaced by folk substitutes, and modern Bulgarian, Serbian, or Russian technical words and modern expressions intentionally were avoided in favor of Western (including American) terms. Literary Macedonian was as different as humanly possible from other Slavic languages, being a veritable linguistic hodgepodge approaching the French meaning of *macedoine* when referring to a mixed salad. Led by Skopje Communist linguist Blaže Koneski, and given international recognition (1952) by Harvard Slavic Professor Horace Lunt, the highly artificial Macedonian literary language provided

the Communist-mandated ethnic validity for an independent Macedonian nationality. Over four decades of state socialization and education efforts may have
succeeded in creating such an entity in actual fact.

Bosnia-Hercegovina also received serious national attention from Tito's regime.
In ethnonational terms, it was exceptional. Its inhabitants were divided among three
religious (civilizational) cultures and, simultaneously, two ethnic groups (Serbs and
Croats). Religion separated out one of the demographic components—the Muslims—from strict ethnic considerations; they were a mixed ethnic bag of Slavic Serbs
and Croats (both of whom primarily were [and are] defined by their particular
Christian religious affiliation). All of the groups shared an overall regional experience
since medieval times, although the participation of each often was unique. The
Bosnian Serbs and Croats fully embraced Western ethnonational culture, while the
Muslims essentially adhered to their traditional theocratic identity. After 1878,
however, the Muslims were forced to adapt to Western European secularized realities.
They formed political parties to represent their interests within an imposed nationalist, pseudoliberal political culture and played that game adroitly—always keeping
on the side of whoever predominated politically in matters affecting them. They
continued that approach under the Communists. Only the Muslims maintained an
awareness of Bosnia as a unique political entity.

Three years after the creation of Communist Yugoslavia, the official census of
1948 contained an ethnonational category for respondents labeled "Muslims,
nationally undeclared." The label demonstrated the Communist regime's complete
misconception of the Islamic religious concept of self-identity. Tito assumed that
Muslims eventually would see themselves as either ethnic Croats or Serbs who
happened to hold to the Islamic faith, so those who had yet to decide on that issue
were given the opportunity to notify the authorities of that fact. By 1961 the
Communists grew more convinced that the Muslims' persistent and pronounced
cultural differences from the Christian populations within the state had to reflect
some sort of ethnonational self-identity. The census for that year listed an ethnic
category of "Undefined Yugoslavs [Muslims in the *ethnic* sense]" specifically for the
Muslims of Bosnia-Hercegovina. The ambiguity in terminology applied to Bosnian
Muslims smacked of the old Ottoman *millet* approach to a somewhat similar
problem of governing a multicultural state. In essence, the Muslims thus were
defined as a unique "nationality" by the Communists solely on the basis of their
religion (much as was the case in Bulgaria as well). The issue was not clarified when,
in 1968, the Bosnian wing of the Yugoslav Communist party came right out and
said so exactly—Muslims constituted a distinct nation. If that were so, then "nation"
could be defined only in Ottoman *millet* terms and not in those of Western
ethnonational culture.

As for the primary Serb-Croat national struggle, which had characterized pre–
World War II Yugoslavia and nearly brought it to dissolution, Tito's violent

eradication of militant Croatian nationalists at the end of the war, his including all of the territories traditionally claimed by Croatian nationalists within the federal Croatian Republic, and his imposition of a strong "security" apparatus successfully suppressed overt expression of Croatian national sentiment until the late 1960s. Decentralization reforms during that decade, however, loosed restraints on intellectual activities, among which were resurrected allusions to pre–Communist era nationalism. Polemical debates in the early 1960s among Serbian and Croatian intellectuals on the nature of "Yugoslavism" led to the expansion of the topic into discussions of broader cultural import by 1967. Serbs and Croats clashed over the status of Serbo-Croatian as a language. The arguments degenerated into fueling older nationalist sentiments, which, in turn, engendered mutual distrust. By 1970 and 1971, a shadow of the old *Ustaše* underground terrorist group (less numerous and well organized than its predecessor) emerged among a small number of extreme Croatian nationalists, who conducted desultory operations within Yugoslavia and even carried out bombing attacks on the international scene. (The 1971 explosion in New York's Kennedy International Airport was one example.) Tito's aggressive security moves quelled the domestic terrorism but did not totally eradicate radical Croatian nationalist sentiment, which continued to seethe below the surface.

While Montenegrins and Slovenes demonstrated little or no signs of nationalist unrest during most of Communist Yugoslavia's existence, the Serbs perceived national problems stemming from Serbia's autonomous provinces of Kosovo and Vojvodina. Until 1966 the Communist administration in the regions-provinces were in the hands of Slavic Serbs, despite the fact that the majority populations were non-Slavs and non-Serbs (Albanians in Kosovo; Hungarians in Vojvodina). A certain level of Serb colonization and discriminatory policies toward non-Serbs similar to the interwar efforts was conducted by the Serbian Republic's Communist regime in both, with the tacit blessing of the central authorities. The situation spawned resentment on the part of the non-Serb majorities, particularly of the Kosovar Albanians, who constituted nearly 90 percent of their region's population. In 1966 Tito decided to extend decentralization reforms, in line with the 1963 constitution, to Yugoslavia's various constituent republics, and, as part of that initiative, Serbia's autonomous provinces were given voting privileges equal to those of the republics at the central federal government level.

Most Serbs privately resented the existence and growing power of the autonomous provinces. The 1966 decision resulted in the ever increasing presence of non-Serbs in the provincial administrations. Especially in Kosovo, the newly installed Communist representatives of the Albanian majority tended to act in a retaliatory fashion toward the resident Slav minority, leading to a steady emigration of Serbs and Montenegrins out of the province during the 1970s. Not unnaturally, leaders among the Kosovar Albanians, using their ethnonational demographic majority as validation, began calling for Kosovo's status to be elevated to that of a separate republic. Their demands grew more strident after Tito (whom many Kosovar Albanians viewed as a benefactor for granting them their autonomous provincial status) died in 1980. The revolving Yugoslav federal presidency initiated to take Tito's leadership place (in which Communist leaders of the respective republics held the top office on an annual, rotating basis) refused to accede to the Kosovar Albanians' desires, since to do so would have violated Communist Yugoslavia's national constitutional foundations.

From the beginning, the legal basis for a recognized republic within Communist Yugoslavia was the "nation"—the group that formed the ethnonational majority for a state. A "nationality," on the other hand, which represented a part of a "nation" that had its own separate state somewhere else, was an ethnonational minority in another "nation's" state. While "nationalities" received recognition and protection under the constitution, they could not be elevated to the level of "nations." Since Kosovo was recognized as a province of Serbia (the state of the Serbian "nation"), the Kosovar Albanians were classified as a "nationality" (because an Albanian "nation"-state already existed in Albania) whose ethnonational existence was recognized and protected by their autonomous status within Serbia. They thus were disqualified from possessing their own Yugoslav republic.

Kosovar Albanian nationalist demands were not stifled by the official opposition of the federal and republican authorities. Nationalist ideals took hold among young Albanian university students, disaffected intellectuals, and workers throughout Kosovo. In 1981 they staged demonstrations and riots, engaging in street battles with the police. Eventually a third of the Yugoslav federal army was deployed in Kosovo to put a lid on the disturbances. In their aftermath, a certain level of nationalist paranoia emerged among the Serb minority in the province. It took on all of the characteristics of the anti-Ottoman nationalist propaganda that traditionally had filled Serbia's textbooks and popular literature for over a century past. Exaggerated reports of Albanian atrocities perpetrated on Kosovar Serbs appeared in the Serbian media throughout most of the 1980s, fueling a growing Serbian nationalist xenophobia throughout Serbia. The nationalist situation in Serbia over Kosovo was destined to play a critical role in the dissolution of Communist Yugoslavia that began with a 1989 Serbian nationalist celebration of the medieval battle at Kosovo Polje.

Communist Collapse

Contrary to the popular Western belief that European communism's collapse primarily resulted from the United States' and NATO's strategic policy of militarily outspending the Soviets, the innate flaws of Communist economic planning and totalitarian political order lay at the heart of its fatal demise. Although Western pressures hastened the outcome, it was the impact of Soviet Premier-President Mikhail Gorbachev's (1985-92) radical Communist reforms on Communist Europe that opened the floodgates of collapse.

By loosening direct party control over the economy and political order, Gorbachev's reforms vented widespread popular frustration with the Communists' failure to deliver their promised beneficial egalitarian society, for which numerous and lengthy "belt-tightening" sacrifices had been made. Popular unrest began in the late 1970s, characterized by an underground dissident movement expressing oppositional views through *samizdat* (a Slavic acronym meaning "self-published") literature and encouraged by the Commission for Security and Cooperation in Europe's Helsinki Final Act (1975), signed by thirty-three European states (including most Communist states), the United States, and Canada. Helsinki recognized as final all existing European borders, declared official détente between the "capitalist" West and Communist East, and pledged all signatories to respect their populations' fundamental "human rights." The failure of signatory Communist regimes to abide by their Helsinki pledges elicited a steady stream of dissidents who used the Helsinki Final Act to validate their opposition to the Communist governments.

The dire early 1980s economic downturn in all Communist states, blatantly caused by central planning, facilitated the headway of the dissident movements. Moreover, post-Helsinki détente increased contacts with the West—films, television programs, news, tourists, consumer goods—providing the populations of the Communist states with barometers for comparing their living standards to those of the non-Communist West with generally disturbing results. Even most Yugoslavs, who enjoyed decades of Western contacts, were disappointed. By the 1980s the older generation of dedicated Communists was dying out, its place taken by younger, more materialistic, and less fanatical bureaucrats and managers with little sincere attachment to the Marxist ideological class struggle. Gorbachev's reforms were injected into an atmosphere of increasing popular skepticism and cynicism regarding Communist realities, which made them unintentionally explosive.

Gorbachev was one of the younger, highly educated Communist leaders convinced that communism could function properly if corruption were eliminated, industrial discipline imposed, and decentralization increased. He originally continued central planning but permitted greater autonomy and increased investments within basic industries. Financial resources were diverted from consumer goods and the military to heavy industry in the hopes that new technologies and manufacturing methods would cut production costs and assure better product quantity and quality. To eliminate micromanaging, he consolidated several ministries into larger "super-ministries" responsible for general policy rather than day-to-day production, and a new quality control agency was established. Gorbachev's planning reforms acquired the name *perestroika* (restructuring).

Since *perestroika* increased labor efforts but reduced consumer amenities, Gorbachev needed to sell his program to the general population through political reform. His political reform initiatives—easing ideological censorship, greater freedom of expression, and competitive party and government elections—became known as *glasnost* (openness). Once *perestroika* and *glasnost* were introduced (1985-86), they took on a logic of their own, despite Gorbachev's efforts to channel them for continuing Communist rule.

The original *perestroika* program failed: The "superministries" micromanaged the economy more than ever; the vague "superministry" command chains bred irresponsibility; the quality control agents interfered in production; existing factory upgrades proved more expensive than building new ones; and reduced consumer goods decreased tax revenues, leading to government deficits. Gorbachev countered the problems with new, more radical initiatives. Open markets were introduced to address planning problems (1988-90), justified by allusions to Lenin's New Economic Program (NEP) of the early 1920s. Whole industries were denationalized, and the economy was reoriented along market values.

Glasnost changed from promoting openness into the Communist system's complete reorganization. The party was reduced to playing a secondary role in government. Top government institutions were overhauled, with legislatures given authentic authority and multicandidate lists introduced for secret ballot elections. The Soviet constitution's clause outlawing criticism of the party and government was repealed.

Political openness prevented Gorbachev from building a consensus for his programs. Old-line Communists were stubbornly critical, while the younger Communists attacked him for reforming too slowly. An unexpected by-product of *glasnost* was the reemergence of nationalism among the Soviets' ethnonationally diverse population, who sensed an opportunity to escape Moscow's control entirely as central authority relaxed. Gorbachev became caught in the dilemma of using either military force or political reconciliation to keep the state together. He soon realized that force alone could prevent the Soviet system's outright collapse, but that its use would discredit his leadership and destroy his reforms.

Carried by events beyond his control, Gorbachev presided over Soviet-style communism's collapse. *Perestroika* pushed the economy into chaos. A failed coup against him (August 1991) by old-line Communists signaled the end of the Soviet system: Although Gorbachev survived, the coup's failure utterly discredited the Communists, reformers and conservatives alike. Soviet communism essentially was dead by the time that Boris Yeltsin (1992-2000) replaced Gorbachev as president.

Gorbachev's reforms made a powerful impact on the European Communist states. In September 1988 he announced that they no longer were required to coordinate their affairs with the Soviet Union nor to expect direct Soviet intervention in them. The Communist leaders of the former "friendly" satellite states were left on their own. Popular discontent and pressures for change, fed by two years of Gorbachev's Soviet reform example, made it too late for them to save their continued undisputed authority. Communist collapse started in Poland with the Solidarity movement (begun 1980) but erupted definitively in Hungary (the most radically reformed and liberal Communist state) during September 1989. Like dominoes, it quickly spread to the other European Communist states. Among those states in the Balkans, communism's collapse varied in time and in speed.

Strongly pro-Soviet Bulgaria dutifully followed Gorbachev's reform lead, although more through lip service than sincere implementation. By 1989 authentic economic reform desperately was needed. The economic growth rate was in steady negative decline, foreign debts escalated, and half of Bulgaria's factories were obsolete. Despite a massive propaganda campaign touting *perestroika,* little actually was undertaken beyond reshuffling ministries and officials. Bulgaria's moribund economy was on the verge of expiring.

Bulgarian dissident activity in 1989, however, was on the rise, demanding that the reform propaganda be realized. Reform clubs were founded and a large independent trade union organized. An ecology movement (Eco-Glasnost), a number of human rights organizations, and a committee espousing religious, moral, and philosophical freedoms were formed. Zhelyu Zhelev, a prominent dissident philosopher, was arrested for circulating appeals for democratic political reforms, and tensions between dissidents and government heightened. Dissident unrest came to a head during the May 1989 Communist-sponsored "Bulgarian unity" mass demonstrations and Muslim-Turkish expulsions.

Public demonstrations of dissident groups, especially Eco-Glasnost, were staged in Sofia demanding free elections and democracy. Communist reformists, fearing a total Communist collapse, forced Zhivkov out the day after (10 November) the Berlin Wall fell and installed Petŭr Mladenov (1989-90) as the Communist reform leader. He rehabilitated the dissidents and permitted the founding of opposition political parties. By late December the anti-Turk campaign officially was terminated and the émigrés were invited to return. (Two-thirds of them eventually did so.) A coalition party called the Union of Democratic Forces (UDF) also was formed, with the freed Zhelev as its leader.

Mladenov called elections for June 1990, too soon for UDF to solidify its organization. The Socialists (the renamed Communists) narrowly won and retained power, bringing about a political stalemate. The UDF refused to participate in a coalition government, and the Socialists refused to make economic reforms without its involvement. Radical Bulgarian nationalists attacked Mladenov for ending the anti-Turk campaign, and the Turks in Bulgaria formed a de facto Turkish-Muslim party to defend their rights.

A 1989 gaffe committed by Mladenov during a street demonstration in Sofia led to his resignation (July 1990), and the national assembly appointed Zhelev to his place, although his prime minister was the leading Socialist, Andrei Lukanov. Lukanov's proposals for radical reforms were opposed by Zhelev and UDF for political reasons, and a statewide trade union strike forced Lukanov out of office (November). The new interim government carried out the Socialists' reform program until new elections were held in 1991: A liberal-democratic constitution was passed; price subsidies were lifted; new independent trade unions were recognized; and foreign loans were secured on the promise of further reforms.

Bulgaria's first post-Communist, democratic elections were held (October 1991) amid drastically rising prices, ballooning unemployment, and little industrial denationalization. Zhelev and UDF won a majority but the Socialists came in a close second. Thereafter, Bulgaria slowly demolished the remnants of the Communist decades, moved toward liberal democracy, and came to terms with its traditional Macedonian and Turkish minority national problems. Those processes, obstructed by stubborn partisan political clashes, have progressed sluggishly but steadily into the present.

By 1989 conditions in Communist Romania were miserable. There were violent street demonstrations in Bucharest and some Transylvanian cities; relations with Hungary were bad; the economy was crippled; and drastic rationing demoralized the population. Ceauşescu's April announcement that the foreign debt had been settled was scant compensation for dreadful living conditions. Communist reformers were harassed by the president's henchmen for objecting to Ceauşescu's autocratic behavior. Although reformers and dissidents founded an underground National Salvation Front (NSF) organization, the security forces kept it in check. While other Communist states attempted to follow Gorbachev's lead, Ceauşescu did the opposite and condemned reform.

Neighboring Hungary's radical reforms attracted increasing numbers of disgruntled Romanians, who fled to Hungary (Spring 1989) in numbers so large that Romania fenced off the border. The Hungarians stoked Romanian discontent by televising interviews with exiled Romanian King Mihai and a dissident Transylvanian Hungarian pastor from Timişoara, László Tökés. In December Ceauşescu's security police tried to deport Tökés but met strong resistance from the Timişoara Hungarians, which escalated into rioting and calls for ending Ceauşescu's regime. When in late December he staged a public rally in Bucharest to condemn the Timişoara demonstrators, Ceauşescu was greeted with catcalls from the crowd. His contemptuous reaction sparked antigovernment demonstrations throughout Romania that, fed by years of misery and repression, turned into a bloody revolution, led by a now-public NSF. Ceauşescu and his wife fled the capital but swiftly were captured, summarily tried, and executed (on live television, broadcast internationally) by enraged rebels on Christmas day (25 December 1989).

The "Christmas Revolution" eliminated Ceauşescu and overthrew the Communist party, but the new interim government, headed by NSF leader and former

Communist Ion Iliescu, embraced the style of Communist authoritarian rule. Some reforms were enacted (1990) but promised elections were put off. Although new opposition parties were permitted, a suspicion that the NSF merely was the Communists under a new name was widespread. When an anti-NSF demonstration was staged in Bucharest (February 1990), Iliescu called in several thousand miners loyal to his party to disperse it by force. In March ethnic tensions between Transylvanian Hungarians and Romanians erupted into open violence. Just months after the Timişoara Hungarians sparked the revolution, they were beaten by nationalist Romanians on the very same streets, and three of them died.

The NSF easily won the first elections (May 1990). The opposition was fragmented and intimidated by the authorities. New President Iliescu received international recognition, despite opposition claims of voter fraud. His regime secured and maintained its grip on power by employing the strong-arm tactics that all previous Romanian governments used since the nineteenth century—beating the political opposition into submission. Differences over economic reforms, however, divided the NSF: Former Communist hard-liners opposed the reformers' attempts to lift price controls, denationalize industry, and permit large foreign investments (all of which ignited popular discontent and public demonstrations, despite the government's repressive tactics).

Soaring prices forced the NSF government to reimpose price controls (late 1990), but the move seemed to signal a reemergence of Communist-like policy. Foreigners balked at providing loans, which prevented the NSF from stemming economic decline during 1991. A radical privatization program was instituted to dispel suspicions of latent communism and emphasize the government's commitment to liberal democracy and capitalism. A new reform constitution modeled on the French (including a strong presidency) was installed (December 1991). Romania continued to suffer economic hardship, strained relations with Hungary, and national concerns regarding independent Moldova (Bessarabia), but tentative moves toward more democratic governance emerged by the late 1990s.

In Yugoslavia by 1989, economic woes reached staggering proportions. Inflation ran at 300 percent; financial irresponsibility was rampant; domestic and foreign debt was crushing; and all economic indicators were in decline. Partly because of Tito's powerful legacy and partly out of pride over their record of independence from the Soviets, the Yugoslav Communists entered the Gorbachev-inspired reform process haltingly and grudgingly. The policies that won such positive acclaim in the West undermined the Communist party's central control as self-management was applied to politics at all government levels. The few Gorbachev-era reforms attempted by the federal authorities were stymied by the republics' failure to ratify them. Following the rise in Serbia of Communist strongman Slobodan Milošević (1987-2000), reforming communism became less of a priority in multinational Yugoslavia than embracing nationalism.

Milošević's public support for Kosovar Serbian nationalists, expressed at the six hundredth anniversary celebration of the Kosovo battle (June 1989), displaced strictly economic factors in Communist policies with more traditional nationalist concerns. Milošević reopened the old political problems regarding Yugoslavia's nature as a unitary nation-state federation of separate, distinct "nations" that Tito's iron will had suppressed. Disputes over the exact relationship between the central federal authorities and the separate ethnonationally defined republics came to the fore. Nationalist issues predominated after Milošević's actions in Kosovo. Nationalism, not communism, became the focus of Yugoslav political consciousness. Communism died. The party's official name change to Socialist (1990) held little real import in the midst of burning national emotions.

During the first half of 1989, Serbia's "Kosovo Question" dominated Yugoslav domestic affairs. Serbian authorities ended the autonomous status of Kosovo and Vojvodina, sparking Kosovar Albanian disturbances that were quelled by "special" police measures (April). Serb-Albanian hostility persisted, heightened by Milošević's anniversary remarks in June. At the same time, Serb-Croat tensions intensified. Clashes between Serbs and Croats in the Serb-inhabited Croatian town of Knin erupted after the Kosovo anniversary celebrations, and Serbs living in Croatian Slavonia declared their autonomy.

In early 1990 piecemeal ethnonationally identified political parties emerged in Croatia and Slovenia, and the Communists disbanded into republican branches, each with new "non-Communist" names. Slovenia held the first republican multiparty elections (April 1990), in which an anti-Communist coalition garnered over half of the votes. In Croatian elections, a highly nationalist party (which adopted many old *Ustaše* symbols), led by former Communist Franjo Tudjman, won a clear victor over the "official" former Communists, and Tudjman was named president of the republic (May 1990).

Republican elections were held in Serbia, Montenegro, Macedonia, and Bosnia-Hercegovina in November and December 1990. In Serbia, where opposition parties technically remained illegal and lacked media access, Milošević's Socialists won handily. In Macedonia, amid widespread "irregularities," a Slav nationalist coalition won a majority, but token Turks and Albanians were included in the new government to placate those minorities. In Bosnia-Hercegovina, ethnonational parties logged votes in proportion to the republic's mix of Muslims, Serbs, and Croats. In Montenegro, the ex-Communists were clear victors and solidified their power. In every election, the party running in opposition to the nationalist and nationalistic former Communist parties was small and fragmented.

Ethnonational tensions within Yugoslavia mounted throughout 1990. In Croatia, the Knin Serbs, fearing rising Croatian nationalism, proclaimed (October) an independent Serbian enclave named Krajina. By early 1991 nationalist tensions escalated further. Slovenia and Croatia threatened to secede from Yugoslavia

(February), and the Knin Serbs seceded from Croatia. Croatia formed its own army to meet the threat of possible intervention by both the "Krajina" Serbs, who were armed by Milošević's Serbian republican authorities, and the Yugoslav army (also under Milošević's sway) in support of the Serbs in Croatia.

May 1991 proved decisive in bringing on outright civil war in Yugoslavia. Slovenia reiterated its intention to secede. A referendum in Croatia returned an overwhelming majority in favor of similar action, while Croatia's "Krajina" Serbs voted to remain within federated Yugoslavia. Under Milošević's influence, federal authorities launched a halfhearted military invasion of Slovenia (June) to prevent its secession but achieved little. Threatened EC sanctions on Yugoslavia resulted in a cease-fire and the Yugoslav forces' withdrawal. Slovenia's de facto independence was secured.

The Yugoslav crisis then shifted to Croatia. In protest over the Serb "Krajina" issue, Tudjman broke off all relations with Serbia (August 1991). Warfare erupted between the hastily organized, ill-armed Croatian military and the regular, highly trained and equipped Yugoslav army (augmented by Serbian ultranationalist paramilitary units) in the Serb-inhabited areas of Croatian Slavonia, where Serbs rejected continued Croat control. Despite repeated EC attempts to negotiate a cease-fire, the Serbs conquered a third of Croatia (areas that were heavily Serb-populated) by late 1991. A United Nations cease-fire finally was imposed, by which time it was obvious to all that Milošević and the Serbian nationalists were intent on realizing the goal of the traditional "Greater Serbia" ultranationalists.

Yugoslavia ceased to exist in December 1991, when the EC, led by Germany, bestowed international recognition on independent Croatia and Slovenia. Emerging nationalist leaders in Bosnia-Hercegovina (Alija Izetbegović heading the Muslims) and Macedonia (Kiro Gligorov, supported by a resurrected IMRO) pushed for their own republics' independence. Albania, in support of Kosovar Albanian nationalists, extended unilateral recognition to an independent sovereign Kosovo. The name "Yugoslavia" continued to be applied to the federal union of Serbia and Montenegro alone. Dominated by Milošević and truncated, Serb-oriented Yugoslavia set out to retain as much Serb-inhabited territory as possible, resulting in the war in Bosnia-Hercegovina (1992-95) and the Kosovo air war (1999). In the process, the world acquired a new term for the ultranationalist genocidal programs that long characterized Balkan nation-state policies: "Ethnic cleansing."

Albania's was the last Balkan Communist regime to fall. The Communists, headed by Ramiz Alia (1985-92), Hoxha's successor, paid little attention to the Gorbachev-era reform movement until Ceaușescu's fall, enacting only limited party and government restructuring. A series of dissident demonstrations (late 1989-early 1990) against police repression, however, coupled with the example of Ceaușescu's fate, awakened Alia to the potential danger facing his regime. He issued a range of so-called reform measures (May 1990), including permission for peasants to sell produce in open markets, and new electoral laws (November) allowed secret balloting from multicandidate (but not multiparty) lists.

The Albanians, their condition nearly as miserable as the Romanians', demanded democratic measures, and public demonstrations in Tiranë (December) forced Alia to accept the formation of non-Communist political parties for participation in planned elections. As 1991 opened, Greeks in southern Albania were fleeing to Greece, the currency was devalued, and the government postponed elections until March, in return for the opposition's agreement to participate in the elections, support a wage freeze, and cancel planned strikes. Antigovernment student demonstrations (February) convinced Alia to declare a state of presidential authoritarian rule until elections took place.

Given the opposition's lack of time to prepare for the elections, the Communists won a parliamentary majority. Their largest single political opposition, the Democratic party, refused to join a coalition government but agreed to serve in the parliament. Alia was appointed president by parliament, while the opposition continued to counter ongoing Communist control through strikes and public demonstrations, which succeeded in bringing down the Communist government (June 1991). An opposition multiparty coalition government of "national stability" then was installed. The Communist party changed its name to Socialist, and, for all intents and purposes, communism ended.

Albania's economy came to a virtual standstill by mid-1991. A needed land privatization plan was enacted to dismantle agricultural collectives, but it failed to legitimize the new owners' rights. Other reforms were half implemented or limited. By September street demonstrations over the sad state of economic life increased, food riots occurred, and public order all but broke down completely. The governing coalition collapsed in December 1991 when the Democratic party pulled out over the government's failure to schedule new elections sooner and prosecute former Communists for alleged corruption. Thereafter, Albania experienced slow and erratic economic recovery and a disruptive major financial disaster tied to a failed pyramid money marketing scheme. Despite the end of communism, Albania remained the poorest and most backward state in the Balkans.

Epilogue

The Communist era ended everywhere in the Balkans by the close of 1991. Just what its successor's name will be currently is unclear. Fourteen hundred years of unique history and three separate civilizational legacies provide the region with a rich pool of cultural traditions for the new era to draw upon. The Balkans' peoples can choose to continue their common authoritarian political approach rooted in the Orthodox-Byzantine and Ottoman past, or they might seriously attempt to make the more recently adopted Western European "enlightened" liberal democratic system work. (If they choose to mix the two, as they did after 1878, there is little reason to believe that things would be significantly different from what occurred in the nation-state nationalist era.) Islamic Ottoman traditions, although frequently blamed for many of the Balkan states' failings since 1878, provide some positive foundations—the *millet* approach, for example—for building the various separate people's tolerance of one another. Current Western European cultural development, in the guise of the European Union, can contribute to that end because of certain resemblances to Islamic structures. (Although arriving at its basis of "supranationalism" [or "postnationalism"] from its own unique cultural and historical experiences, the EU manifests some surprising similarities to the *millet* approach in unifying diverse peoples.) The Balkan peoples, however, may persist in pre-Communist, nation-state nationalist fashion, in which case they will continue to suffer until circumstances force them to change course and adopt alternatives.

Given the decade of nationalist bloodshed, animosities, and "ethnic cleansing" accompanying Yugoslavia's dissolution, "Post-Communist Nationalist" might seem a likely name for the new era (at least at its outset). While the Croat-Serb issue appears resolved as best as can be expected, such is far from the case regarding the tenuous, foreign-imposed cessations of fighting in Bosnia-Hercegovina and Kosovo. It is questionable whether any effective solutions to the nationalist animosities existing in those regions have been achieved. There also is the perennial problem of Macedonia. Greece's nationalist paranoia over the "Slav threat" to its share of the region—aptly demonstrated by its reactions to Macedonian independence in the European Union and the United Nations and the embargo it placed on Macedonia after 1991—appears undampened. Within Macedonia, tensions between the Christian Slav majority and Muslim Albanian minority possess the potential for sparking dangerous clashes threatening the state's existence—tensions that account for Macedonia's ambiguous role during the 1999 Kosovar Albanian refugee crisis. Any explosion of nationalist animosities in Macedonia could raise the nightmare of Greek, Bulgarian, Turkish, and Albanian intervention that might utterly disrupt the Balkans and lead to NATO's fracturing and possibly Western-Russian confrontation.

Pessimism grounded in history aside, there may just as well emerge a new era rejecting the past's divisive, ruinous nationalisms for the possibility of a common multinational future (à la the embryonic European Union). Bulgaria has demonstrated a willingness to move beyond traditional nationalism toward a new multinational European horizon by officially disavowing nationalist irredentism and antiminority discrimination, and has vowed to implement and inculcate those intentions in all forms and levels of educational and cultural expression. Bulgaria's efforts eventually may serve to form the beginnings of a model for the rest of the Balkans. One can hope that the dangerous bane of nationalism will be shed in the new era, and that ethnonational and civilizational tolerance will come to predominate in the minds and hearts of the region's populations. In such a new "internationalist" (or "multicultural") era, the term "Balkans" well might become synonymous with the region's wondrous natural beauty and fascinatingly rich human cultural diversity that, for the past two centuries, have been overshadowed by its troubled nationalist divisiveness.

FURTHER READINGS

General

Abel, Elie. *The Shattered Bloc: Behind the Upheaval in Eastern Europe*. Boston, MA: Houghton Mifflin, 1990.

Barker, Elisabeth. *British Policy in South-East Europe in the Second World War*. Reprint ed. New York: Barnes and Noble, 1976.

Berend, Ivan T. *Central and Eastern Europe, 1944-1993: Detour from the Periphery to the Periphery*. New York: Cambridge University Press, 1999.

Brown, J. F. *Eastern Europe and Communist Rule*. Durham, NC: Duke University Press, 1988.

Burks, R. V. *The Dynamics of Communism in Eastern Europe*. Princeton, NJ: Princeton University Press, 1961.

Dawisha, Karen. *Eastern Europe, Gorbachev, and Reform: The Great Challenge*. 2nd ed. Cambridge: Cambridge University Press, 1990.

Held, Joseph, ed. *Dictionary of East European History since 1945*. Westport, CT: Greenwood, 1994.

Ionescu, Ghita. *The Break-up of the Soviet Empire in Eastern Europe*. Baltimore, MD: Penguin, 1965.

King, Robert R. *Minorities under Communism: Nationalities as a Source of Tension among Balkan Communist States*. Cambridge, MA: Harvard University Press, 1973.

Lendvai, Paul. *Eagles in Cobwebs: Nationalism and Communism in the Balkans*. Garden City, NY: Doubleday, 1969.

Linden, Ronald H. *Communist States and International Change: Romania and Yugoslavia in Comparative Perspective*. Boston, MA: Allen and Unwin, 1987.

Mestrović, Stjepan. *Habits of the Balkan Heart: Social Character and the Fall of Communism*. College Station: Texas A and M University Press, 1993.

Nelson, David N. *Balkan Imbroglio: Politics and Security in Southeastern Europe*. Boulder, CO: Westview, 1991.

Poulton, Hugh. *The Balkans: Minorities and States in Conflict*. New York: Minority Rights Publications, 1991.

Rothschild, Joseph, and Nancy M. Wingfield. *Return to Diversity: A Political History of East Central Europe Since World War II*. 3rd ed. New York: Oxford University Press, 2000.

Seton-Watson, Hugh. *The East European Revolution*. 3rd ed. New York: Praeger, 1956.

Simons, Thomas W., Jr. *Eastern Europe in the Postwar World*. 2nd ed. New York: St. Martin's, 1993.

Starr, Richard F. *The Communist Regimes in Eastern Europe*. 2nd ed., rev. Stanford, CA: Hoover Institution, 1971.

Stokes, Gale. *The Walls Came Tumbling Down: The Collapse of Communism in Eastern Europe*. New York: Oxford University Press, 1993.

Swain, Geoffrey, and Nigel Swain. *Eastern Europe Since 1945*. New York: St. Martin's, 1993.

Albania

Biberaj, Elez. *Albania: A Socialist Maverick*. Boulder, CO: Westview, 1990.

Griffith, William E. *Albania and the Sino-Soviet Rift*. Cambridge, MA: MIT Press, 1963.

Hall, Derek. *Albania and the Albanians*. London: Pinter, 1994.

Hibbert, Reginald. *Albania's National Liberation Struggle: The Bitter Victory*. London: Pinter, 1991.

Pano, Nicholas C. *The People's Republic of Albania*. Baltimore, MD: Johns Hopkins University Press, 1968.

Pipinelis, M. P. *Europe and the Albanian Question*. Chicago, IL: Argonaut, 1961.

Prifti, Peter R. *Socialist Albania since 1944: Domestic and Foreign Developments.* Cambridge, MA: MIT Press, 1978.
Vickers, Miranda, and James Pettifer. *Albania: From Anarchy to a Balkan Identity.* New York: New York University Press, 1997.

Bulgaria

Bell, John D. *The Bulgarian Communist Party from Blagoev to Zhivkov.* Stanford, CA: Hoover Institution, 1985.
Brown, J. F. *Bulgaria under Communist Rule.* New York: Praeger, 1970.
Dellin, L. A. D. *Bulgaria: East-Central Europe under the Communists.* New York: Praeger, 1957.
Devedjiev, Hristo. *Stalinization of the Bulgarian Society, 1949-1953.* Philadelphia, PA: Dorrance, 1975.
McIntyre, Robert J. *Bulgaria: Politics, Economics and Society.* London: Pinter, 1988.
Oren, Nissan. *Revolution Administered: Agrarianism and Communism in Bulgaria.* Baltimore, MD: Johns Hopkins University Press, 1973.

Greece

Averoff-Tossizza, Evangelos. *By Fire and Axe: The Communist Party and the Civil War in Greece, 1944-49.* New Rochelle, NY: Caratzas, 1978.
Bahcheli, T. *Greek-Turkish Relations Since 1955.* Boulder, CO: Westview, 1990.
Close, David H. *The Greek Civil War, 1943-1950.* London: Routledge, 1993.
———. *The Origins of the Greek Civil War.* London: Addison-Wesley Longman, 1995.
Couloumbis, Theodore A. *The United States, Greece and Turkey: The Troubled Triangle.* New York: Praeger, 1983.
Crawshaw, Nancy. *The Cyprus Revolt: An Account of the Struggle for Union with Greece.* London: Allen and Unwin, 1978.
Eudes, Dominique. *The Kapetanios: Partisans and Civil War in Greece, 1943-1949.* New York: Monthly Review, 1973.
Hondros, John L. *Occupation and Resistance: The Greek Agony, 1941-44.* New York: Pella, 1983.
Iatrides, John O. *Revolt in Athens: The Greek Communist "Second Round," 1944-5.* Princeton, NJ: Princeton University Press, 1972.
Jones, Howard. *"A New Kind of War": America's Global Strategy and the Truman Doctrine in Greece.* Oxford: Oxford University Press, 1989.
Legg, Keith R., and John M. Roberts. *Modern Greece: A Civilization on the Periphery.* Boulder, CO: Westview, 1997.
Mazower, Mark. *Inside Hitler's Greece: The Experience of Occupation, 1941-44.* New Haven, CT: Yale University Press, 1993.
McNeill, William H. *The Metamorphosis of Greece Since World War II.* Chicago, IL: University of Chicago Press, 1978.
Murtagh, Peter. *The Rape of Greece: The King, the Colonels and the Resistance.* New York: Simon and Schuster, 1994.
O'Ballance, Edgar. *The Greek Civil War, 1944-1949.* New York: Praeger, 1966.
Pettifer, James. *The Greeks: The Land and People since the War.* New York: Viking, 1993.
Spourdalakis, Michalis. *The Rise of the Greek Socialist Party.* London: Routledge, 1988.
Stavrakis, Peter J. *Moscow and Greek Communism, 1944-9.* Ithaca, NY: Cornell University Press, 1989.
Vlavianos, Haris. *Greece, 1941-49: From Resistance to Civil War.* London: St. Anthony's, 1992.
Wittner, Lawrence S. *American Intervention in Greece, 1943-9.* New York: Columbia University Press, 1982.

Woodhouse, Christopher M. *The Rise and Fall of the Greek Colonels.* New York: Franklin Watts, 1985.
———. *The Struggle for Greece, 1941-1949.* London: Hart-Davis, MacGibbon, 1976.

Romania

Deletant, Dennis. *Ceauşescu and the* Securitate: *Coercion and Dissent in Romania, 1965-1989.* Armonk, NY: M. E. Sharpe, 1996.
Dima, Nicholas. *Bessarabia and Bukovina: The Soviet-Romanian Territorial Dispute.* Boulder, CO: East European Monographs, 1982.
Fischer-Galati, Stephen A. *The Socialist Republic of Rumania.* Baltimore, MD: Johns Hopkins University Press, 1969.
Floyd, David. *Rumania: Russia's Dissident Ally.* New York: Praeger, 1965.
Gallagher, Tom. *Romania after Ceauşescu: The Politics of Intolerance.* Edinburgh: Edinburgh University Press, 1995.
Gilberg, Trond. *Nationalism and Communism in Romania: The Rise and Fall of Ceauşescu's Personal Dictatorship.* Boulder, CO: Westview, 1990.
Giurescu, Dinu C. *Romania's Communist Takeover: The Radescu Government.* Boulder, CO: East European Monographs, 1994.
Illyes, Elemer. *National Minorities in Romania: Change in Transylvania.* Boulder, CO: East European Monographs, 1982.
Ionescu, Ghiţă. *Communism in Rumania, 1944-1962.* London: Oxford University Press, 1964.
King, Robert R. *History of the Romanian Communist Party.* Stanford, CA: Hoover Institution, 1980.
Verdery, Katherine. *National Ideology under Socialism: Identity and Cultural Politics in Ceauşescu's Romania.* Berkeley: University of California Press, 1991.

Yugoslavia

Alexander, Stella. *Church and State in Yugoslavia since 1945.* Cambridge: Cambridge University Press, 1979.
Avakumović, Ivan. *History of the Communist Party of Yugoslavia.* Aberdeen, UK: University Press of Aberdeen, 1964.
Banac, Ivo. *With Stalin against Tito: Conformist Splits in Yugoslav Communism.* Ithaca, NY: Cornell University Press, 1988.
Beloff, Nora. *Tito's Flawed Legacy: Yugoslavia and the West, 1939 to 1984.* London: V. Gollancz, 1985.
Bennett, Christopher. *Yugoslavia's Bloody Collapse: Causes, Course and Consequences.* New York: New York University Press, 1995.
Biberaj, Elez. *Kosova, the Balkan Powder Keg.* London: RISCT, 1993.
Campbell, John C. *Tito's Separate Road: America and Yugoslavia in World Politics.* New York: Harper and Row, 1967.
Cohen, Lenard J. *Broken Bonds: Yugoslavia's Disintegration and Balkan Politics in Transition.* 2nd ed. Boulder, CO: Westview, 1995.
Čuvalo, Ante. *The Croatian National Movement, 1966-1972.* Boulder, CO: East European Monographs, 1990.
Dedijer, Vladimir. *Tito.* New York: Simon and Schuster, 1953.
Djilas, Milovan. *The New Class: An Analysis of the Communist System.* New York: Praeger, 1957.
———. *Rise and Fall.* San Diego, CA: Harcourt, Brace and Jovanovich, 1985.
———. *The Unperfect Society: Beyond the New Class.* Translated by Dorian Cooke. New York: Harcourt, Brace and World, 1969.

———. *Wartime.* Translated by Michael B. Petrovich. New York: Harcourt Brace Jovanovich, 1977.

Doder, Duško. *The Yugoslavs.* London: Allen and Unwin, 1979.

Dyker, David A. *Yugoslavia: Socialism, Development, and Debt.* London: Routledge, 1990

Glenny, Misha. *The Fall of Yugoslavia: The Third Balkan War.* Rev. ed. New York: Penguin Books, 1993.

Hoffman, George W., and Fred W. Neal. *Yugoslavia and the New Communism.* New York: Twentieth Century Fund, 1962.

Irvine, Jill A. *The Croat Question: Partisan Politics in the Formation of the Yugoslav Socialist State.* Boulder, CO: Westview, 1993.

Johnson, A. Ross. *The Transformation of Communist Ideology: The Yugoslav Case, 1948-53.* Cambridge, MA: MIT Press, 1972.

Judah, Tim. *Kosovo: War and Revenge.* New Haven, CT: Yale University Press, 2000.

Karchmar, Lucien. *Draža Mihailović and the Rise of the Četnik Movement, 1941-1942.* 2 vols. New York: Garland, 1987.

Kofos, Evangelos. *Nationalism and Communism in Macedonia.* Thessaloniki: Institute for Balkan Studies, 1964.

Lydall, Harold. *Yugoslavia in Crisis.* Oxford: Clarendon, 1989.

Maclean, Fitzroy. *The Heretic: The Life and Times of Josip Broz-Tito.* New York: Harper, 1957.

Magaš, Branka. *The Destruction of Yugoslavia: Tracking the Break-up, 1980-92.* London: Verso, 1993.

McFarlane, Bruce J. *Yugoslavia: Politics, Economics, and Society.* London: Pinter, 1988.

Milazzo, Matteo J. *The Chetnik Movement and the Yugoslav Resistance.* Baltimore, MD: Johns Hopkins University Press, 1975.

O'Ballance, Edgar. *Civil War in Bosnia, 1992-94.* New York: St. Martin's, 1995.

Palmer, Stephen E., Jr., and Robert R. King. *Yugoslav Communism and the Macedonian Question.* Hamden, CT: Shoestring, 1971.

Pavlowitch, Steven K. *Tito, Yugoslavia's Great Dictator: A Reassessment.* London: C. Hurst, 1992.

———. *Yugoslavia.* New York: Praeger, 1971.

Ramet, Sabrina P. *Balkan Babel: The Disintegration of Yugoslavia from the Death of Tito to the War for Kosovo.* 3rd ed. Boulder, CO: Westview, 1999.

———. *Beyond Yugoslavia: Politics, Economics and Culture in a Shattered Country.* Boulder, CO: Westview, 1995.

———. *Nationalism and Federalism in Yugoslavia, 1962-1991.* 2nd ed. Bloomington: Indiana University Press, 1992.

Roberts, Walter R. *Tito, Mihailović, and the Allies.* Durham, NC: Duke University Press, 1994.

Rubinstein, Alvin Z. *Yugoslavia and the Unaligned World.* Princeton, NJ: Princeton University Press, 1970.

Rusinow, Dennison. *The Yugoslav Experiment, 1948-1974.* Berkeley: University of California Press, 1977.

Sekelj, Laszlo. *Yugoslavia: The Process of Disintegration.* New York: Columbia University Press, 1993.

Shoup, Paul. *Communism and the Yugoslav National Question.* New York: Columbia University Press, 1968.

Silber, Laura, and Allan Little. *Yugoslavia: Death of a Nation.* New York: TV Books, 1996.

Tomasevich, Jozo. *The Chetniks: War and Revolution in Yugoslavia, 1941-1945.* Stanford, CA: Stanford University Press, 1975.

Ulam, Adam B. *Titoism and the Cominform.* Cambridge, MA: Harvard University Press, 1952.

West, Richard. *Tito and the Rise and Fall of Yugoslavia.* London: Sinclair-Stevenson, 1994.

Wilson, Duncan. *Tito's Yugoslavia.* Cambridge: Cambridge University Press, 1979.

Woodward, Susan L. *Balkan Tragedy: Chaos and Dissolution after the Cold War.* Washington, DC: Brookings Institution, 1995.

Zainovich, M. George. *The Development of Socialist Yugoslavia.* Baltimore, MD: Johns Hopkins University Press, 1968.

Selected General Bibliography

General Works

Augustinos, Gerasimos, ed. *The National Idea in Eastern Europe: The Politics of Ethnic and Civic Community*. Lexington, MA: D.C. Heath, 1996.

Bannon, Alfred J., and Achilles Edelenyi, eds. and comps. *Documentary History of Eastern Europe*. New York: Twayne, 1970.

Benbassa, Esther, and Aron Rodrigue. *The Jews of the Balkans: The Judeo-Spanish Community, Fifteenth to Twentieth Centuries*. Oxford: Blackwell, 1995.

Bideleux, Robert, and Ian Jeffries. *A History of Eastern Europe: Crisis and Change*. London: Routledge, 1998.

Brand, Charles M., ed. *Icon and Minaret: Sources of Byzantine and Islamic Civilization*. Englewood Cliffs, NJ: Prentice-Hall, 1969.

Carter, Francis W. *An Historical Geography of the Balkans*. London: Academic Press, 1977.

Carter, Frank, and H. T. Norris. *The Changing Shape of the Balkans*. London: University College Press, 1994.

Castellan, Georges. *History of the Balkans from Mohammed the Conqueror to Stalin*. Translated by Nicholas Bradley. Boulder, CO: East European Monographs, 1991.

Clark, Victoria. *Why Angels Fall: A Journey through Orthodox Europe from Byzantium to Kosovo*. New York: St. Martin's, 2000.

Conte, Francis. *The Slavs*. Boulder, CO: East European Monographs, 1995.

Crampton, Richard J. *Eastern Europe in the Twentieth Century—And After*. 2nd ed. London: Routledge, 1997.

Crampton, Richard J., and Benjamin Crampton. *Atlas of Eastern Europe in the Twentieth Century*. London: Routledge, 1996.

Cvijić, Christopher. *Remaking the Balkans*. London: Royal Institute of International Affairs, 1991.

Djordjević, Dimitrije, and Stephen Fischer-Galati. *The Balkan Revolutionary Tradition*. New York: Columbia University Press, 1981.

Dvornik, Francis. *The Slavs in European History and Civilization*. New Brunswick, NJ: Rutgers University Press, 1962.

Fischer-Galati, Stephen, ed. *Man, State, and Society in East European History*. New York: Praeger, 1970.

Glenny, Misha. *The Balkans: Nationalism, War and the Great Powers, 1804-1999*. London: Viking, 2000.

Held, Joseph, ed. *The Columbia History of Eastern Europe in the Twentieth Century*. New York: Columbia University Press, 1992.

Hösch, Edgar. *The Balkans: A Short History from Greek Times to the Present Day*. Translated by Tania Alexander. New York: Crane, Russak, 1972.

Hupchick, Dennis P. *Conflict and Chaos in Eastern Europe*. New York: St. Martin's, 1995.

———. *Culture and History in Eastern Europe*. New York: St. Martin's, 1994.

Hupchick, Dennis P., and Harold E. Cox. *The Palgrave Concise Historical Atlas of the Balkans*. New York: Palgrave, 2001.

———. *The Palgrave Concise Historical Atlas of Eastern Europe*. 2nd, revised and expanded ed. New York: Palgrave, 2001.

Jelavich, Barbara. *History of the Balkans*. 2 vols. Cambridge: Cambridge University Press, 1985.

Jelavich, Charles, and Barbara Jelavich. *The Balkans*. Englewood Cliffs, NJ: Prentice-Hall, 1965.

Kolarz, Walter. *Myths and Realities in Eastern Europe*. London: Lindsay Drummond, 1946.

Lampe, John, and Marvin R. Jackson. *Balkan Economic History, 1550-1950: From Imperial Borderlands to Developing Nations.* Bloomington: Indiana University Press, 1982.

Longworth, Philip. *The Making of Eastern Europe: From Prehistory to Postcommunism.* 2nd ed. New York: St. Martin's, 1997.

Magocsi, Paul R., and Geoffrey J. Matthews. *Historical Atlas of East Central Europe.* Seattle: University of Washington Press, 1993.

Mazower, Mark. *The Balkans: A Short History.* New York: Modern Library, 2000.

Norris, Harry T. *Islam in the Balkans: Religion and Society between Europe and the Arab World.* Columbia: University of South Carolina Press, 1993.

Okey, R. *Eastern Europe 1740-1985: Feudalism to Communism.* 2nd ed. Minneapolis: University of Minnesota Press, 1986.

Palairet, Michael. *The Balkan Economies, c. 1800-1914: Evolution Without Development.* Cambridge: Cambridge University Press, 1997.

Pavlowitch, Stevan K. *A History of the Balkans, 1804-1945.* London: Longman, 1999.

Portal, Roger. *The Slavs: A Cultural and Historical Survey of the Slavonic Peoples.* New York: Harper and Row, 1969.

Ristelhueber, René. *A History of the Balkan Peoples.* Edited and translated by Sherman D. Spector. New York: Twayne, 1971.

Rupnik, Jacques. *The Other Europe.* London: Weidenfeld and Nicolson, 1988.

Stavrianos, L. S. *The Balkans Since 1453.* New York: Holt, Rinehart and Winston, 1958.

Stoianovich, Traian. *Balkan Worlds: The First and Last Europe.* Armonk, NY: M. E. Sharpe, 1994.

Stokes, Gale. *Three Eras of Political Change in Eastern Europe.* New York: Oxford University Press, 1996.

Stokes, Gale, ed. *From Stalinism to Pluralism: A Documentary History of Eastern Europe Since 1945.* 2nd ed. New York: Oxford University, 1996.

Sugar, Peter F., ed. *Eastern European Nationalism in the Twentieth Century.* Lanham, MD: American University Press, 1995.

Sugar, Peter F., and Ivo J. Lederer, eds. *Nationalism in Eastern Europe.* Seattle: University of Washington Press, 1969.

Todorov, Nikolai. *The Balkan City, 1400-1900.* Seattle: University of Washington Press, 1983.

Todorova, Maria. *Imagining the Balkans.* New York: Oxford University Press, 1997.

Turnock, David. *The Human Geography of Eastern Europe.* London: Routledge, 1989.

———. *The Making of Eastern Europe: From Earliest Times to 1815.* London: Routledge, 1988.

Walters, E. G. *The Other Europe: Eastern Europe to 1945.* Syracuse, NY: Syracuse University Press, 1988.

Winnifrith, T. J. *The Vlachs: The History of a Balkan People.* New York: St. Martin's, 1987.

Wolff, Robert L. *The Balkans in Our Time.* Cambridge, MA: Harvard University Press, 1956.

Albania

Costa, Nicholas J. *Albania: A European Enigma.* Boulder, CO: East European Monographs, 1995.

Hutchings, Raymond. *Historical Dictionary of Albania.* Lanham, MD: Scarecrow Press, 1996.

Jacques, Edwin E. *The Albanians: An Ethnic History from Prehistoric Times to the Present.* Jefferson, NC: McFarland, 1995.

Keefe, Eugene K., et al. *Area Handbook for Albania.* Washington, DC: US Government Printing Office, 1971.

Logoreci, Anton. *The Albanians: Europe's Forgotten Survivors.* Boulder, CO: Westview, 1977.

Marmullaku, Ramadan. *Albania and the Albanians.* Translated by Margot Milosavljević and Boško Milosavljević. London: Hurst, 1975.

Pollo, Stefanaq and Arben Puto. *The History of Albania: From Its Origins to the Present Day.* London: Routledge and Kegan Paul, 1981.

Vickers, Miranda. *Albania: A Modern History.* London: I. B. Tauris, 1994.

Winnifrith, Tom. *Perspectives on Albania.* London: Warwick, 1992.

Bosnia-Hercegovina

Čuvalo, Ante. *Historical Dictionary of Bosnia and Herzegovina.* Lanham, MD: Scarecrow Press, 1997.

Donia, Robert J., and John V. A. Fine, Jr. *Bosnia and Hercegovina: A Tradition Betrayed.* New York: Columbia University Press, 1995.

Friedman, Francine. *The Bosnian Muslims: Denial of a Nation.* Boulder, CO: Westview, 1996.

Lockwood, William G. *European Muslims: Economy and Ethnicity in Western Bosnia.* New York: Academic Press, 1975.

Malcolm, Noel. *Bosnia: A Short History.* New York: New York University Press, 1994.

Pinson, Mark, ed. *The Muslims of Bosnia-Herzegovina: Their Historic Development from the Middle Ages to the Dissolution of Yugoslavia.* 2nd ed. Cambridge, MA: Harvard Middle Eastern Monographs, 1996.

Bulgaria

Anastasoff, Christ. *The Bulgarians: From Their Arrival in the Balkans to Modern Times, Thirteen Centuries of History.* Hicksville, NY: Exposition, 1977.

Crampton, Richard J. *A Concise History of Bulgaria.* Cambridge: Cambridge University Press, 1996.

———. *A Short History of Modern Bulgaria.* Cambridge: Cambridge University Press, 1987.

Detrez, Raymond. *Historical Dictionary of the Republic of Bulgaria.* Lanham, MD: Scarecrow Press, 1997.

Eminov, Ali. *Turkish and Other Muslim Minorities in Bulgaria.* New York: Routledge, 1997.

Karpat, K. H., ed. *The Turks of Bulgaria: The History, Culture and Political Fate of a Minority.* Istanbul: Isis, 1990.

Lang, David M. *The Bulgarians: From Pagan Times to the Ottoman Conquest.* Boulder, CO: Westview, 1976.

Mishev, Dimitŭr. *The Bulgarians in the Past: Pages from the Bulgarian Cultural History.* Lausanne: Central Bookstore of Nationalities, 1919.

Pundeff, Marin V. *Bulgaria in American Perspective: Political and Cultural Issues.* Boulder, CO: East European Monographs, 1994.

Tamir, Vicki. *Bulgaria and Her Jews: The History of a Dubious Symbiosis.* New York: Sepher-Hermon for Yeshiva University Press, 1979.

Tzvetkov, Plamen. *A History of the Balkans: A Regional Overview from a Bulgarian Perspective.* 2 vols. Lewiston, NY: Edwin Mellen, 1993.

Byzantine Empire

Barker, Ernest, trans. and ed. *Social and Political Thought in Byzantium from Justinian I to the Last Palaeologus: Passages from Byzantine Writers and Documents.* Oxford: Clarendon, 1957.

Barker, John W. *Justinian and the Later Roman Empire.* Madison: University of Wisconsin Press, 1966.

Baynes, Norman H. *The Byzantine Empire.* London: Oxford University Press, 1962.

Baynes, Norman H., and H. St. L. B. Moss, eds. *Byzantium: An Introduction to East Roman Civilization.* Oxford: Clarendon, 1961.

Bréhier, Louis. *The Life and Death of Byzantium.* New York: North-Holland, 1977.

Browning, Robert. *The Byzantine Empire.* Revised ed. Washington, DC: Catholic University of America Press, 1992.

Byron, Robert. *The Byzantine Achievement: An Historical Perspective, A.D. 330-1453.* Reprint ed. London: Routledge and Kegan Paul, 1987.

The Cambridge Medieval History. Vol. 4, in 2 pts. Edited by Joan M. Hussey. Cambridge: Cambridge University Press, 1966.

Diehl, Charles. *Byzantium: Greatness and Decline.* Translated by Naomi Walford. New Brunswick, NJ: Rutgers University Press, 1957.

Geanakoplos, Deno J., comp. and ed. *Byzantium: Church, Society, and Civilization Seen through Contemporary Eyes.* Chicago, IL: University of Chicago Press, 1984.

Geanakoplos, Deno J. *Interaction of the "Sibling" Byzantine and Western Cultures in the Middle Ages and Italian Renaissance.* New Haven, CT: Yale University Press, 1976.

Haussig, H. W. *A History of Byzantine Civilization.* Translated by Joan M. Hussey. New York: Praeger, 1971.

Hussey, Joan M. *The Byzantine World.* 3rd ed. London: Hutchinson, 1967.

Kazhdan, Alexander P., et al, eds. *The Oxford Dictionary of Byzantium.* 3 vols. New York: Oxford University Press, 1991.

Lemerle, Paul. *A History of Byzantium.* Translated by Antony Matthew. New York: Walker, 1964.

Magoulias, Harry J. *Byzantine Christianity: Emperor, Church and the West.* Chicago, IL: Rand McNally, 1970.

Mango, Cyril. *Byzantium, the Empire of New Rome.* New York: Scribner, 1980.

Norwich, John J. *Byzantium.* 3 vols. New York: Knopf, 1992-96.

Obolensky, Dimitri. *The Byzantine Commonwealth: Eastern Europe, 500-1453.* New York: Praeger, 1971.

————. *Byzantium and the Slavs.* Crestwood, NY: St. Vladimir's Seminary Press, 1994.

Ostrogorsky, George. *History of the Byzantine State.* Translated by Joan M. Hussey. New Brunswick, NJ: Rutgers University Press, 1957.

Rice, Tamara T. *Everyday Life in Byzantium.* Reprint ed. New York: Dorset, 1987.

Runciman, Steven. *Byzantine Civilization.* 2nd ed. Cleveland, OH: World, 1961.

————. *The Byzantine Theocracy.* Cambridge: Cambridge University Press, 1977.

Treadgold, Warren T. *A History of the Byzantine State and Society.* Stanford, CA: Stanford University Press, 1997.

Vasiliev, A. A. *History of the Byzantine Empire, 324-1453.* 2 vols. 2nd Eng. ed. Madison: University of Wisconsin Press, 1970.

Vryonis, Speros, Jr. *Byzantium and Europe.* New York: Harcourt, Brace and World, 1967.

Whitting, Philip, ed. *Byzantium: An Introduction.* Oxford: Blackwell, 1971.

Croatia

Carter, Francis W. *Dubrovnik (Ragusa): A Classic City-State.* London: Seminar Press, 1972.

Eterovich, Francis H., and Christopher Spalatin, eds. *Croatia: Land, People and Culture.* 2 vols. Toronto: University of Toronto Press, 1964-70.

Goldstein, Ivo. *Croatia: A History.* Montreal: McGill-Queen's University Press, 2000.

Kadić, Ante. *From Croatian Renaissance to Yugoslav Socialism.* The Hague: Mouton, 1969.

Knežević, Anthony. *The Croatian Nation: A Short History.* Translated by Rudolph J. Hrasčanec. Philadelphia, PA: Croatian Catholic Union, 1990.

Mačan, Trpimir, and Josip Sentija. *A Short History of Croatia.* Zagreb: Most, 1992.

Omrčanin, Ivo. *Diplomatic and Political History of Croatia.* Philadelphia, PA: Dorrance, 1972.

Praga, Giuseppe. *History of Dalmatia.* Translated by Edward Steinberg. Pisa: Giardini, 1993.

Preveden, Francis R. *A History of the Croatian People.* 2 vols. New York: Philosophical Society, 1955-62.

Stallaerts, Robert, and Jeannine Laurens. *Historical Dictionary of the Republic of Croatia.* Metuchen, NJ: Scarecrow Press, 1995.

Tanner, Marcus. *Croatia: A Nation Forged in War.* New Haven, CT: Yale University Press, 1997.

Greece

Byron, Robert. *The Station (Athos: Treasures and Men).* London: J. Lehmann, 1949.

Clogg, Richard. *A Concise History of Greece.* Cambridge: Cambridge University Press, 1992.

Crossland, John, and Diana Constance. *Macedonian Greece.* New York: W. W. Norton, 1982.

Dakin, Douglas. *The Unification of Greece, 1770-1923.* London: E. Benn, 1972.

Hasluck, Frederick W. *Athos and Its Monasteries.* London: Kegan Paul, Trench, Trubner, 1924.

Holden, David. *Greece without Columns: The Making of Modern Greece.* Philadelphia, PA: J. B. Lippincott, 1972.

Kourvetaris, Yorgos A., and Betty A. Dobratz. *A Profile of Modern Greece in Search of Identity.* Oxford: Clarendon, 1987.

Michael [Prince, of Greece] and Alan Palmer. *The Royal House of Greece.* London: Weidenfeld and Nicolson, 1990.

Miller, William. *Greece.* New York: Scribner, 1928.

Mouzelis, Nicos P. *Modern Greece: Facets of Underdevelopment.* London: Macmillan, 1988.

Toynbee, Arnold J. *The Greeks and Their Heritage.* Oxford: Oxford University Press, 1981.

Van der Kiste, John. *Kings of the Hellenes: The Greek Kings, 1863-1974.* London: Alan Sutton, 1994.

Veremis, Thanos. *Greece's Balkan Entanglement.* Athens: ELIAMEP-YALCO, 1995.

———. *The Military in Greek Politics.* London: C. Hurst, 1997.

Wace, Alan J. B., and Maurice S. Thompson. *The Nomads of the Balkans: An Account of Life and Customs Among the Vlachs of the Northern Pindus.* London: Methuen, 1914.

Woodhouse, Christopher M. *Modern Greece: A Short History.* 5th ed. London: Faber, 1991.

Macedonia

Brailsford, Henry N. *Macedonia: Its Races and Their Future.* London: Methuen, 1906.

Danforth, Loring M. *Macedonian Conflict: Ethnic Nationalism in a Transnational World.* Princeton, NJ: Princeton University Press, 1995.

Georgieva, Valentina, and Sasha Konechni. *Historical Dictionary of the Republic of Macedonia.* Lanham, MD: Scarecrow Press, 1997.

Mihailoff, Ivan. *Macedonia: A Switzerland of the Balkans.* Translated by Christ Anastasoff. St. Louis, MO: Pearlstone, 1950.

Poulton, Hugh. *Who Are the Macedonians?* 2nd ed. Bloomington: Indiana University Press, 2000.

Pribichevich, Stoyan. *Macedonia: Its People and History.* University Park: Pennsylvania State University Press, 1982.

Shea, John. *Macedonia and Greece: The Struggle to Define a New Nation.* Jefferson, NC: McFarland, 1996.

Wilkinson, H.R. *Maps and Politics: A Review of the Ethnographic Cartography of Macedonia.* Liverpool: University Press of Liverpool, 1951.

Montenegro

Devine, Alexander. *Montenegro in History, Politics and War.* London: Unwin, 1918.

Stevenson, Francis S. *A History of Montenegro.* Reprint ed. New York: Arno, 1971.

Towle, George M. *A Brief History of Montenegro.* Boston, MA: J. R. Osgood, 1877.

Ottoman Empire

Alderson, Anthony D. *The Structure of the Ottoman Dynasty.* Reprint ed. Westport, CT: Greenwood, 1982.

Brown, L. Carl. *The Imperial Legacy: The Ottoman Impact on the Balkans and the Middle East.* Boulder, CO: East European Monographs, 1995.

Erdem, Y. Hakan. *Slavery in the Ottoman Empire and Its Demise, 1800-1909.* New York: St. Martin's, 1996.

Faroqhi, Suraiya. *Approaching Ottoman History: An Introduction to the Sources.* Cambridge: Cambridge University Press, 1999.

Findley, Carter V. *Bureaucratic Reform in the Ottoman Empire: The Sublime Porte, 1789-1922.* Princeton, NJ: Princeton University Press, 1980.

Gibb, H. A. R., and Harold Bowen. *Islamic Society and the West: A Study of the Impact of Western Civilization on Moslem Culture in the Near East.* Vol. 1. *Islamic Society in the Eighteenth Century.* 2 pts. London: Oxford University Press, 1967.

Goodwin, Jason. *Lords of the Horizon: A History of the Ottoman Empire.* New York: Holt, 1999.

Hasluck, Frederick W. *Christianity and Islam under the Sultans.* 2 vols. Oxford: Clarendon, 1929.

Inalcik, Halil, and Donald Quataert, eds. *An Economic and Social History of the Ottoman Empire, 1300-1914.* Cambridge: Cambridge University Press, 1995.

Itzkowitz, Norman. *Ottoman Empire and Islamic Tradition.* 2nd ed. Chicago: University of Chicago Press, 1980.

Karpat, Kemal H. *The Ottoman State and Its Place in World History.* Leiden: E. J. Brill, 1974.

Kinross, [John P. D. B.] Lord. *The Ottoman Centuries: The Rise and Fall of the Turkish Empire.* New York: Morrow Quill, 1977.

Kortepeter, Carl M. *The Ottoman Turks: Nomad Kingdom to World Empire.* Istanbul: Isis, 1991.

Lewis, Raphaela. *Everyday Life in Ottoman Turkey.* London: B. T. Batsford, 1971.

Mansel, Philip. *Constantinople: City of the World's Desire, 1453-1924.* New York: St. Martin's, 1996.

McCarthy, Justin. *The Ottoman Turks: An Introductory History to 1923.* New York: Longman, 1996.

Miller, William. *The Ottoman Empire and Its Successors, 1801-1927.* Cambridge: Cambridge University Press, 1936.

Panaite, Viorel. *The Ottoman Law of War and Peace.* Boulder, CO: East European Monographs, 2000.

Quataert, Donald. *The Ottoman Empire, 1700-1922.* Cambridge: Cambridge University Press, 2000.

Shaw, Stanford J., and Ezel K. Shaw. *History of the Ottoman Empire and Modern Turkey.* 2 vols. Cambridge: Cambridge University Press, 1976-77.

Vucinich, Wayne S. *The Ottoman Empire: Its Record and Legacy.* Reprint ed. Huntington, NY: Krieger, 1979.

Weiker, Walter F. *Ottomans, Turks, and the Jewish Polity: A History of the Jews of Turkey.* Lanham, MD: University Press of America, 1992.

Wheatcroft, Andrew. *The Ottomans.* New York: Viking, 1993.

Romania

Bria, Ion. *Romania: Orthodox Identity at a Crossroads of Europe.* Geneva: WCC Publications, 1995.

Castellan, Georges. *A History of the Romanians.* Translated by Nicholas Bradley. Boulder, CO: East European Monographs, 1989.

Condurachi, Emil, and Constantin Daicoviciu. *Romania.* Translated by James Hogarth. Geneva: Nagel, 1971.

Fischer-Galati, Stephen A. *Twentieth-Century Romania.* 2nd ed. New York: Columbia University Press, 1991.

Georgescu, Vlad. *The Romanians: A History.* Translated by Alexandra Bley-Vroman. Rev. ed. Columbus: Ohio State University Press, 1991.

Iancu, Carol. *Jews in Romania, 1866-1919: From Exclusion to Emancipation.* Translated by Carvel de Bussy. Boulder, CO: East European Monographs, 1996.

Iorga, Nicolae. *A History of Roumania: Land, People, Civilization.* Translated by J. McCabe. London: Unwin, 1925.

Mackenzie, Andrew, ed. *A Concise History of Romania.* New York: St. Martin's, 1984.

Mackenzie, Andrew. *The History of Transylvania.* London: Unified Printers and Publishers, 1983.

Oţetea, Andrei, ed. *A Concise History of Romania.* London: R. Hale, 1985.

Pop, Ioan A. *Romanians and Romania: A Brief History.* Boulder, CO: East European Monographs, 2000.

Seton-Watson, Robert W. *A History of the Roumanians: From Roman Times to the Completion of Unity.* Cambridge: Cambridge University Press, 1934.

Treptow, Kurt W., ed. *A History of Romania.* Iaşi: Center for Romanian Studies, 1996.

Treptow, Kurt W., and Marcel D. Popa. *Historical Dictionary of Romania.* Lanham, MD: Scarecrow Press, 1996.

Serbia

Anzulovic, Branimir. *Heavenly Serbia: From Myth to Genocide.* New York: New York University Press, 1999.

Dragnich, Alex N. *Serbia's Historical Heritage.* Boulder, CO: East European Monographs, 1994.

Judah, Timothy. *The Serbs: History, Myth, and the Destruction of Yugoslavia.* New Haven, CT: Yale University Press, 1997.

Malcolm, Noel. *Kosovo: A Short History.* New York: New York University Press, 1998.

Petrovich, Michael B. *A History of Modern Serbia, 1804-1918.* 2 vols. New York: Harcourt, Brace and Jovanovich, 1976.

Temperley, Harold W. V. *History of Serbia.* Reprint ed. New York: H. Fertig, 1969.

Slovenia

Arnez, John A. *Slovenia in European Affairs: Reflections on Slovenian Political History.* New York: League of CSA, 1958.

Gow, James, and Cathie Carmichael. *Slovenia and the Slovenes: A Small State and the New Europe.* Bloomington: Indiana University Press, 2000.

Plut-Pregelj, Leopoldina. *Historical Dictionary of Slovenia.* Lanham, MD: Scarecrow Press, 1996.

Prunk, Janko. *A Brief History of Slovenia: Historical Background of the Republic of Slovenia.* Translated by Wayne Tuttle and Majda Klander. Ljubljana: Zalozba Mihelac, 1994.

Yugoslavia

Auty, Phyllis. *Yugoslavia.* New York: Walker, 1965.

Clissold, Stephen, ed. *A Short History of Yugoslavia: From Early Times to 1966.* Cambridge: Cambridge University Press, 1966.

Dedijer, Vladimir, et al. *History of Yugoslavia.* Translated by Kordija Kveder. New York: McGraw-Hill, 1974.

Lampe, John R. *Yugoslavia as History: Twice There Was a Country.* Cambridge: Cambridge University, 1996.

Palmer, A. W. *Yugoslavia.* London: Oxford University Press, 1964.

Pavlowitch, Stevan K. *The Improbable Survivor: Yugoslavia and Its Problems, 1918-1988.* Columbus: Ohio State University Press, 1988.

Singleton, Fred B. *A Short History of the Yugoslav Peoples.* New York: Cambridge University Press, 1985.

———. *Twentieth-Century Yugoslavia.* New York: Columbia University Press, 1976.

Tomasevich, Jozo. *Peasants, Politics, and Economic Change in Jugoslavia.* Stanford, CA: Stanford University Press, 1955.

Index

3м